Facilitating Injustice

Facilitating Injustice

*The Complicity of Social Workers in the
Forced Removal and Incarceration of
Japanese Americans, 1941–1946*

YOOSUN PARK

OXFORD
UNIVERSITY PRESS

OXFORD
UNIVERSITY PRESS

Oxford University Press is a department of the University of Oxford. It furthers
the University's objective of excellence in research, scholarship, and education
by publishing worldwide. Oxford is a registered trade mark of Oxford University
Press in the UK and certain other countries.

Published in the United States of America by Oxford University Press
198 Madison Avenue, New York, NY 10016, United States of America.

Library of Congress Cataloging-in-Publication Data
Names: Park, Yoosun, author.
Title: Facilitating injustice : the complicity of social workers in the forced removal and
incarceration of Japanese Americans, 1941–1946 / Yoosun Park.
Description: New York, NY : Oxford University Press, [2019] | Includes bibliographical references. |
Summary: "Social work equivocated. While it did not fully endorse mass removal and incarceration,
neither did it protest, oppose, or explicitly critique government actions. The past should not be judged
by today's standards; the actions and motivations described here occurred in a period rife with fear and
propaganda. Undergoing a major shift from its private charity roots into its public sector future, social
work bounded with the rest of society into "a patriotic fervor" (Specht & Courtney, 1994, p.ix). The history
presented here is all the more disturbing, however, because it is that of social workers doing what seemed
to them to be more or less right and good. While policies of a government at war, intractable bureaucratic
structures, tangled political alliances, and complex professional obligations, all may have mandated
compliance, it is, nevertheless, difficult to deny that social work and social workers were also willing
participants in the events, informed about and aware of the implications of that compliance. In social
work's unwillingness to take a resolute stand against the removal and incarceration, the well-intentioned
profession, doing its conscious best to do good, enforced the existing social order and did its level best to
keep the Nikkei from disrupting it. What might social work in the camps have looked like, had it, instead
of urging caution to deflect attention to its work, instead of denying that its work was coddling the Nikkei,
have attempted, at the very least, to challenge the very logic that made—and continues to make—assisting
the needy and caring for the vulnerable, actions to be mistrusted, defended, and justified? What lessons can
today's social work glean from this history?"— Provided by publisher.
Identifiers: LCCN 2019020540 | ISBN 9780199765058 (hardback) | ISBN 9780190081355 (epub) |
ISBN 9780190081348 (updf)
Subjects: LCSH: Japanese Americans—Evacuation and relocation, 1942–1945. |
Social service—Moral and ethical aspects—United States—History—20th century. |
Social work administration—Moral and ethical aspects—United States—History—20th century. |
United States—Race relations—History—20th century.
Classification: LCC D769.8.A6 P37 2019 | DDC 940.53089/956073—dc23
LC record available at https://lccn.loc.gov/2019020540

1 3 5 7 9 8 6 4 2

Printed by Integrated Books International, United States of America

To beloved teacher, mentor, and irreplaceable friend, Professor Hideki Anthony Ishisaka, born in Amache.

Contents

Contents

Preface

An Occluded History

In 1943, Edward J. Ennis, director of the U.S. Justice Department's Alien Enemy Control Unit, addressed the Seventieth National Conference of Social Work on the issue of enemy aliens in that wartime period. He explained that "within twenty-four hours after the attack on Pearl Harbor 1,000 Japanese aliens had been apprehended, and within a week a total of 3,000 alien enemies of German, Italian, and Japanese nationality were in the custody of the Immigration and Naturalization Service" (1943, p. 291). This initial apprehension of individual aliens was inaugurated in early December 1941. Within three months, the decision was made for the forced removal and incarceration of an entire population. On February 19, 1942, President Franklin Roosevelt issued executive order 9066 (3CFR1092-93), instituting "the greatest planned and controlled migration in our history: the movement of the American Japanese" (Powell, 1943, p. 301). From the last days of February 1942, when the Nikkei residents of Terminal Island became the first group forced from their homes, to March of 1946, when the last of the Relocation Camps was finally closed, the federal government incarcerated approximately 120,000 persons of Japanese ancestry (Burton, Farrell, Lord, & Lord, 2000; Commission on Wartime Relocation and Internment of Civilians, 1982; War Relocation Authority, 1946). Two-thirds of those interned were U.S.-born citizens. The rest were aliens, first-generation Japanese immigrants who, by the provisions of the 1790 Naturalization Act (1 Stat.103) which limited naturalization rights to "free whites," could not become citizens. No other population, alien or citizen, who traced their ancestry to an enemy nation was subjected to wholesale removal and incarceration. "According to the War Relocation Authority, it had, at one time or another, 120,313 individuals in custody. It received 111,236 from the Army, 1,118 from Hawaii, 1,735 who were transferred from INS internment camps, 219 'voluntary residents' (mostly individuals who joined families already in camp), and 24 from various institutions. In addition, 5,981 U.S. citizens were born to incarcerated mothers" (Daniels, Kitano, & Taylor, 1986, p. 73).

Social workers were involved in every part of the process; they were integral cogs in the total engine of forced removal and incarceration. Representatives of

West Coast branches of the American Association of Social Workers (AASW) testified at congressional hearings held on the impending mass removal of the Nikkei (United States Congress—House Select Committee Investigating National Defense Migration, 1942a, 1942b, 1942c). State and county so- cial workers vetted, registered, counseled, and tagged all Nikkei individuals, along with their accompanying luggage, at the many Wartime Civil Control Administration (WCCA) stations, the first stop on the forced removal to mass incarceration (Leahy, 1945, p. 35; Nickel, 1942a). Social workers staffed adminis- trative offices within the War Relocation Authority (WRA) concentration camps in which the Nikkei were imprisoned (Freed, 1944; Gottfried, 1944; Leahy, 1945; Nickel, 1943; Webb, 1946). They worked in the Washington headquarters of the WRA and in the regional offices through which it conducted its "resettlement" program, a planned scattering of the population explicitly intended to prevent their regional concentration (Leahy, 1945).

The history of social work presented in this study is offered as an exemplar for the examination of an enduring tension within social work which often pits its functions in conflict with its purported values and ethics: the profession's dual role as deliverer of social policies and defender of those affected by them. In its unwillingness to take a resolute stand against the removal and incarcer- ation of the Nikkei and in carrying out its "willingly accepted" (DeWitt, 1943, p. 1) government-assigned tasks, social work enacted and thus legitimized the bigoted policies of racial profiling en masse. The profession's contradictory role—facilitating unjust government policies and actualizing social biases while striving to ameliorate their consequences—is, however, not a phenomenon unique to this event or even the past but a recurring and current problematic visible in contemporary social work. Indeed, while the setting for the events chronicled here is a nation at war more than half a century past, the ideas and ideals that fueled and enabled the events—the intersecting discourses of race, racism, culture, and the borders of legal and social citizenship—are all too fa- miliar today. This analysis of the choices made and enacted by the profession and its professionals of that nation in crisis can help to illuminate the necessary task of examining the profession's current approaches, practices, and policies within this troubled nation.

Acknowledgments

This project, many years in the making, would not have been possible without the labor of many. My heartfelt thanks go to research assistants Alex Kim, Andrea Yoshida, and Alicia Simoni who provided invaluable aid in and outside of the archives. Particular thanks are due also to Shea Henly who arrived like a gift from the universe to not only help me through the final tasks necessary to finishing the book, but also turned a much needed pair of keen eyes to read the text through in its entirety. I am ever grateful to Dr. Susan P. Kemp, for nudging me towards history during my doctoral studies, and to Dr. Joshua Miller provided useful feedback on an earlier version of this text. Thanks also goes to the Columbia University Population Research Center where I spent a productive year as a Visiting Scholar, researching and writing parts of this book. Funding from the Lois and Samuel Silberman Fund Faculty Grant Program and the Smith College Brown Foundation Clinical Research Institute made the project possible; both are gratefully acknowledged. Finally, eternal love and appreciation are due to my family: Dr. Andrew G. Rundle, Christopher B. Park, Alexander P. Park, and Sophia B. Rundle, whose love and support propelled me through many crises of confidence, conviction, and will.

Introduction

During my dissertation research into the representation of immigrants in social work discourse in the early years of the profession, I came across a startling article in the pages of *Social Service Review* about the involvement of social workers in the ignominious history detailed in the following chapters. No history of the profession I had ever read had mentioned the disconcerting fact that social workers were involved in all aspects of this history, and, while my subsequent search in the stacks uncovered a handful of articles on the topic written during the war years, I also discovered that none had been written since. Not one of my fellow students knew about the role social workers played in this history. Only one of the many professors I encountered during my studies did; he had been born in a War Relocation Authority (WRA) camp usually called Amache, officially known as Granada. It seemed that social work and social workers' involvement had been forgotten altogether.

Lack of historical knowledge is, of course, in no way idiosyncratic to social workers. The Marxist historian Eric Hobsbawm once wrote that "no one who has been asked by an intelligent American student whether the phrase 'Second World War' meant that there had been a 'First World War' is unaware that knowledge of even the basic facts of the century cannot be taken for granted" (1994, p. 3).[1] But the poverty of knowledge about its own past actions seemed especially troubling for this profession and discipline which prides itself on its dedication to social change and the amelioration of social ills for the benefit of those at its margins. How were we to honestly evaluate our present actions and formulate future plans if we did not even know that our "public past" (1994, p. 3) had included such complicity in injustice?

As I learned in the subsequent years of study, the involvement of social workers had not only been forgotten by social work, but it had never been studied by scholars of the history. The study presented here is an effort to address the lacuna in social work history. As the WRA commented in an internal document circulated at the time of resettlement, the "full story behind the West Coast evacuation has never been adequately told and probably will not be until many years after the return to peace. It is a complex story with many chapters that must necessarily remain hazy in time of total war" (War Relocation Authority, 1942, p. 5).

---

[1] See Park (2006).

The chapters presented here are the tentative first attempts at reconstructing that complex and nearly forgotten history. The facts of the larger history of the forced removal and mass incarceration are well-documented; the body of scholarship and personal accountings and analyses of the events and their aftermath are extensive and far too numerous to list here. I have made no effort to recover those well-established grounds.[2] The narrative arc I have constructed here traces the presence of social work and social workers in the history to establish what social workers did and how they did so. What this means, in concrete terms, is that this particular accounting does not always follow the major event markers usually highlighted in analyses of the larger history of removal and incarceration. Many important facts and events are omitted wholesale or glossed over without detailed explanation. There is no discussion, for example, of the removal and incarceration of the Latin American Nikkei. Major ventures such as the student relocation program, group resettlement to Seabrook Farms, and significant events such as the Manzanar revolt and the Poston strike, have been left out of the discussion. My sole focus was on reconstructing the path of social work through the events and processes of removal, incarceration, and resettlement, though inevitably, even that history is incomplete. Many facets of social work's wartime work—for example, its involvement in the Immigration and Naturalization Service (INS) Detention Stations, Department of Justice Internment facilities, and U.S. Army internment facilities where individually arrested Issei and some family members were detained—have not been examined for this study. Much work remains to be done.

Notes on Terminology

Euphemisms abound in this history.[3] "Evacuation" was the official terminology for the forced removal of an entire racialized civilian population and "relocation" the term for their mass incarceration by the federal government. In all cases, the choice of terminology is a political decision. Should the outbreak of violence which occurred in December 1942 at Manzanar be properly called a riot or an uprising? The choice colors the ways in which the killing of two inmates by soldiers firing into the crowd and the subsequent imposition of martial law can and should be interpreted. The choice of terminology for the population in question, ranging

---

[2] An excellent resource for those wishing for more information on various aspects of the history is Densho, "a free on-line resource about the history of the Japanese American WWII exclusion and incarceration experience" (https://encyclopedia.densho.org/).

[3] See the *Power of words handbook* (2013), by the National Japanese American Citizens League (https://jacl.org/wordpress/wp-content/uploads/2015/08/Power-of-Words-Rev.-Term.-Handbook.pdf).

from "Japanese Americans," which the most progressive tended to use; to the shorthand "Japanese," which rendered both the citizen Nisei and the immigrant Issei equally alien; to the pithy expletive "Jap" used by far too many in the history, shapes the ways in which the removal, incarceration, and the planned scattering of the population post-imprisonment can and should be understood.

The Population

"Evacuees" and "center residents" were the terms most often used by officialdom to describe the displaced and incarcerated. The Issei, the first-generation immigrants from Japan, were also often identified as "Japanese aliens" (see, e.g., Ennis, 1943, p. 291). However correct the term may have been legally, given the racist laws which blocked the Issei from shedding alienage through naturalization, it seems a discourtesy at best to continue to refer to them as "aliens." The commonly used term "American Japanese" to indicate their U.S.-born descendants also replicates the period's exclusionary exoticization of this population, which even *jus soli* citizenship did not forestall. For the purposes of this book, the term "Nikkei" will be used to indicate both Japanese immigrants and U.S.-born Japanese Americans in all instances where the original source is not quoted directly. "Nikkei" is a Japanese term used generally to refer to all Japanese émigrés and their descendants. Its usage as a self-identifier by Japanese Americans is a relatively new phenomenon. As such, it is less burdened by some of the problematic historical discourses of the so-called Japanese immigrants and their descendants. It is a comprehensive term that includes all members of the population, both immigrant and U.S.-born, and it sidesteps the bigoted weight of history.

Japanese language terms marking generational differences in immigration—Issei, Nisei, Sansei, and Kibei—were common terminology in the period examined and will also be used throughout this text. "Issei," or "first generation" were the immigrants to the U.S.; the term "Nisei" marked the "second generation," the children of the Issei who were the first generation of Nikkei born in the United States. The "Sansei," the "third generation" were their children. The term "Kibei" was used to differentiate Nisei who were largely raised and educated in Japan. Born in the United States like all Nisei, the Kibei were, usually for financial reasons, sent by their Issei parents to Japan to be reared by grandparents or other relatives.

The Sites

Terminology for the sites of removal and incarceration is both problematic and confusing. The Wartime Civil Control Administration (WCCA) offices to which the Nikkei were ordered to report to be vetted and registered for removal were variously referred to as Control Stations, Alien Control Stations, and Civil Control Stations. From these Control Stations, the Nikkei were then removed to 17 temporary WCCA "Civilian Assembly Centers," also called "Reception Centers," to await further transportation to more permanent WRA incarceration facilities. In California, these temporary detention centers were located in Fresno, Owens Valley (Manzanar), Marysville, Merced, Pinedale, Pomona, Sacramento, Salinas, Santa Anita, Stockton, Tanforan, Turlock, and Tulare. Puyallup, Washington, and Portland, Oregon, were two sites in the Northwest; Mayer, and Parker Dam were the two sites in Arizona.

The next stop in the removal and incarceration process were ten WRA facilities usually called "Relocation Centers" or "Projects" by those running them. These sites of long-term incarceration were located in California, Arizona, Arkansas, Idaho, Wyoming, Colorado, and Utah. Owens Valley and Parker Dam detention centers became, respectively, Manzanar and Colorado River (also known as Poston) Relocation Centers. Tule Lake camp was redesignated Tule Lake Segregation Center in the Summer of 1943. Many scholars, Nikkei and otherwise, also use the term "concentration camps" (Daniels, 1981; Drinnon, 1989; Feeley, 1999; Hirabayashi, 2008; Nishimoto & Hirabayashi, 1995; Weglyn, 1976) to indicate the ten main WRA facilities; the term was also in use during the wartime period by both the Nikkei and others. In this study, I use the terms "concentration camps" and "incarceration camps" interchangeably. The various official designation for the sites of removal and imprisonment are also used as appropriate to the discussion at hand.

Although the history as a whole is most often known as "the internment," and the WRA relocation facilities are commonly referred to as "internment camps," the WRA camps should not to be confused with the U.S. Justice Department Internment Camps for "enemy aliens." Also confusingly called "Detention Centers," the Department of Justice camps imprisoned individually vetted Nikkei who were designated by the federal government as security risks, as well as their family members, U.S. citizen or otherwise, who elected to be placed with the interned individual. Two "Citizen Isolation Centers"— Moab in southeastern Utah, and Leupp in Arizona—created and run by the WRA were similarly used as detention facilities for Nisei and Kibei marked as "troublemakers" by WRA officials in the aftermath of the Manzanar revolt. For those interested in learning more about the logistics and detailed descriptions of the sites of incarceration, *Confinement and Ethnicity: An Overview of World War II Japanese American Relocation Sites* (Burton et al., 2000) is an excellent resource.

The Social Workers

A difficulty inherent in writing social welfare history lies in determining the borders of social work. Who can be called a social worker? What comprises the social work role and its domains of activity? What, thus, can be legitimately deemed and critiqued as acts of social work? In analysis of the profession's early years, when canons of professional education and the margins of professional identity and purview were even more imprecise than they are today, the designation of a particular history as that of social work is especially difficult. The broad definition offered by social welfare historian James Leiby (1962) serves the purposes of this study: "By social workers I mean people interested in the National Conference of Charities and Corrections [now known as the National Conference on Social Welfare] as well as those who, in the twentieth century, held themselves to be professionals" (p. 30). More specifically, throughout the book, the term "social worker" is used to indicate individuals who had training in social work and were employed to perform work which, in the technical jargon of the period, consisted of some form of scientific "social adjustment program" (War Relocation Authority, 1944a, p. 1) for individuals and/or families. Not all those who performed "social work," however, were trained social workers. Given the massive labor shortages in the war years and the specific difficulty in recruiting trained social workers to work in the remote concentration camps, many functions of the welfare departments were fulfilled by individuals with no education or previous experience in social work. The following chapters attempt to maintain, therefore, a distinction between "social workers" and those performing social work functions.

Excepting the Principle Public Welfare Consultant who served as the Washington "head of the public welfare program for the War Relocation Authority" (United States Civil Service Commission, 1942c, p. 1), social workers in the WRA held job titles of "counselor" of various grades (see Appendix G for job descriptions). In descending order of authority *and* required social work credentials and experience were Head Counselor (War Relocation Authority, 1942a), Senior Counselor (War Relocation Authority, 1942b), Associate Counselor (United States Civil Service Commission, 1942b), Assistant Counselor (United States Civil Service Commission, 1942a), and Junior Counselor (War Relocation Authority, 1944c). The Head Counselor, in charge of the camp social work department, most often called the "Welfare Section," required study in "a recognized school of social work" (War Relocation Authority, 1944b, p. 2) and experience in the social work field. The Junior Counselor job description, at the other end of the professional spectrum, listed one year of study in a recognized school of social work and a year of work experience as "desirable qualifications" (War Relocation Authority, 1944c, p. 3).

In the California State Department of Social Welfare (CSDSW) records, the term "caseworker," "public assistance worker," and "social worker" were used interchangeably. Although it was not possible to ascertain the professional pedigree of most low-ranking workers mentioned in the records, there is no doubt that "social worker" was a term that identified a particular body of professionals involved in the history. In April of 1942, for example, Martha Chickering (1942), then director of the CSDSW, anticipated "over three hundred social workers being withdrawn from the regular State and county public assistance operations" (Chickering, 1942, p. 3) to work in the various Civil Control Stations. So, too, a CSDSW field report indicated that the "entire registration of the more than 4,500 Japanese evacuated from the Civil Control Stations located in Stockton and Lodi was handled by Social Workers on the staff of the San Joaquin County Welfare Department" (Sundquist, 1942, p. 1). Margaret Leahy (1945) reported in *Social Service Review* that the removal was executed by "state and local social workers loaned by the California State Department of Social Welfare" (28). In addition "private social work agencies provided volunteer workers, and representatives of the United States Children's Bureau and the Work Projects Administration gave consultant services" (Leahy, 1945, p. 28).

The social work bona fides of some of the main players in the history were relatively easy to trace. The Nikkei removal (i.e., Alien Enemy Evacuation Program) was a federal program overseen by the Federal Security Agency's Bureau of Public Assistance and administered through state social welfare departments. Jane Hoey, the director of the Bureau of Public Assistance from 1936 to 1953, and thus a primary overseer in the events, was the 1925 Chair of the New York Chapter of the American Association of Social Workers, the 1928 president of the New York State Conference of Social Work, and the 1940–41 president of the National Conference of Social Work. Azile Aaron, the Bureau's West Coast regional representative, oversaw the day-to-day affairs of the Nikkei removal. Both Hoey and Aaron are recognized by the National Association of Social Workers (NASW) as "social work pioneers" (National Association of Social Workers, 2004). Martha Chickering, the director of CSDSW from 1939 until her retirement in 1943, was a professor and the one-time director of the Curriculum in Social Service at the University of California, Berkeley. The University of Southern California's "California Social Work Hall of Distinction" hails her as having made "unique and significant contributions to the emergence of social work education in the state of California, resulting in the establishment of the State's first professional social work education" (University of Southern California School of Social Work, 2005–2006). Annie Clo Watson, executive director of the International Institute of San Francisco and member responsible for Nikkei issues on the CSDSW Committee on Welfare of the State Council of Defense, was the 1945 winner of the Daniel Koshland Jr. Award for Social Work and a one-time president of the Golden Gate chapter of the NASW (University of Minnesota Immigration History Research Center, 2004). The first in the line of several Social Welfare Consultants who worked in the Washington headquarters of the WRA was Grace Longwell Coyle, prominent group work pioneer and Professor of Group Work at Western Reserve University (later, Case Western) School of Applied Social Sciences. She served as the president of the National Conference of Social Work (NCSW) in 1940, the American Association of Social Workers (AASW) in 1942, and the Council on Social Work Education (CSWE) from 1958 to 1960 ("Grace Longwell Coyle," 2018).

Source Materials

Archives

The records of social work and social workers found in the archives outlined here are incomplete, in part because records were produced unevenly in the first place and also because some records have, undoubtedly, been lost in the years hence. There are many more sources, including a host of regional archives, that were not investigated for this study; they remain to be discovered and examined by other scholars. Primary data sources which were examined for this book include the records of the YWCA of the U.S.A., located at Smith College; the records of the War Relocation Authority and the Wartime Civilian Control Administration (WCCA), located at the National Archives and Records Administration (NARA); the records of the California State Department of Social Welfare War Services Bureau and the Governor Earl Warren Papers, located at the California State Archives (CSA); the records of the Oregon State Public Welfare Commission and the Governor Charles A. Sprague Collection, located at the Oregon State Archives; the records of the Public Welfare and Social Security Departments and the Governor Arthur B. Langlie Collection, located at the Washington State Archives; the records of multiple social work agencies and organizations located at the University of Minnesota Social Welfare History Archives (SWHA) and the Immigration History Research Center (IHRC); the Hull House Collection and the records of the Immigrants' Protective League, at the University of Illinois, Chicago; the Grace Coyle Papers at the University Archives, Case Western Reserve University; the Japanese American Relocation Digital Archives and the Japanese American Relocation Reviewed Oral History Collection, at the University of California, Berkeley's Bancroft Library; and Densho: The Japanese American Legacy Project Digital Archives, based in Seattle, Washington.

The California State Archives

The California State Archives (CSA) in Sacramento, California holds the records of the California Department of Social Welfare (CDSW) War Services Bureau, the social work body which administered the removal process in the state of California. These extensive records, hitherto unexamined, were crucial for this study.[4] Departmental records used for this study include general correspondence, interdepartmental and intradepartmental memoranda, staff meeting notes, staff manuals, field reports of supervisors and regional supervisors, and departmental compilations of media clippings. These records detail the role of the CSDSW and that of social workers in the removal, incarceration, and resettlement of the Nikkei. The vast collection includes only a few reports from the other West Coast states; the state archives of Washington and Oregon, also examined for the purposes of the study, themselves contain very few items related to the history. The bureaucratic structure of social work's involvement in the removal and incarceration was consistent across the states. In all affected states, the county welfare departments reported to state offices, and state offices reported to the regional headquarters of the Social Security Board in San Francisco (Leahy, 1945).[5] The State Archives of Washington and Oregon yielded few records of these events, and the miscellaneous copies of correspondence and reports kept in the governors' records and a handful of other collections do not remotely parallel the massive CSDSW collection held by the CSA. The California data and their analysis offered in this article serve, thus, as a representative sample for the role of social workers throughout the coastal regions.

National Archives and Records Administration I and II

The NARA in College Park, MD hold the records of the WCCA, which administered the removal of the Nikkei from the West Coast and operated the detention centers to which they were first incarcerated. NARA offices in Washington, DC, hold the records of the WRA, the federal agency that executed the long-term incarceration and the resettlement of the Nikkei. The WRA kept extensive, if inconsistent, records and also published a series of reports through the U.S. Government Printing Office. The National Archives holdings include

---

[4] See Origel, K., & Woo-Sam, A. (2000). *The World War II Japanese American incarceration: An annotated bibliography of the materials available in the California State Archives* (pp. 1–94). Sacramento: California State Library.

[5] The Social Security Board (SSB), created in 1935 by the Social Security Act, became part of the newly created Federal Security Agency in 1939 and was renamed the Social Security Administration in 1946 (https://www.ssa.gov/history/orghist.html).

administrative files, official publications, reports and surveys, legal papers, correspondence, memoranda, press releases, photographs and scrapbooks, and much more.

Immigration History Research Center, University of Minnesota

The University of Minnesota Library includes the IHRC and the SWHA. The IHRC holdings examined for this study include the records of the International Institute of San Francisco (1922–1992), established in 1918 as an educational program for immigrant women and girls under the San Francisco YWCA, and the records of the American Council of Nationalities Services (ACNS), which include records and publications of its predecessors the Foreign Language Information Service, the Common Council for American Unity, and the American Federation of International Institutes, and the American Council for Nationalities Service. The ACNS and its predecessors were involved in all aspects of immigration and resettlement, including educational services, ethnic presses and radio, social services, and immigration legislation. Finally, the Annie Clo Watson Papers (1934–1960) collection holds the records of a social worker with long associations with the International Institutes and the YWCA.

Social Welfare History Archives, University of Minnesota

The University of Minnesota's SWHA is the major repository for the records of social work and social welfare organizations. Both the SWHA and the IHRC hold surprisingly few items related to this history. The examination of these holdings was, therefore, more of an exercise in verifying that relevant materials did not exist rather than one of discovery. The handful of organizations with records of some involvement and interest in the removal and incarceration processes include the Family Service Association of America (FSSA), the AASW, National Social Welfare Assembly (NSWA), National Refugee Service (NRS), and the Survey Associates records, the collection of the organization behind the journals *The Survey* and *Survey Midmonthly*.

Sophia Smith Collection, Smith College

One of the most informative sources for this study was the YWCA of the U.S.A. records, held in the archives of Smith College. The YWCA was the only social work organization with a significant prewar history with the Nikkei, and the records of multiple committees of the YWCA's National Board show that the organization closely monitored wartime events affecting the Nikkei. The National Public Affairs Committee worked to influence legislation and wartime policies "to guarantee the civil rights of this group" (Briesemeister, 1946, p. 53). The Race Relations Subcommittee of the National Public Affairs Committee led internal efforts to concretize the vision of the YWCA as an "organization in which differences do not divide" (Briesemeister, 1946, p. 5). Finally, the Japanese American Evacuation Project (JAEP), created on April 1, 1942, was "a special emergency piece of work" (YWCA National Board—Community Division Committee, 1942, p. 2) that recreated the Japanese branches in the WRA concentration camps. The reports of the JAEP fieldworkers, frequent and regular visitors to the ten WRA concentration camps, provide a unique perspective on social work in the camps.

Japanese-American Evacuation and Resettlement Study

Berkeley's Bancroft Library also holds material collected and/or generated by the Japanese-American Evacuation and Resettlement Study (JERS). Led by Berkeley sociologist Dorothy Swaine Thomas, JERS was one of three in situ studies of the events undertaken by social scientists.[6] JERS hired multiple, mostly Nisei, fieldworkers to gather data on the individual and institutional processes of mass incarceration. The study published three volumes of findings: *The Spoilage* (Thomas & Nishimoto, 1946/1969), *The Salvage* (Thomas, 1952), and *Prejudice, War, and the Constitution* (tenBroek, Barnhart, & Matson, 1954). Much scholarship about JERS and stemming from it has also been published. These include *Americans Betrayed: Politics and the Japanese Evacuation* (Grodzins, 1974), *Doing Fieldwork: Warnings and Advice* (Wax, 1971), *The Politics of Fieldwork: Research in an American Concentration Camp* (Hirabayashi, 1999), *The Kikuchi Diary: Chronicle from an American Concentration Camp* (Kikuchi, 1973), and *Views from Within* (Ichioka, 1989). The many problems with the study, including the multiple breaches of research ethics inherent in the use of fieldworkers who were inmates living in close proximity with the objects of their

---

[6] The Bureau of Sociological Research (BSR), established at Poston, was another study, one jointly sponsored by the Navy, the Office of Indian Affairs, and the WRA, headed by Alexander Leighton, a psychiatrist and an anthropologist who was also a Lieutenant Commander in the U.S. Naval Reserves (see Leighton, 1945). An anthropologist of the WRA's Community Analysis Section (CAS) carried out research at each of the internment camps (see Embree, 1944).

study within the concentration camps, can be found elsewhere and will not be analyzed here.[7]

Among the mountain of texts produced by JERS, including diaries and journals and staff correspondence, reports, and targeted studies, are several analyses of social work in the camps. Of particular interest to this study were the letters and diaries of Mari Okazaki and Charles Kikuchi, and Tamotsu Shibutani's series called the "Tule Lake Case Documents." Okazaki's involvement with JERS was brief, and her name is often omitted from the list of JERS field workers. The San Francisco native received a degree in education from the University of California, Berkeley, where she was an active member of the campus YWCA chapter. After graduation, she worked at the International Institute as a caseworker and assistant to Annie Clo Watson, Executive Secretary of the organization (Okazaki, 1942a) and the appointed member in charge of Nikkei issues on the CSDSW Committee on Welfare of the State Council of Defense. Watson and Okazaki kept in close contact throughout the war years. Like all other Nikkei personnel detailed to the WCCA, Okazaki was eventually sent to her incarceration site as the control stations finished emptying regions of their Nikkei population and closed down the stations. But prior to her confinement at Manzanar, Okazaki worked as "part of the social work interviewing staff" (Okazaki, 1942b, p. 16) in several WCCA stations in San Francisco, San Mateo, Fresno, Reedley, and other locations along the coast. Her letters and diaries, retained as part of the JERS holdings, provide a rare glimpse into the removal process from the perspective of a Nikkei worker.

Mari Okazaki's decision to work for JERS appears to have been influenced at least in part by the knowledge that Dorothy Thomas could sway the officials to allow the Okazaki family to be sent together to Manzanar from Tanforan, a transfer which had been refused originally. Thomas contacted the Social Security Board and the head of Manzanar on Okazaki's behest. A series of correspondence, including several telegraph messages, between Thomas and Okazaki shows that confirmation of employment with JERS was the basis upon which assignment to Manzanar for herself and her family depended (Okazaki, 1942a). Her employment was, however, short-lived. In a February 1943 letter to Thomas, Okazaki resigned, remarking: "I should not have taken the responsibility of being one of your field workers nor have submitted you to so much trouble in helping me get my family here with me." Because she was reluctant to do the job, which required living among the people while "invading their private lives and

---

[7] See, for example, Lane Ryo Hirabayashi's 1999 book, *The Politics of Fieldwork*; Ichioka's 1989 *Views from Within*; Wax's 1971 *Doing Fieldwork*; and Hansen's 1999 "The Evacuation and Resettlement Study at the Gila River Relocation Center, 1942–1944."

thoughts" (Okazaki, 1942–43, p. 66), she dreaded being seen as an "informer" (Okazaki, 1942–43, p. 68). In 1943, Okazaki left Manzanar on scholarship to attend the New York School of Philanthropy (now Columbia University School of Social Work), where she earned a master's degree in social work in 1947 (New York School of Social Work, 1947).

Charles Kikuchi (1942a) was a 26-year-old MSW student at UC Berkeley prior to his removal to Tanforan detention center, then to Gila River concentration camp. He kept detailed journals of daily life in both camps, producing 32 volumes between May 1942 and April 1943.[8] He worked in Gila River's Welfare Section throughout his imprisonment there and was, between his arrival in early September of 1942 and late November, when an experienced social worker finally arrived at Gila to take over the running of the Section, the best credentialed employee of that department (Kikuchi, 1942b). Few Nikkei had any formal training in social work prior to the war, and Kikuchi's descriptions and frequent criticisms of the WRA and its delivery of social work in the camps are particularly interesting because of his unique position as someone who did have—however limited—some knowledge of social work. Kikuchi left Gila in 1943 for resettlement in Chicago and continued to work as a JERS researcher, chronicling the resettlement process. He eventually completed his social work training, receiving a master's degree in social work from New York University (NYU) in 1947. He worked as a social worker with the Veterans Administration for the rest of his career.

Materials such as: "22. Social welfare; Social Relations Board; student relocation—Poston Relocation Center, 1942–43," credited to Tamie Tsuchiyama (1943), and the report entitled "38. Social Welfare Department, Poston Relocation Center, September 29, 1944," by Richard Nishimoto (1944), were enormously helpful in providing a sense of the workings of the camp from the perspective of Nikkei participant-observers.

Definitively the most troubling, if fascinating, of the JERS documentation on social work are Tamotsu Shibutani's Tule Lake Case Documents (1943a, 1943b, 1943c, 1943d, 1943e, 1943f, 1943g). Shibutani, incarcerated in Tanforan and Tule Lake from 1942 to 1944, obtained a PhD in sociology from the University of Chicago in 1948; his long academic career, which traversed Chicago and UC Berkeley, ended at the University of California at Santa Barbara. The eponymous case documents were, in fact, analyses of client case notes compiled by the Tule Lake Social Welfare department. Pseudonyms are used in all cases referenced in this study.

---

[8] The finding aid for the full series is available at http://pdf.oac.cdlib.org/pdf/ucla/mss/kiku1259.pdf.

Published Sources

Social work's public documents in the relevant period supplement the primary archival sources. Social work publications examined include *The Survey* (including its earlier incarnations as the *Charity Review* and *Charities*), the *Proceedings of the National Conference of Charities and Correction* (1875–1916), the *Proceedings of the National Conference of Social Work* (1916–1924), and writing by social welfare scholars of the period. Social workers did discuss their participation in events and the participation of social workers in a few articles (Ennis, 1943; Freed, 1944; Gottfried, 1944; Hoey, 1942; Lamb, 1942; Leahy, 1946; Nickel, 1942a, 1942b, 1943; Pickett, 1943; Pickett & Morris, 1943; Powell, 1943; Ross, 1944; Schafer, 1943; Webb, 1946). It is difficult to know how to account for this paucity of coverage, but Edith Abbot's editorial comments in *Social Service Review* on the California State Department of Social Welfare Biennial report hints, perhaps, at a rationale—other matters took precedence:

> This Report of the last biennium is important, not because it covers the first six months of the war, including the Japanese evacuation and other important war programs, but because it also reports on the implementing of the federal requirements regarding the merit system. (1943, p. 242)

Also useful were articles published in scientific and social scientific journals of the period and relevant secondary sources drawn from literature on immigration, historical geography, postcolonial studies, urban history, and the history of social work and social welfare. Finally, some passages and ideas from three previously published articles are replicated here with permission (Park, 2006, 2008, 2013).

References

Abbott, E. (1943). Notes and comments by the editor: Foreign relief and rehabilitation. *Social Service Review, 17*(3), 362–367.

Briesemeister, E. (1946). America's children—what happened to us?: Summary report of the Japanese Evacuee Project, January 1942–September 1946, pp. 1–54. Folder 3, Box 721. YWCA of the U.S.A. Records, Sophia Smith Collection. Northampton, MA: Smith College.

Burton, J. F., Farrell, M. M., Lord, F. B., & Lord, R. W. (2000). *Confinement and ethnicity: An overview of Japanese American Relocation sites.* Seattle: University of Washington Press.

Chickering, M. A. (1942). Letter to Richard Neustadt and Azile Aaron, April 13, 1942. Social Welfare—War Services—WCCA—Control Stations—May 1942 (F3729:139). Department of Social Welfare Records, War Services. Sacramento: California State Archives.

Commission on Wartime Relocation and Internment of Civilians. (1982). *Personal justice denied: Report of the Commission on Wartime Relocation and Internment of Civilians.* Washington, DC: U.S. Government Printing Office.

Daniels, R. (1981). *Concentration camps North America: Japanese in the United States and Canada during World War II.* Huntington, NY: R. E. Krieger.

Daniels, R., Kitano, H. H., & Taylor, S. C. (Eds.). (1986). *Japanese Americans: from relocation to redress.* Salt Lake City: University of Utah Press.

DeWitt, J. L. (1943). Letter to Richard M. Neustadt, Regional Director, Federal Security Agency, November 26, 1942. Social Welfare—War Services—WCCA—Control Stations—July 1942–January 1943 (F3729:141). Department of Social Welfare Records, War Services. Sacramento: California State Archives.

Drinnon, R. (1989). *Keeper of the concentration camps: Dillon S. Myer and American racism* (1st ed.). Middleton, CT: Wesleyan University Press.

Embree, J. F. (1944). Community analysis: An example of anthropology in government. *American Anthropologist, New Series, 46*(3), 277–291.

Ennis, E. J. (1943). Alien enemies as a wartime minority. In C. Trumble (Ed.), *Proceedings of the National Conference of Social Work: Selected papers, Seventieth Annual Meeting, War Regional Conferences, New York, St. Louis, Cleveland, 1943* (Vol. 70, pp. 290–300). New York: Columbia University Press.

Feeley, F. M. (1999). *America's concentration camps during World War II: Social science and the Japanese American internment.* New Orleans: University Press of the South.

Freed, A. O. (1944). Our racial refugees. *The Survey, 80*(4), 117–119.

Gottfried, L. V. (1944). Medical social work in the war relocation program. *The Family, 25*(3), 108–113.

Grace Longwell Coyle. (2018). *Encyclopedia of Cleveland History, 2018* (October 29). Retrieved from https://case.edu/ech/articles/c/coyle-grace-longwell.

Grodzins, M. (1974). *Americans betrayed, politics and the Japanese evacuation.* Chicago: University of Chicago Press.

Hansen, A. (1999). The Evacuation and Resettlement Study at the Gila River Relocation Center, 1942–1944. *Journal of the West, 38*(2), 45–55.

Hirabayashi, L. R. (1999). *The politics of fieldwork: Research in an American concentration camp.* Tucson: University of Arizona Press.

Hirabayashi, L. R. (2008). Enduring communities: "Concentration camp" or "relocation center"—what's in a name? Retrieved from http://www.discovernikkei.org/en/journal/2008/4/24/enduring-communities/.

Hobsbawm, E. (1994). *The age of extremes: A history of the world, 1914–1991.* New York: Vintage Books.

Hoey, J. M. (1942). Mass relocation of aliens II. In A. Dunham (Ed.), *Proceedings of the National Conference of Social Work: Selected papers, Sixty-Ninth Annual Conference, New Orleans, Louisiana, May 10–16, 1942* (Vol. 69, pp. 194–199). New York: Columbia University Press.

Ichioka, Y. (Ed.). (1989). *Views from within: The Japanese American Evacuation and Resettlement Study.* Los Angeles: Asian American Studies Center, University of California.

Japanese American Citizens League. (2013). *Power of words handbook: A guide to language about Japanese Americans in World War II: Understanding euphemisms and preferred terminology.* San Francisco, CA: Japanese American Citizens League.

Kikuchi, C. (1942a). Diary 3: July 13–31, 1942, pp. 1–218. Folder W 1.80:03**, Box BANC MSS 67/14 c. Japanese American Evacuation and Resettlement Study, Japanese

American Evacuation and Resettlement records. Berkeley: Bancroft Library, University of California.

Kikuchi, C. (1942b). Diary 9: November 16–December 1, 1942, pp. 1–147. Folder W 1.80:09**, Box BANC MSS 67/14 c. Japanese American Evacuation and Resettlement Study, Japanese American Evacuation and Resettlement records. Berkeley: Bancroft Library, University of California.

Kikuchi, C. (1973). *The Kikuchi diary: Chronicle from an American concentration camp.* John Modell (Ed). Urbana: University of Illinois Press.

Lamb, R. K. (1942). Mass relocation of aliens, I. In A. Dunham (Ed.), *Proceedings of the National Conference of Social Work: Selected papers, Sixty-Ninth Annual Conference, New Orleans, Louisiana, May 10–16, 1942* (Vol. 69, pp. 186–194). New York: Columbia University Press.

Leahy, M. (1945). Public assistance for restricted persons during the Second World War. *Social Service Review, 19*(1), 24–47.

Leahy, M. (1946). Public assistance for restricted persons during the Second World War. *Social Service Review, 19*(1), 24–47.

Leiby, J. (1962). How social workers viewed "The Immigration Problem." *Current issues in social work seen in historical perspective: Compilation of six papers presented at a workshop held during Annual Program Meeting, St. Louis, Mo., January 17–20, 1962* (pp. 30–42). New York: Council on Social Work Education.

Leighton, A. H. (1945). *The governing of men: General principles and recommendations based on experience at a Japanese relocation camp.* Princeton, NJ: Princeton University Press.

National Association of Social Workers. (2004). NASW Social Work Pioneers. Retrieved from http://www.naswfoundation.org/pioneers/.

New York School of Social Work. (1947). *Bulletin of the New York School of Social Work, Columbia University: Report for the year October 1, 1946–September 30, 1947* (Vol. 16). New York: Community Service Society of the City of New York.

Nickel, G. D. (1942a). Evacuation, American style. *The Survey, 78*(4), 99–103.

Nickel, G. D. (1942b). Evacuation: American style, part II. *The Survey, 58*(10), 262–265.

Nickel, G. D. (1943). In the relocation centers. *The Survey, 79*(1), 3–7.

Nishimoto, R. S. (1944). 38. Social Welfare Department, Poston Relocation Center, September 29, 1944, pp. 1–130, Box BANC MSS 67/14 c. Japanese American Evacuation and Resettlement Study, Japanese American Evacuation and Resettlement records. Berkeley: Bancroft Library, University of California.

Nishimoto, R. S., & Hirabayashi, L. R. (1995). *Inside an American concentration camp: Japanese American resistance at Poston, Arizona.* Tucson: University of Arizona Press.

Okazaki, M. (1942a). Okazaki, Mari, correspondence, pp. 1–17. Folder B12.44, Box BANC MSS 67/14 c. Japanese American Evacuation and Resettlement Study, Japanese American Evacuation and Resettlement records. Berkeley: Bancroft Library, University of California.

Okazaki, M. (1942b). Okazaki, Mari, diary excerpts, notes and correspondence, part 1, pp. 1–113. Folder O10.05 (1/2), Box BANC MSS 67/14 c. Japanese American Evacuation and Resettlement Study, Japanese American Evacuation and Resettlement records. Berkeley: Bancroft Library, University of California.

Okazaki, M. (1942–43). Okazaki, Mari, correspondence (see also: B 12.44), pp. 1–68. Folder W 1.30, Box BANC MSS 67/14 c. Japanese American Evacuation and

Resettlement Study, Japanese American Evacuation and Resettlement records. Berkeley: Bancroft Library, University of California.

Park, Y. (2006). Constructing immigrants: A historical discourse analysis of the representations of immigrants in U.S. social work, 1882–1952. *Journal of Social Work*, *6*(2), 169–203. doi: https://doi.org/10.1177/1468017306066673.

Park, Y. (2008). Facilitating injustice: Tracing the role of social workers in the World War II internment of Japanese Americans. *Social Service Review*, *82*(3), 447–483. doi: 10.1086/59236.

Park, Y. (2013). The role of the YWCA in the World War II internment of Japanese Americans: A cautionary tale for social work. *Social Service Review*, *87*(3), 477–524.

Pickett, C. E. (1943). Resettlement of Americans of Japanese Ancestry. In C. Trumble (Ed.), *Proceedings of the National Conference of Social Work: Selected papers, Seventieth Annual Meeting, War Regional Conferences, New York, St. Louis, Cleveland, 1943* (Vol. 70). New York: Columbia University Press.

Pickett, C. E., & Morris, H. L. (1943). From barbed wire to communities. *The Survey*, *79*(8), 210–213.

Powell, J. W. (1943). America's refugees: Exodus and diaspora. In C. Trumble (Ed.), *Proceedings of the National Conference of Social Work: Selected papers, Seventieth Annual Meeting, War Regional Conferences, New York, St. Louis, Cleveland, 1943* (Vol. 70, pp. 301–309). New York: Columbia University Press.

Ross, P. (1944). The War Relocation Authority's program of resettlement of the Japanese. *Compass*, *25*(2), 33–38.

Schafer, P. (1943). A War Relocation Authority community. *Compass*, *25*(1), 16–19.

Shibutani, T. (1943a). Case documents TL-1-6, 8 by family name [indicates pseudonym]— Family organization and disorganization (compiled documents), pp. 1–81. Folder R 21.08:1**, Box BANC MSS 67/14 c. Japanese American Evacuation and Resettlement Study, Japanese American Evacuation and Resettlement records. Berkeley: Bancroft Library, University of California.

Shibutani, T. (1943b). Case documents TL-10, 12-16 by family name [indicates pseudonym]—Family organization and disorganization (compiled documents), pp. 1–79. Folder R 21.08:1**, Box BANC MSS 67/14 c. Japanese American Evacuation and Resettlement Study, Japanese American Evacuation and Resettlement records. Berkeley: Bancroft Library, University of California.

Shibutani, T. (1943c). Case documents TL-17-26 by family name [indicates pseudonym]—Family organization and disorganization (compiled documents), pp. 1–91. Folder R 21.08:4**, Box BANC MSS 67/14 c. Japanese American Evacuation and Resettlement Study, Japanese American Evacuation and Resettlement records. Berkeley: Bancroft Library, University of California.

Shibutani, T. (1943d). Case documents TL-27-30, 32-34 by family name [indicates pseudonym]—Family organization and disorganization (compiled documents), pp. 1–102. Folder R 21.08:5**, Box BANC MSS 67/14 c. Japanese American Evacuation and Resettlement Study, Japanese American Evacuation and Resettlement records. Berkeley: Bancroft Library, University of California.

Shibutani, T. (1943e). Case documents TL-35-38, 40-42, 44-45 by family name [indicates pseudonym]—Family organization and disorganization (compiled documents), pp. 1–86. Folder R 21.08:6**, Box BANC MSS 67/14 c. Japanese American Evacuation and Resettlement Study, Japanese American Evacuation and Resettlement records. Berkeley: Bancroft Library, University of California.

Shibutani, T. (1943f). Case documents TL-53-58, 61-69 by family name [indicates pseu-
donym]—Family organization and disorganization (compiled documents), pp.
1–109. Folder R 21.08:7**, Box BANC MSS 67/14 c. Japanese American Evacuation
and Resettlement Study, Japanese American Evacuation and Resettlement records.
Berkeley: Bancroft Library, University of California.

Shibutani, T. (1943g). Case documents TL-71-72, 101-106, 109-110, 112 by family
name [indicates pseudonym]—Family organization and disorganization (compiled
documents), pp. 1–76. Folder R 21.08:8**, Box BANC MSS 67/14 c. Japanese American
Evacuation and Resettlement Study, Japanese American Evacuation and Resettlement
records. Berkeley: Bancroft Library, University of California.

Sundquist, P. (1942). Report of Perry Sundquist, Public Assistance Supervisor, on oper-
ation of Lodi Control Station (333 No. Washington St., Lodi, Calif.), May 14, 1942 to
May 21, 1942. Social Welfare – War Services – WCCA – Reports – Control Stations –
Lawndale – Riverside – 1942 (F3729:148). Department of Social Welfare Records, War
Services. Sacramento: California State Archives.

tenBroek, J., Barnhart, E. N., & Matson, F. (1954). *Prejudice, war and the Constitution.*
Berkeley: University of California Press.

Thomas, D. S. (1952). *The salvage.* Berkeley: University of California Press.

Thomas, D. S., & Nishimoto, R. S. (1946/1969). *The spoilage: Japanese-American
evacuation and resettlement during World War II.* Berkeley: University of California
Press.

Tsuchiyama, T. (1943). 22. Social welfare; Social Relations Board; student relocation—
Poston Relocation Center, 1942–43 (compiled documents), pp. 1–51. Folder J6.27 (22/
27), Box BANC MSS 67/14 c. Japanese American Evacuation and Resettlement Study,
Japanese American Evacuation and Resettlement records. Berkeley: Bancroft Library,
University of California.

United States Civil Service Commission. (1942a). United States Civil Service Commission
Classification Sheet: Assistant Counselor (P-2-180), War Relocation Authority, Office
for Emergency Management, dated December 31, 1942, pp. 1–2; folder Welfare Section;
Box 2, Records of the War Relocation Authority, 1941–1989, Record Group 210, Job
Descriptions—compiled 1942–1946. ARC Identifier 1543527/MLR Number PI-77 36.
Washington, DC: National Archives and Records Administration.

United States Civil Service Commission. (1942b). United States Civil Service Commission
Classification Sheet: Associate Counselor (P-3-180), War Relocation Authority, Office
for Emergency Management, dated December 31, 1942, pp. 1–2; folder, Welfare Section;
Box 2, Records of the War Relocation Authority, 1941–1989, Record Group 210, Job
Descriptions—compiled 1942–1946. ARC Identifier 1543527/MLR Number PI-77 36.
Washington, DC: National Archives and Records Administration.

United States Civil Service Commission. (1942c). United States Civil Service Commission
Classification Sheet: Public Welfare Consultant (P-6), War Relocation Authority, Office
for Emergency Management, dated August 11, 1942, pp. 1–2; folder, Welfare Section;
Box 2, Records of the War Relocation Authority, 1941–1989, Record Group 210, Job
Descriptions—compiled 1942–1946. ARC Identifier 1543527/MLR Number PI-77 36.
Washington, DC: National Archives and Records Administration.

United   States   Congress—House   Select   Committee   Investigating   National
Defense Migration. (1942a). *National Defense Migration. Part 29, San Francisco
Hearings: Problems of Evacuation of Enemy Aliens and Others from Prohibited
Military Zones [microform]: Hearings before the United States House Select Committee*

Investigating National Defense Migration, Seventy-Seventh Congress, second session, on Feb. 21, 23, 1942. Washington, DC: U.S. Government Printing Office.

United States Congress—House Select Committee Investigating National Defense Migration. (1942b). *National Defense Migration. Part 30, Portland and Seattle Hearings: Problems of Evacuation of Enemy Aliens and Others from Prohibited Military Zones [microform]: Hearings before the United States House Select Committee Investigating National Defense Migration, Seventy-Seventh Congress, second session, on Feb. 26, 28, Mar. 2, 1942*. Washington, DC: U.S. Government Printing Office.

United States Congress—House Select Committee Investigating National Defense Migration. (1942c). *National Defense Migration. Part 31, Los Angeles and San Francisco Hearings: Problems of Evacuation of Enemy Aliens and Others from Prohibited Military Zones [microform]: Hearings before the United States House Select Committee Investigating National Defense Migration, Seventy-Seventh Congress, second session, on Mar. 6, 7, 12, 1942* (ed.). Washington, DC: U.S. Government Printing Office.

University of Minnesota Immigration History Research Center. (2004). Annie Clo Watson Papers, 1934–1960. Retrieved from http://www.ihrc.umn.edu/research/vitrage/all/wa/GENwatson.htm-bio.

University of Southern California School of Social Work. (2005–2006). California Social Work Hall of Distinction. Retrieved from http://socialworkhallofdistinction.org/honorees/item.php?id=26.

War Relocation Authority. (1942). Background for the relocation program: Prepared for information of the staff of the War Relocation Authority. Utah State University Digital Library. Retrieved from http://digital.lib.usu.edu/u?/Topaz,5290.

War Relocation Authority. (1942a). Job description: Head Counselor (CAF- 11), dated November 4, 1942, pp. 1–2; folder, Welfare Section; Box 2, Records of the War Relocation Authority, 1941–1989, Record Group 210, Job Descriptions—compiled 1942–1946. ARC Identifier 1543527/MLR Number PI-77 36. Washington, DC: National Archives and Records Administration.

War Relocation Authority. (1942b). Job description: Senior Counselor (CAF- 9), p. 1; folder, Welfare Section; Box 2, Records of the War Relocation Authority, 1941–1989, Record Group 210, Job Descriptions—compiled 1942–1946. ARC Identifier 1543527/MLR Number PI-77 36. Washington, DC: National Archives and Records Administration.

War Relocation Authority. (1944a). Standard position description: Counselor (P-4-180), pp. 1–3; folder, Welfare Section; Box 2, Records of the War Relocation Authority, 1941–1989, Record Group 210, Job Descriptions—compiled 1942–1946. ARC Identifier 1543527/MLR Number PI-77 36. Washington, DC: National Archives and Records Administration.

War Relocation Authority. (1944b). Standard position description: Counselor (P-4), p. 2; folder, Welfare Section; Box 2, Records of the War Relocation Authority, 1941–1989, Record Group 210, Job Descriptions—compiled 1942–1946. ARC Identifier 1543527/MLR Number PI-77 36. Washington, DC: National Archives and Records Administration.

War Relocation Authority. (1944c). Standard position description: Junior Counselor (P-2), Date Allocated: 10-1-44, p. 2; folder, Welfare Section; Box 2, Records of the War Relocation Authority, 1941–1989, Record Group 210, Job Descriptions—compiled 1942–1946. ARC Identifier 1543527/MLR Number PI-77 36. Washington, DC: National Archives and Records Administration.

War Relocation Authority. (1946). *The relocation program*. Washington, DC: U.S. Government Printing Office.

Wax, R. H. (1971). *Doing fieldwork: Warnings and advice*. Chicago: University of Chicago Press.

Webb, J. L. (1946). The welfare program of the relocation centers. *Social Service Review, 19*(1), 71–86.

Weglyn, M. (1976). *Years of infamy: The untold story of America's concentration camps*. New York: Morrow.

YWCA National Board—Community Division Committee (1942). Minutes of the Community Division Committee Meeting, Tuesday, March 3, 1942, pp. 1–2. Folder 20, Box 719. YWCA of the U.S.A. Records, Sophia Smith Collection. Northampton, MA: Smith College.

1

Discursive Elusions

There are the usual proposals to exclude Asiatic laborers.
—Common welfare: The illiteracy test again before Congress
(1916, p. 651)

The "vexed problem of immigration," as Jane Addams (1909, p. 214) termed it, was a central issue for the emerging social work profession in the late 19th and early 20th centuries. Work with immigrants, who constituted the poorest subsections of the growing urban population and occupied the worst spaces in the burgeoning city landscapes, shaped the nature and the direction of social work in the crucial early years of the profession. From the home visits of the charity organization caseworkers to the neighborhood activism, social research, and public advocacy of the settlement houses, nascent social work interventions, "modern programs for organized and scientific philanthropy," had their origin largely in the "effort to cure the[se] spreading social sores" (Schlesinger, 1921, p. 83) presented by the great tide of immigrants flooding into American cities. The bulk of social work in its growing years, in other words, was work with poor immigrants who congregated in urban slums.

Social work's attention, however, did not extend to Asian immigrants. If European immigration and various aspects of work with those immigrants was a major preoccupation of social workers in the early years of the profession, then the topic of Asian immigration and the issues of Asian immigrants cannot be characterized as anything other than sites of neglect. This neglect is perhaps best exemplified by what is missing from Edith Abbott's two massive tomes on the topic of immigration edited for the University of Chicago Social Service Series: neither the 801-page *Immigration: Select Documents and Case Records* (1924) nor the 862-page *Historical Aspects of Immigration: Select Documents* (1926) devoted a single page to the topic of Asian immigration. The resounding lack of interest in the affairs of Asian immigrants was also evident during the Great Depression years, when volumes were written on the naturalization woes of European immigrants facing the discriminatory practices against noncitizens in the labor market and in federal relief programs. The fact that all Asian immigrants had long been adjudged as a population racially unsuitable for full participation in U.S. society and that this racial exclusion from naturalization

Facilitating Injustice: The complicity of social workers in the forced removal and incarceration of Japanese Americans, 1941–1946. Yoosun Park, Oxford University Press (2020). © Oxford University Press.
DOI: 10.1093/acprof:oso/9780199765058.001.0001

put the United States in the sole company of Nazi Germany, the only other regime in the period to single out race as a measure for the wholesale disenfran-
chisement of populations (Konvitz, 1946), did not appear to have been taken by
social workers as a topic worthy of attention.

In the few occasions in which Asian immigrants did appear in the discourse
of social work, they did so as the archetype of the undesirable alien. They were
useful as counterexamples that underscored some factor of immigrant undesirability as in the following quote from a Federal Commissioner of Immigration
speaking at the annual National Conference of Social Welfare[1]:

> If the immediate development of all material resources were the chief end in
> view, regardless of political or social effects, then the introduction of low-grade
> people, merely because they are cheap laborers, could perhaps be justified, but
> in that event we should admit also the Chinese, who are amongst the most effi-
> cient in the world. (Williams, 1906, p. 289)[2]

The specter of the Oriental could also aid in illustrating the shortcomings of a
different Other:

> Those who from the immigration offices behold the masses of men, brown-
> colored, circumspect, silently awaiting their turn with that air of indifference
> which reminds us of the oriental peoples. (Alvarado, 1920, p. 479)

Presaging the locus of virulent anti-Japanese agitation to come in World War
II, the most venomous attacks hailed from the West Coast, where the comparatively larger numbers of Asian immigrants incited a hostility of far greater urgency and magnitude than in the rest of the nation. The West, as immigration
commissioner William Gates declared at two separate National Conference of
Social Welfare, knew the dangers of the Orientals:

> How many of you know how the Chinaman lives. We are opposed not to the
> Chinese merchant, the Chinese student, but to the Chinese coolie. These men
> come from a country where living is very low. They come in here, and live in
> hovels. I could take you to districts where these people live, and you would be

---

[1] The conference, which began in 1874 as the Conference of the Boards of Public Charities, had
multiple name changes: Conference of Charities (1875–1879), Annual Conference of Charities
and Corrections (1880–1916), the National Conference of Social Work (1917–1956), National
Conference of Social Welfare (1957–1983). To avoid confusion, the conference will be referred to by
its final title, the National Conference of Social Welfare, no matter the year in which the particular
meeting occurred.
[2] From 1902–1905 and 1909–1914, Williams was the federal commissioner of immigration for the
Port of New York, overseeing immigration from his office on Ellis Island.

surprised at the filth and dirt and the cheap methods in which they live. They have no families. They live as single men. They come here and live in a condition by which they can cut wages down to the very lowest and crowd down wages so low that the ordinary white man cannot live. We do not want these conditions on the Pacific Coast. The Chinese coolie and the Japanese coolie bring a condition of things that is much lower than any immigrant which you are getting up on the Atlantic Coast. (Gates, 1905, p. 567)

The moral standards of the Oriental immigrants are low. They have no families. According to the census of 1900, one out of eighteen of the Chinese in this country, and one out of twenty-four of Japanese, are female. Of these women but few are virtuous, most are prostitutes, and some are slaves bought and sold as chattel in this country. The Oriental has planted here the opium habit, now sapping the manhood of the lower strata of the white race. Can the white man build a home, care for wife and weans, perform the duties of an American citizen, and compete for his daily bread with this wifeless, childless, yellow man? (Gates, 1909, p. 231)

That the forced removal and incarceration of the Nikkei in World War II was an actualization of the decades-long history of precisely this kind of racist fear-mongering is difficult to refute. What is unique about Asian immigrants in the early history of social work is that no concerted defense of any kind was ever attempted on their behalf. As the celebrated history of social settlements such as Chicago's Hull House attest, however vilified and feared the latest group of European immigrants of any given period may have been, there was always a progressive wing of social work that mobilized to protect and defend their rights and interests. Anti-Asian racism never provoked such a response in social work. The profession's lackluster response to the plight of the Nikkei during World War II must be placed within this context of a long history of professional apathy; the professional apathy itself must be understood in the context of the nation's long history of Anti-Asian immigration and citizenship laws.

Immigration Exclusion

In 1880, the 7th Annual Conference of Social Welfare established a standing committee on immigration. The first report of the committee, delivered in the following year by Dr. Charles S. Hoyt (1881), secretary of the committee and the New York State Board of Charities, was a clear enumeration of the several issues that would preoccupy the committee and the larger body of social work for years to come.

The Committee, at this meeting, reached the conclusion that, owing to the large number of immigrants now arriving in this country, urgent necessity existed for Federal action to regulate immigration, supervise and protect immigrants, and to guard against the shipment to this country of criminals, and of lunatic, idiotic, crippled, and other infirm alien paupers. (p. 217)

Beginning with this meeting in Boston and continuing well into the next century, the discussion of immigration and immigrants in social work became almost entirely focused on the above-mentioned "classes" of people and the urgent need to exclude them from coming into the country and becoming dependents of the state.

We gladly admit the reputable poor, but the paupers, the vicious, the vagabond, we don't want here at all. We have too many of them now. Go through our poorhouses, jails, hospitals, and insane asylums, and you will find the majority of the paupers there are immigrants, foreigners, many of whom have recently come to this country. (Committee on Immigration, 1881, p. 219)

The fear distilled into law in the following year was the 1882 Act to Regulate Immigration (22 Stat. 214), a reaction to recent increases in the entry of southern and eastern Europeans (i.e., Slavs, Poles, and Russians), deemed less desirable than their northern and western counterparts, and a response to the clamoring of port-of-entry states and local authorities who objected to the costs of caring for indigent, poor, and sick immigrants arriving on their shores.

The year 1882, a peak for Chinese immigration with 39,579 entries, also saw the passage of the Chinese Exclusion Act of May 6, 1882 (22 Statutes-at-Large 58), the first U.S. immigration law to tie eligibility for entry to race or national origin. The ferocity of anti-Chinese sentiment, encapsulated in a series of exclusions laws, was exceptional even in the context of the long story of xenophobia that is the history of U.S. immigration.

Anti-Chinese agitation is unique in the history American nativism for the consistency of its violence, for its success in capturing the major workers' organizations as well as both national political parties, and, ultimately, for its success in winning legislation that singled out one national group for total exclusion. (Jacobson, 2000, p. 81)

The 1882 Exclusion Act, which imposed a ten-year suspension of the entry of Chinese laborers into the United States, with specific exemptions, became reformulated over the next four decades into a total exclusion of all Asian immigration. The "Geary Act" of May 5, 1892, the Act to Prohibit the Coming of Chinese Persons into the United States (ch. 60, 27 Stat. 25), again extended the exclusion measures and attached an additional provision requiring all Chinese in the United States to carry certificates of residence to be obtained within one year of the passage of the Act. Those in violation of the requirement to carry the certificates at all times were liable for deportation, imprisonment, and heavy fines. The Act of April 29, 1902 (c. 641, 32 Stat. 176) extended the existing Chinese exclusion acts for an indefinite amount of time and extended the exclusion to insular territories of the United States, such as Hawaii, "Porto Rico," and the Philippines, which had hitherto been open to Chinese immigration. Though not an immigration law, the Gentleman's Agreement, a series of treaties made between the United States and Japan across 1907–1908, restricted—not excluded—Japanese entry into the United States in return for the guarantee of better treatment for Japanese already in the United States. Japan pledged not to issue new passports for travel to the continental United States, though entry to Hawaii as agricultural workers remained an option.[3]

The "Asiatic Barred Zone Act," the Immigration Act of February 5, 1917 (H.R. 10384; Pub.L. 301; 39 Stat. 874), expanded the exclusions hitherto restricted to the Chinese to all Asians. Immigration from the newly created "Asia-Pacific triangle" was banned, with the exception of the few Japanese exempted from this exclusion by the provisions of the Gentlemen's Agreement and natives of the Philippines excepted because of its status as a U.S. protectorate. The Immigration Act of May 26, 1924 (Pub.L. 68–139, 43 Stat. 153), known also as the Johnson-Reed Act of 1924, eliminated all such exceptions with an explicit ban on the immigration of all aliens ineligible for naturalization. The wholesale exclusion of Asian immigration was rescinded gradually. On December 17, 1943, on the eve of World War II, the racial ban against the Chinese was lifted and a trifling quota of 100 persons per year was allotted to China. Similar quotas for other Asian nations was established after the war through the Immigration and Nationality Act of 1952 (Pub.L. 82–414, 66 Stat. 163),[4] but large-scale Asian immigration would not be permitted until the passage of the 1965 Immigration and Naturalization Act, which removed all national origins quota restrictions and established a seven-category preference system.

---

[3] Wives and family members of those already in the states were exempted from the restriction so that a few Japanese did enter the country from this time until 1924, when all immigration from Asia was barred.

[4] Also known as the McCarran–Walter Act.

The Citizenship Bar

Speaking at the 56th Conference of Social Welfare in 1929, Constantine Panunzio, sociologist and director of San Diego's Neighborhood House and Sociological Laboratory, insisted that the United States had been "generous" in "granting citizenship to the foreign born" (1929, p. 567). This history, marked by a "liberality of attitude and practice prevailed nearly throughout the century" (1929, p. 567), he averred, was absolutely nonracist.

> The phrase "free white persons" in practice applied to status rather than to color or race. This is proved by the facts that Negroes were admitted to citizenship as soon as they were freed from slavery; that citizenship was conferred upon the whole body of inhabitants of territories as they were annexed, regardless of race or color (except in the case of the uncivilized tribes of Alaska—also status); that the citizens of the former Hawaiian republic were made American citizens, as were also the Porto Ricans, many of whom were colored; while partial citizenship was conferred upon the Filipinos. The Chinese were also admitted. (Panunzio, 1929, p. 567)[5]

His transparent distortions notwithstanding, the generosity of the United States in granting citizenship—"generally understood to connote 'full membership' in a state" (Aleinikoff & Klusmeyer, 2001, p. 1)—especially for Asians, was anything but liberal.

There were and are several ways to become a citizen of the United States, including by birth on U.S. soil, through parentage, by individual naturalization, by collective naturalization through treaty, and by collective naturalization through territorial accession into statehood. The right of *jus soli* citizenship for native-born persons of Chinese parentage was not established until the 1898 *United States v. Wong Kim Ark* (169 U.S. 649). The case established citizenship by the fact of birth on U.S. soil for a US-born child of Chinese parents legally residing in the United States as permanent residents at the time of the child's birth.[6] Wong Kim Ark, a native-born person of Chinese parents, left the country for a visit to

---

[5] In the case of Alaska, citizenship was granted to all territorial citizens in 1867. But an exception, not remedied until 1915, was made against territorial citizenship for "uncivilized native tribes" (Van Dyne, 1904, p. 159).

[6] The *Wong Kim Ark* decision also clarified the court's stance on the citizenship of native-born American Indians who, as members of sovereign tribal nations, were not considered citizens of the United States. "As stated in the Wong Kim Ark decision, tribal Indians were excluded from the phrase 'subject to the jurisdiction thereof,' and hence did not acquire United States citizenship jure soli" (Gettys, 1934, p. 21). As absurd as it may sound in retrospect, American Indian tribal members gained the right to US citizenship only through the Act of June 2, 1924. Gettys (1934) quoted Justice Gray again: "The members of these tribes owe immediate allegiance to their several tribes, and were not part of the people of the United States" (p. 22).

China and was denied entry into the United States. upon his return. His case was pursued to the Supreme Court, and, in 1898, Justice Gray delivered the opinion of the court.

> The Fourteenth Amendment affirms the ancient and fundamental rule of citizenship by birth within the territory, in the allegiance and under the protection of the country, including all children born of resident aliens, with the exception or qualifications (as old as the rule itself) of children of foreign sovereigns or their ministers, or born on foreign public ships, or of enemies within and during a hostile occupation of part of our territory, and with the single additional exception of children of members of Indian tribes owing directly allegiance to their several tribes. The Amendment in clear words and in manifest intent, includes the children born, within the territory of the United States of all other persons, of whatever race or color, domiciled with in the United States. (Gettys, 1934, p. 18)

This rare decision made in favor of an Asiatic claimant was not unanimous. The dissent, led by Chief Justice Fuller, opined in essence that the Fourteenth Amendment did not "arbitrarily make citizens of children born in the United States of parents who, according to the law, are and must remain aliens because of their ineligibility" (Konvitz, 1946, p. 109).

This ineligibility, the denial of the right to become a naturalized citizen of the United States, was a linchpin device for both the territorial exclusion of Asian immigrants and their civic and political exclusion from U.S. society.[7] Prior to the 1868 adoption of the Fourteenth Amendment, which declared "all persons born or naturalized in the United States, and subject to the jurisdiction thereof, are citizens of the United States and of the state wherein they reside," the U.S. constitution was "silent as to the meaning of the word citizen, either by way of inclusion or exclusion" (Kansas, 1948, p. 275). The Act of March 26, 1790 (1 Stat. 103), which restricted the right of naturalization to only "free white persons," was the main legal statute defining the parameters of eligibility. It took the Civil War and the Naturalization Act of July 14, 1870 (ch. 254, 16 Stat. 254) to extend naturalization rights to "aliens of African nativity and to persons of African descent"

---

[7] There are many good sources for the history of legal discrimination against Asians. See for example, *Documental History of Law Cases Affecting Japanese in the United States 1916–1924: Japanese Land Cases* (Vol. 2) (The Consulate-General of Japan, 1925b), *Documental History of Law Cases Affecting Japanese in the United States 1916–1924: Naturalization Cases and Cases Affecting Constitutional and Treaty Rights* (Vol. 1) (The Consulate-General of Japan, 1925a), *Oriental Exclusion* (McKenzie, 1927), *Orientals in American Life* (Palmer, 1934), *The Alien and the Asiatic in American Law* (Konvitz, 1946), and *A Legal History of Asian Americans, 1790–1990* (Kim, 1994).

(Van Dyne, 1904, p. 56). Naturalization rights for Asian immigrants were not granted in American law for many years hence.

The 1790 Act did not define "white persons"; no uniform standard of practice governed its interpretation. That the logic of contemporary discourses of race, racial boundaries, and racial definitions were not evident, seamless, and fully accomplished truths but projects in constant flux, in need of readjustment, modification, and realignment, is demonstrated by the fact that decisions and opinions among the lower courts, between lower courts and the higher, among justices in the highest, and within congress and between congressional sessions were often inconsistent and contradictory (Jacobson, 1998; Lopez, 1995). Prior to formal annexation, Hawaiian natives were declared aliens ineligible for naturalization in lower courts,[8] but they were later collectively naturalized by territorial accession. Many Japanese and Indian immigrants were naturalized prior to the 1882 congressional ban on Chinese naturalization specified by the Exclusion Act and two crucial Supreme Court decisions made in the 1920s; the 1910 census, for example, counted more than 400 naturalized Japanese in the United States (Gettys, 1934; Ichioka, 1988).[9]

The 1922 Supreme Court case of Seiji Ozawa (*Ozawa v. United States* 260 U.S. 178), was instrumental in clarifying that the legal definition of "white persons" did not include Japanese immigrants. Mr. Ozawa, a 20-year resident of Hawaii and educated in California, argued that the phrase should be interpreted to mean a person who is assimilable to U.S. society. Mr. Ozawa petitioned for naturalization on the argument that the phrase "free white persons" connoted assimilability rather than racial categorization, and that, as such, he was eligible under the law. The Supreme Court disagreed, insisting that to be "white," one must be "Caucasian." In the words of Justice Sutherland,

> The determination that the words "white persons" are synonymous with the words "a person of the Caucasian race" simplifies the problem, although it does not entirely dispose of it. Controversies have arisen and will do doubt arise again in respect to the proper classification of individuals in border-line cases. The effect of the conclusion that the words "white person" mean a "Caucasian" is not to establish a sharp line of demarcation between those who are entitled and those who are not entitled to naturalization, but rather a zone of more or less debatable ground outside of which, upon the one hand, are those clearly eligible, and outside of which, upon the other hand, are those clearly ineligible

---

[8] On the naturalization of Hawaiians prior to annexation, see *In re kanaka Nian*, 21 Pac.993 (1889).

[9] Chinese petition for naturalization had, however, been denied even before the Exclusion Act of 1882. See *In re Ah Yup*, 5 Sawyer 155 (1878); *In re Gee Hop*, 71 Fed. 274 (1895).

for citizenship. Individual cases falling within this zone must be determined as they arise from time to time by what this Court has called in another connection . . . the gradual process of judicial inclusion and exclusion. The appellant in the case now under consideration, however, is clearly of a race which is not Caucasian, and therefore belongs entirely outside the zone on the negative side. (cited in Gettys, 1934, p. 64)

Barely three months later, however, in the case of *U.S. v. Bhagat Singh Thind* (261 U.S. 204, 213 [1923]), which tested the eligibility of "a high caste Hindu of full Indian blood," the same Justices would shift this earlier opinion that Caucasianness was the indicator of whiteness. Mr. Thind had argued that as an individual whose linguistic and racial roots were, by the agreement of contemporary ethnologists, of Aryan descent tracing their origin back to the regions of Mt. Caucasus, he was indeed Caucasian and therefore included in the eligibility criterion reserved for "white persons." Marian Schisby (1927), of New York's Foreign Language Information Service, explained at the 54th National Conference of Social Welfare that Asian Indians had "protested vigorously against the decision" made against Asian claimants for naturalization.

They contend that Hindus are Aryan and of the Caucasian race, and that a high caste Hindu is, because of the caste system, probably of purer race than are many European peoples to whom American citizenship is granted without question. (p. 580)

The same justices who had adjudicated the Ozawa decision decreed this time that although Indians may in fact be descendants of Caucasian ancestors, they were not "white" in the common and generally known usage of the term. "White" did not equate with "Caucasian" but rather with that which was commonly held to be "white" by the average man on the street, and, since the common parlance did not extend whiteness to "Hindus," they were not eligible for naturalization. Mr. Justice Sutherland again:

The words of familiar speech, which were used by the original framers of the law, were intended to include only the type of man which they knew as white. . . . What, if any, people of primarily Asiatic stock, come within the words of the section, we do not deem it necessary now to decide. There is much in the origin and historic development of the statue to suggest that no Asiatic whatever was included. . . . What we now hold is that the words "free white persons" are words of common speech, to be interpreted in accordance with the understanding of the common man, synonymous with the word "Caucasian" only as that word is popularly understood. As so understood and used, whatever may be the speculations of the ethnologist, it does not include the body of people to whom the appellee belongs. (cited in Gettys, 1934, p. 65)

The Ozawa and Thind decisions resulted in a series of cancellation of naturalization certificates previously granted or upheld through lower court decisions. In repeatedly ruling to deny Asians access to naturalization, moreover, the courts consolidated as juridical truths the powerful discourses of Asian racial inferiority, cultural undesirability, and lack of fitness for inclusion in U.S. society. In doing so, perhaps more importantly, the courts time after time reinforced as established truths the construct of race and racial hierarchy as logical and legitimate taxonomies; the challenge repeatedly made and adjudicated was whether Asians could be included as an acceptable race, *not* whether race was a valid criterion for inclusion.[10]

The Supreme Court never overturned the 1790 law or made interpretations of the "free white" bar in favor of Asians; the right of Asians to become naturalized citizens was ultimately obtained, piecemeal, through Congressional measures enacted well into the 20th century. It was not until 1943, on the eve of World War II and in light of the growing reach of Japanese imperialism in Asia, that Chinese immigrants were finally granted the rights of naturalization. As Adena Rich (1947), the head of Chicago's Immigrants' Protective League, explained,

> It was primarily the war and the need of united fronts in the Pacific that finally impelled action in the Congress with respect to naturalization for persons not "free white or of African nativity or descent." (p. 92)

But the newly granted naturalization rights did not guarantee equal treatment under the law.

> The 1943 amendment extended to Chinese eligibility to United States citizenship and authorized an immigration quota. It did not, however, establish for them the same nonquota and preference-quota categories in relation to United

---

[10] Discourses of racial heredity and blood quantum calculations played out with predictable results in the adjudication of naturalization rights of the offspring of mixed-race unions.

The right to become naturalized depends upon parentage and blood, not upon nationality and status. "Free white persons" includes members of the white Caucasian race as distinct from the blood, red, yellow and brown races. [In re Fisher, 21 F. (2d) 1007.] A person, one-half white and one-half of some other race, belongs to neither of these races, but is literally a half-breed and not a "free white person" under the statute and not eligible to naturalization (In re Knight, 171 F. 299). The son of a full blooded German father and a Japanese mother is not a "white person." It cannot be said that one who is half white and half brown or yellow is a white person as commonly understood. (*In re Knight*, 171 Fed. 299 (1909); cited in Kansas, 1948, p. 285)

States citizenship that were provided for members of the families of other nationalities. (Rich, 1947, p. 92)

Filipinos and Asian Indians were granted naturalization rights in 1946, through the Luce-Celler Act (H. R. 3517; Public Law 483), but, as in the case of the Chinese, it was without the standard nonquota or preference-quota immigration status extended to husbands, wives, parents, and children of European immigrants.

The 1946 Act was also noteworthy for the fact that it made explicit how racial belonging was calculated: "persons who possess either singly or in combination, a preponderance of blood of one or more of the classes specified" or "as much as one-half blood of those classes and some additional blood of one of the classes specified" (Rich, 1947, p. 93). Adena Rich's 1947 characterization of the blood quantum language of the Act as "disquietingly reminiscent of the German pre-war policy of measuring by one-fourth or one-eight or one-sixteenth the blood of those nationals marked for stigma or destruction" (p. 93) is significant for what it occludes: that the United States itself used, during the war years, a blood quantum calculus to determine which mixed-heritage persons of Japanese ancestry would be incarcerated—how much Japanese blood rendered an individual un-American (Spickard, 1989; United States Army, 1943). Although the Army later loosened its policies on the exemptions, at the beginning of the removal process, the only individuals exempt from removal were "imprisoned convicts, patients in asylums, and the few adults with 1/32 or less Japanese ancestry who were able to prove that they had no contact with the Japanese American community" (Hatamiya, 1993, p. 17).

It must be remembered that naturalization rights were extended to other Asians, including Koreans and Japanese, only in 1952 through the Immigration and Nationality Act, also known as the McCarran–Walter Act (Public Law 82–414); "It took Congress 162 years, from 1790 to 1952, to eliminate completely 'color' as a criterion for eligibility to citizenship" (Chuman, 1976, p. 67). The "enemy aliens" of Japanese nationality, incarcerated in concentration camps during World War II, did not have the legal right to become non-alien. To be sure, even birthright citizenship proved no protection for their progeny from the same treatment since, in the final analysis, it was race, not the fact of citizenship that determined their status as enemy. As the social worker Kimi Mukaye noted in a 1927 YWCA publication, "the average American places the American-born in the same category as the native Japanese, and sees them all as aliens" (p. 760).

In a 1921 issue of the *Annals of the American Academy of Political and Social Science* largely dedicated to the "Japanese problem" in the coastal states, California State Controller John S. Chambers (1921) lamented that "California has gone as far as she could go under the federal and state constitutions and the

American–Japanese treaty. If she could have gone further she would have done so" (p. 23) in its persecution of the Nikkei. He explained that one of the next steps to be taken was "the amending of the Constitution of the United States to the effect that children born in this country of parents ineligible to citizenship themselves shall be ineligible to citizenship" (p. 23). Marshall de Motte (1921), Chairman of the California State Board of Control defended this view in the same issue, arguing that children of those "who are incapable of citizenship by our federal laws; incapable of owning land by our state laws" are "incapable by education of true loyalty to our country" (p. 20), the precise argument which would serve as the rationale for the federal government's imprisonment of the Nisei and Sansei who constituted two-thirds of those incarcerated.

Aside from the obvious effect of barring Asian immigrants from participating in the nation's polity, the denial of citizenship had multiple other discriminatory functions. The Married Women's Independent Nationality Act of 1922 (ch. 411, 42 Stat. 1021),[11] commonly known as the Cable Act, was a victory for women's rights activists, including many prominent social workers such as Jane Addams, Sophonisba Breckenridge, and Grace and Edith Abbott, who had for decades marched, lobbied, wrote, and lectured on behalf of suffrage and equal political status for women.[12] The Act established that henceforth, a married woman's citizenship was a status separate from her husband's; a woman's citizenship would not be altered by marriage unless she took affirmative legal action to do so. The law also provided an expedited naturalization mechanism through which eligible American women who had hitherto lost their U.S. citizenship through marriage to an alien could regain it.

The provisions did not, however, benefit all women. Following the discriminatory illogic on which the laws of immigration and citizenship in the early part of the 20th century were built, the law produced starkly different outcomes for women of different races. Jane Addams noted in 1929,

A curious inconsistency of the Cable Act is that it takes away the birthright of an American-born woman if she marries an ineligible, i.e., a man from a country whose people cannot be made citizens, although it is precisely under

---

[11] The Act was supported and welcomed by social work organizations such as the Immigrants Protective League and the National Council of Jewish Women, long involved in aiding women and families affected by the exigencies created by the tangled set of laws on naturalization and immigration (see Park, 2015).

[12] These women were ardent activists for suffrage and citizenship for women (Costin, 1983). Jane Addams and Sophonisba Breckenridge were both active members of the National American Woman Suffrage Association, for which Addams served as the inaugural first vice president (Bellecci-St. Romain, 2004). For examples of original writings, see Grace Abbott's "After suffrage—citizenship" (1920); Jane Addams's (1910) "Why Women Should Vote" (1910), "Votes for Women and Other Votes" (1912), and "Women, War and Suffrage" (1915); and Sophonisba Breckinridge's book, *Marriage and the Civic Rights of Women* (1931).

such circumstances that a woman most needs her citizenship. At present she
literally becomes a woman "without a country." (p. 136)

Excluded from the newly established right of independent citizenship was any
American woman who married an alien, such as an Asian man, who was ineligible for citizenship. Similarly, the right to regain U.S. citizenship through
naturalization that was granted to women who had been expatriated through
marriage with an alien excluded those women who themselves were deemed
ineligible for naturalization. The "curious inconsistency" of the Cable Act
was, in other words, a border drawn precisely along the lines of existing racial
biases codified in the laws and courts of the United States in matters of federal
jurisdictions, such as naturalization, and those of state jurisdiction, such as marriage, and evident in the anti-miscegenation laws that dotted the country. This
provision against marriage to aliens ineligible to citizenship was removed by the
law of March 3, 1931, but, while in existence, the measure added a peculiar twist
to the already convoluted and ever more complicating sets of restrictive laws
and their legal challenges which already existed in this bizarre realm of race and
citizenship.

The effects of the Cable Act cannot be understood without taking into account
the two restrictive immigration acts that bookended its passage: the Emergency
Quota Act of May 19, 1921 (H.R. 4075; Pub.L. 67-5; 42 Stat. 5), the "Act to Limit
the Immigration of Aliens into the United States"; and the Immigration Act of
May 26, 1924 (Pub.L. 68–139, 43 Stat. 153), known also as the Johnson-Reed Act
of 1924. The 1921 Quota Act established the national origins quota system, the
basic structure of the U.S. immigration system which stood until the reforms of
1965 replaced it with the preference category system in place today. Under the
first quota act passed in 1921, a year before the Cable Act, alien wives of U.S. citizens were required to enter the United States as immigrants subject to quota. If
the per-country quota was filled, the wife could not enter the United States. The
law was amended by the Immigration Act of 1924, which made alien wives of
American citizens non-immigrants and therefore not subject to the quota. That
Asian, and therefore "aliens ineligible," wives of US citizens were not covered by
this expansion was established by the U.S. Supreme Court in the 1925 case of
Chang Chan v. Nagle (268 U.S. 346).

For the many East Indians who lost their naturalization certificates due to
the decision of the *Thind* case, the Cable Act also posed a particular difficulty.
Marian Schisby explained at the 54th Conference of Social Welfare.

This situation has produced much dismay among the Hindus in this country,
of whom there are about 3,000, and especially among such of their wives as are
American born. Under the Cable Act an American woman citizen does not,

since September 22, 1922, lose citizenship by marriage to an alien, "unless such alien happens to be ineligible to citizenship." Furthermore, an American born woman who prior to 1922 lost citizenship by marriage to an alien cannot regain it under the Cable Act if her husband is ineligible to naturalization. (p. 580)

But it is *Ex Parte Fung Sing* (6 F.2d 670), adjudicated in July of 1925, that perhaps best illustrates the implausible web of obstacles which the sum of the inventive restriction laws presented for women of Asian descent. Despite her Chinese heritage, Fung Sing was a woman born in the United States and thus a *jus soli* citizen. Her move to China and subsequent marriage to a citizen of that country in 1920 rendered her, however, a subject of China according to U.S. law, if not that of China. Her repatriation to the United States in 1925 following the death of her husband was thus deemed illegal by the District Court for the Western District of Washington. Since she had lost her citizenship through a marriage to an alien ineligible to become a U.S. citizen, she did not qualify for the expedited naturalization enabled by the Cable Act. Once she had lost her *just soli* citizenship—the only possibility for an individual of Asian descent to become a U.S. citizen at the time—she was rendered an alien excluded from entry into the United States by the provisions of the Immigration Act of 1924 on the basis of her racial ineligibility for naturalization.

The citizenship bar also posed limitation on the kinds of employment Asian immigrants could undertake, an important context to understanding the economics of the Nikkei communities in the United States prior to the war. The high concentration of Nikkei, especially the Issei, in family farming occurred in the context of the following restrictions. At the outbreak of World War II, the right to be licensed as an attorney was restricted in all 48 states in the Union to citizens or those who were in the legal process of obtaining citizenship. In the state of California, no aliens ineligible for citizenship could work as collection agents, private detectives, domestic fish breeders, horse race track operators, teachers, certified public accounts, insurance brokers, pharmacists, or registered nurses, among others. In Oregon, no aliens ineligible for citizenship could work as bank directors, barbers, collection agents, embalmers, employment agents, optometrists, pharmacists, airplane pilots, architects, boat pullers, certified public accountants, or realtors, among others. Overall, Asian immigrants, as aliens ineligible for citizenship, could not be licensed or employed as certified public accountants in 47 states, as physicians in 25 states, liquor distributors in 39 states, dentists in 26 states, architects in 22 states, pharmacists in 22 states, optometrists in 18 states, and teachers also in 18 states.

The foregoing are statutory restrictions applicable to private employment or occupations. In addition, similar restrictions are imposed by municipalities as a prerequisite for issuance of licenses for all kinds of businesses, trades, and occupations. Furthermore, citizenship is invariably required for employment on public work, civil service, and by federal, state, county, and municipal governments for employment in the police, fire, education, sanitation, and other departments and boards. (Konvitz, 1946, p. 207)

Asian immigrants' access to not only employment but public relief programs were also restricted: in 26 states from old-age benefits, in 7 states from aid to the needy blind. They were also barred from working on public works projects in 23 states.

Although U.S.-born citizens of Asian descent were not legally barred from employment opportunities, they did face enormous hurdles of discrimination in obtaining both education and employment in many fields, particularly in professional work spheres. Peter Roberts wrote in 1912 about a young "American-born Japanese girl on the Coast, a member of a Presbyterian Church" whose applications to nursing training in two hospitals were "bluntly rejected because of her Japanese ancestry" (Roberts, 1970; 1912, p. 324). Nearly three decades later, William Smith (1939) wrote about a "Seattle-born Japanese" with a degree in electrical engineering who was "turned down repeatedly" by prospective employers "because he was Japanese" (p. 370).

Yet another corollary of the racial bar on naturalization, and one specifically targeting the concentration—and indeed the success of—the Nikkei in agriculture was California's 1913 Webb Alien Land Act, which barred aliens ineligible for citizenship from the right to "acquire, possess, enjoy, transmit, and inherit real property" (Kim, 1994, p. 104).[13] Further restrictions added over subsequent years culminated in the 1923 statute, which prohibited aliens ineligible for naturalization from holding majority interest in collective land ownership, acquiring stock in any corporations, and from leasing land for more than three years (Millis, 1978, 1915). These discriminatory measures were, according to the social work periodical *Survey*, of November 8, 1913, "[d]irected especially against Japanese immigrants and intended to protect the native American farmer from foreign competition" ("Common welfare: California preparing to deal with immigrants," 1913, p. 151). Nikkei farmers' efforts to circumvent the restrictions by buying and leasing land by proxy through their native-born children was also opposed by the state, and the issue was ultimately brought before the California Supreme Court. In the 1922 case of *California* v. *Hayao Yano and Tetsubumi Yano* (188 Cal. 645), the court overturned lower court decisions and established

---

[13] Similar laws were enacted at different times in multiple states: Arizona, Washington, Oregon, Idaho, Texas, Nebraska, Kansas, Montana, Minnesota, New Mexico, Missouri, Louisiana, and the District of Columbia.

that aliens ineligible for citizenship could buy land for their minor children who were U.S. citizens by birth. During the war years, hundreds of *escheat actions*— legal actions taken by a state to acquire title to property for which there is no owner—were initiated by the State of California against the incarcerated Nikkei (Daniels, Kitano, & Taylor, 1986). Upheld through numerous challenges until 1948, the Alien Land laws finally lost enforcement power in that year, when the U.S. Supreme Court ruled in favor of the Nikkei defendant in *Oyama v. State of* California (332 US 633) and opined that the elements of the California Act violated Oyama's Fourteenth Amendment rights. California did not formally repealed the law until 1956.

The Japanese Problem

As the Alien Land Acts attested, the West Coast's antipathies toward the Nikkei played out in the interstices of economic competition and racialized prejudice. As Alexander Goldenweiser (1922) explained at the 49th Conference of Social Welfare, the problem of Asian immigration was one of labor as well as race.

> The oriental problem, while second in importance to that of the Negro, has within recent years rapidly moved to the forefront. Important economic factors as well as racial misunderstandings and antipathies are involved here. (pp. 474–475)

Their "relative low standard of living"—which might otherwise have been described as thrift and industry or simple poverty—was what made the presence of the "Oriental" so "intolerable to American labor" (p. 475). The white antipathy to the Nikkei was categoric, as sociologist Jesse Steiner's (1921) explained:

> A decade or more ago we condemned them as undesirable because they were willing to work for low wages and brought with them such a low standard of living. Today, they are still unpopular and the charges made against them are that they demand high wages, insist upon owning land, are successful in business competition, and desire to establish themselves as residents in white communities. The qualities that would ordinarily command respect become in their case a reproach and intensify our determination to have nothing to do with them. (p. 118)

The trouble was that, despite their small numbers and against many odds, the Nikkei did, through the early decades of the 20th century, compete successfully to become a small but important economic force on the West Coast agricultural landscape. By the eve of World War II, "the intensification of farming methods, frugality and economy of operation, minimization of water consumption, family labor, and special and peculiar skill" (United States Army, 1943, p. 137) enabled the Nikkei community to operate an "estimated 6,000 farms, aggregating some 260,000 acres valued at $73,000,000.00" (United States Army, 1943, p. 136). Their success was such that, "although the Japanese population of the Pacific Coast formed less than 1.2% of the total population, the 6,118 Japanese-operated farms were 2.2% of all farms in these States" (United States Army, 1943, p. 394). Furthermore, Nikkei farmers grew "from 30 to 35% by value of all commercial crops grown in California"; through specialization of crops, they grew "from 50 to 90% of crops like snap beans, celery, strawberries, cauliflower, spinach, and tomatoes. Similar conditions hold for Washington and Oregon" (Miyamoto, 1942, p. 108). In the hyperbolic fear-mongering rhetoric typical of West Coast exclusionists, California State Controller John Chambers (1921) had character-ized the modest and excruciatingly earned successes of the Nikkei farmers as a "bloodless struggle" actualizing a "conquest by colonization" (p. 25) of California and eventually the nation.

> Watch the gopher at work. He starts to bore into a levee, and as he progresses he is joined by more of his kind; then, in due time, the other side of the em-bankment is reached, and a little stream of water passes through. As the dirt crumbles, a flow increases and unless promptly checked the bore soon becomes a wide gap with the water rushing through and overflowing the land. That is the flood that means loss, and perhaps eventual disaster. That is exactly what is hap-pening in the state of California today through the Japanese policy of peaceful penetration. (p. 25)

"We must preserve the soil for the Caucasian race," declared James D. Phelan (1921), the United States Senator from California (p. 17).

The increasingly restrictive immigration legislation targeting Asians, which culminated in the total ban provided by the Act of 1924, meant that the bulk of Japanese immigration to the United States had occurred already by early 20th century. The Nikkei population in the United States in 1940 totaled 126,947 (United States Army, 1943). While this "Japanese population" (United States Army, 1943, p. 384) was small in absolute number, comprising less than one-tenth of 1% of the nation's total population, it was a visible racial minority group considered important in relative terms, outnumbering "all other minor races of recent foreign origin" (United States Army, 1943, p. 384).[14] The immigrant Issei

---

[14] The report states that 77,504 Chinese and 45,563 Filipinos were living in the United States at the time (United States Army, 1943).

comprised one-third of this population; their descendants, citizens of the United States by birthright, comprised nearly two-thirds (United States Army, 1943, p. 389). The population was highly concentrated in the West, with 92.5% living in the eight states (Washington, Oregon, California, Idaho, Montana, Nevada, Utah, and Arizona) comprising the Western Defense Command (United States Army, 1943).[15] The wartime removal and incarceration programs targeted only the West Coast Nikkei, but since 90.4% (113,000) of the population resided in the three Coastal states (14,500 in Washington, 4,000 in Oregon, 93,500 in California), the events, in actuality, affected nearly the whole of the Nikkei population in the nation.

Lieutenant General John Lesesne DeWitt, assigned within a few days after the attack on Pearl Harbor to serve as commanding general of the newly established Western Defense Command (US War Relocation Authority, 1946c), reported to the War Department in February 1942 that the inherent enmity of the Nikkei and the certainty of their threat to national security were matters of racial determination.

> In the war in which we are now engaged racial affinities are not severed by migration. The Japanese race is an enemy race and while many second and third generation Japanese born on United States soil, possessed of United States Citizenship, have become "Americanized", the racial strains are undiluted. To conclude otherwise is to expect that children born of white parents on Japanese soil sever all racial affinity and become loyal Japanese subjects, ready to fight and, if necessary, to die for Japan in a war against the nation of their parents. That Japan is allied with Germany and Italy in this struggle is no ground for assuming that any Japanese, barred from assimilation by convention as he is, though born and raised in the United States, will not turn against this nation when the final test of loyalty comes. It, therefore, follows that along the vital Pacific Coast over 112,000 potential enemies, of Japanese extraction, are at large today. There are indications that these are organized and ready for concerted action at a favorable opportunity. The very fact that no sabotage has taken place to date is a disturbing and confirming indication that such action will be taken. (United States Army, 1943, p. 34)

Under War Department directives, the residents of the areas under the Western Defense Command were classified into five categories: (1) Japanese aliens, (2) American citizens of Japanese lineage, (3) German aliens, (4) Italian aliens, and (5) citizens or aliens suspected "of being actually or potentially

---

[15] There were also 157,905 in Hawaii and 263 in Alaska, both territories not yet incorporated as states in the union (Daniels, 1986).

dangerous either as saboteurs, espionage agents, fifth-columnists or subversive persons" (United States Army, 1943, p. 28). General DeWitt's charge was to "provide for the exclusion of all persons in Classes 1, 2, and 5" (United States Army, 1943, p. 28).

The classification equated all Nikkei, citizen and otherwise, with saboteurs and subversives. Although classified as persons of interest, foreign-born Italians and Germans were not considered for exclusion; US citizens of Italian and German ancestry were not even noted as persons of interest. Given the naturalization bar, citizens of Japanese ancestry were most likely to hold citizenship by virtue of birth on US soil, but at least some citizens of Italian and German ancestry would have been naturalized immigrants. The issues at hand were attachment to the nation and loyalty to the state. The federal government was endorsing, in this racial determination of peril, immigration restrictionists' long-held claim that even relatively recent white immigrants were more likely to be loyal to the United States than life-long citizens of Asian descent, who were racially impossible to assimilate. A study of the Nikkei in California's Great Central Valley published by the Social Science Research Council in 1937 offers what is, perhaps, the most apposite assessment: "The major sin of the rural Japanese, then, appears to have been his success as a wage worker and as a farmer, success which was probably exaggerated by the magnifying power of his striking racial visibility" (Young, 1937/1972, p. 81).

The Tolan Committee Hearings

The racialized threat of disloyalty, the peril that resided in the racialized bodies of the Nikkei, played out also at the Tolan Committee Hearings, a series of congressional hearings chaired by US Representative John H. Tolan of California, which addressed the removal of the Nikkei from the Pacific Coast area.[16] "Testimony on this issue was received from a wide range of groups. Federal, State, and local officials were heard; likewise religious and fraternal groups, representatives of agriculture and organized labor, and spokesmen for Japanese-Americans" (United States Congress—House Select Committee Investigating National Defense Migration, 1942b, p. 139), including various social work groups such

---

[16] Originally established in April of 1940 as the "Select Committee to Investigate the Interstate Migration of Destitute Citizens," the Committee was renamed the "Select Committee Investigating National Defense Migration" in April 1941. The term "Tolan Committee Hearings" generally refer to parts 29, 30, and 31 of the Select Committee's investigations. Begun two days after the Executive Order establishing military areas, before the period of "voluntary evacuation" officially ended, these hearings were held in San Francisco on February 21, 23, and March 12; in Portland on February 26ᵢ, in Seattle on February 28 and March 2, and in Los Angeles on March 6 and 7.

as the American Association of Social Workers (AASW), a precursor to the present-day National Association of Social Workers (NASW).

According to James Rowe (1971), US Assistant Attorney General during the war years, the Hearings were instigated by him in an attempt to counter the push for total removal.

> We tried, and eventually I got Congressman [John Harvey] Tolan to call a congressional committee hearing in California. He had a liberal, courageous committee. Jack Tolan was a man with a lot of courage. . . . But we moved him out there too late to do any real good. (p. 36)

WRA Director Dillon Meyer (1974), interviewed for the same oral history project three years later, confirmed Rowe's recollection of the events:

> John Tolan was a nice chap, a very wonderful fellow, and he was hoping to help. As a matter of fact, Jim Rowe, of the Justice Department, needled Tolan into taking on this committee and trying to do something about it because he saw the trend of things. Well, Tolan tried, but it was too late, and of course, practically everybody that testified before his committee was on the wrong side of the fence as far as we were concerned. (Meyer, 1974, p. 12a)

Indeed, the Hearings, "set up with the idea of helping on the side of the angels" (Meyer, 1974, p. 12a), not only came too late, but produced quite the opposite effect from that which was intended. "We underestimated how much hysteria we were going to get" (p. 39), Rowe remarked. As Meyer noted, much of the testimony given at the Hearings advocated the wholesale removal of the Nikkei. Some witnesses, like Mayor R. Earl Riley, of Portland, Oregon, testified that removal was a way to provide needed protection for the Nikkei (United States Congress—House Select Committee Investigating National Defense Migration, 1942b). Many more, such as California Attorney General Earl Warren, advocated removal as a military necessity. Warren's view that "the Japanese had infiltrated themselves into every strategic spot in our costal and valley counties" (United States Congress—House Select Committee Investigating National Defense Migration, 1942c, p. 10980), and therefore constituted a pressing military threat garnered much support. For many of this persuasion, the idea that "loyalty could be determined by racial or ethnic lines" (United States Congress—House Select Committee Investigating National Defense Migration, 1942b), and that the Nikkei were thus a priori disloyal, was an obvious conclusion.

There was, moreover, no "effective counter-pressure" (p. 36) against the tide pushing for total removal. As Meyer (1974) explained,

a lot of people at that time in California where the emotions had been stirred—
the radio and everybody else, you see, was on the wrong side, to the point where
people who felt strongly about it on the other side, few of them had the courage
to come out and testify. (p. 13a)

In the Seattle hearing on March 11, for instance, only 12 out of the 55 people testifying "were friendly and opposed evacuation and internment" (Schmoe, 1986,
p. 117). Those, such as Oakland attorney Clarence Rust, who did testify against
mass removal, argued that the support for it was motivated by economic, rather
than military, interests.

> The clamor seems to come from chambers of commerce, Associated Farmers,
> and the newspaper, notorious as spokesmen for reactionary interests. In view
> of this fact effort should be made to determine whether there is any connec-
> tion between the clamor for the dispossession of the Japanese farmers and the
> desire of these clamoring interests to get possession of the Japanese farms and
> the elimination of the Japanese competition. (United States Congress—House
> Select Committee Investigating National Defense Migration, 1942b, p. 154)

Richard Neustadt of the Social Security Board supported this read, testifying
that the Board had received numerous proposal from "large-scale agricultural
companies" (United States Congress—House Select Committee Investigating
National Defense Migration, 1942b, pp. 155–156) who pushed for the removal
but also wanted the removed workforce to be placed at their disposal.

> In fact, the picture is one of both wanting their cake and wanting to eat it too.
> The same people who are protesting and demanding that all these people be
> driven out of the State also want all of them to work in the fields and canneries.
> (United States Congress—House Select Committee Investigating National
> Defense Migration, 1942b, pp. 155–156)

But such arguments were few and ineffective, according to Lt. General Dewitt.

> As a matter of fact, 99% of the population are in favor of it, and the 1% are
> the ones that howl, and they don't make any impression. (Office of the
> Commanding General—Headquarters Western Defense Command and
> Fourth Army, 1942a, p. 4)

In a telephone conversation with Lt. General Dewitt, Lt. Colonel Karl Bendetsen
of the Western Defense Command remarked on the surprising paucity of the
protest: "Well, it's coming along all right, I figure. I'm surprised that the thing is

going so smoothly, I thought we'd get a lot more howls and protests" (Office of the Commanding General—Headquarters Western Defense Command and Fourth Army, 1942a, p. 4).

In historian Roger Daniels's (1972) view of the hearings, "by far the strongest statement in support of the Japanese Americans came from A. L. Wirin, counsel for the Southern California Branch of the American Civil Liberties Union, and Louis Goldblatt, Secretary of the State CIO [Congress of Industrial Organizations]" (p. 38). The social work position was what Daniels describes as the "more typical of the left-wing attitude," the view that "restrictions upon the liberty of Japanese were 'unfortunate, but vital'" (p. 70). A "statement of principles" was submitted to the committee by the AASW, which described itself as

> [a] national organization of professional social workers who meet high and certain specifically defined qualifications of academic and professional educa- tion, who have had experience in social planning, case work with individuals, and group work, and who are bound by well-recognized standards of personal performance. (United States Congress—House Select Committee Investigating National Defense Migration, 1942d, p. 11542)

Said to be formulated after more than three months of deliberations on the "re- sponsibility of its members during this time of critical national emergency" (p. 11542), the equivocal stand of the AASW was that it was "not in favor of the indiscriminate evacuation of citizens or noncitizens from this area for the sole reason of nationality or race" (p. 11542). It also affirmed, however, that the "only warranty for accepting the procedure of general evacuation would be the certifi- cation by qualified military or police authority that such evacuation is a military necessity or is required for public safety" (p. 11542).

The testimony of Reverend Thomas Gill, representing the Puget Sound Chapter of the AASW, echoed that stance.

> The judgment as to the reality of need of evacuation at this time is a judgment that calls for ability and opportunity accurately to estimate, not the possi- bility, but the probability, of danger from this group of aliens and racials. So it becomes not a civilian decision, we feel, so much as a police and military deci- sion about the dangers involved. . . . . If you want our civilian opinion, or want my civilian opinion about the necessity for such a mass evacuation, it would still be "no." Nevertheless, we feel that we should reiterate that it is not prima- rily a matter for civilian opinion, except that some particular civilian or group of civilians would have information which was not known to the governmental police and military agencies. (p. 11547)

The statement of Annie Clo Watson, a prominent figure in California social work recognized as an expert on the "American Japanese" (Chickering, 1941, p. 1), perhaps best demonstrates the ambivalent illogic of the social work position.

> The morale and the unity among the American people are, we believe, impor-
> tant factors in the defense of our country. The United States is made up, as is
> perhaps no other country, of minority racial and cultural groups. The degree of
> loyalty of all American minorities has great significance both for actual defense
> efforts and for effective reconstruction when peace comes. We cannot, there-
> fore, be too diligent in safeguarding the deep underlying values of American
> citizenship. One of those values is in willingly surrendering temporarily rights
> of citizenship to urgent military necessity. (United States Congress—House
> Select Committee Investigating National Defense Migration, 1942c, p. 11292)

Given the public and official clamor for mass removal, it is impossible to credit that the AASW or individual social workers expected deference to military judgment to result in an outcome other than wholesale incarceration. The designation of restricted areas, already in place by the time of the hearings, was preceded by the West Coast congressional delegation's February 13, 1942, recommendation to remove all Nikkei from the coast (War Relocation Authority, 1946b). Social workers were "put on the spot" (Johns, 1942, p. 1), as the social worker in charge of aid to evacuated enemy aliens in Tulare county described his difficulties in navigating between the public, who "condemn him for wanting to carry through the assistance plan to enemy-aliens" (Johns, 1942, p. 1) and the California State Department of Social Work (CSDSW), which insisted that he do so. But it is not possible to argue that their testimonies were given in ignorance of the likely outcome. Perhaps, charitably, it can be argued that social workers took a pragmatic view of the hearings, registering their disagreement of the obvious decision in hand, but accepting the inevitable. Perhaps their heads were already turned to planning for that inevitability, focused on the procedures for the removal rather than on fighting what seemed unchangeable. However complex the situation of social work and social workers may have been, and whatever rationale supported their stance, the profession's testimonies read as little more than pro forma registration of moral discomfort.

Tracing absent critiques and missing oppositional arguments is a slippery task. Marginalized discourses may be, by the fact of their marginalization and concealment, difficult discourses to uncover. There may have been—indeed, there no doubt were—social work voices raised in unqualified opposition to mass removal and incarceration. But no recorded social work testimony declared with the conviction of Oakland attorney Clarence E. Rust, who testified that he stood "utterly in opposition to the adoption of a program of hysteria as a national policy. . . . If we are to begin a program which amounts to persecution of sections of our citizenry, because of their race or origin, then Hitlerism has already won America, though the Nazi Army is 4,000 miles away" (United States Congress—House Select Committee Investigating National Defense Migration, 1942b, p. 154).

While the Axis powers against which the United States waged war consisted also of Germany and Italy, at no time were German and Italian aliens seriously considered for mass removal. As James Rowe (1942) explained in the *Common Ground,* the periodical of the Common Council for American Unity,[17] "[t]he huge mass of German and Italian alien enemies (the Japanese centered on the West Coast are regarded as sui generis) are undoubtedly loyal. This is recognized by government and individuals alike. They chose our good earth to live on" (p. 19). To treat the Germans and Italians as were the Nikkei would have meant entertaining the apparently absurd possibility that German nationals such as Thomas Mann, a Nobel laureate, "who is today an alien enemy and possibly subject to evacuation from the West Coast shoreline" (p. 23) should be incarcerated. Chauncey Tramutolo, a former United States attorney speaking on behalf of the Italians of San Francisco explained that such a plan would require the unimaginable outcome of removing and incarcerating Joe DiMaggio's parents.

> Neither of the DiMaggio seniors is a citizen. They have reared nine children, five boys and four girls, eight of whom were born in the United States and the other one is a naturalized citizen. Three of the boys are outstanding persons in the sports world. Joe, who is with the Yanks, was leading hitter for both the American and National Leagues during the years 1939 and 1940. His younger brother Dominic is with the Boston Red Sox and his other brother, Vincent, is with the Pittsburgh team of the National League. All three are so outstanding in their profession that their record is well known to every sports follower. . . . . The senior DiMaggios, though noncitizens, are as loyal as anyone could be. . . . . To evacuate the senior DiMaggios would, in view of the splendid family they have reared and their unquestioned loyalty, present, I am sure you will agree with me, a serious situation. (United

---

[17] The publication, which ran from 1940 to 1949, published multiple articles written by the Nikkei from within and outside the camps, as well as a handful of reports and commentaries such as this by Rowe. Common Council for American Unity was "an organization devoted to the celebration of the US as a product of its diverse immigrant and ethnic populations" (Shaffer, 1998, p. 103). According to Shaffer, the publication initially stood in support of WRA policy, but changed its perspective by the spring of 1943, to "become a leading voice on behalf of Japanese Americans, emphasizing that the definition of Americanism must not be made on a racial basis" (Shaffer, 1998, p. 103).

States Congress—House Select Committee Investigating National Defense Migration, 1942c, p. 11128)

Smith Troy, the Washington State Attorney General, averred at the Seattle Hearings that the public's willingness to incarcerate one population and not others was by no means a matter of racial discrimination.

> Well, frankly speaking, out here we feel that we know the Italian and the German people better. We have been able to come closer to those races than we have with the Japanese. I mean again, no disparagement of races. I don't wish to be misconstrued on that score, but we have to face facts, and for years out here there has always been a distrust of the Japanese. . . . I do think that our first problem is the Japanese. (United States Congress—House Select Committee Investigating National Defense Migration, 1942a, p. 11505)

Robert H. Fouke, representing the California Joint Immigration Committee (formerly the Japanese Exclusion League) testified that for California's many exclusionists, involved for decades in fomenting both anti-Asian sentiment and legislation such as the Alien Land Act, the distrust of the "Japanese" was one of long standing, and the "things that have happened in recent months are events that we predicted would occur or were likely to occur" (United States Congress—House Select Committee Investigating National Defense Migration, 1942c, p. 11069). But it is Lt. General DeWitt's pithy remarks to the Assistant Secretary of War John J. McCloy perhaps best capture the deeply embedded racism at the heart of the matter. Especially for the West Coast exclusionists such as these testifying in the hearings, no matter their years in the United States, record of hard work, economic self-sufficiency, lack of criminality, evidence of cultural integration, or even birthright citizenship, in the final analysis, "a Jap is a Jap" (Office of the Commanding General—Headquarters Western Defense Command and Fourth Army, 1942b, p. 6).

> The five-decade old hostility cultivated by certain sections of the West Coast population toward the Japanese and other Asiatic inhibited stories about them as human beings with names, personalities, and roots in America. Though westerners had known many Japanese personally for some thirty or forty years, they had a mental block which made them think of Japanese as mysterious, inscrutable, and latently dangerous and not as a group made up of persons as individual and different as the ones they did know. (War Relocation Authority, 1946a, p. 15)

References

Abbott, E. (1924). *Immigration: Select documents and case records.* Chicago: University of Chicago Press.

Abbott, E. (1926). *Historical aspects of the immigration problem.* Chicago: University of Chicago Press.

Abbott, G. (1920). After suffrage—citizenship. *The Survey, 44*(19), 655–657.

Addams, J. (1909). Report of the Committee. In A. Johnson (Ed.), *Proceedings of the National Conference of Charities and Correction* (Vol. 36, pp. 213–215). Fort Wayne, IN: Fort Wayne Printing Co.

Addams, J. (1910). Why women should vote. *Ladies' Home Journal, 27,* 21–22.

Addams, J. (1912). Votes for women and other votes. *The Survey, 28*(9), 367–368.

Addams, J. (1915). Women, war and suffrage. *The Survey, 35*(November 6), 148–149.

Aleinikoff, T. A., & Klusmeyer, D. (Eds.). (2001). *Citizenship today: Global perspectives and practices.* Washington, DC: Carnegie Endowment for International Peace.

Alvarado, E. M. (1920). Division X—the uniting of native and foreign-born in America: Mexican immigration to the United States. In A. B. Dinwiddie (Ed.), *Proceedings of the National Conference of Social Work at the forty-seventh annual session held in New Orleans, Louisiana, April 14–21, 1920* (Vol. 47, pp. 479–480). Chicago, IL: University of Chicago Press.

Bellecci-St. Romain, L. (2004). Jane Addams. *The American Feminist* (Summer-Fall), 38–39. Retrieved from http://www.feministsforlife.org/taf/2004/summer-fall/Summer-Fall04.pdf

Breckenridge, S. P. (1931). *Marriage and the civic rights of women: Separate domicile and independent citizenship.* Chicago: University of Chicago Press.

Chambers, J. S. (1921). The Japanese Invasion. *Annals of the American Academy of Political and Social Science, 93,* 23–29.

Chickering, M. A. (1941). "Letter to Miss Annie Clo Watson, International Institute of San Francisco, from Martha A. Chickering, Director, State Department of Social Welfare, Sacamento, California, December 8, 1941." pp. 1. Social Welfare—War Services—Defense, Minority Groups, 1941–1942 (F3729:56). Department of Social Welfare Records, War Services Bureau. Sacramento, CA: California State Archives.

Chuman, F. F. (1976). *The bamboo people: The law and Japanese-Americans.* Del Mar, CA: Publisher's Inc.

Committee on Immigration. (1881). Debate on immigration. In F. B. Sanborn (Ed.), *Proceedings of the Eight Annual Conference of Charities and Correction, held at Boston, July 25–30, 1881* (Vol. 8, pp. 218–219). Boston: A. Williams & Company.

Common welfare: California preparing to deal with immigrants. (1913). *The Survey, 31*(6), 151.

Common welfare: The illiteracy test again before Congress. (1916). *The Survey, 35*(23), 651.

The Consulate-General of Japan. (1925a). *Documental history of law cases affecting Japanese in the United States 1916–1924: Japanese land cases* (Vol. 2). San Francisco: The Consulate-General of Japan, San Francisco.

The Consulate-General of Japan. (1925b). *Documental history of law cases affecting Japanese in the United States 1916–1924: Naturalization cases and cases affecting constitutional and treaty rights* (Vol. 1). San Francisco: The Consulate-General of Japan, San Francisco.

Costin, L. B. (1983). *Two sisters for social justice: A biography of Grace and Edith Abbott.* Urbana: University of Illinois Press.

Daniels, R. (1972). *Concentration camps USA: Japanese Americans and World War II.* New York: Holt, Rinehart and Winston.

Daniels, R., Kitano, H. H., & Taylor, S. C. (Eds.). (1986). *Japanese Americans: From relocation to redress*. Salt Lake City: University of Utah Press.

De Motte, M. (1921). California—White or Yellow? *Annals of the American Academy of Political and Social Science, 93*, 18–23.

Gates, W. A. (1905). Minutes and discussions. In A. Johnson (Ed.), *Proceedings of the National Conference of Charities and Correction at the thirty-second annual session held in the city of Portland, Oregon, July 15–21, 1905* (Vol. 32, p. 567). Columbus, OH: Press of Fred J. Heer.

Gates, W. A. (1909). Oriental immigration on the Pacific Coast. In A. Johnson (Ed.), *Proceedings of the National Conference of Charities and Correction at the Thirty-Sixth Annual Session held in the City of Buffalo, N.Y., June 9th to 16th, 1909* (Vol. 36, pp. 230–232). Fort Wayne, IN: Fort Wayne Printing Co.

Gettys, L. (1934). *The law of citizenship in the United States*. Chicago: University of Chicago Press.

Goldenweiser, A. A. (1922). Some problems of race and culture in the United States. *Proceedings of the National Conference of Social Work, formerly National Conference of Charities and Correction, at the forty-Ninth Annual Session held in Providence, Rhode Island, June 22–29, 1922* (pp. 473–476). Chicago: University of Chicago Press.

Hatamiya, L. T. (1993). *Righting a wrong: Japanese Americans and the passage of the Civil Liberties Act of 1988*. Stanford, CA: Stanford University Press.

Hoyt, C. S. (1881). Report of the Committee on Immigration *Proceedings of the eight annual Conference of Charities and Correction, held at Boston, July 25–30, 1881 F.B. Sanborn* (Vol. 8, pp. 217–218). Boston: A. Williams & Company.

Ichioka, Y. (1988). *The Issei: The world of the first generation Japanese immigrants, 1885–1924*. New York: The Free Press.

Jacobson, M. F. (1998). *Whiteness of a different color: European immigrants and the alchemy of race*. Cambridge, MA: Harvard University Press.

Jacobson, M. F. (2000). *Barbarian virtues: the United States encounters foreign peoples at home and abroad, 1876–1917*. New York: Hill and Wang.

Johns, G. C. (1942). State Department of Social Welfare Official Memorandum, from Gladys C. Johns, Area Supervisor, to Margaret S. Watkins, Supervisor of Field Service, California State Department of Social Welfare, San Francisco, on Enemy-Aliens—Tulare County, San Francisco, CA, 4/18/ 42. pp. 1. Social Welfare—War Services Bureau—Enemy Alien Assistance, Reports, 1942 (F3729: 77). Department of Social Welfare Records, War Services Bureau. Sacramento, CA: California State Archives.

Kansas, S. (1948). *US immigration exclusion and deportation and citizenship of the United States of America*. New York: Matthew Bender.

Kim, H.-C. (1994). *A legal history of Asian Americans, 1790–1990*. Westport, CT: Greenwood Press.

Konvitz, M. R. (1946). *The alien and the Asiatic in American law*. Ithaca, NY: Cornell University Press.

Lopez, I. H. (1995). *White by law: The legal construction of race*. New York: New York University Press.

McKenzie, R. D. (1927). *Oriental exclusion: the effect of American immigration law, regulations and judicial decisions upon the Chinese and Japanese on the American Pacific Coast*. New York: Institute of Pacific Relations.

Meyer, D. S. (1974). War Relocation Authority, the Director's account: An oral history conducted in 1974 by Amelia R. Fry. *Japanese American Relocation Reviewed, Volume II: The Internment* (pp. 1a–55a). Berkeley: Regional Oral History Office, Bancroft Library, University of California.

Millis, H. A. (1915/1978). *The Japanese problem in the United States: An investigation for the commission on relations with Japan appointed by the Federal Council of the Churches of Christ in America.* New York: Arno Press. (Originally published in 1915 by the Macmillan Company.)

Miyamoto, S. F. (1942). Immigrants and citizens of Japanese origin. [Minority peoples in a nation at war.] *Annals of the American Academy of Political and Social Science, 223,* 107–113.

Mukaye, K. (1927). "Young Japan in America." *Woman's Press, XXI*(11), pp. 760–761. YWCA of the USA—Bound Periodicals. Northampton, MA: Smith College.

Office of the Commanding General, Headquarters Western Defense Command and Fourth Army. (1942a). Transcript of telephone conversation between General DeWitt, Commanding Western Defense Command and Fourth Army, and General Benedict, Commanding Communications Zone (Ninth Corps Area), Salt Lake City, Utah, March 14, 1942, 10:32 A.M. Folder 384.4 Val I (AG Records File), ed., pp. 1–4. College Park, MD: National Archives and Records Administration, Archives II Reference Section (Military).

Office of the Commanding General, Headquarters Western Defense Command and Fourth Army. (1942b). Transcript of telephone conversation between General DeWitt, WDC and Fourth Army, and Lt. Colonel Bendetsen, Office of the Provost Marshal General, Washington, DC, March 4, 1942, 11:20 A.M. Folder 384.4 Val I (AG Records File), ed., pp. 1–3. College Park, MD: National Archives and Records Administration, Archives II Reference Section (Military).

Palmer, A. W. (1934). *Orientals in American life.* New York: Friendship Press.

Panunzio, C. (1929). Changing philosophy of the United States toward citizenship by adoption *Proceedings of the National Conference of Social Work at the Fifty-Sixth Annual Session held in San Francisco, California, June 26–July 3, 1929* (Vol. 56, pp. 567–572). Chicago, IL: The University of Chicago Press.

Park, Y. (2015). "A Curious Inconsistency": The discourse of social work on the 1922 Married Women's Independent Nationality Act, and the Intersecting dynamics of race and gender in the laws of immigration and citizenship. *Affilia: Journal of Women & Social Work, 30*(4), 560–579. doi:10.1177/0886109915583546.

Phelan, J. D. (1921). Why California objects to the Japanese Invasion. *Annals of the American Academy of Political and Social Science, 93,* 16–17.

Rich, A. M. (1947). Current immigration problems. *Social Service Review, 21*(1), 85–106.

Roberts, P. (1912/1970). *The new immigration.* New York: Arno Press & The New York Times.

Rowe, J. H. (1942). The alien enemy program: So far. *Common Ground, 2*(2), 19–24.

Rowe, J. H. (1971). The Japanese Evacuation Decision: An oral history conducted in 1971 by Ameila Fry. *Japanese American Relocation Reviewed, volume I: decision and exodus* (pp. i–45). Berkeley: Regional Oral History Office, Bancroft Library, University of California.

Schisby, M. (1927). Hindus and American citizenship. *Proceedings of the National Conference of Social Work at the Fifty-Fourth Annual Session held in Des Moines, Iowa, May 11–18, 1927* (Vol. 54, pp. 579–581). Chicago: University of Chicago Press.

Schlesinger, A. M. (1921). The significance of immigration in American history. *American Journal of Sociology, 27*(1), 71–85.

Schmoe, F. (1983). Seattle's peace churches and relocation. In R. Daniels, S. C. Taylor, & H. H. Kitano (Eds.), *Japanese Americans: from relocation to redress* (pp. 117–122). Salt Lake City, Utah: University of Utah Press.

Shaffer, R. (1998). Cracks in the consensus: Defending the rights of Japanese Americans during World War II. *Radical History Review, 72*(3), 84–120.

Smith, W. C. (1939). *Americans in the making: The natural history of the assimilation of immigrants.* New York and London: D. Appleton-Century.

Spickard, P. R. (1989). *Mixed blood: Intermarriage and ethnic identity in twentieth-century America.* Madison: University of Wisconsin Press.

Steiner, J. F. (1921). Some factors involved in minimizing race friction on the Pacific Coast. *Annals of the American Academy of Political and Social Science, 93,* 116–120.

United States Army. (1943). *Final report, Japanese evacuation from the West Coast, 1942.* Washington, DC: U.S. Government Printing Office.

United States Congress—House Select Committee Investigating National Defense Migration. (1942a). *National defense migration. Fifth interim report of the Select committee investigating national defense migration, House of Representatives, Seventy-Seventh Congress, second session, pursuant to H. Res. 113, a resolution to inquire further into the interstate migration of citizens, emphasizing the present and potential consequences of the migration caused by the national defense program. Recommendations on the mobilization of manpower for the all-out war effort. August 10, 1942.* Washington, DC: U.S. Government Printing Office.

United States Congress—House Select Committee Investigating National Defense Migration. (1942b). *National defense migration. Fourth interim report . . . Seventy-Seventh Congress, second session pursuant to H. Res. 113, Findings and recommendations on evacuation of enemy aliens and others from prohibited military zones.* Washington: U.S. Government Printing Office.

United States Congress—House Select Committee Investigating National Defense Migration. (1942c). *National Defense Migration. Part 29, San Francisco Hearings: Problems of Evacuation of Enemy Aliens and Others from Prohibited Military Zones [microform]: Hearings before the United States House Select Committee Investigating National Defense Migration, Seventy-Seventh Congress, second session, on Feb. 21, 23, 1942.* Washington, DC: U.S. Government Printing Office.

United States Congress—House Select Committee Investigating National Defense Migration. (1942d). *National Defense Migration. Part 30, Portland and Seattle Hearings: Problems of Evacuation of Enemy Aliens and Others from Prohibited Military Zones [microform]: Hearings before the United States House Select Committee Investigating National Defense Migration, Seventy-Seventh Congress, second session, on Feb. 26, 28, Mar. 2, 1942.* Washington, DC: U.S. Government Printing Office.

Van Dyne, F. (1904). *Citizenship of the United States.* Rochester, NY: Lawyers' Co-operative Publishing.

War Relocation Authority. (1946a). *Wartime exile: The exclusion of the Japanese Americans from the West Coast.* Washington, DC: U.S. Government Printing Office.

War Relocation Authority. (1946b). *WRA: A story of human conservation.* Washington, DC: U.S. Government Printing Office.

War Relocation Authority. (1946c). *The relocation program.* Washington, DC: United States Government Printing Office.

Williams, W. (1906). The new immigration: some unfavorable features and possible remedies. In A. Johnson (Ed.), *Proceedings of the Annual Conference of Charities and Correction at the Thirty-Third Annual Session held in the City of Philadelphia, Pennsylvania, May 9–16, 1906* (Vol. 33, pp. 285–299). Columbus, OH: Press of Frederick J. Heer.

Young, D. (1937/1972). *Research memorandum on minority peoples in the Depression.* New York: Arno Press. (Originally published in 1937 by the Social Science Research Council.)

2

The Start of War

No Contact

Few social workers in California, Oregon, and Washington, including state and county welfare workers soon to be confronted with the massive task of facilitating the forced removal of an entire population, had any significant contact with the Nikkei, a population who "had not had a record of dependency upon public or private relief agencies" (War Relocation Authority, 1943, p. 2). A 1915 study commissioned by the Federal Council of the Churches of Christ in America reported that

> [n]ot only are the Japanese industrious; they are well organized to care for those who are unfortunate enough to be in need of assistance, so that few have become dependent upon the public. They have brought with them no problem of dependency and the number of insane have been small. (Millis, 1915/1978, p. 237)

Though Fresno County, California, was an area of high concentration of the Nikkei, they were not one of the 25 nationalities reported to be receiving County Relief aid in 1918 (State Commission of Immigration and Housing of California, 1918). Not a single individual among the total population of 3,000 Nikkei in the county appeared to have received this or any other type of County aid.[1] In a 1930 article on the welfare of minority groups in the Hawaiian "Ghetto and the Slum," University of Hawaii sociologist Andrew Lind explained that, even in Hawaii, where the Nikkei numbers constituted 42% of the total population (Nordyke & Matsumoto, 1977), "the number of cases which demand the attention of the public systems of charity" (Lind, 1930, p. 214) were few. This, according to Lind, was not due to a lack of need in the community, but because "the greater part of such assistance is provided through the informal devices of mutual aid and neighborliness" (p. 214).

The widely accepted sociological analysis that "no Japanese became public charges" (p. 130) because of such intra-ethnic organizations was, however, a

---

[1] The reports shows one Chinese on the Relief rolls. A total of 700 Chinese were estimated in the city of Fresno; no county number given.

Facilitating Injustice: The complicity of social workers in the forced removal and incarceration of Japanese Americans, 1941–1946. Yoosun Park, Oxford University Press (2020). © Oxford University Press.
DOI: 10.1093/acprof:oso/9780199765058.001.0001

distorted view. Immigrants' development and use of mutual aid societies has been much written about (Beito, 1990; Ishisaka & Takagi, 1982; Light, 1972; Portes & Manning, 1986; Reisch, 2008). The social welfare historian James Leiby (1962) remarked on "the range, vitality and importance of the immigrants' own welfare institutions, their own agencies of charitable fellowships and self-help" (p. 41) that flourished in the early decades of the 20th century.

> There were many kinds: burial societies, orphanages, hospitals, labor unions, relief agencies, and many less formal activities associated with social clubs. These were often small and ineffective, of course; sometimes they were efforts by established groups to look out for greenhorns; usually, each new ethnic group insisted on its own. (p. 41)

For white immigrants, mutual aid organizations were temporary measures. As each group successfully melted into the proverbial American pot, "ultimately, these small associations were combined under religious auspices" (Leiby, 1962, p. 41) as Jewish, Lutheran, and Catholic charities that served co-religionists of different white ethnic backgrounds and became part of the social work mainstream. But for the Nikkei, as well for other Asian groups excluded from the American mainstream by law and social practices, aid had to be continually self-generated.

For the Nikkei, as it had for the Chinese immigrants before them, mutual aid associations and other ethnic institutions were necessary buffers to "the powerful forces of racism" (Matsuoka & Ryujin, 1991, p. 230) that threw up discriminatory blocks in all domains of life. Not only unfair laws (some of which will be discussed later) but also quotidian bigotry such as "the fairly general discrimination against Japanese practiced by white barbers in the cities of the Pacific Coast" (Millis, 1915/1978, p. 228), as well as by restaurants, lodging facilities, and movie theaters, required the creation of a separate social economy. Rotating credit associations called *tanomoshi* allowed the Nikkei to obtain capital outside the white banking system (Matsuoka & Ryujin, 1991). "The Japanese boarding-house" (Smith, 1939, p. 97) provided housing for Nikkei migratory workers locked out of other rooming houses and hostels in California and elsewhere. The prefectural societies called *kenjinkai* functioned as bureaus for legal and employment advice and provided a variety of assistance, including financial aid for medical and funeral expenses, that the Nikkei did not have access to elsewhere (Matsuoka & Ryujin, 1991; Park & Miller, 1912/1969). The Japanese Association, for example, was organized in 1900 in San Francisco "to protect the 'rights' of the Japanese" (Park & Miller, 1912/1969, p. 169) during a bubonic plague scare, "when the Japanese and Chinese, being Asiatic races, were dealt with in a different manner from other races" (p. 169). The Association remained active thereafter in light of the "strong anti-Japanese movement which had sprung up" (p. 169).[2] The Japanese Benevolent Society was organized a year later, in 1901, "to make more complete provisions for the care of the sick, injured, and unfortunate than had been made by the several missions, the Japanese Association, the prefectural societies, and trade associations" (Park & Miller, 1912/1969, p. 130). The highly organized system of mutual aid and support among the Nikkei must be understood, in other words, as a product of exigency rather than choice. If assistance and services were to be had, they had to be self-organized.

Japantowns and Chinatowns should similarly be understood as the products of segregation imposed by the legal codes and social mores rather than by Asian immigrants' tendency for un-American "clannishness" (Millis, 1915/1978; Y. Park & Kemp, 2006). The sociologist William Carlson Smith (1939), writing sympathetically about the difficulties faced by the "Oriental races" in assimilating to U.S. society, described that, just as the Chinese had been driven "into a ghetto life in San Francisco from which they have never emerged and where they still maintain ways that are strange and queer," California had "forced the Japanese off the land, into the segregation of 'Little Tokyo' in Los Angeles" (p. 154). But the existence of such neighborhoods—frequently censured as breeding grounds of deviance, vice, and disease (Craddock, 1999, 2000; Park & Kemp, 2006)—were generally decried as evidence of not only of Asians' inability but their inveterate refusal to assimilate, a spurious charge of self-inflicted isolation that would reverberate during the war years as a rationale for the Nikkei's removal and incarceration.

The Exception: The YWCA

Arguably the only consistently proactive social work organization working for the welfare of the Nikkei throughout the forced removal and incarceration was the Young Women's Christian Association (YWCA) and its offshoot organization, the International Institutes. The YWCA was not only a national organization which provided a wide range of social services—using both group work and case work methods—to women of all races, creeds, and nationalities in communities across the nation, but one that publicly and consistently championed the causes of racial equality and cultural pluralism decades before the era of civil rights and the age of multiculturalism. In 1911, on the recommendation of its Bureau of Immigration and the Foreign-Born, the YWCA formed the first International Institute in New York City's immigrant-dense Greenwich Village

---

[2] Its membership was tallied at 1,600 in 1922 (Kanzaki, 1921).

(Mohl & Betten, 1972). Begun as experimental "community centers" (Robertson, 2007, p. 50) serving newly arriving immigrant women, the Institutes was led by Edith Terry Bremer, a young social welfare and settlement worker formerly of the Federal Immigration Commission (Mohl, 1982; Sickels, 1941). Operating from the central tenet that "cultural pluralism [was] good for immigrants and also good for America" (Mohl, 1982, p. 41), it contested the "arrogant assumption that everything American was intrinsically superior to anything foreign" (Edith Bremer, cited in Mohl, 1982, p. 39), the doctrine of assimilation via Americanization which was, whether implicitly or explicitly, a long-standing principle embedded in most social work programs with immigrants (Park, 2006; Park & Kemp, 2006). The Institute saw its "most important function as fostering cultural identity and a positive self-image among immigrant newcomers" (Mohl & Betten, 1974, p. 17) and their descendants; such were the basis on which healthy individual, family, and community development could be established. The Institutes' wide range of casework, group work, community organizing, and public relations services were thus, in contrast to most social work organizations, populated by middle- and upper-class native-born American women and run by "nationality workers" (Mohl, 1982, p. 42), first- or second-generation immigrants who were linguistically and culturally attuned to the clients they served. Branches of the Institute were established in more than 60 industrial cities in the years following World War I. In the 1930s, most branches of the Institutes merged to form an independent national organization called the National Institute of Immigrant Welfare, with Edith Bremer continuing as its head.[3]

If the proto-cultural pluralism of the International Institutes distinguished (in contrast to many other immigrant-focused social services) the YWCA's work with the largely White European immigrants it served, the segregated associations for racial minority women distinguished the YWCA from so many other private charitable organizations of the time that did not serve such populations at all. The first African American YWCA branch opened in Dayton, Ohio, in 1890; the first YWCA for Native American women opened in Chilocco, Oklahoma, in 1894; the Japanese Branch of the Los Angeles chapter opened in 1913. Kimi Mukaye (1927), a Nikkei social worker appointed National Secretary for the YWCA during the war years, explained the establishment of the "Japanese YWCA of Los Angeles."

> In 1922 a spacious building was purchased with several thousand dollars donated by the local Japanese, and was turned into a dormitory for the

---

[3] It became the American Federation of International Institutes in 1943, then merged with the Common Council for American Unity to create the American Council for Nationalities Service, which remains in operation today as the Immigration and Refugee Services of America (Mohl, 1982; Sickels, 1941).

accommodation of the homeless Japanese girl students and professional women in Los Angeles. Prominent Japanese women are chosen as executives of the Japanese Y.W.C.A. and devote their time for the culture and in the interest of the members. (p. 761)

The YWCA had, thus, by the start of World War II, a well-established relationship with West Coast Nikkei communities (Lewis, 2008). At its March 1946 National Convention, the YWCA would reach a unanimous vote to desegregate the entire organization and incorporate these segregated minority associations into the rest of its fold (Lewis, 2008), but in the decades prior to the war, thriving Japanese Associations were in operation in most large cities throughout the Coast and "many of the Nisei (second generation) group have literally grown up within the walls of the Y.W.C.A." (YWCA of the U.S.A., 1942, p. 1). A January 1941 article in the YWCA publication *Woman's Press* described the Los Angeles Japanese branch:

A community of nearly 39,000 Japanese is served by the Japanese Branch. Of this number, better than 24,000 are second-generation Japanese, educated in public schools where they associate with American boys and girls, attend motion pictures, and thoroughly absorb the American viewpoint. The Japanese Y.W.C.A. directly serves 1,800 girls annually, although its influence is felt by a much greater number. (YWCA of the U.S.A, 1941, p. 40)

Katherine Perine (1940), Girl Reserve Secretary of the San Pedro YWCA, described how a mere year before Pearl Harbor, a Girl Reserve club had been established for Nikkei girls who "live on Terminal Island and come to school by way of a ferry boat."

Their fathers are for the most part fishermen. These girls asked the Girl Reserve secretary to help them organize a knitting group. An announcement was made to a group of women that knitting and crocheting teachers were needed. Seven women volunteered to help. For two months the girls and women met together and had a good time learning to knit and crochet. At the end of the time, the girls decided to give a tea for their teachers. The tea was a grand success and all planned by the girls. Later, a chance came to work with a second group of Japanese girls who live on the hills near San Pedro. The girls wanted to learn to dance and wanted the Girl Reserve secretary to help to start a group. The Girl Reserve secretary found a teacher and accompanist who were interested and suggested to them that with such a club there were many things we could teach besides dancing. The girls, who range in age from seventeen to twenty-five, organized their group to meet on Saturday afternoon after they have attended

Japanese school at the community hall. The next week a young Japanese boy came in to say that the boys of this same group wanted to learn to dance. The same teacher was engaged and the boys started their class on Monday nights. The boys are older than the girls. The groups are very eager to learn and they work hard. The teacher has taken a great deal of interest and finds her classes very enjoyable. The boys have invited the teacher and Girl Reserve secretary to come to the hall on Thursday night and watch the jujitsu matches. (p. 487)

Despite these credentials, the YWCA's assertion of deep knowledge of the Nikkei community, that it "knows these people intimately" (YWCA National Board, 1942, p. 2), was not wholly justified. Its familiarity was with the Nisei, who made up the bulk of the YWCA's Nikkei membership, but not with the first-generation immigrant Issei, and, more specifically, the familiarity lay in its contact with the urban, Christian Nisei living in the Japanese enclaves of cities such as Los Angeles and San Francisco. The YWCA's records of its work within the concentration camps shows that it had few established relationships with the rural Nisei and had to strive to gain the trust of the Buddhists. Limited as was the YWCA's knowledge of the Nikkei, however, it was one that no other social work organization could remotely match. As West Coast social work began preparing for the fallout from Pearl Harbor and the U.S. declaration of war on Japan, therefore, the YWCA and the International Institutes were the only social work organizations with both knowledge of the community and contacts within it.

The YWCA had been on alert and focused on the implications of the looming war on the Nikkei community well before the United States formally entered the war. In April 1941, eight months prior to Pearl Harbor, Ruth Crawford Mitchell reported in the *Woman's Press* the growing anxieties of the West Coast Nikkei. "Every time there is a new spy scare or another bombing episode, every time diplomatic envoys exchange demanding notes, Japanese boys and girls feel thousands of curious eyes watching them closely. They keenly feel the unasked question: Are they Japanese or are they Americans? Are they loyal to the country of their birth, or to the land to which they trace their origin?" (p. 165). The first concern in the aftermath of Pearl Harbor was for its Honolulu Association.

The Honolulu Association has an administration building which is approximately seven miles from Pearl Harbor and thirty miles from Schoefield Barracks. There is also a residence which houses a hundred and seventy-five girls in approximately the same location. The Beach House and Camp are even nearer to military fortifications. Cables were sent to each of these Associations as soon as we heard of the bombing of the Hawaiian Islands. . . . Because of the nature the Islands, there are few dugouts cellars. There is little opportunity to evacuate. The last communication from the Honolulu Association before war was declared came from a young leader, an American-born Japanese. (Flack, January 1942)

In the days following, the West Coast YWCAs mobilized to aid its Nikkei members. For instance, shortly after Pearl Harbor, a "letter was sent to all Japanese club members and all Japanese members of the Portland, Oregon, YWCA, expressing the sympathy of the Association and its desire to prevent unnecessary suffering and asking the Japanese to call upon them for help as needed" (Ellis & Ingraham, April 1942, p. 189). The Portland YWCA's leadership also began a correspondence with Earl Sprague, the sympathetic Governor of Oregon (Sprague, 1941a). In a letter dated December 8, 1942, Betty Britton, Secretary of the Young Women's Department; Mildred Bartholomew, Secretary of the Department of Religion and Membership; and Lazelle Alway, Secretary of the Girl Reserve Department explained that the YWCA membership included a large Nisei population and that they had "come to know these girls as individuals and as Americans and to believe in them and in their loyalty during the present crisis" (Britton, Bartholomew, & Alway, 1941, p. 1). They offered their services "both as individuals and as Y.W.C.A. secretaries" to any work that "can help to stabilize these frightened young people" (Britton et al., 1941, p. 2). Sprague (1941a), who had publically declared his confidence in the loyalty of the Nisei in a radio address given on the night of Pearl Harbor, assured the YWCA that he was doing all he could to "protect these people from molestation" (p. 1). In mid-December, Sprague (1941b) directed the State Public Welfare Commission "to set aside sufficient funds to provide for the subsistence of such nationals as may be deprived of their employment during the present war emergency upon an equal basis with other reciprocants for relief" (p. 1).

The YWCA, in contrast to all other social work organizations, was explicit and public about its view of the targeted social, legal, and economic persecution the West Coast Nikkei communities as "a race problem in addition to being a result of war hysteria" (Ellis & Wilkins, 1942, p. 9).

In many parts of our country persons with dark or yellow skins cannot get jobs, cannot train for certain kinds of work in the Army or Navy, cannot eat and cannot sleep where white people eat and sleep. Too easily we forget this pattern of life and it is only when we are jolted by something so immense as the evacuation which is taking place on the Pacific Coast that we remember the injustices meted out to many of our citizens every day. (Ellis & Wilkins, 1942, p. 9)

The historian Sara Lewis (2008) avers that "The events of World War II transform the views of Y leaders about race relations, prompting changes that included the creation of a racially inclusive rhetoric that increasingly fused democratic principles with Christian tenets and a widening definition of interracial relations" (p. 2). As influential as the war years no doubt were, the YWCA's fusion of the ideals of democracy with a progressive stance on race was derived, in large part, from the principles of group work, whose origins can be traced back to the early 20th century settlement movement, as well as to the recreation and progressive education movements of the same period (Andrews, 2001; Breton, 2006; Germain & Gitterman, 1980; Wilson, 1976). Differences in provenance notwithstanding, a principle tenet of group work was the complementarity of the growth and fulfillment of individuals and social change (Alissi, 2001; Coyle, 1952; Newstetter, 1935; Schwartz, 2006). The belief in the power of human association was coupled in group work with "the value orientation of a commitment to social change" (Hartford, 1983, p. 758). The goals of "social responsibility" (Coyle, 1935), "social action" (Fitch, 1940; Maslen, 1941), "civil liberties" (Kaiser, 1948), "democracy" (Lindeman, 1939), and "social reform" (Wilson, 1976) undergirded, in other words, the promotion of the moral, physical, and spiritual welfare of individuals.

The principles and conceptual underpinnings of group work became synthesized in agency-based work such as that of the YWCA (Northern & Kurland, 2001). As Jane Addams noted in 1930, "Certain enthusiasts for creative discussion, such as the national Y.W.C.A. in their widespread organization of committees, boards, and clubs have accepted the growing change of basis in modern life from individual to organized activities" (p. 411). Indeed, the YWCA defined itself as "a group work agency" (Height, 1945, p. 390) which provided "a rich setting for the practice of a type of group work that could count heavily on the side of democracy" (Williamson, 1940, p. 209) and was particularly well-suited to building "democracy as a mode of life" (p. 209). Group work was a major division in which a third of all YWCA staff across the nation were engaged (Hurlin, 1943). As Dorothy Height (1945), an African American social worker who joined the YWCA National Board in 1944 explained, group work was "an educational process aimed at the development, social adjustment and growth of the individual through voluntary group association and the use of this association as a means of furthering other socially desirable ends" (p. 390). The grandest of those socially desirable ends, arguably the ultimate goal of group work, was the practice of true democracy, which required the full and intelligent participation of all members of society unhindered by the shackles of racial inequality and discrimination.

As radical as the YWCA's stance on race relations was in the context of its times, it did not challenge the assimilationist logic of its era. As Ethel Bird of the National Board alluded in 1936, the YWCA envisioned both the minority

Associations and the International Institutes as transitional measures necessitated by the exigencies of the present. "The fact is that the reason for having a Negro branch is exactly opposite for the reason for having an International Institute. In the former case, it is the dominant whites' unreadiness to accept the colored people on equal terms. In the case of the immigrant group it is the unreadiness of the nationality group, their relative security because of language, difference in social customs" (Bird, 1936, p. 1). The YWCA was working to generate social conditions that did not yet exist: a sufficient shift in the general public's prejudiced views on racial minorities to obviate the need for segregated branches and enough acculturation on the part of the White immigrants to obviate the need for the protective Institutes. The ultimate aim was the integration of both racial minorities and new immigrants into an inclusive democracy. But this desired "social integration" (YWCA of the U.S.A., 1942, p. 1) was envisioned as a unidirectional shift. The YWCA saw itself as a link between minority communities and the general "Caucasian community" (YWCA of the U.S.A., 1942, p. 1), but only as one that would shepherd the former to fit into and be accepted by the latter. While the YWCA imagined for the nation a vigorous and vibrant democratic community in which all races would be included as viable and equal participants, it did not imagine that such inclusion could or should fundamentally reshape the community itself; the primacy of the "Caucasian community" was never questioned. It also did not imagine that any minority group might, as would prove to be the case of the Nikkei, resist such an integrationist vision.

Notwithstanding its vocal repudiation of the treatment of the Nikkei, like all social work organizations, however, the YWCA became quickly resigned to mass removal as a *fait accompli* and turned its attention to amelioration rather than opposition.

> The Associations on the Coast have handled the situation, on the whole, extraordinarily well. However certain things must be attended to once evacuation begins in earnest: children must have regular schooling; people who leave must be kept in touch with; Y.W.C.A.'s in reception areas must be asked to look out for these newcomers; their physical health and well-being must be looked after. (YWCA National Board—Civil Liberties Committee of the National Public Affairs Committee, 1942, pp. 1–2)

In a March 6, 1942, "Extra Confidential" memorandum to the Consulting Group on West Coast Situation, a consortium of several California social welfare agencies, Mabel Ellis, a member of the National Board who would head up the as yet unformed Japanese American Evacuation Project, reported on a telephone conversation with Edith Bremer, the Executive Director of the National

Institute of Immigrant Welfare, the umbrella organization for the independent International Institutes.

> Mrs. Bremer telephoned. Miss Watson [Annie Clo Watson] has just reported to her that the San Francisco Committee of Social Agencies reached Chester Rowell[4] on the Japanese situation, and he succeeded in getting in touch with President Roosevelt. The agency representatives met yesterday in San Francisco and decided to "move heaven and earth" to reach the most distinguished California citizens they could get; succeeded in doing so and got the group of distinguished citizens an interview with General de Witt. They urged upon General de Witt two decisions on policy, first; the Federal Government must set up and carry through a plan for evacuation, resettlement, protection and custodian of property, both for American citizens of Japanese parentage, and enemy aliens, whether Japanese, or German, or Italian. Second; they urged that 75 to 100 tribunals be set up immediately to which American citizens of Japanese ancestry could voluntarily submit themselves for investigation of their loyalty to the United States. This group will select from its own membership persons to fly to Washington and talk with President Roosevelt. (Ellis, 1942a, p. 1)

The first point would be accomplished under the aegis of the Fourth Army, the Social Security Board (SSB), and the War Relocation Authority (WRA). The second, "loyalty tribunals," was an enterprise supported by social welfare organizations such as the American Association of Social Workers (AASW) (Price, 1942), which suggested "the setting up of civilian hearing boards which could pass on the loyalty of individual Japanese, whether alien or American born, and give certificates stating their right to remain in the restricted areas" (Ellis, 1942b, p. 1). The individualized adjudication was argued to be a better option than the wholesale presumption of disloyalty—or perhaps the utter impossibility of loyalty—on which the impending removal was believed to be founded. Of course, the prospect of wholesale removal and the blanket presumption of disloyalty for Italians or Germans, a much bigger population of enemy aliens, was never contemplated. The pre-removal individual tribunals never came to fruition. Individual "investigation of loyalty" for the Nikkei did, however, get enacted in the camps through the infamous loyalty questionnaire used to segregate the "disloyal" population to Tule Lake and as part of the regular leave-clearance hearings of the WRA which assessed individual Nikkei applying to leave the camps for work and resettlement (Commission on Wartime Relocation and Internment of Civilians, 1982).

---

[4] The editor of the San Francisco Chronicle, a leading member of the Pacific Coast Committee on American Principles and Fair Play, and a vocal opponent of the Nikkei removal and incarceration.

Clearing the Coast

Becoming Enemy Aliens

The removal of the Nikkei from the West Coast began in February of 1942 under the command of Lieutenant General John Lesesne DeWitt, head of the U.S. Fourth Army and the Western Defense Command. It occurred in two swift but incremental steps. The first was a brief period often referred to as "voluntary evacuation" lasting until March of 1942, during which the Nikkei were "prohibited" from certain waterfront areas and urged to move to the interior regions of the West. The second phase was the mandated removal of all Nikkei from Oregon, Washington, and coastal California. The forced removal, first to 16 temporary detention centers then to 10 long-term incarceration camps, began in March and was accomplished under the aegis of the Army and managed by the SSB.

On December 7, 1941, Japan's First Air Fleet attacked Pearl Harbor, a naval base in the U.S. territory of Hawaii. "Before sunset of December 7, the intelligence authorities had started to pick up individuals on their lists who were suspected of disloyalty" (War Relocation Authority, 1946a, p. 6). By the end of the day, several thousand foreign nationals, including 737 Japanese immigrants, were taken into federal custody (Daniels, Kitano, & Taylor, 1983). On the following day, December 8, 1941, the United States formally entered World War II. On January 14, 1942, Presidential Proclamation 2537 (7 Fed Proclamation. Reg. 329) was issued, establishing regulations pertaining to "alien enemies." The proclamation required all nationals who were from countries at war with the United States and who resided within the continental United States, Puerto Rico, and the Virgin Islands to apply for and acquire certificates of identification. On January 28, 1942, the California State Personnel Board voted to bar all descendants of enemy nations from civil service employment; the policy was enforced only for those of Japanese ancestry (Myer, 1943). On the following day, U.S. Attorney General Francis Biddle issued an order prohibiting all enemy aliens (citizens of nations at war with the United States) from designated areas such as the San Francisco waterfront. On January 31, Biddle added 59 additional prohibited zones in California, to be cleared of enemy aliens by February 15 (Inada, 2000). A curfew, which restricted all Axis aliens from being outside of their registered residence between the hours of 9 P.M. and 6 A.M., and restricted their travel to and from their places of employment or within five miles of their place of residence, was put in place in California on February 4, 1942.

A December 8, 1941, memorandum by Martha Chickering, Director of the California State Department of Social Welfare (CSDSW), indicates that that body immediately began putting together a "Committee on Welfare of the State

Council of Defense" (p. 1) even prior to the declaration of war. Chickering, the Chair of the subcommittee on Welfare, wrote to Annie Clo Watson, the Executive Secretary of the San Francisco International Institute, requesting her service on the committee as the member "responsible for the protection of the welfare of minority groups" (p. 1).[5] Chickering's request to Watson to pay particular attention to the protection of "the American-born Japanese, who regards himself as an American but could well be driven into a bitter attitude toward this country by unwise or hasty action" (p. 1), was a harbinger of things to come, foretelling the military and governmental justification for the mass removal, as well as social work's own equivocal role as both the protector of the Nikkei and the instrument of their delivery into incarceration. Watson, who would take temporary leave of the International Institute from August 1942 to May 1943 to work for the YWCA's Japanese American Evacuation Project (JAEP), readily agreed to serve as the chair of the subcommittee on Minority Groups (International Institute of San Francisco, 1942a).

By late December of 1941, West Coast Nikkei were already living under serious constraints. A December 27, 1941, letter from Watson (1941) to Margaret A. Watkins, CSDSW supervisor of field service, lists the "difficulties of the Japanese in the present emergency" (p. 1) in California. According to Watson, the main concerns for the Nikkei at that point were financial: "The telephone company is asking a special deposit sometimes as high as ten dollars from all Japanese subscribers, whether American citizen or alien"(p. 1). Watson also noted that many Nikkei businesses were forced to close because funds were frozen in "Japanese banks," shut down by government orders for the duration of the war, and that "the public are boycotting businesses that are open" (p. 2). An estimated 1,200 Nikkei truckers could "no longer use their trucks because the 'public liability and property damage' insurance has been revoked" (p. 2). Watson reported that Nikkei children in Sacramento were "afraid to go to school" (p. 1). By February of 1942, Watson reported, "[c]onditions among the Japanese have reached a point of extreme seriousness" (p. 1), with the gravest problems "in San Francisco County, Sacramento County, Alameda County, the Imperial Valley around Fresno and Los Angeles and San Diego counties" (p. 1). By early March of 1942, "[c]ertain definite serious discriminations" (p. 2) had taken place, including revoking of "licenses of certain storekeepers and professional persons" (YWCA National Board—Civil Liberties Committee of the National Public Affairs Committee, 1942, p. 2). The Civil Liberties Committee, the YWCA body reporting on these and other official and civic acts of bigotry, described that "in some places mob law is practically in effect" (p. 2).

---

[5] Watson served as the San Francisco Institute's Executive Secretary for a total of 25 years from 1932 to 1957.

One of the effects of such discriminatory measures was that the well-established systems of mutual aid the Nikkei communities relied on could no longer function. In late February of 1942, the YWCA's Mabel Ellis (1942b) reported that

> [t]he Japanese have been so long apart from the American community that they do not know how to use the American organizations. Since all their own benefit organizations have been closed and their funds frozen they are in a very serious situation. (p. 3)

The minutes of the January 1942 meeting of the San Francisco International Institute Board of Directors provide an inside glimpse into the situation. The Japanese Emergency Relief Committee (JERC), an hitherto independent Nikkei organization, sought the help of the Institute in their effort to have their frozen funds be released to the San Francisco Community Chest.[6] The idea was that those funds could then be funneled to the Institute, which could be the administrative body to distribute those funds to assist the Nikkei during "this emergency" (James, 1942, p. 2). The Japanese Benevolent Society (JBS) similarly sought the Institute's help in "releasing their fund of $750.00 for the salary of the caretaker in the Japanese cemetery" (James, 1942, p. 2). The Institute Board was willing, but the Nikkei organizations' efforts to work around the funding freeze did not prove to be a viable solution. Watson reported at the next Board meeting, held on February 17, that the JBS funds in the Yokohama Specie Bank were frozen for the duration of the war and could not be released to the Chest (International Institute of San Francisco, 1942b). There were no further reports on the fate of the JERC funding in this or subsequent meetings of the Board.

Across the continent in New York City, Tooru Kanazawa (1942), a freelance journalist and a member of a Nikkei organization called the Committee for Democratic Treatment for Japanese Residents in Eastern States, reported that hundreds of Japanese nationals had been picked up for questioning by the FBI on the night of December 7. By the following day when war was declared, "the offices of the Japanese Association and Japanese Chamber of Commerce, the groups to which the Issei would normally turn for assistance in the crisis, were raided and padlocked and their officers taken to Ellis Island" (p. 14) to be interrogated by Hearing Boards. Kanazawa noted that, given "practically ninety per cent of the Nisei here were thrown out of jobs" (p. 14), the "plight of about 300 unattached Issei, who earned a precarious livelihood even in the best of times, is

---

[6] Community Chests in the U.S., precursors of the United Way, were charitable fund-raising organizations that collected money from local businesses and workers and distributed it to charitable community projects.

even more serious. Many face privation and starvation; one committed suicide in a local hotel because he had no hope of help" (p. 14). Ironically, the economic and social sanctions swiftly imposed on the Nikkei drove them from the City, where they would have been exempt from the coming removal and incarceration, "back to their homes on the West Coast" (p. 14) which they would subsequently be forced to leave.

"Alien Enemy Evacuation Program"

On February 13, 1942, the West Coast congressional delegation made a formal recommendation to the President for the removal of all Nikkei from the Pacific Coast. On the next day, Attorney General Francis Biddle established Restricted Area No. 1, "a strip of the California coast 500 miles in length and from 30 to 150 miles wide" within which, effective February 24, a curfew between 9:00 P.M. and 6 A.M. and restricted movements to within five miles of their homes were imposed on all enemy nationalities (War Relocation Authority, 1946b). On February 19, 1942, President Roosevelt signed Executive Order 9066 (3 CFR 1092-93), which authorized the establishment of military areas from which civilians could be excluded. On February 26, 1942, the Western Defense Command designated Terminal Island, located in Los Angeles Harbor and home to approximately 3,500 Nikkei, as a prohibited zone. All Issei males had already been rounded up by the FBI earlier in the month. The remaining Nikkei residents of the island were ordered to leave within 48 hours and to settle themselves in inland areas.

Milton Silverman's report on the "Japanese in California," produced for WRA internal usage dated April 30, 1942, described that most of the Island's Nikkei lived in company housing in a small enclave "in crowded Fish Harbor, in the half dozen square blocks of drab red-walled wooden houses" (p. 4) and had come to the island "long before it became a vital military area" (p. 4). They were not a prosperous group: "A few operated boats—either the small vessels or the big $50, 000 seiners—that usually belong to the cannery. They rarely own their own boats and fishing equipment" (p. 4). A report of the American Friends Service Committee, recounting the efforts of the Friends "to save the net of a Japanese fisherman," provides a glimpse into the crippling economic losses suffered by this community.

> It had cost about $4,000, more than a year's income of this family. The net naturally had to be left behind, and by the time Friends were informed that the owner wished someone to take care of it for him, it had been so exposed to the weather that all they could do was sell it to one of the canneries for the value of the leads and corks. This brought exactly $30. (1942, p. 4)

Silverman described that, by the time of his visit at the end of March, "Terminal Island was deserted, its Shinto temples stripped . . . the small gardens all dying and bedraggled, many of its former inhabitants in concentration camps, others in reception centers for evacuees, it stores shut tight, many of its boats still bearing 'For Sale' signs" (p. 5). The few Nikkei who returned to the island after January 2, 1945, when the exclusion order was rescinded, would find that the village they had called Furusato, variously translated as "hometown," "native place," or "home sweet home," had been totally razed.[7]

Though little used by the Nikkei in actuality, there was, in theory, a federal program of aid available to such populations displaced from prohibited areas. Coordinating the provision of financial aid to the expelled Terminal Islanders as well as to the Nikkei who heeded General DeWitt's advice to leave the coastal areas, to "move out their families voluntarily and thus save themselves even greater troubles in the future, emphasizing to them that it was their patriotic duty to make this move voluntarily and with a minimum of inconvenience to the Government" (War Relocation Authority, 1946b, p. 2), became the job of the California State Department of Social Welfare (CSDSW). On February 7, 1942, Margaret A. Watkins, CSDSW supervisor of field service, notified departmental supervisors that the Alien Enemy Evacuation Program was under way. "Social welfare interviewers" (1942a, p. 1) from the state and county welfare offices would be assigned to the task. The social workers would be on the federal payroll under the aegis of the SSB, and would work out of various U.S. Employment Bureau offices located throughout the state and for the duration of the assignment. Their task was to "conduct interviews with aliens to help in providing solution of problems arising in connection with their removal" (p. 1). The interviewers, Watkins emphasized, must be the "very best available" (p. 2) since "it can be readily be seen that many problems will develop in the removal of this large group of aliens. It will involve the breaking up of families, the leaving of businesses and farms, etc., and the making of adequate plans for their care elsewhere will be very difficult" (p. 1).

The Alien Assistance Services, also called the Social Assistance Program, was part of a federal effort overseen by the SSB and administered via the CSDSW through the various county welfare departments.

> Upon the request of and on behalf of the United States Attorney General, on January 31, 1942, Mr. Paul V. McNutt, Federal Security Administrator and

---

[7] The experience of some of the Terminal Island residents has been captured by the Japanese American National Museum in the Terminal Island Life History Project, a collection of 25 oral history interviews and personal memoirs. The collection is available at the Online Archives of California: http://content.cdlib.org/view?docId=kt367n993t&brand=calisphere&doc.view=entire_text.

Director of Defense, Health and Welfare Services, accepted the responsibility of facilitating the transfer of alien enemies from areas designated by the Attorney General and to relocate and re-establish such aliens in appropriate places and in appropriate activities. (California State Department of Social Welfare, 1942, p. 1 of Part I)

Paul McNutt, in turn, appointed Richard H. Neustadt to serve as the regional director for the Office of Defense, Health, and Welfare Services. Neustadt was charged with administering assistance within the eight-state Western Defense Command, which encompassed Washington, Oregon, California, Idaho, Montana, Nevada, Utah, and Arizona (California State Department of Social Welfare, 1942). Overseeing the day-to-day affairs of the regional office under Neustadt were Azile Aaron, the regional representative of public assistance, and her assistant, Phoebe Bannister. Headquartered in San Francisco, the office oversaw four supervisory areas: Northern California and Nevada, Southern California, Washington, and Oregon (California State Department of Social Welfare, 1942, p. 1 of Part II). This administrative structure remained in place even when the Social Assistance Program shifted out of the "voluntary" phase to manage the processing of the Nikkei for mandatory removal and incarceration.

Backed by $500,000 in federal funds, the Social Assistance Program was designed to "provide financial assistance and other services, on an emergency basis, to enemy aliens and their families whose normal living arrangements have been disrupted as a result of residence in areas now prohibited to them" (California State Department of Social Welfare, 1942, p. 1 of Part II). It provided information and referral to aliens so that they "may conform to existing regulations" and "services in connection with resolving problems of housing, moving, emergency medical care and related contingencies" (California State Department of Social Welfare, 1942, p. 2 of Part I), and it distributed emergency financial assistance. The aid was means-tested. Home visits were recommended "whenever possible in every case when financial assistance is requested" (California State Department of Social Welfare, 1942, p. 6 of Part III). Cash benefits were to be given only "to cover immediate expenses directly attributable to moving" (California State Department of Social Welfare, 1942, p. 2) due specifically to the evacuation orders. Benefits were stringently distinguished from any previous or ongoing social assistance that the families or individuals received from county or state coffers.

In overseeing the assistance program, Neustadt, a government figure noteworthy for his consistent calls for compassion in this era of official bigotry and public hysteria, repeatedly emphasized the need for respectful treatment: "It is highly important that these people be treated with dignity and with courtesy. They should be made to feel that while because of war it is necessary to move them out of the prohibited areas and to prevent their working therein, the United States Government wishes to help them avoid unnecessary hardships in such transfer" (Neustadt, 1942, p. 2). In her February 7 letter to the Social Assistance Program staff, Neustadt's deputy, Azile Aaron reiterated the directives for courteous treatment, emphasizing also that "it will be necessary for you to use judgment and all of your social work skills" (1942, p. 2).

During this "voluntary" period, between mid-February 1942 and March 29, 1943, the workload of the social workers involved in the Alien Enemy Evacuation Program was light. Social workers staffing the Program in Los Angeles County kept a list of the most frequent service requests. Fourth on the list was: "directing Caucasians to Little Tokyo area regarding purchases of reduced priced merchandise" (Copland, 1942, p. 3). Few Nikkei were leaving, and most of those who relocated did not seek aid. In his February 21, 1942, testimony to the Tolan Committee, Neustadt reported that only 140 had applied for financial assistance by that point. He explained, however, that the "small number is not to be taken as a measure of their need" (United States Congress—House Select Committee Investigating National Defense Migration, 1942, p. 11025).

> Rather, it is to be taken as a measure of their pride and their desire to understand the reason for this order and their desire to be as cooperative with the Government as possible. In other words, we know of many cases who will need money, who have strained every resource to move out of the prohibited area, but they prefer to exhaust their own resources before asking for any aid of any kind. (United States Congress—House Select Committee Investigating National Defense Migration, 1942, p. 11025)

It is impossible to definitively determine why so few applied for aid. But several other causal factors, including the near total lack of prewar contact between the Nikkei and mainstream social service organizations, can be conjectured. Though the U.S.-born Nisei and Sansei were eligible for various state and county aid programs, the Nikkei community as a whole had never used government services and, except for those in the direst need, did not do so now. There are also no indications in the records that any proactive efforts were made to make the availability of the evacuation aid known to the Nikkei; it is unclear to what extent the Nikkei community members were aware that such a program existed. Finally, it must be remembered that the aid was strictly means-tested, requiring intrusive measures to determine eligibility. The understandable unwillingness of a minority community already suffering under government censure and hostile scrutiny to seek aid from that very body also must be considered.

Frank Koo Endo, a former resident of Fish Harbor interviewed for the Terminal Island Life History Project, explained that, upon their expulsion from the island, "[p]eople started moving out to Los Angeles and anywhere where friends or relatives lived" (Japanese American National Museum, 2001). The Western Defense Command had mandated their expulsion "but was not suggesting where they might go or how they might get there" (War Relocation Authority, 1946b, p. 2). The displaced Nikkei settled where they could; many interior communities were inhospitable. As soon as the orders for evacuation became public, "from all of the neighboring states began to come violent protests against receiving a population that California, Washington, Oregon and the Army had discredited. Apparently, nobody wanted these refugees" (War Relocation Authority, 1946b, p. 2). At the February Tolan Committee hearings in San Francisco, Neustadt testified that the question of where the Nikkei evacuees were to go had "haunted" him.

> I have seen resolutions of the governors, the chambers of commerce, and all the hospitality centers west of the Rocky Mountain States. They don't want them either. . . . We have had telegrams from all the towns in California protesting. (United States Congress—House Select Committee Investigating National Defense Migration, 1942, p. 11054)

In a midnight telephone conversation with Edith Bremer, the head of the International Institutes, Annie Clo Watson (1942) of the CSDSW Committee on Welfare of the State Council of Defense reported that the reactions came not only from officialdom but the "local communities" who have "held emergency meetings and decided that if the Japanese are not to be trusted in the coastal counties neither can they be trusted in the inland counties" (p. 1). "Vigilantes" were "springing up to prevent the entry of these refugee families into their own counties or town communities. And to insure that they keep moving on" (p. 1). In Watson's analysis, the counties in the southern part of California were "worse than anywhere else" (p. 1). But other reports indicated that the counties of the Central Valley, where a large percentage of the Nikkei already lived and farmed, vied also for the worst status. According to a WRA review dated April 1942, Fresno and Tulare counties had seen the influx of several hundred more Nikkei in the days following the establishment of the military areas.

> They have settled wherever housing facilities were available—in the towns and on farms. In some instances Japanese farm operators have permitted evacuees to settle on their farms. On one farm near Del Rey approximately 100 Japanese—possibly more—are camped. Resentment on the part of the white residents in the area is openly expressed. Their general complaints is there were enough Japanese there before and they object to the area being made "a dumping ground for the Japs from Los Angeles and San Francisco." The

attitude has numerous ramifications. For example, the Tulare County Board of Supervisors several times took action refusing emergency welfare aid to the Japanese evacuees, and Supervisor J. G. Brown of Terra Bella was quoted in the Fresno Bee on April 14, 1942, as saying: "We prefer that the government remove all Japanese from the county. If they love the Japanese enough to send social security workers here to care for them, they may find that the workers would get some of the same treatment as the Japanese." (Dean, 1942, p. 2)

CSDSW Supervisor of Field Service Margaret Watkins' March 20 memorandum to Director Martha Chickering outlined the "need for care of 100 Japanese aliens" who had moved to Hayward County because of Executive Order 9066 of February 19, 1942, which established Prohibited Zone A, and "who, it was reported, were starving" (Watkins, 1942b, p. 2) but was feared "might not receive prompt service" at the County offices. The Central Valley Counties' reluctance and, at times, outright refusal to administer even federally funded aid to the Nikkei was a phenomenon that would recur also in the resettlement period, hampering the Nikkei attempts to make their way back home to the California towns and farms from which they had been removed.

For many of these relocated Nikkei, the so-called voluntary move would prove to have been ultimately futile since they would be "evacuated" from the locations to which they had moved. A report by the CSDSW's Alfred Knight from the Lindsay, California, WCCA station, made in July 1942 during the period of mandated removal, showed that many of the Nikkei in the area were those who had made a "voluntary" move during the period of time when such a move was still permitted.

> The move had been made after consulting the proper authorities to ascertain where they might go. They had spent large sums of money not only in moving, but in relocating, and, of course, found later that they might as well have "not made the effort." However, they showed the usual courtesy found in working with evacuees at Control stations. (Knight, 1942, p. 2)

In its Bulletin of May 12, 1942, the YWCA reported that although "little was accomplished numerically," in the end, the "Y.W.C.A.'s and other agencies tried to find new homes for people known to them" (Ellis & Wilkins, 1942, p. 1) during this period of voluntary evacuation. The YWCA appeared to have been, for example, deeply involved in aiding the Nikkei relocating to Colorado. According to Elsie Harper and Helen Flack of the National Board's Public Affairs Committee, Colorado had an existing population of Nikkei, and it seemed that many of those relocating to Colorado had moved from that state to California and were returning to "memories, friends and relatives" (Harper & Flack, 1942, p. 1). The

Nikkei already living in Colorado at the outbreak of war, however, were "a little nervous for fear too many Japanese people will return, which will make it hard for all of them" (Harper & Flack, 1942, p. 1) because not only the increase in numbers but the inevitable publicity attached to the return would make them a more visible target of "pseudo patriots and . . . other ill-informed people" (Ellis & Wilkins, 1942, p. 1) fomenting racist hysteria.

The Commission on Wartime Relocation and Internment of Civilians estimates that by the end of the voluntary period an estimated 1,963 Nikkei had relocated in Colorado (Commission on Wartime Relocation and Internment of Civilians, 1982).[8] While there was, as elsewhere, vocal opposition to the Nikkei from powerful sources such as the *Denver Post*, and the usual gamut of discriminatory measures such as the revoking of fire and theft insurance on automobiles, the Nikkei found in Colorado a less hostile reaction than they did in inland California and in states such as Utah, Idaho, and Nevada. There was in Colorado, moreover, organized support by the YWCA, whose local associations "dealt actively with the employment, housing, and recreation problems" (Briesemeister & Ingels, 1943, p. 1) that faced the incoming Nikkei. The Denver Association, with its "large group of voting people of Japanese ancestry who have been a part of the Association for the past five years" (Briesemeister, December 1942, p. 540), was particularly proactive in creating wide support within its organization and in creating housing and employment opportunities for the relocated Nikkei.

In the end, approximately 9,000 Nikkei—including those from specifically prohibited areas, such as Terminal Island, where "evacuation" was not voluntary—heeded the call to relocate themselves into the interior areas (United States Army, 1943, p. 43). An estimated 5,000 moved to the interior states, with Colorado (1,963) and Utah (1,519) receiving the largest numbers. The remainder moved within the Coastal states, to face uprooting once again a few months hence, when their new locales became prohibited (Commission on Wartime Relocation and Internment of Civilians, 1982). That so few chose this "voluntary" path is explained in part by Nikkei demographics: "Occupationally, nearly half (45.2%) of the West Coast Japanese were engaged in agriculture" (United States Army, 1943, p. 85). Because Nikkei farms were family enterprises requiring the labors of all family members, the actual numbers involved in farming were probably higher than the Army's estimate. Of course, farmers were not the only segments of the community unwilling and unable to leave their properties and means of livelihood. Given that most Nikkei businesses were in ethnic enclaves with a limited market for resale, liquidating such enterprises, as would be seen in the mandatory phase, would result in heavy losses. Few had liquid

---

[8] The YWCA estimated the number at 3,000 (Briesemeister & Ingels, 1943).

assets since the majority of the population was, thus, bound to land, equipment, crops, or store and stock, and any savings they might have had were frozen in the "Japanese" banks. The AEEP aid provisions were minimal even for moving costs to those without any means, but neither this nor any other program provided any aid to the Nikkei in finding new housing or employment. Relocation was an altogether "impractical" course for all, according to the Commission on Wartime Relocation and Internment of Civilians (1982, p. 94). Those who did relocate during this "voluntary" phase did so because they had no choice but to do so, or, in the Army's analysis, were able to leave because they were "persons with some financial independence" (United States Army, 1943, p. 104) who were to some degree buffered from the inevitable losses.

In the obfuscating language of the Army, the "voluntary" program of removal "met with measurable success" (United States Army, 1943, p. 43). In the incongruous rationale of the Army, whatever its original intent in formulating the program had been, its failure to relocate large numbers of the Nikkei also became the justification for their planned removal and incarceration. In the Army's narrative, the closure of the so-called voluntary program and the shift to the so-called relocation program was precipitated by that failure: "the attitude of the interior states were hostile. This group, considered too dangerous to remain on the West Coast, was similarly regarded by state and local authorities, and by the population of the interior. The evacuees were not welcome. Incidents developed with increasing intensity, with the result that the Assistant Chief of Staff for Civil Affairs, on March 21, recommended to the Commanding General that evacuation be placed on the basis of complete Federal supervision and control" (United States Army, 1943, p. 43).

In her preface to the oral history interview of James H. Rowe, Jr., Assistant Attorney General under Francis Biddle during the war years, conducted for the Japanese American Relocation Oral History Project in 1971, interviewer Amelia Fry explained that, contrary to the popular belief that the removal was a military need, the Justice Department, the FBI, and the Intelligence branches of the Army and the Navy had "all opposed mass evacuation of Japanese-Americans because, in their opinions, such a move would be illegal, unnecessary, and counter-productive for the control of espionage and sabotage since it would disturb established intelligence patterns" (Rowe, 1971, p. 9). The push for removal came from the West Coast congressional delegates; California's attorney general Earl Warren, running for governor in 1942; Western agricultural interests; and Lieutenant General DeWitt and Lieutenant Colonel Karl Bendetsen, two key figures in the Fourth Army, in charge of the Western Defense Command (Commission on Wartime Relocation and Internment of Civilians, 1982).

A February 11, 1942, telephone conversation between Lt. Colonel Bendetsen, calling from General DeWitt's office, and the Assistant Secretary of War John

J. McCloy (Office of the Commanding General—Headquarters Western Defense Command and Fourth Army, 1942, p. 1) indicates that indeed, the path to total removal was already set in place well before the Voluntary Period ended.

MCCLOY: I think that is right; I think, probably if you kick them out of San Diego they would immediately run up to their friends in Los Angeles and just crowd into Little Tokio.

BENDETSEN: Yes, sir. That is the difficulty; they would form a Little Tokio in Los Angeles or some other key point, and then in that case all you'd have would be successive segregation.

MCCLOY: I—we talked to the President and the President, in substance, says go ahead and do anything you think is necessary under the circumstance.

BENDETSEN: Oh, you have already talked to the President and he says go ahead and do whatever you think is necessary?

MCCLOY: That's right. And, if it involves citizens, we will take care of citizens too. He says there will probably be some repercussions but it has got to be dictated by military necessity, but as he puts it, "Be as reasonable as you can."

BENDETSEN: I see, well, would he sign an executive order?

MCCLOY: I think he will.

The Consultative Council on the Problems of Evacuation

The documented history of need experienced by the Nikkei on both coasts renders difficult the interpretation of the brief career of the multiagency group of social work leaders that the Consultative Council of Refugee Agencies (CCRA) brought together in early March. The CCRA was an existing committee "composed of representatives of five national agencies dealing with refugee problems" (Family Welfare Association of America, 1942b, p. 1). Minutes of the CCRA's meeting held on February 11, 1942, at the National Refugee Service (NRS) offices in New York City, show that the meeting was focused on discussions of the "problem of restricted and prohibited areas" (Refugee Consultative Council, 1942a, p. 1). Two attending NRS members, Cecilia Razovsky, Director of the Department of Migration and a prominent figure in Jewish immigrant and refugee work, and Dorothy C. Kahn, the Director of the Department of Economic Adjustment and Family Service and faculty member at the Pennsylvania School of Social Work, had been in Washington the previous week "to discuss" with unnamed figures "plans for the removal of enemy aliens" from designated areas (Refugee Consultative Council, 1942a, p. 1). Much of the information they gathered in DC and disseminated to the Council at the meeting—for example, that "the removal is to be on a case by case basis," or that if "the need for speed and the extension of proscribed areas complicates the problem, the Farm Security Migratory Labor Camps will be used for temporary reception centers rather than CCC Camps" (Refugee Consultative Council, 1942a, p. 1)— would prove to be erroneous. But Kahn's suggestions that the CCRA "should be giving some thought to the matter of what plans it might suggest" (Refugee Consultative Council, 1942a, p. 2) appears to have spurred the sitting Council to convene a meeting of a larger group of national agencies to formulate plans for aiding "enemy aliens affected by the various evacuation measures" (Family Welfare Association of America, 1942b, p. 1).

Held on March 11, 1942, at the New York offices of the Family Welfare Association of America (FWAA) and chaired by Joseph P. Chamberlain, the head of the NRS, the meeting was attended by members of several prominent national private social work agencies: Mabel Ellis of the YWCA National Board, Edith Bremer of the National Institute of Immigrant Welfare (International Institutes), Read Lewis of the Common Council for American Unity (CCAU; formerly the Foreign Language Information Service), Esther Beckwith of the National Council of Jewish Women, Bruce Wohler of the National Catholic Welfare Conference, George W. Rabinoff of the National Social Welfare Assembly, and Harry Lurie of the Council of Jewish Federations and Welfare Funds, among others. Invited but not in attendance were Linton B. Swift of the FWAA, Hanna Ziegler of the Conference of Jewish Social Welfare, Howard W. Hopkirk of the Child Welfare League of America, and Allen Burns of the Community Chests and Councils. The promising gathering of so many prominent social work agencies represented by major players in the field of social work did not, however, appear to have yielded any traceable actions.[9]

The expressed purpose of the expanded group meeting had been to "discuss what private agencies could do to assist in evacuation plans, with the hope that a statement of social work principles to be observed might be adopted which all agencies could send to their locals" (Family Welfare Association of America, 1942b, p. 1). On the first question—what private agencies should do—the surprising conclusion reached at the meeting was that they should curtail, rather than increase, involvement. There was general agreement among the attendees that "clearance between agencies was desirable" (Family Welfare Association of America, 1942b, p. 1). Clearance, however, was not forthcoming. An FWAA Information memorandum for staff, dated February 25, 1942, and broadcasted a couple of weeks prior to the meeting, had noted that the local agencies' offers of service were not met with alacrity by the SSB,

---

[9] Two documents encapsulate the discussions at the meeting: the minutes of the meeting, a four-page document produced by the Refugee Consultative Council (1942b), and the March 13, 1942 Information Memorandum to Staff, a two-page document produced by the FWAA (1942b).

the part of the Federal Security Agency (FSA) charged with providing aid to enemy aliens and others affected by government action. Its report on "the situation on the Pacific Coast" included a note on Freda Mohr of the Jewish Social Service Bureau in Los Angeles, who requested the FWAA's intervention with SSB. Despite her agency's expressed offers to participate "in planning for the evacuation of Japanese emergency in Los Angeles" (Family Welfare Association of America, 1942c, p. 1), Mohr reported that "the local agencies were never taken into the picture" (Family Welfare Association of America, 1942c, p. 1) by the SSB on their plans and activities. Like Mohr's Jewish Social Service Bureau, the NRS had offered its assistance to the regional Director of the SSB in San Francisco (Refugee Consultative Council, 1942a) in mid-February; there were "many problems arising from illness of members of families which have to be evacuated" (p. 2). The NRS was aware also that several other agencies were attempting to provide services, for example, "trying to offer storage room for families to store their goods," knowing it was "extremely difficult for families to find places where their furniture will be safe during their absence" (p. 2).

It is unclear why the SSB refused these offers of help. Many factors were at play. The meeting had taken place in a liminal space between the so-called voluntary evacuation, halted at the end of February, and the first of the series of civilian exclusion orders on March 24 that began the mandatory removal process. At the time of the meeting, the removal was a still-developing phenomenon—a certain prospect, but not yet an actuality. It was as yet unclear to those attending the meeting which areas of the West Coast, and in what order, would be affected by removal orders and whether or not the FSA would be responsible for the provision of aid to the affected as it had been during the "voluntary" period. The rumors that a new agency would be set up to deal with the removal (Family Welfare Association of America, 1942b) were probably about the formation of the WRA—which would not be involved in the removal itself—established on March 18, 1942, a week after the meeting, via Executive Order 9102 (3 CFR 1123). An FWAA Information Memorandum to Staff dated March 13, 1942, two days after the meeting, reported that "during the meeting Miss [Dorothy] Kahn telephoned to Washington and was told that no decision had been reached" on these matters (Family Welfare Association of America, 1942b, p. 1). Perhaps the speed at which plans were formulated and implemented at this stage left the agency itself unable to cope with such offers of help; its own procedures and structures needed to be established on the run. It is also possible that the kinds of help the private agencies offered—geared toward solving the problems of the Nikkei—were not the kinds of issues the SSB found most urgent to solve; its focus was on the efficiency of the removal, not the fallout.

Whatever drove the SSB's actions, the consensus reached at the meeting of these major private agencies was that their offers of involvement impeded the work of the SSB and should be curtailed.

> [T]oo many, rather than too few private agencies and volunteer agencies are concerned in the problem at the moment and in some instances this has been hampering to the official agencies. (Family Welfare Association of America, 1942b, p. 1)[10]

More unaccountable perhaps than the refusal of the SSB to accept aid proffered by social work agencies was that this group of major social work agencies meeting for the ostensible purpose of organizing relief and support for a population undergoing a cataclysm contented themselves with doing so little. It assured itself that the SSB "would call upon the private agencies as needed" (Family Welfare Association of America, 1942b, p. 1) and concluded that nothing further needed to be done. That the wide network of national agencies represented at the meeting could have done much to organize and deliver useful services to the families being wrenched out of their homes and communities, regardless of the reluctance of the SSB to accept those services, is beyond doubt. It did not, however, choose to do so at this meeting.

The second item on the meeting agenda, the "discussion of principles which should be observed in the handling of the whole evacuation program" (Family Welfare Association of America, 1942b, p. 1), provides some points for conjecture on why. Eight items were identified.

1. Interpret to aliens of enemy nationality the plans, regulations and spirit of this removal program
2. Assist in locating relatives, other habitations and in the protection of property rights, business plans, employment and the prevention of exploitation of aliens in respect to the foregoing
3. Lend staff to official agencies for their use temporarily
4. Identify new problems calling for declaration in policy or interpretation by official agencies
5. Assist in avoiding undesirable publicity
6. Use federal rules and regulations regarding travel, curfew, definitions of enemy aliens, etc. as they are issued

---

[10] Organizations in the coastal states, moreover, expressed "considerable irritation with eastern advice being offered to local agencies in the evacuation areas" (Family Welfare Association of America, 1945, p. 1).

7. Refrain from raising questions with state and local official agencies prematurely

8. Pending the designation of a single federal authority, clear all questions of policy and report all new problems to the Sub-Committee on Removal of Aliens of Enemy Nationality of the Consultative Council, 139 Centre Street, New York City. (Refugee Consultative Council, 1942b, pp. 2–3)

None of the eight contested the removal plans; only the second mentions the needs of the Nikkei; the remaining seven are about following the rules and *not* getting in the way of the official engines. The meeting as a whole was focused on determining how "private agencies can assist public agencies in the removal program" (Family Welfare Association of America, 1942b, p. 1), *not* how social work agencies could assist the Nikkei.

Social work was deeply invested in the FSA and the SSB, in whose creation it had been instrumental and in whose success it had a stake (Abramovitz, 1998). "For better or worse, social work had become a part of the machinery of the state" (Abramovitz, 1998, p. 516) during the 1930s, establishing a major professional foothold in public sector work generated by the policies and programs of the New Deal, and it was disinclined, on the whole, to publicly challenge the decisions of the administration which created it (Shaffer, 1998). Social work agencies were also protecting their hard-earned professional standing. Notes appended by Evelyn Hersey of the U.S. Immigration and Naturalization Service, serving as the Council Secretary, indicate that item five on the eight-item discussion points—the need to avoid publicity—"evoked considerable discussion with illustrated materials brought to the group about the difficulties and intense feelings evident in the present situation" (Refugee Consultative Council, 1942b, p. 3). Social work organizations' fear of generating such attention from the media and the general public was a persistent theme throughout the war years. This anxiety was rationalized always as a necessity for social workers to maintain their ability to work for the benefit of the Nikkei. That widespread knowledge of social work involvement was "likely to arouse not only the opposition of reactionary groups but also to make difficult the securing of appropriations in Congress to carry on even the minimum of social work" (Coyle, 1942, p. 1) was not a groundless fear. It is, however, difficult to wholly discount the fact that an element of self-protection was also involved in the calculations. In these war years, rife with fear propaganda, patriotism fervor, and deeply conflicted views on what constituted both, moreover, social work and social workers struggled to define the borders of its professional ethics. The FWAA discussion of client confidentiality and social worker responsibility in its March 1942 newsletter for network agencies, is informative.

1. The information sought by F.B.I. agents is usually factual. It is frequently available from other sources. No instances have come to attention in which it

has been used destructively. If it is not given freely by social agencies, it can be obtained through subpoena of the record.

2. Safeguarding of confidence of clients will continue to be the case workers' responsibility, but public interest in a war period must, at times, supersede this. Case workers cannot refuse information which may contribute to the country's defense. Neither can they lightly disregard the obligation which they have assumed when receiving clients' confidences. When information is given to the F.B.I., it may frequently be possible to inform clients that this has been done and why, or in some instances to explain in advance that this will be necessary. It should be kept in mind that social agencies may, at times also have information which will help to clear clients of suspicion of disloyalty. (Family Welfare Association of America, 1942a, p. 1)

No statement of social work principles ever appears to have materialized from this group. The question as to "whether the group would like to continue to meet as a group on problems of evacuation" was entertained, but "no definite decision was reached in view of the uncertainties of the present situation" (Family Welfare Association of America, 1942b, p. 1), and the group did not meet again.[11] The FWAA continued to periodically disseminate information on the situation through two resources: the "Information Memorandum" sent out to agency staff, and the *Blue Bulletin: Family Welfare and the Home Front*, a newsletter sent out to member agencies. *Common Ground*, the journal of the Common Council for American Unity (CCAU), established by Read Lewis and Louis Adamic, also published several articles on the topic throughout the war.

References

Aaron, A. H. (1942). Letter to all members of the Social Assistance staff, February 7, 1942. pp. 1. Social Welfare—War Services—Instructional Manual, 1942 (F3729:134). Department of Social Welfare Records, War Services Bureau. Sacramento, CA: California State Archives.

Abramovitz, M. (1998). Social work and social reform: An arena of struggle. *Social Work, 43*(6), 512–526.

Addams, J. (1930). *The second twenty years at Hull-House, September 1909 to September 1929, with a record of a growing world consciousness.* New York: Macmillan.

Alissi, A. S. (2001). The social group work tradition: Toward social justice a free society. *Social Group Work Foundation Occasional Papers.*, 1–26. Retrieved from http://digitalcommons.uconn.edu/sw_op/1

---

[11] The archival holdings of both the FWAA and the Common Council for American Unity (CCAU) contain documents that reference this meeting but no record of any subsequent meetings were found in these or any other archival holdings examined for this study.

American Friends Service Committee. (1942). Japanese Student Relocation, pp. 1–4. Folder—1942, Box 17—Pamphlets: Major. American Friends Service Committee—SWPO1, Social Welfare History Archives. Minneapolis: University of Minnesota.

Andrews, J. (2001). Group Work's place in social work: a historical analysis. *Journal of Sociology and Social Welfare, 28*(4), 45–65.

Beito, D. T. (1990). Mutual aid for social welfare: The case of American fraternal societies. *Critical Review: A Journal of Politics and Society, 4*(4), 709–736.

Bird, E. (1936). Letter to Mabel Ellis from Ethel Bird, May 12, 1936, pp. 1–2. Folder 9, Box 527. YWCA of the U.S.A. Records, Sophia Smith Collection. Northampton, MA: Smith College.

Breton, M. (1990). Learning from social group work traditions. *Social Work With Groups, 13*(3), 21–34.

Briesemeister, E. (December, 1942). "A challenge to real democracy: The Japanese in our communities." *Woman's Press, 36*, pp. 540 & 552. YWCA of the U.S.A.—Bound Periodicals, Sophia Smith Collection. Northampton, MA: Smith College.

Briesemeister, E., & Ingels, B. (1943). Report on Rohwer Relocation Center, McGehee, Arkansas, January 8, 1943, pp. 1–10. Folder 11, Box 723. YWCA of the U.S.A. Records, Sophia Smith Collection. Northampton, MA: Smith College.

Britton, B., Bartholomew, M., & Alway, L. (1941). Letter from Betty Britton, Secretary of the Young Women's Department, Mildred Bartholomew, Secretary of the Department of Religion and Membership, and Lazelle Alway, Secretary of the Girl Reserve Department of the Portland, Oregon YWCA to Oregon State Governor Charles A. Sprague, dated December 8, 1941, pp. 1–2. Japanese, relationship during World War II, Box Administrative Correspondence. Governor Charles A. Sprague Collection, Administrative Correspondence. Salem: Oregon State Archives.

California State Department of Social Welfare (1942). Manual of Instruction for Staff. pp. 1–34. Social Welfare—War Services—Instructional Manual, 1942 (F3729:134). Social Welfare—War Services—Instruction Manual, Department of Social Welfare Records, War Services Bureau. Sacramento, CA: California State Archives.

Chickering, M. A. (1941). Letter to Miss Annie Clo Watson, International Institute of San Francisco, from Martha A. Chickering, Director, State Department of Social Welfare, Sacramento, California, December 8, 1941, p. 1. Social Welfare—War Services—Defense, Minority Groups, 1941–1942 (F3729:56). Department of Social Welfare Records, War Services Bureau. Sacramento: California State Archives.

Commission on Wartime Relocation and Internment of Civilians. (1982). *Personal justice denied: Report of the Commission on Wartime Relocation and Internment of Civilians.* Washington, DC: U.S. Government Printing Office.

Copland, B. G. (1942). Alien Assistance Program in Los Angeles County: State Department of Social Welfare Office Memorandum to Miss Margaret S. Watkins, April 3, 1942. pp. 1. Social Welfare—War Services—WCCA—Control Stations—April, 1942 (F3729:138). Department of Social Welfare Records, War Services Bureau. Sacramento, CA: California State Archives.

Coyle, G. L. (1935). Group work and social change. In M. E. Hurlbutt (Ed.), *Proceedings of the National Conference of Social Work: selected papers, sixty-second annual session held in Montreal, Canada, June 9–15, 1935* (Vol. 62, pp. 393–405). New York: Columbia University Press.

Coyle, G. L. (1942). Letter from Grace L. Coyle, Professor of Group Work, Western Reserve University, Cleveland, OH, to George D. Nickel, Personal Finance Companies,

Los Angeles, CA, dated November 27, 1942, pp. 1–2. Folder 1212—Nickel, George—Norman, Sherwood, Box 156—Folders 1208–1214: Working Editorial. Survey Associates Records: SWA01, Social Welfare History Archives. Minneapolis: University of Minnesota.

Coyle, G. L. (1952). PART I: Social group work: An aspect of social work practice. *Journal of Social Issues, 8*(2), 23–34. doi: 10.1111/j.1540-4560.1952.tb01601.x.

Craddock, S. (1999). Embodying place: Pathologizing Chinese and Chinatown in nineteenth-century San Francisco. *Antipode, 31*(4), 351–371.

Craddock, S. (2000). *City of plagues: Disease, poverty, and deviance in San Francisco.* Minneapolis: University of Minnesota Press.

Daniels, R., Kitano, H. H., & Taylor, S. C. (Eds.). (1983). *Japanese Americans: From relocation to redress.* Salt Lake City: University of Utah Press.

Dean, G. D. (1942). Review of anti-Japanese incidents and local sentiment in Fresno and Tulare counties, California: War Relocation Authority Information Service, April 30, 1942, pp. 1–12. Folder: Review of anti-Japanese Incidents, Box 11: Relocation Division—Public Attitudes Files. Records of the War Relocation Authority, 1941–1989, Record Group 210, Washington Office Records—Washington Documents. ARC Identifier 1519285/MLR Number PI-77 2. Washington, DC: National Archives and Records Administration.

Ellis, M. B. (1942a). Letter from Mabel Brown Ellis, Secretary, Committee on Refugees, Young Women's Christian Association, to Miss Jane M. Hoey, Director, Bureau of Public Assistance, dated May 8, 1942, pp. 1–3. Folder 9—Japanese, correspondence, minutes, press releases, clippings, pamphlets, etc. 1942 (1 of 2 folders), Box 222. Immigration & Refugee Services of America: Common Council for American Unity Collection, Immigration History Research Center. Minneapolis: University of Minnesota.

Ellis, M. B. (1942b). Memorandum of Interview with Mr. Milton S. Eisenhower, director, War Relocation Authority from Mabel B. Ellis to Consulting Group on West Coast Situation, date March 23, 1942, pp. 1–2. Folder 20, Box 719. YWCA of the U.S.A. Records, Sophia Smith Collection. Northampton, MA: Smith College.

Ellis, M. B., & Ingraham, M. A. (April, 1942). News and Views: West Coast Evacuations and the YWCA. *Woman's Press, 36,* pp. 189. YWCA of the U.S.A.—Bound Periodicals, Sophia Smith Collection. Northampton, MA: Smith College.

Ellis, M. B., & Wilkins, H. J. (1942). The West Coast evacuation in relation to the struggle for freedom: Public Affairs News Service, Bulletin No. VI—(Series No. 6), May 12, 1942, pp. 1–16. Folder 22, Box 719. YWCA of the U.S.A. Records, Sophia Smith Collection. Northampton, MA: Smith College.

Family Welfare Association of America. (1942a). Family welfare and the Home Front: Blue Bulletin—Series B—No. 9 (For Member Agencies), 3/2/42, pp. 1–3. Folder—F.W.A.A. Bulletin Series B (Inc), Box 87—Pamphlets, Major. Family Service Association of America—SW076, Social Welfare History Archives. Minneapolis: University of Minnesota.

Family Welfare Association of America. (1942b). Information memorandum to staff, re: Evacuation plans on the West Coast, Sub-Committee on removal of aliens of enemy nationalities, March 13th, 1942, pp. 1–2. Folder—F.W.A.A.: Information Memos, 1942, Box 19: Administrative: Finance. Family Service Association of America—SW076, Social Welfare History Archives. Minneapolis: University of Minnesota.

Family Welfare Association of America. (1942c). Information memorandum to staff, re: Japanese evacuation in Oregon, April 18th, 1942, p. 1. Folder—F.W.A.A.: Information Memos, 1942, Box 19: Administrative: Finance. Family Service Association of America—SW076, Social Welfare History Archives. Minneapolis: University of Minnesota.

Family Welfare Association of America. (1945). Information memorandum—Request from UNRRA for personnel to work with displaced persons in German, April 16, 1945, p. 1. Folder—F.W.A.A.: Information Memos, 1945, Box 19: Administrative: Finance. Family Service Association of America—SW076, Social Welfare History Archives. Minneapolis: University of Minnesota.

Fitch, J. (1940). The nature of social action, part I. In G. L. Coyle (Ed.), *Proceedings of the National Conference of Social Work: selected papers, sixty-seventh annual conference, Grand Rapids, Michigan, May 26–June 1, 1940* (Vol. 67, pp. 485–497). New York, NY: Columbia University Press.

Flack, H. N. (January, 1942). Local exchange: In the Hawaiian Islands. *Woman's Press, 36*, pp. 37–41. *Woman's Press*, YWCA of the U.S.A.—Bound Periodicals, Sophia Smith Collection. Northampton, MA: Smith College.

Germain, C. B., & Gitterman, A. (1980). *The life model of social work practice.* New York: Columbia University Press.

Harper, E. D., & Flack, H. (1942). Public Affairs Office memorandum to Mable B. Ellis from Elsie D. Harper & Helen Flack, pp. 1–4. Folder 20, Box 719. YWCA of the U.S.A. Records, Sophia Smith Collection. Northampton, MA: Smith College.

Hartford, M. E. (1983). Group work today—through a rear view mirror, or issues in work with groups in a historical perspective. In N. C. Lang & C. Marshall (Eds.), *Patterns in the mosaic: proceedings of the 4th annual symposium for the advancement of social work with groups* (pp. 737–763). Toronto, Ontario: Committee for the Advancement of Social Work with Groups.

Height, D. I. (1945). The Adult Education Program of the YWCA among Negroes. *The Journal of Negro Education, 14*(3), 390–395.

Hurlin, R. G. (1943). *Salaries and Qualifications of YWCA Professional Workers* (ed.). New York: Russell Sage Foundation.

Inada, L. F. (Ed.). (2000). *Only what we could carry: The Japanese American internment experience.* Berkeley, CA: Heyday Books.

International Institute of San Francisco. (1942a). The International Institute of San Francisco Director's meeting, May 26, 1942, pp. 1–2. Folder 11—Japanese, Americans Relocation Centers and Resettlement, correspondence, reports, brochures, regulations, etc . . . 1942–1945 Box 2. International Institute of San Francisco Collection, Immigration History Research Center. Minneapolis: University of Minnesota.

International Institute of San Francisco. (1942b). Minutes of the Meeting of the Board of Directors, February 17, 1942, pp. 1–2. Folder 11—Japanese, Americans Relocation Centers and Resettlement, correspondence, reports, brochures, regulations, etc . . . 1942–1945, Box 2. International Institute of San Francisco Collection, Immigration History Research Center. Minneapolis: University of Minnesota.

Ishisaka, H., & Takagi, C. (1982). Social work with Asian and Pacific Americans. In J. W. Green (Ed.), *Cultural awareness in the human services* (pp. 122–156). Englewood Cliffs, NY: Prentice Hall.

James, W. L. (1942). The International Institute of San Francisco Meeting of the Board of Directors, January 20, 1942, p. 1. Folder 11—Japanese, Americans Relocation Centers and Resettlement, correspondence, reports, brochures, regulations, etc. . . 1942–1945 Box 2. International Institute of San Francisco Collection, Immigration History Research Center. Minneapolis: University of Minnesota.

Japanese American National Museum. (2001). Terminal Island Life History Project. Retrieved from Japanese American National Museum, http://content.cdlib.org/view?docId=kt367n993t&brand=calisphere&doc.view=entire_text

Kaiser, C. A. (1948). Current frontiers in social group work. In G. Springer (Ed.), *Proceedings of the National Conference of Social Work: selected papers, seventy-fourth Annual meeting, San Francisco, California, April 13–19, 1947* (pp. 418–428). New York: Columbia University Press.

Kanazawa, T. (1942). After Pearl Harbor—New York City. *Common Ground, 2*(1), 13–14.

Kanzaki, K. (1921). Is the Japanese menace in America a reality? *Annals of the American Academy of Political and Social Science, 93*, 88–97.

Knight, A. (1942). Report on Control Station, Lindsay, California, July 29, 1942, pp. 1–3. Social Welfare—War Services—WCCA—Reports—Control Stations—Lawndale-Riverside, 1942 (F3729:148). Department of Social Welfare Records, War Services Bureau. Sacramento: California State Archives.

Leiby, J. (1962). How social workers viewed The Immigration Problem *Current issues in social work seen in historical perspective: Compilation of six papers presented at a workshop held during Annual Program Meeting, St. Louis, Mo., January 17–20, 1962* (pp. 30–42). New York: Council on Social Work Education.

Lewis, A. S. (2008). *The barrier breaking love of God: The multicultural activism of the Young women's Christian Association, 1940s to 1970s.* PhD, Rutgers University, New Brunswick, New Jersey.

Light, I. H. (1972). *Ethnic enterprise in America: Business and welfare among Chinese, Japanese, and Blacks.* Berkeley and Los Angeles: University of California Press.

Lind, A. W. (1930). The ghetto and the slum. *Social Forces, 9*(2), 206–215.

Lindeman, E. (1939). Group work and education for democracy. In P. Kellogg (Ed.), *Proceedings of the National Conference of Social Work: selected papers, sixty-seventh annual conference, Buffalo, NY, June 18–24, 1939* (Vol. 66, pp. 343–347). New York, NY: Columbia University Press.

Maslen, S. (1941). Guideposts to social action. In J. Hoey (Ed.), *Proceedings of the National Conference of Social Work: selected papers, sixty-seventh annual conference, Atlantic City, NJ, June 1–7, 1941* (Vol. 68, pp. 642–651). New York, NY: Columbia University Press.

Matsuoka, J. K., & Ryujin, D. H. (1991). Asian American immigrants: A comparison of the Chinese, Japanese, and Filipinos. *Journal of Sociology & Social Welfare, 18*, 123–133.

Millis, H. A. (1915/1978). *The Japanese problem in the United States: An investigation for the commission on relations with Japan appointed by the Federal Council of the Churches of Christ in America.* New York: Arno Press (Originally published in 1915 by the Macmillan Company).

Mohl, R. A. (1982). Cultural pluralism in immigrant education: The International Institutes of Boston, Philadelphia, and San Francisco, 1920–1940. *Journal of American Ethnic History, 1*(2), 35–58.

Mohl, R. A., & Betten, N. (1972). Ethnic adjustment in the industrial city: The International Institute of Gary, 1919–1940. *International Migration Review, 6*(4), 361–376.

Mohl, R. A., & Betten, N. (1974). Paternalism and pluralism: Immigrants and social welfare in Gary, Indiana, 1906–1940. *American Studies, 15*(1), 5–30.

Mukaye, K. (1927). Young Japan in America. *Woman's Press, XXI*(11), pp. 760–761. YWCA of the USA—Bound Periodicals. Northampton, MA: Smith College.

Myer, D. S. (1943). *Uprooted Americans: The Japanese Americans and the War Relocation Authority during World War II.* Washington, DC: U.S. Government Printing Office.

Newstetter, W. I. (1935). What is social group work. In H. R. Knight (Ed.), *Proceedings of the National Conference of Social Work* (Vol. 62, pp. 291–299). Chicago, Illinois: University of Chicago Press.

Nordyke, E. C., & Matsumoto, Y. S. (1977). The Japanese in Hawaii: A historical and demographic perspective. *Hawaiian Journal of History, 11*(12), 162–174.

Northern, H., & Kurland, R. (2001). *Social work with groups (3rd ed.).* New York: Columbia University Press.

Office of the Commanding General—Headquarters Western Defense Command and Fourth Army. (1942). Transcript of telephone conversation between General DeWitt, Commanding Western Defense Command and Fourth Army, and General Benedict, Commanding Communications Zone (Ninth Corps Area), Salt Lake City, Utah, March 14, 1942. 10:32 A.M., pp. 1–4. Folder: 384.4 Val I.(AG Records File), Box 15: 370.5 Movement to 384.4 Preliminary Evacuation Plans. Western Defense Command and Fourth Army—Wartime Civil Control Administration and Civil Affairs Division, Record Group 499: Records of U.S. Army Defense Commands (World War II), 1942–1946, Western Defense Command and Fourth Army—Wartime Civil Control Administration and Civil Affairs Division 1942–46, Central Correspondence, 1942–46. ARC Identifier 1080573/MLR Number A1 13. College Park, MD: National Archives and Records Administration, Archives II Reference Section (Military).

Park, R. E., & Miller, H. A. (1969; 1912). *Old world traits transplanted.* New York: Arno Press and The New York Times (originally published in 1921 by Harper & Brothers Publishers).

Park, Y. (2006). Constructing Immigrants: A historical discourse analysis of the representations of immigrants in U.S. social work, 1882–1952. *Journal of Social Work, 6*(2), 169–203. doi: https://doi.org/10.1177/1468017306066673

Park, Y., & Kemp, S. P. (2006). Little alien colonies: Representations of immigrants and their neighborhoods in social work discourse, 1875–1924. *Social Service Review, 80*(4), 705–734.

Perine, K. (November, 1940). Y, of course: Two projects with Japanese girls. *Woman's Press, 34*, pp. 487–489. YWCA of the U.S.A.—Bound Periodicals, Sophia Smith Collection. Northampton, MA: Smith College.

Portes, A., & Manning, R. D. (1986). The immigrant enclave: Theory and empirical examples. In J. Lin & C. Mele (Eds.), *The Urban Sociology Reader* (pp. 152–163). London and New York: Routledge.

Price, A. C. (1942). Exhibit 17—Evacuation of enemy aliens and descendants of such aliens: Report by Mr. A. Price, Chairman, Los Angeles County Chapter, American Association of Social Workers, 206 Spring St., Los Angeles, Calif., March 6, 1942. In United States Congress—House Select Committee Investigating National Defense Migration (Ed.), *Select committee investigating national defense migration, House of representatives, Seventy-Seventh Congress, second session, pursuant to H. Res. 113, a resolution to inquire further into the interstate migration of citizens, emphasizing the present and potential consequences of the migration caused by the national defense program. Problems of evacuation of enemy aliens and others from prohibited military zones: Part 31—Los Angeles and San Francisco Hearings—March 6, 7, and 12, 1942.* Washington, DC: U.S. Government Printing Office.

Refugee Consultative Council. (1942a). Minutes of the meeting of the Consultative Council, Wednesday, February 11, 1942, Board Room, National Refugee Service, New York, NY, pp. 1–2. Folder 5—Enemy Aliens—Plans for General Evacuation 1942, Box 221. Immigration & Refugee Services of America: Common Council for American Unity Collection, Immigration History Research Center. Minneapolis: University of Minnesota.

Refugee Consultative Council. (1942b). Minutes of the meeting of the Consultative Council, Wednesday, March 11, 1942, Board Room, National Refugee Service, New York, NY, pp. 1–4. Folder 5—Enemy Aliens—Plans for General Evacuation 1942, Box 221. Immigration & Refugee Services of America: Common Council for American

Unity Collection, Immigration History Research Center. Minneapolis: University of Minnesota.

Reisch, M. (2008). From melting pot to multiculturalism: The impact of racial and ethnic diversity on social work and social justice in the U.S.A. *British Journal of Social Work, 38*(4), 788–804.

Robertson, N. M. (2007). *Christian sisterhood, race relations, and the YWCA, 1906–1946*. Urbana: University of Illinois Press.

Rowe, J. H. (1971). The Japanese Evacuation Decision: An oral history conducted in 1971 by Ameila Fry. *Japanese American Relocation Reviewed, volume I: decision and exodus* (pp. i–45). Berkeley: Regional Oral History Office, Bancroft Library, University of California.

Schwartz, W. (2006). The group work tradition and social work practice. *Social Work with Groups, 28*(3/4), 69–89.

Shaffer, R. (1998). Cracks in the consensus: Defending the rights of Japanese Americans during World War II. *Radical History Review, 72*(3), 84–120.

Sickels, A. L. (1941). Organizations and their work: Bridges of understanding. *Common Ground, 1*(2), 71–74.

Silverman, M. (1942). The Japanese in California: War Relocation Authority Information Service, April 30, 1942, pp. 1–5. Folder: Japanese in California—Silverman, Box 11: Relocation Division—Public Attitudes Files. Records of the War Relocation Authority, 1941–1989, Record Group 210, Washington Office Records—Washington Documents. ARC Identifier 1519285/MLR Number PI-77 2. Washington, DC: National Archives and Records Administration.

Smith, W. C. (1939). *Americans in the making: The natural history of the assimilation of immigrants*. New York and London: D. Appleton-Century Company Incorporated.

Sprague, C. A. (1941a). Letter from Oregon State Governor Charles A. Sprague to Betty Britton, Secretary, Young Women's Department, YWCA, Portland, Oregon, dated December 12 1941, p. 1. Japanese, relationship during World War II, Box: Administrative Correspondence. Governor Charles A. Sprague Collection, Salem, Oregon: Oregon State Archives.

Sprague, C. A. (1941b). Letter from Oregon State Governor Charles A. Sprague to Ralph W. Peoples, Secretary-Treasurer, Oregon State Industrial Union Council, Portland, Oregon, dated December 17, 1941, p. 1. Japanese, relationship during World War II, Box: Administrative Correspondence. Governor Charles A. Sprague Collection, Salem, Oregon: Oregon State Archives.

State Commission of Immigration and Housing of California. (1918). Fresno's immigration problem: With particular reference to educational facilities and requirements. Sacramento: California State Printing Office.

United States Army. (1943). *Final report, Japanese evacuation from the West coast, 1942*. Washington, DC: U.S. Government Printing Office.

United States Congress—House Select Committee Investigating National Defense Migration. (1942). *National Defense Migration. Part 29, San Francisco Hearings: Problems of Evacuation of Enemy Aliens and Others from Prohibited Military Zones [microform]: Hearings before the United States House Select Committee Investigating National Defense Migration, Seventy-Seventh Congress, second session, on Feb. 21, 23, 1942*. Washington, DC: U.S. Government Printing Office.

War Relocation Authority. (1943). The relocation program: A guidebook for the resident of relocation centers, May 1943. Washington, DC: War Relocation Authority.

War Relocation Authority. (1946a). *Wartime exile: The exclusion of the Japanese Americans from the West Coast*. Washington, DC: U.S. Government Printing Office.

War Relocation Authority. (1946b). *WRA: A story of human conservation*. Washington, DC: U.S. Government Printing Office.

Watkins, M. A. (1942a). California State Department of Social Welfare official memorandum: Program for transportation of aliens from restricted districts by Margaret A. Watkins, Supervisor of Field Service, California State Department of Social Welfare, to department staff, February 7, 1942. pp. 1–2. Social Welfare—War Services—Enemy Alien Assistance, Reports, 1942 (F3729:77). Department of Social Welfare Records, War Services Bureau. Sacramento, CA: California State Archives.

Watkins, M. A. (1942b). Personnel Enemy Alien Assistance Program: California State Department of Social Welfare Office Memorandum, to Martha Chickering, March 20, 1942, pp. 1–3. Box Social Welfare—War Services—WCCA—Procedures, 1941-April, 1942 (F3729:144). Department of Social Welfare Records, War Services Bureau. Sacramento: California State Archives.

Watson, A. C. (1941). Letter from Annie Clo Watson, Chairman, Committee on Minority Groups, California State Council of Defense, to Margaret A. Watkins, Supervisor of Field Service, California State Department of Social Welfare, dated December 27, 1941, pp. 1–2. Folder 11—Japanese, Americans Relocation Centers and Resettlement, correspondence, reports, brochures, regulations, etc. . . 1942–1945 Box 13. International Institute of San Francisco Collection, Immigration History Research Center. Minneapolis: University of Minnesota.

Watson, A. C. (1942). Letter to Theodore Waller, Tule Lake Project, War Relocation Authority, from Annie Clo Watson, Secretary, Division of Community YWCA's, September 18, 1942, p. 1. Folder: 523 Americanization and Literacy (Boy Scouts, Girl Reserves, etc.), Box 522: Subject-Classified General Files—Tule Lake Relocation Center Central Files—522 to 535. Records of the War Relocation Authority, 1941–1989, Record Group 210, Subject-Classified General Files of the Relocation Centers—compiled 1942–1946. ARC Identifier 1544889/MLR Number PI-77 48. Washington, DC: National Archives and Records Administration.

Williamson, M. (1940). Group work—experience in democracy. *Woman's Press* (ed., Vol. 34, pp. 208–209). Northampton, MA: Sophia Smith Collection.

Wilson, G. (1976). From practice to theory: a personalized history. In R. W. Roberts & H. Northen (Eds.), *Theories of Social Work with Groups* (pp. 1–44). New York: Columbia University Press.

YWCA National Board. (1942). A proposal for work which the National Board of the Young Women's Christian Association might assume in relation to Japanese reception and resettlement areas in the Western Defense Command, prepared by Helen Flack, Nationality Secretary, Western Region, San Francisco, pp. 1–3. Folder 20, Box 719. YWCA of the U.S.A. Records, Sophia Smith Collection. Northampton, MA: Smith College.

YWCA National Board—Civil Liberties Committee of the National Public Affairs Committee. (1942). Agenda and minutes of the Civil Liberties Committee, March 10, 1942 to March 12, 1942, pp. 1–6. Folder 7, Box 394. YWCA of the U.S.A. Records, Sophia Smith Collection. Northampton, MA: Smith College.

YWCA of the U.S.A. (1942). War Time Program for Women and Girls of Japanese Ancestry: Division of Community Y.W.C.A.'s, dated July 13, 1942, pp. 1–5. Folder 23, Box 719. YWCA of the U.S.A. Records, Sophia Smith Collection. Northampton, MA: Smith College.

YWCA of the U.S.A. (January, 1941). Y, of course: Japanese Americans in time of crisis. *Woman's Press*, 35, pp. 40–43. YWCA of the U.S.A.—Bound Periodicals, Sophia Smith Collection. Northampton, MA: Smith College.

3

The Removal

Logistics of the "Controlled Phase"

On March 24, 1942, Lieutenant General DeWitt issued the first of the series of civilian exclusion orders that would clear the West Coast of the Nikkei by mid-summer. Under the aegis of the Army, the forced removal was accomplished on a block plan, with the 108 exclusion areas into which the coastal areas of the three states were divided cleared of the Nikkei, area by area (United States Army, 1943). The Wartime Civil Control Administration (WCCA), a civilian arm of the Western Defense Command and Fourth Army headed by DeWitt, established 48 WCCA service offices to oversee the management of 123 WCCA temporary Control Stations. The so-called evacuees were registered and tagged at these pop-up stations in Arizona, California, Oregon, and Washington.[1] From the time an exclusion order was issued, the Nikkei in the designated area were theoretically allotted one week in which to settle their affairs and report to the local WCCA Control Station with only what they could carry; in practice, often, the time allotted to them was much shorter. In the WCCA Control Stations, the Nikkei encountered a host of government employees, including consultants from the Federal Reserve Bank and the Farm Security Administration to advise on the management of farm lands and to assist in the disposal or storage of such property as cars, household goods, and farm equipment. Social workers "prepared to assist in family problems and in preliminary plans for housing" (Bendetsen, 1942, p. 2) were on hand at all of the 123 Control Stations, under the direction of Azile Aaron and the Bureau of Public Assistance (BPA) of the Social Security Board (SSB), which was "responsible for the overall supervision of such work in Civil Control stations" (United States Army, 1943, p. 117).

Of the 123 Control Stations, 87 were located in California, 2 in Arizona, 10 in Oregon, and 24 in Washington (Bureau of Public Assistance, 1942). Detailed records of the social work operations in the California stations were kept by the California State Department of Social Welfare (CSDSW) and remain today in the California State Archives in Sacramento; similar records were, unfortunately,

---

[1] The WCCA Control Stations, at which all Nikkei removed from the coastal states were registered and tagged for transport to temporary detention centers, were variously called Civil Control Stations, Alien Control Stations, WCCA offices, WCCA Centers, and Reception Centers.

Facilitating Injustice: The complicity of social workers in the forced removal and incarceration of Japanese Americans, 1941–1946. Yoosun Park, Oxford University Press (2020). © Oxford University Press.
DOI: 10.1093/acprof:oso/9780199765058.001.0001

not found in any of the other state archives. The field reports of social workers cited in the following discussion are, therefore, drawn largely from social workers in California and include only a few reports from the other West Coast states. But because the WCCA organizational and operational structures were identical across the coastal states, with county welfare departments reporting to state offices and the latter reporting to the regional office of the SSB in San Francisco, the California data should be understood as a representative sample of the workings of social workers throughout the coastal regions (Leahy, 1946).

In this so-called controlled phase (United States Army, 1943, p. 114), so-cial workers on loan to the BPA were responsible, as they had been during the "voluntary phase," for the provision of "all necessary social welfare services for the individuals affected by the Exclusion Order" (United States Army, 1943, p. 117). Martha Chickering, the Director of the CSDSW, explained the role of her department.

> The State Department of Social Welfare assumes responsibility for the recruiting of all personnel not already on the Federal payroll or not directly supplied by Federal staff, such personnel to be recruited from either public or private sources depending upon local circumstances. It shall be the responsi-bility of the State Department of Social Welfare to notify the Federal Security Agency as soon as all such personnel has been made available and the Federal Security Agency shall make all arrangements regarding conditions of employ-ment, reimbursement, etc., directly with the persons concerned, except that in the case of employees of the State Department of Social Welfare and the county welfare departments the Federal Government will reimburse the agency for ac-tual salary and expense disbursements as outlined in the State Department of Social Welfare Bulletin #181-A and the contract. (Chickering, 1942, p. 2)

For social work staffing purposes in California, the exclusion regions were di-vided into ten areas.[2] An area supervisor, usually a Federal Security Agency (FSA) employee, was assigned to oversee the provision of services in each area. Social work personnel (also called *public assistance staff*) in each of the WCCA Control Stations established within the exclusion regions consisted of one public assistance supervisor (also called the *team leader*), one or more assistant supervisors, and a number of frontline social workers (also called *interviewers* or

---

[2] For the Army's overall planning purposes, the West Coast was divided into 22 units. "Estimates were made of the Japanese population in each of these areas and a tentative Detention center desti-nation was given. Each of these general-plan areas was considered as comprising a community of Japanese, all of whom were to be moved to the same Detention center and eventually to the same Relocation Center, if the capacity of the Centers and the logistics of movement permitted" (United States Army, 1943, p. 86).

caseworkers). Most of the team leaders were drawn from the supervisory ranks of the CSDSW, "with the exception of those in three or four offices in the San Francisco or Los Angeles areas, of which exception is made because they are already operating units handling a large assignment and should not be disturbed" (Chickering, 1942, p. 1). The assistant supervisors, drawn from both CSDSW and FSA staff, were to be "seated at the 'control desk' to check the record of each alien before such alien leaves the office in order to be sure that all required details in his case have been attended to" (Chickering, 1942, p. 1). The number of frontline social workers was to be determined by need but estimated to be "roughly six social workers to each assistant public assistance supervisor" (Chickering, 1942, p. 1). Many of these social workers—both supervisors and frontline—had been part of the Enemy Alien Public Assistance Program during the "voluntary evacuation" phase. Chickering (1942) surmised in an April 13 letter to Azile Aaron and Aaron's superior, Richard Neustadt, that while the total number of social workers needed in the removal work was not known, "it seems likely that it will be somewhere around two hundred and fifty, making it a possible total of over three hundred social workers being withdrawn from regular State and County public assistance operations for a period of from four to seven weeks, or longer in the case of those persons already in the program" (p. 3) because of their involvement in the voluntary phase of alien assistance work.

The CSDSW's records provide some sense of how this plan worked out on the ground. The South Vermont Avenue Control Station, one of 17 Control Stations in the Los Angeles area, was staffed by "1 Manager, 1 Public Assistant Supervisor, 2 Assistant Supervisors, 6 Social Workers, 2 Federal Reserve Bank Representatives, 2 Farm Security Administration Representatives, 3 Typist's, 3 Clerks" (McDougall, 1942a, p. 1), who registered 800 persons on the first day of its operation and 413 on the following day for a total of 1,213 individuals comprising 305 families. The Stockton Control Station, which operated from May 8 through May 13, and the Lodi Control Station, open for business on May 14 and closed May 21, processed the "some 4,600 Japanese persons" (Sundquist, 1942a, p. 1) according to the Public Assistance Supervisor at both stations. Lodi Control Station was staffed by 21 social workers: one supervisor, 3 assistant supervisors, and 17 frontline workers (McDougall, 1942b). All 17 social workers at Lodi were on loan from the San Joaquin County Welfare Department (Sundquist, 1942b). The Lawndale-Riverside Station, on the other hand, had "six loaned workers from the State Department of Social Welfare; hiring two Japanese workers, one from the International Institute and one from the Young Women's Christian Association; and adding one additional person directly to the Wartime Civil Control Administration payroll" (Ryder, 1942, p. 1).

Each WCCA station hired one or more Nikkei staff to provide linguistic and cultural translation assistance to the social workers interviewing the many

Issei who did not speak or read English. A few Nikkei social workers who were previously employed in state or county offices—or had been employed by the International Institute or the YWCA, as described earlier by Ryder—worked in some Control Stations as assistant supervisors. One supervisor reported that

> the Japanese assistant public assistance supervisor was especially helpful to all agencies in the Control station by her knowledge of her people (for she was a social worker in this community and at present is on the WCCA staff) and her ability to interpret to those who found it difficult to understand the English language. (White, 1942c, p. 2)

Some Nikkei workers were former CSDSW clerical staff whom Chickering (1942) identified as possibilities for staffing the stations as interpreters, receptionists, and stenographers. There were also many Nikkei volunteers. One Control Station report observed, "the language difficulty was solved to a large extent by the cooperation and assistance of the Japanese American Citizens League and the Japanese people themselves" (Ryan, 1942a, p. 1). The volunteers also aided the work of other agencies at the WCCA stations. At the South Normandie Street Station in Los Angeles, according to the Public Assistance Supervisor Florence Pigatti (1942a), the "work of the Employment Service for U.S.E.S. [U.S. Employment Services] seems to be manned largely by volunteer Japanese help" (p. 2).

> Some of the girls typed while sitting on chairs built up with odd cushions and although they seemed weary refused to stop working long past their lunch hour in the 5 PM Mark. Through the efforts of an appreciative, capable manager these alert youngsters were placed on the payroll of the USGS thus delaying their evacuation. There were most thrilled and grateful. (Pigatti, 1942a, p. 2)

All such personnel were, of course, removed to temporary detention centers with the rest of the Nikkei as the Control Stations wrapped up their work.

The Civil Control Stations

To meet the Army's deadlines for swift removal, "As many as 43 Civil Control stations operated simultaneously at the peak of evacuation. At this time an average of 3,750 evacuees per day were being moved from their homes to temporary detention centers, or, in some cases, directly to Manzanar or Colorado River Relocation Centers" (United States Army, 1943, p. 53). The entire "controlled removal" (Bureau of Public Assistance, 1942, p. 28) operation began at the end of March and finished in early August; each station was open for about six days, closing when all Nikkei in the area were registered, tagged, and shipped off to the temporary detention centers, usually referred to as "Assembly Centers." The demand for speed necessitated the use of a diverse group of facilities: "office accommodations ranged from spacious, clean, vacant business property to small, squalid quarters in Produce Row, to church accommodations of various sizes" (Copland, 1942, p. 1). The Huntington Beach Station was in a "lovely new building, clean, and well-equipped" (Irvin, 1942c, p. 1). More usually, the facilities, as in the case of the Oceanside Station, were "not good as far as the staff was concerned as the furniture was poor, there was no heating except by three coal oil stoves and there was a continuous draft through the building. The restroom facilities were deplorable" (Wallace, 1942, p. 1). Similarly, the "Anaheim Civil Control Station was located in an abandoned market which had been permitted to lapse into a bad state of repair. It lacked sanitary conveniences and heating equipment, and the concrete floors made it noisy and cold" (LeHane, 1942, p. 1). In addition to the lack of adequate sanitary facilities, temperature control, and inadequate furniture, the Bakersfield station, located in the Fair Grounds Exhibit Building, featured a problem that several stations shared: "The location of the building was poor in that it was so far from a common carrier that it was impossible for the Japanese to reach the station other than by private transportation" (Larmore, 1942b, p. 1).

Finding means of transportation to the Control Stations—first to report for registration and a day or two later for "entrainment"—was a problem for many rural families who lived a significant distance from their designated Control Station. Public transportation was either nonexistent or nearly so in many areas. In some areas, "ranch owners and managers" (Kallenberg, 1942, p. 233) and other employers brought in their workers. In others locales, neighbors, church groups, the Japanese American Citizens League (JACL), or the Fair Play Committee provided rides (Webb, 1942b). Mostly, however, individuals and families found their own means, and even in cases where the Control Station social workers helped to identify or organize transportation, the Nikkei paid for those means of their delivery into incarceration. The following excerpt from a Lindsay Control Station report described this common phenomenon.

> There were a number of families who needed assistance in planning for transportation. With one group, we worked with them to develop a plan whereby the group was brought for entrainment by a school bus—the group paying the costs. (Knight, 1942b, p. 2)

The ghastly irony, of course, was that many of the Nikkei who owned automobiles had sold them in preparation for the removal, along with whatever else they could unload in the pre-removal fire sales that represented unrecoverable losses for them and windfalls for the buyers. It must be remembered that the terms of the removal and incarceration were unknown at this juncture; the Nikkei had no way of judging how long they would be incarcerated and whether they would ever be allowed to return home again. The historian Roger Daniels (1972) explained.

> Near panic swept the community, particularly where the family head was in custody. Word spread quickly and human vultures in the guise of used-furniture dealers descended on the island. They drove up and down the streets in trucks offering $5 for a nearly new washing machine, $10 for refrigerators. . . . And the Japanese, angry but helpless, sold their dearly purchased possessions because they didn't know what to do . . . and because they sensed the need in the uncertain time ahead for all the cash they could squirrel away. (p. 86)

A Nisei cited in a WRA publication recalled the last days before the removal:

> Everybody took advantage of us. Some people took things when we were not watching. While we were packing inside the house, these people would go around the back and take everything they saw. It was difficult to keep our tempers. For seventeen years, Dad and Mother had struggled to build up their business . . . when they finally succeeded in raising four children and sending them through high school and even had one attending college—BOOM came evacuation and our prosperity crumbled to pieces. (War Relocation Authority, 1946, p. 36)

Relief Provision

Transportation cost to the Control Centers to report for removal was one of three categories of need-based "relief" available to the Nikkei. Funds for the purchase of basic items such as blankets and clothing to be used during the incarceration and for costs of crating household items for storage for the duration of the incarceration were the others (Kallenberg, 1942). In this phase, as during the "voluntary" period, however, there was little disbursement of aid. As CSDSW social worker and an Area Supervisor Bernice Copland (1942) put it, "considering the numbers involved and the availability of relief, there was a surprisingly small amount of relief authorized" (p. 2). The low usage must be interpreted within the context of the fact that the Nikkei were "encouraged to use their own resources" (Kallenberg, 1942, p. 234) and did so.

> Evacuees hesitated to ask, even when in need and in the very short time available for discussion, the social worker had to be skillful in learning their

true financial circumstances, at the same time preserving their self-respect. (Kallenberg, 1942, p. 234)

Unsurprisingly, the disbursements were more frequent in Control Stations in poorer areas where the "nature of the neighborhood, composed as it was of cheap motels and rooming houses, was in itself a substantiation of the need for assistance" (Costigan, 1942, p. 5), and the population, as one social worker characterized, "were less educated, less cultured and less Americanized" (White, 1942b, p. 2). At the San Pedro Control Station, the aid recipients included former merchant marines "who had been out of work and without earnings for months" (Costigan, 1942, p. 5) due to wartime restrictions. The public assistance supervisor from the Santa Barbara County station reported in late April that aid had been provided to a 16-year-old boy who was brought in by the county probation department.

He had turned in his parents for disloyalty and because of this it became necessary for his own protection that the probation department make a plan for him. It seems they have not been able to place him and he has been in the detention home. We purchased a good many articles for him. (Parmley, 1942, p. 1)

The aid disbursed at the San Francisco Control Station covered the more usual range of cases:

. . . a number of county welfare cases, tenement folk, single men from the rooming house district, a group of fishermen unemployed and idle for several months and families new to the district who moved in for the express purpose of being evacuated. (White, 1942b, p. 2)

Requisitions were modest, as Nikkei Assistant Supervisor Mari Okazaki noted in her description of the request of "one of the men with little worldly goods" for "help in purchasing 2 blankets, 2 sheets and toilet paper (1 roll!)" (Okazaki, 1942b, p. 45). The final accounting by the BPA shows that aid was distributed to a total of 872 out of 28,772 cases (or family units). A total of $9,865 was disbursed; thus, to 3% of the total family units, an amount which averages out to nine cents per every individual registered and removed through the Control Stations (Bureau of Public Assistance, 1942).

Family Registration

Determining the need for relief was part of the basic tasks of registration. Social workers interviewed all Nikkei family heads, registering the family by collecting "all necessary social data records" (United States Army, 1943, p. 117) that documented the "family history of the evacuee and his family" (p. 117). Each family head was "carefully questioned as to his business, property, personal and family affairs, to ascertain the problems created by evacuation, and to establish the existing needs for assistance in settling these problems" (p. 117). The determination for direct relief made, social workers sent the family head to other agency representatives at the Control Station for assistance in the disposal of property. Medical examinations by U.S. Public Health Service physicians were mandated for all members of the family. The case number assigned to each family by a social worker during this registration process was the one with which all individuals and accompanying luggage were tagged for removal and was used to identify them throughout their incarceration.

"Interpreting the Evacuation"

Perhaps the most enigmatic of the social work duties during the registration process was to provide, as Margaret Leahy (1946) of the BPA explained, "interpretation to the individual of the reason for the evacuation and of his position in relation to it" (p. 33). The records examined for this study offer no specific information on what kinds of interpretation—or spin—the social workers were able to put on the facts of this program of racially targeted expulsion into an indeterminate incarceration. Leahy explained only that the task was necessary in order that "a clear understanding of the government's plans might relieve tension and anxiety about them" (pp. 33–34). The organizational chaos rampant in so many of the Control Stations make clear that no one, including social workers charged with explaining the government plan, had a clear grasp of the government's plans in so far as such hastily rolled out procedures based on extemporaneously assembled arrangements could be called "plans." The make-shift set-up of the Control Stations did, however, presage the slap-dash and ill-prepared conditions of the incarceration camps, both temporary and long-term, to which the Nikkei were sent off to from the stations. Regardless of the administrative confusion that reigned behind the scenes, that the job of the social workers was "to prepare the Japanese for the kind of living which they will encounter" (p. 3) was also the view of Philip Schafer (1942), a CSDSW social worker who supervised the teams at a several California Control Stations. He averred that this task was "about one of the most important functions of the social worker" (p. 3) and that "the skill which the Public Assistance Workers displays will set the tone and condition the Japanese for the future" (p. 3).

The social work records are unanimous in characterizing this task of conditioning the Nikkei for the future—easing them into their new lives in indefinite federal detention—as a service undertaken to the benefit of the Nikkei. Schafer reported that, after the first few days of the registration, much of the "considerable tension" noted "in the Japanese quarters" prior to registration was alleviated. This was a fact "attributable to the considerate, courteous and objective method of handling the Japanese at the time of registration by the social workers" (p. 3). Jean Kallenberg (1942), an analyst for the BPA, concurred.

> The evacuees were found to be anxious about the new life they were to lead at the Centers—this varied with the kinds of reports received from friends already evacuated, their own degree of security, and so on. The social workers were helpful in anticipating with them individually what they might expect to find, what to take with them in their "suits-cases," as many pronounced the word, which would add to their comfort during a transition stage that loomed very big to them. (p. 233)

At the Hollywood Control Station, Honora Costigan (1942) reported, "[w]orried people were reassured that their destination was as stated, that medical care would be available at Santa Anita and that friends and old neighbors living there would be free to visit within the grounds" (Costigan, 1942, p. 5). Overall, as Jane Hoey reported at the 1942 National Conference of Social Work, the social workers' assigned task of interpretation was considered to be successfully accomplished: the "attitude of the Japanese is good. They have told our workers that they realize why the removal action was taken and are willing to undertake whatever work they are assigned to do" (pp. 196–197).

A different interpretation might, of course, be that the task of spin was not a service provided solely for the benefit of the Nikkei but for the Army and the federal agencies who needed a reassured and compliant population that did not resist or challenge the evacuation orders. The Army's early March 1942 announcement that "Japanese farmers, aliens or citizens, who plowed under growing crops would be arrested and prosecuted as saboteurs" (United States Army, 1943, p. 338) provides a glimpse into the Army's anxieties about the possibilities of violent resistance. According to Roger Daniels (1972), while "resistance, both active and passive, did occur and was more frequent and significant than is generally realized," the more common response was "resignation rather than resistance" (p. 106). Indeed, contrary to the desperate scenarios which occurred only in the Army's imagination, social work supervisors found a self-contained, orderly, and compliant group.

> I cannot speak too highly of the cooperation and splendid spirit shown by the Japanese from the oldest to the youngest. Any bitterness or grief which they may have felt was successfully concealed, and few tears were in evidence even at

the time of entrainment. The whole group was orderly, clean and courteous and followed instructions carefully. Their baggage was well wrapped and of excellent type. Only one disbursing order was issued. (Irvin, 1942a, p. 3)

The Control Station social workers appeared to be both surprised and fascinated by the Nikkei's reactions to the procedures. "Much could be written about such aspects of this evacuation as behavior of the Japanese—their dignity, self-control, and almost docility" (Kallenberg, 1942, p. 232). The interpretations varied, but the view expressed by Mr. S. W. Spangler of the Seattle First National Bank at the Tolan Committee hearings, that it was "exceedingly difficult to divine the oriental" (United States Congress—House Select Committee Investigating National Defense Migration, 1942, p. 142), was a constant and consistent note; there was a distinct tendency by the social workers to stereotype whatever reactions they encountered through a lens of racial and cultural exoticization. Stoicism was perhaps the most frequently noted quality attributed to the Nikkei: "These people seemed to smile, say 'thank you,' and never express themselves" (Pigatti, 1942c, p. 2). Helen Stebbins (1942), supervisor of the Woodland, California, station and arguably the most expressive reporter among the supervisors, described this quality of stoicism with the following story:

> One little boy's dog which had been given to a friend had eluded the friend and came to the station and begged in canine fashion to be allowed to go along. The poundmaster was called and took the dog to his wagon parked behind the station. The background music of the poor pup's wailing along with the tears of the Caucasians who remained behind was almost too much for the workers. The Japanese seldom shed tears, and the visible grief of the white persons and the Japanese standing with fixed smiles were a study in contrasts. (pp. 2–3)[3]

The registrants' lack of complaints about the miserable conditions under which the process of registration took place was often understood as a demonstration of the community's unqualified compliance. Pigatti (1942d) noted that the Nikkei "did not seem to mind the wait" (p. 1) involved in the long queues for registration and for transportation out to the detention centers. She marveled, "[w]hat other group of people would work so hard on their own evacuation—running errands,

---

[3] "Pets—Can't go" (California State Department of Social Welfare, 1942a, p. 2) was the terse directive given in the manual of instruction for Control Station staff provided by the CSDSW. A counterpoint to this narrative of the stoic Nikkei is provided by Ruth Kingman, of the Pacific Fair Play Committee, who recounted that one of the problems encountered by a church group she organized to aid the Berkeley Nikkei during the removal was in finding "people to take the much-beloved pets of the children who were having to depart and who didn't want their cats and dogs to be killed. One of the deaconesses met me at the close of the service. 'I'd be glad to take a Japanese cat,' she said, 'if it will get along all right with my American cat'" (Kingman, 1974, p. 82q).

typing, loading the vans with their baggage, etc. and throughout it all, smiling and saying thank-you without any apparent resentment?" (Pigatti, 1942d, p. 1). But even such uncomplaining compliance and affable cooperation—inexplicable yet reassuring to the workers as a sign that they did not need to question the ethics of their own involvement—was insufficient to allay Pigatti's suspicions of the Nikkei's disloyalty. Reporting on the workings of the Covina Control Station, Pigatti (1942c) bemoaned the lack of more fulsome affirmations of loyalty.

> After having operated in three stations, a person cannot help but form some opinions on the loyalty of Japanese and the necessity for the evacuation. Although discussion was invited, at no time was there any positive expression of loyalty to the United States. Considering the historical background of the Japanese in California, it would seem natural for them to maintain a loyalty to Japan. (p. 2)

For her at least, the Nikkei's lack of effusiveness—whether understood as Oriental inscrutability or stoicism—was validation that the removal was indeed justified. Recognition of the irony that the history of the nation's ill treatment of the Nikkei could be used to justify their incarceration does not seemed to have registered.

The letters of Mari Okazaki, the Nikkei Assistant Supervisor on loan from the San Francisco International Institute noted in the Lawndale-Riverside Station report (Ryder, 1942), provide a different perspective. The San Francisco native was a graduate of the University of California, Berkeley, from which she received a degree in education and where she was an active member of the campus YWCA chapter. At the International Institute, Okazaki worked as a caseworker and assistant to Annie Clo Watson, Executive Secretary of the organization (Okazaki, 1942a) and the appointed member in charge of Nikkei issues on the CSDSW Committee on Welfare of the State Council of Defense.[4] Like all other Nikkei personnel detailed to the WCCA, Okazaki was eventually sent to her incarceration site as the Control Stations finished emptying regions of their Nikkei population and closed down the stations. But prior to her confinement at Manzanar, Okazaki worked as "part of the social work interviewing staff" (Okazaki, 1942b, p. 16) in several WCCA stations in San Francisco, San Mateo, Fresno, Reedley, and other locations along the coast. In 1943, Okazaki left Manzanar, where she and her family were imprisoned, on a scholarship to attend the New York School of Philanthropy (now Columbia University School of Social Work), where she

---

[4] The International Institute, only recently separated from the YWCA where it had originated, had strong ties to its mother organizations—for most of the duration of the war, Watson was loaned out to the YWCA for its work with the Nikkei—and the circle of Nikkei "Y" women was a tight-knit group that received material and psychological support from both organizations throughout the wartime period.

earned a master's degree in 1947 (The New York School of Social Work, 1947). For a brief period during her imprisonment, she was one of 11, mostly Nikkei, field workers employed by the Japanese Evacuation and Resettlement Study (JERS) headed by professor Dorothy Swain Thomas of Berkeley.[5] Okazaki's Manzanar diaries and personal letters are thus part of the massive repository of JERS data; they provide a rare glimpse of the removal process from the perspective of a Nikkei worker.

Okazaki's letters, written to her beau Sam Hohri, a journalist already imprisoned in Manzanar, are indeed lively and upbeat for the most part. But it is a brightness that clearly came at a cost:

> I think today I shall just break down. It's too much to try to cheer the others—there's been too much tragedy and heartbreak that I've tried to soften for others. (Okazaki, 1942b, p. 15)

She found her work in the Control Stations a harrowing experience. Describing a day when she found her colleague Kimi Mukaye, an experienced social worker on loan from the YWCA, dissolved in tears, Okazaki acknowledged the "awful strain of being one of the Japanese workers signing people up" (p. 45) for the removal.

> . . . trying to get their needs met and finally seeing them off with their suitcases, kohris [indistinct], duffle bags and little bitty children—some families with seven or eight—trying to get ambulance cases straightened out—getting families to accept the inevitable staying behind of loved ones in institutions—especially those who could not afford to pay for extra care. (p. 45)

She confessed that "being in the last"—having to work though the removal of all other community members before being shipped out herself—meant that mentally and emotionally, workers like herself and Mukaye "go through everybody else's departure, too" (p. 45). However sanguine she might have appeared to her Caucasian colleagues, she was deeply conflicted about her role in the removal machinery, which she described as "assisting with the sending of almost, crushed personalities thru the last squashing process" (p. 51), and she was indignant about the removal, which she clearly saw as a massive injustice. In a May 5, 1942, letter to Hohri, she described her first glimpses of Tanforan detention center, in which her family would soon be incarcerated and to which she was daily assigning others to be sent:

[5] Okazaki resigned from JERS in February, 1943 citing her discomfiture with "invading the private lives" of those around her (Okazaki, 1942b, p. 66).

If I'm any indication of the rest ... there will always be a smoldering resentment at being forced within those wired, sentry guarded establishments. If they only have one person caught for trying to get out? I'm afraid it will be I in my most lucid moments. It is only those whose minds have just been too smashed up who don't realize the enormity of the injustice done. I don't like doormats and those who go into those darn camps and do not carry feelings of objections are doormats, darn them. Keep on hating it, Sam. Hate is certainly a bad word, but the whole thing is bad. Now you'll probably guess that I've seen Tanforan. Yes, I did and the Mission, El Camino Bus passes not 5 feet away from the place. One can see the young people just sitting—sitting in front of the tar paper barracks and anybody can see them thru the wire as if you were an exhibit at the Fleischaker zoo. Sam, I just sat in the bus, hot tears of anger, humiliation, frustration just rolled down my cheeks—and I hate excessive emotionalism, but I could not be ashamed of crying then. And as I spend my last precious days in the world, signing up people for those darn camps—it's just too much. I can't even work myself out of the mess—stuck down in San Mateo. (p. 51)

Perhaps most telling was her description of a woman, a "mental case" who "absolutely refused to go."

All the cajoling won't let her leave her strawberry patch. She refused to go to the County Hospital for observation, neither will she go to camp. Her hubby and kids think she's a nuisance and want her confined in an institution. It's pitiful that it took a mentally unbalanced person to resist. Maybe she knows better than others—she says she'll die if she goes to camp—and a lot more than she will die, if not physically, then spiritually. (p. 59)

Fear of Separation

One arena in which the Nikkei could not be accused of lacking emotion was in their "fear of being permanently separated from relatives" (Knight, 1942d, p. 2). The "Japanese seem stoical, resigned and little given to emotion," the social workers remarked, except under the threat of family separation when they "could not restrain the tears" (Pigatti, 1942d, p. 2). Given that, at this juncture in the annals of this history, no one knew how long the incarceration would last, what form it would take, or how it would all ultimately end, the Nikkei's fears of prolonged and perhaps permanent separation from family and friends seem all too understandable. But Alfred Knight's remarks that such "attitudes, however, are difficult to explain on a logical basis since human emotions even in aliens do not follow patterns of logic" (Knight, 1942d, p. 2) and that, given the reassurances the social workers provided, the families' fears of separation were unjustified and illogical, captures an underlying vein of exoticization present in the social workers' analysis of even this utterly human reaction. Philip Schafer's (1942) account of the difficulty in recruiting volunteers for advance work parties—to be sent out in advance of the rest of the community to the detention center to aid workers in setting up to receive the masses at the center—illustrates that fears of separation were not unfounded. Schafer explained:

> First, there was considerable difficulty in securing a work-party because the Japanese were afraid that they would be separated from their families, and subsequent events indicated that the group in the community were not to go to Arboga, which is about seven miles distance from Marysville, but to Merced, which is much farther away, and had the work-parties went to Marysville originally they would have been separated from their friends and the community. (p. 4)

The standard policy was to remove families together. Thus, registering any given group of individuals as a family or a "household," as was the official terminology, assured their ability to be removed together and placed in the same incarceration facility. But the Nikkei's extended family networks were an unfamiliar concept to the social workers. In "this connection it should be explained that to the Japanese, the family includes all blood relatives not just the immediate family of parents and unmarried children" (1942a, p. 2), explained Alfred Knight. Pigatti's (1942a) report on the East Twentieth Street station in Los Angeles noted, "[i]t is most interesting how these people cling to their families and relatives even to the degree of cousins. They want most of all to be together" (p. 2). Despite their bemusement, evident in the requests for instructions with a "more practical description of a 'household' or who should be included on the social data card" (White, 1942a, p. 3), the social work staff appeared to have attempted to ensure that individuals who wanted to stay together did so. Jean Kallenberg (1942) reported that a "number of families were allowed to register under one head, thus giving them more of a feeling of security in a strange situation" (p. 234). To this end, sometimes, unrelated people who wished to be sent out together were "registered as a group, with one of them designated as head" (p. 234). The very lack of specific instruction on the composition of a "household" appears to have provided some leeway for the social workers to maneuver. William McDougall (1942a), Public Assistance Supervisor at the South Vermont Avenue Station in Los Angeles, recounted the registration of a "boardinghouse of 25 persons" who "all requested to be registered and transported as a 'family'" (p. 3). Katherine Day (1942b), reported the poignant story of an unrelated couple who came together to register at the Fresno Station.

> One interesting case was that of a man in late middle age who came in to register with an elderly lady. He was no relative to her, but had known her as a neighbor for some years. Fearing that she would be bewildered and lonely at camp, he asked to register with her and be placed in the same quarters so that he could look after her. (p. 1)

The wishes of such individuals to be removed together as a family were not, however, always granted, as evidenced by Kathryn Larmore's (1942a) long tale of a group of 125 workers from the Sierra Vista Ranch in Delano, California, who arrived together to register as a family. The narrative, which aptly illustrates the station administration's utter confusion about the correct procedures for dealing with disputed cases of family registration, was a case which the tested the limits of the social workers' flexibility in this matter on which much margin was usually given. In a team meeting involving the Station managers and the Public Assistance Supervisor overseeing the social work department, among others, the decision was made that the men would be registered in groups of nine, with one man among the nine designated as head of family. This initial decision was made not only because staying together was the men's preference, but because doing so would be more efficient: "the office force would not have a bottleneck at any one point and the flow of work would go more smoothly" (Larmore, 1942a, p. 2). Mr. Newton, the Public Assistance Supervisor, however, was "concerned about this plan" (p. 2) and "pointed out several factors which he felt should be considered" (p. 2), leading to a changed decision that the men should be registered as individuals rather than family groups. The next morning, however, the USES managers, in charge of the total operation of the Control Station "again discussed this large group and again decided to enter them on the Reception Control Sheet as family groups" (p. 2). Mr. Newton, the Public Assistance Supervisor, finally conceded to the decision "on the basis that the men apparently were already informed regarding this plan and seemed perfectly willing to follow through on this arrangement" (p. 2). The confusion, however, did not end with this third decision.

> As a result of the situation, Mr. Fisher [USES manager] telephoned his superior who in turn telephoned his superior in San Francisco, who then telephoned Miss Bannister [Phoebe Bannister of the Bureau of Public Assistance]. About noon Mr. Newton received a telephone call and afterwards instructed PAS [Public Assistance Service—the social workers at the center] that all of the single men registered in groups would have to be re-registered individually. Mr. Newton stated this was "on order" of Miss Bannister. (p. 3)

The various managers and supervisors then took a trip out to the Sierra Vista Ranch to inform the men of this fourth change.

The men were called by the "original family number" and each man returned his original triple tag and was given a new tag. We also try to explain to them what had happened. They were confused and only one man expressed his preference for the new plan. All of the others asked if it now meant that they could not live together and could not relocate together, for this was what they wanted to do. (p. 4)

In the end, the problem was simply punted further down the line; the men were "advised to express a preference for remaining together" (p. 4) to the officials in charge of the temporary detention center to which they were being sent.

Residents of a given area were mandated to report to register at the Control Station created in that locale. Generally, as a matter of logistic efficiency, those registered at a given Control Station were removed together to the same temporary detention center. Those in the same detention centers were then likely to be sent on to the same long-term incarceration camps. For families with members living in different parts of a state or in different states and registering at different Control Stations, there was high likelihood that they would not be sent to the same detention center. Attempting to reunite such scattered family members for the purposes of joint removal was another task for social workers. Jean Kallenberg (1942) recounted the bureaucracy involved in the attempts to reunite one aged couple with their daughter in another state.

Since a travel permit was involved, it was necessary to find out about the soundness of the plan. This verification was done in a day and a half, by wire, the social worker obtaining confirmation by the daughter and employer, encouragement by the district attorney who was a friend of the employer, and agreement by the state department of public welfare. (p. 234)

Public Assistance Supervisor William McDougall (1942b) detailed a case brought to the South Westlake Avenue, Los Angeles, station by a father whose 18-year-old son had been in the county jail serving a six-month sentence for theft. The boy was due to be released in a week's time, after the family's likely departure to the temporary detention center. Social workers made arrangements with the county probation office and obtained a court order for his early release so that he could leave with his family; "social workers met him at the County Probation Office early on May 11 and he was sent to Pomona to rejoin his family" (p. 3). Weddings were a mechanism for creating legal families on the spot to ensure that loved ones were not separated, and arranging emergency marriage ceremonies became a standard part of the social work tasks. Mercedes Davis (1942) of the Modesto, California, station described the hastily organized weddings of two couples who, because of the mandated waiting period for marriage licenses, were only able to obtain their licenses on the very day of their removal. Arrangements were made by the social workers "for one couple to be married at the Control Station just before entrainment. The other couple were married at the courthouse, and the last bus was held a few minutes till they arrived" (p. 3), thus allowing the couples to be removed to the same detention center.

Most Control Stations were open for less than a week, and the time between registration and entrainment for removal was usually only a day or two. Given this tight timeframe in which the social workers had to produce weddings, transfers, and other such outcomes, that they were able to achieve any successes at all is remarkable. Katherine Day (1942a), reporting on the Fresno station, remarked,

> Regardless of the amount of work involved, the public assistance staff willingly made changes at the request of the evacuees up to and including last departure day—realizing that even these seemingly insignificant (with relation to the amount of work involved in changing records and statistics) requests might mean the difference between the personal happiness or unhappiness of the individual evacuee at a particularly distressing time in his life. (p. 3)

Social workers' efforts to ensure that families were sent to the same detention centers did not, however, always produce the desired results. Difficulties often arose because of the intractability of Army procedures, which "usually prevailed in the long run, and frequently ran counter to good social planning" (Day, 1942b, p. 1) recommended by the social workers involved. For example, residents of Florin, California—registered at the Elk Grove station—were sent to different detention centers because the Army's division of the state for the purposes of the exclusion orders divided the town of Florin in half, a fact that directly contradicted the instructions that the social workers had that "every effort be made to keep families together" (Knight, 1942a, p. 2). Edwina Barry's (1942) report on the station noted that "some confusion was caused because there had been hurried moving back and forth across the dividing line prior to the exclusion order" (p. 2) by families and friends attempting to remain together.

Katherine Day (1942a), reporting on the Fresno station, explained that "although many special problems came to light about which nothing could be done, due to Army regulations, etc., every possible resource was exhausted before the public assistance staff was willing to give up" (p. 3). In such cases, the only option for the social worker was "to some extent, to minimize—in accordance with reality, of course" (Day, 1942b, p. 1) the family members' understandable distress. While the stations were managed by USES personnel overseeing a variety of workers, including social workers borrowed from several public sectors, the operation as a whole was a military action, directed by the WCCA, headed by Colonel Karl Bendetsen of the Fourth Army and the Western Defense Command. Outcomes of cases like those just described, in which some non-routine decision had to be made, depended on the character and attitude of the military personnel who were, ultimately, in charge of the proceedings. Florence Pigatti (1942a), reporting on the East Twentieth Street station in Los Angeles, explained that "the careful work of an entire staff can have a sad ending if there is not capable Army leadership in arranging the actual evacuation" (p. 3). Major Shankle, the station's Provost Marshal representative, was an example of capable Army leadership.

> This soldier, with social understanding, obtained over the reluctance of the doctor an evacuation exemption for a mother and her two children who contracted the measles. They were permitted to remain in the closed area in quarantine for five days, later to be moved by the Army. (p. 1)

The Huntington Beach station was also fortunate in its military personnel, according to station supervisor Bessie Irvin (1942c).

> We could not have had better or more courteous service from the two of them. They cleared all questions promptly and went out of their way to see that full consideration was given to certain problem cases. (p. 2)

By contrast, the best that could be said of Lieutenant Hay, the Provost Marshal's representative at the Riverside station, was that he was "present throughout the operation of the station and cooperated with us to the extent of his ability, even though the answer to practically all requests was, 'No'" (Irvin, 1942b, p. 1).

Organizational Chaos

Given the haste with which the removal was executed, the social work encounters—"probably one of the world's most comprehensive short-contact interviewing jobs" (Kallenberg, 1942, p. 234)—were necessarily brief, reported throughout the archives as averaging 30 minutes per family. But many of these brief encounters triggered intensive casework services. Harry White (1942a) of the San Francisco station explained:

> The social problems presented by the Japanese evacuees did not especially differ from those presented by persons with whom the public assistance workers have been dealing with the last few years. These problems, however, intensified by

the speed with which they had to be handled and the limited facts that were as-certainable by the short-contact type of interview. (p. 3)

Social workers did their best, under the circumstances, to maintain a high standard of services utilizing sound casework principles, but "with hundreds pouring in every day, there was understandably little opportunity for imme-diate individualization by them" (Kallenberg, 1942, p. 233). The work often "had to be done superficially" (p. 234) given the time pressure, and, among the staff, "training and skill varied, pressures were tremendous, mistakes occurred, and there were oversights" (p. 234).

However sympathetic to the Nikkei and skilled in casework methods the so-cial workers may have been, the hurriedly assembled teams of workers were, for the most part, poorly trained and ill-informed. They had, at best, one day of training prior to the opening of a station. The problems were particularly acute at the beginning of the removal process, as Mary Bregman (1942), Public Assistance Supervisor of the Long Beach Station explained. Long Beach, oper-ating from March 31 through April 4, was one of the first Control Stations to open for business.

The staff was new—they had had no previous part in this program with the ex-ception of an hour and a half of instruction on the previous day. This applied to practically all members of the team. Even the supervisors had had no previous experience in the operation of a Control Station; therefore, the innumerable questions that were bound to arise had to be answered at this point, this station had to set the precedent for others to follow. (p. 1)

The same names are found repeatedly in the roster of social workers for the various Control Stations, indicating that many social workers who were not attached to particular counties moved from one station that closed to work at the next one that opened. This was especially true for the Public Assistance Supervisors, who tended to be experienced social workers, usually on loan from the CSDSW. Lessons learned from one station, it is to be hoped, produced better services at the next.

How well a station operated, however, depended also on other factors. Mutual recriminations and office politics plagued, for example, the San Jose Station, which opened in mid-May, nearly two months after the Long Beach station. The San Jose station appears to have been a troubled operation from the start, begin-ning with the general staff meeting at which instructions for procedures were to be given.

General meeting was somewhat of a fiasco and degenerated into a debate be-tween Mr. Donnelly, Manager of U.S. Employment Service from Sacramento, and Mr. Johnson who had been at the Byron station in the same capacity. Very few instructions are given to the workers at this meeting and afterward there were complaints from most of them. (Morcom, 1942, p. 1)

In a confidential memo to the CSDSW administration, Margaret Billings (1942a), the station's Public Assistance Supervisor, blamed the station's troubles on the "attitude and activity of the Area Supervisor" Luna Brown, who was "officious and dictatorial with other teams in the station, informing them of their proper function" (p. 1). But in a memo to that area supervisor, Billings (1942b) laid the blame instead on the station manager, a member of the non-social work staff.

> The operation of the San Jose Control Station insofar as it affected the Public Assistance team was so extremely poor a coherent report is difficult to prepare. The cause, as we see it, was utter lack of knowledge or understanding of the manager of his duties and responsibilities. (p. 1)

Contrary to Billings, Margaret Morcom (1942), social work supervisor at the Stockton station, praised the work of Luna Brown, officiously delivered or not, as having provided a necessary corrective to the mismanagement of the USES station manager.

> His entrainment plan was to align everyone up on the sidewalk at the side of the building would stand until they were given a place on the buses. . . . The social workers were not used in the entrainment process except on the second day, when Mrs. Luna [Luna Brown] on her own initiative saw to it that old people, pregnant women, and children were moved to the front of the line and were given places on the buses without a long wait. (p. 2)

Social workers' ability to provide even the most basic casework services apparently required working around not only the military but other public sectors workers. As Mari Okazaki (1942b) described in a letter to a friend, her attempts to circumvent the "mazes of bureaucracy" by utilizing her contacts in the community resulted in a reprimand from her supervisor.

> I was to remember that certain things were done—we did not call on the I.I. [International Institute], etc., etc. Well, gee whiz, if I know my community resources why not use the YM, YW, Friends [American Friends Service Committee], I.I., etc. who want to help and do it in a hurry! This business of referring to HQ's—then interdepartmentally—takes ages—When people have sick members in their family they want to know what to do in case a certain recommendation should be made by the USHS at time of registration. One of

my I.I. cases just had a Caesarian, needs a blood transfusion (some young Nisei could donate and she could get a $50 refund). Everybody calls me up about her—but she has not registered officially with me at 500 Calif. and I have never laid eyes on her so until practically the day she leaves the hospital—hands off for me. The poor lady is in a restricted area hospital and no one can visit her. She's going bats as she doesn't know what post-hospital provisions are made tho [sic] she has 6 weeks exemption [from removal] from the birth date. Whew! (p. 38)

More usually, the difficulties hindering the delivery of sound casework services was an overall procedural confusion and lack of preparation. Dorothy Larmore (1942a), supervisor at the Tulare Control Station, reported that the station set up in the Civic Memorial Auditorium opened at 8:00 A.M. on May 7, but far fewer numbers than expected had reported for registration, due probably to the fact that the military orders to report for registration had only been posted the day before. The postings began at "noon on May 6 and [were] not completed until late at night" (p. 2). Mary Bregman (1942) of the Long Beach station described that, at that station, "the registration forms did not arrive until the afternoon. Meanwhile the Japanese had gathered outside the building before eight A.M. There they waited patiently to register" (p. 1). Larmore (1942a) also reported that the staff at the Tulare station were "not highly organized" (p. 1); they were uninformed of the date of scheduled departure and could not tell the registering families when they should be prepared to leave their homes. The East Twentieth Street station in Los Angeles was a chaotic scene, its staff unapprised about both the time of departure and the destination to which the Nikkei would be sent.

At about 11:30 the same day Col. Severn phoned that the Friday group would go to Manzanar instead of Santa Anita and must leave the Old Santa Fe station at 8:00 A.M. instead of from the Control Station at noon. This time of departure was not known to the Control Station until 2:50 P.M. leaving a very short time to notify people of the change. This was accomplished by 7:30 P.M. largely through the Public Assistance Division. After the entrainment the colonel phoned that only 41 were missing and requested that number be entrained the next morning for Manzanar. The Manager was away so the Public Assistance division with the assistance of an exceptionally capable Japanese paid clerical worker, Miss Fugii, obtained 41 volunteers for Manzanar. The evacuees are to be commended for their response to this sudden change of plans. Many had mixed their baggage and some of it had been sent to Santa Anita. (Pigatti, 1942a, p. 2)

Similarly, at the Control Station in Pasadena, the staff were informed first that the registered families were destined for Pomona Detention center, but the destination was later changed to Tulare, only to be "advised that only 1300 could be sent to Tulare, the remainder to Santa Anita" (Popper, 1942b, p. 2).

Valerie Popper's (1942b) dispassionate appraisal that these changes in destination "caused some confusion" (p. 2) and Graham Tinning's (1942) observation that "[c]onsiderable unrest was caused by the lack of information regarding the destination" (p. 1) at the Palmdale station, no doubt reflected the situation at many other sites. Both statements also cast some doubt on the sanguine views of the social workers' ability to reassure the families, expressed by Philip Schafer (1942) and Jean Kallenberg (1942) and discussed earlier in this chapter. The multiple barriers to good casework, including the very short period between registration and departure—theoretically three days but often less—clearly "did not permit much time for working out some of the family problems that presented themselves" (Cotton, 1942, p. 1). The Madera Control Station's Lexie Cotton (1942) averred, however, that despite the challenges, the "fact that social workers were utilized for interviewing, however, did mean that such problems could be uncovered and called to the attention of the Detention center manager who could work out a long-term plan" (p. 1). This was largely wishful thinking; the temporary detention centers were themselves chaotic settings with wholly inadequate facilities, disorganized administration, and no social work departments or social workers on site to work out such plans.

The hallmark of a well-organized station was prior planning. Cotton (1942), reporting on the Madera Station (in operation May 12–17) explained that, prior to the opening of the Control Station, a proactive county welfare director had inspected and reported on the detention center to which the county population would be sent after registration, making it possible for the workers to "make practical suggestions as to what the families would need at the Center to which they were going" (p. 1). Similarly, Jack Snow (1942) of the Marysville station lauded the "caseworker approach" undertaken by the two assistant supervisors at that station.

> The plans for meeting many specific problems (especially involving health and potential deferments) had been developed by these workers previously, and the registration and subsequent attention represented the final phase of the continuing service. (p. 1)

A Miss Whitehead, a social worker who would go on to assist in developing a library and other recreational provisions and a shopping service at Camp Arboga (Marysville, California, Detention Center) was praised for her "community organization work" (Schafer, 1942, p. 4) done prior to opening of the Control Station.

At the Hayward station, which operated from May 4 through May 9, 1942, the prior planning was done not by social workers but by an extraordinarily efficient chapter of the JACL.[6] According to social work supervisor Mary Dumble (1942):

Prior to the opening of the station, representatives of the JACL had secured printed forms similar to Social Data Registration cards but containing additional items, and had completed these forms in duplicate for every family living in the area. Thus on the day of registration, the head of each family presented to the social worker, a typed form, all the information needed for the completion of the Federal registration forms. This facilitated the work to a marked degree as names and ages were plainly recorded as well as alien registration numbers. These numbers were checked against the alien registration cards for accurate recording. The whole area was divided into districts and a JACL Welfare Chairman had been appointed as the responsible individual in each district. Through them it was possible to send messages to individual families or to publicize instructions regarding entrainment etc. Registration was controlled by the JACL through instructions given by the Welfare Chairman to the people in the district to appear at given hours to complete registration. (p. 1)

Additionally, Dumble reported, there was little need for relief provision at this station, because the JACL "had enough money in the Welfare funds to cover the needs of the people in the area" (p. 2). Conversely, the downside of JACL involvement or control of the registration process was seen at the Elk Grove station. Edwina Barry (1942), characterizing the problem as "the consequences of according special privilege to an organized group" (p. 2), explained the circumstances.

Very definite instructions were given to the public assistance unit by the area supervisor and the office manager to keep 52 families who were members of the JACL together, without regard to the individual family problems or lack of them. This was a definitely complicating factor. When it was found that too many families had been recommended for entrainment on the final day, seventeen families had to have their destination changed from Fresno to Manzanar. Although our interviews had produced information that a number of the JACL families had recently come from Oakland and had no particular ties binding them to the other families, and some had expressed indifference as to their destination, nevertheless, it was insistently repeated that they should go to

---

[6]   The JACL was formed in 1929, as an umbrella organization incorporating existing Nisei groups in California and Washington. Its cooperation with the government in the internment history is "not without controversy" (Lyon, July 25, 2015).

Fresno because the JACL secretary, Mary Sakamoto, had designated them for that destination. Seventeen families, with problems which indicated entrainment on the last day to Fresno, were selected by the clerical staff for arbitrary transfer to Manzanar a day earlier. The list of families selected was handed to the public assistance staff for recommendation, and the unanimous response of the interviewers was that except for the individual JACL families they could not recommend any change in the selection as all other families scheduled for the last day had problems equal to or more serious than those who were selected. The list of families whose entrainment date and destination was changed was handed to the public assistance staff at 9:30 in the morning and all the families to whom the message was taken, with one exception, arrived at the train which left at 3:00 o'clock the same day. One substitution was necessary because the father of the family was delivering checks in payment for last minute labor and could not be located in time. (pp. 1–2)

Difficult Cases

Even in the apparently rare Control Station where sound prior planning, a complement of skilled and sympathetic social work staff, competent station management, and benign and cooperative military oversight all came together, a wide range of presenting issues, all of which had to be resolved nearly instantaneously, challenged both the skill and the ingenuity of the social workers. "If ever there was an opportunity for social workers to use their wits, sound judgment and social work skills this was it. The varied and concentrated forms of problems at this station were tremendous" (1942, p. 1) remarked Long Beach station supervisor Mary Bregman. Her assessment applied, without a doubt, to all Control Stations that dotted the length of the West Coast. Alfred Knight (1942d), a CSDSW social worker who served as a supervisor at the Sacramento and Florin Stations, explained that not all problems "requiring attention were due only to the evacuation" (p. 2). But many were. There were several recorded cases of mentally ill or developmentally disabled individuals who had hitherto been cared for at home and hidden from the community, but whose existence was forced by the present crisis to come "into the open for the first time" (p. 2). In other situations, existing issues became "intensified" (p. 2) by the exigent circumstances. Florence Pigatti (1942a) recounted such a case in Los Angeles.

A brother and sister in their late teens came to the office inwardly seething. They bluntly stated that they were not going to be evacuated. . . . Conference revealed that the mother and her children had been separated from the father for over a year before the evacuation crisis, and that since his return several months previously, life at home was unbearable. They insisted they would not go to any center where he was located and asked to be shot in preference. (p. 2)

While the social workers checked to see if "any possible exemption" or other options could be found so that they would not have to be removed together with the father, the "youngsters requested that the matter be forgotten" (p. 2). The boy later asked for "information as to how to proceed at the Center if matters didn't improve" and was given "suggestions" (p. 2).

The social workers contended also with what Honora Costigan (1942), of the San Pedro and Hollywood stations, described as "a number of unrelated services" such as the request for aid in "phoning the jail to request that a departing Japanese might have a last visit with the Caucasian girlfriend and to leave the gifts she had requested" (p. 5). But the bulk of the "gamut of problems" (Knight, 1942d, p. 2) the social workers discovered fell into a discernible pattern. A handful of the problems that occurred with some frequency and were identified by the social workers to be the most difficult to resolve are examined next.

Miscegenation Cases

Notwithstanding the policy for keeping families together, the social worker's assigned task was, often, to separate families rather than unite them. A standard part of the social work duties was, thus, the task of "attempting to console those whose homes and families were broken up because of the exigencies of the situation" (Knight, 1942d, p. 2). Of these family separation cases, "[m]ixed marriages presented the greatest problem" (Cundiff, 1942, p. 2) and were seen by many field supervisors as examples of the "most interesting human interest story" (Pigatti, 1942c, p. 2). These "Miscegenation Cases" (Webb, 1942a, p. 1), although more numerous in urban stations, presented in stations across the state. At the beginning of the removal process, all persons of Japanese descent with any quantum of Japanese blood, excepting "the few adults with 1/32 or less Japanese ancestry who were able to prove that they had no contact with the Japanese American community" (Hatamiya, 1993, p. 17), were required to register be removed. The invidious choice that mixed-race families had to make was whether the non-"Japanese" members of the family would voluntarily accompany the "Japanese" family members into an indefinite incarceration or remain behind to face what might be a permanent separation. The case of the "L." family, recorded in rather more detail than usual, "illustrates the harsh necessity of breaking up a family" (Knight, 1942d, p. 2).

Mr. L. was a Chinese and his wife Japanese. He did not need to evacuate and planned to remain with his employment in order to maintain an economic basis for reuniting the family whenever this became possible. There were four small children under eight years of age to whom he was very much attached. The family had understood up until the time the Control Station opened that Mrs. L. and her children would not be required to evacuate. The discovery that this could not be done since all persons of Japanese descent were required to leave upset the family very much. Efforts to obtain a deferment failed. All of Mrs. L's family and friends had gone to one detention center and she would have to go to another. It was not found possible to interpret the situation to the family in a way that they would accept other than on the basis of compulsion. The husband wished to keep the oldest two children with him and at the time of entrainment the family showed up with the eldest son, age seven, missing. In talking with him after the busses left it was found that he cared for the boy so much that he could not force him to go. It became necessary to explain to him that there was no other way. Later the Provost Marshal dispatched a soldier with him to take the child to camp with its mother. As a result of last minute efforts it had been possible to arrange for Mrs. L. to go to the same detention center with her mother who will be able to assist with the care of the small children. (Knight, 1942d, pp. 3–4)

In July of 1942, the Army developed criteria for releasing from the detention centers and WRA relocation camps "certain mixed-marriage families and mixed-blood individuals whose background made it reasonably clear that their sympathies were and would remain American" (United States Army, 1943, p. 145).[7] The policies for "Mixed Marriage Leave Clearance," released on July 12, 1942, were as follows:

1. Mixed marriage families composed of a Japanese husband, Caucasian wife and mixed blood children may be released from the center and directed to leave the Western Defense Command area.

2. Families composed of a Caucasian husband who is a citizen of the United States, a Japanese wife and mixed blood children may be released from the center and allowed to remain within the Western Defense Command area providing the environment of the family has been Caucasian. Otherwise the family must leave the Western Defense Command area.

3. Adult individuals of mixed blood who are citizens of the United States may leave the Center and stay within the Western Defense Command area if

[7] The historian Paul Spickard (1989), using data from the WRA's Census Form 26, calculates that the WRA relocation camps were "temporary homes for at least 1,400 intermarried Japanese Americans, a few of their non-Japanese spouses, and at least 700 people of mixed racial ancestry" (p. 53).

their environments have been Caucasian. Otherwise they must leave the Western Defense Command area.

4. Exemptions will not be granted to any family composed of a Japanese and a non-Japanese, where the couple have no unemancipated children. An exception will be made to the rule where it appears that one of the spouses is serving in the Armed Forces of the United States.

5. Families composed of a non-Japanese husband who was not a citizen of the United States, a Japanese wife and mixed blood children may be released from the center on the condition that they leave the Western Defense Command area.

6. Families composed of a Caucasian mother, who was not a citizen of the United States, and mixed blood children may be released from the center on the condition that they leave the Western Defense Command area (Goebel, 1942, p. 1).

In addition to these criteria, certain conditions had to be met: proof of employment or sufficient means to ensure that they would not become public charges and an authorization for residence from the police chief or sheriff of the city or county in which the released individuals intended to live (Goebel, 1942). The categories of families eligible for release but barred from returning to the Western Defense Command area could only "reside in stated inter-mountain states east of Colorado, Wyoming, New Mexico" (Goebel, 1942, p. 1). The Army's final report tallied a total of 465 individuals in mixed-race families who were exempted from removal in the first place or later released and allowed to return to areas within the Western Defense Command area: 206 persons were first sent to detention centers and later released; 259 were granted exemptions or deferments from the removal (United States Army, 1943). Spickard (1986), noting that neither the WRA nor the Army kept specific counts of how many Nikkei were released through the mixed-raced policies, calculates that "several hundred intermarried Japanese Americans and Amerasians were allowed to leave the WCCA and WRA prison camps in 1942 and early 1943" (Spickard, 1986, p. 12), leaving 1,300 intermarried Japanese and 300 people of mixed ancestry incarcerated before the WRA's resettlement program—an all-systems push-out of the camps into communities outside the Western Defense Command—made the mixed-race release procedures irrelevant.

The exemption/release categories were an interesting exemplar of the raciocultural logic of the period. A fundamental premise was that "intermarriers were more likely than other Japanese Americans to be loyal to America" (Spickard, 1989, p. 53). Moreover, and more importantly, according to Spickard, a major goal of the program was to prevent mixed-raced children who had grown up among Caucasians and had previously little contact with Nikkei communities "to be tainted by contact with Japanese people" (p. 53), which incarcerated life in the camps among the Nikkei would inevitably bring. The Army's own estimation of the effect of the program is congruent with Spickard's analysis. The population it released were mostly "American-born, had been through American schools, had not developed Oriental thought patterns or been subjected to so-called Japanese culture" (United States Army, 1943, p. 145). The program had achieved "certain benefits," including the fact that "Mixed-blood children are being reared in an American environment" and that "Mixed-blood adults predominately American in appearance and thought have been restored to their families, to their communities, and to their jobs" (United States Army, 1943, p. 146). As the WRA's attempts in the incarceration camps to "emphasize American-type activities in the program" (War Relocation Authority, 1943, p. 1), such as "social dancing" (Marks, 1943, p. 2), accompanied by a "de-emphasis of Japanese type activities" (War Relocation Authority, 1943, p. 2) such as "Japanese drama," "shogi or go clubs," and the "spread of Japanese language teaching among little children" (Manzanar Relocation Center, 1944, p. 3) would show, the Army was not the only organization to see Japanese-ness as a source of peril.

The exemption/release policies and their underlying logic of racio-cultural reckoning of loyalty and belonging were also profoundly gendered; "there was a not-so-subtle sexism that went with the racism in this selection system" which assumed that "males would dominate the culture and loyalties of their households" (Spickard, 1986, p. 8). The exemptions from removal and policies for release back into the Western Defense Command area never included single Nikkei men nor families headed by Nikkei men. They only provided for "families consisting of a Japanese wife, non-Japanese husband"; "families consisting of a Caucasian mother, citizen of the United States or of a friendly nation, and her mixed-blood children by a Japanese father (either dead or separated from the family)"; "mixed-blood (one-half Japanese or less) individuals, citizens of the United States or of a friendly nation, whose backgrounds have been Caucasian"; "Japanese unemancipated children who are being reared by Caucasian foster-parents"; and, finally, "Japanese wives of non-Japanese spouses serving in the armed forces of the United States" (United States Army, 1943, pp. 145–146).

In the four-month period of registration and removal prior to the Army's announcement of exemption/release policies, the treatment of mixed-race families was uneven. According to Harry White (1942b), social work supervisor at the San Francisco Control Station, the Army's initial order to evacuate all mixed-race Nikkei changed in early May (White, 1942b, p. 2), when some provisions for exemptions were instituted. But social work reports of Control Stations operating after that time indicate that though some exemptions were made, much administrative confusion and inconsistencies were evident in the adjudication of the exemptions. A report on the Santa Rosa Station, which operated from

May 12 to May 17, mentioned that two British citizens, a Nikkei woman "married to a Persian," secured an exemption from removal and a permit to travel to Illinois, an area outside the prohibited zones (Harris, 1942, p. 4). Similarly, a pair of half-Swedish siblings "who had lived all their lives under an English surname" and "appeared thoroughly European and never associated with Japanese" (McDougall, 1942a, p. 4) reluctantly registered at the South Vermont Avenue, LA Station (in operation April 25–May 1) only to obtain an exemption the day before they were scheduled for entrainment.

But in other seemingly similar cases, exemptions were either denied or granted then revoked. An example of the former was the case of nine siblings said to be one-quarter Japanese and their host of children "who were only one-eighth Japanese, and including some who were redheaded and blue-eyed" (Pigatti, 1942b, p. 2). All of the family members who reported for registration at the Covina Station which operated from May 10–20 were denied exemptions. The "cases of three mixed marriages involving a Chinese and two Caucasian husbands" (Pigatti, 1942a, p. 1) exemplified the latter situation in which exemption was granted then revoked. The Army Lieutenant assigned to the LA's East Twentieth Street Station had "cooperated in every way assuming full responsibility for issuing travel permits and for obtaining exemptions" (Pigatti, 1942a, p. 1), only to have the decision revoked by his superiors. Similarly, Opal Cundiff (1942), reporting on LA's South Central Avenue station, which operated from May 1 through May 7, noted that "the registration process was complicated by the shifting policy regarding mixed marriage."

> Ten such marriages were identified. In each instance, the family were registered, at least the persons of Japanese origin. It was understood that the entire family would be exempt from evacuation. On the 2nd day was learned that exceptions would be made on an individual basis by the office of the Provost Marshal after careful investigation. By the third day, members of families of mixed racial origin were reporting that their request for exemption had been denied. After the station closed it was learned that all such exemptions had been denied. (p. 1)

Given such erratic rulings, it is not surprising that some families and individuals opted to avoid registration altogether. Opal Cundiff (1942) reported that one "15-year-old boy with a Japanese father and a German mother deserted the family with the intent of going inland in search of agricultural work. It is reported that he is tall for his age and does not appear Japanese" (p. 2). William McDougall (1942a) of the South Vermont Avenue station in Los Angeles described a family who registered but did not "appear for entrainment" (p. 3). They were believed to have "attempted to solve the problem themselves by leaving the area without permission" (p. 3). The family was composed of a "Polish woman" and "the four children of herself and her Japanese husband," including a 22-year-old son "who was thoroughly European in his appearance" (p. 3).

> The woman had separated from the Japanese husband some two years since although he is known to be in the Los Angeles area. With the family lived a 23-year-old Texas girl named Willie. Although Willie has a husband in Texas, she fled to California in search of employment. Her eldest son having fallen in love with Willie, the mother felt that practically, if not morally, the better arrangement would be for Willie to move in with the family, which she promptly did. The social problem presented for adjustment was the disposition of Willie who is reputedly so bashful as to be unable to answer questions of an interviewer and totally unable to support herself by work, although in good physical health. The family was registered without Willie, who being unrelated and entirely white obviously could not go to the Detention center. Willie's case was referred to the Los Angeles County General Relief Division at 434 S. San Pedro Street. This family did not appear on entrainment today, nor has anyone appeared at the Los Angeles County Office seeking Willie's returned to Texas. (p. 3)

Harry White (1942a), reporting on the San Francisco Station that operated May 6–11, calculated that "in three out of eight cases" of mixed-race families registered at that station, "the non-Japanese spouse accompanied the family to Tanforan" (p. 2). Opal Cundiff (1942), reporting on the West Los Angeles station that operated from April 21 to 28, noted that two Caucasian mothers accompanied their families into incarceration (p. 2). Warren Webb (1942a) of the Sanger Station described the station's sole "miscegenation family" (p. 1) as a situation "complicated by children with the exempt parent in a quandary as to what to do" (p. 1). This family consisting of a Caucasian wife and a Nikkei husband, two white children from her former marriage, and three mixed-race children from the couple's marriage opted to remain together and be removed as a family. When reminded of her option to remain behind with her two white children, the wife "stated that she did not wish to be separated from any of her children" (p. 1).

The social work reports do not evidence any overt signs of disapproval about the fact of mixed marriages. Consider Valerie Popper's (1942a) description of "the separation of a Caucasian mother from her 19-month-old baby" taken with "its Japanese father and grandmother" (p. 3) to Pomona detention center as one of "the many tragedies incident to carrying out the program" (p. 3). The social workers did, however, regard mixed families' choice to remain together as unsound decisions. The records do not articulate why the "net result" of such decisions was deemed "far from satisfactory from a social point of view" (White, 1942a, p. 2) and what constituted the "[m]any problems" that "may be expected from this group of evacuees in the detention centers" (White, 1942a, p. 2). They may have been simply anticipating what the Army's final report described to have been a common experience of such families.

> The adults were ostracized and the half-caste children ridiculed. Their presence in the Detention centers was the source of constant irritation to the Japanese, provoked bad feeling and added to the difficulties of administration. Although non-Japanese spouses were eligible to reside in the Centers, many of them found life in a totally Japanese community unbearable, and left, thus breaking up the family group. (United States Army, 1943, p. 145)

Social workers were also reluctant to remove "Japanese" individuals, full-blooded or otherwise, who had lived primarily among other populations. This was the case of a "Japanese" woman from Fortuna, California, who "at the age of seven years, was adopted by an American couple in Honolulu" (Todd, 1942, p. 1). Married twice, both times to Caucasian men, she had three children and had lived with her husband for a number of years in an all-Caucasian community, "having been accepted in the community" of Caucasians "as the only known Japanese resident in the county" (Todd, 1942, p. 1). Despite her "strong aversion" to "living among persons of her own race" (Todd, 1942, p. 1) and the fact that her registration occurred well after the Army's policy change, she was denied exemption, much to the regret of the social workers. The case of a "19-year-old part Japanese girl" married to a "Mexican" man who "did not wish to go to camp with his wife, as he felt that he would definitely be cut out of place there" (Day, 1942b, p. 1) was another example. She was "Mexican" on her father's side and "had always associated with Mexican people and did not relate herself in any way to the Japanese group" (Day, 1942b, p. 1). Her first request for exemption was denied, again despite the fact that the request was made after the policy change. But because the social workers felt that from "a social point of view" exemption "was the best plan for the family," a special effort was made and a second request was pushed further up the chain of command. The social workers' sympathies for "the girl's terror of being separated from her husband and thrust into a completely alien environment" (Day, 1942b, p. 1) were evident in the report which regretted that no answer to the second request had been received at the time of entrainment.

Medical Deferments and Exemptions

Deferment was the Army policy for individuals with temporary illness, contagious disease, and near-term pregnancy, with removal to the detention centers being delayed until "recovery was complete or when the physical condition, for which deferment had been granted, so improved as to permit evacuation with complete safety to the individual" (United States Army, 1943, p. 125). Exemption from removal was the policy for individuals with long-term illnesses and those requiring special medical care with diagnoses "such as pulmonary tuberculosis and insanity" (United States Army, 1943, p. 125), as long as they remained institutionalized. As part of the registration process, social workers identified individuals with possible medical or mental health problems and referred them to be examined by a U.S. Public Health Service (USPHS) physician. According to Warren Webb (1942a), writing about the Sanger station, social workers "had been instructed to pay close attention to family members who might be suffering from mental and nervous conditions that would make adjustment to group living difficult" (p. 1). The task of the USPHS physician was to determine whether the individuals referred by the social workers qualified for exemption, deferment, or for special aid during their travel to the detention center. William McDougall (1942a) described the medical inspection process at a Los Angeles Control Station.

> Dr. Meeham of the United States Public Health Service called on Tuesday, April 28, and examined the 40 cases which had been noted by the Assistant Supervisor of Public Assistance as worthy of his attention. Approximately one-half of these were determined summarily by the Doctors as being able to proceed to Santa Anita, while the remaining cases revisited at their homes. The final result of this medical inspection was that 7 persons were determined as being unable to go to Santa Anita. Of these only four were permanent convalescent cases and 3 are post-operative cases and will soon be ambulatory and able to join their families. (p. 1)

Valerie Popper's report of the Pasadena station included another description.

> Two home visits were made. A letter was received from a woman stating that she was too ill to come to register and her mother too old. The doctor visited and reported that the daughter was in an advanced stage of pulmonary tuberculosis and the mother senile. A social worker, Federal Reserve and Farm Security representative called on the family. Arrangements were made for the care of the property, interested neighbor's promise to pack the personal belongings. (Popper, 1942b, pp. 1–2)

The 83-year-old mother and the tubercular daughter were to be sent to two separate institutions. Dealing with the outcome of all such determinations was the social work task: special transportation (such as ambulances or Pullman cars) to the detention centers had to be organized for bed-ridden or otherwise incapacitated individuals; supplies and accommodations had to be organized for infants and others in need of special diets and other specialized care during travel; temporary deferment arrangements and care plans had to be made for pregnant women too near term to be removed immediately; sanatoria and hospital admissions had be secured for those being left behind to be institutionalized.

As in all sectors of the control center operations, disorganized management, incompetent or indifferent staff, and confusion about policies appear to have been the standard operating norm. The social work reports included many thinly veiled and not so veiled criticisms of USPHS incompetence and lack of concern for the patients and families. Luna Brown (1942) reported that at the San Jose Control Station,

> [t]he County Health officer designated by the United States Public Health Service did not contact the Manager until two hours after the Control Station registration had started. The nurse assigned to the Control Station had received no instructions. The San Jose Public Health officer who assisted the nurse during the two days of registration had been assigned without instructions. The doctor and nurse did not know what forms were to be filled out. The Manager was unable to advise so the Provost Marshal gave instructions as to procedures much of which instructions were incorrect. (p. 1)

At the Vacaville station where the "medical officers either had not received adequate instructions or those instructions were not understood" (Schafer, 1942, p. 1), the medical inspection "was exceptionally casual and it was reported that cases of mumps and measles developed during the entrainment process with the delivery occurring very shortly after arrival at the Detention center" (Schafer, 1942, p. 5). The more capable physician assigned to the San Francisco station, said to be "an improvement over the United States Public Health doctor who was employed at Station #21" (White, 1942b, p. 1), LA's South Normandie Street station, netted a "substantial increase" of medical cases "undoubtedly due to a more thorough coverage" (White, 1942b, p. 2).

It was necessary for social workers to "word their questions about health carefully" during their interviews because the Nikkei were "inclined to say it was good even though it was not; they seemed throughout not to want to deviate from what they thought would be acceptable. Tuberculosis is very common among them" (Kallenberg, 1942, p. 233). An alternative explanation for the Nikkei reluctance to disclose illnesses is that they did not want to risk being separated from their families. From the Army's perspective, the exemptions and deferments were benevolent exceptions "made in the interest of justice" (United States Army, 1943, p. 145).

There were Japanese in hospitals too ill to be moved without danger to life. There were Japanese children in orphanages, for whom proper facilities were not available in the Detention centers. There were Japanese in institutions who required special attention, which the Detention centers were not equipped to provide, and those who were imprisoned. (United States Army, 1943, p. 145)

For many families, however, the medical exemptions were sources of distress; they effected devastating separations that, in some instances, turned out to be permanent.

Exemptions from removal were granted to individuals such as penitentiary inmates or those with long-term illnesses who were already institutionalized at the time of registration and to "those requiring special medical care, such as pulmonary tuberculosis and insanity" (United States Army, 1943, p. 125) identified during registration, all for as long as they remained institutionalized. Medical institutions, however, did not welcome Nikkei patients. A report from the Tulare County Control Station indicated that "any and all Japanese persons" (Johns, 1942a, p. 5) were unwelcome in County institutions. Warren Webb (1942b) of the Clovis Control Station reported that the local County Hospital "was not anxious to take one Japanese tuberculosis patient into the institution" and explained that there was "reluctance to admit a Japanese when there were white persons on the waiting list" (p. 1). The Yuba City Control Station detailed social workers' unsuccessful efforts to place an individual in the Industrial Home for the Blind. "Apparently, that institution did not wish to accept a Japanese" (Ryan, 1942a, p. 2). Institutions were, in fact, doing their best to rid themselves of the Nikkei patients they already had. The Lincoln Control Station reported that there was a "strong drive on the part of sanatorium directors to release persons of Japanese origin as quickly as possible" (Knight, 1942c, p. 2) to join the queue for removal. Such report also puts under question whether the 14 tubercular patients the Weimar Sanatorium in Place County, California, deemed ready for release, were indeed medically sound. Given the demonstrated aversion of such institutions for them, it is also likely that at least some of the Nikkei patients wished to leave, whether or not they were medically fit to do so. In any case, Weimar Sanatorium was informed that the Control Station would not accept such patients without "proper verification that there were adequate medical facilities and that the centers involved were prepared to receive the persons released" (Knight, 1942a, p. 2), an unlikely outcome given the poor conditions of the detention centers. Knight's report did not include information on the final decision made about these patients.

Even in the most serious cases in which institutionalization made medical sense, families did not wish to leave a child, a sibling, or a parent in the custody of strangers who clearly did not wish to care for them. The families had no hope of visiting those left behind in the foreseeable future, no ability to oversee and intervene in their future treatment, and knew, in many cases, that they might not see that family member ever again. K. C. Simmons (1942) of the South Mariposa, Los Angeles, station reported that a bed-ridden man suffering from severe rheumatism was "issued an exemption slip" (p. 2) to be institutionalized.

> However, when the ambulance called for that man there was no one at home, and a check revealed the fact that the man was sitting with his family in their car in the line-up ready for evacuation. He had decided that he preferred the hardships of travel to life in an institution. (p. 2)

Alfred Knight (1942b), writing about the Lindsay Control Station, detailed the handling of three cases where families opposed exemptions.

> All of them are "hopeless cases" with little that can be done for them, medically speaking. Their families were anxious that these individuals go with the regular entrainment, even though it endangered life. Partly because of the emotional reaction, Dr. Malcom and Dr. Vieu were willing that the individuals attempt the trip with the others. On July 12th Dr. Raymond F. Kaiser of the USPHS was at the Lindsay station. He asked the PAS [Public Assistance Supervisor] if there were any medical problems, and when he read the diagnosis on this group he made a written recommendation that they were "not to be allowed to accompany the movement" but were to be temporarily detained at the County Hospital. Later he recommended that the group be sent in a week or two by air conditioned Pullman to Colorado River Relocation Center. Although the families felt keenly about the matter, they finally conceded it would be better for those who were ill, but their fear was that they would not be reunited within the near future. During the week of July 20, 1942 we have had some contact with these cases. The doctor has reported the patients ready to go, but the local WCCA office has found it difficult to make the recommended and necessary travel arrangements. We hope it may be settled within the next week or two. (p. 1)

While some families had to leave behind members who had long been institutionalized prior to the removal order, for other families, the removal order created the exigency mandating institutionalization. An example for the former was found in the case of a family that had to leave behind a parent, "aged 79, brain tumor, paralysis" (Johns, 1942b, p. 3) in the county hospital. The case of a 16-year-old boy who had suffered spinal meningitis as a child and had "attacks about once a month during which time he becomes violent and abusive" (Larmore, 1942a, p. 5) illustrated the latter. The boy had been cared for at home prior to the removal order—his condition unknown to those outside the family—but his residence in the camps was deemed inadvisable by the public health physician and the social workers on hand. Since an emergency commitment in a medical facility was impossible to accomplish in the limited time between the family's registration at the Control Station and their scheduled entrainment, the social work solution was to transfer the boy to the Tulare County Probation Office with the understanding that he would be "admitted to a State Institution in approximately two weeks' time" (Johns, 1942a, p. 3). Even in these cases where the wishes of a family may have leaned, ultimately, toward institutionalization, they were invidious choices the families struggled to make.

> One of the most touching cases was that of the N. family. Several weeks before the Control Station opened the adult sons of the family came to the public assistance representative of the WCCA office with their problem. They had an older brother who was blind, and had never developed mentally or physically so that while he was older than they he was no larger than a boy of ten. The family had kept its secret so well that no one in the community knew of the older brother's existence. Going to camp meant that the secret would have to be faced and the boys felt they could not do this. They preferred to try running away. Every effort was made to reach a solution but with little success. The parents were deeply attached to the older son and started blaming the other sons for wanting to be rid of him. When the Control Station opened the problem had not been solved but some progress had been made in establishing relationship with the family. The solution was ready made because of the requirement that the son be institutionalized since he could not go with the family to the detention center. The decision coming as it did from the outside was accepted by the family without blame being attached to anyone of them. The mother packed the boy's things and brought him out in the ambulance where the family gathered to say goodbyes which he could not understand. (Knight, 1942a, p. 3)

A report for the Needles Control Station outlined the problems of a family with a "sub-normal child" (Meyer & Popper, 1942, p. 2). The family had been granted a travel permit to move out of the restricted area during the "voluntary evacuation" period, but the child became ill and unable to travel before they could complete the move. The physician who examined the child declared her fit to go to camp with the family, but also proposed, "if the father and mother so desired arrangements could be made to send her to an institution" (Meyer & Popper, 1942, p. 2). The family was willing to do so but "only if the mother could accompany the child or if they were sure that they would permitted to visit her from time to time" (Meyer & Popper, 1942, p. 2). Being informed, of course, that both conditions "would be impossible," they ultimately decided to take the child with them into incarceration (Meyer & Popper, 1942, p. 2).

Not only exemption but determination of deferment, which allowed the patient and the families to be reunited once the temporary illness resolved, was a source of anguish for families. Alfred Knight wrote of a family registering at the Lincoln Control Station:

> When Mrs. T. and her children were being examined by the doctor in the Control Station her three year old daughter began to cough and it was found she had the whooping cough. When the need to hospitalize the child was explained to her she became frantic and refused to consider such a move. It was learned that while the child was three years old she had not been weaned and had never been away from the mother. Not only the mother but the whole family felt that the child was being taken away from them. The problem of interpreting to the family the reason for the hospitalization was handled by one of the assistant supervisors who was herself a Japanese. The result was the acceptance of the situation by the family who willingly brought the child to the ambulance. Hours of effort went into this but the results she obtained were gratifying. (Knight, 1942a, p. 3)

It is difficult not to speculate on the content of that interpretation conducted in Japanese. It is possible that the Nikkei social worker simply explained that the child's deferment was to prevent the spread of whooping cough among the community going into mass living. But the mother's frantic worry was not necessarily about the need to hospitalize her child but the fact that hospitalization entailed leaving her three-year-old child behind in the care of hostile strangers. The family had no real alternative but "acceptance of the situation" which demanded a surrender of their child to the authorities. How "willingly" such an acceptance and delivery was made by the parents, however "gratifying" the results may have been to the social workers, seems eminently questionable.

In very rare cases a family member was allowed to stay behind with the deferred patient. Florence Pigatti (1942c) reported one such case in Covina, where a mother was "given a temporary exemption by the Army so that she might remain in the closed area with her two children who had just contracted the measles" (p. 2) and could not be moved immediately. Bessie Irvin (1942a) recounted two other cases, one of "a man with a broken back who was not expected to live" and another of "a woman with a brain tumor, a mental case, whose daughter had been nursing her for the past seven years" (p. 1), where a family member was allowed to stay behind temporarily. But, in most instances, parents were forced to leave behind ailing children, husbands to leave behind pregnant wives, and children to leave behind frail parents in the uncertain guardianship of inimical institutions.

The dispassionate social work reports of the forced separations, offering few details or outcomes, are a frustrating read. Honora Costigan (1942) of the Hollywood station sympathized with a father who "entrained with his 2 ½-year-old daughter, while the mother was sent to the County hospital to await the birth of her second child" (p. 2). Florence Pigatti (1942a) opined that arguably "the saddest task was the separating of parent and child when in a few cases the latter had the measles or was too ill to travel, or separation of husband and wife because she was to be confined shortly" (p. 2). More often than not, however, the catastrophic circumstances of family anguishes were rendered into a handful of staccato lines.

> Case consists of Japanese family of four. Mother carcinoma, father advanced active TBc. No previous medical care. Supported by children who worked as farm laborers. Medical examination of older son revealed advanced active TBc. Hospitalized in sanatorium. Mother deceased 3 days after interview. Father placed in a local hospital and remaining child checked for TBc and placed with relatives. (Schafer, 1942, p. 8)

Did the father and the two remaining children ever meet again? How did they fare through these calamities? Similarly, Honora Costigan's pithy encapsulation of a long span of a man's life:

> Another registrant had worked in a home for 15 years and had never, according to his employer, been willing to take vacation or time off, although she had urged him to do so. He never complained to her about his health, but in registration brought a report from his doctor. When examined by Dr. W. Frank, U.S. Public Health Service, he was given a medical exemption and moved to a rest home. (Costigan, 1942, p. 1)

What condition, serious enough to garner exemption, had the man endured without complaint? Had his endurance been due to his devotion to his employer or servitude to his employment? Was he glad for the exemption? What did the social workers make of these and many other cases about which volumes of tragedies could be written but were reported so sparingly and equably? The sparse, bureaucratic contents of the supervisors' reports—no doubt hastily written—give few hints about how individual social workers rationalized their part in this large-scale uprooting of entire communities and the need to impose and enforce such family separations that the uprooting engendered. For the most part, the social work reports describe these feats of institutionalizations, admittedly difficult to pull off in the time and circumstances given, as well-concluded and sensitively handled accomplishments. Their perspectives are perhaps better represented in

the actions recorded but not discussed. A small but tantalizing trace of the ambivalence and the need for rationalization that the social workers *must* have felt
may be evident in the scrupulousness with which they obtained and recorded
the "consent" of family members for every institutionalization and other such
actions leading to separation, in full knowledge that the family could not alter or
refuse any part of the decision handed to them.

Orphans, Foster Children, and Adoptions

According to the final military report of the evacuation (1943), another group of
institutionalized individuals exempted from removal "in the interest of justice"
was "Japanese children in orphanages, for whom proper facilities were not available in the Detention centers" (p. 145). Prior to the war, three institutions housed
the majority of Nikkei orphans in the United States: the Japanese Children's Home
and the Maryknoll Home, both located in southern California, and the Salvation
Army Japanese Children's Home in San Francisco (Nobe, 1999). Technically, the
children housed in these institutions were exempted from the Army's removal
process; though the children were ultimately removed to Manzanar, the removal
did not occur until three weeks after Manzanar, which opened as a temporary
WCCA detention center, had been transferred to the WRA to function as a
long-term incarceration camp. The Manzanar Children's Village, an institution
created within the camp to house and care for these children, opened its doors
on June 20, 1942. Despite the Army's stated policy for exempting this population, the SSB and the CSDSW had anticipated that the children's would eventually be removed. The loss of Nikkei staff, through both individual detention
in Department of Justice internment camps and thorough the mass removal
to WRA incarceration camps, would leave the orphanages unable to function
(Nobe, 1999). A letter dated March 20, 1942, from Margaret Watkins (1942), supervisor of field services at CSDSW to Martha Chickering, its director, indicates
that the two organizations had begun planning. In mid-April, Lillian and Harry
Matsumoto, the heads of the Japanese Children's Home, accompanied by "a representative of some Commission of Social Welfare of Washington DC and a
leading social worker from LA" (Kikuchi, 1942, p. 2) visited Manzanar to investigate the possibilities of moving the orphanage to the camp. In a letter to Margaret
D'Ille, the social worker at the head of Manzanar's Welfare Department, written a
couple of days before her departure from the CSDSW and her role as its director,
Martha Chickering (1943) explained that the department had, without success,
"tried very hard to get those children made wards of a court before they went
to Manzanar" to provide the children "some continuing legal protection" (p. 1).
In the end, a total of 101 Nikkei children—some orphans and others children

left guardianless due to various exigencies of the war—spent the war years at the Manzanar Children's Village.

In a memorandum sent out to all SSB regional directors about the responsibilities of the BPA for providing Temporary Aid necessitated by Enemy Action to Civilians, Oscar M. Powell, Executive Director of the SSB declared the following:

> All services on behalf of children shall be consistent with the standards for child care developed by the child welfare division of the state, and should utilize the specialized services of personnel operating under the State child welfare program as well as other specialized personnel available in other agencies of the community and, if necessary, of other communities. (Powell, April 29, 1942, p. 16)

But the policy articulating the need to provide a high quality of care for children was not always applied to those of Japanese heritage. The Control Station reports detail multiple cases of children in various forms of care or guardianships who were summarily removed from those care arrangements and packed off to the camps or put into institutions. As described previously, the granting of medical deferments and exemptions usually entailed the separation of families. The effects were no different in many of the cases involving orphans and children in foster care. Exemptions in these cases, moreover, were as idiosyncratically determined as they were in other types of cases. It is impossible to know what combination of factors—the particular sympathies of individuals such as the Provost Marshal in whose hands the ultimate decision lay, the varied willingness and/or ability of the social workers to push for particular outcomes—resulted in the granting or denial of exemptions. But few exemptions were granted overall. The case of a "half Japanese-half white abandoned child on whom adoption proceedings has [sic] been instigated by a Filipino married to a Caucasian" (Stebbins, 1942, p. 2) was one. A last-minute exemption was granted so that the 22-month-old child, who had been with the foster family since she was a month old, could remain with the parents who had decided that "rather than give up the child, which they loved as their own, they would break up their home and the [Caucasian] mother would accompany the baby into the Japanese Detention center" (Stebbins, 1942, p. 2). At the Woodland Control Station, on the other hand, the Provost Marshal refused exemption for a 23-month-old "half Caucasian half Japanese" child who was in the process of being adopted by a "Mexican Caucasian family" (Schafer, 1942, p. 6). The "fourteen-year-old crippled child who had been under the care of Caucasians for the past ten years" (Pigatti, 1942c, p. 2) would have been exempted under the rules published in July of 1942. At the Covina station in May, however, no exemption could be obtained, and she was taken from the Caucasian family with whom she had lived for a decade and "ordered placed in the county hospital" (Pigatti, 1942c, p. 2) for the duration of the war. In late April, a five-year-old boy who "had lived for years in an Italian foster home" (Larmore, 1942c, p. 2) was also denied exemption, taken out of his long-term foster home to be placed in the Maryknoll orphanage for Japanese children, and presumably removed to the Manzanar Children's Home with the rest of the children from that institution.

Entrainment

Once the brutally swift and fraught registration process was completed, with various deferments, exemptions, and other adjudications made and the families and their luggage tagged for removal, the process of "entrainment" began. Though called such because trains were frequently used, in actuality, communities were moved to the detention centers via multiple modes including cars, buses, and ambulances. In 52 of the 108 Exclusion Areas, the Nikkei were allowed to drive themselves in to the detention center, in a "strange cavalcade" (Kallenberg, 1942, p. 234) of supervised convoys "escorted by military police, and a nurse or doctor" as well as an "Army towcar" (United States Army, 1943, p. 125). The Nikkei-owned cars were impounded once they reached the center.

Kathryn Larmore's (1942b) report on Tulare Detention center provides a snapshot of the range of complications encountered in organizing the transportation for the removal of whole communities.

Transportation, not only to the Control Station but for the entrainment, presented a large problem with the Kern County group. In the Delano area many of the men had been interned [arrested by the FBI and incarcerated in internment, rather than relocation, camps]. In addition to this the advance work done had resulted in many of the private cars being sold so that there were only approximately fifteen automobiles available to the group. During registration each head of the family was asked whether assistance was needed in securing transportation. It was necessary to work out a plan for transportation, both medical and entrainment. With the Delano group the area supervisor, the Secretary of the JACL and Mr. Johnson, head of the FRB, made arrangements with the board of education whereby school buses might be used for both trips. With the Bakersfield and Taft groups we worked with Reverend Throckmorton of the American Methodist Church, and Reverent Mathews of the Taft Methodist Church. Lieutenant Hull made arrangements with the Santa Fe Railway whereby the train would be on a siding by 3:00 P.M. of the day preceding entrainment. In this way it was possible for the Japanese groups to bring in their baggage and load it the day before they left. On Sunday night many of the Japanese from Taft and the rural area around Bakersfield also came in and slept in the train as the early entrainment and the loading of baggage presented such a big problem. (p. 4)

Organizing the transportation to the detention centers was a task further complicated by the need to account for the welfare of the many elderly and ill. While the official photographic records of the removal process and incarceration settings taken by WPA photographers such as Dorothea Lange and Ansel Adams tend to show only the smiling images of the young and vigorous, it should be remembered that infants and children, as well as the frail, the aged, and ill were also part of the forced exodus. Some of the "most difficult health problems" (Larmore, 1942b, p. 5) among the group sent by Pullman from the Tulare station were a paralyzed 62-year-old woman, a woman with a fractured pelvic bone, a 77-year-old man with hypertension, a woman with pneumonia just released from hospital, and a woman in her eighth month of pregnancy. Larmore, the social work supervisor at the station noted that initially, "the UPHS questioned the necessity of a doctor and nurse being in attendance on the trip" to Parker Detention camp, but changed its views so that, in the end, a doctor and a nurse were assigned to each Pullman journey. The doctor on one of those trips reported that there were several cases of "heat prostration" and one case of previously unreported epilepsy encountered during the journey.

He also reported that lunches had not been provided for everyone. Also, the delay in starting had delayed arrival so that the group were on the train from 7:00 A.M. to 6:30 P.M. with only one box lunch. Fortunately there was a crate of oranges on the train from which the doctor and nurse made orange juice for the elderly, the sick, and the children. (An interesting sidelight is that Dr. Buss's brother was connected with the Philippines and is now "among those captured"). (pp. 7–8)

The journey was difficult not only for the elderly and ill. In her narrative report to the CSDSW, Yuba City WCCA Public Assistance Supervisor Eileen Ryan related that an assistant supervisor from the station accompanied the Nikkei on their rail trip from the Yuba control center to the Merced Detention center, a distance of some 160 miles. Several long excerpts from the assistant supervisor's "interesting account of her trip" on a "very dirty" (in Ryan, 1942b, p. 1) train were included in the report.

We had not ordered a Pullman thinking we could make everyone comfortable in the coaches. It turned out, however, that we had one woman who had a nervous disorder and became ill when she sat up long, especially in travelling.

A place where she could lie down was improvised in the smoker but there were no pillows or blankets available to make any of our elderly people comfortable. The only provisions the WP [Western Pacific] could make for warming babies bottles was a bucket of hot chemical water out of an engine which we obtained at Sacramento during the hot afternoon.... The trip took from 11:30 A.M. to 7:30 P.M. and some of the evacuees were on the train twelve hours as it was 10 o'clock before they were all detrained and put in buses for the camp. At Stockton we switched to Santa Fe tracks and sat in the yards there for an hour. After that, the train crawled along stopping frequently at blocks, and freight yards. It took five hours from the time we arrived in Stockton until we reached Merced, a distance of about sixty-five miles by highway. There were no M.P.'s from the Merced camp to do the detraining and so those who had accompanied the train had to remain on duty. One of the two buses taking the evacuees to camp broke down, and it was some time before another was obtained. The camp personnel was very fine however, encouraging and helping everyone and, even taking our invalid, blind man and mothers with unfed babies to camp in their own cars. There had been no way to warm bottles from Sacramento on and we had, of course, expected to be at camp before the second feedings were necessary. Some of the milk had soured and a thermos had been broken, so even cold milk could not be given some of the babies and their mothers were very worried. Many questions were asked about the delays, but the people were not fretful or complaining about them—they were good sports and helpful to each other throughout. Some of the young people even tried to start some singing to keep up morale but the noise of the train made it almost impossible. The M.P.'s were grand, helping to keep the children entertained and being very patient with them. One break, in our favor, occurred because lunches had been ordered twice, from both Yuba City and San Francisco, and we had 1000 instead of 500. The Lieutenant and the train agent were very disturbed at the time, but it turned out to be providential, for lunches were distributed again at six o'clock, and the people at least did not have to go hungry for hours. The box lunch consisted of two cold meat sandwiches, a slice of apple pie, an orange, and a 1/2 pint of milk apiece. The trip was an experience I am very grateful for having had. Apart from my personal feeling about it, however, I would strongly recommend that a nurse, or probably preferably a social worker who is acquainted with some of the passengers, accompany any long-distance trip of evacuees. There are many small jobs she can do, encouragement she can give. I think the Japanese were pleased there was someone there to whose attention they could bring their problems and of whom they could ask questions. To summarize, it seemed to me the delay on the Santa Fe was outrageous, but if it was necessary, we should at least have been prepared for it. Adequate arrangements for warming bottles on the train, 15 or

20 pillows and a few blankets would have made a big difference in the peace of mind or comfort of some of our passengers, and I would recommend that on other trips these be requested when arrangements are made for the train, as there is very little can be done about it afterwards. (Ryan, 1942b, p. 2)

Area Supervisor Philip Schafer's report to his supervisor, Public Assistance Representative Azile Aaron, contained a similar description narrating, in all likelihood, the same journey and identifying the Public Assistance Assistant Supervisor as a Miss Whitehead.

We had a phone report subsequent to the entrainment by Miss Whitehead who went with the Japanese to the Detention point that there was considerable confusion and delay in arrival at the Detention center. The Japanese spent over twelve hours on the train and did not arrive until 10 P.M., during which time all of the milk for the children spoiled and considerable hardship was experienced. Only by accident there were twice as many luncheons provided which served to feed the people in the evening. The lieutenant in charge of the party reported that he had responsibility for troop trains but not for women and children and would have been lost without the assistance of the Public Assistance Worker and the nurse who accompanied the train. (Schafer, 1942, p. 5)

In a letter to a college friend, Emi Kimura, a student at San Jose State College and a member of the YWCA leadership at the College, described the "amply ghastly" train journey to the Santa Anita Detention center.

Today I learned that a friend of ours, who was on the train that pulled out just before us, died in Santa Barbara. He was ill to begin with and suddenly became worse in the middle of the night. He was taken to the hospital in Santa Barbara, but his family was not allowed to get off the train—the poor military Police on our train hadn't been to sleep since Wednesday, since he was on duty getting people down. (Kimura, 1942, p. 1)

One of the social work duties was to accompany MPs on trips to bring in various individuals who were registered but did not report for entrainment. On the morning of an entrainment at the Pasadena station, for example:

. . . a family arrived stating the mother who is senile, refused to get up and go. Thereupon, the police gave escort and an M.P. and a social worker went out to get the woman who looked to weigh about 70 pounds. She enjoyed the fast ride and especially the sirens. (Popper, 1942b, p. 3)

In some stations, social workers directed the entire process of entrainment. The social work view was, of course, that entrainment functioned far better in stations in which a "social worker was responsible for assembling each group and for counting the individuals onto the bus" (Underhill, 1942, p. 1). The Lodi station was one example where an assistant social work supervisor was tasked with the job of assigning to each family "the hour of departure and the number of the bus" (Sundquist, 1942b, p. 1) that would remove them. At the Stockton Control Station, conversely, the entrainment was overseen by a USES manager, "a very nervous and arbitrary person" (Morcom, 1942, p. 2) whose overall incompetence was a source of much frustration for the station social workers.

> His entrainment plan was to align everyone up on the sidewalk at the side of the building would stand until they were given a place on buses. . . . The social workers were not used in the entrainment process except on the second day, when Mrs. Luna [SW supervisor] on her own initiative saw to it that old people, pregnant women, and children were moved to the front of the line and were given places on the buses without a long wait. (Morcom, 1942, p. 2)

The miscommunication, missteps, incompetence, and arcane Army logic that had made the removal process as a whole a chaotic mire also played out fully in the entrainment. Valerie Popper's (1942b) conclusion that the bureaucratic muddles caused "some confusion" (p. 2) was an absurd understatement. Truncating the reporting timeline meant that the already monumental task of contracting whole lives into a couple of suitcases needed to be done in hours rather than days. The careful planning by families and social workers to keep friends and relatives together was often undone in the last-minute scramble. The social work staff at the East Twentieth Street station in Los Angeles were apprised of the date of entrainment and changes to the destination of its registrants—from Santa Anita to Manzanar—so late that families were given little more than 12 hours of notice to settle their affairs and report for removal (Pigatti, 1942a). Edwina Barry of the Elk Grove station described the plight of several families informed of 11th-hour changes to their destination and given, in some cases, less than two hours to report for removal.

> This group was transferred from Fresno to Manzanar by Army orders. Workers arrived at 12 noon at the home to advise them of change of departure to 2 P.M. that date. The family had arranged for Friday entrainment. . . . A truck had been hired for Friday to convey their baggage to the depot. Family had not packed completely. . . . The girls and mother were rather hysterical, not crying, but laughing and wailing and insisting to the last they could not be ready. . . . They

were seen later on the train and were all dressed up and quite calmed down. (Barry, 1942, p. 6)

Another family was notified at 10:30 on a Thursday morning that they had three and a half hours to prepare themselves to leave on the train to Manzanar (instead of Santa Anita as they had previously been informed). Social workers informed a family demurring "that a crippled daughter and grandmother were all added burden to the family in trying to pack in a hurry and leave on such a short notice" that "they had no other alternative" (Barry, 1942, p. 9). Another group who "asked what would happen if they did not go" at the given time was told that "the FBI would probably have to investigate" (Barry, 1942, p. 13), the implication being that the noncompliant would be deemed specific threats to national security with the likelihood of being sent to a Department of Justice internment camp. "Considerable unrest was caused by the lack of information regarding the destination" (Tinning, 1942, p. 1) of families entraining from the Palmdale station, who were not informed of their destination until they arrived for entrainment on the day of removal. Pasadena residents who had been informed during the registration that they would be sent to Pomona detention center were then told that their destination had changed to Tulare, only to be told that only 1,300 could be sent to Tulare, with the rest bound for Santa Anita (Popper, 1942b). The last-minute changes, which only served to deepen already acute fears of loss and separation, countermanded social workers' efforts to reassure the Nikkei that the uncertain futures to which they were being led were not so.

The families so hastened, threatened, and corralled to report for entrainment were then, in many cases, condemned to "hours and hours of sitting. Hours and hours of waiting around" (Kingman, 1974, p. 10b) while the multiple problems in transportation puzzles were worked out. In some areas, church groups organized volunteers to provide refreshments to the waiting Nikkei. Entrainments at both the Normandie and Vermont stations in Los Angeles were attended by members of the Methodist Church who distributed approximately 1,200 bagged lunches to the departing community members (Pigatti, 1942a). At the Lindsay station from which the departure "was scheduled in the evening making it difficult for the families to have their evening meal and the Army was not providing a meal until the following morning" (Knight, 1942b, p. 2), church groups requested and received permission from the Army to provide fruit, sandwiches, and drinks. Such demonstrations of "Christian brotherhood" (Pigatti, 1942a, p. 3) were often met with derision and protest from other members of the local communities. After the first Anaheim station entrainment, an article published in the local newspaper "roundly criticized the Protestant churches for serving coffee and cocoa to the departing Japanese, and pointing out that this service was overlooked when U.S. armed forces departed" (LeHane, 1942, p. 2). At the

Lindsay station entrainment the protest came "particularly from the American Legion" (Knight, 1942b, p. 2), forcing the military representative to explain that the churches had volunteered such services; "that the Army had not requested refreshments to be served, but that the Government wished the movement to be handled humanely and with consideration" (Knight, 1942b, p. 2). The representative of the Provost Marshall declined to interfere beyond providing this notice, informing both sides that the issue should be settled between them, and, in the end, the food was served to the waiting Nikkei and the remainders put on the trains for use during the journey. Ruth Kingman, Executive Secretary of the Pacific Fair Play Committee,[8] recalled witnessing the entrainment from the Berkeley Control Station.

> I remember the last person to leave Berkeley, on the last bus, the last person to get on. It was a man, a middle-aged man, a businessman, who carried his crippled mother over his shoulders—like a baby—just carried her on to the bus leaving for Tanforan. And that was the last person of Japanese ancestry to leave Berkeley. (Kingman, 1974, p. 12b)

Sanger, Reedley, and Visalia, the last of the California WCCA Control Stations, completed their tasks and closed operations on August 11, 1942 (California State Department of Social Welfare, 1942b, p. 3).

References

Barry, E. C. (1942). Report to the Area Supervisor, Elk Grove Civil Control Station, May 24 through May 30, 1942, pp. 1–13. Social Welfare—War Services—WCCA—Reports—Control Stations—Anaheim-Isleton, 1942 (F3729:147). Department of Social Welfare Records, War Services Bureau. Sacramento: California State Archives.

Bendetsen, K. R. (1942). The story of Pacific Coast Japanese evacuation: An address delivered before the Commonwealth Club of San Francisco on May 20, 1942 (pp. 1–8). San Francisco: United States Army, Western Defense Command and Fourth Army.

[8] An "independent committee of influential individuals" (Wollenberg, 2012, p. 26) prominent in multiple fields, the Fair Play committee was originally constituted in September 1941 as the Northern California Committee for Fair Play for Citizens and Aliens of Japanese Ancestry. It was renamed the Committee on National Security and Fair Play in February 1942, and, in January of 1943, again changed its name to become the Pacific Coast Committee on American Principles and Fair Play in until its dissolution in December 1945. Members included Robert Gordon Sproul, the President of the University of California (UC); Monroe Deutsch, the Provost of the UC system; the economist Paul Taylor, UC faculty and husband of the photographer Dorothea Lange; Chester Rowell, Editor of the *San Francisco Chronicle*; and Ray Lyman Wilbur, President of the San Francisco Federal Reserve Bank. The committee's purpose was to influence public opinion and public policy for "fair play" for the Nikkei (Wollenberg, 2012).

Billings, M. (1942a). San Jose Control Station, May 24–29, 1942: State Department of Social Welfare Office Memorandum to Margaret S. Watkins from Margaret Billings, filed July 6, 1942, p. 1. Social Welfare—War Services—WCCA –Control Stations—Sacramento—Yuba City, 1942 (F3729:149). Department of Social Welfare Records, War Services Bureau. Sacramento: California State Archives.

Billings, M. (1942b). San Jose Control Station, May 24–29, 1942: State Department of Social Welfare Office Memorandum to Miss Luna Brown Area Supervisor, Bureau of Public Assistance, San Francisco, California, from Margaret Billings, filed June 30, 1942, pp. 1–8. Social Welfare—War Services—WCCA –Control Stations—Sacramento—Yuba City, 1942 (F3729:149). Department of Social Welfare Records, War Services Bureau. Sacramento: California State Archives.

Bregman, M. G. (1942). Japanese Evacuation—Long Beach Control Station, pp. 1–2. Social Welfare—War Services—WCCA—Reports—Control Stations—Lawndale-Riverside, 1942 (F3729:148). Department of Social Welfare Records, War Services Bureau. Sacramento: California State Archives.

Brown, L. (1942). Report on Operations of the San Jose Civil Control Station, May 30, 1942, pp. 1–3. Social Welfare—War Services—WCCA –Control Stations—Sacramento—Yuba City, 1942 (F3729:149). Department of Social Welfare Records, War Services Bureau. Sacramento: California State Archives.

Bureau of Public Assistance. (1942). Removal of enemy aliens and other persons from prohibited areas: A statistical summary of persons in Regions XI and XII, February–August 1942. *Social Security Bulletin, 5*(10), 27–30.

California State Department of Social Welfare. (1942b). Tabulation of control stations—public assistance supervisors—summary reports, pp. 1–3. Social Welfare—War Services—WCCA—Reports—Control Stations—Anaheim-Isleton, 1942 (F3729:147), Department of Social Welfare Records, War Services Bureau. Sacramento: California State Archives.

Chickering, M. A. (1942). Letter to Richard Neustadt and Azile Aaron from Martha A. Chickering, Director, Department of Social Welfare, Sacramento, California, April 13, 1942, pp. 1–3. Social Welfare—War Services—WCCA—Control Stations—April, 1942 (F3729:138), Department of Social Welfare Records, War Services Bureau. Sacramento: California State Archives.

Chickering, M. A. (1943). Letter to Mrs. Margaret D'Ille, Counselor, Manzanar Relocation Center, Manzanar, California, from Martha A. Chickering, Director, State Department of Social Welfare, Sacramento, California, October 27, 1943, p. 1. Folder: 61.520—Child Welfare—Children's Village, Box 224: Manzanar Relocation Center—Central Files—50.026 to 62.014. Records of the War Relocation Authority, 1941–1989, Record Group 210, Subject-Classified General Files of the Relocation Centers—compiled 1942–1946. ARC Identifier 1544889/MLR Number PI-77 48. Washington, DC: National Archives and Records Administration.

Copland, B. G. (1942). On Alien Control Centers: State Department of Social Welfare Office Memorandum to Miss Margaret S. Watkins, Los Angeles, May 9, 1942. Social Welfare—War Services—WCCA—Control Stations—May, 1942 (F3729:139). Department of Social Welfare Records, War Services Bureau. Sacramento: California State Archives.

Costigan, H. (1942). Letter to Miss Winifred J. Ryder, Social Security Board, Los Angeles, California, from Miss Honora Costigan on the Hollywood WCCA Office, May 4, 1942, pp. 1–2. Social Welfare—War Services—WCCA –Control

Stations—Anaheim—Isleton, 1942 (F3729:147). Department of Social Welfare Records, War Services Bureau. Sacramento: California State Archives.

Cotton, L. (1942). Report on Operation of the Madera Civil Control Station, May 12— May 17, 1942, pp. 1–2. Social Welfare—War Services—WCCA—Reports—Control Stations—Lawndale-Riverside, 1942 (F3729:148). Department of Social Welfare Records, War Services Bureau. Sacramento: California State Archives.

Cundiff, O. (1942). Evacuation #31, 839 S. Central Avenue, Los Angeles, California: Memorandum to Miss Winifred Ryder May 1–May 7, 1942, pp. 1–5. Social Welfare—War Services—WCCA—Reports—Control Stations—Lawndale-Riverside, 1942 (F3729:148). Department of Social Welfare Records, War Services Bureau. Sacramento: California State Archives.

Daniels, R. (1972). *Concentration camps U.S.A.: Japanese Americans and World War II.* New York: Holt, Rinehart and Winston.

Davis, M. (1942). Report on the Operation of the WCCA Control Station at Modesto, May 8–13, 1942, pp. 1–3. Social Welfare—War Services—WCCA—Reports—Control Stations—Lawndale-Riverside, 1942 (F3729:148). Department of Social Welfare Records, War Services Bureau. Sacramento: California State Archives.

Day, K. (1942a). Report of the Operation of the Fresno WCCA Station, May 12 through May 17, 1942, pp. 1–3. Social Welfare—War Services—WCCA—Reports—Control Stations—Anaheim-Isleton, 1942 (F3729:147). Department of Social Welfare Records, War Services Bureau. Sacramento: California State Archives.

Day, K. (1942b). Supplemental Report of Fresno WCCA Station: State Department of Social Welfare Office Memorandum to Margaret S. Watkins from Katherine Day Public Assistance Supervisor, WCCA Station, Sacramento, Report on Alien Control Stations, Sacramento and Florin, June 23, 1942. Social Welfare—War Services—WCCA— Reports—Control Stations—Sacramento—Yuba City, 1942 (F3729:149). Department of Social Welfare Records, War Services Bureau. Sacramento: California State Archives.

Dumble, M. F. (1942). Hayward Civil Control Station, May 4–9: Report of Public Assistance Supervisor, pp. 1–4. Social Welfare—War Services—WCCA—Control Stations—Anaheim—Isleton, 1942 (F3729:147). Department of Social Welfare Records, War Services Bureau. Sacramento: California State Archives.

Goebel, H. P. (1942). Mixed Marriage Policy: Memorandum to Captain Astrup, from Herman P. Goebel, Jr., Major, Cavalry, Chief of Regulatory Section, July 16, 1942, pp. 1–2. Folder: 020.46 Welfare, Box 106: Subject-Classified General Files—Colorado River Central Files—020.31 to 030.32. Records of the War Relocation Authority, 1941– 1989, Record Group 210, Subject-Classified General Files of the Relocation Centers— compiled 1942–1946. ARC Identifier 1544889/MLR Number PI-77 48. Washington, DC: National Archives and Records Administration.

Harris, J. (1942). Civil Control Station, Santa Rosa: Letter to Mr. Philip Ruby, Area Supervisor, from Martha A. Chickering, by Jeannette Harris, May 22, 1942, pp. 1–5. Social Welfare—War Services—WCCA –Control Stations—Sacramento—Yuba City, 1942 (F3729:149). Department of Social Welfare Records, War Services Bureau. Sacramento: California State Archives.

Hatamiya, L. T. (1993). *Righting a wrong: Japanese Americans and the passage of the Civil Liberties Act of 1988.* Stanford, CA: Stanford University Press.

Hoey, J. M. (1942). Mass relocation of aliens II. In A. Dunham (Ed.), *Proceedings of the National Conference of Social Work: Selected papers, Sixty-Ninth Annual Conference,*

New Orleans, Louisiana, May 10–16, 1942 (Vol. 69, pp. 194–199). New York: Columbia University Press.

Irvin, B. C. (1942a). Alien Evacuation, Arroyo Grande Station, April 24–30, 1942: State Department of Social Welfare Memorandum to Miss Margaret S. Watkins, from Gladys C. Johns, by Bessie C. Irvin, filed May 14, 1942, pp. 1–3. Social Welfare—War Services—WCCA—Reports—Control Stations—Anaheim-Isleton, 1942 (F3729:147). Department of Social Welfare Records, War Services Bureau. Sacramento: California State Archives.

Irvin, B. C. (1942b). Alien Evacuation, Riverside Control Station, May 20–25, 1942, pp. 1–2. Social Welfare—War Services—WCCA—Reports—Control Stations—Lawndale-Riverside, 1942 (F3729:148). Department of Social Welfare Records, War Services Bureau. Sacramento: California State Archives.

Irvin, B. C. (1942c). Operation of Control Station, Huntington Beach, California, May 11–17, 1942: State Department of Social Welfare Memorandum to Miss Margaret S. Watkins, from Gladys C. Johns, by Bessie C. Irvin, filed May 19, 1942, pp. 1–3. Social Welfare—War Services—WCCA—Reports—Control Stations—Anaheim-Isleton, 1942 (F3729:147). Department of Social Welfare Records, War Services Bureau. Sacramento: California State Archives.

Johns, G. C. (1942). Report from Mrs. Gladys C. Johns, Area Supervisor, Control Station, Memorial Auditorium, Tulare, California, June 10, 1942. pp. 1–7. Social Welfare—War Services—WCCA—Reports—Control Stations—Sacramento—Yuba City, 1942 (F3729:149). Department of Social Welfare Records, War Services Bureau. Sacramento, CA: California State Archives.

Johns, G. C. (1942b). State Department of Social Welfare Office Memorandum to Miss Margaret S. Watkins, Los Angeles, California, 7-29-42. Social Welfare—War Services—WCCA—Reports—Control Stations—Sacramento—Yuba City, 1942 (F3729:149). Department of Social Welfare Records, War Services Bureau. Sacramento, CA: California State Archives.

Kallenberg, J. (1942). In times like these: Some aspects of controlled evacuation of Japanese on the West Coast. *The Family: Journal of Social Case Work, 23*(6), 232–234.

Kikuchi, M. (1942). Memorandum to Mr. Kidwell, from Miya Kikuchi, Family Relations, Manzanar Relocation Center, Manzanar, California, April 27, 1942, pp. 1–3. Folder: 18.200—Social Welfare Cases, Box 220: Manzanar Relocation Center—Central Files—50.026 to 62.014. Records of the War Relocation Authority, 1941–1989, Record Group 210, Subject-Classified General Files of the Relocation Centers—compiled 1942–1946. ARC Identifier 1544889/MLR Number PI-77 48. Washington, DC: National Archives and Records Administration.

Kimura, E. (1942). Letter from Emi Kimura, a member of the YWCA Cabinet at San Jose State College to Dear Jean, the Student Secretary at San Jose State College, received June 15, 1942, pp. 1–2. Folder 9—Japanese, correspondence, minutes, press releases, clippings, pamphlets, etc. 1942 (1 of 2 folders), Box 222. Immigration & Refugee Services of America: Common Council for American Unity Collection, Immigration History Research Center. Minneapolis: University of Minnesota.

Kingman, R. (1974). The Fair Play Committee and Citizen Participation: An oral history conducted in 1974 by Rosemary Levenson. *Japanese American Relocation Reviewed, Volume II: The Internment* (pp. 1b–97q). Berkeley: Regional Oral History Office, Bancroft Library, University of California.

Knight, A. (1942a). Letter to Miss Phoebe H. Bannister, Federal Security Agency, Division of Public Assistance, San Francisco, California, from Alfred Knight, Public Assistance Supervisor, Control Station #102, Lincoln, California, July 15, 1942, pp. 1–2. Social Welfare—War Services—WCCA—Reports—Control Stations—Lawndale-Riverside, 1942 (F3729:148). Department of Social Welfare Records, War Services Bureau. Sacramento: California State Archives.

Knight, A. (1942b). Report on Control Station, Lindsay, California, July 29, 1942, pp. 1–3. Social Welfare—War Services—WCCA—Reports—Control Stations—Lawndale-Riverside, 1942 (F3729:148). Department of Social Welfare Records, War Services Bureau. Sacramento: California State Archives.

Knight, A. (1942). Letter to Miss Phoebe H. Bannister, Federal Security Agency, Division of Public Assistance, San Francisco, California, from Alfred Knight, Public Assistance Supervisor, Control Station #102, Lincoln, California, July 15, 1942. pp. 1–2. Social Welfare—War Services—WCCA—Reports—Control Stations—Lawndale-Riverside, 1942 (F3729:148). Department of Social Welfare Records, War Services Bureau. Sacramento, CA: California State Archives.

Knight, A. (1942d). Sacramento and Florin Alien Control Stations: Statement Department of Social Welfare Office Memorandum to Margaret Bullard, from Alfred Knight, Sacramento, California, June 5, 1942, pp. 1–4. Social Welfare—War Services—WCCA—Reports—Control Stations—Anaheim-Isleton, 1942 (F3729:147). Department of Social Welfare Records, War Services Bureau. Sacramento: California State Archives.

Larmore, K. M. (1942a). Control Station, Civic Memorial Auditorium, Tulare, California: State Department of Social Welfare Office Memorandum to Margaret S. Watkins, from Gladys C. Johns, by Kathryn Larmore, May 8, 1942, pp. 1–2. Social Welfare—War Services—WCCA –Control Stations—Sacramento—Yuba City, 1942 (F3729:149). Department of Social Welfare Records, War Services Bureau. Sacramento: California State Archives.

Larmore, K. M. (1942b). Control Station, Memorial Auditorium, Tulare, California: State Department of Social Welfare Office Memorandum to Margaret S. Watkins, from Gladys C. Johns, by Kathryn Larmore, June 10, 1942, pp. 1–7. Social Welfare—War Services—WCCA –Control Stations—Sacramento—Yuba City, 1942 (F3729:149). Department of Social Welfare Records, War Services Bureau. Sacramento: California State Archives.

Larmore, K. M. (1942c). Control Station, Ventura, California: State Department of Social Welfare Office Memorandum to Margaret S. Watkins, from Gladys C. Johns, by Kathryn Larmore, April 29, 1942, pp. 1–6. Social Welfare—War Services—WCCA – Control Stations—Sacramento—Yuba City, 1942 (F3729:149). Department of Social Welfare Records, War Services Bureau. Sacramento: California State Archives.

Leahy, M. (1946). Public Assistance for restricted persons during the Second World War. Social Service Review, 19(1), 24–47.

LeHane, M. (1942). Report of Operation of Civil Control Station, Anaheim, California, May 21 through 17, 1942, pp. 1–2. Social Welfare—War Services—WCCA—Reports—Control Stations—Anaheim-Isleton, 1942 (F3729:147). Department of Social Welfare Records, War Services Bureau. Sacramento: California State Archives.

Lyon, C. M. (July 25, 2015). Japanese American Citizens League. Retrieved from http://encyclopedia.densho.org/Japanese American Citizens League/.

Manzanar Relocation Center. (1944). Minutes of the meeting of the Coordinating Council Meeting, November 28, 1944, pp. 1–3. Folder: 60.120 Youth Coordinating

Council, Box 225: Manzanar Relocation Center Central Files 50.026 to 62.014 (1942 to 1943). Records of the War Relocation Authority, 1941–1989, Record Group 210, Subject-Classified General Files of the Relocation Centers—compiled 1942—1946. ARC Identifier 1544889/MLR Number PI-77 48. Washington, DC: National Archives and Records Administration.

Marks Jr., E. B. (1943). Memorandum to John H. Provinse, Chief, Community Services Division, WRA, Washington, DC, April 2, 1943, pp. 1–3. Folder: Provinse, John—Jan.–April, 1943, Box 35: Washington Office Records—Chronological File; General—Alphabetical—PF-John Provinse. Records of the War Relocation Authority, 1941–1989, Record Group 210, General Outgoing Correspondence, compiled 1942–1946. ARC Identifier 1534421/MLR Number PI-77 18. Washington, DC: National Archives and Records Administration.

McDougall, W. R. (1942a). Narrative Report of Civil Control Station, 2314 South Vermont Avenue, Los Angeles, California, April 25–May 1, 1942, pp. 1–4. Box Social Welfare—War Services—WCCA—Reports—Control Stations—Lawndale-Riverside, 1942 (F3729:148). Department of Social Welfare Records, War Services Bureau. Sacramento: California State Archives.

McDougall, W. R. (1942b). Public Assistance Supervisor's Report of Operation of W.C.C.A. Station at 360 South Westlake Avenue, Los Angeles, May 11, 1942, pp. 1–3. Social Welfare—War Services—WCCA—Reports—Control Stations—Lawndale-Riverside, 1942 (F3729:148). Department of Social Welfare Records, War Services Bureau. Sacramento: California State Archives.

Meyer, V., & Popper, V. (1942). Report on WCCA Control Station, 719 Front Street, Needles, July 16, 1942, pp. 1–2. Social Welfare—War Services—WCCA—Reports—Control Stations—Lawndale-Riverside, 1942 (F3729:148). Department of Social Welfare Records, War Services Bureau. Sacramento: California State Archives.

Morcom, M. K. (1942). Report on Stockton Control Station, May 20, 1942, pp. 1–2. Social Welfare—War Services—WCCA—Control Stations—Sacramento—Yuba City, 1942 (F3729:149). Department of Social Welfare Records, War Services Bureau. Sacramento: California State Archives.

Nobe, L. N. (1999). The Children's Village at Manzanar: The World War II eviction and detention of Japanese American orphans. Journal of the West, 38(2), 65–71.

Okazaki, M. (1942a). Okazaki, Mari—Correspondence, pp. 1–17. Folder B12.44, Box BANC MSS 67/14 c. Japanese American Evacuation and Resettlement Study, Japanese American Evacuation and Resettlement records. Berkeley: Bancroft Library, University of California.

Okazaki, M. (1942b). Okazaki, Mari, diary excerpts, notes and correspondence, part 1, pp. 1–113. Folder O10.05 (1/2), Box BANC MSS 67/14 c. Japanese American Evacuation and Resettlement Study, Japanese American Evacuation and Resettlement records. Berkeley: Bancroft Library, University of California.

Parmley, E. (1942). WCCA Evacuation, Santa Barbara County: State Department of Social Welfare Memorandum to Margaret S. Watkins, from Gladys C. Johns, by Elizabeth Parmley, filed April 27, 1942, pp. 1–2. Social Welfare—War Services—WCCA—Control Stations—Sacramento—Yuba City, 1942 (F3729:149). Department of Social Welfare Records, War Services Bureau. Sacramento: California State Archives.

Pigatti, F. G. (1942a). Report of Operation of WCCA Station No. 32 at 822 E. 20th Street, L.A., May 15 1942, pp. 1–2. Social Welfare—War Services—WCCA—Reports—Control Stations—Lawndale-Riverside, 1942 (F3729:148). Department of Social Welfare Records, War Services Bureau. Sacramento: California State Archives.

Pigatti, F. G. (1942b). Report on WCCA Station No. 55, 340 North Valencia Street, Covina, California, 5-20-42, pp. 1-3. Social Welfare—War Services—WCCA –Control Stations—Anaheim—Isleton, 1942 (F3729:147). Department of Social Welfare Records, War Services Bureau. Sacramento: California State Archives.

Pigatti, F. G. (1942c). Report on WCCA Station No. 55, 340 North Valencia Street, Covina, California, 5-20-42, pp. 1-2. Social Welfare—War Services—WCCA—Reports—Control Stations—Anaheim-Isleton, 1942 (F3729:147). Department of Social Welfare Records, War Services Bureau. Sacramento: California State Archives.

Pigatti, F. G. (1942d). Reporting on Evacuation from W.C.C.A. Station, 3500 S. Normandie, Los Angeles, California, May 15, 1942, pp. 1-3. Social Welfare—War Services—WCCA—Reports—Control Stations—Lawndale-Riverside, 1942 (F3729:148). Department of Social Welfare Records, War Services Bureau. Sacramento: California State Archives.

Popper, V. (1942a). Memorandum to Miss Winifred J. Ryder: Wartime Civil Control Station at 2923 East Second Street, Los Angeles, June 3, 1942, pp. 1-3. Social Welfare—War Services—WCCA—Reports—Control Stations—Lawndale-Riverside, 1942 (F3729:148). Department of Social Welfare Records, War Services Bureau. Sacramento: California State Archives.

Popper, V. (1942b). Wartime Civil Control Station, 38 East California St., Pasadena, California: Civil Exclusion Order No. 54, May 9–14, 1942, pp. 1-3. Social Welfare—War Services—WCCA—Reports—Control Stations—Lawndale-Riverside, 1942 (F3729:148). Department of Social Welfare Records, War Services Bureau. Sacramento: California State Archives.

Powell, O. M. (April 29, 1942). Memorandum from Oscar M. Powell, Executive Director to Regional Directors: Plan for carrying out responsibilities assigned to the Bureau of Public Assistance for providing Temporary Aid necessitated by Enemy Action to Civilians, pp. 1-26. Box Child Welfare Division Correspondence. Public Welfare Commission Records. Salem: Oregon State Archives.

Ryan, E. (1942a). Yuba City Control Station: Memorandum to Mr. Philip Schafer, Federal Area Representative, Social Security Board, San Francisco, California, from Miss Eileen Ryan, Public Assistance Supervisor, June 2, 1942. pp. 1-2. Social Welfare—War Services—WCCA –Control Stations—Sacramento—Yuba City, 1942 (F3729:149). Department of Social Welfare Records, War Services Bureau. Sacramento: California State Archives.

Ryan, E. (1942b). Yuba City Control Station Report to State Department of Social Welfare, pp. 1-3. Social Welfare—War Services—WCCA –Control Stations—Sacramento—Yuba City, 1942 (F3729:149). Department of Social Welfare Records, War Services Bureau. Sacramento: California State Archives.

Ryder, W. J. (1942). Control Station Operation—707 South Spring Street—March 30 through April 4, 1942, pp. 1-5. Box Social Welfare—War Services—WCCA—Reports—Control Stations—Lawndale-Riverside, 1942 (F3729:148). Department of Social Welfare Records, War Services Bureau. Sacramento: California State Archives.

Schafer, P. (1942). Report on Wartime Civil Control Station at Vacaville, Sacramento, Loomis, Newcastle, Yuba City, Chico, Woodland, and Isleton: Memorandum to Azile H. Aaron, Public Assistance Representative, May 22, 1942, pp. 1-8. Social Welfare—War Services—WCCA—Control Stations—Sacramento—Yuba City, 1942 (F3729:149). Department of Social Welfare Records, War Services Bureau. Sacramento: California State Archives.

Simmons, K. C. (1942). Project #18—Exclusion Order #11,961 South Mariposa Street, Los Angeles, April 23–April 29, 1942, pp. 1–4. Social Welfare—War Services—WCCA—Reports—Control Stations—Lawndale-Riverside, 1942 (F3729:148). Department of Social Welfare Records, War Services Bureau. Sacramento: California State Archives.

Snow, J. (1942). Summary Report of Marysville Civil Control Station, July 4–12, 1942, pp. 1–2. Social Welfare—War Services—WCCA—Reports—Control Stations—Lawndale-Riverside, 1942 (F3729:148). Department of Social Welfare Records, War Services Bureau. Sacramento: California State Archives.

Spickard, P. R. (1986). Injustice compounded: Amerasians and Non-Japanese Americans in World War II concentration camps. *Journal of American Ethnic History*, 5(2), 5–22.

Spickard, P. R. (1989). *Mixed blood: Intermarriage and ethnic identity in twentieth-century America*. Madison: University of Wisconsin Press.

Stebbins, H. I. (1942). Narrative report of the Operation of the Woodland Wartime Civilian Control Station, Exclusion Order #78 by Helen I. Stebbins, Public Assistance Supervisor, May 16 to 21, 1942, pp. 1–3. Folder: 149, Box Social Welfare—War Services—WCCA—Reports—Control Stations—Sacramento—Yuba City, 1942 (F3729:149). Department of Social Welfare Records, War Services Bureau. Sacramento: California State Archives.

Sundquist, P. (1942a). Letter to Mr. C.A. Stuart, Director, San Joaquin County Welfare Department, from Perry Sundquist, Public Assistance Supervisor, Lodi Control Station, May 22, 1942. Social Welfare—War Services—WCCA—Reports, General, 1942-43 (F3729-146). Department of Social Welfare Records, War Services Bureau. Sacramento: California State Archives.

Sundquist, P. (1942b). Report on operation of Lodi Control Station: Memorandum from Perry Sundquist, Public Assistance Supervisor, to Mrs. Margaret Morcom, Area Supervisor—May 14, 1942 to May 21, 1942 inc., pp. 1–2. Social Welfare—War Services—WCCA—Reports—Control Stations—Lawndale-Riverside, 1942 (F3729:148). Department of Social Welfare Records, War Services Bureau. Sacramento: California State Archives.

The New York School of Social Work. (1947). *Bulletin of the New York School of Social Work, Columbia University: report for the year October 1, 1946–September 30, 1947* (Vol. 16). New York: Community Service Society of the City of New York.

Tinning, G. (1942). Narrative Report on Palmdale Station #84, May 21–25, 1942, p. 1. Box Social Welfare—War Services—WCCA—Reports—Control Stations—Lawndale-Riverside, 1942 (F3729:148). Department of Social Welfare Records, War Services Bureau. Sacramento: California State Archives.

Todd, D. (1942). Civil Control Station, 181 Smith Street, Ukiah, California: State Department of Social Welfare Office Memorandum to Margaret Watkins, from Doris Todd, May 27, 1942, pp. 1–2. Social Welfare—War Services—WCCA –Control Stations—Sacramento—Yuba City, 1942 (F3729:149). Department of Social Welfare Records, War Services Bureau. Sacramento: California State Archives.

Underhill, B. S. (1942). Report of Public Assistance Supervisor, Selma Civil Control Station, American Legion Hall, Selma California, May 21, 1942. Social Welfare—War Services—WCCA—Reports—Control Stations—Sacramento—Yuba City, 1942 (F3729:149). Department of Social Welfare Records, War Services Bureau. Sacramento: California State Archives.

United States Army. (1943). *Final report, Japanese evacuation from the West Coast, 1942*. Washington, DC: U.S. Government Printing Office.

United States Congress—House Select Committee Investigating National Defense Migration. (1942). *National defense migration. Fourth interim report ... Seventy-Seventh Congress, second session pursuant to H. Res. 113, Findings and recommendations on evacuation of enemy aliens and others from prohibited military zones.* Washington: U.S. Government Printing Office.

Wallace, S. F. (1942). Report of Operations of Civil Control Station at Oceanside, California, May 11 through May 17th, 1942, pp. 1–2. Social Welfare—War Services—WCCA—Reports—Control Stations—Lawndale-Riverside, 1942 (F3729:148). Department of Social Welfare Records, War Services Bureau. Sacramento: California State Archives.

War Relocation Authority. (1943). Community Activities semi-annual report: July through December 1943, pp. 1–6. Folder: Semi-Annual Reports—Community Management Division Reports of Health Section & Reports of Welfare Section, Box 5: Washington Office Records—Documentary Files—Semi-Annual Reports: Operation D Division, Community Mgmt. Div., Administrative Mgmt. Division. Records of the War Relocation Authority, 1941–1989, Record Group 210, Headquarters Basic Documentation Reports, compiled 1942–1946. ARC Identifier 1526983/ MLR Number PI-77 3. Washington, DC: National Archives and Records Administration.

War Relocation Authority. (1946). *Wartime exile: The exclusion of the Japanese Americans from the West Coast.* Washington, DC: U.S. Government Printing Office.

Watkins, M. A. (1942). Personnel Enemy Alien Assistance Program: California State Department of Social Welfare Office Memorandum, to Martha Chickering, March 20, 1942, pp. 1–3. Box Social Welfare—War Services—WCCA—Procedures, 1941–April, 1942 (F3729:144). Department of Social Welfare Records, War Services Bureau. Sacramento: California State Archives.

Webb, W. (1942a). Report of Operation of WCCA Station, Sanger, California, July 27 through August 8, 1942, pp. 1–3. Social Welfare—War Services—WCCA—Control Stations—Sacramento—Yuba City, 1942 (F3729:149). Department of Social Welfare Records, War Services Bureau. Sacramento: California State Archives.

Webb, W. (1942b). Report of Operations of Clovis WCCA Station, July 8 through July 15, 1942, pp. 1–2. Social Welfare—War Services—WCCA—Reports—Control Stations—Anaheim-Isleton, 1942 (F3729:147). Department of Social Welfare Records, War Services Bureau. Sacramento: California State Archives.

White, H. B. (1942a). Report of San Francisco Control Station, Exclusion Order No. 20, pp. 1–5. Social Welfare—War Services—WCCA –Control Stations—Sacramento—Yuba City, 1942 (F3729:149). Department of Social Welfare Records, War Services Bureau. Sacramento: California State Archives.

White, H. B. (1942b). Report of San Francisco Control Station, Exclusion Order No. 41, pp. 1–4. Social Welfare—War Services—WCCA –Control Stations—Sacramento—Yuba City, 1942 (F3729:149). Department of Social Welfare Records, War Services Bureau. Sacramento: California State Archives.

White, H. B. (1942c). Report of San Francisco Control Station: Exclusion Order No. 20, pp. 1–5. Social Welfare—War Services—WCCA—Control Stations—Sacramento—Yuba City, 1942 (F3729:149). Department of Social Welfare Records, War Services Bureau. Sacramento: California State Archives.

Wollenberg, C. (2012). Dear Earl, The Fair Play Committee, Earl Warren, and Japanese internment. *California History, 89*(4), 24–60. doi: 10.2307/41853220

4

Incarceration

Temporary Detention Centers

When the Japanese finally arrived in the assembly center, a surprisingly large number were bitter and sullen. (Silverman, 1942a)

One of the fellows on the train was saying that the little kids in one of the assembly centers have been wanting to go home—to America; they think they're in Japan. (Kimura, 1942, p. 1)

Center Conditions

The temporary detention centers—usually referred to "assembly" or "reception" centers—awaiting the Nikkei at the end of the difficult journeys were insalubrious environments. Hastily built on existing sites such as race tracks and fair grounds, the temporary camps boasted few facilities and no amenities, "poorly organized, unsanitary, and no adequate facilities for any good use" (cited in Ryan, 1942, p. 3), as one "evacuee" described the Merced facilities.

> The 20 by 25 feet hovel that greeted us on arrival was a discouraging and a bare sight for this travel weary evacuee; no, not even a stray nail in the wall on which to hang our clothes. Cement flooring, plywood partitions, no ceiling, no privacy!" (cited in Ryan, 1942, p. 3)

Housing in Puyallup, Washington, and Santa Anita, California, was cramped spaces that ordinarily held livestock. As the historian Roger, Daniels (1972) asserts, the centers were not "generally brutal" environments, more "like a century-old American institution, the Indian reservation" (p. 105) rather than the concentration camps that operated throughout Nazi-occupied Europe. As he also noted, however, it "was probably more than the housing shortage that inspired them to select sites that had been intended to house livestock" (p. 89). There were alternatives such as "college dormitories soon to be vacated" (p. 89) which could have been used instead. The fact that it was the loss of access to the

Facilitating Injustice: The complicity of social workers in the forced removal and incarceration of Japanese Americans, 1941–1946. Yoosun Park, Oxford University Press (2020). © Oxford University Press.
DOI: 10.1093/acprof:oso/9780199765058.001.0001

racetracks and fairgrounds, rather than the fact of their usage to illegally detain human beings, that incensed the local populations around the centers was an indication that such alternatives would not have found political or popular support. An early report of the War Relocation Authority (WRA) noted in April of 1942 that the "people of Pasadena and Arcadia are blaming the Japanese for closing Santa Anita" (Silverman, 1942a, p. 2), as did those of Salinas about the rodeo grounds which had been similarly converted. For the people of Seattle and its environs, "one of the main concerns connected with the assembly center was whether the Japanese would be removed and the ground cleared in time to hold the famous Puyallup Valley Fair" (Simms, 1944, p. 4).

Recalling her visit to the Tanforan Center at Christmas time, Ruth Kingman (1974), Executive Secretary of the Pacific Fair Play Committee, recalled the conditions being "to say the least, disgracefully uncomfortable" (p. 12b).

> It was a race track and these people lived in the horses' stalls. And all of the remaining vestiges of the horses' occupancy were not necessarily gone. There would be a family, say of three, or four; father, mother, two small children, maybe a tiny baby. And, of course, one couldn't help but be a little ambivalent about this. You felt so sorry for them. I mean having to live that way when they were American citizens who'd never done anything but go to school—that sort of thing. I mean while we weren't worried about them we felt sorry for them. . . . One of the things that bothered the older women down there more than anything else and also when they got to Topaz, was that, as the Army calls them, latrines had no dividing curtains at all. Now this, for a Japanese woman, was just about as hard as anything she could ever be asked to undergo. (pp. 12b–13b)

A large degree of latitude, however, was afforded the Army's oversight of the centers, even by individuals such as Kingman who had seen the conditions of the detention camps first-hand and exhibited sympathy for its inmates. The Army had, Kingman averred, needed to move at lightning speed to accomplish a highly unusual task.

> [T]his was a job that the Army had been given to do and in American history there had never been anything like this. They were not equipped to handle men and women and babies. On a large basis like this, all in a hurry. They were not accustomed to providing for the needs of women and children. (p. 13b)

But, as Carey McWilliams (1942b), another a member of the Fair Play Committee, commented, such excuses might explain the initial conditions of the centers, but did not account for the fact that the problems were not resolved over time.

I have been reluctant to say or do anything with reference to the conditions in the camps as I naturally assumed that there would be much confusion at the outset and that a reasonable opportunity should be afforded responsible officials to work out satisfactory program. But the reports I have been receiving indicate to me that conditions are not improving. The camp at Pomona is apparently a nightmare. Even making allowances for the inherent difficulties involved, some of the confusion and lack of planning seems inexcusable. (p. 1)

The Army's own assessment of the conditions was not entirely sanguine, as the following excerpt from an internal report on the Puyallup detention center indicates.

Living quarters in Areas A, B, C and outside in D are satisfactory. It is hard to give a word picture of the quarters in D that have been built under the seats in these huge wooden grandstands, but in the runways quarters have been built, they have concrete floors—are cold and clammy, no outside entrance or windows; therefore, will require lights in daytime. Barracks face inward on long narrow aisles. In case of fire, which is a menace, especially here, would probably be tragic. I say this because the heat provided is these old type kerosene wick burning, light, moveable heaters. (Office of the Commanding General—Headquarters Western Defense Command and Fourth Army, 1942a, p. 6a)

The fact was that the detention centers were "provisions for a transitory phase" (United States Army, 1943, p. 78) within the scheme of the Army's removal plans and were designed to provide only "the minimum essentials for the health and maintenance of health and morale" (p. 78). The bar, in other words, had been set very low. Milton Silverman (1942b), a journalist hired by the WRA to produce background reports on the removal process, reported that facilities at the Salinas Center—"very much like the Santa Anita, Tanforan, Fresno and other assembly centers," though "more attractive than Tanforan, less crowded than Santa Anita" (p. 9)—were abysmal.

The shower rooms there (constructed on the basis for American soldier encampments) were over-head showers with faucets to the shower head. These were completely out of reach. I couldn't reach the darn things. The Japanese are all pretty short and they couldn't reach them. Finally, one was put in (there are perhaps 50 shower heads in each building) and put an extension on it, although I have not checked this thoroughly as yet. They have all been using it. It's the only one they can reach. Then there was the little item of neglecting to put on

"Hot" and "Cold" on faucets. Darned inconvenient. The latrine situation is un-believably filthy. At Santa Anita at least there was porcelain plumbing. These are wooden cess-pools, dirty, poorly-ventilated, dark. (p. 9)

Silverman's report concluded that such conditions, moreover, made the centers "Typhoid specials" (p. 9). Although major outbreaks of typhoid or such commu-nicable diseases did not occur in the centers, the inadequate state of health care provided in the centers was a matter noted by many. Silverman reported that, despite the fact that hospital facilities existed at the Salinas detention center "only by title" (p. 4), five Nikkei patients "pretty sick" (p. 4) with tuberculosis had been taken out of the county hospital and moved to it. Dr. Martha Elliot of the U.S. Children's Bureau, on assignment to inspect detention center conditions, vis-ited Santa Anita, Puyallup, and Portland in the Spring of 1942. In her report on the conditions and recommendations for improvement sent to the WRA and to the War Department, Elliot deplored the total lack of maternal and child health physicians and emphasized the need for "women doctors and social workers" (Ellis, 1942b, p. 1). She warned that "proper precautions" were not being taken in bottle feeding preparations for babies, resulting "in much diarrhea," and noted that food in the centers was also "inadequate for older children" (Ellis, 1942b, p. 1).

Social Welfare in the Detention Centers

In the detention centers, as they had during the removal process, many of the Nikkei worked tirelessly to make the best of the unenviable situation in which they found themselves. One young Nikkei from Colusa, California explained.

So they gave us a lemon! So, we've started a lemonade stand! Curtains were hung to add that homely touch; closets were crudely fashioned. Drapes were strung across the room to foil any would be "peeking tom"; tables and benches now grace our humble abode. Leave it to the Japanese ingenuity and a little "elbow grease." (cited in Ryan, 1942, p. 3)

Despite the homemade furniture built from scavenged wood and other homey touches scraped together in an effort to create more tolerable surroundings, "still, home was never like this" (cited in Ryan, 1942, p. 3). The discomforts of camp living, where the basic functions of life were conducted en mass in crowded dining halls, latrines and showers without walls or doors, and in cramped living quarters in which entire families were pressed into tiny unpartitioned spaces, created new strife and amplified whatever discord may have already existed among families and neighbors. The urgent need for social services, however obvious, went largely unheeded.

Several centers did have, at least on paper, welfare bureaus offering a wide variety of social services. Tulare Center's welfare bureau boasted a "Family Welfare Unit, which takes care of problems pertaining to births, marriages, deaths, serious illness and relocation of evacuees" as well as a "Juvenile Department dealing with delinquency and moral problems" ("Social Welfare Bureau organized," 1942, p. 2). Fresno's welfare bureau was reported to have staff providing "information on changes for alien registration and selective service, notarizing of signatures, and health adjustments will be available in these offices" ("Seichi Mikami heads new welfare office," 1942, p. 5). The Merced Center's counterpart dealt with issues of "delinquency, adjustment, committee, morals, parent education, clinic care, hospitalization, etc." ("Commissioners appointed," 1942, p. 1). Pomona Center's "social welfare committee, a friendly body for promoting goodwill and harmony for the community at large" was to "aid in family relations, character building, relief, delinquencies, public health, and to act as a clearing house for general complaints" ("Welfare board named," 1942, p. 1).

Whether and how any such services were provided by the welfare offices staffed mostly by untrained workers and wielding few resources is difficult to fathom. Social Work Today's May 1942 report of welfare services being provided by "trained Japanese" ("News of alien evacuation," p. 34) in the centers specifically cited Manzanar's Miya Kikuchi, "an experienced social worker," who was "to deal with all welfare work, and any friction among or within families" ("News of alien evacuation," 1942, p. 34). CSDSW Director Martha Chickering's accounting during the removal phase had tallied only a handful of trained social workers among the California Nikkei. Grace Coyle, the WRA's first hire to organize social services in the long-term incarceration camps identified "only 7 Japanese-Americans who have had professional experience and training in case work and only 7 with experience in group work" (Ellis, 1942d, p. 2). Miya Kikichi was a rarity, in other words, and Manzanar's ability to establish a welfare office under the aegis of a trained social worker was a distinct anomaly. More typical was the set-up at Tulare, where the social welfare bureau was organized with "amateurs in positions requiring skill and judgment" (Sakoda, 1942a, p. 79). According to the camp newsletter, a "former insurance man" ("Social Welfare Bureau organized," 1942, p. 2) was appointed its head. James Sakoda (1942b), a member of the Japanese American Evacuation and Resettlement Study (JERS),[1] appraised the

---

[1] The multidisciplinary research project led by Berkeley sociologist Dorothy Swaine Thomas employed multiple Nikkei field researchers (and non-Nikkei researchers) to gather data during their removal, incarceration, and resettlement periods. The researchers kept detailed camp diaries in which they recorded their observations and experiences.

Nikkei workers attending the camp's ongoing Social Work Discussion Group as such amateurs: "while several had lived among Caucasians a great deal, the intellectual and educational level was probably only slightly superior to the high school level" (p. 3). The Tanforan welfare office was the only other that boasted a trained social worker named Kimi Mukaye, staff member of the YWCA prior to the war. Unfortunately, Mukaye's "prime function," according to Charles Kikuchi (1942b), another JERS researcher and an MSW student at Berkeley prior to removal, was "making up order forms for the people who need clothing" (p. 91).

> All of the other social problems are handled, many badly, by the police, house managers, council, administration, churches, school and rec dept. It is usually an incidental factor. The House Managers think they solved a social problem by recommending that a man be sent to another camp because he beat up his wife recently. They did not see that the conflict was more basic than that, a case that needed intensive handling by a very experienced worker. (p. 91)

A Mr. Green, a "clerical stooge" in Kikuchi's estimation, who intended to "put the division in with the barbers, beauty operators and shoemakers down in mess hall 19" (1942a, p. 185), rather than Mukaye, was the head of the Tanforan Welfare Bureau.

Given the economic devastation wreaked on the community by the exclusion orders, the need for financial aid that soon surfaced among the incarcerated Nikkei was unsurprising. Many had lost the bulk of their assets in the fire sales precipitated by the exclusion. Others had had few assets to begin with and exhausted the little they had in preparing for the removal and in buying basic necessities, such as toiletries, within the camps. No system of aid had, however, been established at the centers. Tanforan began operations as a detention center in late April of 1942. Charles Kikuchi (1942a) who, like Mari Okazaki and other JERS research assistants, kept extensive journals of daily life in the camps, reported in early July of that year that one community leader estimated at least "50 cases of destitution" (p. 194), an estimation the center administration discounted. In Diary 9, capturing the events between November 16 and December 1, 1942, Kikuchi described the situation of a 74-year-old man in desperate need. "He and his wife, 73, are near the end of the trail. His wife just sits on the bed and stares. It's scary" (Kikuchi, 1942f, p. 89). Kikuchi explained that a "grant" had been "approved" by the center administration for this couple, but the news provided little comfort. The officials supplied no specifics on what that grant would consist of or when it would arrive. The routine administrative chaos in the center obvious to all inmates meant that no one trusted that a timely disbursal of the grant would be made.

A system of grants for basic clothing was eventually established in late July. Kikuchi (1942a) explained that the need for replacement clothing and shoes was "one of the most acute problems" (p. 194). The limit on luggage to only what one could carry meant that "people did not bring enough clothes in many cases or else they have worn out what they did have" (Kikuchi, 1942b, p. 95) by mid-summer. The established grant scale per month (Kikuchi, 1942a, p. 194) was:

Adult male—$3.82
Male age 6–18—$2.15
Children age 1–5—$2.60
Adult female—$ 4.61
Female age 6–18—$2.85
Infant to age 1 year—$2.25

Everyone was technically eligible for the grant. Because limited funds were appropriated for the program, however, the welfare department worked to "discourage people from taking the full allotment" (Kikuchi, 1942c, p. 111). The clothing grant was established, moreover, after a portion of the camp population had been transferred to the longer term WRA concentration camps. That population thus began their incarceration in the long-term camps lacking even the most basic supplies, such as shoes and winter clothing. As they had in the detention centers, however, functioning welfare programs would take months to develop in the WRA camps. Aid would not reach the impoverished for months to come.

The WRA Concentration Camps

On March 18, 1942, Executive Order 9102 established a civilian agency called the War Relocation Authority under the aegis of the Office of Emergency Management in the Executive Office of the President (United States Army, 1943). The task of the new "rather substantial permanent organization" (Office of the Commanding General—Headquarters Western Defense Command and Fourth Army, 1942b, p. 4) was to "deal with the many aspects of the evacuation problem" (p. 4). The general history of the WRA, including its establishment, operations, and its main protagonists has been extensively documented elsewhere and will not be repeated here. On the establishment of the agency, it suffices to note that the camp sites were chosen and built, in the words of the WRA Assistant Director Robert Cozzens (1974), with "unbelievable" speed.

When you think that we started in March 1942 and two or three weeks later we were established. In November, it was Thanks-giving Day, the last people arrived in centers, 110,000 people. The centers were built, the people were all moved, the centers were equipped, the schools were built, and everything else was finished by that time—hospitals, everything. Now that's speed. I don't care what lines you take; and it was not easy. (p. 13)

A non-negotiable criterion guiding the WRA in site selection, according to Milton Eisenhower, its first director, was that the camps had be built on public lands in order "that improvements made at public expense will not pass into private hands" (McWilliams, 1942a, p. 72). It was a policy, as Carey McWilliams noted, that functioned to "narrow the range of possible desirable locations" (p. 72). The ten chosen sites, all located thus on lands under the control of the Department of Interior—"on federal land, or Indian reservations, or things of that kind" (Cozzens, 1974, p. 8)—represented some of the most inhospitable terrain in the nation. YWCA fieldworker Lilian Sharpley (1943) described Topaz concentration camp as being "located on the most God forsaken spot" (p. 1) she had ever visited. Marnette Wood Chestnutt (1943), another YWCA worker, visiting Jerome Relocation Center in January, was moved to write:

That these evacuees have been put on such poor land, today mud ankle deep everywhere, next summer heat unrelieved by trees or shaded porches, is a crime against justice and mercy. That Arkansas should have entered into the arrangement makes me bow my head in shame. Beauty of natural surroundings might compensate somewhat, at least at times assuage the hurt, but the ugliness of the out of doors there today took the courage of a martyr to bear. (p. 2)

Setting Up Social Services

The WRA reported in 1943 that a Welfare Section had been established at all ten incarceration camps. The department would:

assist families and individuals with the problems involved in housing, cash clothing allowances, public assistance, reuniting of members of families separated in the course of the evacuation, and social and individual problems such as delinquency, family difficulties, problems of foster care, broken homes, and other problems beyond the scope of the evacuees to solve. (War Relocation Authority, 1943e, p. 1)

It would also coordinate with federal and state authorities for the provision of care to persons—the elderly, the disabled, or dependent, etc.—requiring specialized care and treatment which could not be accomplished within the camps. Organizing the continued care or removal to the camps for the hundreds of exempted individuals who had been left behind in institutions such as hospitals and prisons as their status changed would also be the responsibility of the department (War Relocation Authority, 1943e). The glossy vision of social services conjured in the announcement was, however, far from the ill-planned, underfunded, poorly staffed, and inconsistently administered departments that were on the ground.

The establishment of social services in the camps was a protracted process. The WRA had been established as an agency in March of 1942; Tule Lake, the first of the WRA incarceration camps to open, began operations on May 27, 1942, and Manzanar and Poston, which had served as detention centers, began operating as long-term incarceration camps on June 1, 1942. As fast as the WRA moved to create the camps, it had not moved fast enough to have either the staff or the structures in place to serve the needs of a population being shipped in from the temporary detention centers. No system of aid or services was put in place in any of the camps until the end of that calendar year, and no aid was disbursed until the start of the next year. In a retrospective analysis of the Heart Mountain Welfare Section, Head Counselor Adeline Kell (1945) described that, in 1942 and into the first months of 1943, the department functioned like "an emergency program" within "a community that has experienced a disaster which has disrupted the habits of living of an entire population" (p. 2). Heart Mountain began operations on August 11, 1942. It was nearly a year after, once "practical patterns of daily living and community relationships had been established" (p. 2) in the makeshift community, that the Welfare Section gradually evolved into a "program similar, in many respects, to that of a public welfare program in an ordinary community" (p. 2), though there were other duties such as the management of "housing services, issuance of gate passes, burial services, wedding services, transfers between centers, family reunions, and relocation counseling" (p. 2) that a public welfare program on the outside would not have had on its roster of responsibilities. Kell's narrative attributes a veneer of sense and method to a development process that most other accounts describe as an unmitigated muddle, as slapdash an affair as the development of the rest of the camp structures and systems. A telling detail is that a consistent title for the department was not settled upon until well into 1943, when the name Welfare Section began to be used uniformly across the camps. Scant services had been provided by the camp division functioning under various titles such as the Bureau of Family Services, Social Services, Public

Welfare, Family Welfare, and the Office of Welfare and Housing in the different camps, which were guided by no uniform protocol or central oversight.[2]

William Tuttle (1945) reported that when he arrived to take up the position of Head Counselor[3] of Gila River in November 1942, no Welfare Section actually existed in the camp which had opened on July 20 of that year. The Welfare Section at Rohwer, a camp which began operations on September 18, 1942, was not organized until April of 1943, when Wilma Dusseldorp was appointed Head Counselor. According to Dusseldorp (1945), only a semblance of services "limited to clerical work incident to processing the payment of clothing allowances, investigation of applications for public assistance by unsupervised counseling aides, and review and action on requests for inter-center transfers"(p. 1) had been provided prior to the establishment of that office. J. Lloyd Webb (1945), Dussedorp's counterpart at Jerome, described that its Welfare Section had not been "unified in nature of function, organization of staff, or supervision during the first six months of its life" (p. 1). It did not appoint personnel until April of 1943, and the many indications of "the lack of unity and organization of the Section prior to April 1943 suggest that only a limited amount of attention was given to the direction and organization of the Section" (p. 6) until that time. A "Social Service Unit," which was "both desired and organized by the evacuees with a minimum of encouragement and cooperation from the administrative staff" (p. 2), had been established on November 3, 1942, and had provided a variety of services "with practically no equipment and a staff of four evacuees" (p. 2). Minidoka's "checkered history of Welfare Section" (Kimmerling, 1945, p. 1) began with a period of confusion in which no one, including the camp administration, appeared to know the department's remit; all manner of seemingly unrelated tasks were assigned to the Welfare Section while the Section itself struggled "with a new and sometimes unwieldy staff" (Kimmerling, 1945,

---

[2] Grace Coyle, the first social worker hired by the WRA to design social services in the camps, had done so under the official title "Consultant on Recreation, Social Work, and the Interests of Women and Children Under the Division of Community Management." In her analysis, "what was needed in the Washington office was a person familiar with case work and public welfare" (p. 1) because the management of welfare programs would be the central task of the camp departments. Coyle, therefore, pushed to have Selene Gifford, her successor, be brought in under a different title: "Consultant on Public Welfare."

[3] The position of Head Counselor, the Chief of a camp Social Welfare Section, was "Counselor (CAF-9)" working the supervision of the Chief of Community Services and "responsible for establishing, directing, and maintaining a complete counseling an individual and family welfare program, including the selection and training of Japanese Counseling Aides" (War Relocation Authority, 1942a, p. 1). A master's degree in social welfare from "an accredited school of Social Service" with courses in "Social Welfare Casework, Family Problems, Social Adjustment, And in Public Welfare Organization and Administration" (War Relocation Authority, 1942a, p. 2) was required. Two years of social work experience, one of which was "in a supervisory capacity in social welfare work in which a thorough working knowledge of government aid, family problems, and social adjustment has been gained" (War Relocation Authority, 1942a, p. 2) was necessary.

p. 1) with little training and less clarity about what the limits of their jobs should be. Jerome's J. Lloyd Webb (1945) described, similarly, that that camp's Welfare Section lacked a clear vision of the "function, organization of staff, or supervision during the first six months of its life" (p. 1). Heart Mountain's Head Counselor Adeline Kell (1945) explained in her final report to the WRA that accurate case load statistics for the duration of the camp were difficult to ascertain because accounting procedures had not been developed in the early periods of the Welfare program.[4] Even more unfortunately, social services at Heart Mountain, which received its first inmates on August 12, 1942, had operated under the aegis of Internal Security, the camp's police force, until October 13, 1942, when it was reorganized as the Welfare Section under the Community Management Division (Kell, 1945). Central Utah, usually called Topaz, which began operations on September 11, 1942, was the only outlier in creating a social service office at "about the same time that the vanguard of Topaz evacuees reached this desolate wilderness of dust, burning sun, and tar paper buildings" (Pratt, 1945, p. 1). George H. LeFabregue, its first Head Counselor, was said to have "arrived literally in a cloud of dust, but full of enthusiasm, about September 12, 1942 and in true 'LaFabregue' fashion no time was lost in setting into motion the wheels of the Welfare Department" (Pratt, 1945, pp. 1–2).

A set of correspondence between George D. Nickel, on assignment for the social work periodical *The Survey* to produce a series of articles on the removal process, and Kathryn Close, an associate editor at the periodical, provide another glimpse into the development of the Welfare Section. Nickel visited camps and interviewed several WRA employees during his research for the series. His conclusion was that "welfare is being pretty much de-emphasized" (p. 1) by the WRA. He reported in early December of 1942 that no one in the WRA West Coast regional office or Gila concentration camp, which he had visited in person, seemed to have much information on the particulars of the welfare program in the camps. It was also possible, he speculated, that whatever policy the headquarters may establish in the end, "may not be carried out as such in the centers—for I think I detected in my conversations with administrative staff a feeling against setting up anything resembling a strong welfare program in the centers" (p. 2). Upon the advice of his editor, Nickel wrote to Grace Coyle, the social worker who had been hired by the WRA to design social services in the camps, to request more information. Coyle, a prominent group work pioneer and Professor of Group Work at Case Western School of Applied Social Sciences, had been on the payroll for a short two-month span at the WRA headquarters but was no longer in the position by the time Nickel contacted her. She was curiously reluctant to

---

[4] Given the heterogeneous reporting procedures followed by the various welfare heads for their final closing reports, it is likely that the same was true for all the camps.

provide information, insisting that her experience with the WRA was "now so far in the past" (Coyle, 1942, p. 1) to be of no value. While Coyle's disavowal may not make sense on a normal time scale, given that she was writing about an organization that threw up in a matter of weeks the physical and administrative structures of incarcerating more than 100,000 people of all ages, there was much to her contention that "conditions have changed undoubtedly so much" (Coyle, 1942, p. 1) at that organization in the three months since her departure.[5]

The frenetic speed with which the WRA needed to move to invent itself into existence explains, to some degree, the confusion that reigned in the development of social welfare in the camps. The low rates of relief requested and disbursed during the removal process, and the total absence of information from the detention centers where needs were not systematically tracked, may have lulled them into complacency about the coming need. There was also the undeniable reality that the WRA did not know what services would be needed or the extent to which those services would be needed because setting up a structure to deliver social services to an entire population in captivity had not been attempted before by it or any other organization. But Annie Clo Watson's conclusion in May of 1942 that "failure as yet of all private agencies both in northern and in southern California to achieve a constructive working relationship with the War Relocation Authority" (Watson, 1942b, p. 1) may be because social services was not a high priority for the WRA should also be taken seriously. Records of the YWCA show that that organization's and other private organizations' efforts to volunteer its services to the WRA had been rebuffed. Grace Coyle had warned the YWCA "against pressing too hard for consideration of our desire to be of service, since too much pressure has been brought to bear by other groups and the War Relocation Authority is rather resistive to such efforts" (Ellis, 1942d, p. 2). Mabel Brown Ellis of the YWCA, reporting in May of 1942 that an offer of a donation of recreational equipment to the WRA by a committee formed in the Bay Area had gone unheeded, had surmised that "the authorities are so overwhelmed with the problem of providing basic necessities that they cannot pay very much attention to the working out of ideal conditions in the temporary places of detention (Ellis, 1942c, p. 1).

If recreational equipment could be relegated to the nonurgent category of items needed only to create "ideal conditions," the shoes, coats, eye glasses, and other such items that so many of the incarcerated Nikkei needed in short order could not. A different explanation for the WRA's reluctance for the involvement

[5] Coyle, remarkably, does not seem to have ever written about her experience with the WRA. Although her tenure at the WRA was short, she had worked for the organization at its crucial starting point, creating the beginning structures for social service delivery in the camps. The Grace Coyle archives at Case Western University, however, do not contains a single document on the topic.

of outside agencies despite its inability to provide such items of basic necessity long after the opening of the camps was that it was ambivalent about providing aid, especially the kinds of material aid that usually counted as "welfare" or "relief." As was discussed in previous chapters, the Nikkei had had little contact with social workers prior to the forced removal. The WRA's praise (1943e) of the Nikkei as a population without a history of "dependency" (p. 2), who displayed a "considerable resistance" (p. 2) to public assistance, was accompanied by the prediction that the need for relief would increase in proportion to diminishing resources. More importantly, as need increased, "their independence" (p. 2) would be replaced by a habit of dependence. This moralizing judgment of the psychological dependence to come shadowed all work undertaken by the Welfare Section; aid could not be avoided, but it also could not go uncensured. The concentration camps, in the WRA's imagination, were "communities where evacuees might live and contribute, through work, to *their own support* pending their gradual reabsorption into private employment and normal American life" (War Relocation Authority, 1943c, p. 2). The camps, in other words, would not be welfare states, and the Nikkei would be pushed to be self-sufficient, regardless of the fact that they were prisoners from whom the very right to independence and faculty for self-management had been forcibly abrogated.

The stigmatization of welfare—and of charity before the development of systems of public welfare—was a phenomenon of long and wide standing. That dependency was an inevitable outcome of relief but was, nevertheless, "a defect of individual character" (Fraser & Gordon, 1994, p. 320), was not, of course, a view held uniquely by the WRA. As enemy aliens too dangerous to be kept in "ordinary American communities" (War Relocation Authority, 1943c, p. 2), the Nikkei were, moreover, the ultimate "undeserving." In her reply to Nickel, dated November 27, 1942, Grace Coyle insisted that for social services to be possible in the WRA camps, they needed to operate sub rosa.

> I had considerable feeling when I was out there that it was just as well not to publicize the social work aspects of this program because there were so many groups on the coast who wished to attack the WRA, and who would seize upon evidence of a social work point of view as the ground for attack. In fact, one of the local papers in a town near a center accused the WRA of having "a social service viewpoint" and it was one of the worst things they could say against it. Under these circumstances, too much publicity is likely to arouse not only the opposition of reactionary groups but also to make difficult the securing of appropriations in Congress to carry on even the minimum of social work which is now included. The attitude on the coast and in Congress was such that it seemed wise to call the social worker Assistant to the Chief of Community Management rather than any other title. That is, of course, strictly confidential

and should never be used in any way which might seep out to the papers. I hope very much, therefore, that you will consult with the publicity division of the WRA and with Miss Gifford as to the strategy of such an article. It might well be focused on certain aspects of community life, the development of the public schools, of libraries, or recreation activities with no mention of social work services and with a great stress on the economy with which the program is being managed, especially in its use of Japanese rather than Caucasian lead-ership. It is very much more important to have the program go on than to have *Survey* readers exactly informed, and under present circumstances it may not be possible to do both. I know you will treat this whole matter with wisdom and perspective. (Coyle, 1942, p. 1)[6]

Staffing the Camp Welfare Sections

On July 24, 1942, several months before Coyle's correspondence with Nickel, Mabel Brown Ellis of the YWCA had met with Coyle to discuss the future of social work in the camps. Coyle had informed Ellis that each camp would have a Chief of Community Services under whose authority divisions such as health, education, internal government, internal security, and community activities would operate (Ellis, 1942d). John H. Provinse, an anthropologist with a special-ization in Native American societies, had recently been appointed to the role in the Washington headquarters. Ellis (1942d) reported:

Miss Coyle has succeeded in getting the War Relocation Authority to plan for a trained social worker as the Assistant to the Chief of Community Services in each Center. This job will pay $3200. The person appointed will carry respon-sibility for child welfare and family welfare and for the handling of public assis-tance grants, etc. She will also be expected to train Japanese aides to function in these fields. Miss Coyle has selected 40 to 50 names from the Civil Service lists and has been interviewing people who have had satisfactory professional expe-rience and training for these positions. (p. 1)

Coyle's plan to place a trained social worker as the Assistant Chief of Community Services never materialized, though eventually a social worker would be hired to

---

[6] Nickel sent Coyle's letter to his *Survey* editor. Her response was the following: "Thank you for sending me a copy of Miss Coyle's letter, which I found extremely interesting—especially the part about concealing the fact that there is any social work in the camp. I would not know what to say about this. It seems to me that a journalist has to put down what he finds. If the WRA does not want this known, I am sure they will see that it is censored out of the article" (Close, 1942, p. 1).

head up the Welfare Section created within the Community Service Division in each camp.

In his correspondence with his *Survey* editor, George Nickel had predicted that in those camps where there were "good social workers on the administrative staff (not necessarily employed as social workers)" a reasonable welfare program would be established. In camps without such personnel, "welfare matters are apt to be handled in hit or miss fashion" (p. 1). Finding those good social workers with suitable experience and a willingness to work in the camps became the major difficulty in executing Coyle's plan. It was a problem that would plague the division as long as the camps were in operation. The 1943 WRA announcement on the establishment of camp Welfare Sections included the caveat that while social work positions had been created on paper, those positions had not been filled (War Relocation Authority, 1943e).

The relocation camps were difficult places to staff. The war had precipitated acute labor shortages in multiple domains across the nation. The serious shortfall in trained social workers was a phenomenon that predated the war and was greatly exacerbated by it. Social work was one of the fastest growing professions in the decades before the war (American Association of Social Workers, 1943). Between 1930 and 1940, the profession had added approximately 32,000 workers—a 55% increase. But the demand for trained workers—stimulated by the creation of new types of social work jobs and the expansion of existing jobs— far exceeded the number of graduates from schools of social work ("Editorial notes," 1942; Family Welfare Association of America, 1942). The deficit was only intensified by the exigencies of war. According to the American Association of Social Workers (AASW) (1943), approximately 5,000 new "war-connected" (p. 14) social work jobs had been created. These included the more than 200 new positions created in the Office of Defense Health and Welfare Services and 25 positions with the Office of Civilian Defense, as well as the dozens of positions in the WRA, which was recruiting experienced social workers for all of its ten incarceration camps (American Association of Social Workers, 1943). While the war heightened the already existing shortage, there was also a countervailing "draining off of trained and experienced personnel and potential personnel" (American Association of Social Workers, 1943, p. 14) drafted into armed forces, recruited away by various industries in constant need of new labor sources, and lost to new occupational opportunities for women that emerged due to the war. The resulting shortage was believed to be as large as 9,000–10,000 social workers nationwide (American Association of Social Workers, 1943).

Recruiting and retaining trained and experienced social workers in the context of this national shortage was a persistent problem for the WRA from the opening of the camps to their closing. The Minidoka Welfare Section reported that "[o]ne of the most difficult things to accomplish was the building up of the professional staff" (Kimmerling, Fite, & Abbott, 1945, p. 19). Despite urgent need, "new staff members were not recruited as rapidly as anticipated" (Kimmerling et al., 1945, p. 20) and the unfortunate "tendency on the part of the Center Administration seemed to be toward filling positions with local people whether or not they were trained for the work" (Kimmerling et al., 1945, p. 19). Even when qualified and available personnel were found, the bureaucratic machinery turned slowly, and "it took months to have them approved and processed for employment" (Kimmerling et al., 1945, p. 19).

There is ample evidence that, throughout the existence of the camps, both officials in Washington DC and individuals within the camps did conduct aggressive outreach to identify and recruit qualified social workers. The WRA quarterly report covering the period between October 1 and December 31, 1942, indicates that a member of the Washington staff "made two trips to middle western and eastern cities in an attempt to locate qualified persons who might be interested" (War Relocation Authority, 1942b, p. 24). Recruitment materials were distributed "through the National Conference of Social Work and the Chicago Chapter of the American Association of Social Workers and articles have been written for the *Public Welfare News* and other social work publications" (War Relocation Authority, 1944a, p. 1) and sent out to numerous social welfare agencies (Fite, 1945; Lane, 1945; Smithburg, 1945).

The limited gains made through these efforts were, however, continually eroded by factors such as the draft, which "made serious inroads on existing staff" (War Relocation Authority, 1943d, p. 5), taking both the Head and the Assistant Head of the Welfare Section at one camp at the same time (War Relocation Authority, 1945). Targeted recruitment of experienced social workers by more glamorous—and less obviously ethically compromised—organizations such as the United Nations Relief and Rehabilitation Administration (UNRRA) in charge of aiding persons displaced by the war in various European nations, also took a toll (War Relocation Authority, 1945). Selene Gifford, Head of the Welfare Section in the DC headquarters was one such social worker lured away.[7] As the war progressed and camp closure became the central imperative for the WRA, the camp staff were also diverted by the WRA itself to various regional

---

[7] The following is an excerpt from Gifford's resignation memo to John H. Provinse, Chief of the Community Services Division, which oversaw Welfare: "You and I have had many discussions concerning the request of the United Nations Relief and Rehabilitation Administration that I join their staff for duty either in this country or abroad. After considerable thought, and certainly with mixed emotions, I have decided to accept their offer. This decision is not without some feeling of regret.... It has been a pleasure to help in the development of a Welfare Section for the Authority. We have tried to quietly but consistently strive for basic organization and plans which would serve as the underpinning for eventual liquidation and be ready to give the individualized service based upon overall planning which that move will necessitate. At that eventual date the problems which have been dormant and more or less lost in these temporary communities will come up one by one and must be met in view of liquidation" (Gifford, 1944, p. 1).

resettlement offices (War Relocation Authority, 1945). The loss of personnel through these and other various reasons is encapsulated in a report from the Minidoka Welfare Section.

> During the year there was a total of eleven appointive staff members, six of whom terminated their services for the following reasons: One Junior Counselor was called by Selective Service; an Assistant Counselor and a Junior Counselor were transferred to the Relocation Division; two (husband and wife), an Assistant Counselor and a half-time Junior Counselor resigned when the former was called by UNRRA; the Head Counselor was transferred to the Washington Office as Public Welfare Consultant, after she was called east for family reasons which necessitated her remaining near Philadelphia for several months. (In June she resigned to work with UNRRA). (Kimmerling et al., 1945, p. 20)

The WRA's dire need for skilled social workers in the latter period of the camps' operations is outlined in an April 1945 letter from Marie D. Lane, Selene Gifford's replacement who would also be scouted by the UNRRA,[8] to Miss Margaret Rich, Executive Secretary of the Pittsburgh Family Welfare Society.

> Although you may already have been contacted by this office in reference to vacancies in the social work staff at the Relocation Centers, I am writing anyway in the hope that you may know of people—caseworkers, or supervisors—who might be interested in working with the Japanese group for the next six to eight months. There never has been a period in the brief history of WRA when casework attitudes and thinking were more necessary in the project than they will be in these last months, when thousands of dependent families and individuals will need help in planning for resettlement against the closing date, December 31st. I am enclosing a statement of the welfare program, and descriptions of the positions now open. If you know of interested people, will you please pass this material on to them, and suggest that they write me at the above address. If there is a group—even a small one—interested and wishing to know more about the work at the Centers, we can arrange to send one of the Consultants from the office to talk with them. (1945, p. 1)

A similar request from A. Lidie Fite (1945), in the Washington office, to Mrs. Jennie Schott, Director of the Department of Public Assistance in Montgomery

---

[8] Marie Dresden Lane went on to serve as the chief of the welfare division at the International Refugee Organization (IRO), which took over many of the functions of UNRRA when the latter was disbanded in 1947.

County, Pennsylvania, requested a "loan" of social workers and laid out the promise of a transfer to other governmental agencies to those willing to come on board and remain until the closure of the camps.

> Considering your acquaintance among social workers, I thought you might be
> able to suggest a few who would be interested in the experience of working on
> the centers in the busy and exciting period between now and December 31.
> I feel that the experience has been an invaluable one for me, and I can recom-
> mend it for both adventure and opportunity for real service. While the posi-
> tion is a temporary one, WRA staff members who are qualified for positions
> in other governmental agencies are being given some preference in transfer to
> those agencies when this project ends. If you are so fortunate as to have a staff
> member or two you could loan to WRA for the duration of the project, the
> lack of permanency would be solved for the worker, your agency would gain in
> the future by having a worker experienced in working with the Japanese group,
> and we would be most grateful to you, since social welfare principles cannot
> be maintained on the centers unless more people with those viewpoints can be
> secured. (p. 1)

The WRA (1943d) identified the "isolation of the centers from the best sources of supply" (p. 5), namely the Midwest and the East Coast, as the major hurdle in recruitment. Many other factors were also at play. The remoteness of the camp locations meant that most applicants had to take the jobs sight unseen, "without an opportunity to talk personally with the appropriate staff member at the center" (p. 5), an unappealing prospect for most. There were also objection to the "nature of the program" (War Relocation Authority, 1944b, p. 1), on both sides of the po-litical divide. Some were reluctant because they saw the camps as sites of unjust incarceration, and others were unwilling to work for the maintenance of Nikkei whom they saw as the enemy. The possibility of transfer notwithstanding, there was also the "uncertainty of tenure" (p. 1) of employment attached to a program whose end, contingent on the length of the war, was uncertain. At the start of the program, at least, there was also a "salary problem" (War Relocation Authority, 1942b, p. 24), the result of not only an underestimation of "the administrative responsibilities actually involved in the position" (p. 24), as the WRA character-ized, but also, without a doubt, a gross miscalculation on the part of the WRA of the difficulties they would encounter in recruiting qualified social workers. Adjustments were made to change job classifications, and the attendant compen-sation rise did result in comparatively high salaries for the WRA field positions. They did not, however, offset the many other factors, including the uncongenial settings of the camps and the objectionable conditions of the facilities therein, that hindered the recruitment and retention of a professional social work staff. The Minidoka Welfare Department reported, for example, that applicants for positions in the department "seemed to feel that Minidoka was too far away from the population centers to offer desirable leisure time activities. Single persons were housed in rather crude dormitories with little chance for outside recreation" (Kimmerling et al., 1945, p. 6).

As Dorothy Thomas and Richard Nishimoto (1946/1969) of the JERS described, the camps were in remote and inhospitable settings.

> Each of the ten sites were relatively isolated. The six western projects were wind and dust swept. Tule Lake, Minidoka, and Heart Mountain were subject to severe winters. Poston and Gila, both in the Arizona desert, had temperatures well above 100 degrees for lengthy periods, and Rohwer and Jerome experienced the excessive humidity and mosquito infestations of swampy delta land. (pp. 28–29)

The WRA camps, just as hastily and shoddily thrown up as the temporary detention centers had been, were predictably ill-equipped for the hostile environments in which they were built. In a July 19, 1943, memorandum to J. Lloyd Webb, the head of the Jerome's Community Welfare Section, Joseph L. McSparran, Chief Medical Officer of the camp in Denson, Arkansas, noted the urgent need for electric fans for the camp's many chronic invalids.

> There is a certain number of bed-ridden and helpless chronic invalids in the community. Some of them are in the Old Peoples Home and others in various apartments throughout the area. These unfortunate people are suffering greatly from the excessive heat of the summer climate and are urgently in need of electric fans. I recommend that such apparatus be secured as quickly as possible for the relief of these people. (McSparran, 1943, p. 1)

Winter brought a different set of problems. Staff housing in the camps was undoubtedly superior to that afforded the inmates. But the camps, still under construction months after they began operations, were uncomfortable settings even for the staff. Robert Cozzens (1974) described his move to serve as the director of the Gila camp in Arizona in the Fall of 1942.

> I was called down there when Mr. [Eastburn] Smith, our director at Gila, left the job. We lived in an unfinished wing of the hospital. There was no heat. We had three rooms that had no partitions in them, just studs—no walls. That's where we lived for quite some time. Finally we had a freeze. It went

down to sixteen degrees in the morning and stayed at around thirty-one or thirty-two degrees all day long for a week. Babies were turning absolutely blue. I don't know whether Babe [Mrs. Cozzens] realizes just what happened there or not, but the Army told us when we built that camp to use gas heaters. The camp was designed for gas heaters, and pipes put in. We'd already started to move in. Then they cancelled the order for gas and said we couldn't have it except for cooking and that the Los Angeles industries were going to need it all. So we couldn't have any natural gas for heating. They let us have natural gas for the ranges that had been purchased for the mess halls, but we couldn't use any for heat in the mess halls or any of the apartments. The pipes and everything had already been put in! We had to use oil heaters and they had to be manufactured. It took us over two months. In the meantime, we let contracts for putting concrete oil tanks in each block and bought hundreds of little gallon cans that each family could have to go get oil from the tanks. We had a hand pump on each tank so they could get a gallon of oil to take home, but we had no heaters. . . . We put a couple of stoves in each hall and they used the scrap lumber for fuel. The blocks at Gila were about 375 people. They'd build bonfires outside and they'd get in these rec halls with two little heaters and stand close together in order to get warm. It was a pitiful thing, and it went on for six weeks or about that long. It was just a miserable thing! (pp. 15–16)

Another factor working against recruitment was the hostile public reaction against the WRA and those opting to work with the Nikkei within the organization (Kimmerling et al., 1945). The camp staff, officially called "Appointed Personnel" or "AP," but commonly referred to simply as the "Caucasians" (Briesemeister, 1942a, p. 1), were resentful, on the one hand, of being "constantly on the spot from the point of view of the colonists who are critical of the administration" (Briesemeister & Wilbur, 1945, p. 2) and, on the other hand, of being criticized by the public at large for "coddling and pampering" (Tozier, 1945, p. 10) the Nikkei. The accusations of coddling, which became "loudly vocal whenever any story breaks that would indicate 'softness' in dealing with the Japanese" (Ellis, 1942a, p. 1), moved various legislative committees in Congress to investigate the WRA to substantiate those views (Tozier, 1945). A Gila River Caucasian staffer disclosed that he was reluctant to divulge the nature of his employment to people on the outside because they "invariably started an argument with him, called him un-American, etc." (Briesemeister, 1943, p. 10). Minidoka Director Harry Stafford's insistence that war hysteria being omnipresent, the public viewed the Nikkei and the WRA employees who worked with them "with an equal amount of distrust or suspicion" (Stafford, 1945, p. 5) was a factor working against the recruitment of social workers.

Problems in Service Delivery

The WRA's inability to recruit and retain sufficient numbers of qualified social workers created multiple problems. Due to the lack of pertinent staff in the Washington headquarters, the long-delayed *Welfare Handbook* of a policy and practice guidelines for carrying out the work of the department in the camps, was still incomplete in mid-1944, two years after the opening of the camps (War Relocation Authority, 1944c). According to Jerome's Head Counselor (Webb, 1945), the Washington headquarters were unable to provide even standard job descriptions for the various positions within the department until mid-November of 1943, more than a year after the camps opened. The Welfare Sections in the concentration camps were, in other words, providing social services to an unfamiliar client population with little institutional guidance and few trained workers in a wholly new practice terrain in which all rules and regulations were being invented as the need for them was discovered. William Tuttle (1945), Head of the Gila River Welfare Section, recalled that while the Welfare Section did not yet exist and had to be created upon his arrival, "exact staff needs were not known as no one had any idea about what type of problems would come to the attention of the Welfare Section" (p. 1). The office, moreover, was to serve a client population who "had no past experience with Welfare agencies" and thus did not know what they should seek from it and what it could deliver to them (p. 1). The camp Welfare Sections were, to be sure, confronted with novel questions idiosyncratic to the truly peculiar circumstances in which the Nikkei lived and the Sections functioned: Could incarcerated families be considered eligible for Public Assistance since food and shelter, at least nominally, were already being provided for? What entity had guardianship of an orphaned child from California now incarcerated in a camp in a different state? What bodies needed to be involved in decisions about that child's adoption by a Caucasian family in a third state?

It was the Welfare Section personnel who "most frequently discovered the need for change in housing, health conditions, mental conditions requiring attention, and who generally perceived the earliest signs of delinquency in young boys and girls" (War Relocation Authority, 1942b, p. 24). But, as Rohwer Welfare Head Wilma Van Dusseldorp (1945)[9] recounted, the identified need for services far outstripped the capacity of the office in which she was the lone professional social worker. The provision of high-quality services were "wholly impossible due to lack of qualified staff, as well as inappropriate and inadequate physical accommodations" (p. 6). The volume of services, moreover, had to be curtailed

[9] Dusseldorp had been a prominent social worker in Atlanta, Georgia, where she helped establish the Atlanta Relief Commission (Ferguson, 2002).

to the point that her "staff had to consciously avoid entering situations calling for more service than the available staff service could meet" (p. 17). Addressing on-going issues such as "delinquency, broken homes, unattached children, and other similar problems" (p. 17), which might be considered core social work domains, were set aside in favor of "more pressing needs" (p. 17) such as the filing of Public Assistance applications for individuals and families in desperate need for basic aid. Welfare sections were also assigned tasks, such as the delivery of draft notices and the investigation and determination of exemption petitions, which ethically compromised its workers.

Dusseldorp described her plight as the lone professional social worker employed in the Camp.

> The pressure for interviewing service that came each day to the desk of the only professional worker, with a desk amid many clerical workers, so occupied the worker's time, that there was limited opportunity to spend with the Counseling Aide staff in becoming familiar with what they were doing and to guide them. There was no time for the home visiting except during evenings after dinner. Many of the requests could have been met satisfactorily had there been opportunity to organize the counseling aide service to better advantage. Such interviewing as was done at the desk, or in the evenings, was too sketchy to serve as a foundation for continued service to an increasing number of complicated social problems. There were long delays in answering correspondence coming from other centers, and in making investigations involving contacts with two or more persons involved in a single situation. There was no stenographic service available to the Welfare Section during the first couple of months after its organization, and all correspondence had to be written in long hand. Due to this lack of stenographic assistance, it was not possible to record interviews held in case histories. (p. 6)

The inevitable outcome of the "[f]requent postponements, inability to follow through on indicated successive interviews, and sometimes the total dropping of a problem calling for immediate attention" meant the "creation of doubts within the residents' minds concerning the worker's sincerity and interest in their problems" (p. 6). In a client population with little previous contact with social workers and already wary of both the efficacy and the motivations of the Caucasian personnel, the delays and bungling responses of the Welfare Sections also resulted in clients who "become restless and have a tendency to become angry" (Colorado River Relocation Center, 1942, p. 3). The YWCA worker Ethlyn Christensen's (1944) assessment of the Heart Mountain Welfare Section, that the "department is short staffed and carrying a terrifically heavy load" (p. 4), was the consistent condition across the camps.

Trained Social Workers

The handful of experienced social workers, such as Dusseldorp, on staff was un-evenly distributed among the camps, and their tenures tended to be short. For a brief while, the Poston, Arizona, camp had a Miss Ruth Green, "who had con-siderable experience in group work in Washington, D.C." (Balderston, 1945, p. 5). Tule Lake had "a very good Social Welfare Department with a staff of six trained case workers" (Briesemeister, 1944, p. 1), according to the YWCA's Esther Briesemeister, a frequent visitor to the camps.[10] Minidoka's department reported itself as also being fortunate in its staff, boasting "a very happy com-bination of supervisors in the Counseling Section" (Kimmerling et al., 1945, p. 40), including an experienced child welfare worker and a psychiatric social worker who had worked "in one of the outstanding organizations of the Middle West" (p. 40), as well as a counselor with "long experience in Public Assistance" (p. 40) who was working in the camp during her summer break from her training at the University of Pittsburgh School of Social Work. The YWCA's Marion Brown Reith (1943a) assessed George Lefabregue, the head of the Topaz Welfare Section, as a "man of real social concern, doing an excellent job with his resi-dent staff" (p. 6). Lorne Bell, Director of Community Service, the division which administered the Welfare Section, was said to exhibit "good organization and ef-ficiency" (p. 6). Lilian Sharpley, another YWCA worker who had visited Topaz a few months before Reith, was similarly impressed with Mr. Lamb, the Chief of the Community Activities section, in charge of the recreational and group work programs, which included the various YWCA activities. Sharpley (1943) described him as a "young fellow with social work training and experience, in-telligent and understanding of the problems the Japanese people have, caught as they are in this situation" (Sharpley, 1943, p. 4).

The Welfare Section at Heart Mountain camp in Wyoming was led by a Miss Virgil Payne, a graduate of the New York School of Social Work. Payne had orig-inally come to Heart Mountain as a temporary consultant in October 1942, two months after the opening of the camp, to organize the office then called the "Social Service Department." Esther Briesemeister (1942a) had noted in December of 1942 that Payne, the only "trained caseworker on the project" was

---

[10] The YWCA field team members, headed by Esther Briesemeister, were consistent visitors to the camps in the course of their ongoing work to establish and support YWCA chapters. As representa-tives of an external organization which had a relatively long history of work with Nikkei women and girls and with a sterling national reputation for good work, they were trusted for the most part by both the AP and the inmates. They were keen observers of camp life, and their skillful and deliberate avoidance of involvement in camp politics gave them a uniquely unencumbered perspective from which to assess the AP and their relationship with the Nikkei. While much of the YWCA's analysis was focused on the question of who among the AP would be useful allies in their own work in the camps, their recorded views on various staff make for an interesting and enlightening read.

an "exceptionally fine person interested in the whole problem and one of the few Caucasians who is living on the project" (p. 1). Payne would leave the position in August, 1944, 18 months before the camp closed its doors, to become the Assistant Relocation Supervisor of the Great Lakes Area in Cleveland. [11] "Miss Payne was, according to all reports, the most popular Caucasian staff member had ever been on the project and her departure was occasion for a community-wide demonstration in her honor" (Christensen, 1944, p. 3). Adeline S. Kell, who took over the role from Payne until the closing of the center in November 1945, was not so well received. Prior to the WRA, Kell had been the Social Welfare Director of the WPA in Kentucky and a Welfare Consultant in the Social Protection Division of the Federal Security Agency. The YWCA's Ethlyn Christensen, reporting on a Fall visit to the Heart Mountain, noted:

Miss Kell was finding it extremely difficult to fill the vacancy left by Miss Payne. She had brought with her an assistant from New York City, leaving the three Caucasian staff members who had served with Miss Payne in the position of Junior counselors. She also introduced new methods of work in the office and inaugurated new casework procedures. The Japanese staff members resented all this and many resigned. Residents who came to the Social Welfare office complained of red tape, delays in rejection of requests for assistance. Everywhere I heard expressions of dissatisfaction with Miss Kell and there was even more intense feeling against her assistant, Miss Czoda. They were by far the most unpopular staff members on the project. Miss Kell was aware of some of this. She explained to me that there was a difference in her approach and Miss Payne's. Miss Payne had been with the project since it opened and of necessity had approached the situation from the point of view of giving disaster relief. Miss Kell said she faced a situation in which the emphasis was on relocation and doing everything possible to hasten people's departure from the center. Her record, therefore, was one of more rejections to requests for some kinds of services. I felt that Miss Kell was an able social worker and that she was conscientiously trying to do a good job, but she lacked warmth in her approach to the evacuees and they miss the genuine friendliness and confidence in them which Miss Payne demonstrated. (Christensen, 1944, p. 3)

Likewise unpopular was Tule Lake's Mrs. Halle, an experienced social worker described by James Sakoda (1942b), a JERS fieldworker and a member of her staff, as "a rather nervous woman, with some sense of insecurity" who "did not have much understanding of the Japanese people" (p. 5).

[11] Payne became, in 1952, the National Director of the newly formed Florence Crittendon Homes Association, a national organization which provided services to single mothers.

Complaints that came to her she often thought unreasonable, she did not sym-
pathize with the people. In the discussion of the food shortage, her answer was
that the people should realize that people on the outside are suffering, too. For
instance, they had sugar rationing, while here that was not done. . . . When
someone suggested that the meeting be adjourned once because it was becoming drawn-out and it was chilly, she retorted, "You can always walk out if
you want, you know." Her discussions centered around problems which had
come up in the Welfare Department, and about which she had complaints to
make. The group did not respond favorably to her. (p. 5)

Winona Chambers (1944), a YWCA worker reporting on a May 1944 visit to
meet with various YWCA groups at Rohwer, pithily assessed the two recently
hired social workers: "one from Cleveland Public Relief News, excellent but on
leave for only 2 months; the second, impossible and more permanently employed" (p. 3). J. Lloyd Webb (1945), head of the department at Jerome, had one
Junior Counselor "who had some training and experience in social work" (p. 7).
Though she had no experience as a supervisor, she was responsible nevertheless
for "demonstrating methods of counseling, case diagnosis, and case recording
for the benefit of the inexperienced counseling aides. She was also asked to act as
leader in group meetings for training and orientation" (p. 7).

Aside from these occasional and informal assessments, the social work bona
fides of the Welfare Section AP are difficult to ascertain. The final reports of camp
Welfare Sections do include some accounting of the personnel, providing some
sense of the scale of the operation as a whole. Poston Relocation Center, for example, was the largest of the ten camps with three units separated from each
other by approximately three miles. Its Welfare Section, with an office at each of
the units, began with one Caucasian personnel in 1942 and grew to a total of 18
by May of 1945 (Butler, 1945, p. 2). As was the case in all of the camps, a host of
"evacuee staff," varying in number from 10 to 60, worked in various capacities in
the Section. The Heart Mountain Welfare Section employed one Counselor who
was the head of the Section and one Assistant Counselor. Six Junior Counselors
were added beginning in April 1944, and six Counselor Aides, most of whom
were transferred from the Education Section, were added beginning in June of
1945 (Kell, 1945).[12] These two groups of later additions were likely to have been
brought on to manage the push for resettlement. The reports do not identify
which of the staff were trained as social workers.

Among the many untrained workers assigned to the Minidoka welfare department were three teachers—one of whom had been a missionary and teacher in

---

[12] See the Minidoka Welfare Section Final Report by Adeline S. Kell (1945) for a fairly detailed accounting of the duties attached to the various positions.

Burma—reassigned from the camp schools to the welfare department. There was also a young college graduate who "had no practical experience" (Kimmerling et al., 1945, p. 40). In a July 29, 1944, memorandum to John H. Provinse, Chief of the Community Services Division at Washington headquarters, Vera H. McCord (1944), Acting Head of Poston's Welfare Section, makes clear her disapproval of the use of untrained and "unqualified staff members" occupying "top welfare jobs" (p. 1). "Both are excellent people," McCord insisted, "but their strength is not in supervision of a Welfare program. Neither had ever seen a family case record before employment on this job; they themselves need constant supervision and guidance" (p. 2). Given its ongoing inability to recruit and hire a sufficient number of trained and experienced social workers, all of the WRA camps resorted to the use of such inappropriate personnel.

"Evacuee Staff"

As Esther Briesemeister (1942b) noted in one of her many reports, mainline social work tasks such as addressing "problems arising around the families" (p. 5) in the camps were often handled by Christian and Buddhist ministers rather than the Welfare Sections. The serious and continual shortage of trained social workers coupled with the understandable distrust of most AP by the Nikkei were two explanations for this phenomenon. But another important factor was that many of the day-to-day tasks of the welfare departments in the camps were carried out by "evacuee staff." In all of the camp Welfare Sections, tasks which should have been carried out by trained social workers were being assigned to Nikkei staff who, for the most part, had themselves never before encountered a social worker except in the removal process and often did not have professional work experiences of any kind. Claud Pratt, the head of the Topaz Welfare Section, reported that, by late September of 1942, a total of 26 Nikkei staff worked in the four major divisions comprising the department: Family Counseling, Youth Counseling, Legal Counseling, and Medical Counseling. Ten of the 26 Nikkei staff were employed as counselors: 10 "Field Workers (Jr. Counselors)" and 6 "Supervisors (Sr. Counselors)" (Pratt, 1945, p. 2). The number in the Poston Welfare Section varied from 10 to 60, with 5 to 10 working as Counseling Aides, 30 to 40 as Clerical Workers, and the rest in various other roles (Butler, 1945). At Heart Mountain, an average of 15–35 Nikkei staff "participated in policy-making, community interpretation, counseling services, clerical activities, interpreting, and the control of properties" (Kell, 1945, p. 3).

Adeline Kell's positive frame that the Nikkei staff in her Heart Mountain department, whose qualifications covered "a wide range of pre-evacuation educational training and working experiences" and included "persons who were recognized by the residents as community leaders, such as educational and religious leaders and councilmen" (Kell, 1945, p. 3), is contradicted by all other reports. Esther Briesemeister (1942a), reporting on her visit to Heart Mountain in mid-December 1942, described the Nikkei workers in that camp's Welfare Section as "inexperienced and untrained" (p. 1). Briesemeister worried that these untrained workers were quite often "put into a position of advising" on difficult matters such as resettlement possibilities requiring the separation of families when they "do not have enough knowledge to do so" (p. 1). College graduates were "very rare" (1943a, p. 9) in the Gila River department, reported Charles Kikuchi, who himself worked in that camp's Welfare Section as the Chief Case Work Supervisor, despite his single year of training as an MSW student at Berkeley before removal.

> We get a couple of applications a day from people who want to do social work. A lot of them give as qualification that they can speak Japanese so that they are able to get on with the Issei. A lot of them are young kids or else old ladies. Only a limited few of these applicants have any experience or training of any sort. Some of the girls have been connected with the church activities and they present this as proof that they are qualified social workers. (Kikuchi, 1942d, p. 94)

J. Lloyd Webb (1945) noted, similarly, that none among the Jerome's department's Nikkei workers "had ever had training or experience as professional counselors or social workers" (p. 14). He worried that their lack of case work skills and knowledge made it "difficult for them to individualize" (p. 14) and make tailored judgments appropriate to specific cases and individual situations. Writing up case records was "unfamiliar and most difficult" (p. 14) tasks for the counseling aides, and taking part in case discussions "of policies and personal and family problems" (p. 14) was an entirely new experience. Webb noted that even the basic structures and rationale of a welfare department were unfamiliar to most of the counseling staff.

> To sum up the difficulties of the counseling aide staff might be to say that they had probably never thought of counseling or social service as an institutionalized or professional function and apparently never fully accepted the possibilities of institutionalized counseling even as a result of their experience at Jerome. Social service meant performing tangible aids in terms of material assistance or speaking or writing for the needy parties. It never quite encompassed service by a professional relationship between people. This was still left to the family group, baishaku, or the neighborhood sage, such as the secretary or chairman of the Association. (p. 14)

The problems inherent in running a social welfare department with a large cadre of untrained and unavoidably conflicted workers were handled by the heads of the departments in one of two ways. One method was to attempt to avoid assigning cases "of continuing difficult social problems" (p. 14) to the Nikkei staff. Webb explained:

> Some might be able to do competent brief service counseling, but it would be preferable to use them as actual aides to competent appointed case workers, probably not more than one per worker. In this capacity they could help a great deal with the routine part of the work by interpretation and could also attain a real appreciation for the possibilities of social counseling. To give them a case load with complicated social problems and with even the best of supervision is almost too much. (p. 14)

To what degree Webb was successful in organizing the staff in this way was not reported. What most departments appeared to have done, whether in addition to or instead of the kind of deliberate case allocation Webb described, was to attempt to train the Nikkei workers in case work theories and methods. Poston welfare head Lou Butler (1945) reported, for example, that Nikkei staff in her department meet twice weekly, from March to August of 1943, for "what they called a 'class'" (p. 4). At these meetings, "supervisors and other staff members participated in the discussions and appointed personnel and evacuee officials spoke to the group and led some of the discussions" (p. 4). Topics for the meetings included:

1. Social work agencies and their functions
2. WRA Administrative Instructions
3. Project Policies and procedures
4. The Inter-Faith Council and the Christian Church, Rev. Kowta
5. The Buddhist Church, Rev. Tsunoda
6. Public Health, Miss Rood
7. Polio, Miss Vlehos
8. Community Activities, Dr. Balderston
9. Mental Hygiene, Dr. Leighton[13]
10. Poston Red Cross, Mr. Motoki
11. Vocational Counseling, Mrs. Hayes
12. Evacuee Property
13. Leave Procedures
14. Student Relocation

---

[13] Presumably, Alexander H. Leighton, a psychiatrist and a member of the Navy Reserve Medical Corps who was the Community Analyst at Poston and the head of the Bureau of Sociological Research located in Poston.

15. Social work techniques
16. Case records (p. 4)

In May of 1943, the Welfare Section at Granada also reported that training for Nikkei case aides was being planned. Sarah Brown (1943), Associate Counselor in the department, wrote to Poston to request that department's help in locating materials such as reading lists, "especially any current articles pertinent to the practice of 'generic' social services" (p. 1) and any social case material suitable for training the case aides as well as the more experienced staff members in her department. Writing that she was planning to adapt her teaching material to the needs of the young people at Granada and "to the life of our people in this community, and to whatever it may mean to the Evacuees as they go out from this Center" (p. 1), Brown looked to exchange resources with Poston. The Granada course of training included also a series of discussions led by the heads of various departments in the camp and aiming to provide a better understanding of the "function of the Welfare Section in relation to other departments in the Center" (Moore, 1943, p. 1).

While these training programs may have helped, they were not solutions. For Webb (1945), the training of the Nikkei staff was "the most challenging problem, the one requiring most attention, and the one probably least well done" (p. 11) by the Jerome department. The reading of "selected Administrative Manual material, some simple literature on case work and general social service objectives"[14] was insufficient to the need, and Webb's attempts to institute biweekly case conferences for the case aides and himself "never quite worked because of perpetual exigencies of an administrative nature" (p. 11). The trainings at Gila River, given by Section Head William Tuttle and open to all who worked in some capacity with community members, were generally ill-attended. Charles Kikuchi (1943b) stated critically that Tuttle's solution to the difficulty in finding college-educated Nikkei staff was to "lower the standards" for education and add more lectures to the "in-training program" (p. 5). The problem was that "nobody even attends. The wardens who were handling juvenile delinquency have all quit coming" (p. 5) because, as one warden explained: "It puts me to sleep. I don't learn a thing from him" (p. 5). Kikuchi confessed that most Section staff, including himself, "always 'manage' to have a heavy case load on the days of the lecture" to avoid attending (p. 5).

The Welfare Sections relied on the Nikkei staff members' bilingualism and knowledge of community networks. But many Nisei workers had "an inadequate knowledge of Japanese" (Colorado River Relocation Center, 1942, p. 3). Kikuchi

---

[14] Some readings that Webb recommended for staff were: Bertha C. Reynolds, Learning and Teaching in the Practice of Social Work (1943); Virginia Robinson, A Changing Psychology and Social Care Work (1934); Ballo May, The Art of Counseling (1939); Karl De Schweinitz, The Art of Helping People Out of Trouble (1924); and Joanne C. Colcord, Your Community: Its Provisions for Health Education Safety and Welfare (1939) (Webb, 1944, p. 1).

(1942e), confessing that his limited Japanese proficiency made him "feel so inadequate," explained that "Most of the people can understand me a little, but they take refuge by developing an inability to understand when they don't want to answer a question" (p. 58). Beyond the issue of oral proficiency, the Nikkei staff were also facing a larger linguistic challenge that went unnoticed in the official documents—that of translating a set of ideas and practices from one language into another which did not have equivalencies. James Sakoda (1942a) described in his Tulare diaries the struggles of two Nisei workers putting together a case report. The difficulty lay in not only the unfamiliar narrative structure required by the case report but that they had "difficulty in finding an American equivalent" (p. 79) for many of the expressions their clients used to describe their situations. A related difficulty was the task of "community interpretation" (Kell, 1945, p. 3) with which the Nikkei staff were tasked—a two-way tuition in which the Nikkei workers schooled community members to behave as proper social work clients and educated Caucasian workers to understand Nikkei family and community dynamics. Robert Billigmeier (1943), a Caucasian fieldworker for JERS at Tule Lake, concluded that the "Caucasians, no matter how understanding and no matter how sympathetic, cannot quite grasp some of the issues involved" (p. 122).

> For example Miss Montgomery of the social welfare department makes a sincere effort to understand the problems that confront her department. But it is hard for someone not steeped in Oriental culture to grasp the nature of the Japanese family unit. She finds it difficult to understand a 29 year old Nisei man who cannot make a decision until he has talked the problem over with his parents. (p. 122)

Many of the Nikkei workers were young enough and inexperienced enough to not have ever faced the task of fully analyzing those dynamics for themselves. It was their job, however, to make sense of them for their Caucasian supervisors, some of whom, like Dorothy Montgomery, were at least sympathetic to the need to understand, but also to many others who were not.

As Adeline Kell (1945) observed, moreover, to "engage in social welfare work without special training for such work is difficult under normal conditions; it was extremely difficult to do so when the case aides were struggling with their own serious problems of life as evacuees" (p. 3). For example, the young counseling aide who had been sent out to advise parents on whether they should allow their child to leave the camp alone to attend one of the East Coast universities willing to take a Nikkei student could very well have been facing the same quandary in his or her own family. The case aides also had to contend with the fact that, for many of the older generations of Nikkei who were leaders of family and community groups, the need to seek and receive guidance and resources from young Nisei workers was a prohibitive difficulty. It was, conversely, an uncomfortable prospect for many of the young workers to play their part in that dynamic and do so with a semblance of confidence and authority (Colorado River Relocation Center, 1942). Perhaps most importantly, the fact that Nikkei staff members were an incarcerated population, living in a close and closed community, both as members of that community and as ill-paid employees of the organization that superintended their imprisonment, cannot be forgotten.

Community Relations

The complicated and conflicted role of the Nikkei workers in the Welfare Sections should be understood in the context of the generally fraught dynamic that existed between the Nikkei inmates and the Caucasian staff. Head Counselor Mrs. Halle was heartily disliked by both Nikkei staff and clients not only for her heavy-handed rule of the Tule Lake social welfare department, but also because she displayed "the condescending attitude unconsciously taken by so many of the Caucasian staff members" (Sakoda, 1942c, p. 2). According to visiting YWCA staff, the AP–Nikkei relations ranged from the "particularly fine attitude" (Briesemeister, 1942c, p. 1) found in Minidoka, to Poston, where "they were not good except in rare instances" (Briesemeister & Lyle, 1942, p. 20), to Tule Lake, where the relations were said to be frankly "bad" (Briesemeister & Wilbur, 1945, p. 1). According to Toru Matsumoto (1945), Director of Resettlement for the Home Missions Council of North America, who toured the camps on behalf of that organization in the later years of the war, relations at even Minidoka could not be characterized as friendly.

> If anyone still thinks that the W.R.A. Administration Personnel (called A.P.'s for short) and the evacuees are good friends, he will be forced to change his notion completely the first day at Minidoka. Joe Kitagawa calls the best evacuee attitude "antagonistic cooperation." (p. 4)

There was a marked "gap between the appointed personnel and the evacuees" (p. 3) and "a very clear-cut line between these two groups" (Briesemeister, 1942d, p. 6) at all camps. Conflict, though of varying in intensity, was endemic to all camps.

In the YWCA fieldworkers' assessment, two related factors shaped the quality of the Nikkei–AP relations: the level of "informal contacts so valuable in building rapport" (Reith, 1943b, p. 1) between the two groups and the attitude of the staff toward the inmates.[15]

---

[15] The Community Analysis Section (CAS) of the WRA was designed to moderate the attitude of the staff toward the inmates. In a confidential report filed by Annie Clo Watson for the YWCA,

There were few points of informal contact between the two groups who lived apart and conducted their personal lives in separate spheres in these abnormal communities. Virgil Payne, Head Counselor at Heart Mountain, "an exceptionally fine person interested in the whole problem," was one of the "few Caucasians who is living on the project" (Briesemeister, 1942a, p. 1) rather than in the nearby towns of Cody and Powell where most of the teachers and administrative staff lived (Briesemeister, 1942a, p. 1). Maruko Kato (1942), Secretary of Manzanar's YWCA Girls Council wrote enthusiastically about Mrs. Bruce, the wife of Dr. William Bruce, Head of the Community Enterprises Section at Manzanar, as not only being an active member in the camp's Junior Matrons Club but as one of only two Caucasian mothers whose children attended the camp schools alongside the Nikkei children. Shared spaces mattered, opined Marianne Robinson (1943) who ran the nursery school programs at Tule Lake, where the Caucasians and the Nikkei used the same dining facilities.

> Fortunately because we eat in the same mess hall I see most of the women with young children and have quite a bit of opportunity to talk with them, reassure them about future possibilities for the school and related matters in their homes. (p. 148)

The WRA agreed that in camps with shared spaces—mixed housing, integrated schools, and less-segregated facilities—"social relations seem to be considerably better" (War Relocation Authority, 1943b, p. 1) than in more segregated camps. In Poston Head Counselor Lou Butler's (1945) view, while the camp's isolated location was the strongest factor in her department's recruitment and retention difficulties, "personal factors" were also at play: "Those who enjoyed sharing with the residents the recreational, religious and social activities planned by and for the community, seemed better able to make a happy adjustment in this isolated center" (p. 3). Those who did not enjoy such contact with the Nikkei population did not last.

Segregation, however, was not solely a matter of personal preference. Most of the Minidoka AP lived in the nearby towns of Cody and Powell, a matter

Watson describes a conversation with Selene Gifford, eventual Head of the WRA Welfare Section at the Washington headquarters, in which she explained the formation of the CAS. Gifford explained that because the "Caucasian leadership did not understand the Japanese" there was growing tension between the two groups. "A Dr. Embry, social anthropologist, has been engaged by WRA to help 'explain' the Japanese culturally to the Americans." Further, since Dr. Embree knew the Japanese in Japan but not in the U.S. context, the "suggestion was made that Dr. Jesse Steiner of Washington University (Seattle) might be helpful in presenting facts regarding the American setting and including the American Japanese" (Watson, 1942a, p. 1). The presence of these social scientists in the WRA's CAS, well-meaning and sympathetic as some such as Embree might have been, did not appear to have affected the desired improvements in relations.

of choice for some but not for others who could not because the camp did not have enough space to house them. Gila River, for one, had "many rules and regulations" (Briesemeister, 1943, p. 2) instituted by the administration to specifically prevent social interactions between the Caucasians and inmates. Reverend Shunji Nishi, writing about his tour through Gila River, Poston, Topaz, and Heart Mountain, characterized Gila as the "most rigid" among the four in their segregation policies and Poston the "most lenient" (n.d., p. 12).[16] At Gila, even visitors of Japanese ancestry such as himself, "representing national organizations trying to assist WRA" (p. 12) were not permitted to stay in quarters reserved for visitors or eat in the AP-only dining hall. Conversely, Caucasian visitors were "strongly discouraged" (p. 12) from entering evacuee dining halls or staying in the Nikkei quarters. Despite such strictures, the liberal AP at Gila and other camps did have social contact and formed friendships with the Nikkei. Those relationships, however, were formed "almost wholly with highly assimilated evacuees" (Billigmeier, 1944, p. 22). Across the board, from the visiting YWCA workers to the camp staff, there was a clear sense among the Caucasian workers that the most productive, promising, well-adjusted, and helpful members of the community were educated, middle-class Nisei who were Americanized. There was, as Billigmeier (1944) put it,

> the distinct tendency to regard evacuees as good in proportion to their assimilation. A "good" evacuee is one who has shown himself wholly assimilated. If an evacuee "can't stand the Japs" that is often accepted as an indication that the individual is a very good evacuee. (p. 20)

The motley mix of "social workers, missionaries, school teachers, other government people" (p. 21) who came to work in the camps did so for widely divergent reasons. Esther Briesemeister (1946), a frequent visitor to all ten camps, characterized the Caucasian personnel who staffed the camps.

> Some were interested in the sociological aspects of the problems and many came on the staffs with this interest, to accumulate data for future papers, etc. Another rather large group represents the former WPA and other emergency government agency employees who transferred to these projects. A few came primarily for the increase in pay which it offered them and had little interest in the whole program. Another rather small group are the Pacifists who felt that working in the centers offered them an opportunity to serve and to make their contributions at this time. (p. 8)

---

[16] The document cited is undated and does not provide Nishi's affiliations. Nishi, an Episcopalian priest was, in all likelihood, working for the Federation of Churches.

Given the disparate reasons that brought the various APs to work in the inhospitable and conflict-ridden camps, it was unsurprising that their attitude toward the Nikkei inmates also varied. Anthony O'Brien, Attorney for the Tule Lake camp, placed this "division among the staff as to their attitude in handling the evacuees" (cited in Glick, 1943, p. 1) into three categories: (1) those who were overly solicitous toward the Nikkei, (2) those who were entirely prejudiced against the Nikkei, and (3) those who took the middle ground.

"Damned Sociologists"

In the first category were "persons who approach the problem from a definite sociological viewpoint" (cited in Glick, 1943, p. 1), a perspective commonly ascribed to social work and social workers in this period. Attorney O'Brien explained:

> The extreme of this group feels that there are no bad persons among the evacuees; that they are misguided and misunderstood; that they have been persecuted and that everything should be done to prevent any disciplinary action that might in any way further hinder the activities of the people. (cited in Glick, 1943, p. 1)

A "pattern of benevolent attitudes" toward the Nikkei displayed by such staff, referred by some as "them damned sociologists" (Billigmeier, 1944, p. 1), resulted in "project-wide disrespect for law and order" (cited in Glick, 1943, p. 1); such attitudes were not tolerated by camp administration. O'Brien cited the example of two Tule Lake school teachers who made the radical request to live in camp housing among the Nikkei and to be paid the same nominal salary as they; these two were forced to resign and left the camp in disgrace (cited in Glick, 1943).

A June 1943 WRA report noted that the inmates' "sensitivity to any evidence of racial feeling is acute" enough to spot any instance of prejudice "with amazing perception" (War Relocation Authority, 1943a, p. 12). The report also insisted, however, that there was "equal acuity, it should be added, in rejecting as useless any sentimental actions or expressions of the 'Angel of Mercy' variety'" (p. 12). The "sentimentalist attitude" of the teachers "who loudly proclaim their desire to live the life of the residents, sharing their fortunes" (War Relocation Authority, 1943a, p. 12), derided by O'Brien, was said to be "generally stigmatized as undignified, condescending and charitable" (p. 12) also by the Nikkei. While the notion that the Nikkei were sensitive to the condescension of charity is in itself credible, the accuracy of the administration's categorization of the kinds of personnel and types of behaviors that the Nikkei rejected as condescension is less so. In Robert Billigmeier's (1944) assessment, Tule Lake's liberal AP derided by O'Brien were "not so deeply involved intellectually and emotionally in the problems at Tule Lake that they have lost their objectivity" (p. 19). They were, however, comprised generally of "those individuals who have given good evidence of their interest in the welfare of the Japanese-Americans, Issei and Nisei, and have developed a wide circle of friends and acquaintances among them" (p. 1). Tori Matsumoto (1945) described the case of one such "sympathetic" AP at Minidoka.

> When the school children learned that their sympathetic principal was to be dismissed on the ground that he was too sympathetic, they signed a petition to the Project Director. The Director called the idea of "petition" un-American and refused to accept the petition. (p. 5)

At the other extreme from the "damned sociologists" were those AP who simply saw all inmates as "Japs" and saw "the relocation center as an internment camp where people dangerous to our national safety must be herded and pre-sided over with a strong hand" (Billigmeier, 1944, p. 10). While "the intensity of feeling against the colonists" varied among this group, there were many staff members who "might best be described by the current term 'Jap-hater'" (p. 2). They "expressed freely deep prejudices against the evacuees or have displayed animosity to them" (p. 2). Toru Matsumoto (1945) averred that damage "beyond repair" was caused by a Minidoka school teacher's calling the children "No good Japs" (p. 5). Such "name calling by the A.P.," he elaborated, was commonplace and such causes of discord were present at "almost every point of contact between the A.P. and the evacuees" (p. 5). The "very different view-point" (Reith, 1943b, p. 1) that a staff member such as Hugo Walter, Gila River's Head of Community Activities, was said to bring to the mix stood in stark contrast to this group who "favored the theory that the best way to govern the 'Nips' and 'Japs,' as some of the staff called the residents, was to issue orders, 'be tough with them' (Yasumura, 1945, p. 2).

"Jap-Haters"

"Caste attitudes" (Embree, 1943, p. 4) was the euphemism frequently used by the WRA to describe this manifestation of white supremacy among the Caucasian staff. The anthropologist John Embree of the Community Analysis Section explained that "caste attitudes" were

> related to a factor inherent in the situation, i.e., the fact that the WRA admin-istrative staff is 'Caucasian,' while the evacuees are 'Oriental.' Too often this gives rise to attitudes of superiority on the part of the administrative personnel. Citizen evacuees feel the distinction keenly. (p. 4)

In his report on the Tule Lake Caucasian Staff, Robert Billigmeier (1944) explained the phenomenon of "caste mentality."

> There are a number of Caucasians on the staff who have found a stimulus in the realization that they are members of the dominant racial group. It is true that a semi-caste situation is intimated in the conditions of the relocation centers— the forced confinement of the evacuees, differential in living conditions, wages, administrative control by Caucasians, etc. A large number of Caucasians have come to accept that situation as good and reasonable, giving substance to their feelings of superiority! (p. 5)

In Minidoka Director Harry Stafford's (1945) view, it was difficult to find a contingent of workers who did not exhibit blatant racism. It was "extremely difficult to recruit a large number of Caucasian people who can make the adjustments necessary for the administration of a humane policy of decency with proper respect for their fellow men regardless of race, creed or color" (p. 5). Reading between the lines of the memorandum on terminology sent out to department heads by W. Wade Head, Director of the Poston camp in Colorado, a large dose of ignorance as well as a deeply embedded racism were rife among the staff, including the writer himself.

> It is inaccurate to refer to the persons who have been evacuated from the West Coast as "Japanese." The Japanese are the people who live in Japan. The persons who have been evacuated from the West Coast are people of Japanese ancestry; but they are not "Japanese" in all cases. With a few exceptions, they have come to the United States because they want to live here and two-thirds of them are citizens of the United States. It is even more objectionable of course, to refer to the evacuees as "Japs." They do not like that word; nor would you if you were an American of Japanese ancestry. "Japs" means the subjects of the Japanese Emperor, and living in Japan. (Head, 1943, p. 1)

Billigmeier reported that the administrative directives on terminology had little effect. While some of the "large number of Caucasians who have shown little disposition to observe the niceties of language or to take into consideration the sensitivity of many evacuees to the matter of race" did come to realize the need to follow the regulations in public settings, "a considerable number" stilled referred to the Nikkei as "Japs" and worse.

> Often the reference is even more offensive. For example, Mr. Bergman, a plumber from Tule Lake employed on the project, has the habit of calling the evacuees "monkeys," not only in reference to evacuees when in the presence of

Caucasians but even in addressing the evacuees them-selves. He has absolutely no regard for their feelings. (Billigmeier, 1944, p. 7)

"The Practical Administrator"

Standing somewhere between the "damned sociologists" and the "Jap-haters" in Attorney Anthony O'Brien's taxonomy of AP attitudes was the "practical administrator" (cited in Glick, 1943, p. 1).

> He realizes that these people have rights, that they are human beings, and that they have been "pushed around" by everyone, particularly in the West Coast Region. On the other hand, he realizes that if he has to administer a project of 15,000 or 16,000 people that there must be law and order and that there must be discipline. He further realizes that these people are to be rehabilitated in other sections of the country that they must take with them a moral and civil responsibility so that they may become worthwhile members of the new community. (cited in Glick, 1943, p. 1)

To much of the general public and some of the camp administrators, social workers were undoubtedly a part of the overly sympathetic contingent with a tendency to "coddle" the Nikkei. The social workers, however, saw themselves as the ultimate "practical administrators" whose work could be a "constructive influence" (Flack, 1942, p. 1) because they were level-headed and prudent. Manzanar's Margaret D'Ille, a social worker with ten years of experience in Japan as Executive Secretary of the YWCA (Woodsmall, 1942), for example, was praised for exhibiting "an unusual combination of sympathy and understanding with objectivity and common sense" (Woodsmall, 1942, p. 2). Hugo Walter, the Head of Community Activities at Gila River, a person with "a real concern for the colonists" was seen as "doing his utmost" to build a friendly relationship with the Nikkei, but doing so "in a quiet way" (Reith, 1943b, p. 1). Thus, no Caucasian social worker involved in this history ever made radical demands, took up activist causes, or created administrative waves, whatever their assessment of the policies and procedures of the camp structures and management might have been.

The Nikkei were said to be astute observers of the attitudes of the AP, "quick to sense whether or not the personnel were sympathetic or hostile toward them" (Briesemeister, 1946, p. 11), though, given the many reports of unambiguous racism perpetrated by the AP and exhibitions of "caste attitudes" by them, "amazing perception" (War Relocation Authority, 1943a, p. 12) hardly seems to have been necessary. Aside from the explicit use of racist epithets and other less candid acts of prejudice, there were tangible institutional practices that made clear to both the Nikkei and the Caucasians that there was indeed a caste system in place. JERS researcher Tamie Tsuchiyama (1942) provided one example in her analysis of the housing situation in Poston.

> The whole matter is symbolized by the distribution of the last eight coolers to arrive. Three went to the personnel mess and five went to the hospital. No other mess had coolers. It was felt by many people that the hospital needed more, especially the children. Whether or not the two babies who died were really killed by the heat, everyone who passes the personnel mess will think that it was so. A story like this will spread all over the community and people will fasten on it because it expresses in vivid and dramatic form what they have already felt from a multitude of smaller discriminations—such things, for example, as the organization chart which has a J after some names and a W after others. Little symbols may carry great significance. (p. 7)

Charles Kikuchi (1942e) provided similar examples from Gila River.

> The Empire Hotel furniture from San Francisco is being put into the administration quarters now. The Navy bought the hotel and they auctioned off all of the furniture for $150,000 to the WRA. It is being divided up among the relocation centers for administration living quarters purposes. The food that they eat in their messhalls is also of much better quality. That is discrimination, and for that reason they should not advertise the fact that they are going through the same hardships as the evacuees. Their barracks are much better constructed than ours—not that old beaverboard that couldn't stand a hard blow—and the floors are laid with good lumber. We sleep on army canvas cots on the crack-filled floors. No armchairs or any furniture is provided us. Undoubtedly they will get an air-cooling system when it gets hot. (p. 28)

The Nikkei ability to fathom such distinctions was notable to the administration because the Nikkei were "especially good at setting up a passive resistant non-cooperative attitude that made it impossible for certain branches of the Administration to function" (Briesemeister, 1946, p. 11) when those offices were staffed by personnel deemed prejudiced. Things did not get done, or got done slowly or differently from what the administration wished. Billigmeier (1944) reported a not-so-passive instance at Tule Lake where the Nikkei employees went on strike—a not infrequent occurrence in the camps—refusing to work under a furniture factory supervisor who "was not willing to respect them as human beings and treat them accordingly" (p. 9). When he was replaced by another manager "willing to grant them the respect they wanted" (p. 9) and "exercised his authority with special care" (p. 9), the workers immediately returned to work. Billigmeier's interpretation of the strike was not, of course, one universally shared. For those camp administrators who found the inmates' resistance a daily problem to manage, the widespread anti-administration sentiment among the Nikkei and the action or inaction prompted by it were "conclusive evidence that the individuals are anti-America and therefore pro-Japan" (p. 17); they were justifiably incarcerated.

In Billigmeier's final analysis, the fundamental difference between the liberal and authoritarian elements among the Caucasians was that the former were "determined to keep the relocation center community as much like outside communities as possible" (p. 10) whereas the latter believed the camps should operate as a penal operation guarding captives of war. But neither was correct in its conceptions of the camps and its inmates. The authoritarian rules, which insisted on the treatment of the Nikkei as alien prisoners, erased the fact that two-thirds of the community were U.S.-born citizens and that the entirely of the population had neither been tried nor found guilty of any crimes or wrongdoings. To attempt to operate the camps as if they were normal communities, as the liberal rule endeavored, required the willful discounting of the fact that the community consisted of an incarcerated population living in barb-wired concentration camps. Whether for their restraint or for their righteousness, both sides believed they deserved gratitude from the Nikkei. One administrator, who had come to the camp with an expressed interest in the Nikkei and an understanding of them as a "downtrodden people" (p. 13), came to resent and dislike them because he found them not only "uncooperative, and difficult to manage" but "ungrateful" (p. 13) in the face of the benevolence of a Caucasian who granted them a modicum of civility.

References

American Association of Social Workers. (1943). Essential services and training need in social welfare: A Report of the Wartime Committee on Personnel in the Social Services, March 1943, pp. 1–17. Folder 831—National Committee on Wartime Personnel, 1942–1946, Box 76—Folders 828–838, Contents: Membership Committee, 1937–1946. NASW: AASW—SWC1, Social Welfare History Archives. Minneapolis: University of Minnesota.

Balderston, W. (1945). Colorado River Relocation Center Community Activities Section final report, November 16, 1945. War Relocation Authority, Colorado River Relocation Center, Poston, Arizona (pp. 1–30). Retrieved from http://content.cdlib.org/view?docId=ft0779n5gc&brand=calisphere&doc.view=entire_text

Billigmeier, R. H. (1943). Diary 2, Sept. 1942-Feb. 1943, Mar. 20, 1943, Tule Lake Relocation Center, pp. 1–122. Folder R 20.03:2, Box BANC MSS 67/14 c. Japanese American Evacuation and Resettlement Study, Japanese American Evacuation and Resettlement records. Berkeley: Bancroft Library, University of California.

Billigmeier, R. H. (1944). Caucasian Staff at Tule Lake Relocation Center, pp. 1–27. Folder R 20.01, Box BANC MSS 67/14 c. Japanese American Evacuation and Resettlement Study, Japanese American Evacuation and Resettlement records. Berkeley: Bancroft Library, University of California.

Briesemeister, E. (1942a). Report on Heart Mountain Relocation Center, Heart Mountain, Wyoming, December 17, 1942, pp. 1–2. Folder 23, Box 724. YWCA of the U.S.A. Records, Sophia Smith collection. Northampton, MA: Smith College.

Briesemeister, E. (1942b). Report on Minidoka Relocation Center, Hunt, Idaho by Esther Briesemeister, dated November 3, 1942, pp. 1–7. Folder 15, Box 724. YWCA of the U.S.A. Records, Sophia Smith Collection. Northampton, MA: Smith College.

Briesemeister, E. (1942c). Report on Minidoka Relocation Center, Hunt, Idaho by Esther Briesemeister, dated November 5, 1942, p. 1. Folder 15, Box 724. YWCA of the U.S.A. Records, Sophia Smith Collection. Northampton, MA: Smith College.

Briesemeister, E. (1942d). Report on Tule Lake Relocation Center, Newell, California, October 30, 1942, pp. 1–6. Folder 1, Box 724. YWCA of the U.S.A. Records, Sophia Smith Collection. Northampton, MA: Smith College.

Briesemeister, E. (1943). Report on Gila River Relocation Center, Rivers, Arizona, dated February 16, 1943, pp. 1–12. Folder 5, Box 723. YWCA of the U.S.A. Records, Sophia Smith Collection. Northampton, MA: Smith College.

Briesemeister, E. (1944). Future work at Tule Lake based on past visitation reports: Memorandum from Esther Briesemeister, Secretary, Japanese Evacuee Project to Miss Grace Stuff, Executive, Division of Community YWCAs, September 25, 1944, pp. 1–3. Folder 7, Box 724. YWCA of the U.S.A. Records, Sophia Smith Collection. Northampton, MA: Smith College.

Briesemeister, E. (1946). America's children—what happened to us?: Summary report of the Japanese Evacuee Project, January 1942–September 1946, pp. 1–54. Folder 3, Box 721. YWCA of the U.S.A. Records, Sophia Smith Collection. Northampton, MA: Smith College.

Briesemeister, E., & Lyle, B. (1942). Report on Visit to Colorado River Relocation Project, Poston, Arizona—October 16–20, 1942, pp. 1–22. Folder 8, Box 723. YWCA of the U.S.A. Records, Sophia Smith Collection. Northampton, MA: Smith College.

Briesemeister, E., & Wilbur, H. (1945). Report on Tule Lake Center, Newell, California, February 15–21, 1945, marked Confidential—not to be circulated pp. 1–3. Folder 8, Box 724. YWCA of the U.S.A. Records, Sophia Smith Collection. Northampton, MA: Smith College.

Brown, S. A. (1943). Letter to Mr. Wade Head, Director, Colorado River Relocation Center, Poston, Arizona, from Sara A. Brown, Associate Counselor, Public Welfare Section, Granada Relocation Center, Amache, Colorado, May 18, 1943, p. 1. Folder: 510—Public Welfare, Box 154: Granada Relocation Center—Central Files— 502.6 to 513. Records of the War Relocation Authority, 1941–1989, Record Group 210, Subject-Classified General Files of the Relocation Centers—compiled 1942–1946. ARC Identifier 1544889/MLR Number PI-77 48. Washington, DC: National Archives and Records Administration.

Butler, L. E. (1945). Story of the Family Welfare Section, May 1942 to May 1945, pp. 1– 17. Calisphere, Japanese American Relocation Digital Archives, Box Poston, Arizona. Berkeley: Bancroft Library, University of California.

Chambers, W. H. (1944). Report of local visit: Rohwer Relocation Center, McGehee, Arkansas, May 4–6, 1944; filed May 24, 1944, pp. 1–5. Folder 11, Box 723. YWCA of the U.S.A. Records, Sophia Smith Collection. Northampton, MA: Smith College.

Chestnutt, M. W. (1943). Letter to Belle Ingels, YWCA, from Marnette Wood Chestnut, Hot Springs, Arkansas, dated January 31, 1943, pp. 1–2. 10, Box 723. YWCA of the U.S.A. Records, Sophia Smith Collection. Northampton, MA: Smith College.

Christensen, E. (1944). Report on visit to Hearts Mountain Relocation Center, Heart Mountain, Wyoming, October 25–November 1, 1944, pp. 1–14. Folder 24, Box 724. YWCA of the U.S.A. Records, Sophia Smith Collection. Northampton, MA: Smith College.

Close, K. (1942). Letter from Kathryn Close, Associate Editor, Survey Associates, Inc., New York, NY, to George D. Nickel, Personal Finance Companies, Los Angeles, CA, dated December 3, 1942, p. 1. Folder 1212—Nickel, George—Norman, Sherwood, Box 156—Folders 1208–1214: Working Editorial. Survey Associates Records: SWA01, Social Welfare History Archives. Minneapolis: University of Minnesota.

Colorado River Relocation Center. (1942). Family Welfare Meeting, December 21, 1942, pp. 1–7. Folder 040.46 Welfare, Box 108: Subject-Classified General Files—Colorado River Central Files—040.22 to 050.11. Records of the War Relocation Authority, 1941–1989, Record Group 210, Subject-Classified General Files of the Relocation Centers—compiled 1942–1946. ARC Identifier 1544889/MLR Number PI-77 48. Washington, DC: National Archives and Records Administration.

Commissioners appointed. (1942, June 23). The Mercedian, pp. 1–4. Retrieved from http://ddr.densho.org/ddr-densho-191-3/

Coyle, G. L. (1942). Letter from Grace L. Coyle, Professor of Group Work, Western Reserve University, Cleveland, OH, to George D. Nickel, Personal Finance Companies, Los Angeles, CA, dated November 27, 1942, pp. 1–2. Folder 1212—Nickel, George—Norman, Sherwood, Box 156—Folders 1208–1214: Working Editorial. Survey Associates Records: SWA01, Social Welfare History Archives. Minneapolis: University of Minnesota.

Cozzens, R. B. (1974). Assistant National Director of the War Relocation Authority: An oral history conducted in 1974 by Rosemary Levenson. Japanese American Relocation Reviewed, Volume II: The Internment (pp. 1–105). Berkeley: Regional Oral History Office, Bancroft Library, University of California.

Daniels, R. (1972). Concentration camps U.S.A.: Japanese Americans and World War II. New York: Holt, Rinehart and Winston.

Dusseldorp, W. V. (1945). Historical Statistical—Functional Report of Welfare Section, Wilma Van Dusseldorp—Head Counselor. War Relocation Authority, Rohwer Relocation Center, McGehee, Arkansas (Calisphere, Japanese American Relocation Digital Archives ed.). Berkeley: Bancroft Library, University of California.

Editorial notes. (1942). The Family: Journal of Social Case Work, 23(1), 32–33.

Ellis, M. B. (1942a). Confidential letter written May 8, 1942 by Mabel Ellis, marked Copy of handwritten letter received Saturday morning, May 9, 1942 air-mail special delivery, to Miss Stuff from Miss Ellis, pp. 1–3. Folder 22, Box 719. YWCA of the U.S.A. Records, Sophia Smith Collection. Northampton, MA: Smith College.

Ellis, M. B. (1942b). Interview with Dr. Martha Eliot, Assistant Chief, U.S. Children's Bureau, May 8, 1942, Washington, DC: Memorandum to YWCA, Consulting Group on West Coast Situation from Mabel B. Ellis, pp. 1–4. Folder 22, Box 719. YWCA of the U.S.A. Records, Sophia Smith Collection. Northampton, MA: Smith College.

Ellis, M. B. (1942c). Letter from Mabel Brown Ellis, Secretary, Committee on Refugees, Young Women's Christian Association, to Miss Jane M. Hoey, Director, Bureau of Public Assistance, dated May 8, 1942, pp. 1–3. Folder 9—Japanese, correspondence, minutes, press releases, clippings, pamphlets, etc. 1942 (1 of 2 folders), Box 222. Immigration & Refugee Services of America: Common Council for American Unity Collection, Immigration History Research Center. Minneapolis: University of Minnesota.

Ellis, M. B. (1942d). Report of conference with Grace Coyle, July 24, 1942: Memorandum to West Coast Consultants from Mabel Brown Ellis, July 30, 1942, pp. 1–2. Folder 23, Box 719. YWCA of the U.S.A. Records, Sophia Smith Collection. Northampton, MA: Smith College.

Embree, J. (1943). Causes of unrest at Relocation Centers: Community Analysis Report No. 2, February 1943, pp. 1–6. Folder 16, Box 722. YWCA of the U.S.A. Records, Sophia Smith Collection. Northampton, MA: Smith College.

Family Welfare Association of America. (1942). Family welfare and the Home Front: Blue Bulletin—Series C—No. 4 (For Member Agencies), 10/14/42, pp. 1–3. F.W.A.A. Bulletin Series C (Comp), Box 87—Pamphlets, Major. Family Service Association of America—SW076, Social Welfare History Archives. Minneapolis: University of Minnesota.

Ferguson, K. J. (2002). *Black politics in New Deal Atlanta*. Chapel Hill: University of North Carolina Press.

Fite, A. L. (1945). Letter from A. Lidie Fite, Public Welfare Consultant, WRA to Mrs. Jennie Schott, Director, Department of Public Assistance, Montgomery County, Pennsylvania, April 5, 1945, p. 1. Folder: F, Box 1: Washington Office Records—Appointed Personnel—Miscellaneous, A—Shin. Records of the War Relocation Authority, 1941–1989, Record Group 210, Records Relating to Appointed Personnel, compiled 1942–1945. ARC Identifier 5752766/MLR Number UD 9. Washington, DC: National Archives and Records Administration.

Flack, H. N. (1942). Letter to Dillon S. Meyer, Director, WRA, from Helen N. Flack, Division of Community YWCA's, May 28, 1942, p. 1. Folder: 523.6—YWCA Box 38: Subject Class. Gen. Files of the SF Regional Office, 1942, 521.22 to 530. Records of the War Relocation Authority, 1941–1989, Record Group 210, Subject-Classified General Files—compiled 1942–1942. ARC Identifier 1543537/MLR Number PI-77 38. Washington, DC: National Archives and Records Administration.

Fraser, N., & Gordon, L. (1994). A genealogy of dependency: Tracing a keyword of the U.S. welfare state. *Signs: A Journal of Women in Culture and Society, 19*(2), 309–336.

Gifford, S. (1944). Resignation: Memorandum to John H. Provinse, Chief, Community Services Division, from Selene Gifford, Public Welfare Consultant, Welfare Section, WRA, Washington, DC, May 23, 1944, pp. 1–2. Folder: Provinse, John—#3—November 1943–May 1944, Box 35: Washington Office Records—Chronological File; General—Alphabetical—PF-John Provinse. Records of the War Relocation Authority, 1941–1989, Record Group 210, General Outgoing Correspondence, compiled 1942–1946. ARC Identifier 1534421/MLR Number PI-77 18. Washington, DC: National Archives and Records Administration.

Glick, P. M. (1943). Minor crime wave: Memorandum to John H. Provinse, Chief, Community Services Division, from Philip M. Glick, Solicitor, WRA, Washington, DC, October 11, 1943, pp. 1–2. Folder: Provinse, John—#2—May-October, 1943, Box 35: Washington Office Records—Chronological File; General—Alphabetical—PF-John Provinse. Records of the War Relocation Authority, 1941–1989, Record Group 210, General Outgoing Correspondence, compiled 1942–1946. ARC Identifier 1534421/MLR Number PI-77 18. Washington, DC: National Archives and Records Administration.

Head, W. W. (1943). Use of terms Japanese, Camp, and Internment: Memorandum to Department Heads, from W. Wade Head, Project Director, Colorado River Relocation Center, p. 1. Folder 120.1 Complaints and Criticism, Box 112: Subject-Classified

General Files—Colorado River Central Files—110.41 to 130. Records of the War Relocation Authority, 1941–1989, Record Group 210, Subject-Classified General Files of the Relocation Centers—compiled 1942–1946. ARC Identifier 1544889/MLR Number PI-77 48. Washington, DC: National Archives and Records Administration.

Kato, M. (1942). Letter from Maruko Kato, Secretary, Y's Girls' Council to Miss Esther Briesemeister on Minutes of the Y's Girls' Council Meeting, dated October, 1942, pp. 1–7. Folder 14, Box 723. YWCA of the U.S.A. Records, Sophia Smith Collection. Northampton, MA: Smith College.

Kell, A. S. (1945). Welfare Section Final Report by Adeline S. Kell, Counselor, Term of Service August 28, 1944 to Center closure. War Relocation Authority, Heart Mountain Relocation Center, Heart Mountain, Wyoming (Calisphere, Japanese American Relocation Digital Archives ed., pp. 1–12). Berkeley: Bancroft Library, University of California.

Kikuchi, C. (1942a). Diary 2: June 2—July 13, 1942, pp. 1–218. Folder W 1.80:02**, Box BANC MSS 67/14 c. Japanese American Evacuation and Resettlement Study, Japanese American Evacuation and Resettlement records. Berkeley: Bancroft Library, University of California.

Kikuchi, C. (1942b). Diary 3: July 13—31, 1942, pp. 1–218. Folder W 1.80:03**, Box BANC MSS 67/14 c. Japanese American Evacuation and Resettlement Study, Japanese American Evacuation and Resettlement records. Berkeley: Bancroft Library, University of California.

Kikuchi, C. (1942c). Diary 4: August 1—31, 1942, pp. 1–182. Folder W 1.80:04**, Box BANC MSS 67/14 c. Japanese American Evacuation and Resettlement Study, Japanese American Evacuation and Resettlement records. Berkeley: Bancroft Library, University of California.

Kikuchi, C. (1942d). Diary 6: October 1—14, 1942, pp. 1–127. Folder W 1.80:06**, Box BANC MSS 67/14 c. Japanese American Evacuation and Resettlement Study, Japanese American Evacuation and Resettlement records. Berkeley: Bancroft Library, University of California.

Kikuchi, C. (1942e). Diary 8: November 1—15, 1942, pp. 1–175. Folder W 1.80:08**, Box BANC MSS 67/14 c. Japanese American Evacuation and Resettlement Study, Japanese American Evacuation and Resettlement records. Berkeley: Bancroft Library, University of California.

Kikuchi, C. (1942f). Diary 9: November 16–December 1, 1942, pp. 1–147. Folder W 1.80:09**, Box BANC MSS 67/14 c. Japanese American Evacuation and Resettlement Study, Japanese American Evacuation and Resettlement records. Berkeley: Bancroft Library, University of California.

Kikuchi, C. (1943a). Diary 12: January 8–31, 1943, pp. 1–207. Folder W 1.80:012**, Box BANC MSS 67/14 c. Japanese American Evacuation and Resettlement Study, Japanese American Evacuation and Resettlement records. Berkeley: Bancroft Library, University of California.

Kikuchi, C. (1943b). Diary 13: February 1–27, 1943, pp. 1–245. Folder W 1.80:013**, Box BANC MSS 67/14 c. Japanese American Evacuation and Resettlement Study, Japanese American Evacuation and Resettlement records. Berkeley: Bancroft Library, University of California.

Kimmerling, C. (1945). Personal narrative report of the Welfare Section by Constance Kimmerling, Head Counselor, April 13, 1945 to November 1, 1945, dated November 15, 1945. War Relocation Authority, Minidoka Relocation Center (Calisphere, Japanese

American Relocation Digital Archives ed., pp. 1–8). Berkeley: Bancroft Library, University of California.

Kimmerling, C., Fite, A. L., & Abbott, C. W. (1945). Report of the Welfare Section, August 1942 to November 1945. War Relocation Authority, Minidoka Relocation Center (Calisphere, Japanese American Relocation Digital Archives ed., pp. 1–69). Berkeley: Bancroft Library, University of California.

Kimura, E. (1942). Letter from Emi Kimura, a member of the YWCA Cabinet at San Jose State College to Dear Jean, the Student Secretary at San Jose State College, received June 15, 1942, pp. 1–2. Folder 9—Japanese, correspondence, minutes, press releases, clippings, pamphlets, etc. 1942 (1 of 2 folders), Box 222. Immigration & Refugee Services of America: Common Council for American Unity Collection, Immigration History Research Center. Minneapolis: University of Minnesota.

Kingman, R. (1974). The Fair Play Committee and Citizen Participation: An oral history conducted in 1974 by Rosemary Levenson. *Japanese American Relocation Reviewed, Volume II: The Internment* (pp. 1b–97q). Berkeley: Regional Oral History Office, Bancroft Library, University of California.

Lane, M. D. (1945). Letter from Mrs. Marie D. Lane, Head, Welfare Section, WRA to Miss Margaret Rich, Executive Secretary, Family Welfare Society, Pittsburgh, Pennsylvania, April 23, 1945, p. 1. Folder: F, Box 1: Washington Office Records—Appointed Personnel—Miscellaneous, A—Shin. Records of the War Relocation Authority, 1941–1989, Record Group 210, Records Relating to Appointed Personnel, compiled 1942–1945. ARC Identifier 5752766/MLR Number UD 9. Washington, DC: National Archives and Records Administration.

Matsumoto, T. (1945). Report of visits to four Relocation Centers (Granada, Minidoka, Heart Mountain & Rohwer), March 9–April 1, 1945, pp. 1–21. Folder 11—Japanese, Americans Relocation Centers and Resettlement, correspondence, reports, brochures, regulations, etc. . . 1942–1945 Box 222. Immigration & Refugee Services of America: Common Council for American Unity Collection, Immigration History Research Center. Minneapolis: University of Minnesota.

McCord, V. H. (1944). Colorado River Center: Memorandum to John H. Provinse, Chief, Community Services Division, from Vera H. McCord, Acting Head, Welfare Section, WRA, Washington, DC, July 29, 1944, pp. 1–2. Folder: Provinse, John—#4—June–December, 1944, Box 35: Washington Office Records—Chronological File; General—Alphabetical—PF-John Provinse. Records of the War Relocation Authority, 1941–1989, Record Group 210, General Outgoing Correspondence, compiled 1942–1946. ARC Identifier 1534421/MLR Number PI-77 18. Washington, DC: National Archives and Records Administration.

McSparran, J. L. (1943). Electric fans for chronic invalids: Memorandum to J. Lloyd Webb, Counselor, Community Welfare Section, from Joseph L. McSparran, Chief Medical Officer, Jerome Relocation Center, Denson, Arkansas, July 19, 1943, p. 1. Folder: 61.510—Welfare (General), Box 198: Jerome Center, Denson, Arkansas—Central Files—61.310 to 61.510. Records of the War Relocation Authority, 1941–1989, Record Group 210, Subject-Classified General Files of the Relocation Centers—compiled 1942–1946. ARC Identifier 1544889/MLR Number PI-77 48. Washington, DC: National Archives and Records Administration.

McWilliams, C. (1942a). Japanese evacuation: Policy and perspectives. *Common Ground*, 2(2), 65–72.

McWilliams, C. (1942b). Letter from Carey McWilliams, California State Department of Industrial Relations, Division of Immigration and Housing, to Dr. Robert K. Lamb, House Office Building, Washington, DC, dated May 19, 1942, pp. 1–2. Folder 9— Japanese, correspondence, minutes, press releases, clippings, pamphlets, etc. 1942 (1 of 2 folders), Box 222. Immigration & Refugee Services of America: Common Council for American Unity Collection, Immigration History Research Center. Minneapolis: University of Minnesota.

Moore, J. J. O. (1943). Letter to Mr. Tomlinson, Chief Police Department, from John J. O. Moore, Counselor, Public Welfare Section, Granada Relocation Center, Amache, Colorado, June 7, 1943, p. 1. Folder: 510—Public Welfare, Box 154: Granada Relocation Center—Central Files—502.6 to 513. Records of the War Relocation Authority, 1941–1989, Record Group 210, Subject-Classified General Files of the Relocation Centers— compiled 1942–1946. ARC Identifier 1544889/MLR Number PI-77 48. Washington, DC: National Archives and Records Administration.

News of alien evacuation. (1942). *Social Work Today: A Journal of Progressive Social Work Thought and Action, 9*(6), 20, 34.

Nickel, G. D. (1942). Letter from George D. Nickel, Personal Finance Companies, Los Angeles, CA, to Kathryn Close, Associate Editor, Survey Associates, Inc., New York, NY, dated December 18, 1942, pp. 1–2. Folder 1212—Nickel, George—Norman, Sherwood, Box 156—Folders 1208–1214: Working Editorial. Survey Associates Records: SWA01, Social Welfare History Archives. Minneapolis: University of Minnesota.

Nishi, S. F. (n.d.). Report on trip to West Coast and Relocation Centers (Poston, Gila, Topaz, Heart Mountain), submitted by Rev. Shunji F. Nishi, pp. 1–20. Folder 5, Box 720. YWCA of the U.S.A. Records, Sophia Smith Collection. Northampton, MA: Smith College.

Office of the Commanding General—Headquarters Western Defense Command and Fourth Army. (1942a). Puyallup Assembly Center, pp. 1–10. Folder: 332.3 Puyallup Assembly Center Box 58: 323.3 Puyallup Assembly Center to 323.3 Santa Anita Assembly Center. Western Defense Command and Fourth Army—Wartime Civil Control Administration and Civil Affairs Division, Record Group 499: Records of U.S. Army Defense Commands (World War II), 1942–1946, Western Defense Command and Fourth Army—Wartime Civil Control Administration and Civil Affairs Division 1942–46, Central Correspondence, 1942–46. ARC Identifier 1080573/MLR Number A1 13. College Park, MD: National Archives and Records Administration, Archives II Reference Section (Military).

Office of the Commanding General—Headquarters Western Defense Command and Fourth Army. (1942b). Transcript of telephone conversation between General DeWitt, Commanding Western Defense Command and Fourth Army, and General Benedict, Commanding Communications Zone (Ninth Corps Area), Salt Lake City, Utah, March 14, 1942, 10:32 A.M., pp. 1–4. Folder: 384.4 Val I.(AG Records File), Box 15: 370.5 Movement to 384.4 Preliminary Evacuation Plans. Western Defense Command and Fourth Army—Wartime Civil Control Administration and Civil Affairs Division, Record Group 499: Records of U.S. Army Defense Commands (World War II), 1942–1946, Western Defense Command and Fourth Army—Wartime Civil Control Administration and Civil Affairs Division 1942–46, Central Correspondence, 1942–46. ARC Identifier 1080573/MLR Number A1 13. College Park, MD: National Archives and Records Administration, Archives II Reference Section (Military).

Pratt, C. H. (1945). Closing report of the Welfare Section, from Sept. 11, 1943 to Center Closing, dated December 20, 1945. War Relocation Authority, Central Utah Project, Topaz, Utah (Calisphere, Japanese American Relocation Digital Archives ed., Vol. Bancroft Library, pp. 1–10). Berkeley: Bancroft Library, University of California.

Reith, M. B. (1943a). Report on Topaz WRA Project, Topaz, Utah, June 7–10, 1943, pp. 1–6. Folder 21, Box 724. YWCA of the U.S.A. Records, Sophia Smith Collection. Northampton, MA: Smith College.

Reith, M. B. (1943b). Report on visit to Gila River, April 3–6, 1943 by Mrs. Marian Brown Reith, Asilomar Region, pp. 1–4. Folder 5, Box 723. YWCA of the U.S.A. Records, Sophia Smith Collection. Northampton, MA: Smith College.

Robinson, M. (1943). The War Relocation Authority, Tule Lake, California: Extracts from letters by Marianne Robinson, '39, Vol. XXVII, No. 3, February, 1943, pp. 147–149. Folder 3, Box 724. YWCA of the U.S.A. Records, Sophia Smith Collection. Northampton, MA: Smith College.

Ryan, E. (1942). Yuba City Control Station Report to State Department of Social Welfare, pp. 1–3. Social Welfare—War Services—WCCA –Control Stations—Sacramento— Yuba City, 1942 (F3729:149). Department of Social Welfare Records, War Services Bureau. Sacramento: California State Archives.

Sakoda, J. M. (1942a). Diary 2: Tulare Assembly Center, May 25–June 14, 1942, pp. 1–88. Folder B12.20 (2/2), Box BANC MSS 67/14 c. Japanese American Evacuation and Resettlement Study, Japanese American Evacuation and Resettlement records. Berkeley: Bancroft Library, University of California.

Sakoda, J. M. (1942b). Social Group: Social Workers Discussion Group; Records Office; miscellaneous, pp. 1–34. Folder R 20.86:13, Box BANC MSS 67/14 c. Japanese American Evacuation and Resettlement Study, Japanese American Evacuation and Resettlement records. Berkeley: Bancroft Library, University of California.

Sakoda, J. M. (1942c). Social Welfare Department, Tule Lake Relocation Center, November 11, 1942, pp. 1–130. Box BANC MSS 67/14 c. Japanese American Evacuation and Resettlement Study, Japanese American Evacuation and Resettlement records. Berkeley: Bancroft Library, University of California.

Seichi Mikami heads new welfare office. (1942, June 3). *Fresno Grapevine*, pp. 1–6. Retrieved from http://ddr.densho.org/ddr-densho-190-4/

Sharpley, L. (1943). Report on Topaz Relocation Center, Delta, Utah: Dates of visit— March 15–17, 1943; date of filing report—March 22, 1943, pp. 1–5. Folder 21, Box 724. YWCA of the U.S.A. Records, Sophia Smith Collection. Northampton, MA: Smith College.

Silverman, M. (1942a). Assembly Centers: Salinas, April 30, 1942, pp. 1–6. Folder: Salinas—Silverman, Box 11: Relocation Division—Public Attitudes Files. Records of the War Relocation Authority, 1941–1989, Record Group 210, Washington Office Records—Washington Documents. ARC Identifier 1519285/MLR Number PI-77 2. Washington, DC: National Archives and Records Administration.

Silverman, M. (1942b). Meeting with Mr. Ferguson, Mr. Bates, Mr. Tozler and Mr. Silverman: Transcription of a verbal report given by Mr. Silverman on his findings in Salinas and Monterey area in connection with evacuation of Japanese to Salinas Assembly Center, dated May 2, 1942, pp. 1–9. Folder: Salinas Center—Verbal, Box 11: Relocation Division—Public Attitudes Files. Records of the War Relocation Authority, 1941–1989, Record Group 210, Washington Office Records—Washington

Documents. ARC Identifier 1519285/MLR Number PI-77 2. Washington, DC: National Archives and Records Administration.

Simms, D. H. (1944). Survey of Public Opinion in Western States on Japanese Evacuation, Washington: War Relocation Authority Information Service, May 18, 1942, pp. 1–28. Folder: Oregon, Box 11: Relocation Division—Public Attitudes Files. Records of the War Relocation Authority, 1941–1989, Record Group 210, Washington Office Records—Washington Documents. ARC Identifier 1519285/MLR Number PI-77 2. Washington, DC: National Archives and Records Administration.

Smithburg, M. (1945). Letter from Mary Smithburg, Placement Officer, WRA to Miss Letty Wagner, c/o Travelers Aid, Camden, New Jersey, July 31, 1945, pp. 1–2. Folder: W, Box 2: Washington Office Records—Appointed Personnel—Miscellaneous, S-Z. Records of the War Relocation Authority, 1941–1989, Record Group 210, Records Relating to Appointed Personnel, compiled 1942–1945. ARC Identifier 5752766/MLR Number UD 9. Washington, DC: National Archives and Records Administration.

Social Welfare Bureau organized. (1942, May 16). *Tulare News*, pp. 1–6. Retrieved from http://ddr.densho.org/ddr-densho-197-3/

Stafford, H. L. (1945). Project Director's narrative: Minidoka Relocation Center, Hunt, Idaho. War Relocation Authority, Colorado River Relocation Center, Poston, Arizona (Calisphere, Japanese American Relocation Digital Archives ed., pp. 1–6). Berkeley: Bancroft Library, University of California.

Thomas, D. S., & Nishimoto, R. S. (1946/1969). *The spoilage: Japanese-American evacuation and resettlement during World War II*. Berkeley: University of California Press.

Tozier, M. M. (1945). Roundtable Conference of Building Better Race Relations: Education of public opinion toward Minority groups, November 24, 1945, pp. 1–16. Folder 13, Box 537. YWCA of the U.S.A. Records, Sophia Smith Collection. Northampton, MA: Smith College.

Tsuchiyama, T. (1942). 13. Housing (compiled documents), pp. 1–76. Folder J6.27 Box BANC MSS 67/14 c. Japanese American Evacuation and Resettlement Study, Japanese American Evacuation and Resettlement records. Berkeley: Bancroft Library, University of California.

Tuttle, W. K. (1945). History of Gila Welfare Section by W. K. Tuttle, Head, Welfare Section. War Relocation Authority, Gila River Relocation Center, Rivers, Arizona (Calisphere, Japanese American Relocation Digital Archives ed., pp. 1–10). Berkeley: Bancroft Library, University of California.

United States Army. (1943). *Final report, Japanese evacuation from the West Coast, 1942*. Washington, DC: U.S. Government Printing Office.

War Relocation Authority. (1942a). Job Description: Counselor (CAF-9), pp. 1–2. Folder: Welfare Section, Box 2. Records of the War Relocation Authority, 1941–1989, Record Group 210, Job Descriptions—compiled 1942–1946. ARC Identifier 1543527/MLR Number PI-77 36. Washington, DC: National Archives and Records Administration.

War Relocation Authority. (1942b). Third Quarterly Report: October 1 to December 31, 1942, pp. 1–71. Folder: Second Quarterly Report—WRA Printed—July 1 to Sept. 30, 1942, Box 1: Washington Office Records—Documentary Files—Quarterly Reports 1942. Records of the War Relocation Authority, 1941–1989, Record Group 210, Headquarters Basic Documentation Reports, compiled 1942–1946. ARC Identifier 1526983/MLR Number PI-77 3. Washington, DC: National Archives and Records Administration.

War Relocation Authority. (1943a). Project Analysis Series No. 9, June 23, 1943: Preliminary Survey of Resistances to Resettlement at the Tule Lake Relocation Center, pp. 1–15. Folder 3, Box 724. YWCA of the U.S.A. Records, Sophia Smith Collection. Northampton, MA: Smith College.

War Relocation Authority. (1943b). Registration at Central Utah: 14–17, February 1943, Project Analysis Series No. 1, Community Analysis Section, pp. 1–12. Folder 21, Box 724. YWCA of the U.S.A. Records, Sophia Smith Collection. Northampton, MA: Smith College.

War Relocation Authority. (1943c). *Relocation of Japanese-Americans*. Washington, DC: War Relocation Authority, U.S. Government Printing Office.

War Relocation Authority. (1943d). Report of the Welfare Section: July 1 to December 31, 194, pp. 1–6. Folder: Semi-Annual Reports—Community Management Division Reports of Health Section & Reports of Welfare Section, Box 5: Washington Office Records—Documentary Files—Semi-Annual Reports: Operation D Division, Community Mgmt. Div, Administrative Mgmt. Division. Records of the War Relocation Authority, 1941–1989, Record Group 210, Headquarters Basic Documentation Reports, compiled 1942–1946. ARC Identifier 1526983/MLR Number PI-77 3. Washington, DC: National Archives and Records Administration.

War Relocation Authority. (1943e). Welfare Activities, pp. 1–4. Folder: Health Section— Community Management Division, Box 4: Community Management Division— Monthly Vocational Training (1944–45), Education, Welfare and Housing, Health, Internal Security, Religion. Operational Division—Engineering and Agriculture. Records of the War Relocation Authority, 1941–1989, Record Group 210, Washington Office Records—Washington Documents. ARC Identifier 1519285/MLR Number PI-77 2. Washington, DC: National Archives and Records Administration.

War Relocation Authority. (1944a). Report of the Welfare Section, January 1–June 30, 1944, pp. 1–6. Folder: Semi-Annual Reports—Community Management Division Reports of Health Section & Reports of Welfare Section, Box 5: Washington Office Records— Documentary Files—Semi-Annual Reports: Operation D Division, Community Mgmt. Div, Administrative Mgmt. Division. Records of the War Relocation Authority, 1941–1989, Record Group 210, Headquarters Basic Documentation Reports, compiled 1942–1946. ARC Identifier 1526983/MLR Number PI-77 3. Washington, DC: National Archives and Records Administration.

War Relocation Authority. (1944b). Report of the Welfare Section, July 1–December 31, 1944, pp. 1–6. Folder: Semi-Annual Reports—Community Management Division Reports of Health Section & Reports of Welfare Section, Box 5: Washington Office Records—Documentary Files—Semi-Annual Reports: Operation D Division, Community Mgmt. Div, Administrative Mgmt. Division. Records of the War Relocation Authority, 1941–1989, Record Group 210, Headquarters Basic Documentation Reports, compiled 1942–1946. ARC Identifier 1526983/MLR Number PI-77 3. Washington, DC: National Archives and Records Administration.

War Relocation Authority. (1944c). Welfare: January–June, 1944, pp. 1–4. Folder: Semi-Annual Reports—Community Management Division—Reports of Health Section & Reports of Welfare Section, Box 5: Washington Office Records—Documentary Files— Semi-Annual Reports: Operation D Division, Community Mgmt. Div, Administrative Mgmt. Division. Records of the War Relocation Authority, 1941–1989, Record Group 210, Headquarters Basic Documentation Reports, compiled 1942–1946. ARC

Identifier 1526983/MLR Number PI-77 3. Washington, DC: National Archives and Records Administration.

War Relocation Authority. (1945). Semi-Annual Reports: Welfare Section, January 1–June 30, 1945, pp. 1–6. Folder: Semi-Annual Reports—Community Management Division Reports of Health Section & Reports of Welfare Section, Box 5: Washington Office Records—Documentary Files—Semi-Annual Reports: Operation D Division, Community Mgmt. Div, Administrative Mgmt. Division. Records of the War Relocation Authority, 1941–1989, Record Group 210, Headquarters Basic Documentation Reports, compiled 1942–1946. ARC Identifier 1526983/MLR Number PI-77 3. Washington, DC: National Archives and Records Administration.

Watson, A. C. (1942a). 'CONFIDENTIAL' report filed November 16, 1942, p. 1. Folder 1, Box 528. YWCA of the U.S.A. Records, Sophia Smith Collection. Northampton, MA: Smith College.

Watson, A. C. (1942b). Memorandum on the Japanese Problem, May 5, 1942, p. 1. Folder 22, Box 719. YWCA of the U.S.A. Records, Sophia Smith Collection. Northampton, MA: Smith College.

Webb, J. L. (1944). Letter to Mrs. George Campster, Chairman, Home Service, Drew County, Arkansas Chapter, American Red Cross, from J. Lloyd Webb, Counselor, Community Welfare Section, Jerome Relocation Center, Denson, Arkansas, April 28, 1944, p. 1. Folder: 61.510—Welfare (General), Box 198: Jerome Center, Denson, Arkansas—Central Files—61.310 to 61.510. Records of the War Relocation Authority, 1941–1989, Record Group 210, Subject-Classified General Files of the Relocation Centers—compiled 1942–1946. ARC Identifier 1544889/MLR Number PI-77 48. Washington, DC: National Archives and Records Administration.

Webb, J. L. (1945). Final report: Community Management division, Welfare Section. War Relocation Authority, Jerome Relocation Center, Jerome, Arkansas (Calisphere, Japanese American Relocation Digital Archives ed., pp. 1–37). Berkeley: Bancroft Library, University of California.

Welfare board named. (1942, June 9). Pomona Center News, pp. 1–6. Retrieved from http://ddr.densho.org/ddr-densho-193-5/

Woodsmall, R. L. (1942). Impressions of the Japanese Relocation Center at Manzanar, California: World's YWCA, Washington, DC, dated December 1, 1942, pp. 1–5. Folder 14, Box 723. YWCA of the U.S.A. Records, Sophia Smith Collection. Northampton, MA: Smith College.

Yasumura, J. (1945). Report on the closing of Minidoka Relocation Center by Jobu Yasumura, Department of Cities, American Baptist Home Mission Society, dated November 5, 1945, pp. 1–9. Folder 17, Box 724. YWCA of the U.S.A. Records, Sophia Smith Collection. Northampton, MA: Smith College.

5

Social Work in the Camps

Part I: Public Assistance

A Day in the Life of a Camp Social Worker

Among the multitude of War Relocation Authority (WRA) documents held by the National Archives in Washington, DC, are copies of nine letters written by Lou E. Butler, social worker and head of the Poston Welfare Section. The official closing reports of the camp Welfare Sections provide a general overview of the history of the departments as they unfolded in the various camps. The internal reports made by the YWCA fieldworkers to its National Board, garnered from the unique position they enjoyed in the camps as privileged outsiders, provide a more candid assessment of the workings of the sections and their staff. The nine letters written across the span of her tenure at Poston by Butler to be circulated among her friends and family are, however, the only detailed personal narrative of a Caucasian social worker who worked inside the camps. Butler, a social worker to be counted on the "sympathetic" side among the Appointed Personnel (APs), began her comparatively long tenure at Poston in late February 1943, approximately 10 months after its opening, and she stayed through its closing in October 1945. In her first letter, dated February 28, 1943, addressed to her sister Edith, she described her arrival in Poston "after a three-day journey by train from Lansing" (Butler, 1943a, p. 1).

> Between Tucson and Phoenix, a Phoenix resident introduced me to various shrubs and trees which we could see from the train window: such as the creosote bush, sage, paloverde which has no leaves but leaf-green branches, mesquite, eucalyptus, castor bean, cottonwood. At Phoenix, one of the social workers from the Social Security Board came down to the depot and we had a visit between trains. My supervisor had written that "the truck would meet the train at Parker." A nice elderly lady who sat across the aisle from me and with whom I had dinner on the train said she going to Poston also and was to be met by someone at the request of OWI. So when we left the train at Parker we were looking for a professional person and a truck driver. We spotted them immediately. A young lawyer carried off my elderly friend and the truck driver picked up my bags. The "truck" was a covered wagon type of

Facilitating Injustice: The complicity of social workers in the forced removal and incarceration of Japanese Americans, 1941–1946. Yoosun Park, Oxford University Press (2020). © Oxford University Press.
DOI: 10.1093/acprof:oso/9780199765058.001.0001

military transport. The passengers, 2 Caucasian women, 1 Caucasian man, and 4 Japanese-Americans—2 men, 1 woman, and a little boy—faced each other, sitting on benches. The driver checked us off on a list he carried. We drove 17 miles to the camp, arriving about 11:30 P.M., stopping twice, once for a burro and once for the sentry who flashed his light in our faces and asked each his business and checked the driver's list. When we reached the barracks the driver referred again to his list to see where to leave each of us. He told me I was to sleep in E-3, meaning Barrack E, Room 3. (Butler, 1943a, p. 1)

Butler described herself as the "head of the Family Welfare Section," whose official title was "Supervisor of Public Assistance and Housing" (Butler, 1943b, p. 5). Room 3 was in a barrack containing 11 bedrooms and a shared bathroom in Poston I, one of the three subcamps that comprised the Colorado River Relocation Center at Poston, Arizona.

The room is quite cold but I am comfortable under three heavy wooden blankets. It is still dark as we are on the very western edge of the Mountain Time belt. I close the window and turn on the light. The appearance of the room is familiar by this time. It is approximately eight by sixteen feet with a door into the hall in the middle of one side and two windows on the other side. At either end is a single bed. There is one large easy chair, a small chair, a table, a four-drawer chest, a mirror and a large floor lamp. We have electricity. The floor is of fairly good boards, apparently oiled, the walls are plasterboard and so is the ceiling. There is a ventilator in the ceiling, connected I think with the cooling system in the summer. There is a kerosene heater, too, which is quite effective if used. I seldom use it because I leave too suddenly in the morning and return too late at night. I am told that much of the furniture is from some hotel taken over by the Army. I grab my towels (furnished) and my soap (I'm glad I brought some; it's hard to get here) and go four doors down the hall to the bathroom. There are 19 women in this barrack (20 at times when I have a transient room-mate). In the bathroom there are 5 lavatories, 5 stools, and in an adjoining room, (no door), there are four showers. Still compared to the residents, who have to go out-of-doors to get to the large latrine, one for each block, we feel quite luxurious. I, at least, usually have the shower room to myself, thanks to my preference for a 7:15 A.M. shower. There is running hot, (very hot), and cold water. It is hard and I am always dusty so I lather myself well and use a sharp shower. (Butler, 1943b, p. 2)

Breakfast was served in the mess hall reserved for APs, a block from her barracks.

7:45 A.M. I am dressed and ready for the outside world with my heaviest coat, (just right). As I open the barrack door I face east and see the bright streamers of morning coming apparently out of a black mountain. The air is crisp. I join a straggle of women and men walking north to the mess-hall, one block from my barrack. Each of us holds a meal ticket which we show to a checker inside the hall. She checks my number off a page covered with numbers, thus charging my meal against my salary, to be deducted before I am paid, as is my room rent. I pass on into the mess-hall and select a table at which sit a few of my friends, but not too many, as service is quicker if not too many are ahead of me. I greet my friends, who are already eating, and begin too without ceremony to help myself to food. I choose a small orange from a platter heaped with oranges and half-grapefruit. A brisk young Japanese man or girl offers hot coffee. I decline but ask for hot cereal, please. Before my orange is finished the cereal is there and the waiter says, "May I have your order, please?" Breakfast has just begun. The waiter recites, "hot cakes, sausage, (or salt pork), eggs, toast, warmed-over potatoes." I see that some women as well as men take it all, but, being a trifle more delicate, I ask for a poached egg on toast, (emphasizing one egg and one piece of toast of I'm likely to get two eggs and two or three slices of toast), or sometimes I take hot cakes and sausage. Milk is placed on the table in square waxed paper containers and we help ourselves, with one eye on the sign on the blackboard which says, "Only one glass of milk per person." Occasionally it reads, "Milk for children only." Yes there are children, too. Two of the nicest children are the daughters of an Indian couple who themselves are very good looking. This being Indian Bureau, there are several Indians on the staff. (Butler, 1943b, p. 2)

By 8:15 A.M., Butler had finished breakfast and walked across "the street" to her office in the Administration Building:

This building is composed of a number of barracks placed side by side and end to end, finally forming a T, with the top of the T facing the street. I enter the door in the center of the T-top and go down the long hall to the very bottom of the T-stem. Here it is quiet as a welfare office should be. My office is on the north side of the building, with two windows on the north. My desk is in front of one of the windows. There are five other workers in the room, two Caucasian and three Japanese. Among the six of us, one Caucasian and two Japanese speak Japanese, while two Caucasians and one from Japan speak only English. One corner of the room is walled off as a storeroom for clothing and yardage sent from various parts of the U.S. Across the hall are our clerical force, a receptionist file clerk and typist and two stenographers. They work for Miss [Nell] Findley, Chief of Community Services, and for the Family Welfare Section. There is a small waiting room space in the room. (Butler, 1943b, p. 2)

Her morning is spent "with appointments and conferences with the workers in this camp, both interviewers and clerks" (Butler, 1943b, p. 3) and in conferring with Nell Findlay, a social worker from Hawaii who served as the Chief of Community Services, to whom Butler reported. At 12:30, the Caucasian staff left for lunch.

> A sample lunch might be lettuce and tomato salad with Thousand Island dressing, broccoli or mustard greens or spinach, some other cooked vegetable, potatoes, meat balls, or pork and beans or kidney beans, milk, and pie, probably rhubarb or apple. The only thing lacking is water, which we have to ask for if we get it at all. I usually take a long drink at the cooler before going to lunch. The one mail a day is now delivered to the pigeon holes at the end of the dining room. And we are delighted when we find our names on letters. One day there were hundreds of mail order catalogues received at the post office, about three dozen came to our mess hall. (Butler, 1943b, p. 3)

The "Japanese workers" left the office for lunch a half-hour earlier, at noon, since their mess hall was not so conveniently located and they had "a distance to go to lunch" (Butler, 1943b, p. 3).

At its peak, the combined population of Poston's three subunits reached 17,814, making it the third largest city in Arizona at the time.

> A sample block contains 19 buildings; 12 apartment buildings containing 4 apartments each, 2 barracks for single persons, a man's and women's wash room, a laundry, dining hall, recreation hall. The laundry and washrooms are located in the service court area which forms the center of each block. The recreation hall is on the corner directly across from the dining hall. Each block is numbered, each building shown on one corner the number of the block and over the door the number of the building and the letter of the apartment. Camp 1, or Unit 1, was planned for 60 blocks. [end page 3] However, it was not completed. 36 blocks are living quarters for evacuees; 2 blocks, (not arranged as the living quarters described above), are administration offices and barracks for the appointed personnel; 2 blocks are hospital quarters; 4 blocks are warehouse and maintenance; in 2 blocks the schools are being built of adobe blocks. At present, the recreation halls are being used for schools and churches. The whole is a mile or more square with the highway running through one corner near the administration buildings. Across the highway are farm buildings and the offices of the Army engineers and military police. Units II and III are similar and each about half as large. There is a large canteen, (general merchandise store), in each Unit and several small canteens dispensing soap, (when they can get it), newspaper, milk, (insofar as quota permits), and soft drinks. In each

Unit there is a workshop called "Industry" where workers make gift articles, ranging from simple cards and carved wood items to small and large paintings. Each Unit, also, has it "Internal Security" unit, (police), and fire departments, a post office and an employment office. Units II and III are more fortunate than Unit I, in that they have a whole block reserved for school buildings. There are two libraries in each Unit, one a school library and the other a city free library. At this time the libraries are fairly well established, except that they have few magazine subscriptions. When school started last fall, the teachers had to teach without books for a time, which taxed their ingenuity and, I guess, their balance. The head of the music department had no music except what he brought with him. (Butler, 1943b, pp. 3–4)

Built on 71,000 acres inside the Colorado River Indian Reservation despite opposition from the tribal council, "overruled by the Office of Indian Affairs and the Army" (Fujita-Rony, July 14, 2015), Poston was the largest of the ten WRA incarceration camps. Its desert location made it the hottest, with a vast range of temperatures from day to night. "Before morning, I will be glad of my three blankets. At this moment I am glad of a cotton dress with short sleeves" (Butler, 1943b, p. 4), Butler remarked of the late March weather. There were also dust storms that blew through the camps: "the wind from the west gathers up the dust from the 'subjugated' fields and from the streets and the firebreaks and blows it through everything, windows, doors, and apparently, walls. Then suddenly the air is clear and quiet. But the dust is piled on our desks and clothes" (1943b, p. 4).

Butler spread her time across the three subcamps, generally spending four days per week in Camp I and two days in Camps II and II, about three miles distant from each other by an unpaved road.

[S]oon they hope to give it a hard top so it won't all blow away. We pass some of the "subjugated" land, that is, it is cleared and leveled. This piece is not yet planted, so we are likely to get into clouds of dust. We pass the hog farm, too, and we know it without looking out from under the canopy. (Butler, 1943b, p. 3)

A hourly bus service—using trucks, given the unpaved roads—ran between the camps every hour, except when gasoline was unavailable.

There are no sidewalks such as you have in mind. However, the adobe has been piled up and leveled off so that there is a raised place on each side of the street on which we can walk should the street suddenly turn into a river. The soil in the streets is adobe and can be a nice hard walk, but it can also be a mighty slippery surface and, at times, dusty. (Butler, 1943b, p. 5)

Twice a week, from 9 to 11, "a class in family welfare" (Butler, 1943b, p. 3) was held in Camp II for about 16 inexperienced employees of the family welfare department from the three camps. Alongside these trainings, which Butler hoped would aid her staff in finding better opportunities in the world outside, the "regular work" of the department was carried out.

> Public assistance, with monthly interview; Clothing allowances with monthly vouchers; Transfers of persons and families to and from other centers; Soldiers asking furlough extension; Babies and children needing special attention; Internees visiting sick relatives; Other internees paroled and coming home to their families. (Butler, 1943c, p. 4)

Lou Butler worked till 5:30 in the afternoon "every day, including Saturday" (Butler, 1943b, p. 3) and there was "just time to go over to the barrack and wash before dinner" (Butler, 1943b, p. 3) back in the Caucasian mess hall.

> After dinner when I don't work, I join some of my friends for a walk. We may walk to the hill nearby, where the sand is like beach sand and there is a cross set up for exercises. Here we have a lovely view of the sunset which is usually lovelier in the east than in the west, with the eastern mountains turning gradually from pink to lavender to blue, the mountain tops becoming more clearly etched against the light blue sky, as the sun sinks. Sometimes the sunset is more spectacular, colors flaming across the western horizon, with clouds like bright red powder puffs hanging motionless above us. (Butler, 1943b, p. 3)

On other evenings, she might accompany a YWCA visitor to a club meeting held at the home of a Nikkei member or visit "a Japanese friend in the resident's area" where there were "family apartments, usually four to a barrack" with "gardens, flowers and vegetables between the barracks and on the wide firebreaks which separate rows of blocks" (Butler, 1943b, p. 3).

Financial Need

In similar barracks in ten camps across seven states in vastly different climates and terrains, Butler and social workers like her carried out the programs of the Welfare Section; some tasks such as leave clearance, citizenship renunciation, and intercamp transfers were peculiar to the abnormal community life in incarceration, while others were tasks whose basic outlines would have been familiar to social workers in any community of comparable size in the nation. Primary among the latter was public assistance, which came in three forms: cash assistance, clothing allowance, and unemployment benefits. Notwithstanding Butler's consistently upbeat and often lyrical descriptions of camp life and surroundings, the concentration camps were grueling places for their inmates to endure, not the least because of their "radically abnormal" (Webb, 1946, p. 72) economic structure and the Kafkaesque system of public assistance developed to uphold those structures.

According to Jane Hoey (1943), the Chief of the Social Security Board's Bureau of Public Assistance, the war brought a rise in economic security to many families around the nation. The War Manpower Program created new job possibilities for those previously considered unemployable: "handicapped workers, older men and women, and minority groups" (p. 43). The high wages paid by war industry and the rising value of agricultural products were, additionally, "enabling many families to attain a much higher standard of living in spite of increased costs" (p. 43). The war had, conversely, brought economic devastation to the Nikkei. What savings and resources they had and were able to salvage from the catastrophic fire sales of the removal period had been exhausted in the months of confinement in the detention centers. Many came to the long-term incarceration camps financially depleted. Shotaro Frank Miyamoto (1942), a Japanese American Evacuation and Resettlement Study (JERS) fieldworker at Tule Lake, observed that many arrived "with only a few hundred dollars savings at most, or with nothing at all at worst" (p. 2). One of "a considerable number of people" without "adequate means to provide for all their minimum needs" (p. 33) as the WRA characterized in its second quarterly report covering the July–September period of 1942, was a 68-year-old man, without family or friends, who had been living in Modesto County hospital for two years prior to his removal to Gila. He had arrived to the camp with nothing but the clothes he had on: "The only blankets he had were the govt. issue" (Kikuchi, 1942a, p. 106).

The concentration camps were costly places to live. JERS fieldworker Tamotsu Shibutani's (1943) statement that "contrary to the popular belief, one cannot live free in Tule Lake" (p. 77) was true for all of the camps. While subsistence food, rudimentary shelter, and basic medical care were provided, private funds were necessary to purchase and enable much else required for daily living. In an article published in *Social Service Review*, Jerome Welfare head Lloyd Webb (1946) enumerated some of the necessities the Nikkei had to provide for themselves.

> ... clothing, personal incidentals, household furnishings and equipment (army cots, pads, and blanket were provided), cleaning supplies, household linens, participation in community activities (church, gifts, recreation, club or organization fees), communication and correspondence items (radio, newspapers, magazines, postage, writing materials, school supplies), medicine chest, and life insurance. (p. 78)

Funds were also necessary to purchase food to supplement the poor diet provided by the camp (Briesemeister, 1946; War Relocation Authority, 1945). Letters of complaint about the inadequacy of the camp food submitted by the Nikkei to various authorities—including Eleanor Roosevelt (Takamura, 1942)—contradicted the Department of State's (1945) assurance that the food in the camps was adequate to need. A letter of request for better food written by a group of residents of Poston (Residents of Colorado River Relocation Center, 1943) to the camp administration noted that while the menus published by the WRA as being served in the camps were undoubtedly "excellent," there was a vast gulf between "the quality and quantity of the served food and the quality and quantity of the food as stated in the menus" (p. 3). In the assessment of those letter writers, "approximately 90% of the residents have lost weight amounting from 10 to 15 pounds since entering this center" (p. 3).

The Report of the Commission on the Wartime Relocation and Internment of Civilians (CWRIC; 1982), the nine-member bipartisan federal commission appointed in 1980 to examine the government's role and determine reparations, found that many of the camp inmates were indeed unable to afford basic needs. Gila River's Welfare Section reported that when public assistance funds finally became available at the end of December, 1942, they were used "in nearly all cases" (Tuttle, 1945, p. 3) for basic necessities; "the barest essentials in the Sears catalogue, such as shoes for the children, were out of reach" (p. 167) for many. Meeting "outside obligations" (p. 167) such as taxes, mortgage payments, or insurance costs was impossible. The plight of a Christian minister from San Francisco recounted by Charles Kikuchi (1942c) in his November 1–15, 1942 diary was an example. The minister was "worried about what to do with the churchfull of stuff he has in his church" (p. 13), consisting of household goods entrusted to him by community members who were now incarcerated in several different camps. He had employed a local policeman to watch over the church in his absence, but several months into incarceration no longer had the funds to pay for the policeman's services or to keep up the mortgage payments he had been making on the church for the past 20 years. There was "nobody there to sort the things out" (p. 13) back at home.

Income earned in the camps was totally inadequate to offset the cost of living in them. The set monthly salaries for Nikkei work in the camps were initially divided into three categories: $12 (equivalent of $174.18 in 2018) for trainees and apprentices, $16 ($232.24 in 2018) for most of the workforce, and $19 ($275.79 in 2018) for professional workers such as doctors and pharmacists; the bottom salary category was later eliminated.[1] As a point of comparison,

---

[1] Converting 1943 dollars to 2018 equivalents, using the American Institute for Economic Research cost of living calculator (https://www.aier.org/cost-living-calculator).

the job of Counselor, the head of the Welfare Section, carried a salary of $3,800 ($55,157 in 2018) per year, or about $317 ($4,601.26 in 2018) per month, plus overtime. Project Attorneys and Caucasian Medical Officers were paid $5,600 ($81,284.16 in 2018) per annum, or about $467 ($6,778.52 in 2018) per month. Capped at the top inmate rate of $19 per month, Nikkei doctors who did the same job as the latter received approximately $276 ($3,309 in 2018) per year, about 5% of the salary paid to the Caucasians. The "insulting" (Commission on Wartime Relocation and Internment of Civilians, 1982, p. 167) salary gap was, according to Winifred Wygel (1943) of the YWCA, "one of the hardest blows the intellectual Japanese have had" (p. 7) in the camps. Not only were the Nikkei indefinitely stalled in furthering whatever educational and career ladder they were on prior to their incarceration, they were on a downward economic trajectory while the Caucasian staff in the camps had "gone up the economic scale as a result of promotion to their jobs in the relocation in almost the same measure that the evacuees had come down" (Leighton, 1945, p. 107). This was a reality "well recognized" by the Nikkei (Leighton, 1945, p. 107).

The unjust salary system "caused severe financial hardship" (Commission on Wartime Relocation and Internment of Civilians, 1982, p. 167). An income study fielded in December 1942 at Rohwer showed that "the average per capita income of employed residents, and their dependents, was $9.75 a month" (Dusseldorp, 1945, p. 10). Many Nikkei households were, however, unable to earn even that nominal income. There were families in which "the only person able to work is interned or institutionalized" (D'Ille, 1943, p. 2) elsewhere. There were many who were too "old and ill" (D'Ille, 1943, p. 2) to work, and others, such as "widows with young children unable to work" (D'Ille, 1943, p. 2) because of their child care obligations. Even those families with a working parent or even two often struggled to get by on the derisible salaries; families large by today's standards, with four to six children, were all too common. There was for the Nikkei workers, moreover, months-long bureaucratic delays in payment of those meager salaries in all the camps (Leighton, 1945; Spicer, Hansen, Luomala, & Opler, 1969). For all these reasons, as Manzanar social worker Margaret D'Ille's (1943) put it, "For the first time in the history of the Japanese people in America, 'Grants in Aid' became necessary for certain families" (p. 2).

Reluctance for Aid

Public assistance was a new phenomenon for the community as a whole; individuals and families receiving state or county aid of any kind had been rare among the Nikkei prior to removal, and while the poverty engendered by the displacement and incarceration made aid unavoidable for many, the deep and real reluctance to accept government assistance was slow to ebb and would never be entirely jettisoned. The identification of people in need often came through *block managers*—Nikkei community members appointed by the administration as leaders of a set of barracks—who brought to the attention of the Welfare Sections the many individuals and families in desperate straits but greatly reluctant to apply for aid. The case of Mrs. W., a pregnant young mother of a small child, was an example. The application for assistance for the woman had to eventually be made without her consent by her block manager. Though she was in dire need, she was unwilling to apply for aid lest she "disgrace the family of her husband" (Shibutani, 1943, p. 3), incarcerated in a Department of Justice internment camp. Though "she was at first resentful that anyone should offer relief," Mrs. W. agreed eventually to accept the grant "provided it was called something other than relief" (p. 3) and even then "only after the block manager assured her that it was the responsibility of the government to make up for any inconvenienced by evacuation" (p. 3). The amount she received—$7.25 a month—was meager enough for her to still have to rely on the help of relatives to make ends meet.

Part of the resistance against applying for aid was that doing so meant that the applicant had to "submit to a means test and to answer questions about personal financial matters" (Webb, 1946, p. 79). Jerome's J. Lloyd Webb conjectured that "the same resistance to having financial status checked is probably universal among those whose applications for assistance follow other ill-fortune" (Webb, 1946, p. 79).

> But those who require assistance from the department of public welfare have not been so pre-dominantly self-sufficient as had been the evacuees. Public assistance was regarded by the evacuees as a possible source of compensation for the damages incurred by evacuation. Hence, there was a stronger resistance than was ordinarily found to any tendency toward preciseness in verifying resources. (Webb, 1946, p. 80)

That public assistance was reparation rather than unearned charity was a belief that the Nikkei workers of the Welfare Sections shared, and assuring reluctant community members that they should understand it as such was a common tactic used by Nikkei workers to convince them to accept desperately needed assistance. The case of Mr. S., a 71-year-old Issei "under hospital care for a 'nervous breakdown'" (Kikuchi, 1943d, p. 44), was an example. The plight of the itinerant farm worker without any family was another case which became known to the social work department through the intervention of a block manager. Charles Kikuchi reported that it was only "after a great deal of persuasion," including a promise of total confidentiality and assurance that "he did not need to feel any shame since the government had provided for these cases" (p. 44), that Mr. S. agreed to sign the application form for assistance.

Public Assistance Grants

As had been the case for the social service offices in the detention centers, "the need for Public Assistance grants" was the "first general type of problem brought to the attention of the department" (Kimmerling, Fite, & Abbott, 1945, p. 22) in the long-term incarceration camps. Unfortunately for those in need, aid did not quickly materialize. No funds had been allocated for such grants at the start of the camps, and no real plans had been made to establish the welfare offices which would administer such grants. All that the so-called social work offices in various camps could do for several months into their operations was to keep files on the people in need of assistance grants. In the last week of August 1942, the WRA established, in theory, a public assistance grants program for "deserving evacuees" who could not be expected to work and were ineligible for unemployment compensations.

> These would include: (1) evacuee who is unable to work because of illness or incapacity; (2) dependents of physically incapacitated evacuees; (3) orphans and other children under the age of 18 without means of support; (4) heads of families which have a total income from all sources inadequate to meet their needs. (War Relocation Authority, 1942, p. 34)

Actual disbursal of funds for public assistance, however, did not occur until months later. According to Gila River Welfare Head William Tuttle (1945), funds became available for disbursal only at the end of December of 1942, five months after the camp began operations and four months after the supposed establishment of the assistance program. The first disbursements at Topaz, which began operations on September 11, 1942, were made in January of 1943 (Pratt, 1945); at Poston, which opened on June 1, 1942, the first disbursal of aid occurred eight months later, in February of 1943 (Butler, 1945).

The roster of aid recipients reported at Poston was typical for all the camps: women whose husbands were incarcerated in internment camps and who could not work due to ill health or because of child care needs; large families with one wage earner whose income was insufficient to the need; families with unusual expenses, "such as special shoes, braces, layettes, and travel expense for off-project medical care" (Butler, 1945, p. 7); and frail or disabled elderly single men with no families to rely on. The last group was in particularly dire financial straits. The WRA reported that, in the last quarter of 1943, "the average size of the family unit receiving assistance grants during the period [July 1–December 31, 1943]" was 1.78, the small number indicating "that a large number of such units are single unattached individuals. It is probably safe to assume that need for assistance among this group is largely due to age or disability or both" (War Relocation Authority, 1943d, p. 5). By April of 1943 at Topaz, some 150 of such "unattached, mostly elderly, men" (Pratt, 1945, p. 8) were identified as regular recipients, alongside a few families. By the summer of that year, the roster of the "old, infirm and otherwise unemployable" (Pratt, 1945, p. 8) receiving aid had grown to about 240 cases comprised of 400 recipients of aid totaling approximately $3,100 per month.[2]

Charles Kikuchi (1942d) was particularly affected by the plight of such men that he encountered as a worker in the Gila Welfare Section: "The more I see of these single men, the more I realize how poor they are" (p. 90). Many of these aged men, Kikuchi (1942b) explained, had immigrated alone and had "worked for years as farm laborers and have nothing to show for it" (p. 76). Though their labor had contributed "a great deal to the development of California—in the fields and on the railroads" (Kikuchi, 1943a, p. 91), they had been too poor to return to Japan to find a bride or to send for one and were now in their old age, unable to work and without family support. Writing in reaction against the oft-heard characterization of Issei men—especially family-less men without the anchors of U.S.-born children—as instigators of pro-Japanese agitation, Kikuchi described the desperate straits of the occupants of a single men's barracks he visited in the course of his work.

I am beginning to doubt the fact that it is the single men that are so dangerous. They give vent to all sorts of feelings, but they look so damned old and worn out that they are almost harmless. In that room full of old Issei, almost all of them looked as if they were all dried up. They have worked hard all of their lives and they appear to be simple persons. It may be that I have not run across too many of these so-called agitators. I don't doubt that a lot of these simple persons can be led by them on an emotional basis. Mr. F., age 65, is perfectly harmless. He can barely totter around. For the past 25 years, he has worked as a farm laborer near Delano. He just isn't the type to be dangerous. Mr. K., age 74, is another. He has absolutely no relatives. For many years, he worked on the farms near Vacaville. Now he is practically penniless. What would he do if he went to Japan? Mr. H. is 63 but he looks 80. He was sick in bed until about a week ago.

---

[2] At Heart Mountain, where the population peaked at 10,767, an estimated 1,774 families (5,322 individuals) were said to have received one or more public assistance grants between September of 1942 to the start of November of 1945 (Kell, 1945). The average at Gila River was about 350 families per month (Tuttle, 1945).

Hasn't a cent so he started to work as a thinner on the farm, but he can't stand this sort of hard work for long. He says that he took the job so that he could get some work corps clothes and not have to apply for relief. Mr. T., age 67, is a gnarled old man who looks absolutely helpless. For many years he has been earning his living from season to season cutting celery near Stockton. This year he did not get any work due to the war conditions so he hasn't a cent. Mr. T., 58, has stomach ulcers and he is receiving medical care from the hospital. He did not have doctor's care before because he had no money. In Vacaville, he worked on a Japanese farm and he relied upon Japanese patent medicines to apply for his ulcers. He was able to make a little money picking apricots or something just before evacuation so that he has a little money left. But he absolutely refused to take any assistance. "Don't need any now. Go to work when I get well." But it is doubtful if his condition will improve much. Mr. S., age 64, was a farm laborer in Parlier. He only has a few dollars left. All he wants is a pair of underwear. He was very ashamed to even ask for that. Mr. N., 63, worked in a farm near Vacaville. He worked here for one month as a ground keeper, but this position was eliminated. All he wants is a pair of pants as he does not know when the October checks will come in. (Kikuchi, 1942c, pp. 102–103)

Cash Assistance

The camps did not follow a uniform standard in determining eligibility for assistance and the amount to be granted to individual cases, a fact known to the Nikkei across the various camps, who were well "aware of the differences in the methods of granting public assistance" (Kimmerling et al., 1945, p. 22). Instructions provided by the WRA were "very broad in character" (Tuttle, 1945, p. 1).

> There were no absolute limitations placed on the use of funds for grants to meet needs of exceptional circumstances except that in most centers the project director or an assistant project director retained the authority to disapprove a recommendation by the welfare counselor. (Webb, 1946, p. 79)

Those Welfare Sections that had the support of the camp upper administration, or at least an administration that did not interfere, thus had fairly broad discretion in determining their own practices. William Tuttle reported that, at Gila River, "a good deal of discussion with regard to policy making was left to the section at the center" (p. 1), allowing the policies to be "developed by trained Welfare people" (p. 1). Topaz, where special grants for items such as eye glasses or baby layettes "were given freely upon application" (Pratt, 1945, p. 8), and where there "was never any attempt to establish budgets" (p. 8) and those who met basic criteria for assistance were "given the maximum grant" (p. 8), presumably had a similarly cooperative or noninterfering administration.

In the "absence of detailed instructions concerning eligibility for public assistance grants" (Shirrell, 1942b), Tule Lake's Welfare Section requested the WRA Regional office to provide more detailed instructions. The request was answered with the decree that "determination of degree of need was an administrative function of the project" (Shirrell, 1942b, p. 1). Working from the principle that public aid policies "should not require applicants to impoverish themselves before becoming eligible" (Shirrell, 1942b, p. 1), Tule Lake established comparatively liberal policies. The possession of some liquid assets ($100 per individual or $500 per family) would not constitute ineligibility for aid, and even if an applicant had an income from work or other sources, the applicant would "be entitled to a public assistance grant in an amount equal to the difference between income and the amount that he would be receiving under public assistance grant if the latter would be greater" (Shirrell, 1942a, p. 1). Only half of the income from a working child younger than 16 years of age would be calculated into the family budget for grant calculations.

Conversely, at Minidoka, which had the lowest average for assistance grants among the camps, "need" was "interpreted in a very restricted sense" (Kimmerling et al., 1945, p. 22). The WRA Manual, which came out in 1943, specified that cash assistance should not exceed $4.75 ($68.95 in 2018 dollars) per month for men, $4.25 ($61.69) per month for women, $2.50 ($36.29) per month for children aged 13–17, and $1.50 ($21.77) per month for children under 13 (War Relocation Authority, 1943e, section 30.4.12). In disregard of these instructions, the Minidoka upper administration set an "arbitrary amount" of $3.00 ($43.55) for all cases. The grant applicants, furthermore, had to specify the items for which they were requesting funds and submit receipts for their purchases, a procedure not required by the WRA manual. The Nikkei staff "reported that many evacuees were so humiliated by the procedure that they went without necessities rather than apply for assistance" (Kimmerling et al., 1945, p. 22). The Welfare Section's requests to camp administration for permission to follow the higher rates set by the headquarters manual were continually rebuffed. In an effort to convince the administration to change its policy, the Welfare Section conducted a living cost study which "revealed that even the amounts allowed in the Manual were not sufficient to meet the needs of residents who had no income from other sources" (Kimmerling et al., 1945, p. 22). The study was completed in August of 1943 and submitted to the camp director in September. The higher rates were finally approved in November.

The Rohwer Welfare Section overseen by Wilma Dusseldorp also operated a flat grant program, but at about double the amount set at Minidoka. Because "it was not considered feasible to give full public assistance grants as described in the administrative instruction plus full clothing allowance to dependent individuals" (Dusseldorp, 1945, p. 10), a set amount of $6.00 or $.6.50 per month was given to cover both grants and clothing allowance combined. The flat grants at Rohwer worked in the following way for families who were unable to work: (1) families of adults who could not work and did not have children under 18 were granted $6.00 ($87.09) a month per person; (2) families with children under 18 or over 18 but still in school were given $6.50 ($94.35) a month per person; (3) families with a working child, but no adult worker, were given grant amounts to equal $6.00 per month per person (or if there were other minor children, $6.50 a month per person), after accounting for the full income of the working child (Dusseldorp, 1945). Under the structure outlined in the WRA manual, the top possible grant-in-aid would have been $8.00 ($116.12) per month, accounting for both cash assistance and a clothing allowance, which was set at $3.50 for persons 16 years of age or older, $3.00 for persons aged 1 to 16 years, and $2.00 for persons under 1 year of age. Those eligible were individuals employed or exempted from the work requirement because of illness or the need to care for dependents (War Relocation Authority, 1943e, section 30.4.51). Rohwer's flat grant, though set at double the amount given at Minidoka, thus still came in under the rate set by headquarters, which had itself been determined by the Minidoka Welfare Section as being insufficient to meet basic needs.

Clothing Allowance

By the close of 1942, the Nikkei had been living in incarceration for several months, and the limited amount of clothing they had been allowed to bring had quickly become worn through in the hard-scrabble environments of the camps. Coats, boots, and other winter clothing necessary to endure the harsh winters of camps in Colorado, Wyoming, Utah, and Arizona were not items that the majority of the population had on hand to bring in the first place, and since they had been given no information on where they would be incarcerated for the duration of the war, they could not have packed in anticipation. Private funds were depleted while the price of commodities in the wartime economy soared (Residents of Colorado River Relocation Center, 1943) and winter was on hand. The WRA did not, however, consider clothing a basic necessity to be provided to all inmates. The clothing allowance grant it instituted in the last quarter of 1942 was constructed as a part of public assistance, a supplementary grant doled out in addition to cash assistance to only those eligible to receive it. The WRA manual stated: "Each evacuee who is employed or eligible for extended illness compensation shall receive a supplementary allowance for clothing for himself and each of his dependents" (War Relocation Authority, 1943e, section 30.4.51). Those who did not meet these qualifications would have to obtain clothing with whatever personal resources they had. The one exception to this rule, according to Poston's Lou Butler (1943d) was that those "over 65 years of age may have coats regardless of whether they were working or not" (p. 1).

The clothing allowance in J. Lloyd Webb's assessment was "hardly sufficient to maintain the simplest wardrobes" (Webb, 1946, p. 80). It "was never great enough to meet adequately the needs of center residents" (p. 9) according to Topaz Head Counselor Claud Pratt (1945). As they were about the inadequacy of the camp diet and the abysmal barracks in which they were forced to live, the Nikkei were vocal in demanding changes to the clothing allowance policy. They insisted that the allowance limits be increased to reflect the actual prices in the wartime economy and that clothing should be issued to everyone regardless of their employment status (Residents of Colorado River Relocation Center, 1943). The camp Welfare Sections tended to concur. William Tuttle noted in mid-March of 1943 that "since the present clothing allowance schedules were esti-mated in the summer of 1942 prices have increased, quality has deteriorated and there is a tendency for cheaper clothing to disappear from the market" (Tuttle, 1943, p. 1). His review of studies by the Heller Committee for Research in Social Economics of the University of California made clear that the "present schedules are quite inadequate and should be revised upward" (Tuttle, 1943, p. 1) if the clothing allowance was to be "realistic in terms of actual cost" (Tuttle, 1943, p. 1). The Welfare Section in Washington, DC, headquarters also agreed. That office learned that the recommended clothing budget for Crystal City Family Internment Camp, run by the Department of Justice, was higher than that of the WRA, and consultations with various government offices such as the Social Security Board convinced it that an increase was necessary. During the first quarter of 1943, recommendation for an increase was made by the Washington office to WRA Director Dillon Meyer (War Relocation Authority, 1943b). The Director's decision, reported a year later, was "that it was not desirable to increase the cash clothing allowances at this time" (War Relocation Authority, 1944, p. 3).

Unemployment Benefits

Employment, to which the clothing allowance was hitched, was not a certainty in the camps. The WRA had envisioned self-sufficient communities in the camps. Full employment of the Nikkei was to be the bulwark against their descent into becoming a "permanently dependent population like the Indians" (Commission on Wartime Relocation and Internment of Civilians, 1982, p. 165). The WRA's belief that "prolonged idleness" in incarceration would create dependency among the Nikkei was a notion well supported by social workers who had forecasted it at the beginning of the war (California State Department of Social Welfare, 1942–43; Hoey, 1942) and would consider it accomplished at its close (Choda, 1946; Gerrild, 1944; Reith, 1943). The imperative for work, valorized as a moral and psychological necessity for the good of the Nikkei themselves, undergirded all aspects of the welfare system created in the camps. As discussed in the previous chapter, the WRA was ambivalent about providing aid, especially the kinds of material aid that usually counted as "welfare." Even when the camp social workers and departments believed that the terms and conditions for relief set by headquarters were too strict or too parsimonious, the basic premise that dependency was a phenomenon to be feared and aid should be reserved for those who endeavored against it remained uncontested.

The Nikkei did indeed work—in offices, hospitals, mess halls, factories, and farms within the camps. By 1943, an estimated 85% of all vegetables consumed in the camps (and an additional 2.5 million pounds sold to outside markets) was produced in the camp farms, hacked out of the inhospitable terrain by Nikkei labor (Commission on Wartime Relocation and Internment of Civilians, 1982). The great bulk of the work required to keep the camps operating was supplied by the Nikkei; no camp could have functioned without it. Work was mandated and valorized, and a Byzantine tangle of contradictory stances and policies was constructed to buttress this morality. Eligibility for crucial elements of public assistance was contingent upon it. To be deserving of aid, one had to be a worker or at least fail in finding employment. The labor economy that the WRA created, however—with abusive wages and little choice of occupation—did nothing to promote work or provide incentives to engage in it. As J. Lloyd Webb put it, with "private property, enterprise, and higher compensation for greater production" largely prohibited, the "[e]conomic structure and incentives at the centers were radically abnormal" (1946, p. 72).

There was, moreover, a scarcity of jobs in the camps. The bizarre economic snarl the WRA created mandated that everyone work, but it failed to make work available to everyone. In the second quarter of 1943, the WRA radically shifted its policy on work, retreating from its boast that "jobs would be provided for everyone who wished to work" (Spicer et al., 1969, p. 88), to mandate instead an overall reduction in camp employment. The policy about-face was, it insisted, necessary to combat the too common practice of overstaffing and the "slack work habits" (Commission on Wartime Relocation and Internment of Civilians, 1982, p. 167) that developed from it. The Nikkei surmised, in contrast, that limiting work was part of the administration's "moves aimed toward making the centers less pleasant places to live in" (Spicer et al., 1969, p. 213) in order to induce greater cooperation with its resettlement push—its new directive to empty the camps of their inmates through a scheme of "relocation" to Eastern and Midwestern locales, in full force by this time. This interpretation was supported by the fact that the employment division in the camps soon became transmogrified into the Relocation Section responsible for the resettlement program (Pratt, 1945). In utter contradiction to all the haste with which the Nikkei had been removed from the coastal states as palpable threats to national security, the WRA had instituted various measures to move the Nikkei out of the camps almost as soon as the camps opened. in the early Fall of 1942, when the WRA instituted its program for "permanent relocation" (Briesemeister, 1946, p. 38). A Relocation Division was established in each camp, and regional Relocation Offices to facilitate the process were opened in target areas such as Chicago, Denver, Cleveland, and Salt Lake City (War Relocation Authority, 1943c). Henceforth, all activities within the camps would be geared to support this goal (see Chapters 8 and 9 for fuller discussion on relocation/resettlement).

The new mandate for a reduction in camp employment restricted the number of employed people in families to only one worker for a two-person family and two workers for families comprising more than two persons. Administrative reports filed for Tule Lake (Bigelow, 1944) shows that, in August of 1944, 61 families determined to have "too many workers" (p. 5) had "refused to cooperate" (p. 5) with the administration's request to voluntarily terminate the employment identified as surplus. The report indicated that those 61 families would be given one more opportunity to do so; failure to comply would result in all workers in the family being terminated from their jobs. Neither the voluntarily nor involuntarily unemployed workers, moreover, would receive unemployment compensation under the new rule. The employment reduction mandate also included the call to clear out the unemployment compensation rolls (Commission on Wartime Relocation and Internment of Civilians, 1982; War Relocation Authority, 1942). Under the terms of the employment and compensation policy of September 1, 1942, which established the camps' unemployment compensation mechanisms, compensation was to be given to any inmate who "applies for work and is assigned to a job or who is laid off through no fault of his own" (War Relocation Authority, 1942, p. 33). Under the new rule, eligibility was restricted to only those who were unable to work due to illness or incapacity (War Relocation Authority, 1943a). There is evidence that this stringent policy, adopted officially in the Spring of 1943, had already been in practice prior. A December 31, 1942, memorandum from John C. Henderson, the Employment and Housing Officer at Tule Lake, explained the basis on which unemployment benefits would be determined in that camp.

> Unemployment compensation for evacuee workers is effective from October 1, 1942. Generally speaking, only those persons who were employed on October 1st or later and who were forced to stop work permanently or temporarily because of illness or injury on the job are eligible to unemployment compensation.

There have at all times been jobs available for all persons who were desirous of work, and those persons who declined to accept jobs because they desired to wait for some other job which they considered preferable are not eligible to unemployment compensation. According to revised Administrative instructions an injured or ailing worker is to be kept on the timekeepers payroll for fifteen days after his last day's work. Thereupon, he is to be terminated and instructed to report to the Placement Office with a termination slip and a doctor's certificate reflecting his incapacity for work. The Placement Officer will review the facts and certify such employee as being eligible for unemployment compensation. (cited in Kikuchi, 1943b, p. 7)

Since eligibility for the clothing allowance was tied to work, the draconian workforce reduction played out on the ground as a socialistic policy accounted to have resulted in a wider distribution of those resources. Tule Lake reported that, in the third quarter of 1944, a total of "533 adjustments" in employment status gave "more families at least one worker and the accompanying privileges of clothing allowances for all" (Bigelow, 1944, p. 5). On the other hand, welfare departments overall anticipated a rise in total welfare usage since a reduction in employment in conjunction with a reduction in unemployment benefits could only result in more need (War Relocation Authority, 1943a). The reality was that no more resources were added to the pool available to the Nikkei. Rather than the wider and better distribution of resources that the WRA insisted it was, the shift in employment policy was, at best, an alternative distribution of poverty.

Dependent Allowance

A dependent's allowance for families of active soldiers and veterans' benefits for the families of deceased soldiers were two possible sources of funds that were not administered by the WRA. Eligibility for both were, nevertheless, predicated on the faulty assumption that basic support was already provided by the WRA. Nisei eligibility for the draft was reinstituted in January 1944 in a volte-face from the early years of war, when Nikkei soldiers were summarily dismissed from service (Spicer et al., 1969). The Servicemen's Dependents Allowance Act of 1942 established grants of "flat, fixed schedule of amounts" (Grossman, 1943, p. 217) which were given, according to First Lieutenant Harry Grossman of the War Department Office of Dependency Benefits, "without a means test to the persons who will normally be dependent" (Grossman, 1943, p. 217) on soldiers. There was to be, furthermore, "no discrimination between the dependents of one soldier and the dependents of another soldier" (Grossman, 1943, p. 217). The War Department's determination of benefits for the families of Nikkei soldiers fighting for the nation that imprisoned them belied both directives. Calculated on the basis that the WRA already "provided maintenance for evacuees" (Kimmerling et al., 1945, p. 23), the War Department was "inclined to either reject their applications, or to allow them only minimum grants" (Kimmerling et al., 1945, p. 23). The Veterans Administration, in charge of administering needs-based survivor benefits to families of soldiers killed in the war, took the position that as long as the family "resides in a relocation center their needs are being met by the Federal Government and they are not eligible" (Residents of Colorado River Relocation Center, 1943, p. 1). According to the Minidoka Welfare Section (Kimmerling, 1945), if that office believed a rejected case "warranted reconsideration by the War Department a letter stating the situation of the evacuee and the limitations of W.R.A. provisions" provided by the Welfare Section usually resulted in "favorable reconsideration" of the application for the Servicemen's Dependents benefit. "Whenever possible," however, the benefit was "used to stimulate relocation" by the Welfare Section, with "the Counselor pointing out that larger grants would necessarily be made to families without other means of livelihood" (p. 23). Since families could also reapply for the VA survivor benefits when they left the camps, it was also likely to have been used as an incentive for resettlement, the WRA's primary goal in the months to come.

Red Tape and Administrative Chaos

The fact was that even the begrudgingly doled and unequivocally insufficient aid was difficult to obtain. The case of a Seattle family recounted by Tamotsu Shibutani (1943), is illustrative of the reprehensible effects of the snarled aid structure created in the camps. The family, headed by a widow, was unusual for the fact that they had been on county relief prior to the removal, a fact which rendered their social status in the camp "at the bottom of the ladder" (Shibutani, 1943, p. 74), but made their financial straits in the camps all the more understandable. The widow was unemployed, counseled by the doctors at the camp hospital to refrain from working because of her health, and the family "soon began to feel the pinch of the cost of living in Tule Lake" (p. 77). Unemployment compensations, for which she would have been technically eligible, had not been institutionalized in the camps and would not materialize for many months still. In early October of 1942, she applied to the social welfare department for aid, requesting funds only for shoes and clothing for her school-aged children.

> Unfortunately, at the time of her application, the Social Welfare Department was still fighting with the Fiscal Division over the forms to be used in applications for Public Assistance Grants, and all payments had been delayed.

Furthermore, it was necessary for her to get a medical statement from the base hospital and this required an additional week. In the meantime, the needs of her family increased day by day. Finally, on October 15, after much discussion, the public assistance grants were paid for the first time. (pp. 77–78)

The grant of $2.50 she received "obviously was not enough, but it was all that the department could give her under the existing regulations" (p. 78). Grants were, as this case illustrates, more often than not delayed in reaching the recipients, languishing in a tangle of administrative chaos and red tape. As Shibutani averred "many families suffered unnecessarily" (p. 71) because of the combined effects of "the delays in the payment of wages, the setting up of public assistance grants, and the setting up of the procedures for unemployment compensation" (p. 71).

The case of the H. family was another example. The family had arrived in Tule Lake in late June of 1942 and came to the attention of the Welfare Section in October of that year. The 24-year-old son had begun to work as a carpenter's apprentice at $12 a month as soon as he had arrived in the camp, but, like all other Nikkei workers in all camps, had not yet been paid for those months of work. The 68-year-old father had been paralyzed since before the removal and was unable to work. The 58-year-old mother, suffering from rheumatism, was also unable to work, not only because of her ailment but because she was the primary caregiver for her husband who had spent the first few months of his tenure at Tule Lake in the camp hospital but had since been discharged to his family. In October, three months after their arrival, the family was still waiting for the son's salary, their sole income, as well as the clothing allowance attached to it. They reluctantly applied for a grant for the purchase of a coat for the father, who needed to be taken to the latrines outside since even the promised bedpans also had not arrived. A sum of $7.50 was granted to the family by the Welfare Section. When the son's salaries were finally paid in November, however, the family lost their eligibility for aid.

"Some family were really down to their last penny when they came into the Welfare Department for help" (Sakoda, 1942, p. 11). But, in many cases, little could be done to help them. By mid-September, a large volume of requests for assistance sent in by block managers had piled up in the Tule Lake Social Welfare Section according to James Sakoda (1942), but none of the sources of possible relief was actually up and running.

While these requests were piling up, Mrs. Halle [Welfare Section head] found that she was not able to get the money from the WRA to pay these grants. Previously a few needy cases had been taken care of by asking for credit of the canteen, but even this credit had not been paid as yet. (Sakoda, 1942, p. 11)

By the middle of October, the unemployment compensation mechanism promised to have been functioning since the beginning of the September also had not yet materialized, as Mr. T., who had been advised against work by the camp doctors and was thus eligible for unemployment, had cause to discover. At the urging of their block manager, Mr. T.'s wife finally applied to the Welfare Section for assistance for him, only to be told by the section staff that she must first register at the employment office. In that office, however, she was duly informed that "the procedure for unemployment compensation had not yet been set up" (Shibutani, 1943, p. 71), and no funds could even be promised, much less disbursed.

At the time of Sakoda's reporting in October of 1942, no Nikkei worker had yet been paid for his or her labor. But even if the funds for public assistance grants had been available, no one who was owed wages from the WRA would have received any because, however implausibly, their unpaid wages counted as income and made them ineligible for aid. This was the situation in which Mr. I., who had applied to the welfare office on October 1 for a grant, found himself. To begin with, because "the office was in the midst of internal conflict" (Shibutani, 1943, p. 105), the grant application went unattended for nearly a month.

> Finally, on October 26, his block manager became very irritated and threatened to complain to the administration unless something was done about this now destitute family. The block manager and a social worker sat down to figure up the amount of money that Mr. H. was entitled to in public assistance grant and discovered to their amazement that he was not eligible to any because he presumably had an "income"—the salary from the work he and his son had done which had not yet been paid. (p. 105)

Similar was the case of a family headed by Mrs. K., a 36-year-old Issei mother with four children (aged 5–11) and a husband institutionalized in a state asylum back in California. She had received aid from the county welfare department until soon after Pearl Harbor in December, 1942, when she was abruptly dropped from the relief role. The penniless family had arrived in Tule Lake on June 26, 1942, and Mrs. K. began work as a utility room attendant on her block for $12 a month.

> It was not until August that she discovered that she cannot support four children on $12 a month. On October 5, 1942 she finally applied for relief at the Social Welfare Department. Her block manager, who went to the office with her, reported that her children were inadequately clothed and had no underwear and no coats for the winter weather. (p. 84)

But because Mrs. K. was owed $60 in clothing allowance and salary, she was in-
eligible for public assistance grants though neither the salary nor the clothing
allowance had yet been paid.

Censure of Aid

The delays in processing and payment could be explained by the inter- and
intradepartmental confusion and conflict recounted earlier, the glaring gaps in
eligibility could be attributed faulty policies set by the WRA headquarters, the
WRA's parsimonious policies blamed on the unwillingness of the federal government to fund the camps adequately, and so on up the chain of command. But
that a deeply held censure of aid—lest it breed dependency, lest it fund the undeserving, lest the Nikkei become coddled—existed on the part of the Caucasian
administrators also cannot be left out of the mix. In Charles Kikuchi's (1943b)
view, while the Caucasian supervisors hid "behind the defense of 'red tape,'" they
themselves created it due their "overcautious" (p. 199) approach to aid. Since
"a lot of the policy is left to the discretion of the WRA officials" (p. 177) in the
camps, a more liberal practice was possible if the supervisors had been willing
to operate from the perspective that the department's "object is to help the community, not to be a detective agency" (p. 177). Kikuchi (1943c) believed that the
practices of administrators such as Mr. Gabe, the Assistant Chief of Community
Service at Gila River, tasked with approving the aid requests put through by the
social work department, indicated otherwise.

> All he has to do is to sign the vouchers. But he sticks his big nose into things
> and he is getting more unpopular because of the fine interpretations which
> he draws. He writes a memo to Tuttle on almost every case. I saw a couple of
> dumb ones today. He told of a case of an aged man who applied for assistance.
> The man has a Caucasian wife in L.A. who is working. According to Gabe, this
> makes the man ineligible and he should ask his wife for money. This is silly. If
> this were true, we would have to put in a strict relative responsibility clause
> as one of the conditions for eligibility. It would cut our list of clients in half.
> Another Gabe brainstorm is that all people getting glasses and teeth should get
> a minimum and uniform ones so that they won't all order the higher cost ones.
> He thinks the evacuees only deserve the cheapest. (pp. 219–220)

Giving credence to Kikuchi's sense that more generous practices were possible
where there was will was Shibutani's (1943) report that many long-delayed grants
at Tule Lake were suddenly paid out a mere week after the restrictive regime of the
much-disliked Mrs. Halle ended with her abrupt departure and a Miss Hoshino

was assigned temporary supervisor. Under Miss Hoshino's recommendation, previously rejected cases, such as that of the F. family, consisting of a widower with an elderly father and nine young children (aged 2–7), were reversed by the camp director Elmer Shirrell. The two older men and the oldest son had all begun working in June but, along with the rest of the camp, had not been paid well into October. The family had applied to the Social Welfare Department for assistance several times but had been turned away. The income calculations based on the as yet theoretical wages of the three employed members of the family made them ineligible for grants. The issue was finally brought, on October 29, three weeks after Halle's departure, to the attention of the camp director Elmer Shirrell, "who apparently had not realized how much effect the delay in the payment of salaries had on the lives of large families" (Shibutani, 1943, p. 95). Shirrell delivered a set of reprimands to personnel and authorized a grant of $12.50 for the family (Shibutani, 1943, p. 95). While the Director of a camp did have the final authority to approve or deny aid, a reputation for such indulgence toward the inmates did not, apparently, advance career prospects within the WRA. Shirell was removed from his post in December 1942 and replaced by Harvey Coverley, who had previously been the Acting Director of Manzanar and Assistant Director of the WRA Regional Office in San Francisco. In her December 4 diary entry, Mrs. Shirrell, distraught with the news that they were to leave Tule Lake, recorded: "Why we don't know. He was told the military authorities think he's too lenient with the Japanese" (Japanese American Evacuation and Resettlement Study—Compiler, n.d., p. 40).

Whether to increase the pressure for resettlement, because Congress was reluctant to continue to fund the WRA, or a combination of the two, the already inadequate public assistance available to the Nikkei only decreased as the months and years of incarceration passed. One of the mechanisms through which the WRA effected its belt tightening was an instrument called "A Working Supplement on Public Assistance" developed in the later years of the war. One positive change the Supplement wrought was the elimination of the requirement for medical certification of unemployability for applicants over the age of 65. It was a policy change welcomed by all on the ground since it meant a great reduction in paperwork for the administration, an easing of the workload of the already overstretched health services and social services in the camps, and one less hurdle for those applicants themselves. As a whole, however, the Working Supplement reduced eligibility (Pratt, 1945). It limited to three months the period that a family with a wage-earner resettled on the outside could receive cash assistance. It also narrowed the eligibility for "special grants" for items such as baby layettes and eye glasses (Pratt, 1945). Heart Mountain's Adeline Kell (1945) reported that, in the last quarter of 1944, the assistance rolls were culled to eliminate from the list any inmate who received income from outside benefits such as Social Security, Railroad Retirement Benefits, Servicemen's Dependents Allowances, or from sources such as rentals and leases or annuities. These measures were protested not only by the recipients but by Nikkei Welfare Section staff and community leaders who argued "that grants should be issued for the purpose of enabling recipients to save their current income for future use" (Kell, 1945, p. 5), a perspective fundamentally at odds with the administration's view that public assistance was for minimal subsistence and to be granted only when all personal and familial resources were depleted.

Resistance

Such views on the nature of aid, identification of problems, and the definition of "constructive outcomes" held by the Nikkei workers and contradicting their own, was usually interpreted by Caucasian social workers as examples of "emotional conflicts occasioned by the fact that they were identified closely with the clients they served in a relocation center" (p. 4). They were one of the "serious handicaps" (p. 4) hampering the proper functioning of Nikkei personnel in the Welfare Sections. The Caucasian supervisors saw the conflict of identification— the rub between the role of the worker and that of community member—as a detriment to an objective stance necessary to achieving "constructive" outcomes and a certain indication of the Nikkei workers' lack of professionalism. Though well aware of their own dearth of training and professional knowledge, many of the Nikkei workers saw the issue differently. As Rohwer Head Counselor Wilma Van Dusseldorp rued, Nikkei counseling aides invariably insisted: "we can't represent the administration . . . we only explain the administration" (1945, p. 12) and resisted the form of professionalism the administration worked to instill. From the perspective of the Nikkei workers, the emotional conflict they experienced arose from the need to absorb and process the demands of a job that did not always and obviously put the welfare of their community as its primary objective. The "constructive" outcomes the Caucasian workers sought to achieve were not necessarily beneficial to their community, in their view. That these workers were "constantly subjected to community pressures" (Kell, 1945, p. 4) was no doubt true, but to imagine them only as naïfs floundering out of their depth and confused by blurred boundaries would, nevertheless, be an unfair assessment of their acuity and agency. For better or worse, many of the Nikkei workers found ways to circumvent the system that they saw as reprehensible in order to accomplish the outcomes *they* believed to be constructive. Charles Kikuchi (1943b) explained.

I have learned enough by now not to make an issue of it. There are ways that I can get around these policies without violating my position as a Social Worker. (p. 116)

Tamotsu Shibutani (1943) averred that the Nikkei social work staff, for example, "often lied in order to get money for their clients" (p. 21). They defied policies and practices and took such action not simply because they were pressured to do so by the clients but because they believed many policies and practices were unjust, misguided, or simply mishandled by the Caucasians in charge (Kikuchi, 1942d; Shibutani, 1943). In Diary 13, detailing his observations between February 1 and 27, 1943, Kikuchi described his handling of a case of a destitute couple whose eligibility for aid was disputed by welfare head William Tuttle.

He [the husband] came into the assembly center financially destitute. Only recently, he has been able to get up and around a bit. He has been in the U.S. for the past 37 years and he speaks fair English. His wife has been working as a block janitress. She was pregnant. After work yesterday, she began to suffer labor pains. At 4:00 A.M. this morning she was taken to the hospital & at 7:00 A.M. a baby girl was born. In this case, as in others, Tuttle would hesitate about granting an emergency sum of money because of the red tape. I will find out tomorrow if he will sign it. Perhaps, I will have Kimi [Mukaye] send it through without discussing it with him. The family is clearly eligible on an emergency basis, but Tuttle will want to give them an advance only & deduct it from her $16.00 salary later on. I took some baby clothes out to him from the clothing box at housing. All of this is new stuff. Helen & I decided that I should not enter it on the case record because Tuttle doesn't believe that this is the right philosophy of relief. But the baby can't wait until the wages for the past month comes in so that the father can buy some baby clothing. This is what would be called a violation of "agency policy" on the outside. The only difference is that we are not supposed to be a "relief" department in the way Tuttle wants it. (Kikuchi, 1943c, p. 14)

The general inefficacy of the administration and its staff was a conclusion also reached by JERS researcher Robert Billigmeier's (1944) analysis of the Caucasian staff at Tule Lake. According to Billigmeier, a "long list could be compiled" (p. 16) on the problems caused by WRA policies and the incompetent staff who carried them out.

Promises were made by various administrators who were not able to live up to their promises. The Assistant Project Director has a long record of lamentable lack of honesty and common sense. Many administrators have carried out their functions with little efficiency. (p. 16)

For Nikkei workers such Charles Kikuchi, James Sakoda, and others, far more fundamentally problematic than their ineffectiveness was the Caucasian supervisors' inability to see "that social work in the Project might possibly be different from social work being practiced on the outside" (Sakoda, 1942, p. 3). Whereas the Caucasians endeavored to run the department along the lines of a welfare agency on the outside, these Nikkei workers believed that line of logic to be deeply flawed. It was a total misunderstanding of the circumstances in which the Nikkei workers and their clients lived; a discounting of the fact that they were prisoners of the government, a population who had never before received its aid and were now having to do so only because of its unjust actions. To an elderly couple with " 'typical Japanese pride" who "refused aid on the basis that they would be disgraced" by doing so, Kikuchi (1942b) explained that the aid disbursed by his office was "not really relief since we are all technically on relief as wards of the government" (p. 60). While the argument failed to dissuade the couple from first exhausting their small remaining savings before considering government aid, his insistence "that it was their right to receive any advantages to which they were eligible" (p. 60) was not merely a method of persuasion but a statement of his understanding of the role of social work in the camps. The aid was, in his view, a right not charity: "The people are not 'relief' clients here" (Kikuchi, 1943b, p. 177) but victims of a gross injustice.

Kikuchi's growing approbation of Head Counselor William Tuttle corresponded with his assessment of Tuttle's slackening adherence to rules: "I am convinced now that Tuttle really has the welfare of the people at heart and he is proceeding from this basis. Previously, he was a stickler to technicalities" (Kikuchi, 1943e, pp. 33–34). Kikuchi's argument—difficult to refute—was that since the "whole WRA is experimental" (1943b, p. 177), the administration of its various parts ought also to be inventive enough to meet the highly unusual and fast-changing circumstances of the camps. Given the unique circumstances of social work in the camps, moreover, it was insensible to hold on to a mode of social work practice "that is not applicable to the situation here" (1943b, p. 177), an idea that "doesn't have evacuation as a basis" (p. 177). Tuttle had been too "full of the welfare procedures that apply to a regular welfare department" (p. 116)—that is, the methods appropriate to "a relief department that thinks the client is going to spend all his grant on liquor" (1943c, p. 126), but one that did not "take into consideration the influences and circumstances of a mass evacuation" (1943b, p. 116).

James Minoru Sakoda (1942), JERS researcher and a staff member of the Tule Lake Welfare Section, provided similar criticism of Mrs. Halle, the first Head

Counselor at Tule Lake. She, too, was an intransigent upholder of inapt rules that did not fit the peculiar circumstances of the camps. Sakoda asserted that Halle attempted to replicate at Tule Lake the kind of ill-functioning welfare department "that she had seen actually practiced during her career as a social worker" (Sakoda, 1942, p. 4) on the outside, driven by the "suspicion that the people would take advantage of the Social Welfare Department if she did not stick to regulations" (p. 15).

> Mrs. Halle had been a practical social worker and probably had been too long in the field to see some of the larger aims of a Social Welfare department. She could only think in terms of rules set up by the WRA, and did not attempt to see problems in terms of the needs of the people. Workers complained that cases were turned down bluntly by her because there were no precedent set or because the case, while needy, did not conform to the requirement stipulated by orders from [the regional headquarters in] San Francisco. (p. 3)

Along with "her unstable personality" (p. 1), the "most important contributing cause to the conflict which characterized the department throughout the initial period of adjustment was Mrs. Halle's lack of understanding and sympathy with the Japanese people" (p. 1), in Sakoda's view. Described as an awkward, nervous woman in her late thirties, "constantly smoking a cigarette" (p. 2), Mrs. Halle was, in Sakoda's estimation, a disorganized and ineffective manager. While "Part of her distrust of workers on her staff was probably justified because of their lack of training" (p. 2), she was a rule-bound supervisor whose "lack of sympathy with the Japanese people," evidenced in her inflexibility, often resulted in "argument whenever someone came to see her about a problem" (p. 3).

Tamotsu Shibutani (1943), another JERS fieldworker at Tule Lake, who conducted a massive review of the department's case files for the study, noted that, under Halle's rule, a "person had to be completely destitute, unemployable, and without any friends or relatives who could help before he was eligible" (Shibutani, 1943, p. 21) for relief. The case of a couple from Salinas with four children ranging from age 5 to 11 was illustrative of this stringent application of eligibility. The family had arrived at Tule Lake in late June of 1942. Due to an appendix operation, the husband, who worked as a dishwasher at the bottom-rung monthly salary of $12 was "unable to do heavy work" (p. 21) which might have earned a higher income. The wife was employed as a waitress in the dining hall, presumably at the same low salary. Because the camp administration had not yet worked out the mechanism for payroll disbursement in the camps, they, like all other inmates, had not yet been paid even these low salaries. Finding themselves unable to meet the family's needs, the husband applied to the Welfare Section for assistance in early October.

In his application for relief he stated that he had no savings and that he dreaded the coming winter cold since he had no winter clothing for the children. He felt that even if the WRA paid him all his clothing allowance and all back salary he could not adequately clothe his family. The WRA owed the family $67. Mrs. Halle would not approve the grant, however, on the grounds that both the man and wife are able to work and thought [his] brother, who was a block manager and family also living in the same block, that they therefore could help him. The family was dropped from the roll and had to manage best they could by borrowing from relatives. (p. 45)

Mrs. Halle's "very narrowly" (p. 78) constructed definition of the administrative policy on relief also demanded that all recipients of aid submit itemized accounting of the funds spent on the highly restricted number of goods defined by her as "essential." If any grant recipients were found to have used the funds to purchase nonessentials such as "fruits for the ill or for the children" (p. 21), they were immediately struck off the relief roll. Such "strange regulations" were only removed when Mrs. Halle "broke down under the strain" (Sakoda, 1942, p. 12) of the job and left, in mid-October, for a month's leave of absence from which she evidently did not return.

References

Bigelow, J. (1944). Tule Lake: Monthly Administrative Report Summaries, July, September, November 1944. War Relocation Authority, Tule Lake Relocation Center, Tule Lake, California (Calisphere, Japanese American Relocation Digital Archives ed.). Berkeley: Bancroft Library, University of California.

Billigmeier, R. H. (1944). Caucasian Staff at Tule Lake Relocation Center, pp. 1–27. Folder R 20.01, Box BANC MSS 67/14 c. Japanese American Evacuation and Resettlement Study, Japanese American Evacuation and Resettlement records. Berkeley: Bancroft Library, University of California.

Briesemeister, E. (1946). America's children—what happened to us?: Summary report of the Japanese Evacuee Project, January 1942–September 1946, pp. 1–54. Folder 3, Box 721. YWCA of the U.S.A. Records, Sophia Smith Collection. Northampton, MA: Smith College.

Butler, L. E. (1943a). Letter No. 1. Round Robin from Colorado River WRA Project, Poston, Arizona, February 23, 1943, p. 1. Folder: Copies of Circular Letters (1–9) Feb. 28, 1943–Dec. 1945 Box 3. Records of the War Relocation Authority, 1941–1989, Record Group 210, Office Files of Miss Lou Butler, Head Counselor of the Welfare Section of the Community Management Division at the Colorado River Relocation Center, compiled 1942–1945. ARC Identifier 5752763/MLR Number UD 6. Washington, DC: National Archives and Records Administration.

Butler, L. E. (1943b). Letter No. 3. Round Robin from Colorado River WRA Project, Poston, Arizona, March 25, 1943, pp. 1–5. Folder: Copies of Circular Letters

(1–9) Feb. 28, 1943–Dec. 1945 Box 3. Records of the War Relocation Authority, 1941–1989, Record Group 210, Office Files of Miss Lou Butler, Head Counselor of the Welfare Section of the Community Management Division at the Colorado River Relocation Center, compiled 1942–1945. ARC Identifier 5752763/MLR Number UD 6. Washington, DC: National Archives and Records Administration.

Butler, L. E. (1943c). Letter No. 6. Round Robin from Colorado River WRA Project, Poston, Arizona, November 14–21, 1943, pp. 1–7. Folder: Copies of Circular Letters (1–9) Feb. 28, 1943–Dec. 1945 Box 3. Records of the War Relocation Authority, 1941–1989, Record Group 210, Office Files of Miss Lou Butler, Head Counselor of the Welfare Section of the Community Management Division at the Colorado River Relocation Center, compiled 1942–1945. ARC Identifier 5752763/MLR Number UD 6. Washington, DC: National Archives and Records Administration.

Butler, L. E. (1943d). Narrative Report, Family Welfare Department, Community Services Division, Colorado River War Relocation Project, Poston, Arizona, May, 1943, pp. 1–4. Folder: Community Management Division—Welfare Section—Family Welfare Monthly Report, Box 5. Records of the War Relocation Authority, 1941–1989, Record Group 210, Office Files of Miss Lou Butler, Head Counselor of the Welfare Section of the Community Management Division at the Colorado River Relocation Center, compiled 1942–1945. ARC Identifier 5752763/MLR Number UD 6. Washington, DC: National Archives and Records Administration.

Butler, L. E. (1945). Story of the Family Welfare Section, May 1942 to May 1945, pp. 1–17. Calisphere, Japanese American Relocation Digital Archives, Box Poston, Arizona. Berkeley: Bancroft Library, University of California.

California State Department of Social Welfare. (1942–43). Evacuation of Japanese in California. Social Welfare—War Services—WCCA—Reports, General, 1942–43 (F3729-146). Department of Social Welfare Records, War Services Bureau. Sacramento, CA: California State Archives.

Choda, B. (1946). A counseling program in a relocation center. *The Family, 27*(4), 140–145.

Commission on Wartime Relocation and Internment of Civilians. (1982). *Personal justice denied: Report of the Commission on Wartime Relocation and Internment of Civilians.* Washington, DC: U.S. Government Printing Office.

D'Ille, M. (1943). Memorandum to Mrs. Lucy W. Adams, Chief of Community Services Division, from Margaret D'Ille, Counselor, Community Welfare, Manzanar Relocation Center, Manzanar, California, March 9, 1943, pp. 1–2. Folder: 18.200—Social Welfare Cases, Box 220: Manzanar Relocation Center—Central Files—50.026 to 62.014. Records of the War Relocation Authority, 1941–1989, Record Group 210, Subject-Classified General Files of the Relocation Centers—compiled 1942–1946. ARC Identifier 1544889/MLR Number PI-77 48. Washington, DC: National Archives and Records Administration.

Department of State. (1945). Memorandum re: requests and complaints from the residents of Poston to the Spanish Consul, February 12, 1945, pp. 1–4. Folder 120.2 Public Reactions, Box 112: Subject-Classified General Files—Colorado River Central Files—110.41 to 130. Records of the War Relocation Authority, 1941–1989, Record Group 210, Subject-Classified General Files of the Relocation Centers—compiled 1942–1946. ARC Identifier 1544889/MLR Number PI-77 48. Washington, DC: National Archives and Records Administration.

Dusseldorp, W. V. (1945). Historical Statistical—Functional Report of Welfare Section, Wilma Van Dusseldorp—Head Counselor. War Relocation Authority, Rohwer

Relocation Center, McGehee, Arkansas (Calisphere, Japanese American Relocation Digital Archives ed.). Berkeley: Bancroft Library, University of California.

Fujita-Rony, T. Y. (2015, July 14). Poston (Colorado River). *Densho Encyclopedia of the Japanese American Incarceration.* Retrieved from http://encyclopedia.densho.org/Poston_(Colorado_River)/

Gerrild, J. (1944). Goro John Fujiwara, committed from Prowers County, February 15, 1944 to Colorado State Hospital, Pablo, Colorado: Memorandum from Jacob Gerrild, counselor, Public Welfare Section, to Mr. H. F. Halliday, Assistant Project Director, Granada Relocation Center, Amache, Colorado, February 22, 1944, pp. 1–2. Folder: 510—Public Welfare, Box 154: Granada Relocation Center—Central Files—502.6 to 513. Records of the War Relocation Authority, 1941–1989, Record Group 210, Subject-Classified General Files of the Relocation Centers—compiled 1942–1946. ARC Identifier 1544889/MLR Number PI-77 48. Washington, DC: National Archives and Records Administration.

Grossman, H. (1943). Administration of family allowances for men in military service. *Cornell Law Review, 29,* 217–232. Retrieved from http://scholarship.law.cornell.edu/clr/vol29/iss2/7

Hoey, J. M. (1942). Mass relocation of aliens II. In A. Dunham (Ed.), *Proceedings of the National Conference of Social Work: Selected papers, Sixty-Ninth Annual Conference, New Orleans, Louisiana, May 10–16, 1942* (Vol. 69, pp. 194–199). New York: Columbia University Press.

Hoey, J. M. (1943). The conservation of family values in wartime. *The Family: Journal of Social Case Work, 24*(2), 43–49.

Japanese American Evacuation and Resettlement Study—Compiler. (n.d.). Shirrell, Mrs. Elmer, diary, pp. 1–130. Box Japanese American Evacuation and Resettlement Study, Japanese American Evacuation and Resettlement records. Berkeley: Bancroft Library, University of California.

Kell, A. S. (1945). Welfare Section Final Report by Adeline S. Kell, Counselor, Term of Service August 28, 1944 to Center closure. War Relocation Authority, Heart Mountain Relocation Center, Heart Mountain, Wyoming (Calisphere, Japanese American Relocation Digital Archives ed., pp. 1–12). Berkeley: Bancroft Library, University of California.

Kikuchi, C. (1942a). Diary 6: October 1–14, 1942, pp. 1–127. Folder W 1.80:06**, Box BANC MSS 67/14 c. Japanese American Evacuation and Resettlement Study, Japanese American Evacuation and Resettlement records. Berkeley: Bancroft Library, University of California.

Kikuchi, C. (1942b). Diary 7: October 15–November 1, 1942, pp. 1–131. Folder W 1.80:07**, Box BANC MSS 67/14 c. Japanese American Evacuation and Resettlement Study, Japanese American Evacuation and Resettlement records. Berkeley: Bancroft Library, University of California.

Kikuchi, C. (1942c). Diary 8: November 1–15, 1942, pp. 1–175. Folder W 1.80:08**, Box BANC MSS 67/14 c. Japanese American Evacuation and Resettlement Study, Japanese American Evacuation and Resettlement records. Berkeley: Bancroft Library, University of California.

Kikuchi, C. (1942d). Diary 9: November 16–December 1, 1942, pp. 1–147. Folder W 1.80:09**, Box BANC MSS 67/14 c. Japanese American Evacuation and Resettlement Study, Japanese American Evacuation and Resettlement records. Berkeley: Bancroft Library, University of California.

Kikuchi, C. (1943a). Diary 11: December 18, 1942–January 8, 1943, pp. 1–218. Folder W 1.80:011**, Box BANC MSS 67/14 c. Japanese American Evacuation and Resettlement Study, Japanese American Evacuation and Resettlement records. Berkeley: Bancroft Library, University of California.

Kikuchi, C. (1943b). Diary 12: January 8–31, 1943, pp. 1–207. Folder W 1.80:012**, Box BANC MSS 67/14 c. Japanese American Evacuation and Resettlement Study, Japanese American Evacuation and Resettlement records. Berkeley: Bancroft Library, University of California.

Kikuchi, C. (1943c). Diary 13: February 1–27, 1943, pp. 1–245. Folder W 1.80:013**, Box BANC MSS 67/14 c. Japanese American Evacuation and Resettlement Study, Japanese American Evacuation and Resettlement records. Berkeley: Bancroft Library, University of California.

Kikuchi, C. (1943d). Diary 14: March 1–31, 1943, pp. 1–295. Folder W 1.80:014**, Box BANC MSS 67/14 c. Japanese American Evacuation and Resettlement Study, Japanese American Evacuation and Resettlement records. Berkeley: Bancroft Library, University of California.

Kikuchi, C. (1943e). Diary 15: April 1–30, 1943, pp. 1–129. Folder W 1.80:015**, Box BANC MSS 67/14 c. Japanese American Evacuation and Resettlement Study, Japanese American Evacuation and Resettlement records. Berkeley: Bancroft Library, University of California.

Kimmerling, C., Fite, A. L., & Abbott, C. W. (1945). Report of the Welfare Section, August 1942 to November 1945. War Relocation Authority, Minidoka Relocation Center (Calisphere, Japanese American Relocation Digital Archives ed., pp. 1–69). Berkeley: Bancroft Library, University of California.

Leighton, A. H. (1945). *The governing of men: General principles and recommendations based on experience at a Japanese relocation camp*. Princeton, NJ: Princeton University Press.

Miyamoto, S. F. (1942). Prevalent fears in Tule Lake Community, pp. 1–33. Folder R 20.34, Box BANC MSS 67/14 c. Japanese American Evacuation and Resettlement Study, Japanese American Evacuation and Resettlement records. Berkeley: Bancroft Library, University of California.

Pratt, C. H. (1945). Closing report of the Welfare Section, from Sept. 11, 1943 to Center Closing, dated December 20, 1945. War Relocation Authority, Central Utah Project, Topaz, Utah (Calisphere, Japanese American Relocation Digital Archives ed., Vol. Bancroft Library, pp. 1–10): Berkeley: Bancroft Library, University of California.

Reith, M. B. (1943). Report on Tule Lake Visit, March 1–11–12, 1943, pp. 1–14. Folder 3, Box 724. YWCA of the U.S.A. Records, Sophia Smith Collection. Northampton, MA: Smith College.

Residents of Colorado River Relocation Center. (1943). Requests made by Camp residents of Poston, Arizona, December 21, 1943, pp. 1–3. Folder 120.1 Complaints and Criticism, Box 112: Subject-Classified General Files—Colorado River Central Files—110.41 to 130. Records of the War Relocation Authority, 1941–1989, Record Group 210, Subject-Classified General Files of the Relocation Centers—compiled 1942–1946. ARC Identifier 1544889/ MLR Number PI-77 48. Washington, DC: National Archives and Records Administration.

Sakoda, J. M. (1942). Social Welfare Department, Tule Lake Relocation Center, November 11, 1942, pp. 1–130. Box BANC MSS 67/14 c. Japanese American Evacuation and Resettlement Study, Japanese American Evacuation and Resettlement records. Berkeley: Bancroft Library, University of California.

Shibutani, T. (1943). Case documents TL-53-58, 61–69 by family name [indicates pseudonym]—Family organization and disorganization (compiled documents), pp. 1–109. Folder R 21.08:7**, Box BANC MSS 67/14 c. Japanese American Evacuation and Resettlement Study, Japanese American Evacuation and Resettlement records. Berkeley: Bancroft Library, University of California.

Shirrell, E. L. (1942a). Eligibility for Public Assistance Grants—Project Instructions No. 23: Memorandum to all employees, November 17, 1942, pp. 1–2. Folder: 580—Community Services 1942 Box 35: Subject Class. Gen. Files of the SF Regional Office, 1942, 580. Records of the War Relocation Authority, 1941–1989, Record Group 210, Subject-Classified General Files—compiled 1942–1942. ARC Identifier 1543537/MLR Number PI-77 38. Washington, DC: National Archives and Records Administration.

Shirrell, E. L. (1942b). Memorandum to Mr. E. R. Fryer, Regional Director from Elmer L. Shirrell, Project Director, Tule Lake Project, on eligibility for public assistance grants, dated November 19, 1942, p. 1. Folder: 580—Community Services 1942 Box 35: Subject Class. Gen. Files of the SF Regional Office, 1942, 580. Records of the War Relocation Authority, 1941–1989, Record Group 210, Subject-Classified General Files—compiled 1942–1942. ARC Identifier 1543537/MLR Number PI-77 38. Washington, DC: National Archives and Records Administration.

Spicer, E. H., Hansen, A. T., Luomala, K., & Opler, M. K. (1969). *Impounded people: Japanese Americans in the Relocation Centers.* Tucson: University of Arizona Press.

Takamura, J. (1942). Letter to Eleanor Roosevelt from John Takamura, Minidoka War Relocation Center, Twin Falls, Idaho, September 15, 1942, p. 1. Folder: 103—Complaints—General—(March–August), Box 4: Subject Class. Gen. Files of the SF Regional Office, 1942, 102 to 103. Records of the War Relocation Authority, 1941–1989, Record Group 210, Subject-Classified General Files—compiled 1942–1942. ARC Identifier 1543537/MLR Number PI-77 38. Washington, DC: National Archives and Records Administration.

Tuttle, W. K. (1943). Rummage sale for clothing on hand: Memorandum to Mr. Morton J. Gaba, from Mr. Tuttle, Counselor, Social Service Department, Gila River Project, Rivers, Arizona, March 16, 1943, p. 1. Folder: 580—Community Service and Welfare, Box 144: Gila River Relocation Center—Central Files—571 to 580. Records of the War Relocation Authority, 1941–1989, Record Group 210, Subject-Classified General Files of the Relocation Centers—compiled 1942–1946. ARC Identifier 1544889/MLR Number PI-77 48. Washington, DC: National Archives and Records Administration.

Tuttle, W. K. (1945). History of Gila Welfare Section by W. K. Tuttle, Head, Welfare Section. War Relocation Authority, Gila River Relocation Center, Rivers, Arizona (Calisphere, Japanese American Relocation Digital Archives ed., pp. 1–10). Berkeley: Bancroft Library, University of California.

War Relocation Authority (1942). Second Quarterly Report: July 1 to September 30, 1942, pp. 1–81. Folder: Second Quarterly Report—WRA Printed—July 1 to Sept. 30, 1942, Box 1: Washington Office Records—Documentary Files—Quarterly Reports 1942. Records of the War Relocation Authority, 1941–1989, Record Group 210, Headquarters Basic Documentation Reports, compiled 1942–1946. ARC Identifier 1526983/MLR Number PI-77 3. Washington, DC: National Archives and Records Administration.

War Relocation Authority (1943a). Quarterly Report: Welfare Section—April 1 to June 30, 1943, dated September 28, 1943, pp. 1–3. Folder: Semi-Annual Reports—Community Management Division Reports of Health Section & Reports of Welfare Section, Box 5: Washington Office Records—Documentary Files—Semi-Annual Reports: Operation

D Division, Community Mgmt. Div, Administrative Mgmt. Division. Records of the War Relocation Authority, 1941–1989, Record Group 210, Headquarters Basic Documentation Reports, compiled 1942–1946. ARC Identifier 1526983/MLR Number PI-77 3. Washington, DC: National Archives and Records Administration.

War Relocation Authority (1943b). Quarterly Report: Welfare Section—January 1 to March 31, 1943, pp. 1–3. Folder: Semi-Annual Reports—Community Management Division Reports of Health Section & Reports of Welfare Section, Box 5: Washington Office Records–Documentary Files—Semi-Annual Reports: Operation D Division, Community Mgmt. Div, Administrative Mgmt. Division. Records of the War Relocation Authority, 1941–1989, Record Group 210, Headquarters Basic Documentation Reports, compiled 1942–1946. ARC Identifier 1526983/MLR Number PI-77 3. Washington, DC: National Archives and Records Administration.

War Relocation Authority. (1943c). The relocation program: a guidebook for the resident of relocation centers, May 1943. Washington, DC: War Relocation Authority.

War Relocation Authority (1943d). Report of the Welfare Section, July 1–December 31, 1943, pp. 1–6. Folder: Semi-Annual Reports–Community Management Division— Reports of Health Section & Reports of Welfare Section, Box 5: Washington Office Records—Documentary Files—Semi-Annual Reports: Operation D Division, Community Mgmt. Div, Administrative Mgmt. Division. Records of the War Relocation Authority, 1941–1989, Record Group 210, Headquarters Basic Documentation Reports, compiled 1942–1946. ARC Identifier 1526983/MLR Number PI-77 3. Washington, DC: National Archives and Records Administration.

War Relocation Authority (1943e). WRA Administrative Manual, pp. 1–30. Folder: WRA Administrative Manual (Set 1), Box 1. Records of the War Relocation Authority, 1941–1989, Record Group 210, Headquarter Records—Management Files— WRA Administrative Manuals. ARC Identifier 1542506/MLR Number PI-77 29. Washington, DC: National Archives and Records Administration.

War Relocation Authority (1944). Report of the Welfare Section, January 1–June 30, 1944, pp. 1–6. Folder: Semi-Annual Reports—Community Management Division Reports of Health Section & Reports of Welfare Section, Box 5: Washington Office Records— Documentary Files—Semi-Annual Reports: Operation D Division, Community Mgmt. Div, Administrative Mgmt. Division. Records of the War Relocation Authority, 1941–1989, Record Group 210, Headquarters Basic Documentation Reports, compiled 1942–1946. ARC Identifier 1526983/MLR Number PI-77 3. Washington, DC: National Archives and Records Administration.

War Relocation Authority (1945). Semi-Annual Reports: Welfare Section, January 1– June 30, 1945, pp. 1–6. Folder: Semi-Annual Reports—Community Management Division Reports of Health Section & Reports of Welfare Section, Box 5: Washington Office Records—Documentary Files—Semi-Annual Reports: Operation D Division, Community Mgmt. Div, Administrative Mgmt. Division. Records of the War Relocation Authority, 1941–1989, Record Group 210, Headquarters Basic Documentation Reports, compiled 1942–1946. ARC Identifier 1526983/MLR Number PI-77 3. Washington, DC: National Archives and Records Administration.

Webb, J. L. (1946). The welfare program of the relocation centers. Social Service Review, 20(1), 71–86.

Wygel, W. (1943). Report on Manzanar, July 22–27, 1943, pp. 1–11. Folder 16, Box 723. YWCA of the U.S.A. Records, Sophia Smith Collection. Northampton, MA: Smith College.

6

Social Work in the Camps

Part II: "Abnormal Communities"

Problems in "Mass Living"

The Japanese American Evacuation Project

On April 1, 1942, the National Board of the YWCA voted to establish and finance the Japanese American Evacuation Project (JAEP), "a special emergency
piece of work" which would "transplant its Japanese Branch to these new communities and continue a program there" (YWCA National Board—Community
Division Committee, 1942, p. 2) in the ten WRA concentration camps. The
major concerns the JAEP were to address were (1) "the psychological effect
upon the Japanese who have been forced to leave their homes, businesses,
friends, etc., and the effect upon American citizens of Japanese parentage who
have been uprooted, despite their loyalty to the United States" and (2) "the ultimate concern of living re-adjustments after war, for the Japanese" (YWCA
National Board—Race Relations Subcommitee of the National Public Affairs
Committee, 1942, p. 1). West Coast Associations had brought to the National
Board's attention the anticipated psychological costs of the removal. The Los
Angeles Japanese branch reported that "the younger girls are so concerned
about the long-time results of this evacuation. They fear that they will become
an 'outcast group' so that when they are free again to move about the country
such fear and animosity will have grown up about them that they will be ostra-
cized" (Ellis & Ingraham, April 1942, p. 189). The JAEP's "first emphasis was on
helping the evacuees improve their living conditions within the centers, helping
them to adjust to new conditions" (YWCA National Board—Community
Division Committee, 1944, p. 2).

To this end, its proposed programs were: the "supervision of housing units
for single and unattached women and girls" (YWCA of the U.S.A., May 1942,
p. 260) to provide "protection and security which would normally come through
a family unit (YWCA National Board, 1942, p. 2); "counseling, providing trained
leadership (speaking the Japanese language) to deal with personal and family
problems which are bound to arise" (YWCA National Board, 1942, p. 2); and the
"development of an educational and recreational program in the realm of arts,

*Facilitating Injustice: The complicity of social workers in the forced removal and incarceration of Japanese Americans,
1941–1946.* Yoosun Park, Oxford University Press (2020). © Oxford University Press.
DOI: 10.1093/acprof:oso/9780199765058.001.0001

family relationships, work problems, religion and health" (YWCA of the U.S.A., May 1942).

The YWCA chapters, eventually established in all ten relocation camps and one Department of Justice internment camp in Crystal City, Texas, replicated local associations and clubs, including Girl Reserves for young girls, and business clubs and young matron's clubs for the older girls and women. Through JAEP programs, the YWCA aimed to thwart the tedium of incarcerated life and the various social ills predicted to arise from the "abnormal communities" (Briesemeister, 1946, p. 21) of the camps in which the "stabilizing influence" (YWCA of the U.S.A., 1942b, p. 1) of family life were severely compromised. The YWCA surmised that the lives of women, without household duties to anchor their lives and "lack of interesting work to replace the usual home responsibilities" (Lyle, 1943, p. 1), were particularly altered in the unhealthy "mass living" (Briesemeister & North, 1942, p. 2) situation of the camps. The JAEP intended for the clubs to provide "a constructive influence in the building of morale, the development of leadership, personal growth and the taking of responsibility as citizens of the community" (YWCA National Board, 1942, p. 3).

The YWCA workers saw the camps as an unhealthy environment not only for the Nikkei but also for the Caucasian staff employed in them. Lilian Sharpley (1943) noted that, at Topaz, most of the Caucasian women worked, but those "Caucasian women who didn't work had nothing to occupy their time since all eat in the dining hall" (p. 4); they did not have housework to occupy their time. Such women, she opined, "probably need a Y. [YWCA services and programs] as badly as the residents" (p. 4). According to Mrs. Roscoe Bell, an employee in the Housing Unit of the Welfare section and the wife of the Topaz Chief of Community Services, "competition, departmental jealousy, and pettiness were rife" among the staff, and "the discord and lack of cooperation among the Japanese was a reflection of the disunity among the Caucasians" (cited in Sharpley, 1943, p. 4). Esther Briesemeister's (1946) assessment that the Nikkei "residents" perspectives "become very narrow with a great deal of emphasis put on their own individual problems" (p. 20) clearly applied also to the Caucasians. Sharpley's (1943) reflections on Topaz, that she had "never seen a place where a group work program was needed so badly—for morale, group understanding of problems and leadership development" (p. 4)—was a commentary not only on the state of the Nikkei inmates also on but that of the Appointed Personnel (AP) Caucasians and the divided community that the two groups comprised.

JAEP was directed by Helen Flack, described as "a Western woman who understands local attitudes" (Watson, 1942, p. 1). Staff dedicated to the program, including Betty Lyle, an established Girl Reserves leader, and Esther Briesemeister, experienced in working with older girls and women, were "the best the Association has to offer" (Watson, 1942, p. 1), according to Annie Clo

Watson, who, for the bulk of the war, would take leave from her job as the head of the San Francisco International Institute to work on the JAEP. Though not administratively tied to the program but playing a key role was Mable B. Ellis, former Secretary of the Committee on Refugees, assigned by the National Board in March to "act as liaison officer between the National Board and the Federal Government and within the National Board itself at the point of service to 'those who because of racial and nationality background will have the greatest difficulties at this time'" (YWCA of the U.S.A., 1942a, p. 1).

In July of 1942, Ellis, in her role as liaison to the federal government, met to discuss the YWCA's goals for the camps with Grace Coyle, the consultant hired by the War Relocation Authority (WRA) to design social services in the camps. Ellis's report (1942) sketches a hesitant Coyle, who hoped that "something can be done by private organizations" (p. 2) such as the YWCA, but was skeptical of both the YWCA's motives and capabilities. Coyle iterated the "fear felt by some of the War Relocation Authority staff of so-called proselytizing or attempts to exploit the Japanese for the sake of boosting the prestige of the private agency" (p. 2). Emphasizing the WRA's desire "to have the Japanese themselves determine what is to be done in the relocation Centers" (p. 2), she warned against "pressing too hard" (p. 2) to be allowed in the camps and made it clear "that Caucasian consultants would be allowed in the Relocation Centers for short periods only and not too often" (p. 2).

Ellis, however, had arrived armed with written requests for YWCA services from Nell Findley, a social worker serving as the Chief of Community Services at Poston, and Elmer Shirrell, her counterpart at Tule Lake (Ellis, 1942). By policy, the camp chapters were self-generated. The "national YWCA did not send a representative to any relocation center until a request had come from the residents stating their desire to have a YWCA and asking for the services of the national staff. A visit to the center was then put into the travel schedule and the secretary working in these communities began an active correspondence with those most interested in starting the organization" (Briesemeister, 1946, p. 12). The visits began with meetings with members of the administration such as the Project Director, Director of Community Services, Director of Community Activities, and the Superintendent and Principals of the of camp schools, as well as with Nikkei religious and secular leaders. "This made it possible to gauge community attitudes in preparation for the meeting where representatives from the various community groups were to discuss the possibility of starting a YWCA" (p. 12). Such meetings, moreover, established crucial relationships that would allow the fieldworkers to continuously track the shifting "community patterns" (p. 12) within the camps. As Briesemeister explained, "a worker had to try to keep up with political and social developments. The authority to represent the majority of the people rests in a variety of different places. It was important to know who the 'behind the scenes' groups were if possible" (p. 21).

Coyle also forewarned that the YWCA would have great difficulties in finding able personnel among the incarcerated Nikkei; she had identified only seven with professional experience and training in casework and seven more with experience in group work. Nikkei leadership for YWCA programs would indeed prove an ongoing difficulty, especially as the WRA's resettlement program began funneling the skilled and confident Nisei out of the camps. While they remained in the camps, however, the YWCA's work was facilitated by the many Nikkei and Caucasian administrative staffers (or their wives) who came to the camps with established YWCA ties. These included Varina Merritt, a former YWCA board member in the San Francisco Bay Area and the wife of Manzanar Center Director. Margaret D'Ille, a Japanese-speaking social worker who eventually became the Director of Manzanar's Welfare Division, had a decade of experience as Executive Secretary for YWCA in Japan (Woodsmall, 1942). Granada's Catherine Ludy, a junior high school teacher, and Grace Lewis, a high school teacher, were former Girl Reserve club advisers (North, 1942). Mrs. Herbert Walther, wife of Granada's junior high school principal, had been a Public Affairs chairman in the Denver Association (Briesemeister, 1942). Many such women, "vitally interested in this whole question of democracy and its apparent breakdown in regard to the Japanese evacuation" (Briesemeister, 1942, p. 4), were scattered throughout the ten camps and were tapped to provide leadership and guidance.

There were also many Nikkei women with YWCA ties. Several leaders from the Los Angeles Japanese Branch were at Granada: Mrs. Takayama, a former member of the board of directors (Briesemeister, 1944a), Sumi Kashiwagi and Mrs. Yamasaki who had served as "Chairman of the Committee of Management" (Mukaye, 1942, p. 4), and Hana Uno, a Girl Reserves Advisor (North, 1942). Sophie Torimui, a Girl Reserves Secretary at the same Los Angeles branch, was at Heart Mountain (Nakamura, 1942). Granada also boasted Yuri Domoto, a former caseworker in the Alameda (California) County Welfare Department who had been an active member the Student YWCA at UC Berkeley (Mukaye, 1942). Six women at Jerome had been involved with the YWCA (Briesemeister, 1943b). An estimated 300 former members of the San Francisco YWCA, and 25–50 members of the University of California YWCA were imprisoned at Topaz (Hayashi, 1942).

The core YWCA programs consisted of multiple membership groups for various age groups of "girls from twelve years of age up—Girl Reserve program for school girls, business and industrial program for girls above high school age and home women's program" (Flack, 1942, p. 1). Multiple groups such as Girl Reserves, business and professional clubs, matrons' groups, and in some camps such as Granada, dedicated groups for Issei women, were established in the camps. The YWCA's method was to aid the club members in developing a program of activities "based on interests and initiative of the group in the realm of arts, family relationships, work problems, religion, health and recreation" (Flack, 1942, p. 1); the JAEP fieldworkers provided ongoing support through frequent visits and continuous correspondence. At its first-year anniversary in July 1943, the Manzanar YWCA reported a total of 30 clubs in operation (Kusayanagi, 1943). The Girl Reserves, the largest of the groups, emphasized members' "character development while in their most impressionable ages" (Morimitsu & Waller, 1942, p. 7) in order to aid them to "discover inner security and confidence" (Reith, 1943b, p. 3). Unlike the Girl Reserves, the matrons' groups at the various camps were usually composed of a mixed group of "the wives of the administrative workers and the colonists" (Amache Young Women's Christian Association, 1942, p. 1). Often hosted by a female staff member or the wife of an administrator in her home, they were likely the only settings in which the Nikkei and the Caucasians met regularly on at least theoretically equal footing within the camps. The business and professional clubs were for older girls and women interested in pursuing professional careers. The members at Topaz, for example, were said to be "a highly skilled group—teachers, social workers, stenographers etc." (Sharpley, 1943, p. 3), many of whom were employed in the camp's social welfare department (Reith, 1943a, p. 2) and interested in preparing for jobs outside.

While total club membership numbers are difficult to estimate, some sense of the scale can be gauged from the archived records: in the summer of 1942, early in its development, the Tule Lake chapter reported that a total of 90 girls were involved in the Reserves (Morimitsu & Waller, 1942, p. 7). Sally Kusayanagi (1943), the General Secretary of the Manzanar YWCA, reported that, a year after its inception, membership totaled 539. Approximately 80 women reportedly attended the Young Matron's Meeting at Manzanar in late July of 1942; an estimated 300 attended the Older Women's Meeting in early August (Briesemeister & Flack, 1942). Amache reported in June of 1943 that a total of 407 girls and women were members of various YWCA groups (Amache Young Women's Christian Association, 1943, p. 2).

"Undesired and Undesirable Proximity"

One indication of the JAEP's influence in the camps was its remarkable ability to claim dedicated spaces in the overcrowded camps. Despite extreme shortages in housing stock which beleaguered every camp, the JAEP managed to push for the establishment of separate dormitories for single girls and women in several camps. The JAEP also successfully lobbied to carve out dedicated facilities in each camp for "club meetings, informal social activities, small discussion groups, and etc." (Briesemeister, 1943d, p. 4). Furnished usually through in-kind donations from outside associations, funding from the YWCA National Board, and the labor and creativity of the Nikkei membership, the clubhouses became multifunctional spaces. At Manzanar, the "clubhouse is used all of the time, either by YWCA groups or other community groups. It is the scene of many weddings, receptions, etc." (Briesemeister, 1943c, p. 2). Tule Lake had two "1/ 2 buildings in different sections of the community" (Briesemeister, 1943d, p. 3) furnished with the help of the San Francisco YWCA (Reith, 1943b, p. 13). The curtains "made of two shades of blue denim" (Briesemeister, 1943a, p. 1) hung in the Amache (Granada) clubhouse, "by far the most attractive and best equipped YWCA building," (Briesemeister, 1943a, p. 1), were sent by the YWCA in Pueblo, Colorado. The Denver YWCA's Thursday Night Club provided construction paper and other office supplies. "I was there four nights and the building was filled to capacity each evening," with a variety co-ed programs for youth and adults, noted Briesemeister (1943a, p. 1). These spaces, the "brightest spots in the community and the only places with comfortable chairs, gay curtains and a sense of home" (Briesemeister, 1943c, p. 2) were all the more important because the spaces outside of them were so abysmal.

The inmate housing at the camps was not only makeshift but grossly overcrowded. "Monterey sardines," JERS researcher Tamie Tsuchiyama put it, had "nothing on the Japanese families when it comes to being packed in" (1942, p. 3). In most camps, the task of managing the various issues related to housing both AP and the Nikkei fell to the welfare departments. Given the inadequate facilities—in both quality and quantity—in the camps, Housing Services was an ongoing struggle for the department's personnel. Noting that the "girls making the housing assignments are almost physical wrecks," Charles Kikuchi (1942a) described a few of the housing issues that came into the Gila Welfare Department in September of 1942.

Mr. K's family wants a room nearer the toilet. The wife is ill and she cannot walk a half block to the latrine. Mr. M. and Mr. O.'s family are now quarreling. 7 grown-ups in one room, three of whom are invalids. Mr. O. has a rasping cough at night and it keeps all parties within awake at night. Mr. O. claims that it is Mr. M's fault, because he grinds his teeth loudly. Mrs. A. is a mental case. She has a doctor's note to have an apartment for her family alone, but there are no available apartments yet. The other family never knew them before and they are afraid that she may commit violence upon their young child. And so it goes on an endless stream. Something will have to be done to give all individual families separate apartments, but this is impossible with the present proposed population. (p. 11)

Tamie Tsuchiyama's description of the barracks at Poston, included in his analysis of the housing sitution, was a blueprint for how quarters were allotted to the inmates across the camps.

> A barrack is usually divided into four apartments, and of these, 3 apartments are 24' long by 20' wide while the fourth is 28' long by 20' wide. A 24' by 20' apartment has a square footage of 480 square feet. A standard army steel cot is 2.5' wide and 6.75' long, or 16.875 square feet. Now there is usually a space of a 2' × 6.75' flooring reserved between each bed. If there were 8 persons assigned, to an apartment of 20' x 24' it means a total of 135 square feet for beds and a total of 108 square feet reserved as space between beds, adding to the total figure 243 square feet given to bed space alone, and which is more than 1/2 of the entire floor space of the apartment. Granting that the 8 people can easily sleep in the 243 square feet thus allotted, how can they be expected to live in the small space that is the balance of the 480 square feet? (p. 3)

It was an arrangement that violated the occupancy standards of the United States Housing Authority published in 1940. "Even allowing for flexibility to meet changing conditions, it is obvious that minimum standards of privacy by any standard are being flagrantly violated at the centers," was a conclusion reached by the Community Management Division which oversaw Welfare and Housing (War Relocation Authority, n.d.-a, p. 1).

The overcrowded quarters were, moreover, in poorly built structures equipped with only the most rudimentary fittings. Bill Tanaka (1942), a block manager at Poston, reported in October of 1942 that, four months after opening, the barracks still lacked anything resembling real floors, ceilings, and wall coverings to keep out the elements. There was "unbearable heat in the barracks; dust and soot all over everything; flies, crickets, dragon flies, etc., buzzing in and out the open windows and doors" (Tanaka, 1942, p. 1). Such spaces "could hardly be called homes, even temporary homes" (Tanaka, 1942, p. 1). The flagrant violation of housing standards, moreover, was not a temporary phenomenon. Many of the problems identified by Tanaka remained still in 1944, according to Phyllis Kinoshita, author of a memorandum entitled "Crisis in housing situation" (p. 1) in Poston. She reported that nearly 500 families shared quarters with other families: 394 cases of two families sharing space, 82 cases in which three families shared, and 16 cases in which four families were cramped together, usually without partitions of any kind to divide the shared space. There were points in the history of Minidoka, (Kimmerling, Fite, & Abbott, 1945), when even such shared quarters might have been preferable to the reality of living in facilities intended as recreation halls, separated only by makeshift barriers that did not "afford proper privacy nor warmth" (p. 14).

Such "unendurable housing situation" (Kinoshita, 1944, p. 1) which forced families to live huddled together was "a constant source of irritation and friction within these households" (p. 1). They incited "hatred and contempt between strange families, immediate families, and life-long friends due to lack of privacy and also due to "paper thin" walls" (Tanaka, 1942, p. 1). For the many families at Minidoka—numbering 96 at the start of 1944—who were forced to share housing, "jealousy arose, which led to serious family disturbances. In all cases there was unrest and embarrassment due to this condition" (p. 14). The conditions were "directly related to the morale of the evacuees" (C. Kikuchi, 1942d, p. 89) and affected "family adjustment" (Kimmerling et al., 1945, p. 14). "Crowding" families into unpartitioned apartments lacking any facility for privacy, moreover, was especially problematic for those with adult or teen-aged children, who inevitably "went outside of the home to find recreation and in a sense, privacy or escape from the crowded home" (p. 14), likely into the feared realm of juvenile delinquency.

> Housing conditions, it was generally agreed, contributed to child welfare problems. Lack of privacy in the home, the need of a proper place for young people to entertain friends in the evening, and the separation of family units at meal time, all had a tendency to weaken parental control. Parents were very much concerned over this situation. It was the topic of frequent discussion, both in case conferences and in group meetings. (Department of State, 1945, p. 1)

Given, as Kinoshita declared, the "conclusive peril to the morale and general welfare of the people" (1944, p. 1) that the overcrowded barracks represented, the task of sorting housing assignments and problems assigned to camp Welfare Sections did make some sense. But because the constant shortage in housing gave the department little room, literally, to maneuver any changes in assignments of quarters, whatever problems it caused in families, housing services was a loathed assignment for its personnel. Charles Kikuchi (1942b) bemoaned that some "come in and plead for a room; others are very belligerant and demanding; other get threatening. But what can we do for these cases when there is no room?" (p. 31). An excerpt from the proceedings of the Block Manager's meeting of September 18, 1942, at Poston cites a housing worker who reported that 12 apartments were kept for use in the case of "serious social problems" (Tsuchiyama, 1942, p. 39) but far more were needed. As of that date, there were 173 applications for small apartments that the department "considered urgent" (Tsuchiyama, 1942, p. 39). Kinoshita's report on Poston in 1944 noted that there was not a single unused quarter to which "maladjusted families and emergency cases can be moved" (p. 1), though there were a number of cases in which some change was obviously necessary.

Custodial Care

Construction of hospitals, like most camp facilities, had not been completed by the opening of the camps and functioned only "on an emergency basis" (YWCA National Board—Race Relations Subcommitee of the National Public Affairs Committee, 1946, p. 2) for many months after. The WRA's Semi-Annual Report for the second half of 1943 noted that the crisis of care for the elderly and the ill was worsening in the camps, "aggravated by the departure of younger family members on relocation and the increasing shortage of professional health personnel" (War Relocation Authority, 1943d, p. 70). The WRA's Resettlement Program—a planned ejection of the incarcerated population out of the camps and into the Midwest and East—took a toll on not only family care but on the crucial staff power provided by Nikkei physicians and nurses, even as "increasing number of tuberculosis cases have been discovered in the centers" (M. Kikuchi, 1942a, p. 3).

> Heretofore, with a number of these persons cared for in family barracks, the small number who lacked such family care could be cared for in the hospital. However, by the close of 1943, hospital facilities could neither be expanded to provide for additional patients of this type nor be considered adequate to retain such patients already hospitalized. (War Relocation Authority, 1943d, p. 70)

According to G. D. Carlyle Thompson, the WRA's Chief Medical Officer, hospitals were necessary in the camps because their remote locations made them "without resources of city and county facilities usually available to cities of comparable population" (Thompson, 1943b, p. 1). Utilization rates of the hospitals in the concentration camps, where people were forced to live "without running water, toilet facilities or cooking facilities" (Thompson, 1943b, p. 1), with "no corner drug stores" (Thompson, 1943b, p. 1), were also higher than in "a normal community" (Thompson, 1943b, p. 1). The WRA calculated that, in the second quarter of 1942 (July 1 though September 30) the time period just after most camps began operations, approximately 5,800 individuals were admitted to camp hospitals, 750 were referred to external resources, and 125,000 outpatient visits, excluding dentistry and optometry, were logged (War Relocation Authority, 1942, p. 19).

The busy camp hospitals were, however, persistently understaffed. Thompson described, in June of 1943, the acute problem at the hospital in Manzanar, a camp whose population peaked at 10,046.

First, there is no surgeon at Manzanar fully competent to undertake a wide variety of major surgery. The physicians are able to perform simple abdominal work but because of their limited skill the time required for any particular operation is several times that of a skilled surgeon. Secondly, with the loss of all qualified X-Ray and laboratory technicians, it became and still is necessary for the physicians to perform certain essential work in these fields. By no means can they have time to perform all of the work that should be done. Third, the number of registered nurses at Manzanar as of the date of the report was one registered nurse for 34 hospital patients. We have been attempting to not exceed 1 to 21. Fourth, there is the factor of considerable isolation at Manzanar with no nearby assistance. (Thompson, 1943a, pp. 1–2)

The lowest ratio for safe nursing care, by the WRA's own admission, was one nurse to 21 patients (War Relocation Authority, 1943d, p. 71). The staffing problem was even worse at Rohwer, Minidoka, and Heart Mountain (Thompson, 1943a). Recruitment efforts for both doctors and nurses were plagued by the same issues as those for social workers. Given the national labor shortage, competent nurses and physicians were in high demand in much more appealing locales and settings. "Many rejections are based purely on the fact of the Japanese aspect of the work. Others are the rural locations" (p. 2). Consequently, noted Thompson, those medical professionals the WRA did manage to bring on were "not likely to be of the highest caliber" (p. 2).

Despite these acknowledged difficulties, Thompson insisted that no patient "considered in need of hospital care is denied admission because of the lack of hospital beds" (p. 3). The determination of that need was, however, a point of conflict. Charles Kikuchi (1942c), for one, reported that he frequently encountered clients who needed hospitalization but had been denied it by the hospital. One such case was a frail 68-year-old man, "alone in the world" (p. 168), who had been resident at the Stockton, California, hospital for several months prior to removal to the Fresno detention center, and he spent the duration there in hospital before being transferred to Gila River. In mid-November of 1942, Kikuchi reported that the man was suffering from persistent asthma which made him cough "incessantly day and night" (p. 168).

He went up to the doctors for hospitalization but they only gave him some medicine for a cold and refused to take him in. I sent in a note to them asking them to check up on the case from a medical standpoint. The doctors have so many cases that they are reluctant to accept only the most serious cases for hospitalization. (p. 168)

He was finally admitted to hospital in early December, 20 days after Kikuchi's referral.

On November 23, Mrs. Hoffman, the Public Health nurse, sent a note to Dr. Sleath saying that the man was visited and cough medicine given. An X-ray was taken of his chest to determine if he had chronic asthma. Finally, on December 4, the man was admitted to the hospital. He was put in the T. B. Ward because he had tuberculosis. (Kikuchi, 1943a, p. 125)

The issue was close to home for Kikuchi. His father, who had suffered a stroke in Tanforan and had been sent out of that detention center to be treated as an inpatient at San Luis Obispo hospital. He had finally been transferred to the Hospital at Gila to join his family who were moved from the detention center to the WRA incarceration camp several months before. Soon after his arrival, even before the medical records from San Luis Obispo Hospital had arrived, the Gila hospital moved to discharge him to the care of his family. He was "absolutely helpless and bedridden" (Kikuchi, 1943c, p. 2), but the hospital was short staffed. Kikuchi worried that the family did not have "any equipment at all to give him proper care—sheets, bedpans, hospital beds, etc." (p. 3) in the barracks and that the burden care would overtax his mother, who herself suffered from dubious health.

The need to develop special housing facilities for patients like Charles Kikuchi's father and other "blind, semi-invalids, and feeble aged" (M. Kikuchi, 1942b, p. 2) individuals requiring some level of institutional care, quickly became obvious in all the camps. Those in this category at Manzanar included a blind man who was temporarily housed in the hospital but needed a long-term plan of care and a paralyzed woman whose care, provided for by kindly neighbors, would discontinue when those neighbors began work (Payne, 1944). Those noted by Marie Dresden Lane (1944), the Washington Head of Welfare at the WRA, in a November 1944 memo to Bureau of Public Assistance (BPA) Director Jane Hoey, had all been cared for in institutions prior to the removal: a man with chronic arthritis who had resided in Bakersfield Old Age Home in California; another who had been paralyzed by a stroke in 1941 and had lived as a patient in the Visalia County Hospital; an elderly woman with senile dementia who had lived in the LA County Hospital for 20 years prior to removal; and another with partial paralysis who had been a patient in Monterey County Hospital in Salinas for several years prior to removal.

Housing the numerous "bachelors"—elderly Issei men without families—was a difficulty in all the camps where barracks allotment, however inadequate, was designed for family clusters and no single spaces were available. The usual solution was to group several men to live together in shared, unpartitioned barracks. But because it was not always feasible to house together only "those congenial to each other" (Kimmerling et al., 1945, p. 14), "[m]any distressing conditions arose from this situation" (Kimmerling et al., 1945, p. 14).[1] More importantly, these predominately "elderly and often disabled" (Dusseldorp, 1945, p. 16) single men required care but were without family support. In the incarceration camps, short on hospital beds and professional services and reliant on families for the care of the aged and infirm, they were a problematic population. Rohwer Head Counselor Wilma Dusseldorp (1945) recounted that Nikkei community leaders and Welfare Section staff were concerned about "the unmet needs" (p. 16) of the bachelors from the earliest days of the department's operations. Some of the men were bed-ridden and needed "services such as appropriately prepared diet, help with housekeeping, laundry work and recreation" (p. 16). One Nikkei Counseling Aide's survey of the community, accomplished with the cooperation of Block Managers, identified more than 500 who were "either disabled through age or physical disability, or in need of some special services which the Center did not provide" (p. 16).

The solutions were slow in development. Minidoka was the first to designate, in the winter of 1942, two residential blocks for the use of "families needing frequent or regular hospital treatment, and who were not ill enough to be hospitalized" (Kimmerling et al., 1945, p. 14). It was only in the latter half of 1943 that Manzanar and Poston developed similar "Convalescent Barracks, Hostels or Custodial Barracks near the hospitals and under the hospital's direction" (War Relocation Authority, 1943d, p. 70) designed to provide "minimum sanitary facilities and small serving kitchens for groups of 20 to 30 patients" (War Relocation Authority, 1943d, p. 70) who needed supervised care but were not acutely ill. The creation of the Custodial Care Hostel at Heart Mountain was still stalled in 1944. In March of that year, Virgil Payne, head of the Social Service Unit, reported that the Nikkei Community Council had written to the Washington office reproving the long delay and specifying that work on the Care Hostel was at a standstill because labor was continuously being funneled instead to "provide fancy apartments for the Administrative homes" (Payne, 1944, p. 1). Similarly, at Rohwer, for the span of a year from the Spring of 1943 to that of 1944, the Welfare Section submitted several memoranda, to both the Chief of

---

[1] Kimmerling reported that single older women in the camp, a "more delicate problem" (1945, p. 14) than the men, were far fewer in number and the group barracks created for them did boast partitions.

the Community Management Division and the Project Director, noting the need and recommending the creation of a "Nursing Home."

> Having once established the fact that budget limitations did not permit the building of a structure to be used as a Nursing Home, the only alternative was that of remodeling at least one barrack for the housing of those residents in need of, and desiring, special services that could be made available to them if they lived in the same block. (p. 16)

The plan of converting existing barracks space was a controversial one because it required the move of multiple families already occupying the targeted block. In April of 1944, after many conferences with community representatives, the Camp Director finally chose a block of barracks to be converted into a space for custodial care. After a great deal of confusion and conflict and an initial refusal by the block residents to move, as well as the usual delays in construction, the care facility was finally opened for occupation at the end of the Summer of 1944. A Nikkei couple who had operated a nursing home for elderly men in Los Angeles prior to removal were hired as resident managers.

> By September, 1944, the new plan was fully operating; the one barrack for boarding home cases, under the administration of the Hospital; three other barracks housing the feeble men in need of laundry service and special diets. Representatives of several church groups, and other organizations, took an interest in helping to furnish and decorate the Infirmary, as the nursing unit was called, and assisted in developing some recreational activities for the occupants of the other barracks. Admissions to the Infirmary were approved by the Medical Social worker, admission to the other barracks was approved by the Housing Unit of the Welfare Section. (p. 18)

The medical social worker whose approval was necessary for admission to the infirmary was attached to the Health, rather than the Welfare Section, of the camp. In the second semi-annual report for 1943, the WRA (1943d) reported that nine of the ten camps had instituted a medical social work program. The medical social workers in the program coordinated services between the health and other divisions within the camp and took over many tasks from the medical staff: sending medical reports to welfare and employment divisions, conducting "marriage certificates interviews," and working with "crippled children which included everything from ordering special shoes to helping with arrangements for a special class in the hospital" (Thompson, 1943b, p. 4). The medical social workers also seem to have made great efforts to organize recreational activities— soliciting ideas and donations of materials from several sources for arts and crafts projects and puzzles and Bingo games—for hospitalized patients (Pirrone, 1944; Scott, 1944; Shipps, 1943), including the tubercular, who were often deeply isolated from the community.

Several experienced social workers were on staff in the camps. Miss Teresa Pirrone at Granada, had two years of postgraduate work in medical social work at Western Reserve University and three years of experience in the Social Service Department at University Hospitals. Mrs. Josephine L. Wilson at Gila River had approximately nine years of experience in general social work prior to completing her master's degree in medical social work at Washington University. Minidoka's Miss Dorothy Cram was also a graduate of the MSW program at Washington University and was on leave from the University of Oklahoma, where she had been teaching medical and psychiatric social work and had worked for a year as the head of social work at the Iowa tuberculosis sanatorium (Shipps, 1943). Two Nikkei women, unnamed in the reports, were in charge of medical social work at Tule Lake and Topaz, supervised by a Caucasian staff person per WRA policy (Thompson, 1943c).

Treating "Mental Cases"

In writing about the many conflicts arising from the housing crunch, Minidoka's Welfare Department (Kimmerling, Fite, & Abbott, 1945) observed that it was easy to see that "case-work and careful counseling was necessary in order to adjust any of these conditions to a point where living was tenable" (p. 15). In some cases, the client's situation could be "bettered through adjustment of living conditions" (p. 15) within the limits of the possibilities within the camps. But although custodial living spaces could be created, orphans could be moved to barracks with or near those "who were acquired to care for them" (p. 15), and some family troubles were ameliorated through judicious changes in living arrangements, there were also many cases in which a housing shift was insufficient to the need. The camps, like any other sizeable communities, contained their share of people suffering from a variety of mental illnesses.

According to Berta Choda (1946), one time Assistant Counselor of the Heart Mountain Welfare Section, "Serious emotional problems and mental breakdowns among the evacuees were not infrequent" (p. 143). The "mental cases" the camp hospitals diagnosed included a wide variety of conditions "ranging all the way from minor personality maladjustments to definite psychosis" (Kimmerling et al., 1945, p. 29), including "nervous breakdown" (Shibutani, 1943e, p. 40), "suicidal ideation" (Shibutani, 1943e, p. 37), "manic depression" (C. Kikuchi, 1942a, p. 117), "menopausal psychosis" (Carstarphen, 1943, p. 1), "dementia praecox" (Shibutani, 1943e, p. 40), and "chorea dementia" (Kikuchi,

1943c, p. 294). A common diagnosis was "psycho-neurotic breakdown" (War Relocation Authority, 1943a, p. 12). The WRA reported in June of 1943 that Tule Lake's Social Welfare Department tallied more than a dozen such cases "all of them interestingly enough exhibiting symptoms of a persecutory nature" (p. 12). The report cited as primary examples a number of women whose husbands were incarcerated in Department of Justice internment camps, whose conditions were described as "delicate emotional problems in which caste-feeling and persecutory elements are both present" (War Relocation Authority, 1943a, p. 12). An example of a case of "caste-feeling" was a "mentally well-balanced and emotionally stable" woman who "confided that she hates to 'look at' Caucasians when she talks to them now, and finds it most embarrassing" (War Relocation Authority, 1943a, p. 12). An example of a case showing "persecutory elements" was an "obviously unbalanced woman" who confessed to feeling "that people generally are talking about her and laughing at her: that all have lost their sense of courtesy and politeness and that she is becoming 'white' and unrecognizable" (War Relocation Authority, 1943a, p. 12).

These were problems that "might have been helped by psychiatric treatment or consultation" (Kimmerling et al., 1945, p. 29). The camps, however, were without facilities or providers for such treatment. Psychiatric diagnoses at the camp hospitals were made by the various general practitioners, obstetricians, and other physicians who were on hand. Some "mental cases" arrived in the camps already labeled as such by hospitals or social welfare departments in detention centers which had also lacked clinical expertise. In reviewing the case records of a woman who had been diagnosed with "a persecution complex" (p. 75) while she was at Tulare detention center, Charles Kikuchi concluded that the workers involved "had made all sorts of diagnoses and even had figured out the nature of her mental illness without benefit of any professional help. It seemed to me that they only reflected their own prejudices in this case" (p. 75).

As in most cases of nontangible problems, the needs of the "insane" tended to be discovered indirectly, through housing services or in the process of "discussions about other needs" such clothing or cash assistance, which the inmates felt "they could apply for . . . more readily" (Kimmerling et al., 1945, p. 29) than for help for mental conditions. The referrals also came through the internal security personnel called in to deal with domestic disputes or other incidents of violence or conflict. Neither the untrained and inadequately staffed Welfare Sections nor the equally overtaxed and underresourced Health Sections were, however, equipped to provide necessary care. That "the diagnostic and treatment skills of the welfare and health departments were severely challenged" (Choda, 1946, p. 142) was an understatement. Minidoka's Welfare Section (1945) deemed that the "most serious lack in case-work facilities, aside from the inadequacy of staff, was the absence of psychiatric facilities" (p. 30).

There was only one psychiatrist in the State of Idaho and he was with the Veteran's Administration. An attempt was made, through the Washington Office, to arrange a plan for sharing the services of this psychiatrist, but it was never effected. (p. 30)

The only way for a patient at Minidoka to access psychiatric services was to be committed to an outside institution.[2]

The Welfare Sections were short on workers trained in even basic casework. There were no psychiatric social workers among the staff of the welfare departments; only one medical social worker across all camp hospitals had any training in psychiatric social work. Charles Kikuchi (1943a) recounted that a friend who led a boxing club for boys had come seeking advice about a young "kleptomaniac" shunned by the others. Kikuchi, a supervisor in the social work department and one of the most experienced among its staff despite only having spent one year as an MSW student, advised his friend that "the boy was in need of psychiatric care and a close follow up of the family situation" (p. 94). Kikuchi admitted that he "would not know what to do with the case" (p. 94) since he could not provide "intensive care and follow it up" (p. 94). Without a psychiatrist, moreover, all he could do was "read the books and keep one step ahead" (p. 94) of the coach as he worked with the boy to change his behavior.

Few means were available to the social workers in managing mentally ill clients: (1) to confine them in their barracks to isolate them from the community; or, (2) in hopes of avoiding identified points of conflict, move them out of one barrack to a different one or to a different camp to be cared for by a different set of relatives; or, (3) finally, send them out of the camp for institutionalization on the outside. None of these options was easy to accomplish. The disposition of the case of a young boy "mentally confused, disoriented as to time and, partially, as to place" and "entertaining ideas of suicide" (Shibutani, 1943e, p. 37) was an example of the first. Noting that the boy asked him "several times about the best methods and if I possessed a 'gat' with which he could blow out his brains," Tule Lake Chief Medical Officer, A. B. Carson's "snapshot impression" was that the boy suffered from "a hebi-phrenic type of schizophrenia" (Shibutani, 1943e, p. 37). The boy was sent home from the hospital and, a few weeks later, had

---

[2] Amache camp was reported to have convened an internal medical board to review cases of "the insane" and "the problem of protection, both to the patients, the center and those people contiguous to the patient" (War Relocation Authority, 1943a, p. 12). Their task was "to make factual and scientific determination of his or her status with recommendation and ultimate disposition" (War Relocation Authority, 1943a, p. 12). Given the staffing problems in both Welfare and Health, it is unclear who comprised the board and how scientific determinations were made; the medical board seems another example of a camp program that looked far better on paper than on the ground.

"another spell and was confined to his apartment for a week. A few weeks later when his condition improved, he was assigned to the mess division, helping the truck drivers to supply food to the mess hall—nothing else seems to have been done" (Shibutani, 1943e, p. 34).

The case of Mr. M., a married man with seven children, was an example of the second option of housing shift as intervention. He came to the attention of the administration because of an incident during which he "broke the partition between his room and that of his wife and became violent. His daughter jumped out of the window and ran to the warden's headquarters" (Shibutani, 1943c, p. 60) for help. Mr. M. was arrested by the camp police and sent to the hospital for observation. The perpetually understaffed camp hospitals was, as usual, short of bed space and both unable and unwilling to keep such patients long term; it recommended sending him out of the camp to be institutionalized. But because the family objected and insisted that he be kept in the camp—and also, presumably, because convincing a state institution to accept a Nikkei patient was not a simple matter for the administration—Mr. M. was ultimately released back to the family. The police, understandably, felt that "the care of the insane" (Shibutani, 1943c, p. 60) should not be its responsibility, as it often became when patients such as Mr. M. were released back into the general population without treatment. But the only measure taken, ultimately, was to move him to a different block, away from his family quarters. The last report on Mr. M. "was that he is still unbalanced" (Shibutani, 1943c, p. 60).

As discussed previously, changing housing arrangements was difficult to effect in the camps. The case of 31-year-old Mr. A., noted as a "mental case," was one in which housing modification was desperately needed but unavailable. Mr. A. had come to Poston under the care of Mr. K., an unrelated man with a seven children, who had looked after Mr. A since his parents "disowned him as a hopeless case" (Tanaka, 1942, p. 2). The kindly arrangement which appeared to have worked in normal circumstances became impossible to maintain in the tiny unpartitioned quarters in which the K. family of eight and Mr. A. were cramped together. Although creating a partitioned room within the family quarters was the desired solution, it was not possible to accomplish because materials to build the partition were unobtainable. Mr. A. was moved instead to separate quarters to live by himself "with nobody looking after him" (Tanaka, 1942, p. 2). During the day, Mr. A.'s new quarters were used by another patient, a 41-year-old married woman who lived with her husband and four children and was said to have been "suffering from nervousness due to menopause" (Tanaka, 1942, p. 2) for several years. Block Manager Bill Tanaka reported that the woman's condition, which had been manageable prior to the removal from her California home, deteriorated in the camp.

Since coming here, it has been aggravated, because of the unnecessary crowded quarters. It was during the worst dust storm when the roofs were blown off, that the anxiety over the safety of the children further accentuated her nervousness. Now her condition is getting worse instead of improving, and the hospital has refused to let her stay because of the shortage of single rooms. Now, during the day she is staying in the room which Mr. A. now occupies, because every little noise, as the rattle of the door, irritates her. In the evenings she returns to sleep with the family. This is another case waiting for that much needed partitions. I was informed that unless I separated and placed her in a quiet room she would go insane, so I have made the best possible arrangement under the circumstances. The cause for her illness and suffering lies partly in the children also. If they should be out playing or dancing, she would go out and get them, even in her nightgown. Then she would scold them and sometimes strike them not knowing what she was doing, because of her illness. So the separation would benefit her and the children as well. Her children are all very young, still being in the teen ages. (p. 2)

"Mental Disease has been one of the most difficult problems to handle in many of the Centers, even for the less severe cases when involuntary commitment to an institution may not be justified" (p. 4), according to Chief Medical Officer G. Carlyle Thompson (1943b). Committing patients to state hospitals, even when such a course was justified, was not an easy matter. Institutions in the states in which the camps were located were "for the most part unwilling to undertake the burden" (Rowalt, 1943, p. 1), both because the patients were "Japanese" and because they were technically nonresidents of states in which they were imprisoned. No state was willing to bear the cost of their treatment. The WRA reported in 1943 that its negotiations with mental institutions in the three West Coast states, from which most of the Nikkei had been removed, were expected to produce an agreement of transfer through which those Nikkei patients committed to institutions in the state of their incarceration would be returned—or deported, as it were—to those in the states from which they were removed (Rowalt, 1943; Thompson, 1943b). When the patients were returned to their original state of residence, they would remain "the custodial responsibility of the War Relocation Authority but not the financial responsibility of the Authority" (Gifford, 1944, p. 1).

These deportation proceedings were wrenching matters for the patients and their families. In October of 1943, Colorado State Mental Hospital was holding four patients committed from Granada Camp, usually referred to as Amache. The families of the patients were informed of their deportation to California with only a day or two notice in terse letters stating that the patients were being discharged from the hospital and sent to the charge of the sheriff of the

California county from which they had been removed. Amache Welfare Section's efforts to delay the deportation to allow time for the families to visit the patients were denied by the doctor in charge of the state hospital who "stated this move was being carried out as per the initial agreement with the WRA" (Neher, 1944, p. 1). California remained an exclusion zone to which the Nikkei could not return unless, ironically, it was as a prisoner to be incarcerated for a crime or a patient to be institutionalized. California medical institutions holding Nikkei patients had been all too eager to release them for removal; many had refused to take in new Nikkei patients. The families would not, therefore, have had any assurance that their family members would be well-treated; given the exclusion order, they could not visit to see for themselves or know how long the imposed separation would last. "Because it was impossible for members of these families to visit their relatives" institutionalized in excluded areas, as Manzanar social worker Margaret D'Ille observed, "the strain upon the families is severe" (D'Ille, 1943, p. 2).

Disputes about payment responsibility were, of course, a major part of the deportation measures and related jurisdictional struggles.[3] The case of Ms. S., a young woman released from Manzanar and resettled in Salt Lake City to attend university, is an apt example. For a while, Ms. S. had been making excellent grades at the school while working "satisfactorily" as a live-in domestic help in a Caucasian household, but she became ill and was committed to the state mental hospital in Provo. The hospital, according to John Moore, Counselor at the Amache Welfare Section, recommended insulin treatments but would not provide the treatment "until they know who will pay for them" (Moore, 1943, p. 2). The state hospital had been corresponding with the WRA for months on the matter without a conclusion being reached; neither wanted responsibility for her care. Utah State Social Welfare Department and local representative of the BPA insisted that "the case is one involving permanent care and therefore not eligible under the agreement" (Moore, 1943, p. 2) the hospital had made with

---

[3] Finding institutional support for disabled children appeared to have been similarly difficult. "So far state schools for the deaf have been unwilling to accept evacuees and no satisfactory plan has been developed for providing training or other assistance for them" (War Relocation Authority, 1943b, p. 2). By the end of 1944, the WRA reported that some progress had been made in a few camps. The Utah School for the Deaf had agreed to accept one deaf girl from the Topaz camp, with funding coming from the Millard County, Utah, Department of Public Welfare from Social Security Board funds. With the assistance of the state, the Granada camp created a recreational program for the blind, "including instruction of the family as to constructive treatment of the handicapped person" (War Relocation Authority, 1944, p. 4). Jerome had finally secured the agreement of the Louisiana State Board of Education to accept four deaf children at the State School for the Deaf and one blind child at the State School for the Blind, though the agreement did not come easily and, as a segregated state, which "reserve[s] the right, of course, to receive into the schools only children of the white race," the Board made clear that it was "making a concession in agreeing to take Japanese children" (Phillips, 1944, p. 1).

the WRA about the care of its inmates. The WRA representative in Utah took the position that the commitment was not permanent and that the hospital, with payment coming from the state or the Public Assistance Bureau, should "provide at least three months treatment" (Moore, 1943, p. 2). The WRA headquarters held that individuals such as Ms. S., who had left the camps on "indefinite leave" status, were "no longer the responsibility of WRA, but are in the same position as any other resident of the community" (Moore, 1943, p. 2). Conversely, the BPA insisted that it had been assured that "persons who do not adjust in the community" (Brown, 1943, p. 1) could be returned to the camps from which they were released.

One way to circumvent the jurisdictional struggle and the resulting deportation was to pay for care as a private patient, a course few families in the camps could afford. Lucy Brown, Associate Welfare Consultant for the WRA headquarters, described Mr. F., the father of a young man about to be deported to California from the Colorado State Hospital as "very anxious" (Brown, 1943, p. 2) to prevent the move. The son was "especially attached to his father, and it is believed that the separation would result in a set-back in his condition" (Brown, 1943, p. 2). The family was attempting to raise funds by applying for servicemen's dependency benefit for the father under the patient's brother, a sergeant in the U.S. Army. While the deportation order was imminent, the usual turn-around for decisions on dependency benefits, regularly denied families in camps as was previously discussed, was more than three months. The records examined did not include information on the final disposition of either of these cases.

While the cause of mental illness may not be laid at the foot of war, removal, and incarceration, it is not a stretch to suggest that the stresses and tensions arising from those events and conditions triggered and aggravated existing disorders and underlying vulnerabilities. In the "abnormal communities" of the concentration camps, the care of the ill, moreover, became exponentially more difficult. Families who had long cared for mentally ill family members at home could no longer do so in the overcrowded camps, which also did not offer any viable alternatives to in-home care. The fact of incarceration in remote states rendered ill and institutionalized individuals deportable aliens to be shipped back to the very places from which they were forcibly removed and to which families could not follow to provide oversight and support. The fiscal wrangles over jurisdiction among localities and systems ensured that, even in committed care, treatment was withheld and deferred. The economic ruin that the forced removal and incarceration wrought in so many families meant they were without funds to interject private care. The Nikkei were trapped in a setting which not only exacerbated existing issues and propagated new ones "that would probably never have arisen under normal living conditions" (Briesemeister, 1944b, p. 1), but also stripped them of any control over the care of their most vulnerable members.

Family Troubles

That "the type of living that was necessary" (Kimmerling et al., 1945, p. 10) in the camps had become detrimental to family life was a conclusion universally agreed upon by all who had first-hand knowledge of the situation and had cause to comment. In a confidential memorandum to the YWCA National Board written in the Fall of 1944, the JAEP's Esther Briesemeister (1944b) lamented:

> The very nature of center life—its crowded living conditions, inadequate facilities, and above all, the lack of privacy—intensifies the complexity of the social welfare problem. This environment not only aggravates existing problems but breeds new ones that would probably never have arisen under normal living conditions. Marital difficulties, juvenile delinquency, inter-family quarrels, all find encouragement within the single-room apartment that contains married and unmarried, young and old, stable and unstable in undesired and undesirable proximity. (p. 1)

The retrospective history of the Minidoka Welfare, written on the eve of the camp closure, reached similar conclusions:

> Parents lost a great deal of their authority over children due to break in family relations occasioned by eating in common mess halls, using common toilets and bath, and the loss of habitual forms of recreation. These conditions led some of the children to seek new friends and new recreation and break away from many of the ties of home, which had been a disciplinary force before this time. Husband and wife relationships were often strained by these same conditions which eliminated many social controls that are operative in a normal community. (Kimmerling et al., 1945, p. 10)

The families who "lost their sense of stability" and were unable to "adjust themselves to the rapidly changing situations" (Kimmerling et al., 1945, p. 10) needed a depth of support that the Welfare Sections were unable to provide. Counseling families around issues of "delinquency, personal maladjustment, family difficulties and broken homes" was said to be "a major responsibility" (Pratt, 1945, p. 9) for the Topaz Welfare Section which had, on paper, a special Child Welfare Unit as well as a Family Unit with a caseworker assigned to specific blocks of housing units. Since, however, the section often had only one or two professional social workers on staff, neither unit functioned as it was designed to do. The untrained "evacuees assigned to the Child Welfare Unit could hardly be expected to carry on any intensive case work treatment" (Pratt, 1945, p. 9), according to Section Head Claud Pratt. At Rohwer, there was "no provision for general counseling on family relationship, juvenile delinquency, or other social problems" (Dusseldorp, 1945, p. 5). Despite the best of will to provide such services, the staffing problems made it "increasingly evident that counseling service had to be limited to the most pressing problems" (Dusseldorp, 1945, p. 17). Even the known cases of "delinquency, broken homes, unattached children, and other similar problems" (Dusseldorp, 1945, p. 17) had to be deliberately ignored because the staff were occupied with other matters. The Jerome section's final accounting contained a similar admission: "there were all too many opportunities for constructive work following careful social diagnosis, which was never accomplished" (Webb, 1945, p. 26). While many child welfare problems, for example, were known to the department, "few were adequately explored and practically none were sufficiently treated" (Webb, 1945, p. 26), admitted Section Head J. Lloyd Webb. The Jerome section did not have a social worker with experience in child welfare until nearly the end of the camp's operations, and "practically no outside children's resources seemed to exist" (Webb, 1945, p. 26) that could be accessed by or for the camp inmates. The staff the section did employee "was neither equipped nor inclined to search out and uncover private social problems" (Webb, 1945, p. 26) for which they were untrained to address and too busy to pursue. Only the Poston Welfare Section is on record for having an experienced child welfare worker on staff for a significant period of time (Butler, 1945, p. 10). The Heart Mountain Welfare Section stands alone in reporting that it rendered "intensive case work services to a substantial number of individuals and families" (Kell, 1945, p. 7) on family issues including problems of delinquency, neglect, marital disharmony, and emotional instability. The claim is difficult to credit given the staffing problems with which all of the Welfare Sections struggled throughout their existence in the camps.

Juvenile Delinquency

Of the many kinds of problems predicted to result from the abnormal pattern of family life in incarceration, juvenile delinquency was arguably that most feared by the WRA staff. Reports of the supposed rise of juvenile delinquency abound in the reports of various branches of the WRA (War Relocation Authority, 1942, 1943c). They also appeared in the deeply confidential—"not to be circulated outside the building" (Briesemeister, 1944b, p. 1)—reports made by Esther Briesemeister to the YWCA National Board. That the rate of juvenile delinquency had "increased tremendously after December 7th" (in Leighton, 1942–43, p. 56) was considered axiomatic, but there is no evidence that an epidemic of criminality among the youth ever materialized. While individual instances of serious crime and delinquency did undoubtedly occur as they might in any sizeable grouping of people, the claim that delinquency was "rampant, some-times in quite serious form" (Marks Jr., 1943, p. 1) was never substantiated. The Caucasians' anticipation of chaos fomented by disaffected, undisciplined youth was more reflective of their own fears and biases than the behavior of the Nikkei youth. No data indicate that, on a large scale, there were problems more alarming than boys engaged in minor bouts of vandalism and other kinds of adolescent troublemaking (Briesemeister, 1944b; Marks Jr., 1943), "a great deal of gambling among the young people" (Marks Jr., 1943, p. 1), or "instances in which children had been reported for stealing" (Dusseldorp, 1945, p. 5). For the most part, the troubles caused by the so-called delinquents seem to have been of the variety described at Rohwer.

> It was explained that for several successive nights, boys had maliciously broken out window panes in the school block in 18 and had cut up two new tennis nets which were on the playground. The rude behavior of young boys at the USO picture shows recently was also discussed. It was stated that young boys of Junior High School age had been causing difficulty on the high school grounds by marking up the buildings with chalk. (Gifford, 1943, p. 1)

The WRA created both prevention and intervention programs and structures, such as the Youth Guidance Unit, the Juvenile Board, and the Guidance Committee (Manzanar Relocation Center, 1944; War Relocation Authority, 1943c). Interdepartmental meetings were held to clarify the tangle of roles and responsibilities allotted across departments such as Welfare, Education, and Internal Security (Powell, 1942; War Relocation Authority, 1943c). As well-intended as the groups and committees may have been, these efforts functioned far less impressively than their titles may suggest. Continuous coordinated efforts between the three relevant sections were crucial but "not being devel-oped" (Powell, 1942, p. 1) or, once developed, not maintained. At Gila River, for example, most work around delinquency was initially assigned to the Internal Security Section staff, young Nikkei men who had attended a training course on delinquency given by William Tuttle, the WS Head Counselor, noted for his abstruse and ineffectual lectures. In June of 1943, a committee composed of staff from Internal Security, Welfare, Churches, Schools, and Community Activities and headed by Tuttle was set up for the purposes of discussing proper methods of delinquency prevention and treatment and to make recommendations for the handling of individual cases. By the Fall of that year, however, the respon-sibility defaulted entirely to the Welfare Section, with a single appointed case-worker assigned the "responsibility for carrying delinquents and adopting whatever treatment methods which were deemed desirable" (Tuttle, 1945, p. 6). The Minidoka Welfare Section worked with the Education and Internal Security

Sections "as closely as limitations of personnel would permit" (Kimmerling et al., 1945, p. 10); those limitations were significant. Internal Security was as poorly staffed as Welfare and was ill-equipped to work with youth. John Powell (1943), the Acting Chief of Community Management at Poston, noted, in December 1943, that his "acquaintance with the average run of police officers on the other Projects is not reassuring as to their capacity to fit in with the professional approach to counseling and prevention" (p. 3). The punishment meted out by parents under community scrutiny, however, tended to be "severe" to the point that they "might have been more detrimental than the original crime" (p. 5). In Rohwer Head Counselor Wilma Dusseldorp's (1945) view, there were no good alternatives. The approach of the Chief of Community Management, to whom she and Internal Security reported, was problematic—"strongly moralistic, not infrequently associated with religious doctrine" (p. 5).

Training Social Work Clients

The Welfare Sections did not, unsurprisingly, enjoy a reputation as a viable source of help for family issues. That there was, as Jerome's J. Lloyd Webb (1945) reported, "no articulated criticism from any quarter as to failure in this area of service" (p. 26) was more likely an indication of the community's low expectations than a reflection of its satisfaction with services rendered. Only the direst of circumstances brought families into the Welfare Sections to seek even the most concrete of aids such as cash and clothing assistance; seeking the department's aid in resolving family problems was an even less obvious course for the Nikkei, especially the Issei. It was through "private self-reliance, family ingenuity, pride, and repression" (p. 26), rather than any real social work services from the Welfare Sections, that the majority of the Nikkei families tended to manage their troubles. In Webb's accounting, nearly all "family and personal problems were introduced under cover of a request for information or some tangible service" (p. 26), such as transfer to join family members in a different camp or a shift in housing assignment. To put it differently, social workers only came to know those problems existed in the course of working out those tangible services, not because families sought their help for those issues. To varying degrees, the Nikkei staff of the Welfare Sections shared this community ethos for private resolutions. Dusseldorp (1945) reported that Nikkei Counseling Aides "tended to indicate skepticism about the need for such service" (p. 5) as family counseling, insisting that "the Japanese family takes care of all family relationship problems" and that they have "too much pride" (p. 5) to turn to social agencies for their intimate family troubles. The aides offered examples from their own families in which incidents of discord were resolved with the help of both immediate and extended family members or with the help and counsel of trusted friends, all without the involvement or even knowledge of the Welfare Section. Belief in the efficacy of professional counseling was held only by a handful of Nikkei workers like Charles Kikuchi, who had been educated in social work and had prior exposure to case work methods and ideals.

The seriously underresourced welfare office, where reasonable "quality of service was wholly impossible" not only due to lack of qualified staff, but because of the "inappropriate and inadequate physical accommodations" (Dusseldorp, 1945, p. 6), did nothing to boost the community's already low regard for social work and its workers. The dearth of professional staff meant even problems "calling for immediate attention" (Dusseldorp, 1945, p. 6) were neglected—subject to postponement, confusion, and frequently forgotten altogether. The lack of clerical aid, specifically stenographic service during the first few of months of the section's operations, meant that it was difficult to record detailed case histories affecting the office's ability to follow through with cases. All of these problems contributed to the understandable "creation of doubts within the residents' minds concerning the worker's sincerity and interest in their problems" (Dusseldorp, 1945, p. 6) among a client population who doubted the utility of social services in the first place. In the overcrowded camps where space was premium, moreover, the welfare offices were as congested as the barracks themselves. Clients "frequently complained that the nearness of families together caused embarrassing questions and gossip as a result of home visits" (Webb, 1945, p. 26) by social workers. The department offices, which also lacked partitions and discrete spaces, were little better for confidential interviews. The only way to have a semblance of privacy, according to Dusseldorp (1945), was to interview clients while walking around outside, though during certain times of the day, even the roads were crowded with people.

A common method employed by families who could not avoid seeking professional services was to use an intermediary chosen by the family to serve as spokespersons on their behalf. Dusseldorp (1945) explained that, in the early months of the department's existence, Nikkei Counseling Aides reporting cases of families in need of family or child counseling "invariably introduced a resident who expected to serve as 'go-between' for the family involved, and through whom the Counseling Aide recommended that all interviewing be done" (p. 12). Extending the traditional practice of using go-betweens, who served as both counsel and negotiator, to interactions with the Welfare Sections was an understandable move for the families: it allowed them to access services while maintaining their distance from the source of those services and retain at least a nominal sense of anonymity. At Tule Lake, the department nearly always worked through an intermediary in "cases of family disorganization" (Shibutani, 1943a, p. 78) involving Issei family members.

All negotiations were made through intermediaries so that if some error takes place the person involved would not lose face. In a sense two factions were like armed camps and all official pronouncements for from one side to the other went through a third party. (Shibutani, 1943a, p. 78)

This three-party system, however useful it may have been for the families involved, was entirely at odds with the casework principle of individual engagement, in which home visits were de rigueur and face-to-face interactions with the client a necessary component of the method. Dusseldorp (1945), for one, held that maintaining "the more direct way in which social case workers took responsibility for helping people" (p. 12) was an unquestionable necessity. The Counseling Aide's "chief defense" for the intermediary—that "the Japanese are used to that" (p. 12)—was immaterial in her view since "that may be true as they lived in Japan, but they live in America now" (p. 12). Teaching the Nikkei to "become able to take responsibility for learning about American customs and how to use public services to their own advantage" (p. 12) was a necessary task for the social workers and a benefit conferred to the Nikkei. The policy for dealing with Issei clients who used intermediaries was a "denial of service, by way of a carefully planned interview and translated by the best interpreters available to present the nature of the Welfare Section Service" (p. 12). Clients were informed, in other words, that the only way they could receive the department's services was to follow the methods it considered appropriate. Such "orientation services" given to Nikkei clients and staff were a corrective measure "comparable to Americanization courses" (p. 12), according to Dusseldorp. The Nikkei needed to assimilate to function properly as clients *and* Americans.

Defining "Family"

Within the structure of the WRA, not only the traditional methods of resolving family problems but the very conception of what constituted a family was challenged. Charles Kikuchi (1942a) explained, that the Nikkei "have a different conception of the family unit than the Americans" (p. 71); it included a far wider circle of relatives than the nuclear family. The distinction was nowhere more evident than in the requests for intercamp transfers brought to the Welfare Sections.

So many cases come in to us and they want grandfathers, uncles, cousins, nephews, etc. to be joined with them. I had to go to about four families today to inform them that the W.R.A. policy of immediate family was different from the Japanese interpretation which includes all in-laws and even distant relatives. They just don't seem to understand it. (C. Kikuchi, 1942b, pp. 65–66)

Technically, intercamp transfers were allowed only to reunite separated family members. For the purposes of these transfers, "family" was defined by the WRA as "that group domiciled together as a family immediately prior to evacuation, plus other members dependent upon the family group for principal support, or contributing principal support to the family group at that time" (War Relocation Authority, n.d.-b, p. 1), a definition that did not fit many requesting reunification. Although they may not have lived together for many years, JERS researcher James Sakoda (1942) surmised, many extended family members "felt that under present uncertain conditions it was best for members of a family or relatives to keep together as much as possible"(p. 17) and requested to be reunified; the majority of such requests were rejected. Sakoda, a staff member of the Tule Lake Welfare Section, reported in November of 1942 that only about a 100 of the 300–400 family transfer requests made had been granted. Kikuchi (1942a) noted from his perspective as a supervisor in the Gila River Welfare Section that the Issei heads of families whose requests for transfers had been refused by the administration saw the policy as an abrogation of the government's original promise to keep families together (p. 71).

Of course, not all members of a family, by either the WRA definition or the more expansive one Kikuchi described, desired to live in close proximity. The administration, discovering that some individuals on whose behalf a transfer request had been made did not want to be transferred to their relatives or have their relatives transfer to them, instituted a policy to have all requests countersigned at both ends of the transfer by relevant parties (Sakoda, 1942). Many Caucasian staff saw the desire for family proximity not only as a cultural eccentricity but a phenomenon showcasing a problematic dynamic between the assimilated younger generations and the "Japanese" older generation. While the Issei–Nisei divide did no doubt hold some explanatory power for conflicts between parents and children, as Poston Head Counselor Lou Butler commented, however, disagreements between parents and children were "universal" (Butler, 1943, p. 1). Generational differences in outlook existed in all families. Family relations and situational complications within those relationships varied in Nikkei families as they did in all families.

When a whole family lives in one room, this conflict is intensified, as the youth have to entertain their guests in the presence of their parents and their conversation is sometimes displeasing to the elders, who try to change the youth and so on. One Issei even told me that older Japanese do not want self-government, which the Nisei are trying to organize here, with the help of the Caucasian Administration and an Issei advisory board—that some do not believe in democracy. I asked one of our social workers what she thought of the statement, she replied that it was true of some, possibly a majority of Issei, but not all. She said her parents had been here 40 years and had partaken in community affairs and would have been citizens if permitted, they believed emphatically in a democratic form of government and had always stood behind their children, had confidence in the children and encouraged them to make their own decisions. Consequently, the children had confidence in their parents and kept nothing from them, talked over everything with their parents. She realized that not all Japanese families were like this, that there was disagreement between parents and children in many families. (Butler, 1943, p. 2)

The tendency, however, was toward a reductionistic explanation of differential assimilation. Manzanar's Head Counselor Margaret D'Ille, a Japanese-speaking social worker with a decade's experience as Executive Secretary for YWCA in Japan, saw family problems at Manzanar as arising "largely between the conflicts of the Japanese ideas of the family as a unit and the American accent upon the importance and responsibility of the individual" (D'Ille, 1943, p. 1). YWCA field-worker Lazelle Alway (1943) attributed the increased level of family tensions at Tule Lake to the many cases of "American-Japanese girls having to live in close proximity of a husband's family, where she must learn to accept the Japanese tradition of the husband's family dictating to her" (p. 7).

Marital Problems

The supposed assimilative divide between the generations did not explain the many cases of divorce and separation among the Issei with which the Welfare Sections contended. Marital problems often came into the Welfare Sections as requests for transfer: "for example the woman who sought a transfer to another center to get away from her husband," or, conversely, "the husband who came in to see about getting an intruder into his family removed to another center" (Pratt, 1945, p. 9). Minidoka's Welfare Section, the only department to report that requests for aid with "marital problems" were brought directly to it from an early period in the department's functioning, pointed to "a triangle marital dispute" (Kimmerling et al., 1945, p. 22) ending in murder as an impetus for such direct requests for intervention. The triangle, which had involved three Issei, "brought quite a number of husbands and wives to the department who had strained marital relations and were in fear of physical violence on the part of the spouse or a third party" (Kimmerling et al., 1945, p. 22). In writing about similar "difficult love affairs" that had ended in several separations and one murder at Manzanar, Margaret D'Ille (1943) blamed the "lack of absorbing jobs, the absence of many husbands in internment camps and housing problems" (p. 1). In nearly all such cases that the department handled, "long-standing disagreements have been revealed which were hidden and only came to light in the great strain of this camp" (p. 1).

In analyzing the many cases of marital troubles documented by the Tule Lake Welfare Section, JERS fieldworker Tamotsu Shibutani (1943d) came to similar conclusions. In his view, two factors explained why the "final break" (p. 84) in long-troubled relationships occurred in the camp. First, the congested housing instigated and intensified existing conflicts, not the least because the close barracks and the enclosed camps where "rumors and gossip spread unusually fast" (Shibutani, 1943a, p. 26) made escape from scrutiny and judgment impossible. "People are close enough to know their neighbors well and to make things extremely uncomfortable for those whom they wish to ostracize" (Shibutani, 1943a, p. 26). Second, a significant factor for the women concerned was the camp economy. The YWCA had surmised that the lives of women, without household duties to anchor their lives and "lack of interesting work to replace the usual home responsibilities" (Lyle, 1943, p. 1), would be altered adversely in the unhealthy "mass living" of the camps. In Shibutani's analysis, whether for good or ill, the removal of the daily grind of household work opened up women's—especially Issei women's lives—to the possibility of independence. The basic subsistence of food and shelter provided by the camps, alongside the plausibility of working to earn independent wages or to receive public assistance to aid them financially, allowed them, ironically, to imagine the feasibility of separation and divorce. In Shibutani's (1943d) cautious phrasing, the "fact that the women define the camp situation in such a way that they conceive to themselves as being financial independent of their husbands may have been of some significance" (p. 84) to their decision to break from long-standing marriage difficulties. Tamie Tsuchiyama, a JERS researcher at Poston, related a similar observation.

> One Issei woman reported that her friends (Issei woman from the rural districts) are saying that they are thankful to have been evacuated. "They are saying, "Arigatai! Arigatai!" (I am thankful. I am thankful.) In this connection I remember that John Powell recently told me that the evacuation resulted in the emancipation of Japanese women. (Tsuchiyama, 1943, p. 48)

While made theoretically feasible, separation and divorce were not easily accomplished in the camps. Divorce was not only a socially but financially expensive venture for the family involved; "even in Tule Lake where the Attorney did not charge a fee, the Court expenses totaled over $100" (Shibutani, 1943c, p. 71), a vast sum in a setting where no Nikkei was allow to earn more than $19 per month. Divorce in incarceration was further complicated by the fact that the laws of the various states in which the camps were located had different procedures and wait times. While the benefits of state residence did not extend to the inmates, as discussed in Chapter 5, the laws apparently did. Charles Kikuchi noted, in January of 1943, that there were no provisions established for divorce at Gila River. Arizona required a year's residence in the state before filing for divorce, and the only aid the Welfare Section could offer a wife seeking divorce from an abusive husband was to "separate them for a while" (Kikuchi, 1943b, p. 106) within the camp. Only those inmates of the two California camps, Manzanar and Tule Lake, who had been removed from that state were able to sue for divorce, according to Miya Kikuchi (1942b), staff member of the Manzanar Welfare Section and the head of the camp YWCA chapter.

> Where divorce has been found necessary, the suits can be prepared in the Legal Aid Department, but the evidence is reviewed by the Judge in Inyo County and sent to the Court in Los Angeles. Decisions can be rendered in Los Angeles, since the residents of Manzanar are still residents of Los Angeles. (p. 2)

The Welfare Sections held a great deal of power over the lives of men and women who found themselves in these difficult circumstances. Without social work's endorsement for divorce, one was unlikely to be able to change residence to get away from a problematic relationship or to go to a more desirable one. WRA Administrative Bulletin No. 52 stipulated that divorce cases had to be first cleared through a Welfare Section before they could be processed by the Office of the Project Attorney (Shibutani, 1943c). The "recommendation of Social Welfare is next to final (Project director's word is final) in decisions relating to dispositions of domestic problems" (p. 5). The social Welfare Sections tended to push reconciliation. While intermediaries were negotiating terms for divorce between a Nisei wife and an Issei husband in a "long-term unhappy marriage which wife wants to leave" (Shibutani, 1943a, p. 78), the Tule Lake social welfare department "consistently counsels [the] wife to reconcile" (Shibutani, 1943a, p. 78). The case of Mrs. L., who came into the Jerome office to request a move for herself and her young son was another example. Disregarding her specific request for transfer, the Welfare Section "soon discovered that the need was not for transfer, but for help in solution of difficulties between the husband and wife, who were still together" (Webb, 1945, p. 26). Head Counselor Webb reported that, after some social work visits to the couple, "the transfer was not consummated. The Welfare Section managed to prevent this home from splitting" (Webb, 1945, p. 26).

Reconciliation seemed to have been impelled even in cases of domestic violence. The complicated and infuriating story of Tule Lake's Mrs. M. is an illustration. Mrs. M. had been separated from her husband for five years prior to the removal but was assigned to share quarters with him at the camp with their 11-year-old son. She was pregnant with the child of Mr. S., a widow with a

14-year-old daughter, who was also imprisoned at Tule Lake. In early October 1943, she went to the Legal Aid department for advice in getting a separation from her husband and was referred to the Welfare Section, where she reported a long history of domestic violence perpetrated by her husband. She requested that he be removed from their quarters or, alternatively, she be permitted to live with a friend who was willing to take in her and her son. She was, however, "told by the social worker to consider the fact that the boy needed his father's influence" and though she "objected and said that her son was happier away from his father" (Shibutani, 1943b, p. 38), she was advised to reconsider the matter before returning to the office. Mrs. M. returned to the office two days later to again request a housing change, but, on that day, the Legal Aid department had informed the Welfare Section that it was "advisable though not necessary to have Mr. M.'s agreement before arranging for separate housing quarters for his wife" since the "child to be born would be illegitimate if not accepted" (Shibutani, 1943b, p. 40) by him. Mrs. M.'s request was again put aside, and a social worker duly called on the husband to see if he would agree to let his wife move. In the ensuing month, the husband vacillated between agreeing to let her move—on the conditions that his wife leave without any possessions except the clothes she stood in—then revoking that agreement. Finally, on November 10, a group meeting, to which Mrs. M. does not appeared to have been invited, was called with the husband, the father of the unborn child, several administrators, and a social worker. At this meeting, Dr. Jacoby, the Head of Community Services, the division in which the Welfare Section operated, "ordered Mr. M. to allow his wife to have separate quarters at least when the baby was born" (Shibutani, 1943b, p. 43). In the end, in December of that year, two months after Mrs. M.'s first reporting of domestic abuse and the desire to leave to escape it, the Welfare Section transferred both the husband and the lover out of Tule Lake and to other camps.

That the Welfare Sections' push for reconciliation was influenced at least in part by the structural constraints of the overcrowded camp is difficult to refute. Moving unhappy people to different quarters was a difficult matter and clearly an option that social welfare departments did not wish to endorse or encourage. Shibutani's report that a married but long-estranged couple's separate living arrangements came under Welfare Section scrutiny, "since housing was scarce and since more people were expected in the center" (Shibutani, 1943c, p. 4), is one indication of the weight that housing difficulties had on departmental adjudications. Not only intracamp moves but intercamp transfers were often infeasible—the family at the receiving end did not always want to accept the responsibility of an additional family member into already overloaded quarters, and no camp had extra housing available to accommodate new arrivals. Keeping couples in place, therefore, was the least troublesome solution for the administration. An intracamp move or an intercamp transfer were undertaken for only the most acute cases—in which threat of serious violence and community up-heaval loomed.

The handling of marital dispute by social welfare staff also shows, however, that the push for reconciliation was not only due to logistic difficulties but also because divorce was seen as an undesirable outcome to be prevented if at all possible. Given the social mores of the times, the measured approach of Gila River Welfare Head William Tuttle, a social worker by training and experience, is notable. In a letter to the son of a woman who wished to separate from her husband and transfer to her son's camp to live with him, Tuttle stated that, aside from the basic facts about the case he had related, "we have no opinion one way or the other as to what should be done and await your decision" (Tuttle, 1943, p. 2). The explicitly neutral position Tuttle presented was quite in contrast to the views expressed by Welfare Section staff who clearly held rigid views about marriage and marital relations and saw divorce, separation, and infidelity as actions to be condemned and those involved as people to be censured and even punished. The following two cases, perhaps the most egregious examples of this perspective at work, were handled by Caucasian staff who were not trained social workers.

That occasional bouts of wife-beating did not appear to have been considered an acute problem meriting housing reassignment is illustrated in the case of Mrs. J., handled by John Landward, an Administrative Assistant, who acted as the head of the Gila River Welfare Section until the arrival of William Tuttle in late November of 1942. Mrs. J's brother had written to Landward requesting that his sister who was "brutally mistreated" (Landward, 1942, p. 1) by her husband at Gila be transferred to Tule Lake where he, the brother, was incarcerated. In reply to the brother, Landward acknowledged that the accusation of abuse had been confirmed. There were, however, "a number of other factors involved in the case" (p. 1). Mrs. J. was having an extramarital affair and that affair, the topic of much community gossip, had "made neighborhood social relations disagreeable" (p. 1) not only for her and her husband, but for the unrelated people with whom they were quartered. As the brother could "readily understand," Landward explained, the "treatment which he [the husband] subsequently accorded [the wife] was motivated by his anger and jealousy" (p. 1), and he could not "feel that [the husband] is entirely to blame for his attitude towards his wife" (p. 1). Thus, while he had obtained from the husband the promise of better behavior, he had also counseled the wife to "honestly play her part in her marriage relationship" (p. 2) and extracted a promise from the lover that he would cease to interfere in the couple's marriage. Landward concluded sententiously:

It may be in the future, that I shall be urged to have [Mrs. J.] and her two children transferred to Tule Lake if living conditions with her husband become unbearable. However, if such should be the case, it is not because I hold her blameless. It will merely be due to the fact that this will be the only solution in my judgment. (p. 2)

The actions of Miss Cheney, an untrained staff member of the Poston Welfare Section described simply as "unqualified" (McCord, 1944, p. 1) by Vera McCord, Acting Head of that Section, was arguable more censorious than those of Landward. Miss Cheney, in the course of interviewing a family on another matter, had discovered that a couple housed together in the camp was not legally married. While the State of California did not recognize common-law marriages, the Community Council at Poston had voted to allow co-habitation of couples who were already doing so prior to removal (Glick, 1943). Miss Cheney, however, insistent that the couple should be induced to marry or be separated, consulted the Project Attorney to "determine what legal action could be taken against the parties" (p. 1). The Project Attorney, Phillip Glick, explained to Miss Cheney that if the "Project Director thought such conduct inimical to the welfare of the Project he could inflict punishment but that the community sentiment did not regard this conduct as immoral" (p. 1). Undeterred, Miss Cheney wrote a memorandum to the Project Director citing the couple as detriments to the morals of the young people in the community. No action appears to have been taken by the director on the matter.

Unmarried Mothers, Orphans, and Adoptions

Unmarried mothers and children born out of wedlock, viewed as a consequence of the many kinds of family disintegration, were another set of complications for the Welfare Sections to manage. If, as the JERS researcher Shotaro Miyamoto (1942) averred, the "chief method of moral control in the Japanese communities has been through parental authority in ordering and forbidding certain forms of behavior," that those "normal channels of articulation are not present" (p. 12) in the abnormal settings of the camps was a fact acknowledged by all. Women's sexuality was, of course, a surveilled and guarded domain, even when the "trouble" of pregnancy did not result. The sole charge against one young Nisei woman, considered so much of a "very serious problem" by her family, the Welfare Section, and Internal Security, that she was ordered returned to Tule Lake camp from resettlement in Chicago, was "consorting with soldiers at camp and with various men in Chicago" (p. 15). When out-of-wedlock births did occur, the standard practice was to separate the mother and the child to avoid the "disaster of the unmarried mother having to live in the community and near her child" (Alway, 1943, p. 7). Given the enormous difficulties involved in effecting intercamp transfers, and even more so in doing so quickly, such separations were not always accomplished. Ray G. Johnston, Rohwer Project Director, wrote to his counterpart in Jerome about a widow with a baby born out of wedlock, requesting that the two camps enact a quid pro quo exchange.

> We believe that it will be better for all concerned if the baby can be taken care of temporarily away from this center, and we would like to ask that the Jerome Welfare Section assume responsibility for securing a foster home until the mother has more time to make a definite decision as to permanent plans for the baby. . . . It is our understanding from Miss Bayless that Jerome will probably be asking a similar service of Rohwer Center at an early date, and our Welfare Section will be glad to cooperate in the matter. (Johnston, 1944, p. 1)

Even in cases in which such temporary arrangements could be made to avert the "disaster" of an unwed mother being on view, Welfare Sections struggled to arrange temporary foster care for the separated child and found permanent adoptions nearly impossible to effect. Not all state public welfare agency were willing to assist the camp Welfare Sections in arranging adoptions. Another significant hurdle was that while it was "desirable to place babies with families of the same racial group" (Alway, 1943, p. 7), few such adoptive families for Nikkei children were available on the outside. Indeed, few families were willing to adopt a "Japanese" child across racial lines.

The feasibility of adoption was a matter of concern for the welfare departments not only because of the occasional need to place children born out of wedlock, but also because of the children held in the Manzanar Children's Village, the euphemistically named orphanage in incarceration run by an appointed Superintendent reporting to the Head of the Welfare Section. The Children's Village had been created to house and care for Nikkei children removed from the three orphanages in California which had held them: the Salvation Army Orphanage at San Francisco, the Maryknoll Father's Orphanage in Los Angeles, and Shonien Japanese Children's Home in Los Angeles.[4] While the majority of the children at the Village had come directly from the three California orphanages, the Village also housed children newly orphaned since the removal, as well as "temporary orphans" (Nobe, 1999, p. 66) without guardians. Some of the temporary orphans were children whose only parent was incarcerated in a Department of Justice Internment camp, children who needed temporary care while parents were ill or otherwise unable to provide care, and children born out of wedlock in the camps for whom other arrangements had not materialized.

---

[4] See Irwin (2008), *Twice Orphaned*; Kuramoto (1976), *A History of the Shonien, 1914–1972*; and Nobe (1999), "The Children's Village at Manzanar."

The Village was superintended by Harry Matsumoto, a young Nisei who had been running the Japanese Children's Home in Los Angeles since the war began. He had been assisting Shonien founder Joy Kusumoto for several years when the war broke out, and Kusomoto became one of many prominent community members to be arrested by the FBI and incarcerated in a Department of Justice Internment camp. His new bride Lilian, a graduate of the UC Berkeley Graduate School of Social Work, had originally been hired as the Shonien's first trained caseworker (Irwin, 2008; Kuramoto, 1976). Since all funds in Nikkei banks had been frozen for the duration of the war, Shonien had kept its doors open only through the infusion of emergency operational funds by the LA Community Chest (Kuramoto, 1976). It soon became clear, despite hopes otherwise, that the orphans would not be part of the group exempted from removal. The Army insisted, as the YWCA's Winifred Wygel (1943) noted acerbically, that "the great states of California, Oregon and Washington needed to be protected also from the orphans of Japanese-American heritage who were in various orphan asylums" (p. 4). At a conference of representatives from more than a dozen public and private social service agencies serving children, the decision was made to recreate an orphanage at Manzanar. Miya Kikuchi (1942a), a worker in the proto-Welfare Section at Manzanar, then called the Family Relations department, recalled the first scouting visit "to examine the possibilities and advisability of moving the orphanage" by the Matsumotos and "a representative of some Commission of Social Welfare of Washington DC and a leading social worker from LA" (p. 2). The Children's Village was in operation from June 1942 until September 1945 in a set of self-contained buildings equipped with their own kitchen, mess hall, bathing facilities, and sleeping quarters for the children and the core staff, located a mile from the administrative center of the camp. It held an average of 65 children in its care, according to Margaret D'Ille in early March of 1943 (Manzanar Public Welfare Department, 1943).

References

Alway, L. (1943). Travel Report, Tule Lake Relocation Center, August 2-4, 1943, dated August 25, 1943, pp. 1-1-8. Folder 3, Box 724. YWCA of the U.S.A. Records, Sophia Smith Collection. Northampton, MA: Smith College.

Amache Young Women's Christian Association. (1942). Matron's Group meeting, Amache Young Women's Christian Association, Amache, Colorado, November 24, 1942, 7-10:00 p.m., pp. 1-2. Folder 9, Box 724. YWCA of the U.S.A. Records, Sophia Smith Collection. Northampton, MA: Smith College.

Amache Young Women's Christian Association. (1943). Report of the Amache YWCA, Granada Relocation Center, Amache, Colorado, June, 1943, pp. 1-7. Folder 9, Box 724. YWCA of the U.S.A. Records, Sophia Smith Collection. Northampton, MA: Smith College.

Briesemeister, E. (1942). Report on Interviews with Center Administration, Granada Relocation Center, Amache, Colorado, November 22, 1942, pp. 1–4. Folder 9, Box 724. YWCA of the U.S.A. Records, Sophia Smith Collection. Northampton, MA: Smith College.

Briesemeister, E. (1943a). Report on Granada Relocation Center, Amache, Colorado, May 6–10, 1943, pp. 1–3. Folder 12, Box 724. YWCA of the U.S.A. Records, Sophia Smith Collection. Northampton, MA: Smith College.

Briesemeister, E. (1943b). Report on Jerome Relocation Center, January 6, 1943, pp. 1–3. Folder 10, Box 723. YWCA of the U.S.A. Records, Sophia Smith Collection. Northampton, MA: Smith College.

Briesemeister, E. (1943c). Report on Manazanar Relocation Center, March 17 through March 23, 1943, pp. 1–10. Folder 15, Box 723. YWCA of the U.S.A. Records, Sophia Smith Collection. Northampton, MA: Smith College.

Briesemeister, E. (1943d). Report on Tule Lake Relocation Center, March 28 through April 3, 1943, pp. 1–4. Folder 3, Box 724. YWCA of the U.S.A. Records, Sophia Smith Collection. Northampton, MA: Smith College.

Briesemeister, E. (1944a). Report on Granada Relocation Center, Amache, Colorado, March 26–April 2, 1944; report filed May 17, 1944, pp. 1–3. Folder 13, Box 724. YWCA of the U.S.A. Records, Sophia Smith Collection. Northampton, MA: Smith College.

Briesemeister, E. (1944b). Report on Tule Lake Relocation Center, Newell, California, August 30–September 8, 1944, marked "Confidential—not to be circulated outside the building," pp. 1–6. Folder 7, Box 724. YWCA of the U.S.A. Records, Sophia Smith Collection. Northampton, MA: Smith College.

Briesemeister, E. (1946). America's children—what happened to us?: Summary report of the Japanese Evacuee Project, January 1942–September 1946, pp. 1–54. Folder 3, Box 721. YWCA of the U.S.A. Records, Sophia Smith Collection. Northampton, MA: Smith College.

Briesemeister, E., & Flack, H. (1942). Report of the first visits to Manzanar Relocation Camp, California: Helen Flack—July 26, 1942; Esther Briesemeister and Helen Flack—August 3–7, 1942; Esther Briesemeister—August 8–12, 1942, pp. 1–11. Folder 13, Box 723. YWCA of the U.S.A. Records, Sophia Smith Collection. Northampton, MA: Smith College.

Briesemeister, E., & North, L. (1942). Advisors meeting, Granada Relocation Center, Amache, Colorado, November 21, 1942, pp. 1–3. Folder 9, Box 724. YWCA of the U.S.A. Records, Sophia Smith Collection. Northampton, MA: Smith College.

Brown, L. W. (1943). Letter to Miss Selene Gifford, c/o Project Director, Tule Lake Relocation Center, Newell, California, from Lucy Brown, Associate Public Welfare Consultant, August 2, 1943, pp. 1–3. Folder: Gifford, Selene, Box 17: Washington Office Records—Chronological File; General—Alphabetical—GF-GRE. Records of the War Relocation Authority, 1941–1989, Record Group 210, General Outgoing Correspondence, compiled 1942–1946. ARC Identifier 1534421/MLR Number PI-77 18. Washington, DC: National Archives and Records Administration.

Butler, L. E. (1943). Letter No. 2. Round Robin from Colorado River WRA Project, Poston, Arizona, March 11, 1943, pp. 1–2. Folder: Copies of Circular Letters (1–9) Feb. 28, 1943–Dec. 1945 Box 3. Records of the War Relocation Authority, 1941–1989, Record Group 210, Office Files of Miss Lou Butler, Head Counselor of the Welfare Section of the Community Management Division at the Colorado River Relocation Center, compiled 1942–1945. ARC Identifier 5752763/MLR Number UD 6. Washington, DC: National Archives and Records Administration.

Butler, L. E. (1945). Story of the Family Welfare Section, May 1942 to May 1945, pp. 1–17. Calisphere, Japanese American Relocation Digital Archives, Poston, Arizona. Berkeley: Bancroft Library, University of California.

Carstarphen, W. T. (1943). Hospitalization of the insane; special reference to the Colorado Sate Hospital, Pueblo, Colorado: Memorandum to W. Ray Johnson, Community Service, from W. T. Carstarphen, Chief Medical Officer, Granada Relocation Center, Amache, Colorado, December 22, 1943, pp. 1–3. Folder: 521—Correspondence on Crippled, Blind, & Mental, Box 135: Granada Relocation Center—Central Files—514 to 624. Records of the War Relocation Authority, 1941–1989, Record Group 210, Subject-Classified General Files of the Relocation Centers—compiled 1942–1946. ARC Identifier 1544889/MLR Number PI-77 48. Washington, DC: National Archives and Records Administration.

Choda, B. (1946). A counseling program in a relocation center. The Family, 27(4), 140–145.

Department of State. (1945). Memorandum re: Requests and complaints from the residents of Poston to the Spanish Consul, February 12, 1945, pp. 1–4. Folder 120.2 Public Reactions, Box 112: Subject-Classified General Files—Colorado River Central Files—110.41 to 130. Records of the War Relocation Authority, 1941–1989, Record Group 210, Subject-Classified General Files of the Relocation Centers—compiled 1942–1946. ARC Identifier 1544889/MLR Number PI-77 48. Washington, DC: National Archives and Records Administration.

D'Ille, M. (1943). Memorandum to Mrs. Lucy W. Adams, Chief of Community Services Division, from Margaret D'Ille, Counselor, Community Welfare, Manzanar Relocation Center, Manzanar, California, March 9, 1943, pp. 1–2. Folder: 18.200—Social Welfare Cases, Box 220: Manzanar Relocation Center—Central Files—50.026 to 62.014. Records of the War Relocation Authority, 1941–1989, Record Group 210, Subject-Classified General Files of the Relocation Centers—compiled 1942–1946. ARC Identifier 1544889/MLR Number PI-77 48. Washington, DC: National Archives and Records Administration.

Dusseldorp, W. V. (1945). Historical Statistical—Functional Report of Welfare Section, Wilma Van Dusseldorp—Head Counselor. War Relocation Authority, Rohwer Relocation Center, McGehee, Arkansas (Calisphere, Japanese American Relocation Digital Archives ed.). Berkeley: Bancroft Library, University of California.

Ellis, M. B. (1942). Report of conference with Grace Coyle, July 24, 1942: Memorandum to West Coast Consultants from Mabel Brown Ellis, July 30, 1942, pp. 1–2. Folder 23, Box 719. YWCA of the U.S.A. Records, Sophia Smith Collection. Northampton, MA: Smith College.

Ellis, M. B., & Ingraham, M. A. (April, 1942). News and Views: West Coast Evacuations and the YWCA. Woman's Press, 36, pp. 189. Smith College, YWCA of the USA—Bound Periodicals, Sophia Smith Collection. Northampton, MA: Smith College.

Flack, H. N. (1942). Letter to Dillon S. Meyer, Director, WRA, from Helen N. Flack, Division of Community YWCA's, May 28, 1942, p. 1. Folder: 523.6—YWCA Box 38: Subject Class. Gen. Files of the SF Regional Office, 1942, 521.22 to 530. Records of the War Relocation Authority, 1941–1989, Record Group 210, Subject-Classified General Files—compiled 1942–1942. ARC Identifier 1543537/MLR Number PI-77 38. Washington, DC: National Archives and Records Administration.

Gifford, S. (1943). Baby beds—Rohwer: Memorandum to John H. Provinse, Chief, Community Services Division, from Selene Gifford, Public Welfare Consultant, Welfare Section, WRA, Washington, DC, July 16, 1943, p. 1. Folder: Provinse,

John—#2—May-October, 1943, Box 35: Washington Office Records—Chronological File; General—Alphabetical—PF-John Provinse. Records of the War Relocation Authority, 1941–1989, Record Group 210, General Outgoing Correspondence, compiled 1942–1946. ARC Identifier 1534421/MLR Number PI-77 18. Washington, DC: National Archives and Records Administration.

Gifford, S. (1944). Letter to Jane Hoey, Director, Social Security Board, from Selene Gifford, Head of Welfare Section, War Relocation Authority, dated April 18, 1944, p. 1. Folder: Social Security Board, Box 40: Washington Office Records—Chronological File; General—Alphabetical—SN-STATE DEPT. Records of the War Relocation Authority, 1941–1989, Record Group 210, General Outgoing Correspondence, compiled 1942–1946. ARC Identifier 1534421/MLR Number PI-77 18. Washington, DC: National Archives and Records Administration.

Glick, P. M. (1943). Excerpts from the August 28 report of Ted Hass, Project Attorney at Poston: Memorandum to John H. Provinse, Chief, Community Services Division, from Philip M. Glick, Solicitor, WRA, Washington, DC, September 9, 1943, p. 1. Folder: Provinse, John—#2—May-October, 1943, Box 35: Washington Office Records—Chronological File; General—Alphabetical—PF-John Provinse. Records of the War Relocation Authority, 1941–1989, Record Group 210, General Outgoing Correspondence, compiled 1942–1946. ARC Identifier 1534421/MLR Number PI-77 18. Washington, DC: National Archives and Records Administration.

Hayashi, D. (1942). Organizational meeting of the YWCA: Second meeting, Topaz, November 14, 1942, pp. 1–2. Folder 20, Box 724. YWCA of the U.S. Records, Sophia Smith Collection. Northampton, MA: Smith College.

Irwin, C. (2008). *Twice orphaned: Voices from the Children's Village of Manzanar.* Fullerton, CA: Center for Oral and Public History.

Johnston, R. G. (1944). Letter to Mr. E. B. Whitaker, Project Director, Jerome Relocation Center, Denson, Arkansas, from Ray G. Johnston, Project Director, Rohwer Relocation Center, McGhehee, Arkansas, February 19, 1944, pp. 1–2. Folder: 61.513—Family Reunion—Crystal City, Box 200: Jerome Center, Denson, Arkansas—Central Files—61.512to 62.010. Records of the War Relocation Authority, 1941–1989, Record Group 210, Subject-Classified General Files of the Relocation Centers—compiled 1942–1946. ARC Identifier 1544889/MLR Number PI-77 48. Washington, DC: National Archives and Records Administration.

Kell, A. S. (1945). Welfare Section Final Report by Adeline S. Kell, Counselor, Term of Service August 28, 1944 to Center closure. War Relocation Authority, Heart Mountain Relocation Center, Heart Mountain, Wyoming (Calisphere, Japanese American Relocation Digital Archives ed., pp. 1–12). Berkeley: Bancroft Library, University of California.

Kikuchi, C. (1942a). Diary 5: September 2–30, 1942, pp. 1–182. Folder W 1.80:05**, Box BANC MSS 67/14 c. Japanese American Evacuation and Resettlement Study, Japanese American Evacuation and Resettlement records. Berkeley: Bancroft Library, University of California.

Kikuchi, C. (1942b). Diary 6: October 1–14, 1942, pp. 1–127. Folder W 1.80:06**, Box BANC MSS 67/14 c. Japanese American Evacuation and Resettlement Study, Japanese American Evacuation and Resettlement records. Berkeley: Bancroft Library, University of California.

Kikuchi, C. (1942c). Diary 8: November 1–15, 1942, pp. 1–175. Folder W 1.80:08**, Box BANC MSS 67/14 c. Japanese American Evacuation and Resettlement Study, Japanese American Evacuation and Resettlement records. Berkeley: Bancroft Library, University of California.

Kikuchi, C. (1943a). Diary 11: December 18, 1942–January 8, 1943, pp. 1–218. Folder W 1.80:011**, Box BANC MSS 67/14 c. Japanese American Evacuation and Resettlement Study, Japanese American Evacuation and Resettlement records. Berkeley: Bancroft Library, University of California.

Kikuchi, C. (1943b). Diary 12: January 8-31, 1943, pp. 1–207. Folder W 1.80:012**, Box BANC MSS 67/14 c. Japanese American Evacuation and Resettlement Study, Japanese American Evacuation and Resettlement records. Berkeley: Bancroft Library, University of California.

Kikuchi, C. (1943c). Diary 14: March 1-31, 1943, pp. 1–295. Folder W 1.80:014**, Box BANC MSS 67/14 c. Japanese American Evacuation and Resettlement Study, Japanese American Evacuation and Resettlement records. Berkeley: Bancroft Library, University of California.

Kikuchi, C. (1942d). Diary 8: November 1-15, 1942. pp. 1–175. folder W 1.80:08**, Box BANC MSS 67/14 c. Japanese American Evacuation and Resettlement Study, Japanese American Evacuation and Resettlement records. Berkeley, CA: Bancroft Library, University of California.

Kikuchi, M. (1942a). Memorandum to Mr. Kidwell, from Miya Kikuchi, Family Relations, Manzanar Relocation Center, Manzanar, California, April 27, 1942, pp. 1–3. Folder: 18.200—Social Welfare Cases, Box 220: Manzanar Relocation Center—Central Files—50.026 to 62.014. Records of the War Relocation Authority, 1941–1989, Record Group 210, Subject-Classified General Files of the Relocation Centers—compiled 1942–1946. ARC Identifier 1544889/MLR Number PI-77 48. Washington, DC: National Archives and Records Administration.

Kikuchi, M. (1942b). Memorandum to Mr. Kidwell, from Miya Kikuchi, Family Relations, Manzanar Relocation Center, Manzanar, California, April 30, 1942, pp. 1–2. Folder: 18.200—Social Welfare Cases, Box 220: Manzanar Relocation Center—Central Files—50.026 to 62.014. Records of the War Relocation Authority, 1941–1989, Record Group 210, Subject-Classified General Files of the Relocation Centers—compiled 1942–1946. ARC Identifier 1544889/MLR Number PI-77 48. Washington, DC: National Archives and Records Administration.

Kimmerling, C., Fite, A. L., & Abbott, C. W. (1945). Report of the Welfare Section, August 1942 to November 1945. War Relocation Authority, Minidoka Relocation Center (Calisphere, Japanese American Relocation Digital Archives ed., pp. 1–69). University of California, Berkeley: Bancroft Library.

Kinoshita, P. (1944). Crisis in housing situation of Unit I: Memorandum to Executive committee and Civic Planning Board, from Housing Department, Unit I, pp. 1–4. Folder 020.46 Welfare, Box 106: Subject-Classified General Files—Colorado River Central Files—020.31 to 030.32. Records of the War Relocation Authority, 1941–1989, Record Group 210, Subject-Classified General Files of the Relocation Centers—compiled 1942–1946. ARC Identifier 1544889/MLR Number PI-77 48. Washington, DC: National Archives and Records Administration.

Kuramoto, F. (1976). A History of the Shonien, 1914–1972: An account of a program of institutional care of Japanese children in Los Angeles. San Francisco: R and E Research Associates.

Kusayanagi, S. (1943). Letter from Sally Kusayanagi regarding the first anniversary of the Manzanar YWCA, dated July 23, 1943, p. 1. Folder 16, Box 723. YWCA of the U.S. Records, Sophia Smith Collection. Northampton, MA: Smith College.

Landward, J. (1942). Letter to Mr. Harry Iida, Tule Lake Relocation Center, Newell, California, from John Landward, Gila River Project, Rivers, Arizona, October 28, 1942, pp. 1–2. Folder: 580—Community Service and Welfare, Box 144: Gila River Relocation Center—Central Files—571 to 580. Records of the War Relocation Authority, 1941–1989, Record Group 210, Subject-Classified General Files of the Relocation Centers—compiled 1942–1946. ARC Identifier 1544889/MLR Number PI-77 48. Washington, DC: National Archives and Records Administration.

Lane, M. D. (1944). Memo to Jane Hoey, Director, Social Security Board, from Marie Dresden Lane, Head of Welfare Section, War Relocation Authority, dated October 10, 1944, pp. 1–2. Folder: Social Security Board, Box 40: Washington Office Records—Chronological File; General—Alphabetical—SN-STATE DEPT. Records of the War Relocation Authority, 1941–1989, Record Group 210, General Outgoing Correspondence, compiled 1942–1946. ARC Identifier 1534421/MLR Number PI-77 18. Washington, DC: National Archives and Records Administration.

Leighton, A. H. (1942–43). Staff meetings—Poston Relocation Center (Ariz.) (Compiled), pp. 1–33. Folder J10.05 (1/2), Box BANC MSS 67/14 c. Bureau of Sociological Research (Poston, Ariz.), Japanese American Evacuation and Resettlement records. Berkeley: Bancroft Library, University of California.

Lyle, B. (1943). Summary Report of the Japanese American Project, August 1942–September 1943, pp. 1–7. Folder 2, Box 720. YWCA of the U.S. Records, Sophia Smith Collection. Northampton, MA: Smith College.

Manzanar Public Welfare Department (1943). Memorandum of a talk between Mrs. D'Ille, Counselor, Manzanar Relocation Center and Miss Ellen Marshall, Acting Director of Social Work for Children's Aid Society of California, pp. 1–2. Folder: 61. 520—Child Welfare—Children's Village, Box 224: Manzanar Relocation Center—Central Files—50.026 to 62.014. Records of the War Relocation Authority, 1941–1989, Record Group 210, Subject-Classified General Files of the Relocation Centers—compiled 1942–1946. ARC Identifier 1544889/MLR Number PI-77 48. Washington, DC: National Archives and Records Administration.

Manzanar Relocation Center (1944). Minutes of the meeting of the Coordinating Council Meeting, November 28, 1944, pp. 1–3. Folder: 60.120 Youth Coordinating Council, Box 225: Manzanar Relocation Center Central Files 50.026 to 62.014 (1942 to 1943). Records of the War Relocation Authority, 1941–1989, Record Group 210, Subject-Classified General Files of the Relocation Centers—compiled 1942–1946. ARC Identifier 1544889/MLR Number PI-77 48. Washington, DC: National Archives and Records Administration.

Marks Jr., E. B. (1943). Memorandum to John H. Provinse, Chief, Community Services Division, WRA, Washington, DC, April 2, 1943, pp. 1–3. Folder: Provinse, John—Jan.–April, 1943, Box 35: Washington Office Records—Chronological File; General—Alphabetical—PF-John Provinse. Records of the War Relocation Authority, 1941–1989, Record Group 210, General Outgoing Correspondence, compiled 1942–1946. ARC Identifier 1534421/MLR Number PI-77 18. Washington, DC: National Archives and Records Administration.

McCord, V. H. (1944). Colorado River Center: Memorandum to John H. Provinse, Chief, Community Services Division, from Vera H. McCord, Acting Head, Welfare Section, WRA, Washington, DC, July 29, 1944, pp. 1–2. Folder: Provinse, John—#4—June-December, 1944, Box 35: Washington Office Records—Chronological File;

General—Alphabetical—PF-John Provinse. Records of the War Relocation Authority, 1941–1989, Record Group 210, General Outgoing Correspondence, compiled 1942–1946. ARC Identifier 1534421/MLR Number PI-77 18. Washington, DC: National Archives and Records Administration.

Miyamoto, S. F. (1942). Prevalent fears in Tule Lake Community, pp. 1–33. Folder R 20.34, Box BANC MSS 67/14 c. Japanese American Evacuation and Resettlement Study, Japanese American Evacuation and Resettlement records. Berkeley: Bancroft Library, University of California.

Moore, J. J. O. (1943). Transfer of cases from the Colorado State Hospital at Pueblo to California Institutions: Memorandum to Mr. James G. Lindley, Project Director, from John J. O. Moore, Counselor, Public Welfare Section, Granada Relocation Center, Amache, Colorado, October 20, 1943, pp. 1–2. Folder: 521—Correspondence on Crippled, Blind, & Mental, Box 135: Granada Relocation Center—Central Files—514 to 624. Records of the War Relocation Authority, 1941–1989, Record Group 210, Subject-Classified General Files of the Relocation Centers—compiled 1942–1946. ARC Identifier 1544889/MLR Number PI-77 48. Washington, DC: National Archives and Records Administration.

Morimitsu, A. T., & Waller, T. (1942). Tule Lake Relocation Center Community Activities Report, for the period May 27, 1942 to July 20, 1942, dated July 25, 1942 pp. 1–13. Folder 1, Box 724. YWCA of the U.S. Records, Sophia Smith Collection. Northampton, MA: Smith College.

Mukaye, K. (1942). Report on Granada Relocation Center, Granada, Colorado, October 11, 1942 pp. 1–4. Folder 9, Box 724. YWCA of the U.S. Records, Sophia Smith Collection. Northampton, MA: Smith College.

Nakamura, M. L. (1942). Letter from Mary Lucy Nakamura, Girls Clubs, Heart Mountain, Wyoming, to Miss Esther Briesemeister, dated November 5, 1942, pp. 1–3. Folder 23, Box 724. YWCA of the U.S. Records, Sophia Smith Collection. Northampton, MA: Smith College.

Neher, L. M. (1944). Amache Patients in the Pueblo State Institution for the Insane: Memorandum to Mr. Lindley Project Director, from L. M. Neher, M.D., Acting Chief Medical Officer, Granada Relocation Center, Amache, Colorado, May 19, 1944, pp. 1–2. Folder: 521—Correspondence on Crippled, Blind, & Mental, Box 135: Granada Relocation Center—Central Files—514 to 624. Records of the War Relocation Authority, 1941–1989, Record Group 210, Subject-Classified General Files of the Relocation Centers—compiled 1942–1946. ARC Identifier 1544889/MLR Number PI-77 48. Washington, DC: National Archives and Records Administration.

Nobe, L. N. (1999). The Children's Village at Manzanar: The World War II eviction and detention of Japanese American orphans. Journal of the West, 38(2), 65–71.

North, L. (1942). The educational system at Granada Relocation Center, Amache, Colorado, November 23, 1942, pp. 1–4. Folder 9, Box 724. YWCA of the U.S.A. Records, Sophia Smith Collection. Northampton, MA: Smith College.

Payne, V. (1944). Weekly report—week ending March17, 1944: Memorandum to Reports Division from Social Service Department, Heart Mountain Relocation Project, Heart Mountain, Wyoming, pp. 1–5. Folder: Welfare—General, Box 159: Heart Mountain Relocation Center—Central Files—Hearings and Reports to Community Activities (General). Records of the War Relocation Authority, 1941–1989, Record Group 210, Subject-Classified General Files of the Relocation Centers—compiled 1942–1946.

ARC Identifier 1544889/MLR Number PI-77 48. Washington, DC: National Archives and Records Administration.

Phillips, S. (1944). Letter to R. E. Arne, Assistant Project Director, Community Management Division, Jerome Relocation Center, Denson, Arkansas, from Spencer Phillips, Superintendent, Louisiana State School for the Deaf, Baton Rouge, March 24, 1944, pp. 1–2. Folder: 61.510—Welfare (General), Box 198: Jerome Center, Denson, Arkansas—Central Files—61.310 to 61.510. Records of the War Relocation Authority, 1941–1989, Record Group 210, Subject-Classified General Files of the Relocation Centers—compiled 1942–1946. ARC Identifier 1544889/MLR Number PI-77 48. Washington, DC: National Archives and Records Administration.

Pirrone, T. (1944). Letter to Katherine M. Scott, Medical Social Worker, Heart Mountain Relocation Project, Heart Mountain, Wyoming, from Miss Teresa Pirrone, Assistant Counselor-Medical Social Worker, Public Welfare Section, Granada Relocation Center, Amache, Colorado from October 17, 1944, pp. 1–2. Folder: Hospital (General) 1944 to 45, Box 159: Heart Mountain Relocation Center—Central Files—Hearings and Reports to Community Activities (General). Records of the War Relocation Authority, 1941–1989, Record Group 210, Subject-Classified General Files of the Relocation Centers—compiled 1942–1946. ARC Identifier 1544889/MLR Number PI-77 48. Washington, DC: National Archives and Records Administration.

Powell, J. W. (1942). Formation of Guidance Committee: Memorandum to Duncan Mills, Project Director, Colorado River Relocation Center, from John Powell, Assistant Project Director, February 22, 1945, p. 1. Folder 020.4 Community Management, Box 106: Subject-Classified General Files—Colorado River Central Files—020.31 to 030.32. Records of the War Relocation Authority, 1941–1989, Record Group 210, Subject-Classified General Files of the Relocation Centers—compiled 1942–1946. ARC Identifier 1544889/MLR Number PI-77 48. Washington, DC: National Archives and Records Administration.

Powell, J. W. (1943). Jurisdiction of the Community Management Division: Memorandum to W. Wade Head, Project Director, Colorado River Relocation Center, from John Powell, Acting Chief of Community Management, December 21, 1943, pp. 1–4. Folder 020.4 Community Management, Box 106: Subject-Classified General Files—Colorado River Central Files—020.31 to 030.32. Records of the War Relocation Authority, 1941–1989, Record Group 210, Subject-Classified General Files of the Relocation Centers—compiled 1942–1946. ARC Identifier 1544889/MLR Number PI-77 48. Washington, DC: National Archives and Records Administration.

Pratt, C. H. (1945). Closing report of the Welfare Section, from Sept. 11, 1943 to Center Closing, dated December 20, 1945. War Relocation Authority, Central Utah Project, Topaz, Utah (Calisphere, Japanese American Relocation Digital Archives ed., Vol. Bancroft Library, pp. 1–10). Berkeley: Bancroft Library, University of California.

Reith, M. B. (1943a). Report on Topaz WRA Project, Topaz, Utah, June 7–10, 1943, pp. 1–6. Folder 21, Box 724. YWCA of the U.S. Records, Sophia Smith Collection. Northampton, MA: Smith College.

Reith, M. B. (1943b). Report on Tule Lake Visit, March 1–11–12, 1943, pp. 1–14. Folder 3, Box 724. YWCA of the U.S.A. Records, Sophia Smith Collection. Northampton, MA: Smith College.

Rowalt, E. M. (1943). Hospitalization of mental cases: Memorandum to all project directors, from E. M. Rowalt, Acting Director, WRA, stamped April 26, 1943, p. 1. Folder: Administrative Notices (6 of 7), Box 1: Administrative Notices. Records of the War Relocation Authority, 1941–1989, Record Group 210, Washington Office Records—Washington Documents. ARC Identifier 5634012/MLR Number P 4 (formerly UD 5). Washington, DC: National Archives and Records Administration.

Sakoda, J. M. (1942). Social Welfare Department, Tule Lake Relocation Center, November 11, 1942, pp. 1–130. Box BANC MSS 67/14 c. Japanese American Evacuation and Resettlement Study, Japanese American Evacuation and Resettlement records. Berkeley: Bancroft Library, University of California.

Scott, K. M. (1944). Letter to Miss Teresa Pirrone, Medical Social Worker, Public Welfare Section, Granada Relocation Center, Amache, Colorado from Katherine M. Scott, Medical Social Worker, Heart Mountain Relocation Project, Heart Mountain, Wyoming, November 13, 1944, p. 1. Folder: Hospital (General) 1944 to 45, Box 159: Heart Mountain Relocation Center—Central Files—Hearings and Reports to Community Activities (General). Records of the War Relocation Authority, 1941–1989, Record Group 210, Subject-Classified General Files of the Relocation Centers—compiled 1942–1946. ARC Identifier 1544889/MLR Number PI-77 48. Washington, DC: National Archives and Records Administration.

Sharpley, L. (1943). Report on Topaz Relocation Center, Delta, Utah: Dates of visit—March 15–17, 1943; date of filing report—March 22, 1943, pp. 1–5. Folder 21, Box 724. YWCA of the U.S.A. Records, Sophia Smith Collection. Northampton, MA: Smith College.

Shibutani, T. (1943a). Case documents TL-1-6, 8 by family name [indicates pseudonym]—Family organization and disorganization (compiled documents), pp. 1–81. Folder R 21.08:1**, Box BANC MSS 67/14 c. Japanese American Evacuation and Resettlement Study, Japanese American Evacuation and Resettlement records. Berkeley: Bancroft Library, University of California.

Shibutani, T. (1943b). Case documents TL-10, 12-16 by family name [indicates pseudonym]—Family organization and disorganization (compiled documents), pp. 1–79. Folder R 21.08:1**, Box BANC MSS 67/14 c. Japanese American Evacuation and Resettlement Study, Japanese American Evacuation and Resettlement records. Berkeley: Bancroft Library, University of California.

Shibutani, T. (1943c). Case documents TL-17-26 by family name [indicates pseudonym]—Family organization and disorganization (compiled documents), pp. 1–91. Folder R 21.08:4**, Box BANC MSS 67/14 c. Japanese American Evacuation and Resettlement Study, Japanese American Evacuation and Resettlement records. Berkeley: Bancroft Library, University of California.

Shibutani, T. (1943d). Case documents TL-27-30, 32-34 by family name [indicates pseudonym]—Family organization and disorganization (compiled documents), pp. 1–102. Folder R 21.08:5**, Box BANC MSS 67/14 c. Japanese American Evacuation and Resettlement Study, Japanese American Evacuation and Resettlement records. Berkeley: Bancroft Library, University of California.

Shibutani, T. (1943e). Case documents TL-71-72, 101-106, 109-110, 112 by family name [indicates pseudonym]—Family organization and disorganization (compiled documents), pp. 1–76. Folder R 21.08:8**, Box BANC MSS 67/14 c. Japanese American Evacuation and Resettlement Study, Japanese American Evacuation and Resettlement records. Berkeley: Bancroft Library, University of California.

Shipps, H. K. (1943). Memorandum to Miss Selene Gifford, Head, Welfare Section, from Helen K. Shipps, Medical Social Consultant, WRA, Washington, DC, June 3, 1943, pp. 1–2. Folder: Gifford, Selene, Box 17: Washington Office Records—Chronological

File; General—Alphabetical—GF-GRE. Records of the War Relocation Authority, 1941–1989, Record Group 210, General Outgoing Correspondence, compiled 1942–1946. ARC Identifier 1534421/MLR Number PI-77 18. Washington, DC: National Archives and Records Administration.

Tanaka, B. (1942). Inadequate housing: Memorandum to Mr. Wade Head, Project Director, Colorado River Relocation Center, from Bill Tanaka, Block Manager of #46, October 6, 1942, pp. 1–2. Folder 020.46 Welfare, Box 106: Subject-Classified General Files—Colorado River Central Files—020.31 to 030.32. Records of the War Relocation Authority, 1941–1989, Record Group 210, Subject-Classified General Files of the Relocation Centers—compiled 1942–1946. ARC Identifier 1544889/MLR Number PI-77 48. Washington, DC: National Archives and Records Administration.

Thompson, G. D. C. (1943a). Health Personnel shortage: Memorandum to John H. Provinse, Chief, Community Services Division, from G. D. Carlyle Thompson, Chief Medical Officer, WRA, Washington, DC, June 7, 1943, pp. 1–3. Folder: Provinse, John—#2—May–October, 1943, Box 35: Washington Office Records—Chronological File; General—Alphabetical—PF-John Provinse. Records of the War Relocation Authority, 1941–1989, Record Group 210, General Outgoing Correspondence, compiled 1942–1946. ARC Identifier 1534421/MLR Number PI-77 18. Washington, DC: National Archives and Records Administration.

Thompson, G. D. C. (1943b). Quarterly Report, January 1st–March 31, 1943, pp. 1–4. Folder: Semi-Annual Reports—Community Management Division—Reports of Health Section & Reports of Welfare Section, Box 5: Washington Office Records—Documentary Files—Semi-Annual Reports: Operation D Division, Community Mgmt. Div., Administrative Mgmt. Division. Records of the War Relocation Authority, 1941–1989, Record Group 210, Headquarters Basic Documentation Reports, compiled 1942–1946. ARC Identifier 1526983/MLR Number PI-77 3. Washington, DC: National Archives and Records Administration.

Thompson, G. D. C. (1943c). Semi-Annual Report, July 1–Dec. 30, 1943, pp. 1–4. Folder: Semi-Annual Reports—Community Management Division—Reports of Health Section & Reports of Welfare Section, Box 5: Washington Office Records—Documentary Files—Semi-Annual Reports: Operation D Division, Community Mgmt. Div., Administrative Mgmt. Division. Records of the War Relocation Authority, 1941–1989, Record Group 210, Headquarters Basic Documentation Reports, compiled 1942–1946. ARC Identifier 1526983/MLR Number PI-77 3. Washington, DC: National Archives and Records Administration.

Tsuchiyama, T. (1942). 13. Housing (compiled documents), pp. 1–76. Folder J6.27 Box BANC MSS 67/14 c. Japanese American Evacuation and Resettlement Study, Japanese American Evacuation and Resettlement records. Berkeley: Bancroft Library, University of California.

Tsuchiyama, T. (1943). Attitudes—Poston Relocation Center, 1942–43 (compiled documents), pp. 1–92. Folder J6.27 (03/27), Box BANC MSS 67/14 c. Japanese American Evacuation and Resettlement Study, Japanese American Evacuation and Resettlement records. Berkeley: Bancroft Library, University of California.

Tuttle, W. K. (1943). Rummage sale for clothing on hand: Memorandum to Mr. Morton J. Gaba, from Mr. Tuttle, Counselor, Social Service Department, Gila River Project, Rivers, Arizona, March 16, 1943, p. 1. Folder: 580—Community Service and Welfare, Box 144: Gila River Relocation Center—Central Files—571 to 580. Records of the War Relocation Authority, 1941–1989, Record Group 210, Subject-Classified General

Files of the Relocation Centers—compiled 1942–1946. ARC Identifier 1544889/MLR Number PI-77 48. Washington, DC: National Archives and Records Administration.

Tuttle, W. K. (1945). History of Gila Welfare Section by W. K. Tuttle, Head, Welfare Section. War Relocation Authority, Gila River Relocation Center, Rivers, Arizona (Calisphere, Japanese American Relocation Digital Archives ed., pp. 1–10). Berkeley: Bancroft Library, University of California.

War Relocation Authority (1942). Third Quarterly Report: October 1 to December 31, 1942, pp. 1–71. Folder: Second Quarterly Report—WRA Printed—July 1 to Sept. 30, 1942, Box 1: Washington Office Records—Documentary Files—Quarterly Reports 1942. Records of the War Relocation Authority, 1941–1989, Record Group 210, Headquarters Basic Documentation Reports, compiled 1942–1946. ARC Identifier 1526983/MLR Number PI-77 3. Washington, DC: National Archives and Records Administration.

War Relocation Authority (1943a). Project Analysis Series No. 9, June 23, 1943: Preliminary Survey of Resistances to Resettlement at the Tule Lake Relocation Center, pp. 1–15. Folder 3, Box 724. YWCA of the U.S.A. Records, Sophia Smith Collection. Northampton, MA: Smith College.

War Relocation Authority (1943b). Quarterly Report: Community Welfare Section, January 1- March 31, 1943, pp. 1–3. Folder: Semi-Annual Reports—Community Management Division—Reports of Health Section & Reports of Welfare Section, Box 5: Washington Office Records—Documentary Files—Semi-Annual Reports: Operation D Division, Community Mgmt. Div., Administrative Mgmt. Division. Records of the War Relocation Authority, 1941–1989, Record Group 210, Headquarters Basic Documentation Reports, compiled 1942–1946. ARC Identifier 1526983/MLR Number PI-77 3. Washington, DC: National Archives and Records Administration.

War Relocation Authority (1943c). Quarterly Report: Welfare Section—April 1 to June 30, 1943, dated September 28, 1943, pp. 1–3. Folder: Semi-Annual Reports— Community Management Division Reports of Health Section & Reports of Welfare Section, Box 5: Washington Office Records—Documentary Files—Semi-Annual Reports: Operation D Division, Community Mgmt. Div., Administrative Mgmt. Division. Records of the War Relocation Authority, 1941–1989, Record Group 210, Headquarters Basic Documentation Reports, compiled 1942–1946. ARC Identifier 1526983/MLR Number PI-77 3. Washington, DC: National Archives and Records Administration.

War Relocation Authority (1943d). Semi-Annual Report, July 1–Dec. 31, 1943, pp. 1– 90. Folder: Semi-Annual Report, July 1–Dec. 31, 1943, Box 3: Washington Office Records—Documentary Files—Semi-Annual Reports, 1943 & 1944: Semi-Annual Reports, Evacuee Employment; Annual reports, 1943 &1944; History of WRA, Ruth McKee; Annual Report of the Director of WRA; Semi-Annual Reports, Oswego 1944. Records of the War Relocation Authority, 1941–1989, Record Group 210, Headquarters Basic Documentation Reports, compiled 1942–1946. ARC Identifier 1526983/MLR Number PI-77 3. Washington, DC: National Archives and Records Administration.

War Relocation Authority (1944). Semi-Annual Reports: Report of the Welfare Section, July 1- December 31, 1944, pp. 1–6. Folder: Semi-Annual Reports— Community Management Division—Reports of Health Section & Reports of Welfare Section, Box 5: Washington Office Records—Documentary Files—Semi-Annual Reports: Operation D Division, Community Mgmt. Div., Administrative Mgmt.

Division. Records of the War Relocation Authority, 1941–1989, Record Group 210, Headquarters Basic Documentation Reports, compiled 1942–1946. ARC Identifier 1526983/MLR Number PI-77 3. Washington, DC: National Archives and Records Administration.

War Relocation Authority (1943). Evacuee Housing. pp. 1–3. Folder: Health Section—Community Management Division, Box 4: Community Management Division—Monthly Vocational Training (1944–45), Education, Welfare and Housing, Health, Internal Security, Religion. Operational Division—Engineering and Agriculture. Records of the War Relocation Authority, 1941–1989, Record Group 210, Washington Office Records—Washington Documents, ARC Identifier 1519285 / MLR Number PI-77 2 Washington, DC: National Archives and Records Administration.

War Relocation Authority (n.d.-b). Interim policy on Special Transfers to and between relocation centers, pp. 1–2. Folder: Circular Letters, Box 1: Miscellaneous Records 1942-48. Records of the War Relocation Authority, 1941–1989, Record Group 210, Headquarters Records; Miscellaneous Records, 1942-48. ARC Identifier 5634526/MLR Number P 15 (formerly UD18). Washington, DC: National Archives and Records Administration.

Watson, A. C. (1942). Letter to Theodore Waller, Tule Lake Project, War Relocation Authority, from Annie Clo Watson, Secretary, Division of Community YWCA's, September 18, 1942, p. 1. Folder: 523 Americanization and Literacy (Boy Scouts, Girl Reserves, etc.), Box 522: Subject-Classified General Files—Tule Lake Relocation Center Central Files—522 to 535. Records of the War Relocation Authority, 1941–1989, Record Group 210, Subject-Classified General Files of the Relocation Centers—compiled 1942–1946. ARC Identifier 1544889/MLR Number PI-77 48. Washington, DC: National Archives and Records Administration.

Webb, J. L. (1945). Final report: Community Management division, Welfare Section. War Relocation Authority, Jerome Relocation Center, Jerome, Arkansas (Calisphere, Japanese American Relocation Digital Archives ed., pp. 1–37). Berkeley: Bancroft Library, University of California.

Woodsmall, R. L. (1942). Impressions of the Japanese Relocation Center at Manzanar, California: World's YWCA, Washington, DC, dated December 1, 1942, pp. 1–5. Folder 14, Box 723. YWCA of the U.S.A. Records, Sophia Smith Collection. Northampton, MA: Smith College.

Wygel, W. (1943). Report on Manzanar, July 22–27, 1943, pp. 1–11. Folder 16, Box 723. YWCA of the U.S.A. Records, Sophia Smith Collection. Northampton, MA: Smith College.

YWCA National Board (1942). A proposal for work which the National Board of the Young Women's Christian Association might assume in relation to Japanese reception and resettlement areas in the Western Defense Command, prepared by Helen Flack, Nationality Secretary, Western Region, San Francisco, pp. 1–3. Folder 20, Box 719. YWCA of the U.S.A. Records, Sophia Smith Collection. Northampton, MA: Smith College.

YWCA National Board—Community Division Committee (1942). Minutes of the Community Division Committee Meeting, Tuesday, March 3, 1942, pp. 1–2. Folder 20, Box 719. YWCA of the U.S.A. Records, Northampton, MA: Smith College.

YWCA National Board—Community Division Committee (1944). Minutes of the Community Division Committee Meeting, Tuesday, January 4, 1944, pp. 1–2. Folder 20, Box 719. YWCA of the U.S.A. Records, Sophia Smith Collection. Northampton, MA: Smith College.

YWCA National Board—Race Relations Subcommittee of the National Public Affairs Committee (1942). Minutes of the Race Relations Section—Public Affairs Committee, April 22, 1942, p. 1. Folder 1, Box 395. YWCA of the U.S.A. Records, Sophia Smith Collection. Northampton, MA: Smith College.

YWCA National Board—Race Relations Subcommittee of the National Public Affairs Committee (1946). Minutes of Race Relations Subcommittee, April 17 1946, Mrs. Frances K. Chalmers, presiding, pp. 1–4. Folder 3, Box 395. YWCA of the U.S.A. Records, Sophia Smith Collection. Northampton, MA: Smith College.

YWCA of the U.S.A. (1942a). Outline of a plan of work for Miss Mabel Ellis during the West Coast Evacuation Emergency: Prepared and discussed in Executive Staff Group, March 19, 1942, p. 1. Folder 3, Box 716. YWCA of the U.S.A. Records, Sophia Smith Collection. Northampton, MA: Smith College.

YWCA of the U.S.A. (1942b). War Time Program for Women and Girls of Japanese Ancestry: Division of Community Y.W.C.A.'s, dated July 13, 1942 pp. 1–5. Folder 23, Box 719. YWCA of the U.S.A. Records, Sophia Smith Collection. Northampton, MA: Smith College.

YWCA of the U.S.A. (May, 1942). News and Views: funds appropriated for work with Japanese Evacuees. pp. 260. Smith College, YWCA of the USA—Bound Periodicals. Northampton, MA: Sophia Smith Collection.

7

The Emotional Crisis of Registration

"Loyalty Questionnaire"

Among the sea of institutionally created troubles that befell Nikkei families in incarceration, arguably the most catastrophic was the family conflict and separation generated by the "loyalty questionnaire," an administrative debacle which churned violently through the ten camps, splitting apart families and communities for generations to come. The questionnaire began life as a War Department project devised to uncover "tendencies of loyalty or disloyalty" (Commission on Wartime Relocation and Internment of Civilians, 1982, p. 190) among the Nisei. In a total reversal from its policy barring the Nisei from all military service instituted early in the War, the department planned to create a segregated combat team comprised of Nisei volunteers and to register the age-eligible remainder for the draft.[1] The survey was to provide them with information to weed out the disloyal. In early January of 1943, the War Relocation Authority (WRA) learned of the imminent implementation of the questionnaire and proposed enlarging the project to include not only the draft-age Nisei, but "anyone who had reached seventeen years of age by February 1, 1943" (War Relocation Authority, 1943c, p. 4), citizen or not, incarcerated in its camps. The WRA would use the survey results to expedite the "Leave Clearance" process, its existing methods for vetting those who applied to leave the camps for seasonal work or for resettlement and in furthering its "all-out relocation policy program" (Meyer, 1974, p. 28a), a scheme for the "permanent relocation" (Briesemeister, 1946, p. 38) of the Nikkei outside the camps. The "mass registration"—the execution of the 28-item questionnaire—begun in February 1943 was the "most important step in this process" (War Relocation Authority, 1943c, p. 15) that the agency had thus far undertaken. The WRA had, according to its post-registration propaganda materials, "realized the necessity of taking adequate precautions to safeguard national security" before letting them out, having "recognized from the beginning that some of the evacuees had stronger ties with Japan than with the United States" (War Relocation Authority, 1943c, p. 15).

The first 25 questions solicited information on "such matters as education, previous employment, relatives in Japan, knowledge of the Japanese language,

---

[1] In the end, the Army recruited 1,208 volunteers.

Facilitating Injustice: The complicity of social workers in the forced removal and incarceration of Japanese Americans, 1941–1946. Yoosun Park, Oxford University Press (2020). © Oxford University Press.
DOI: 10.1093/acprof:oso/9780199765058.001.0001

investments in Japan, organizational and religious affiliations, and other pertinent matters" (War Relocation Authority, 1943c, p. 15) including dates and
purpose of foreign travel, lists of customarily read magazines and newspapers,
and lists of sports and hobbies. The answers were then "scored according to categories of 'Americanness' and 'Japaneseness' that each response" (Lyon, 2014,
May 12) was deemed to have indicated. The last two questions in the questionnaire were the infamous Questions 27 and 28. Number 27 asked the draft-age
males' willingness to serve in combat for the U.S. military "wherever ordered"
(War Relocation Authority, 1943c, p. 26). All others were asked if they would
be willing to serve ACs or the Army Nurse Corp if the occasion arose. Number
28 asked whether the respondent was willing to "swear unqualified allegiance
to the United States of America and faithfully defend the United States from
any or all attack by foreign or domestic forces and foreswear any form of allegiance or obedience to the Japanese emperor or any other foreign government,
power, or organization?" (War Relocation Authority, 1943c, p. 26). The question
was later revised by Washington headquarters to: "will you swear to abide by the
laws of the United States and to take no action which would in any way interfere
with the war effort of the United States?" By that time, however, the damage had
been done.

The details of the Registration have been discussed thoroughly by many elsewhere (see Hayashi, 2004; Muller, 2007; Weglyn, 1996) and will not be belabored
here. It suffices to note that the very existence of the questionnaire elicited
strong reactions; the two last seemingly straightforward questions imposed on
the Nikkei decisions of gut-wrenching complexity. The Community Analysis
Section at Manzanar explained the negative reactions the questionnaire generated among the immigrant Issei. [2]

> The crux of the whole problem is that the aliens were asked a question to which
> they felt they could not, in safety to their future and conscience, say "yes." (War
> Relocation Authority, 1943e, p. 2)

The respondents were asked not only to swear allegiance to the United States,
which categorically "refuses them naturalization and citizenship" (War
Relocation Authority, 1943e, pp. 1–2) on the basis of race, but also to forswear
allegiance to Japan, the country of their citizenship. It was an act which would
leave them stateless, in all likelihood.

---

[2] John de Young and Morris E. Opler were the Community Analysts at Manzanar. This first-
person narrative does not indicate which of the two authored it.

It must be realized that these aliens are well aware of the resolutions of legislatures and a group and individual demands that they be returned to Japan as soon as possible. Many, despite an earnest desire to end their days in this land, have been led by circumstances to the conclusion that they will never again be able to earn a livelihood in this country, and assume that they will therefore be forced to seek a refuge in Japan. Naturally they wondered whether such a renunciation of Japan would not jeopardize their Japanese citizenship or subject them to punishment or disability at the hands of the Japanese government should they come within its jurisdiction, and they reacted accordingly. The negativistic attitude sets in. (War Relocation Authority, 1943e, p. 2)

For the Nisei—U.S.-born citizens—the questionnaire as a whole was another "repugnant" (War Relocation Authority, 1943e, p. 6) reminder of the fact that, despite their citizenship and without any cause, they had been summarily branded disloyal at the start of the war. It was another indication "that our government was making race and not national or international law the criterion of their status" (War Relocation Authority, 1943e, p. 6). The push to forswear loyalty to an emperor to whom they had never held allegiance, moreover, seemed an entrapment which sought tacit admission of previous disloyalty (Commission on Wartime Relocation and Internment of Civilians, 1982).

They did not fail to note that they were being asked to assent to a loyalty oath such as is ordinarily administered to foreigners when they naturalize. (War Relocation Authority, 1943e, p. 6)

Even William Huso (1945), the Head of Relocation at Gila River, one of the Appointed Personnel (AP) whose writings indicate a distinct antagonistic tendency toward the Nikkei, agreed that "there was something very vague and tricky about the question" (p. 9). Young men were also concerned that indicating their willingness to serve in combat on Question 27 was, in effect, volunteering to do so (Lyon, 2015, July 17). Japanese American Evacuation and Resettlement Study (JERS) researcher James Minoru Sakoda (1943b) explained the reluctance of some of the Nisei to being drafted.

Practically none of the Nisei, for instance, would have refused to be drafted and fight for the United States prior to evacuation, in spite of the discrimination they had received both inside and outside of the Army. Now that they had been removed from their houses on the Coast, and placed in government camps, many refused to take the chance to being drafted, even going to the extent of declaring themselves to be disloyal to the United States. (p. 88)

Another factor behind their reluctance to go to war was fear for Issei parents who would be left behind. "What will happen to the family of a Nisei who is drafted? Will they be sent to Japan? Will they be kept here? Will they be forced to re-settle?" (Billigmeier, 1943, p. 119).

Constructing Disloyalty

Like so many programs of the WRA, registration was hastily conceived, inad-equately planned, and poorly executed; from the content of the questionnaire to its administration in the camps, every facet of Registration was an object lesson in how not to do survey research. The questionnaire, imposed with few explanations about its purpose and no answers about its consequences, was bewildering to all, including the staff administering it. A June 1943 report by the WRA's Community Analysis Section described:

> Accompanying the emotional crisis of registration at all projects was an al-most unbelievable amount of confusion and misunderstanding of the purposes of registration and even of the significance of various questions in the questionnaires. Confusion was most marked among the evacuees but it is important to recognize that it was also great among the appointed staff at some projects. (War Relocation Authority, 1943a, p. 17)

The confusion among the staff, who "knew nothing about the real motivation which surrounded the coming of this registration" (Huso, 1945, p. 8), resulted in many inconsistencies "in the manner in which registration was presented to center residents, in the manner in which registration was conducted, in the methods used by the administration to deal with crisis situations, indeed in the kinds of crises which arose at various projects" (War Relocation Authority, 1943a, p. 17). In many camps even "contradictory interpretations, and some-times direct violations of instructions" (War Relocation Authority, 1943a, p. 8) were evident. Because staff were uncertain whether registration was a compul-sory or voluntary endeavor, for example, the questionnaire was first presented in some camps as the latter then changed to the former when few complied (War Relocation Authority, 1943a). In part due to factors such as the secrecy imposed on the proceedings by the War Department, but principally because of the "ra-pidity with which the program was put into operation," the plans for "one of the most significant steps in WRA history, was not fully understood by many WRA employees" in the camps as well as in the Washington headquarters (War Relocation Authority, 1943a, p. 8).

In his Tule Lake diaries, JERS researcher Robert Billigmeier (1943) noted that Harvey Coverley, the new camp Director who had replaced "Jap-loving" (p. 116) Elmer Shirrell, denied "that the registration program lacked the proper publicity" (p. 115). This, despite the fact that one of the major examples of "misinformation was the project director's belief that the Army registration was ordered by the Selective Service" (War Relocation Authority, 1943a, p. 24) rather than the War Department, and on that basis, arrested the male citizens who refused to register. Contrary to Coverley's view, as well as the WRA's post-hoc propaganda that the conflicts incited by the registration and the need for segregation of the loyal from the disloyal was an "inevitable result of public reaction to the indiscriminate intermingling of evacuees who are loyal to Japan and those who are loyal to the United States" (War Relocation Authority, 1943d, p. 14), Billigmeier and many others insisted that the registration did not uncover existing problems but generated them, in large part. In Billigmeier's view, "the manner in which the matter was introduced" and carried out by the administration was, in fact, "a very large factor in the negative response" it garnered.

> There were no careful explanations of the program in the beginning. No one anticipated the questions and issues that might be expected to arise. No one on the project seemed able to answer these questions when they did arise. (Billigmeier, 1943, p. 115).

By February of 1943, when registration began, the Nikkei had been incarcerated in one atrocious setting or two for nearly a year, living precarious lives without certainty about their present or the future. As discussed in the previous chapter, many were in dire financial straits while jobs, pay, public assistance, unemployment benefits, medical care, and even food and clothing were in short supply and while rules and regulations about them changed constantly and incoherently. Registration erupted in this "atmosphere of insecurity and suspicion" (War Relocation Authority, 1943a, p. 7), and, in the vacuum of real information about its purpose and consequences, and in light of the inconsistent and contradictory messages about it conveyed by the AP, the "issues grew and accumulated other issues like a rolling stone. This phenomena has been witnessed time and time again in the project experience" (Billigmeier, 1943, p. 115).

In the final count, 87% of those who were eligible to register answered "yes" to the two questions and did so without qualification. A total of 9,935, answered "no" on at least one of the two questions or had qualified their answer in some way—indicating, for example, that they would serve in the military if they and their families were freed from the camps—or had altogether refused to participate in the registration. About 5,300 out of the 9,935 had answered "no" to both questions (Commission on Wartime Relocation and Internment of Civilians, 1982). While the Western Defense Command "interpreted the results as a vindication of its position that there were many disloyal evacuees" and its push for removal and incarceration had been justified, many other saw different reasons for the answers.

According to the Manzanar Community Analysis report, however, the "no" answers by the Nikkei, "like that of some young ladies, should not always be taken at face value" (War Relocation Authority, 1943e, p. 6). For many, the "no-no" answers were a form of political protest, lodged "against the injustice of their treatment as citizens and against racial prejudice" (Hankey, 1943a, p. 10). Jerome's Head Counselor similarly opined that "for all realistic purposes" the questionnaire could not be called a test of "loyalty" since in "a good many cases (the great majority, I suspect) the final decision had relatively little to do with affection for Japan or disaffection for the United States" (Webb, 1944, p. 1). Instead, according to the official WRA report on the registration, the "no" answers were much more likely an indication of resentment arising out of the experiences of removal and incarceration; a general lack of trust and confidence in the WRA, the government in general, and especially the military; and, finally, the respondents' uncertainty about their future status and welfare in the United States (War Relocation Authority, 1943a). Given the hostile treatment accorded them by the government and the general public, many respondents assessed their chances for social and economic recovery in the postwar years to be at best uncertain. Their "no" vote was an "index of their faith and their future and rehabilitation in America than of loyalty" (War Relocation Authority, 1943e, p. 4), or the lack thereof. This was particularly true for the Issei.

> Many of these aliens have seen the stakes and fruits of the life of toil disappear in a few turbulent months. They're now an average well past their prime in years. Their total discouragement at their dispossession and insecurity is a reaction from their past thrift and industry. This loss of faith and confidence is and will continue to be one of the most appalling consequences of evacuation. (War Relocation Authority, 1943e, p. 3)

A request for expatriation by a Nisei documented by Richard Nishimoto, JERS fieldworker and a Block Manager at Poston, serves as an exemplar that the phenomenon was not limited to the Issei.

> Mr. Y. and his family apparently suffered a great deal of loss in property and money as a result of evacuation, and although he does not feel embittered, he does feel that America is not the country in which to start over again. He stated that his father worked for nearly forty years establishing the farm for his

children, that he does not wish to make the same mistake but intends to go to Japan where he feels the future will be much more secure. (Nishimoto, 1943, pp. 17–18)

"No response to an important question can be dissociated from recent, bitter experiences. It is naïve to expect it; it is cynical to pretend to expect it" (War Relocation Authority, 1943e, p. 3), averred the June 1943 Community Analysis report. It seemed the WRA was both naïve and cynical. By its own admission, the plan for the registration "was not predicated on full understanding of the prevailing attitudes of the center residents. Since there was very little expectation of resistance to registration, no adequate provisions were made to meet it" (War Relocation Authority, 1943a, p. 8). What the WRA had utterly failed to grasp was that the incarcerated Nikkei "felt that they had been discriminated against in the evacuation, that they had blundered in failing to protest it, that their future in the United States was being threatened from many quarters, that WRA and the government generally could not be trusted, and that the Army, in particular, was responsible for their present situation" (War Relocation Authority, 1943a, p. 7). The WRA's cynicism, on the other hand, lay in its post-questionnaire actions. Despite its knowledge that its procedures, and therefore its findings, were deeply flawed, the WRA acted on the registration data as valid information on loyalty. It insisted that the "information obtained from these questionnaires has been extremely useful in identifying strongly pro-Japanese or potentially dangerous individuals who are denied the privilege of leave under our regulations" (War Relocation Authority, 1943c, p. 15). This information thus gathered triggered a deeper dive into the lives of those so identified as pro-Japanese.

In addition, we have gathered extensive information from other sources pertaining to the back-grounds and attitudes of the individual evacuees. In many cases information has been sought from former employers, former neighbors, municipal officials and others in the communities where the evacuee lived before the evacuation. We have consulted the files of Federal intelligence agencies, including the Federal Bureau of Investigation for any information available there on the people in the centers whose eligibility for leave was receiving our attention. (War Relocation Authority, 1943c, p. 15)

The records of various departments such as internal security, employment, and, no doubt, social welfare, were also tapped to "obtain information regarding the conduct of individual evacuees since they came under the supervision of the War Relocation Authority" (War Relocation Authority, 1943c, p. 15). The end result of these investigations was, on the one hand, "dockets of information" on individuals to be used in determining eligibility for indefinite leave, thus allowing the WRA to assure the public that "those released from relocation centers have been carefully checked for loyalty more than any other group in our country's population, citizen or alien" (War Relocation Authority, 1943c, p. 15). On the other hand, this was a program of segregation developed by the WRA at the urging of the War Department (Lyon, 2015, July 29) to separate "those who wish to follow the American way of life" (War Relocation Authority, 1943d, p. 2) from "those whose interests are not in harmony with those of the United States" (War Relocation Authority, 1943d, p. 2).

The Segregation Program

> The segregation process is based primarily on the choice of the individual evacuee, as expressed in words or in acts. Some of the evacuees have said they prefer to live in Japan; others, while not expressing desire to live in Japan, have refused to pledge loyalty to the United States; still others, by their acts in the relocation centers or before evacuation, have indicated that their interests lie with Japan rather than with the United States. In one way or another, these people have made their own choices. The War Relocation Authority is assuming the grave responsibility of interpreting what those choices were.
> —War Relocation Authority (1943d, p. 13)

Under the Segregation Program, Tule Lake was designated as a Segregation Center to which all those "found not to be loyal or sympathetic to the United States" (War Relocation Authority, 1943d, p. 11) would be removed, to be held until they could be repatriated, in the case of Japanese nationals, or expatriated in the case of U.S. citizens. It was chosen as the site of segregation for several reasons: because it was the largest of the camps and it had garnered the most number of "no-no" votes as well as the largest number of outright refusals to answer the registration questionnaire (War Relocation Authority, 1943g). Those already imprisoned at Tule Lake "found to be American in their loyalties or sympathies" would be transferred out to other camps "or, preferably, given permission to relocate outside" (War Relocation Authority, 1943d, p. 11) of the camps through its Leave Clearance procedures. The "segregant" population was comprised in large part of individuals whose answers to the two "loyalty" questions had not been entirely in the affirmative. But the program designed to sweep the camps clear of the "disloyal" also included in the segregation population those individuals who had previously registered their desire to repatriate to Japan; individuals who had been previously denied Leave Clearance by the Director of WRA "on the basis of some accumulation of adverse evidence in their records"

(War Relocation Authority, 1946, p. 64), whatever their registration answers had been; and, finally, immediate family members of any of the preceding categories who, however they may have answered the questionnaire, opted to follow family members into segregation at Tule Lake. While social work departments in the camps would be in charge of tallying and preparing the intercamp transfers, the actual transportation of an estimated 20,000 persons to and from Tule Lake would be executed by the Army, "with the cooperation of the Office of Defense Transportation and the Association of American Railroads" (War Relocation Authority, 1943d, p. 14).

The registration had garnered many more negative responses than expected. The WRA, which had continuously been accused by politicians and the media of harboring and coddling the enemy, feared that large numbers of segregants would justify those criticisms of its policies and programs. In her documentation of the segregation procedures at Gila River, JERS researcher Rosemary Hankey explained that it was, thus, the "hope of some members of the administration that the people who had applied for repatriation or expatriation out of economic and physical fears would cancel their requests" (Hankey, 1943a, p. 6). They believed that many of those who answered the two questions in the negative were "not categorically disloyal" (Hankey, 1943a, p. 6), but had been pressured to do so by family members and pro-Japanese elements in the camps. To their consternation, however, "additional application for repatriation continued to pour in" (Hankey, 1943a, p. 6), not only at Gila River but in all of the camps. In light of both its fears for negative publicity and its hopes for changed answers that would reduce the number of segregants, the WRA instituted two different types of individual vetting procedures: segregation hearings conducted by an appointed Board of Review and interviews conducted by camp Social Welfare sections. The purpose of the Segregation Board of Review hearings was to determine if the registrants who did not answer the two questions affirmatively "knew the meaning of what they did when they did it or whether they still want to be Japanese" (War Relocation Authority, 1943g, p. 10). The welfare meetings were designed to take place after the segregation hearings. Family members of those identified as "segregants" by the Board of Review would be interviewed individually to determine whether or not they wished to accompany the segregants to Tule Lake and beyond.

A Board of Review for Segregation made up of a "careful selection of responsible and respected men who have a reputation among the evacuees for fair-mindedness" (War Relocation Authority—Compiler, 1943, p. 46) was duly appointed by the director of each camp. Its task was to hold individual hearings for those who had not indicated a positive, unqualified answer for Questions 27 and 28; in WRA Director Dillon Meyer's words, "for those who have refused to pledge loyalty to the United States or good behavior while in this country"

(War Relocation Authority—Compiler, 1943, p. 15). The hearings were to "take fully into account the conditions under which the individual registered" (War Relocation Authority, 1943a, p. 33) and to make certain that an individual's negative answer or refusal to comply with the registration reflected "true feelings" (War Relocation Authority—Compiler, 1943, p. 15) rather than a momentary lapse of judgment or a decision made under duress. Anyone who indicated a willingness to change their position to "pledge loyalty or good behavior" (War Relocation Authority—Compiler, 1943, p. 15) during the hearing would be allowed to do so and sent on to the Leave Clearance Section of each camp to undergo another hearing to determine his or her eligibility for release and resettlement outside. All those unwilling to change their answers and pledge loyalty, or who were otherwise determined by the Segregation Board to be disloyal, would be designated a "segregant" to be shipped off to Tule Lake. According to summary notes of the two-day Segregation Conference of WRA Officials, held in Denver, Colorado, at the end of July 1943, while there were "tactful ways in which an evacuee can be influenced" (War Relocation Authority, 1943g, p. 14), the Segregation Board "should clearly not argue in helping the evacuee make up his mind" and attempt to shape his or her decision. As Rosalie Hankey explained about the way the hearings played out on the ground at Gila River, these instructions "not to argue with the evacuees, nor to attempt to change their minds" were "ignored in a considerable number of cases where some especially conscientious committeemen went to great pains to try to influence certain Nisei to change their minds" (Hankey, 1943a, pp. 9–10). Few minds were changed in the process.

Welfare Section Interviews

Welfare Sections were responsible for identifying and compiling a comprehensive list of those who needed to be interviewed, not an insignificant task unto itself. The next task, once this was done, was to conduct interviews with each family member (aged 15 or older) to determine whether that individual wished to accompany the segregant family member or members to Tule Lake (War Relocation Authority—Compiler, 1943). All persons definitely leaving for segregation had then to be contacted to arrange the details of transfer: the "routing of trucks for picking up freight, baggage and persons being transferred out" (Kimmerling, Fite, & Abbott, 1945, p. 11); preparation of train lists, organizing of special transport for the frail and the ill, and in planning for the actual entrainment en route to Tule Lake (Kell, 1945); documenting all decisions to be reported up the chain of command; and keeping all other camp departments abreast of the changes in counts and revised counts of both those staying and leaving (Webb,

1945). Arrangements, additionally, had to be made for the care of dependent family members who had relied on the support and care of those who were leaving, and housing had to be arranged for new arrivals transferring in from Tule Lake (Kell, 1945). All this, of course, was in addition to the "routine work of providing counsel in connection with the family and social problems, arranging shifts in housing assignments, and handling the distribution of clothing allowances and public assistance grants" (War Relocation Authority, 1943f, p. 1) with which the Welfare Sections already struggled to manage.

The sheer volume of those opting for segregation, "an enormous surprise to the administration" (Hankey, 1943a, p. 3), made the task of interviewing family members a vast enterprise unto itself. The work enormously amplified the duties of the department "to the point where both Caucasians and Japanese worked day and night" (Hankey, 1943a, p. 25). More than 2,000 interview/counseling sessions were conducted with 509 families comprised of 1,440 individuals in Poston alone (Butler, 1945). In one of the nine "round robin" letters she wrote to be circulated among her friends and family, Poston Welfare Head Lou E. Butler mentioned that, on June 25, "the Project Director handed the Family Welfare Division (of which I am the head), his file on repatriation and expatriation and asked us to 'carry on'" (Butler, 1943b, p. 1). She explained that the file containing a list of persons "who had (presumably), applied for repatriation or expatriation" contained more than 700 names, with new names coming in to the department continuously, and the department was "over our heads long before we had finished analyzing the job to be done and organizing procedure" (Butler, 1943b, p. 1). Another set of interview candidates referred to the department in mid-July was a group of Kibei who had expressed their decision to expatriate.

> While this group numbered about 85, their referral alone resulted in about 400 interviews during the next two weeks, a volume which we had not foreseen. The large number of interviews was largely a result of our policy to have more than one interview with the prospective applicant and also to have interviews with the family group together and with any other member of the family who wished to discuss the matter. (Butler, 1943b, p. 1)

WRA headquarters had authorized temporary hires to fill the staffing gap, but it also instituted tight deadlines that made hiring new staff an impossibility. Most Welfare Sections resorted to temporarily borrowing existing staff from other departments, especially the Education Sections, to accomplish the segregation work (War Relocation Authority, 1943h).

Jerome's J. Lloyd Webb (1945) reported that, as was true for much of the work carried out by the Welfare Section, the work on segregation was a hurried endeavor guided by few instructions from the administration and marked by a distinct "lack of planning" (p. 27). Once the list of segregants was compiled, Welfare Sections were given less than a week to complete the process of interviewing and counseling the families. Webb noted that while the interviews conducted en masse in the block mess halls was completed in the time allotted with the temporary help of 12 hastily oriented high school teachers, "it could not be claimed that the quality of these interviews was comparable to the speed with which they were completed" (p. 27). As James Sakoda observed (1943b) from his perspective at Tule Lake, it was "probably not an exaggeration to say that the scope of the program was staggering, and not surprising that there were signs of disorganization throughout the program" (p. 99).

Like the Segregation Board, social work interviewers were enjoined to refrain from attempting to influence decisions. Public Welfare Consultant Selene Gifford, the WRA's head of social welfare, reminded the officials at the Denver meeting on segregation that the interviews conducted by the Welfare Sections would take place after the segregation determination had been made by the board. It was important to remember that the "Welfare Section in its interviews gets into no discussion at all about the right or wrong of that decision" (War Relocation Authority, 1943g, p. 12). The role of the Welfare Section interviewers was "only for helping the members of the families who are affected by this decision to make their plans on what they want to do" (War Relocation Authority, 1943g, p. 12). Helping families clarify what they wanted to do, however, was no small matter. The reason the Welfare Section interviews would be "so complicated," Selene Gifford predicted, was that the families had "many choices open to them." (War Relocation Authority, 1943g, pp. 12–13), with none of those choices being painless. There were many "split" families—families in which one or more but not all members had applied for repatriation or expatriation, had answered in the negative or at least qualified their answer, or had refused to register altogether. Each member of each of those families was to be interviewed by the Welfare Sections and asked to choose what his or her course would be. Family members who had not been flagged as disloyal, whether through the registration questionnaire or otherwise, could opt to go through Leave Clearance procedures and, if cleared, leave the camp for resettlement on the outside. The West Coast exclusion still remained in place, and they could not return to the coastal states but were, theoretically, free to resettle anywhere else in the nation. They could also maintain status quo and opt to remain in the camp as long as the camps were open, or to follow the "segregant" family member to Tule Lake. All of the options required each member of a split family to choose one family member over others, between family and principle, or, as YWCA fieldworker Lazalle Alway remarked after a visit to Tule Lake in August of 1943, "between family and country, without any real assurance that the country for which they give up family ties will offer any kind of happiness let alone security" (Alway,

1943, p. 6) and without any knowledge of how long or how permanent any separation might be.

The end result of the thousands of interviews conducted by the welfare departments was that the bulk of the "split" families opted to be transferred together as a unit to Tule Lake, regardless of their differences. Poston Welfare Head Lou Butler (1943b) explained:

> Family solidarity was one of the securities left to them. They would say, "We must stick together." A boy would say, "I'm sticking to my dad." Parents would say, "We can't let our son go to Tule Lake alone, we will have to go with him." They might add, "We thought we had brought him up to be a good United States citizen and wanted him to be loyal, but he got in with a bad group who said, 'See what your citizenship has done for you.'" (p. 2)

Of the total of 509 families interviewed by the Welfare Section at Poston, only 19 families opted to send a family member alone to Tule Lake; in 8 families, one or more members of the family accompanied the segregant; the rest opted to go to Tule Lake as intact units. None of these decisions was easily made. Gifford had warned the officials gathered at the Denver segregation conferences that families, "will have difficulty in making up their minds as to what is best for them to do" (War Relocation Authority, 1943g, p. 14). The only thing that the Welfare Sections could do in the situation was to have on hand as much information as possible "so that every single phase of our policy and our attitude is known to the interviewer so that questions can be answered and then the family make the decision" (War Relocation Authority, 1943g, p. 13).

> The attitude I think we should take toward people in interviewing should be one of simply being helpful. We are there to help them in whatever way we can. They have a problem. We try to get the answers for them. Many of them will have questions about the kind of place that Tule Lake is going to be. The welfare interviewer should be in a position to tell them. (War Relocation Authority, 1943g, p. 14)

Butler (1945) reported that, indeed, the families interviewed "debated the question, asked for information and returned for further conference" (p. 12).

Regardless of how the families chose to go forward, the "tragedies of broken family ties" (Alway, 1943, p. 6) were inherent to these processes which pitted loyalty to one part of a family against that to others. As JERS fieldworker James Sakoda (1943a) put it, "In words alone, family splits do not sound so very bad. But when one witnesses the anguish that the parties involved have to face, it looms as a tragedy of major proportion" (p. 17). In one family, the mother applied for expatriation in order to go to her oldest child who was in Japan, living with a grandmother. The rest of the family "held out a long time" (Butler, 1943b, p. 2) against her wishes but in the end accompanied her to segregation at Tule Lake, prepared to follow her to Japan. The 14-year-old daughter of another family came into the Welfare Office the day before her family's scheduled departure for Tule Lake, enquiring about the possibility of separating from her family to re-settle outside once they reached Tule Lake. She explained that she had agreed to go with the family as far as Tule Lake but not to Japan. The WRA segrega-tion policy held that no one segregated at Tule Lake, voluntarily or otherwise, would be eligible for Leave Clearance (War Relocation Authority—Compiler, 1943). Butler (1943b) also recorded the situation of a friend and co-worker in the Welfare Section whose 21-year-old brother had answered "no" and ultimately "dragged parents and three unwilling sisters with him to the Segregation Center" (Butler, 1943b, p. 2). The JERS researcher Tamie Tsuchiyama described a young couple who had given opposite answers during registration but opted to remain together.

The wife answered "no" and is going to Tule Lake now. Her husband, however, answered "yes" in February, and when he learned that she could change her answers before the Review Board, he tried every method to make her change her answers. She did not give in and her husband is accompanying her to Tule Lake. (Tsuchiyama, 1943, p. 19)

Conversely, the "no" vote of a 21-year old son divided a family who did not wish to go to Tule Lake but also did not wish him to go unaccompanied.

His father insisted that all the members should accompany the boy, while the others did not want to go. The father stuck to his opinion and applied to the Family Welfare Department to accompany his son alone leaving his family here. Finally his son and his family friends prevailed upon him and he with-drew his application to go to Tule Lake. (Tsuchiyama, 1943, p. 19)

Butler's description of one family's dilemma provides a glimpse into the tangled dynamics of a family faced with a set of wrenching decisions.

A man and his wife had lived in this country 40 years with no intention of re-turning to Japan ever, with years of planning for their children's future in this country. One son had volunteered and was in the armed services; a daughter was making good at a job in Minnesota; but one son had applied for expatria-tion. There were two school children. Those parents were in the office a dozen times. Once they had had a letter from the son who was expatriating. He advised them to apply for repatriation, join him and he would take care of them. Next, they had a letter from the son in the armed services begging them not to repatriate, he would take care of them. Then came a letter from the daughter in Minnesota asking them to send the younger daughter to her and she would take care of her sister so she wouldn't have to go. Then the younger girl came into the office to discuss the feasibility of going to Minnesota. As you see, the problem is complicated by the feeling of economic insecurity on the part of the parents. (Butler, 1943b, p. 2)

The complicating factor of finances, though underplayed in the official reports of the WRA, was an important factor in many families' decision to opt for segregation. Whether or not their actual desire was repatriation or expatriation to Japan, a significant reason for many who chose segregation "was the desire for security and safety which some of the evacuees hoped to find in Tule" (Hankey, 1943a, p. 7). Economic insecurity was also at the heart of their opposition to resettlement. There was "much adverse popular sentiment in the camps towards relocation" (Butler, 1943a, p. 3)—that is, resettlement on the outside—where the thoroughly impoverished families would have to endeavor to reestablish their lives, and it manifested for many as the decision for segregation. The fear that they may be forced out of the camps empty-handed into resettlement in unknown and likely hostile locales was, in other words, a reason for choosing segregation, a choice that must be understood not so much as the Nikkei's rejection of the United States as the Nikkei's appraisal of their rejection by the United States. It is easy to forget that the WRA's goal for instituting registration had been to boost its ability to speed up the cumbersome Leave Clearance process by investigating the entirety of the population in one fell swoop. Resettlement had been the WRA's preferred outcome for the Nikkei, and it was an option pushed at every juncture of the registration process and loomed over the subsequent procedures for segregation. Many opting for segregation believed, whatever may happen in the long run in a future no one could predict with any confidence, at least "they could not be forced to relocate to the hostile 'outside' if they were potential repatriates" (Hankey, 1943a, p. 8) segregated for the time being at Tule Lake. "Repatriation or expatriation are regarded as a feasible alternatives to relocation, and in their eyes a better one" (Butler, 1943a, p. 3), given the prospect of destitution, discrimination, and yet another displacement, which resettlement signified, especially for the older members of the community. Rosalie Hankey (1943b) explained the phenomenon:

The overpowering desire of these people is to escape somehow from this troubled and insecure life. Outside they will be separated from their families, they will be separated from their own kind. They know that they will not be well received; they have heard frightening reports of violence, at the beginning of the war they were told that they had to evacuate "for the duration for their own security," they were told they would be in relocation centers for the duration. Now rather than face hardship, persecution and the separation from their own people they prefer to be segregated. In Tule Lake they feel they will be safely taken care of; they will be with their families and with other Japanese. (p. 11)

Tule Lake

On September 14, 1943, the WRA began the mass transfers in and out of Tule Lake. Segregants and "voluntary segregants" accompanying them to Tule Lake left the various camps and neighbors and whatever semblance of home they had managed to create in their barracks quarters. Ushered by social workers, as they had been on their first removal from their homes, they climbed onto the backs of trucks to begin what was for most of them a third journey into the unknown since the outbreak of war.

There was a great commotion with bidding of farewell and well-wishing for their future with a considerable display of emotion. Many were weeping; some were crying audibly. The segregants themselves after they had gotten on the truck were weeping. They stood erect on the truck and bowed profusely many times. (Tsuchiyama, 1943, p. 20)

The Segregation Program was, according to a WRA press release, the first time that any population in the United States had been "sorted and segregated on the basis of national loyalty" (War Relocation Authority—Compiler, 1943, p. 56). Tule Lake, renamed the Tule Lake Center—rather than Tule Lake Relocation Center—chosen because it had suffered "the most turbulent registration" (Briesemeister, 1943, p. 1) and had netted the largest number of renunciates among the ten camps—which had all reverberated with conflict and tension— had been refitted to receive the segregants.

A man-proof fence is going up around the project at the present time. There are some six tanks which are going to be used regarding the dangerous residents. All of this is simply absurd, but nonetheless, the matter is factual. The atmosphere is not conducive to constructive thinking and there is a tendency on the part of all of us to become mired by these brutal facts. (Mayeda, 1943, p. 1)

The YWCA's Esther Briesemeister (1943), reporting during a visit to the camp about three weeks after the registration began, noted that "the community was still in a disorganized state" (p. 1) with schools closed and community meetings prohibited and several hundred still refusing to register. Briesemeister opined that while Tule Lake had indeed seen "more than its share of labor disturbances" (p. 1) in the past and had held a consistent reputation as an uneasy place, it was not, as many insisted, because it was a hotbed of disloyalty. The explanation, in her view, was that Tule Lake and its population had a "more exploited past" (p. 1), including incarceration in the "worse assembly centers for the majority of the population" (p. 1) prior to their arrival at Tule Lake. Its inmates had, "by consequence, the more poignant sense of insecurity as regards both the present and the future" (p. 1).

From the perspective of at least some of the Welfare Sections sending segregants to Tule Lake, the process ultimately "went through without any trouble at all, much to the surprise of a good many people in WRA" (Pratt, 1945, p. 4). On the receiving end at Tule Lake, to which a total of 9,903 individuals were transferred in (and 8,808 transferred out), the reality was not quite so sanguine (Commission on Wartime Relocation and Internment of Civilians, 1982). Selene Gifford, the organizational head of the Welfare Section normally stationed in Washington DC, spent August and September at the camp, overseeing the movement of inmates transferring in and out of the camp (War Relocation Authority, 1943h). But her presence, however helpful it may have been to the camp's Welfare Section, could not ameliorate persistent problems such as the housing shortage, greatly aggravated by the need to slot in new arrivals among the approximately 6,000 Tuleans remaining in place. Temporary dormitory spaces had to be devised and jobs had to be found for the new arrivals. Perhaps the "greatest repercussion" (Sakoda, 1943b, p. 66) of segregation, however, was on those individuals at Tule Lake categorized "loyal." While those in similar circumstances in other camps remained in place, the "loyal" Tuleans were mandated to transfer out. The move was an unwelcome prospect for a population which had already been displaced at least twice before, from home to detention center and then to the long-term incarceration camp. They had labored for months to transform their grim barracks into more amenable quarters, and Tule Lake, "in spite of the unpleasantness caused by the registration issue" (Sakoda, 1943b, p. 66) had become home base, a now-familiar surrounding preferable to a venture into another unfamiliar destination.

The Welfare Section was inundated with anxious individuals seeking information on "which center they would be sent to, whether they would have a choice of centers, or not" (Sakoda, 1943b, p. 66), and to register their destination preference, hoping to influence the decision on their next destination. Once the Welfare Section instituted a course of interviews for segregation purposes, individuals were asked to provide the office with a list of preferred destinations, under the threat that the office would make the choice for them if they did not do so. A series of Welfare Section interview notes retained by JERS (Sakoda, 1943c) contain many tersely recorded exchanges with those who protested the mandate to move:

> Resistance. He does not wish to move because of his health. He does not want to give a choice of centers. However, he does not say that he will refuse to leave. (p. 54)

> Resistance. Second interview. He has given the impression that those above 65 would be given a choice as to whether they could stay or leave. He insists rather strongly that he just won't leave, although he doesn't have good reasons for doing so. It was a mistake to have given the impression that he had a free choice. (p. 54)

> Husband paralytic, but recommended for removal. Feels it will upset her husband to move. Determined to stay. Feels she has been tricked into leaving. (p. 33)

> 73 years old. Wishes to stay, too old and weak to travel. (p. 52)

> Insists on staying. Main reason: support of small children. Also, wife's parents are both sick and to be segregated. However, they have a son to take care of them. Would not budge when told of possibility of forced out of housing by incoming residents. Willing to take the chance of missing out on his choice. Calm, not afraid at all. (p. 59)

Included were also notes such as: "Requested Granada. Changed to Rohwer. Was put on train to Granada" (Sakoda, 1943c, p. 58); "Wants to go to Colorado. . . . Told: Not enough room. Wait for Utah schedules. Resigned. Goes away" (Sakoda, 1943c, p. 59). The final decision clearly lay within the Welfare Section and not with those to be transferred out. As was true for other camp inmates, the fear of being forced out of the camps to resettle outside was a reigning concern and a factor influencing many to insist on staying at Tule Lake, from which resettlement was off the table. Indeed, while the WRA reassured the Nikkei that no one would be forced to resettle, the WRA's preference was to have as many people in the solidly "loyal" category opt to resettle rather than transfer to another camp. The administration's push for resettlement "only increased the belief on the part of the people that the segregation program was only another means of relocating people" (Sakoda, 1943b, p. 99), that is was another "scheme on the part of the WRA to force people to leave the center" (p. 73).

While the approximately 6,200 newly transferred inmates from Tule Lake settled into their new camps with relative ease, Tule Lake entered a period of even greater turmoil.[3] As Topaz Head Counselor Claud Pratt (1945) recounted, there was "considerable trouble with the group that was finally collected at Tule Lake," trouble that the WRA fervently hoped would not "spread to the other centers and will not affect too disastrously the intensified relocation program that we are developing for the people at the other centers" (p. 4). A series of labor disputes resulting in strikes and violence culminated with the installation of a military guard in early November and the creation of the "stockade," a prison created within the camp to isolate those determined by the Army and the WRA to be a threat to the security of the camp. Martial law was eventually lifted in mid-January 1944, but the stockade, which held hundreds of "detainees" in harsh conditions without due process of any kind—without stated charges, hearings, or trials—remained in place beyond that date (Niiya, 2001).[4] The WRA resumed control of the camp in which not only the always strained AP–inmate relations had worsened by a magnitude, but open conflict among the Nikkei— between the old and new, the young and old, and across the spectrum of political differences—was rife. But even as, eventually, daily life at Tule Lake also settled into a consistent rhythm for most, the fate of those on the repatriation/expatriation list, still remained unresolved.

By the end of 1942, the WRA had logged 2,255 applications for removal to Japan: 58% were from Issei requesting repatriation; 42% were expatriation requests from U.S. citizens, more than half of whom were minors under age 18 (Ng, 2002). By 1944, the WRA had recorded more than 19,000 applications for repatriation/expatriation, three-quarters of which came from the segregants at Tule Lake (Lyon, August 4, 2014; Ng, 2002). Repatriation during the wartime period was an exchange program through which nationals of countries at war were traded. The WRA manual of evacuee transfer operations explained that the "selection of persons for exchange is determined on the basis of lists supplied by the Japanese Government" (War Relocation Authority—Compiler, 1943, p. 43). In June of 1942, 54 Nikkei under Wartime Civil Control Administration jurisdiction had been repatriated to Japan on the S.S. Gripsholm (Butler, 1943a). In September of 1943, the Gripsholm sailed again with a group of repatriates, some of whom had been under the jurisdiction of the WRA. The Welfare Sections in camps such as Manzanar, Poston, and Gila River, in the midst of the registration crisis and the subsequent need to organize inmates for journeys into segregation,

---

[3] Six camps received transfers from Tule Lake. None was transferred to Manzanar, Colorado River, and Gila River (War Relocation Authority, 1946).

[4] The stockade did not close until August of 1944 through the intercession of the ACLU of Northern California.

were also tasked with preparing other families and individuals for this voyage (War Relocation Authority, 1943f). The Welfare Sections were responsible for verifying the applications on file and interviewing those whose names were forwarded by the Japanese Government as possible exchanges. Some of those who had applied for repatriation had changed their minds meanwhile, and others on the Japanese list were discovered to have never requested the move in the first place. The JERS fieldworker Rosalie Hankey described the situation of one young woman who was on the Japanese list against her wishes. Gila Head Counselor William Tuttle, according to Hankey (1943a), "was at this time approaching the breakdown he later suffered, and from which it took him weeks to recover. He was emotionally disturbed over several cases in which individuals were being made to suffer needlessly because of the *Gripsholm* matter" (p. 20). The young woman had received notice in November of 1942 that her parents in Japan had requested her repatriation and had consulted John Landward, the incompetent then in charge of the Welfare Section which had yet to hire a trained social worker. Landward's counsel was that "since this had been done, she must now apply for repatriation" herself. She did so, but in February 1943, upon finding out that Landward's information had been wrong, petitioned to cancel her application. The petition was presumed to have been lost.

> Since then she has married. Now her name appeared on the *Gripsholm* list. Since she is the wife of one of Tuttle's most capable evacuee employees Tuttle was particularly concerned. He got in touch with Washington and was told that she must accompany the group leaving Gila for New Jersey and her case will be adjusted when she arrived in Jersey City. The young woman was terrified, fearing, perhaps with good reason, that on her arrival at New Jersey she might be forced aboard the boat and sent to Japan willy nilly. She is a United States citizen. (p. 21)[5]

According to Poston's Lou Butler (1943a), the social workers' "responsibility in regard to the invitations from Japan was to discuss the invitation with those invited, giving them all the information we had which would help them to arrive at a decision but in no way to influence their decision!" (p. 1). The Welfare Sections then prepared those slated to go, advising them on what and how to pack or leave behind, arranging physical examinations with the Health Section, and preparing the necessary documentation. Butler explained that not all those the Poston Welfare Section sent off would actually make it on to the ship.

---

[5] She was given permission to remain in the United States.

There were lists of high priority, low priority, and no priority. Those whose names were so low that the boat was filled before their names were reached are now at Tule Lake Center waiting for another opportunity. We are informed that it was necessary to have some extra people on hand at the sailing in case someone fell sick or for some other reason was unable to sail. It was imperative that the boat should be filled to capacity and that those to sail should be chosen in order of priority. This, because at the 1942 sailing of the *Gripsholm*, so many declined that the Japanese government was displeased. One reason it has taken so long to arrange a second exchange is that the Japanese government was suspicious and displeased because of the large number of those invited who preferred to stay in the United States. They still have faith that they have a future here after the war is over. For the same reason, our records had to be very accurate and show signed statements from those who declined invitations from Japan. In fact, we are told that when the Japanese Exchange Vessel had gotten about half way from Japan to the exchange point, it was stopped and held at some Chinese port until we could satisfy them that one man invited had really declined. They demanded to know why he was not on board the *Gripsholm*. We had wired and telephoned to Washington and the man had wired and airmailed the Spanish Embassy saying he had never applied and never had any intention or desire to apply for repatriation. Japan just could not believe it. But finally the Spanish convinced them, or at least persuaded Japan to let the exchange proceed. (p. 3)

At this point in the war, no one was prepared to lay wagers on how and when the war would end and what would happen to the repatriates/expatriates who had not been exchanged by the end of the war. At the National Social Welfare Assembly–hosted Working Conference on Problems Relating to Resettlement of Japanese-Americans held in January 17, 1946, four and a half months after the end of the War, Evelyn Hersey, a social worker employed by the U.S. Immigration and Naturalization Service, explained what did happen. In the closing months of 1945, the Immigration and Naturalization Service had sent off on several ships to Japan more than 7,100 "Japanese and their families" (National Social Welfare Assembly, 1946, p. 69) who had opted for repatriation. All ships had sailed with nurses and a Japanese-speaking social worker on board and "proper recreational facilities" (National Social Welfare Assembly, 1946, p. 69) provided by the National Catholic Welfare Fund and several other organizations. About 400 "die-hards" (War Relocation Authority, 1946, p. 74) from Tule Lake, along with a thousand others from the Department of Justice Internment camps had sailed on the November 25 departure. The December 29 departure included a much larger group: more than 3,500 from Tule Lake and approximately 700 from the internment camps. The February 25 departure included 400 from Tule Lake and approximately 200 from the Department of Justice internment camps. In total, according to Hersey, "approximately 8,000 people of Japanese descent, including about 4,700 from WRA centers" had been sent to Japan (War Relocation Authority, 1946, p. 74) by this mid-January 1944 date. With the bulk of the putatively "voluntary" repatriates/expatriates shipped off, what remained to be dealt with were the deportees.

In July of 1944, Congress had responded to the insistently rising repatriation and expatriation requests with the passage of the Denaturalization Act of 1944 (Public Law 78-405), which made possible the renunciation of citizenship by individuals residing on U.S. soil (War Relocation Authority, 1946). During the Winter and Spring of 1944 and 1945, approximately 5,700 individuals applied to renounce their citizenship under the provisions of this new law; the bulk of the applicants were segregants held at Tule Lake (War Relocation Authority, 1946). In fact, all but 128 of the more than 6,000 applications received by the Justice Department in the final count were from Tule Lake. One explanation for the large numbers is that most "had renounced their citizenship under duress" (Lyon, August 4, 2014). Tremendous pressures were exerted by "radical pro-Japanese organizations that greatly increased their militant activities, violence and threats to secure renunciations" (Niiya, 2001, p. 346) within Tule Lake. Families, moreover, had been swept up in the fury of panic over announcements made by the WRA in December 1944: (1) all camps were to close within a year, and (2) the West Coast exclusion would be lifted and the three coastal states would be open to Nikkei return (Niiya, 2001). Both announcements renewed fears about forced resettlement and spurred applications for renunciation. Most, however, almost immediately began seeking ways to cancel their applications or to restore their renounced citizenship. Evelyn Hersey, speaking at the National Social Welfare Assembly conference on resettlement explained it thus:

A great many of those people are very sorry they have given up American citizenship. Many of them seem to have done it fairly lightly. We get letters saying, "Please I would like my citizenship back. I want to go to New York." (Laughter) They seem to have no comprehension that they have done something that affects them the rest of their lives. (National Social Welfare Assembly, 1946, p. 72)

However hasty the decision to renounce may have seemed, it must be understood as one step in the context of months of debate and strife among families, friends, and neighbors; not a step taken lightly but one seen as an inevitability. Once a family had begun going down a path marked as "disloyalty" in refusing registration or separation, opting to be segregated, etc., that final step, which took no more than a remote declaration by letter, did not, perhaps, seem as weighty as it might have otherwise. Then, as Hersey herself suggested, there was the "question of whether the thing was presented to him in such a way so that he understood what he was doing" (National Social Welfare Assembly, 1946, p. 73). The Denaturalization Act was unprecedented, as had been registration and the segregation, and whether the Act was constitutional was still under question.

By mid-January 1944, the "completely involved, completely unsolvable, and extremely painful problem of the renunciants" (National Social Welfare Assembly, 1946, p. 71) concerned a group of approximately 6,000. Evelyn Hersey declared "Solomon, himself, could never find any kind of a formula to untangle that psychological mess in any logical way" (National Social Welfare Assembly, 1946, p. 71). Given the morass of anger, fear, and, indeed, love, that had driven the renunciants to go down that path in the first place, and the racism, intransigence, and befuddlement among the government agencies and agents that created that morass and consistently added fuel to that fire, the problem did seem insurmountable. The Justice Department was adamant that restoration was impossible and that deportation rather than resettlement awaited the renunciants. But American Civil Liberties Union attorney Wayne Collins did eventually challenge this view. By the time Hersey spoke at the Resettlement Conference held on January 17, 1946, nearly a thousand cases had been appealed to the Civil Liberties Union and were already in courts under the direction of this "San Francisco lawyer" (National Social Welfare Assembly, 1946, p. 72). He was able to bring about sizeable reductions in the deportation orders for the renunciants, successfully blocking the removal of about two-thirds of the total list. It was not until the mid-1960s that the decades-long legal battles resulted in the return of citizenship for most, though not all, of this group. The WRA Community Analysis section's June 1943 internal report on the registration debacle, marked "not to be published," noted that "shock and after-effects of registration are still with us and have created serious rifts between evacuees and staff at some projects" (War Relocation Authority, 1943b, p. 8). The after-effects of the registration, segregation, and the choices made by individuals and families during this turbulent period affected those families and their communities for decades to come.

References

Alway, L. (1943). Travel Report, Tule Lake Relocation Center, August 2–4, 1943, dated August 25, 1943, pp. 1–8. Folder 3, Box 724. YWCA of the U.S.A. Records, Sophia Smith Collection. Northampton, MA: Smith College.

Billigmeier, R. H. (1943). Diary 2, Sept. 1942–Feb. 1943, Mar. 20, 1943, Tule Lake Relocation Center, pp. 1–122. Folder R 20.03:2, Box BANC MSS 67/14 c. Japanese American Evacuation and Resettlement Study, Japanese American Evacuation and Resettlement records. Berkeley: Bancroft Library, University of California.

Briesemeister, E. (1943). Report on Tule Lake Relocation Center, March 28 through April 3, 1943, pp. 1–4. Folder 3, Box 724. YWCA of the U.S.A. Records, Sophia Smith Collection. Northampton, MA: Smith College.

Briesemeister, E. (1946). America's children—what happened to us?: Summary report of the Japanese Evacuee Project, January 1942–September 1946, pp. 1–54. Folder 3, Box 721. YWCA of the U.S.A. Records, Sophia Smith Collection. Northampton, MA: Smith College.

Butler, L. E. (1943a). Family Welfare Section Meeting, Colorado River War Relocation Project, Poston, Arizona, March 31, 1944, pp. 1–5. Folder: Community Management Division—Welfare Section—Family Welfare Monthly Report, Box 5. Records of the War Relocation Authority, 1941–1989, Record Group 210, Office Files of Miss Lou Butler, Head Counselor of the Welfare Section of the Community Management Division at the Colorado River Relocation Center, compiled 1942–1945. ARC Identifier 5752763/MLR Number UD 6. Washington, DC: National Archives and Records Administration.

Butler, L. E. (1943b). Letter No. 6. Round Robin from Colorado River WRA Project, Poston, Arizona, November 14–21, 1943, pp. 1–7. Folder: Copies of Circular Letters (1–9) Feb. 28, 1943–Dec. 1945 Box 3. Records of the War Relocation Authority, 1941–1989, Record Group 210, Office Files of Miss Lou Butler, Head Counselor of the Welfare Section of the Community Management Division at the Colorado River Relocation Center, compiled 1942–1945. ARC Identifier 5752763/MLR Number UD 6. Washington, DC: National Archives and Records Administration.

Butler, L. E. (1945). Story of the Family Welfare Section, May 1942 to May 1945, pp. 1–17. Calisphere, Japanese American Relocation Digital Archives, Box Poston, Arizona. Berkeley: Bancroft Library, University of California.

Commission on Wartime Relocation and Internment of Civilians. (1982). *Personal justice denied: Report of the Commission on Wartime Relocation and Internment of Civilians.* Washington, DC: U.S. Government Printing Office.

Hankey, R. (1943a). Chronological Account of Segregation—Gila River Relocation Center, pp. 1–30. Folder K8.01, Box BANC MSS 67/14 c. Japanese American Evacuation and Resettlement Study, Japanese American Evacuation and Resettlement records. Berkeley: Bancroft Library, University of California.

Hankey, R. (1943b). Interviews on Segregation, pp. 1–78. Folder K8.02, Box BANC MSS 67/14 c. Japanese American Evacuation and Resettlement Study, Japanese American Evacuation and Resettlement records. Berkeley: Bancroft Library, University of California.

Hayashi, B. M. (2004). *Democratizing the enemy: The Japanese American internment.* Princeton, NJ: Princeton University Press.

Huso, W. (1945). A history of Relocation at the Gila River Relocation Center. War Relocation Authority, Gila River Relocation Center, Rivers, Arizona, dated December 21, 1945 (Calisphere, Japanese American Relocation Digital Archives ed., pp. 1–148). Berkeley: University of California, Bancroft Library.

Kell, A. S. (1945). Welfare Section Final Report by Adeline S. Kell, Counselor, Term of Service August 28, 1944 to Center closure. War Relocation Authority, Heart Mountain Relocation Center, Heart Mountain, Wyoming (Calisphere, Japanese American Relocation Digital Archives ed., pp. 1–12). Berkeley: Bancroft Library, University of California.

Kimmerling, C., Fite, A. L., & Abbott, C. W. (1945). Report of the Welfare Section, August 1942 to November 1945. War Relocation Authority, Minidoka Relocation Center (Calisphere, Japanese American Relocation Digital Archives ed., pp. 1–69). Berkeley: Bancroft Library, University of California.

Lyon, C. M. (August 4, 2014). Denaturalization Act of 1944/Public Law 78–405. *Densho Encyclopedia of the Japanese American Incarceration*. Retrieved from http://encyclopedia.densho.org/Denaturalization Act of 1944/Public Law 78%E2%80%93405/

Lyon, C. M. (May 12, 2014). Loyalty Questionnaire. *Densho Encyclopedia of the Japanese American Incarceration*. Retrieved from http://encyclopedia.densho.org/Loyalty questionnaire/

Lyon, C. M. (July 17, 2015). Questions 27 and 28. *Densho Encyclopedia of the Japanese American Incarceration*. Retrieved from http://encyclopedia.densho.org/Questions 27 and 28/

Lyon, C. M. (July 29, 2015). Segregation. *Densho Encyclopedia of the Japanese American Incarceration*. Retrieved from http://encyclopedia.densho.org/Segregation/

Mayeda, H. (1943). Excerpt from letter from Harry Mayeda, Tule Lake Center, Newell, California to Mrs. Marian Brown Reith, dated September 10, 1943, p. 1. Folder 4, Box 724. YWCA of the U.S.A. Records, Sophia Smith Collection. Northampton, MA: Smith College.

Meyer, D. S. (1974). War Relocation Authority, the Director's account: an oral history conducted in 1974 by Amelia R. Fry. *Japanese American Relocation Reviewed, Volume II: The Internment* (pp. 1a–55a). Berkeley: Regional Oral History Office, Bancroft Library, University of California.

Muller, E. (2007). *American inquisition: The hunt for Japanese American disloyalty in World War II*. Chapel Hill: University of North Carolina Press.

National Social Welfare Assembly. (1946). Proceedings of the Working Conference on Problems Relating to Resettlement of Japanese-Americans held under the auspices of National Social Welfare Assembly, January 17, 1946, pp. i–173. Folder 159—SWD4, NSWA; NSWA—Relocation and Resettlement of Japanese-Americans, 1942–1947, Box 16: Folders 158–169. National Social Welfare Assembly Records—SW0004, Social Welfare History Archives. Minneapolis: University of Minnesota.

Ng, W. L. (2002). *Japanese American internment during World War II: A history and reference guide*. Westport, CT: Greenwood Press.

Niiya, B. (Ed.). (2001). *Encyclopedia of Japanese American history: An A to Z reference from 1868 to the present*. Los Angeles: Japanese American National Museum.

Nishimoto, R. S. (1943). 15. Expatriation & repatriation, pp. 1–26. Folder J6.15 (15/43), Box BANC MSS 67/14 c. Japanese American Evacuation and Resettlement Study, Japanese American Evacuation and Resettlement records. Berkeley: Bancroft Library, University of California.

Pratt, C. H. (1945). Closing report of the Welfare Section, from Sept. 11, 1943 to Center Closing, dated December 20, 1945. War Relocation Authority, Central Utah Project, Topaz, Utah (Calisphere, Japanese American Relocation Digital Archives ed., Vol. Bancroft Library, pp. 1–10). Berkeley: Bancroft Library, University of California.

Sakoda, J. M. (1943a). James Minoru Sakoda on segregation, field notes from Tule Lake, pp. 1–101. Folder R 20.91, Box BANC MSS 67/14 c. Japanese American Evacuation and Resettlement Study, Japanese American Evacuation and Resettlement records. Berkeley: Bancroft Library, University of California.

Sakoda, J. M. (1943b). The Segregation Program in Tule Lake, pp. 1–129. Folder R 20.90:1, Box BANC MSS 67/14 c. Japanese American Evacuation and Resettlement Study, Japanese American Evacuation and Resettlement records. Berkeley: Bancroft Library, University of California.

Sakoda, J. M. (1943c). Welfare appointment and interview notes with related material— Tule Lake Relocation Center (compiled), pp. 1–104. Folder R 20.92**, Box BANC MSS 67/14 c. Japanese American Evacuation and Resettlement Study, Japanese American Evacuation and Resettlement records. Berkeley: Bancroft Library, University of California.

Tsuchiyama, T. (1943). 21. Segregation—Poston Relocation Center (compiled documents), pp. 1–120. Folder J6.27 (21/27), Box BANC MSS 67/14 c. Japanese American Evacuation and Resettlement Study, Japanese American Evacuation and Resettlement records. Berkeley: Bancroft Library, University of California.

War Relocation Authority. (1943a). Army and Leave Clearance Registration at War Relocation Centers, Community Analysis Section, pp. 1–83. Folder E7.10, Box BANC MSS 67/14 c. Japanese American Evacuation and Resettlement records. Berkeley: Bancroft Library, University of California.

War Relocation Authority. (1943b). Evacuee resistance to relocation—reasons for the Relocation Program: Community Analysis Report No. 5, June 1943, marked "not for publication," pp. 1–9. Folder 16, Box 722. YWCA of the U.S.A. Records, Sophia Smith Collection. Northampton, MA: Smith College.

War Relocation Authority. (1943c). General information (Registration Program) pp. 1–38. Folder E7.00, Box BANC MSS 67/14 c. Federal Government Records, Japanese American Evacuation and Resettlement records. Berkeley: Bancroft Library, University of California.

War Relocation Authority. (1943d). General information (Segregation Program), pp. 1–72. Folder E6.00, Box BANC MSS 67/14 c. Federal Government Records, Japanese American Evacuation and Resettlement records. Berkeley: Bancroft Library, University of California.

War Relocation Authority. (1943e). Registration at Manzanar: Community Analysis Section, Manazar Relocation Center, Project Analysis Series #3, April 3, 1943, pp. 1–7. Folder 15, Box 723. YWCA of the U.S.A. Records, Sophia Smith Collection. Northampton, MA: Smith College.

War Relocation Authority. (1943f). Report of the Welfare Section: July 1 to December 31, 194, pp. 1–6. Folder: Semi-Annual Reports—Community Management Division Reports of Health Section & Reports of Welfare Section, Box 5: Washington Office Records—Documentary Files—Semi-Annual Reports: Operation D Division, Community Mgmt. Div, Administrative Mgmt. Division. Records of the War Relocation Authority, 1941–1989, Record Group 210, Headquarters Basic Documentation Reports, compiled 1942–1946. ARC Identifier 1526983/MLR Number PI-77 3. Washington, DC: National Archives and Records Administration.

War Relocation Authority. (1943g). Segregation Conference of WRA Officials, Denver, Colorado July 26–27, 1943, pp. 1–33. Folder E6.01, Box BANC MSS 67/14 c. Federal Government Records, Japanese American Evacuation and Resettlement records. Berkeley: Bancroft Library, University of California.

War Relocation Authority. (1943h). Semi-Annual Report: July 1 to Dec. 31, 1943. 1–90.

War Relocation Authority. (1946). *WRA: A story of human conservation.* Washington, DC: U.S. Government Printing Office.

War Relocation Authority—Compiler. (1943). General information (Segregation Program), pp. 1–72. Folder E6.00, Box BANC MSS 67/14 c. Federal Government Records, Japanese American Evacuation and Resettlement records. Berkeley: Bancroft Library, University of California.

Webb, J. L. (1944). Letter to Mrs. George Campster, Chairman, Home Service, Drew County, Arkansas Chapter, American Red Cross, from J. Lloyd Webb, Counselor, Community Welfare Section, Jerome Relocation Center, Denson, Arkansas, April 28, 1944, p. 1. Folder: 61.510—Welfare (General), Box 198: Jerome Center, Denson, Arkansas—Central Files—61.310 to 61.510. Records of the War Relocation Authority, 1941–1989, Record Group 210, Subject-Classified General Files of the Relocation Centers—compiled 1942–1946. ARC Identifier 1544889/MLR Number PI-77 48. Washington, DC: National Archives and Records Administration.

Webb, J. L. (1945). Final report: Community Management division, Welfare Section. War Relocation Authority, Jerome Relocation Center, Jerome, Arkansas (Calisphere, Japanese American Relocation Digital Archives ed., pp. 1–37). Berkeley: Bancroft Library, University of California.

Weglyn, M. (1996). *Years of infamy: The untold story of America's concentration camps.* Seattle: University of Washington Press.

8

Resettlement

Part I: The Scattering

"All-Out Relocation Policy Program"

In October of 1942, mere months after the opening of the camps, the War
Relocation Authority (WRA) instituted an "all-out relocation policy program"
(Meyer, 1974, p. 28a), a scheme for the "permanent relocation" (Briesemeister,
1946, p. 38) of the Nikkei outside the camps, which the agency had always
insisted were temporary establishments. Indeed, the WRA had, almost as soon
as the camps opened, instituted various measures to move the Nikkei out of
them. Workers were released on a temporary basis to large agricultural interests
in the inter-mountain states desperate for workers, for example, to harvest sugar
beets (United States Civil Service Commission, 1943). Through the National
Japanese American Student Relocation Council (NJASRC) organized by the
American Friends Service Committee, a number of college-age youth left for
those schools in the East and the Midwest willing to accept Nikkei students.[1]
The Leave Clearance Program, through which all those leaving the camps had
to be vetted, was a cumbersome process which moved slowly and yielded scant
result overall. The new push for permanent relocation was activated in early
1943 with the registration programs, which allowed the WRA to conduct background checks en masse and to compile a database that separated out those eligible for leave from those ineligible to leave. While it had created lasting turmoil
and strife among families and friends, the registration and its loyalty questionnaire had functioned as the Army intended: Nisei men began leaving for war,
both as draftees and as volunteers in the all-Nikkei 442nd Regimental Combat
Team (War Relocation Authority, 1946f). As the WRA had intended, the end
result of the registration process saw the establishment of Relocation Sections
in each camp. Regional Relocation Offices were created in target areas such as
Chicago, Denver, Cleveland, and Salt Lake City (War Relocation Authority,
1943f) to manage the program in cooperation with state and local social welfare departments, private social agencies, and religious and civic organizations.

---

[1] The NJASRC operated from May 29, 1942, to June 30, 1946. A total of 3,613 Nisei students were
accepted by 680 institutions (Nisei Student Relocation Commemorative Fund, n.d.).

Facilitating Injustice: The complicity of social workers in the forced removal and incarceration of Japanese Americans,
1941–1946. Yoosun Park, Oxford University Press (2020). © Oxford University Press.
DOI: 10.1093/acprof:oso/9780199765058.001.0001

Social workers staffed the relocation offices in the camps and in the regional centers (War Relocation Authority, 1946f).

The Washington headquarters set a punishing schedule for resettlement. "An ideal relocation program would have everyone relocated before June 30, 1944, that is, within the next year. To do this would require the relocation of Center residents at the rate of about 7500 per month" (War Relocation Authority, 1943c, p. 1). To accomplish this goal, resettlement "became the end and aim of all activities" (Kimmerling, 1945, p. 1), a singular focus that "overshadowed and permeated every other activity in every division and section" (Kimmerling, Fite, & Abbott, 1945, p. 50), including social welfare. That which the WRA called routine welfare tasks—"public assistance grants, administration of cash clothing allowances, housing assignments, and counseling regarding family problems" (War Relocation Authority, 1944d, p. 13)—continued to be administered by the Welfare Sections. But the focus of the social welfare work shifted. Services were now provided "with a weather-eye cocked," in Minidoka Head Counselor Constance Kimmerling's expression, as to "how they might contribute to the general plan of helping families return to a more normal way of living in a more normal community of their own choosing" (p. 1). A return to the normal was not, however, how the Nikkei tended to view resettlement. Especially for the Issei, the unfamiliar cities and towns urged by the WRA as resettlement locales were most definitely not communities of choice. Many held out for the war to end and the West Coast to reopen, reluctant to begin new lives in unknown settings and hoping to return to the remnants of the communities whence they came. The West Coast exclusion put in place by Executive Order 9066 in February of 1942, however, would not be rescinded until the very end of 1944. Return to the small farming and fishing communities to which they had given a lifetime of labor and had, in turn, provided them with some insulation from the routine prejudice and discrimination of daily life in a nation that saw them as alien, even if they still existed, was not on the table.

The simple fact was that the resettlement the WRA intended was the absolute obverse of the return to familiar ways, means, places, and people that so many of the Nikkei longed for. Presaging the nation's refugee resettlement policies in the years to come, the WRA's plan for the post-incarceration "resettlement" of the Nikkei was a planned scattering of the population across the country. Its explicit goal was the prevention of regional concentrations and the reformulation of enclaves—to prevent the recreation of "Japanese" spaces and ways.

In the words of Charles F. Ernst (1943) of the American Public Welfare Association, the goal was "not to colonize certain parts of the United States but rather to spread the evacuees all over the United States" (p. 2). The resettlement program's three objectives were "to get the evacuees out of the centers, to disperse them, and to integrate them into the communities where they settled"

(War Relocation Authority, 1946f, p. 218). As Dillon Meyer noted in the 1944 Annual Report, the WRA policy had been "from the beginning to discourage the concentration of the evacuees in large numbers in any one community" (Meyer, 1944, p. 282). The scheme for the "decentralization of the Japanese-American group" (Minneapolis Relocation Committee, 1943, p. 1) was squarely predicated on assimilation. "If they could be widely scattered, they would become integrated with the American majority more rapidly and fully" (War Relocation Authority, 1946f, p. 218). Through resettlement, in other words, the Nikkei would be re-made Americans rather than Japanese. To this end, the crucial element in the WRA claim that its policy was "to assist families to go to places of their own choice if feasible" (Lane, 1946, p. 129) was the last two words: "feasibility" was in-terpretable, and the choice of interpretation lay with the WRA. When, despite its concerted efforts for a national dispersal, "the people from the centers showed a strong disposition to congregate in certain localities" (Meyer, 1944, p. 282) where family and friends had gone before, the WRA limited choices "by restricting per-mission to relocate in the Inter-Mountain and the Western Plains Slates to the members of families already relocated in those areas, and through stressing the relocation program in the Middle West and East" (Meyer, 1944, p. 282).

Integration and Assimilation

Most of the locations targeted for resettlement had no prior histories of Asian settlement and offered uncertain receptions to the Nikkei. In these areas, the fear of generating "undue community antagonism to the resettlement plan or to indi-viduals of Japanese ancestry coming into the community" (National Social Case Work Council, 1943, p. 3), consistently cited by social work organizations as one rationale for the need for a wide dispersal, was not altogether unjustified. The YWCA's Betty Lyle reported in the Fall of 1943 that "although resettlement is progressing well, adverse community sentiment is still a great handicap" (p. 5). "The concentrations aroused local opposition particularly in the Inter-Mountain region" (1944, p. 282), according to WRA head Dillon Meyer. The program as a whole underscored the pragmatic benefits of a thinly scattered population, more likely to be settled quietly and quickly before anyone noticed and objected to its presence.

Social work organizations were in full agreement with the WRA's perspec-tive that all workers and organizations involved in the resettlement efforts must "work quietly" (Ellis, 1942b, p. 1). Avoiding "an over-sympathetic approach or one that over-emphasizes civil liberties aspect of the situation" (Ellis, 1942b, p. 1) was necessary to prevent the reinvigoration of the oft-levied accusations of "coddling" (Tozier, 1945). At the October 21, 1942, meeting of the National

Social Case Work Council convened to discuss how it could aid the resettlement program, leaders of multiple national social work agencies in attendance were cautioned that their local agencies must work "quietly with the other agencies on this program, recognizing the need for avoiding conspicuous or emotional efforts" (National Social Case Work Council, 1943, p. 3) which would bring attention and inevitably incite opposition. In reaction to the suspension of the West Coast exclusion in early 1945, Charles Wollenberg, Martha Chickering's replacement as the head of the California State Department of Social Welfare similarly warned his staff that "the less that attention is called to the subject of the returning Japanese-Americans, the better will their return to the community be served" (Underhill, 1945, p. 1).

According to an internal WRA document entitled "Background for the Relocation Program" marked "Not for Publication," the Nikkei tendency to congregate together—their failure to assimilate and integrate—had generated the need to incarcerate them. "The so-called 'Japanese problem' in this country stems largely from the fact that our Japanese population has always been concentrated to a great extent along the Pacific Coast" (War Relocation Authority, n.d.-b, p. 65). "It was recognized," averred the WRA in another document, that "their concentration on the West Coast was a factor back of the decision to evacuate them" (War Relocation Authority, 1946f, p. 218). Dispersing the hitherto regionally concentrated Nikkei across the national landscape, the WRA argued, would allow them to become a known factor.

> The prevailing national prejudice against Japanese Americans as a collective abstraction would decline as Americans in many different communities saw them in the flesh and came to know them as persons. (War Relocation Authority, 1946f, p. 218)

But, in order to ensure that to know them would be to like them, it was imperative that the Nikkei behave in ways that did not incite fears and antagonism; the resettled Nikkei themselves needed to attract less attention. Thus, conspicuous reminders of their presence in the new communities—such as "Talking in a language other than English" (p. 5) and "Living in 'colonies' or traveling in large groups of persons of Japanese ancestry" (p. 6) were to be avoided. Mari Okazaki, the former assistant to the head of the San Francisco International Institute, noted in a National Social Welfare Assembly Bulletin that "neat formulas have been suggested as to the relative numbers of Japanese and non Japanese who should make up any group" (Okazaki, 1946, p. 4) by various interested organizations.[2]

---

[2] Okazaki was a staff member of the San Francisco International Institute prior to removal. She worked in several WCCA control stations during the removal and was employed for a brief time as a JERS fieldworker. She left Manzanar to attend the New York School of Philanthropy, now Columbia

The problematization of immigrant enclaves as unwholesome settings for its residents and a source of danger to the public at large is a phenomenon of long standing in both social work and the public sphere. The idea that such enclaves are created by immigrants unwilling to assimilate to American ways and values is an entrenched part of this discourse (Park & Kemp, 2006). Integration, built on the underlying principle of assimilation, was an unquestioned good in the eyes of all organizations involved. "In discussion of program and objectives in every agency the question of 'social integration' inevitably and naturally arises. It was 'the generally accepted goal'" (Okazaki, 1946, p. 4), understood as an outcome that "would bring many obvious benefits" (War Relocation Authority, 1946f, p. 218) to the Nikkei. Many organizations such as the Girl Scouts, the National Recreation Association, the YWCA, the Baptist Home Mission, and many others adopted a national policy of integration, to fold its Nikkei members into "normal" activities rather than in segregated branches or program. For these organizations, the move was a progressive act fueled by "the worthy desire to avoid 'segregation'" (Okazaki, 1946, p. 4) and the firm belief that the social integration of the Nikkei would not only aid the Nikkei but, in doing so, advance the greater societal goal of building an ever more inclusive democracy.

The benefit to the Nikkei was purported to be many. John Powell, Poston's Acting Chief of Community Management, explained at the 1943 National Conference of Social Work that resettlement was an opportunity to turn the "internment" experience into "a channel of permanent advantage to the Japanese Americans themselves, and into a triumphant example of successful assimilation of what has been a 'problem' group" (p. 302). According to the multi-agency Committee on Resettlement of Japanese Americans (Hall, 1946), the experience as a whole could be rationalized this way.

> Japanese-Americans are now scattered all over the United States. This dispersal is a bi-product of evacuation and the relocation program carried on by the untiring efforts of the War Relocation Authority. It is one of the good things that resulted from evacuation. (p. 2)

In an oral history interview conducted in 1974, former WRA Assistant Director Robert Cozzens called the resettlement program "the greatest thing that ever happened to the Japanese people in America" (p. 50).

> They were happy. They were all located in three states before that, in concentrated areas, living in—oh, I wouldn't say squalor, but very poorly. Very, very

University School of Social Work, where she received her master's degree in 1947 (New York School of Social Work, 1947). See Chapter 3 for more information.

poorly. Living in shacks and things of that kind. After the war, when they came back, even the poorer or medium-class Japanese, came back to live like part of the general population. They lived as Japanese before. They came back living a life similar to the American people. And the kids liked hamburgers, instead of sukiyaki and a lot of other things. Because they'd lived all over the United States. (p. 50)

While nothing in its archived records indicates that it viewed the resettlement in such triumphalist terms, the YWCA, arguably the most progressive of the social service organizations involved in the resettlement endeavor, shared the belief that resettlement would thus benefit the Nikkei. "Our goal is integration of persons of Japanese ancestry" (1945, p. 1), declared the YWCA's National Board Race Relations Subcommittee. The YWCA (1945) saw integration—a term it used interchangeably with assimilation—as a necessary part of successful resettlement for the Nikkei *and* the nation at large. In "helping Japanese-American citizens and their families to take their places again in normal community life" resettlement was "rendering significant service to this nation in the struggle to preserve the values long cherished as the American way of life" (Roe, 1944, p. 2). Interpreting the events as a facet of the nation's race prejudice, the YWCA did not share the commonly held belief that the Nikkei's isolation was self-imposed or that it was responsible for their incarceration. Indeed while most social work organizations saw the events as an understandable, however unfortunate, fallout of the war, the YWCA understood it as "a race problem in addition to being a result of war hysteria" (Ellis, 1942a, p. 9) and an "immense" (Ellis, 1942a, p. 9) contradiction of the nation's democratic principles. Undergirding the YWCA's distinct perspective that work with the Nikkei in the camps "seems not to be a thing merely that we can do; it seems a thing we must do" (Ellis & Wilkins, 1942, p. 15) was an established anti-racism stance (Lewis, 2008). It was central to the organization's willingness to publicly identify the wartime treatment of the Nikkei as a manifestation of the larger societal problem of racism within the United States and connected both, explicitly, to the nation's rationale for fighting the war.

The means must have something to do with the end, if we are successfully to reach the goal desired; and talk of a whole group of peoples as the "yellow peril" and "yellow bellies," and of the continent of Australia, which our troops are helping to defend, as "a white man's country" have little to do with the ends we envision. Such talk as that, attitudes like that, raise legitimate question as to whether the struggle is a clash of rival imperialism fighting to preserve the status quo, with a double standard of democracy which limits its true applications to white men only, or in truth a struggle to preserve and extend democracy for all people.... And such talk as that—together with the American brand of anti-Semitism together with such acts as lynchings and race riots and all our other forms of racial discrimination—serves to aid the partners in the Axis when they try to convince the darker peoples of the world that America and the United nations cannot be given full credence when we state our war aims in terms of democracy. (Ellis & Wilkins, 1942, p. 14)

As earnestly held and comparatively progressive as the YWCA's stance on race relations was in the context of its times, it nevertheless did not fundamentally contest the racial logic of its era. The YWCA's vision for the Nikkei was an assimilationist path. While it worked tirelessly to create social conditions which would allow the integration of racial minorities such as the Nikkei into an inclusive democracy, the YWCA's desired "social integration" (Bird, 1942, p. 1) was a unidirectional shift. While it imagined for the nation a vigorous and vibrant democratic community in which all races would be included as viable and equal participants, it did not imagine that such inclusion could or should fundamentally reshape the national community itself; the primacy of the "Caucasian community" was never questioned. In its work with the Nikkei and other racial minority groups, YWCA saw itself as a link between those and the general "Caucasian community" (Bird, 1942, p. 1), but only as that which would shepherd the former to fit into, and be accepted by, the latter. The Japanese American Evacuation Project (JAEP) worker Winfred Wygel's praise of the girls of the Manzanar YWCA: "so many of them are lovely, even beautiful. So many look more American than Japanese" (Wygel, 1943, p. 10), hints at an underlying belief that the Nikkei's potential to be absorbed into the American fold and become assets to "a country which is trying the greatest experiment in mixed population in history" (Wygel, 1943, p. 10) depended on their ability to be, and to act, less Japanese. The progressivism of the YWCA, like that of other social service organizations involved, did not preclude the fundamentally racist belief that being Japanese and being American were mutually exclusive states. The Army's policy for exempting from incarceration certain mixed-race individuals who, having lived exclusively among Caucasians, "had not developed Oriental thought patterns or been subjected to so-called Japanese culture" (United States Army, 1943, p. 145), had followed the same racist logic (Spickard, 1986).

The YWCA, however, saw its approach to assimilation as being qualitatively different—both more nuanced in understanding and pragmatic in application— from the usual. The JAEP's Esther Briesemeister (1946) criticized the view of "some community people" who believed "it is wrong for the Japanese Americans to gather in groups and advocate that upon arrival into the new community they seek their association with Caucasians and others" (p. 44). Dismissing as unrealistic the reductive approach that other organizations had taken in recommending that "not more than three Nisei should ever be seen on the street together" or "six should be the limit of attendance at 'all-Japanese' gatherings," Annie Clo Watson (1943b) explained the YWCA's position that "assimilation is a psychological and sociological process that does not take place overnight or according to nice rules" (p. 3). While "the avoidance of segregation in the assimilation of the Japanese is the objective most earnestly to be sought after" (p. 3), the YWCA's usual pragmatic position was that assimilation was not a process that could be hurried or imposed at will. But these comparatively nuanced views of assimilation held by the organization's National Board and JAEP staff did not always materialize in practice. The YWCA's assessment of the Nisei was that they "already belong here by birth and education, by culture and custom. It is ours to absorb them" (Wygel, 1943, p. 10). While it was a far more progressive view than most of the nation, and more than even most social work organizations were willing to shout out loud, it was still a view predicated on the belief that absorption was unidirectional; less Japanese was more American. That their absorption by the Caucasian mainstream was not necessarily the goal of the Nisei was an idea difficult for even the YWCA to grasp. Arline Brauer, a "YWCA groupworker" (Yatsushiro, 1946, p. 1) in Denver "was quite puzzled at the fact that the Nisei, especially girls, just won't mix with Caucasian groups no matter how hard she tries to integrate the Nisei into the latter groups. Instead, she stated, the Nisei prefer to be among themselves and stage activities among themselves" (Yatsushiro, 1946, p. 4).

When the West Coast exclusion was finally rescinded at the end of 1944 and the Nikkei began to return to their former communities from the camps as well as from the various resettlement sites to which they had been relocated in the early months of 1945, the cracks in the integration schema began to show more clearly. T. S. Sasaki (1946a), on tour through California for the WRA's Resettlement Study, reported on a controversy in the Boyle Heights area of Los Angeles. Mrs. S., a middle-aged Nikkei woman who professed to have "lost faith in the white race," explained:

> The YWCA building in Boyle Heights was set aside to house all races while we, the Japanese, who own the building have no say in the matter. We had an agreement with the YW when we left that we intended to take it back when we came back. But instead, the YW went ahead on their program of integration and without consulting us. (p. 1)

Her claim that "You can multiply the same situation any number of times," was corroborated by Mr. I., a board member of the Union Church, located in the heart of Little Tokyo.

The integration program is a good thing, but it will take years before it can be totally successful. The Japanese are not ready for it ... the Church Board wants an "integration" program while the Japanese are still suffering from the effects of being segregated in camps. Many of us still want things Japanese, whether it is people, food, picture shows, etc. We cannot offer them that, and the people do not come. (p. 2)[3]

Minutes of a meeting of the Committee on Resettlement of Japanese Americans, a multiagency collective, indicate that the Nikkei resistance to compulsory integration was an issue that plagued not only the YWCA.

The church situation is complicated and full of problems which cannot be ignored. The question of integration vs. segregation is the basis of most difficulties. The Seattle Council of Churches went on record as recommending union services for Issei, and this plan is being tried until May when all denominations will meet to decide what they will recommend for the future. The Methodists have reactivated their own churches on the west coast but in Seattle the Methodist minister is conducting union services for Issei. The Baptist Home Mission Council has agreed with other denominations not to open segregated churches but one group of Nisei in Seattle want a segregated church and a second do not. One Caucasian minister favors a Nisei church. The Issei who have been attending union services in Caucasian churches are backing the Nisei who want a segregated church. The executive of the American Baptist Home Mission Council will be in Seattle May 1st to try to help resolve the conflict. (Committee on Resettlement of Japanese Americans, 1946b, p. 2)

The Salvation Army in California was also unwilling to reopen the Japanese facility for worship and aid that it had operated before the war.

No attempt will be made to reorganize on the segregation bases. Rather it is hoped that the Japanese-American will accept the services voluntarily and with an understanding of the agency's ability to help along with members of the community. (War Relocation Authority, 1946b, p. 15)

While they acknowledged that people could not be "forced to become a part of the community" (Committee on Resettlement of Japanese Americans,

---

[3] See Brant T. Lee's discussion of the selling of the building that housed the San Francisco Japanese YWCA. He raises an interesting question of who actually owned the buildings, given the Alien Land Law which prohibited the Issei from owing land in California and many other states; see Lee, B. T. (2001). A racial trust: the Japanese YWCA and the Alien Land Law. *UCLA Asian Pacific American Law Journal, 1,* 1–61.

1945c, p. 8), social work organizations believed it was necessary to shepherd them toward it. The self-imposed segregation of the Nikkei prior to removal, compounded by the "spiritual isolationism" fostered by life in incarceration, had led the Nikkei to "like to live a life 'unto themselves'" (Committee on Resettlement of Japanese Americans, 1945c, p. 10). Social workers had an obligation to correct this tendency, and the Nikkei had an obligation to integrate into "the total on-going life of the community" (Committee on Resettlement of Japanese Americans, 1945c, p. 8).

> If the Nisei is to share the privilege of being an American, he must also share the responsibility of acting as one. He must be willing to live with the members of the community as well as among them. (Committee on Resettlement of Japanese Americans, 1945c, p. 8)

In an article written on behalf of the International Institutes and published in the National Social Welfare Assembly Bulletin, Mari Okazaki (1946) averred that integration was a more complex issue than this stance seemed to acknowledge. Whereas the common social work approach lodged the onus of integrative resettlement squarely on the Nikkei, it should be understood as "a social process involving the cultural and psychological patterns not only of the Japanese but the non-Japanese in a complex American community" (p. 4), which required changes in both.

Making Americans Through Group Work:
The Community Activities Division

Long before such forces of integration came to play out in resettlement areas across the nation, the WRA had reached the conclusion that a program for Americanization to prepare the Nikkei for the coming integration into "normal society" must begin within the camps. The recreation programs of the Community Activities Section were originally conceived as an offering of salubrious pastimes with which the incarcerated population could fill the long days in incarceration, a preventative measure against the delinquency and criminality which inactivity and tedium were predicted to inevitably breed.

> Where good leadership is available CA [Community Activities] has done a good deal to combat delinquency bred of slum housing and other conditions existing on the projects. At Tule Lake several months ago there was considerable trouble with gangs of young boys. The "Termites" were a particularly obstreperous group. The organization of special boxing classes by CA, with expert

instructors, has all but eliminated this type of operation. A strong Boy's Club program in Heart Mountain is also minimized gang disturbances, I am informed. (Marks, 1943, p. 2)

Reporting on a July 24, 1942, meeting with Grace Coyle, the group work maven and the original Social Welfare Head at the Washington headquarters of the WRA, the YWCA's Mable Ellis (1942c) relayed that while Coyle hoped that some programming could be delivered through the public school system as well as through adult education classes, no funds had been earmarked for the "recreation (group work)" (p. 1) programs in the camps.[4] The expansion of Community Activities as a division of significance with a professional staff carrying out a critical mission came only with the recognition that "Inherent in the objectives of the Community Activities program at the centers is the relocation objective" (War Relocation Authority, 1944b, p. 3). The "fear of relocation officers that a good activities program hindered relocation" (War Relocation Authority, 1944a, p. 3)—that the Nikkei were too entertained by fun in the camp to want to leave—was outweighed by the belief that "deliberate planning of group activities to encourage people to decide to relocate and to prepare them for successful resettlement in normal communities on the outside" (War Relocation Authority, 1944b, p. 1) would benefit the resettlement project.

There was an "urgency for developing activities and interests facing out on the American scene" (War Relocation Authority, 1943d, p. 1). To put it differently, the central resettlement goals of integration and assimilation could be promoted through the provision of a "healthy community activities program" that would "counter Japanizing influences, especially among the younger project residents" (War Relocation Authority, n.d.-a, p. 1). A major purpose of the community activities was, in other words, "to conserve and extend the Americanism" (Morimitsu & Waller, 1942, p. 1) of the Nisei, which the Caucasian staff declared endangered. WRA Welfare Head of Marie Dresden Lane remarked to the National Social Welfare Assembly in 1946 that, as the resettlement proceeded apace and more and more Nisei left the camps, the younger children left in the camps with their grandparents and other Issei "underwent a deAmericanization" (National Social Welfare Assembly, 1946, p. 11) process. According to Community Activities staff Edward Marks Jr. (1943), in camps "where the number of Buddhists is large and fluency in English is low," the children were "subjected to an undesirable degree to the old world, Issei type of recreation influence" (p. 2). He feared that American activities such as "social dancing, for example, cannot help but be more and more

---

[4] Coyle, professor of group work at Case Western Reserve University, was, "by 1940 one of the nation's foremost advocates of social group work, the social work profession's equivalent of social psychology" (Graebner, 1986, p. 143).

restrictive as time goes on" (p. 2). Manzanar Director, Ralph Merritt pointed out, "there would be no Japanese drama, no shogi or go clubs" (Manzanar Relocation Center, 1944, p. 3) in the "normal" world outside the camps; there was a need "for Americanization by those who intend to go back into California" (Manzanar Relocation Center, 1944, p. 3) and other locales of resettlement.

Along with offering straightforward lectures and courses on Americanization—reported to have been regularly attended by more than 200 adults at Topaz alone (War Relocation Authority, 1943b)— Community Activities "maintained and strengthened" (War Relocation Authority, 1943a, p. 1) youth interest and involvement "in baseball, football, basketball, and other characteristically American sports and recreational activities" (War Relocation Authority, 1943a, p. 1). The WRA firmly believed that "participation in such Programs facilitates the relocation program by providing opportunities for identification with activities which may be continued outside the centers" (War Relocation Authority, 1944c, p. 1). The "de-emphasis of Japanese type activities" (War Relocation Authority, 1943a, p. 2) was accomplished in part by the simple expedient of restricting funding for running "Sumo, Go, and Shogi and other Japanese-style activities" (War Relocation Authority, 1943a, p. 1). The WRA also credited the segregation program achieved at the end of Registration for culling out "those who were more interested in strictly Japanese cultural activities" so that the "general character of the recreational program became more American in type" (War Relocation Authority, 1943a, p. 2) as the years progressed. The shift in the character of the programming, however, also required deeper changes. A shift in the philosophical approach to the Section's work was described by the WRA as an adjustment in "emphasis from planned recreational activities to group work programs" (War Relocation Authority, 1943a, p. 2). To lead that shift in focus, an experienced group worker was hired for the newly upgraded position of Community Activities Advisor (Provinse, 1943, 1944).[5].

The origins of group work can be traced back to a handful of early 20th-century liberal movements, including the settlement and the progressive education movements (Andrews, 2001; Breton, 1990; Germain & Gitterman, 1980; Wilson, 1976). Group work was first established as a medium of service in organizations that focused on character-building, recreation, and informal education: settlement houses, the Y's, Jewish centers, clubs, and Scouts. Social group work as a theory of social work practice and a professional identity emerged out of the practice of such agency-based programs beginning in the 1920s. While

[5] John H. Provinse, Chief of Community Management Division, who oversaw both the Welfare and Community Activities sections, wrote to Grace Coyle, former WRA Welfare advisor, seeking recommendations for suitable, experienced group workers for this and other Community Activities positions.

professionals identified with the emerging field held a wide range of interests and disciplinary allegiances, a unifying principle across the spectrum was the belief that the individual was intrinsically tied to the greater goal of the growth and wellbeing of society (Alissi, 2001; Coyle, 1952; Newstetter, 1935; Schwartz, 2006). The cultivation of moral, physical, and spiritual welfare of individuals through structured group activity was the means for cultivating social responsibility and, ultimately, social change toward an ever more vigorous democracy. However benevolent such goals of social improvement may be judged, group work functioned thus as a form of social control, a method of social engineering. The multitude of group work programs promoted by the camp Community Activities Sections were, inevitably, "permeated by the methods of democratic social engineering" (Graebner, 1986, p. 139). The explicit objective of group work for the WRA was to teach the Nikkei "the techniques of participating in groups in order to give them experience in adjusting in new communities" (War Relocation Authority, 1943a, p. 2). Group work programs— through the medium of recreation, sports, club activities—were to provide the Nikkei, in other words, a socialization to a specific way of life and set of behaviors and beliefs. The programs were intended to reshape the Nikkei into less Japanese and recognizably more American members who could take their place in "normal" communities.

The work of the YWCA under the aegis of Community Activities provides a clear illustration of the forces of group work social engineering at work. The programmatic shift from recreation to group work made the cultivation and maintenance of the support and involvement of "national private agencies" practicing group work "one of the primary aims" (Marks Jr., 1943, p. 3) of the Section.[6] YWCA chapters, eventually established in all ten relocation camps and one internment camp in Crystal City, Texas, replicated local associations and clubs, including Girl Reserves for young girls and business clubs and young matron's clubs for the older girls and women.[7] The clubs were intended to provide "a

[6] "At the instigation of the Washington Community Activities office there was organized a committee of representatives from the national agencies interested in and contributing services to the Community Activities program of the War Relocation Authority. This committee included representatives from the following agencies: The Camp Fire Girls, the Young Men's Christian Association, the Young Women's Christian Association, the Children's Bureau, the Associated Youth Serving Organizations, the Boy Scouts, the Girl Scouts, the Recreation Division of the Federal Security Agency, and the National Recreation Association. This group, recognizing that their combined services to the residents of the centers could be strengthened by channeling their efforts, decided to sponsor a series of Group Activities Conferences at a number of the relocation centers. As a result, such training programs were held, each one lasting approximately for a two-week period. The conferences were held at the Rohwer Relocation Center, the Gila River Relocation Center, and the Manzanar Relocation Center" (War Relocation Authority, 1944b, p. 2).

[7] The YWCA's work was facilitated by the many Nikkei and Caucasian administrative staffers (or their wives) who came to the camps with established YWCA ties. These included Varina Merritt, a former YWCA Board member in the San Francisco Bay Area and the wife of Manzanar Center Director. Margaret D'Ille, a Japanese-speaking social worker who eventually became the Director of Manzanar's Welfare Division, had a decade of experience as Executive Secretary for the YWCA in

constructive influence in the building of morale, the development of leadership, personal growth and the taking of responsibility as citizens of the community" (YWCA National Board, 1942, p. 3). Club activities were varied, with "a great deal of emphasis on social recreation group activities" (Lyle, 1943, p. 2). Ethlyn Christensen (1944) reported that a children's Halloween party at Heart Mountain organized by the camp YWCA "using group work methods and techniques" (p. 6) was attended by an estimated 2,000 children and won the group "recognition throughout the center" (p. 6). Observing that the attendees of dances held in the camp high school seemed to have "lost some of the buoyancy of young people" (p. 6), Christensen also organized dance lessons for the youth.

> I discovered a couple who were good at doing the jitterbug and I suggested to Miss Kawakame and our club advisors that they organize some dancing classes and ask this couple to give instructions. Young people are going to need the security of feeling they can dance like those outside the centers. (I was surprised to find that I was encouraging anyone to learn to jitterbug). (p. 6)

More often, the programs were small-scale events like the Granada Young Matrons meetings of "refreshments and a program with discussions" (Wygel, 1943, p. 5), casual occasions in which relationships were built and "many thoughts and ideas are exchanged on clothing, diet, housing, behavior and various other problems of the children" (Amache Young Women's Christian Association, 1942, p. 1). Poston social worker Lou E. Butler's detailed description (1943) of a similar meeting of the Business and Professional Club provides an affecting glimpse into the creative efforts of the women to enhance their grim surroundings:

> There were 12 or 15 girls present. The subject discussed was interior decorations. All were interested in the simple suggestions exchanged to help make the

---

Japan (Woodsmall, 1942). Granada's Catherine Ludy, a junior high school teacher, and Grace Lewis, a high school teacher, were former Girl Reserve club advisers (North, 1942). Mrs. Herbert Walther, wife of Granada's junior high school principal, had been a Public Affairs chairman in the Denver Association (Briesemeister, 1942). Many such women, "vitally interested in this whole question of democracy and its apparent breakdown in regard to the Japanese evacuation" (Briesemeister, 1942, p. 4), were scattered throughout the ten camps and were tapped to provide leadership and guidance. There were also many Nikkei women with previous YWCA experiences. Several leaders from the Los Angeles Japanese Branch were at Granada: Mrs. Takayama, a former member of the board of directors (Briesemeister, 1944a); Sumi Kashiwagi and Mrs. Yamasaki who had served as "Chairman of the Committee of Management" (Mukaye, 1942, p. 4); and Hana Uno, a Girl Reserves advisor (North, 1942). Sophie Torimui, a Girl Reserves Secretary at the same Los Angeles branch, was at Heart Mountain (Nakamura, 1942). Granada also boasted Yuri Domoto, a former caseworker in the Alameda (California) County Welfare Department who had been an active member of the Student YWCA at UC Berkeley (Mukaye, 1942). Six women at Jerome had YWCA experience (Briesemeister, 1943). Topaz had an estimated 300 former members of the San Francisco YWCA and 25–50 members of the University of California YWCA (Hayashi, 1942).

barracks apartments more comfortable and homelike. The leader of the discussion is a Japanese-American girl who teaches art in the elementary schools.
Some of the suggestions were—use of corrugated pasteboard on the walls to
cover the cracks and make the rooms warmer in winter and cooler in summer;
the use of Standard Oil Co. pictures on the walls; the careful placement of furniture to make the room larger or to help screen off the bedroom space from the
living space; the use of cups and other dishes as decoration. The girl in whose
home we met had some colorful dishes and she had them placed in an orange
crate nailed to the wall as to form shelves. (p. 1)

The clubs also engaged in service work. They operated U.S.O. canteens established in several camps for Nikkei soldiers on leave, made decorative curtains
for camp hospital wards (Amache Young Women's Christian Association, 1943,
p. 3), and organized fundraisers, such as one the Topaz Senior Girl Reserve event
Marion Brown Reith (1943) described.

About thirty enthusiastic girls gather at 4 o'clock. They were jubilant over the
success of the pie and punch sale. They had made 110 pies with hard work and
material saved from the mess hall. They netted $65 and were presenting it to the
Scholarship Aid Fund. (p. 2)

Advocacy and community organizing were also part of the program: the Issei
women's group at Granada "affected the move of a whole block which was
later used for school—they're beneficial influence caused the removal of these
residents without opposition" (Amache Young Women's Christian Association,
1942, p. 1). Educational programs on topics designed to aid in improving camp
life and prepare for the outside abounded in the camps: lectures on health issues by the camp doctors; American history lessons for the Issei; sex education
for teenagers; girls' discussions groups on personality, appearance, and etiquette;
courses on group work; adolescent psychology; and discussions on the ideal
community, resettlement, and family relations for the older population were all
reported as having taken place or being planned in the camps.

The YWCA's progressive stance on race, illustrated in the insistence that the
nation could not "battle for democracy while denying it in clinging to practices
of racial superiority" (Ellis & Wilkins, 1942, p. 14) was derived, at least in part,
from the principles of group work, in which the belief in the power of human
association was coupled with "the value orientation of a commitment to social
change" (Hartford 1983, p. 758). The YWCA defined itself as "a group work
agency" (Height, 1945, p. 390). As Dorothy Height, an African American social
worker who joined the YWCA National Board in 1944 explained, group work
was "an educational process aimed at the development, social adjustment and

growth of the individual through voluntary group association and the use of this association as a means of furthering other socially desirable ends" (Height, 1945, p. 390). The grandest of those socially desirable ends—the ultimate ideal of group work—was the practice of true democracy, which required the full and intelligent participation of all members of society unhindered by the shackles of racial inequality and discrimination.

The YWCA's view of the Nikkei and the methods to be used in working with them differed often from those of the WRA. In their basic goals for the future of the Nikkei—assimilative resettlement as the ideal—the two organizations were, however, entirely aligned. The YWCA's many group work programs for leadership, recreation, and socialization, however welcome they were to the incarcerated Nikkei, were geared, ultimately, to serve the purposes of assimilationist resettlement, to strip away the influence of "Japanese culture" and instill an American sensibility so that they could be absorbed into "normal" communities. The YWCA's efforts to ensure that its membership in the camps maintained a link to normal communities through various types of Nikkei–Caucasian "exchange of association" (Amache Young Women's Christian Association, 1942, p. 1) were intended to achieve this exact effect. The benefit of "keeping alive old connections and establishing new relationships with the membership and the ongoing activities of YWCAs which are within reasonable reach of the relocation centers" (Watson, 1943a, p. 198) was that "this relationship with the outside group is a definite help in relocating people from the centers" (Briesemeister, 1946, p. 12). The YWCA fieldworkers who made, for example, 61 visits between August 1942 and September 1943 (Lyle, 1943) to the camps, were a primary source of such a relationship. Girl Reserves in seven camps participated in a "Letter-Friend" (Lyle, 1943, p. 3) pen-pal project with 57 of their counterparts in 21 states. The YWCA also established friendly visiting relations with local associations which had been kept informed about the Nikkei and the camp chapters through the YWCA's national Public Affairs Bulletins.

> At the G.R. [Girl Reserves] rally in the center, about 80 Caucasians from the surrounding communities attended among whom were the parents. The mothers were invited to a matron's meeting the next afternoon scheduled in the center. In the heavy rain many women came to this meeting and had a very enjoyable afternoon exchanging news and getting acquainted. The center women are now invited to the Christmas Bazaar which will be held by the Caucasian women. Material for the kindergarten were sent in by these women. (Amache Young Women's Christian Association, 1942, p. 1)

The YWCA fieldworkers also arranged for dozens of Nikkei girls and women from various camps to attend YWCA gatherings, such as regional and national conferences and leadership workshops, an endeavor that required the not negligible task of engineering the cooperation of both the WRA and local Associations. These projects, described in characteristic YWCA rhetoric as "leadership from the centers . . . finding ways to make contributions to outside Associations" (Lyle, 1943, p. 3), were said to have made deep impressions on the participants.

> Statements from the delegates themselves show how much the experience meant to them in the way of restoring their faith and hope and courage, their sense of personal dignity and worth. It was also effective in raising the morale in the whole population of the center and encouraging the relocation program. (Lyle, 1943, p. 3)

Miya Kikuchi, the enthusiastic head of the Manzanar YWCA and a staff member of the camp Welfare Section, "had been released" (Woodsmall, 1942, p. 4) to attend a YWCA conference in Chicago.

> You can easily realize how our young people after sitting for five or six months in this hot desert center have come gradually to just sit back and vegetate. Many have lost all ambition or interest. Many are fearful of venturing forth from the protection and drab dreariness of this place. All of them feel that the whole world has forgotten them and cares nothing about them. However, I ensure that my report of this trip will give them courage and relight a spark of interest hold them to once again take up the threads of life. Old people can be helped through my visit to dispel their fears and letting the young people go out into the world. It will brighten the lives and heighten the hopes and interests of everyone. I am not saying this as just wishful thinking. (Kikuchi, 1942, p. 7)

Whether or not reports such as hers had the kind of revivifying effect Kikuchi claimed, the experiences of the travelers were closely noted by the camp community, especially as the prospect of leaving the camps for "permanent relocation" began to loom large. A young Nikkei delegate to an April 1943 leadership workshop in Jackson, Mississippi, wrote that the first question "everyone asked" when she returned from her trip was "'How did they like you?' They are eager to know how we were greeted" (Briesemeister, 1946, p. 30) by the outside world. The controlled ventures outside by a hand-picked group of Nikkei women aided not only in raising community morale and providing personal satisfaction to those involved, but in moderating the Nikkei's fear of a hostile outside reception. Familiarizing the YWCA base outside the camps to Nikkei women aided in "building constructive community attitudes regarding the Japanese" (Flack, 1943, p. 1) necessary to the eventual, successful integration of the Nikkei into the outside world. For the camp administration whose success would "be measured by decrease in Center population" (Briesemeister, 1942, p. 1) through resettlement, and the YWCA staff, heavily invested in ensuring for the Nikkei the smoothest transition and integration into the outside world, the possibility that not only the YWCA members but the camp community as a whole might be "heartened and made less afraid of relocation because of the way in which the [five] delegates were received in the outside world" (Alway, 1943, p. 5) was a significant incentive.

Resistance: "Resettlement Is a Fighting Word"

It is necessary to underscore that resettlement, an endeavor actively supported and aided by not only the YWCA but also by a host of social welfare organizations that had little presence during the early years of the removal and incarceration, was a project that provoked profound dread and anger in much of the Nikkei population in the camps. As discussed in the previous chapter, opposition to looming resettlement was one of the factors that impelled many to opt for segregation and even repatriation or expatriation to Japan. At Tule Lake, it was reported that, "resettlement is a fighting word" that incited "distrust, grim forebodings and vague apprehensions" (War Relocation Authority, 1943e, p. 1). At Minidoka, the best that could be said about the Nikkei attitude toward resettlement was "antagonistic cooperation" (Matsumoto, 1945, p. 3).

The Nikkei in the camps were well aware that there was "considerable negative propaganda" (Lyle, 1943, p. 5) against them generated by "yellow peril" genre films and grim news reports from the Pacific theater of war. That the conservative governors of states such as New Jersey and Ohio, and even the liberal mayor of New York City "objected, in one way or another, to Japanese being resettled within their bailiwicks" (Daniels, 1972, p. 151) was a known factor. The negative experience of some early ventures in resettlement also did little to reassure the reluctant. There was, for example, a well-publicized incident in Great Meadows, New Jersey, where the WRA had resettled five Nikkei farmers to work as share croppers for a single employer. The workers were forced to return to the camp in less than a month because the employer quickly rescinded his offer under pressures from neighbors vehemently opposed to the presence of Nikkei in their community (YWCA National Board—Race Relations Subcommitee of the National Public Affairs Committee, 1944). The case of two men from Poston who had left on indefinite leave to work at a ranch in Delaware became another public relations fiasco for the WRA. The men, who were also forced to return less than a month after they left the camp, reported that because the local bank had refused to lease to the rancher the building which was to house them, they were forced to live in a toolshed by day and an office by night, to sleep in cots and cook "over the heater in the office. Just like hobos" (Crawford, 1942, p. 2). They had felt unsafe in venturing out from even those confined spaces, moreover, because the local newspaper's reporting of the men as the first of a mass of "prisoners of war being released in the state of Delaware and tens of thousands" (Crawford, 1942, p. 1) had riled the community. A year later when the resettlement program was in full swing and many had been settled in new locales reports from the outside remained troubled. A Heart Mountain inmate resettled in Salt Lake City reported, for example, that while she and her family were glad to have left the camp and planned to remain in Salt Lake until they could return to California, life was not easy. It was difficult to make ends meet and the housing market was generally tight and specifically ill-disposed to the Nikkei. The business community in the city was so alarmed about the influx of the Nikkei that they were attempting to pass a city ordinance that would block aliens from obtaining business licenses of any kind (Payne, 1944, p. 2).

Public Proclamation Number 21, issued on December 17, 1944, rescinded the mass exclusion of the West Coast. Many who had resisted resettlement in other parts of the country and many who had left the camps to go to those locales began to return to their former communities in the three coastal states. Their reception in these states justified all the fears, economic and otherwise, which had made resettlement an alarming prospect for so many (see Sakoda, 1989). As WRA head Dillion Meyer (1945) explained, in many parts of the three coastal states, "hostility toward the evacuated people and opposition to their return assumed serious and rather widespread proportions" (p. 278). There were orchestrated boycotts of Nikkei-grown crops at produce markets, formation of new organizations and resolutions put forth by existing organizations opposed to the return of the Nikkei, hostile editorials and paid advertisements published in local newspapers, anti-Japanese signs posted in shop windows, and attempts by union members to incite strikes against the employment of the Nikkei (1945). By June of 1945, there were 70 reported incidents of violence; hate crimes including arson, shootings, bombing, and a wide array of vandalism and property damage were waged against Nikkei who returned to their prewar homes and communities.

The blatant unwillingness of law enforcement officials to prosecute known perpetrators and to levy appropriate sentences when they were prosecuted finally moved the U.S. Secretary of the Interior Harold L. Ickes to publicly denounce a California justice of the peace who had imposed a suspended sentence on a man convicted of shooting into the home of a returned Nikkei and to call for more vigorous local law enforcement (Meyer, 1945, p. 279). Alongside the extralegal violence and discrimination perpetrated by the citizenry and tacitly supported by law enforcement, the legislatures of the coastal states began passing laws geared to hamper the return and reestablishment of Nikkei communities. Oregon "adopted a law making the possession or ownership of land by Japanese and other aliens ineligible for citizenship a criminal offense" (Meyer, 1945, p. 286). In 1945, the California Legislature appropriated $200,000 for use by the attorney general's office in the enforcement of the Alien Land Laws. At least 80 cases of escheatment action were initiated during exclusion years (Myer, 1971; Niiya & Robinson, July 1, 2015). Thirteen similar suits were filed in Washington state (Meyer, 1945). Such were the conditions of the "normal communities" to which the Nikkei were being pressured to resettle.

Social Service Organizations on the Outside

The YWCA was the only organization, aside from the Federal Council of Churches, invited by the WRA's Relocation Division to tour target resettlement areas and "sample the reaction of the middle west to the idea of receiving the Japanese and giving them jobs" (Briesemeister, 1946, p. 38).[8] The WRA counted specifically on the cooperation of the YWCA, a strong presence in all ten of the camps, in both encouraging the Nikkei to leave the centers and in aiding them in their resettlement processes on the outside. In a letter to Esther Briesemeister, John Provinse, Head of the WRA Community Services Division, outlined a number of ways in which the YWCA could "assist in the relocation program" (1945, p. 1). The first was the "continued group work training at the center" by the YWCA, indicating that the various morale-building, social skills–accruing group work activities that the camp chapters engaged in through their club programs and "exchange of association" with outside groups were indeed assessed by the WRA to be helpful to the resettlement scheme. John H. Provinse (1945) also suggested that the YWCA fieldworkers should explicitly encourage relocation by "pointing out" to the Nikkei that "acceptance is good and opportunities are many for the evacuees who leave the centers" (p. 2). On the outside, the WRA needed the YWCA's aid in "building constructive community attitudes regarding the Japanese" (Flack, 1943, p. 1), which the organization had already been specifically preparing for through its exchange of association program and the National Board's continuous public relations efforts.

The WRA also requested the YWCA's aid in "getting the cooperation of community people in helping Japanese to work out their own problems and helping

---

[8] Protestant churches were active supporters of the Nikkei in the war years. See pages 112–113, *Personal Justice Denied: Report of the Commission on Wartime Relocation and Internment of Civilians.*

them become a part of the total community into which they move" (Flack, 1943, p. 1). Along with the Federal Council of Churches, the YWCA played a leadership role on the ground in resettlement locations. It provided services and resources directly to the resettling Nikkei.

> As early as last spring the Chicago and Denver Associations began to receive incoming evacuees. They provided emergency housing, found employment in homes, organized recreation in various ways to help the newcomers and their new city to become mutually acquainted. In the service they were associated with other agencies and churches. Fifteen additional associations are now preparing for similar participation in the resettlement program, others are employing evacuees as stenographers and in various capacities and still others are standing ready to receive referrals of incoming women and girls, to give them the kind of assistance offered to all other women and girls and to include them in regular activities. (Watson, 1943a, p. 199)

It also "pioneered" (p. 199), according to Annie Clo Watson (1943a) the task of organizing national and local social welfare coalitions, providing administrative, financial, and material support "in early cooperative preparation in several Middle Western communities for reception of evacuees" (p. 199). Since the WRA considered its responsibilities to the Nikkei to end "when jobs are found" (Flack, 1943, p. 1), there was also a longer term need for the YWCA to pay attention to the "adjustment problems of individuals as they move into new situations" and ensure that "ways be provided whereby the evacuees can find their normal place in their new communities" (Flack, 1943, p. 1).

Committee on the Resettlement of Japanese Americans

The Committee on Resettlement of Japanese Americans, "a working unit of the Home Missions Council of North America," (n.d., p. 1), was originally created in October 1942 by the combined efforts of the Federal Council of Churches and the Home Missions Council. Representatives of thirteen of the Council's Protestant denominations, the Federal Council of the Churches of Christ in America, the Foreign Missions Conference of North America, the American Friends Service Committee, the YMCA, and the YWCA were members of this original committee whose "purpose was to cooperate with the War Relocation Authority in opening up communities for the settlement of Japanese Americans evacuated to the Relocation Center" (p. 1). In November of 1945, the Committee sponsored a national conference in New York City, an informational meeting to provide information on issues pertinent to the resettlement endeavor and to

enlist the cooperation of the national organizations invited.[9] A second conference, a "Working Conference on Problems Relating to Resettlement of Japanese
Americans," rather than an informational meeting, was held on January 17 of
the following year. Marie Dresden Lane, then Head of the WRA Welfare Section
provided an update on the state of the affairs, and pressing problems such as
housing, employment, public relations were discussed. Out of this smaller gathering, a stable working group called the "Committee on the Problems related
to the Resettlement of Japanese Americans" was created under the auspices of
the National Social Welfare Assembly (called the National Social Work Council
until early 1945). The Committee, which later dropped the "problems related to"
portion of the title and became the "Committee on the Resettlement of Japanese
Americans," was chaired by Esther Briesemeister of the YWCA's JAEP. Livingston
L. Blair of the American National Red Cross; Sallie E. Bright of the National
Public Council for Health and Welfare Services; Sara H. James, Assistant Chief of
the Field Department of the Social Security Board's Bureau of Public Assistance;
Violet M. Sieder of the Community Chests and Councils of America; Jobu
Yasumura of the American Baptist Home Mission Society; and Robert Dolins,
WRA Relocation Area Supervisor, served as committee members.

The working group produced a series of informational guides for use by
local social service agencies and resettlement committees on various issues
pertinent to resettlement and distributed these to the wide network of health
and human service agencies and organizations—ranging from the Red Cross
and Girl Scouts to the Community Chests and Charities and the International

---

[9] The registration list at the National Conference on Japanese Americans on November 8, 1945,
which appears to have been an informational meeting, reads like a Who's Who of U.S. social service
and religious organizations, most of which appears to have one or more top officials: American Baptist
Home Mission Society, American Civil Liberties Union, American Friends Service Committee,
Board of National Missions of the Evangelical & Reformed Church, Brethren Service Committee,
Camp Fire Girls Inc., Child Welfare League of America, Common Council for American Unity,
Community Chests and Councils, Inc., East and West Association, Family Welfare Association of
America, Federal Council of Churches of Christ in America, Girl Scouts of America, Home Missions
Council of North America, Intercultural Education Workshop, Japanese American Citizens League,
National Association for the Advancement of Colored People, The National Board of the YWCA,
Child Labor Committee, National Committee on Post-War Immigration Policy, Conference of
Catholic Charities, Federation of Settlements Inc., Japanese American Student Relocation Council,
National Organization for Public Health Nursing, National Social Work Council, National Student
Council, YWCA, New York School of Social Work, Nisei Work (Japanese American News Corp),
Pacific Coast Committee on American Principles and Fair Play, Presbyterian Board of Christian
Education, Presbyterian Church Commission for Japanese Service, Protestant Episcopal Church,
Religious News Service, Union Theological Seminary and New School for Social Research, United
Council of Church Women, Women's Division of Methodist Church, Women's International League,
the Salvation Army, Foreign Missions Conference of North America, Committee on Friendly
Relations Among Foreign Students, Federal Council of Churches, Brethren Service Committee,
Woman's International League Peace and Freedom, Japanese American Committee for Democracy
Member, American Council on Race Relations (Committee on Resettlement of Japanese Americans,
1945b).

Institutes—that were members of the National Social Welfare Assembly. Educating relevant organizations and agencies to develop the proper attitude toward Japanese Americans, functioning as a central source of information for best practices to aid local resources, and organizing well-functioning coalitions were the major goals of the group (Committee on Resettlement of Japanese Americans, 1946c). Concerned that, in many localities, there was "failure on the part of local groups outside to 'get together' and forget petty differences and work out a cooperative program in this emergency" (Committee on Resettlement of Japanese Americans, 1945a, p. 3), the Committee urged communities to organize resettlement committees, preferably under the aegis of an existing umbrella organization such as a community welfare council. Such a committee should "serve as the primary local force aiding resettlers to attain social and economic adjustment in the community and to mobilize community resources to meet their needs" (Committee on Resettlement of Japanese Americans, 1946c, p. 1).

In a June 1946 publication of the National Social Welfare Assembly, the Committee provided an example of how resettlement work developed in a large city of almost two million, where only a handful of Nikkei had lived prior to the war. The development of a structure of coordination for the various components of resettlement was, evidently, an organic process.

A few Japanese-Americans from the relocation centers began to resettle in the city in the spring of 1943. By July 1943 the number had increased so much that interested citizens gathered together to discuss best ways of meeting the needs of the newcomers, The result was the organization of a committee, which called itself the "Citizens Cooperative Committee." This group gave immediate attention to the resettler's housing needs and later opened a hostel. However, this committee did not develop much beyond a housing committee and too few organizations were represented on it; also it did not adequately develop its relationships with the various social agencies. The Nisei began to express the need for social and recreational activities. This resulted in the organization of a special subcommittee on which the Nisei were represented. The subcommittee later developed into the "Nisei Council." In the middle of 1944 attempts were made to broaden the base of the committees work in order to provide social agency assistance and better job offers, but these efforts met with little success because the representation on the committee was too limited. In May 1945 the Council of Social Agencies agreed to sponsor a meeting of persons representing the community's social resources, to hear and participate in the discussion of the needs of the resettlers. Up to this time the War Relocation Authority had been operating directly with many individual social agencies for services that were not being handled through the local committee. Representatives from a variety of organizations attended the meeting and after discussion it was agreed that considerable exchange of information was needed and that machinery should be set up for coordinated planning. (Committee on Resettlement of Japanese Americans, 1946c, p. 3)

The types of private organizations working on the ground in resettlement localities varied from place to place. A review of the many lists developed by the Resettlement Committee and the WRA indicate, however, that some national organizations were omnipresent. The YWCA and the American Federation of International Institutes and National Travelers Aid Association—two organizations that grew out of the YWCA—were prominent in all locations in which chapters existed and, along with the local Council of Social Agencies, often functioned as the coordinating body. Family Welfare Councils, chapters of National Council of Christians and Jews, Family Service Society, and American Friends Service Committees also served as coordinating organizations in multiple locations (War Relocation Authority, 1946a, p. 6). Religious organizations such as the National Federation of Churches, Home Missions Council of North America, National Catholic Welfare Conference, and the Salvation Army, and civic organizations such as American Civil Liberties Union (ACLU) and the National Urban League were also a heavy presence. Group work–oriented recreational membership organizations such as Girl Scouts, Boy Scouts, Camp Fire Girls, and the YMCA were also active in many communities (War Relocation Authority, 1946a).

Housing and Employment Problems

Along with social and recreational programs intended to address the psycho-emotional adjustment issues emerging from the experience of forced removal and mass incarceration, these organizations also offered housing and employment aid. Housing shortage was a national crisis. According to the U.S. Department of Housing, the housing stock in the nation had been substandard and insufficient prior to the war (Committee on Resettlement of Japanese Americans, 1946a). The war had greatly worsened the existing problem. The booming war industry in major cities attracted floods of newcomers who needed to be housed. Marriage and birth rates, and thus family units requiring separate housing, spiked during the war years.

By the beginning of 1946, nearly two million families were living doubled up, millions more were living in substandard dwellings and thousands of the veterans returning each week were rejoining their families or getting married and looking for places to live. (Committee on Resettlement of Japanese Americans, 1946a, p. 1)

The situation was particularly dire for the resettling Nikkei: "because of racial restrictions they have more than the usual difficulty in obtaining housing" (California State Department of Social Welfare, 1946a, p. 2). So many had, additionally, been thoroughly impoverished by the forced removal and incarceration and had few funds with which to buy homes or pay the inflated rental costs in cities bustling with war workers and returning soldiers. Those few who had managed to hold on to homes on the West Coast feared that they would be unable to evict sitting tenants, and those who did manage to find their way back to their houses found it difficult—both because of discrimination and the threat of arson—to buy fire insurance for their homes (Nishi, n.d.). Those who were attempting to rent had also to contend with discriminatory landlords and racist neighbors. A Japanese American Evacuation and Resettlement Study (JERS) report noted several cases in Chicago where resettlers did find housing only to be told later "to move out because of the pressure from neighbors" (Miyamoto, 1942, p. 7) or were asked by the landlord "not to have evacuee visitors in their home" (Miyamoto, 1942, p. 7).

Resolving the housing crunch was a long-term problem which could only be solved though the building of sufficient new stock (Committee on Resettlement of Japanese Americans, 1946a). The resettlers who were being cajoled, urged, and ultimately closed out of the camps required a more immediate solution. In some communities, direct appeals to rooming house and apartment owners did garner some cooperation (Committee on Resettlement of Japanese Americans, 1946a). When efforts "to educate less sympathetic" (Committee on Resettlement of Japanese Americans, 1945c, p. 3) landlords and listing agents failed, their names were kept on a list of sources to be avoided. In many areas, the WRA, in close cooperation with local service organizations, instituted a variety of temporary measures. Temporary "hostels" were established by local chapters of the YWCA, the International Institute, American Friends Service Committee, and other such social service organizations; by civic organizations such as the Councils for Civic Unity or Race Relations; by various Buddhist, Protestant, Jewish, and Catholic groups; or by the local umbrella Resettlement Committee comprised usually of a mix of social service and religious organizations (War Relocation Authority, 1946c, 1946d, 1946e). Such rooming house facilities were soon "bulging at the seams" (California State Department of Social Welfare, 1946b, p. 1), afforded little privacy, and were costly and impractical options. A WRA report on the conditions in Los Angeles noted that a family of four living in a hotel in "Little Tokyo" on a $275 monthly income, was paying $60 per month for the room. All of the rest of the income was "being spent for the bare necessities (Sasaki, 1946b,

p. 15) because the attendant cost of living was high: the family had to eat their meals out since there were no cooking facilities and clothes had to be sent out to be cleaned because there were no laundry facilities. The YWCA (1945) lamented that the "actual living condition to which the evacuees are forced to return now are much worse" (p. 2) than even the objectionable conditions of the camps. The crowded hostels, "becoming cores for "Little Tokyos" (p. 2), moreover, kept the Nikkei segregated from normal society, a circumstance in absolute conflict with the YWCA conviction that the "only solution is the integration of these people" (p. 2). Hostels, in other words, were an unfortunate extension of camp life, only with "more limited facilities than the centers provided" (YWCA National Board—Race Relations Subcommittee of the National Public Affairs Committee, 1945, p. 2).

In parts of the West Coast, where the housing situation was even more dire than in the Midwestern and Eastern cities, "emergency shelter for many of the families was provided in surplus barracks and temporary war housing" (Committee on Resettlement of Japanese Americans, 1946a, p. 1). The WRA was ultimately successful in acquiring several army facilities, though it required "a battle to get them" according to WRA Chief Dillon Meyer (1974, p. 52). In San Francisco, Camp Kohler and Camp Funston were both used for a time in this capacity, and the barracks at Hunters Point were converted for use by 117 families by the Federal Public Housing Authority (FPHA) using WRA funds (War Relocation Authority, 1946g). The barracks at Lomita Air-Strip, just outside of the city of Torrance, had housed approximately 200 enlisted men during the war and became emergency housing for 600 Nikkei. According to Jobu Yasumura (1945) of the American Baptist Home Mission Society, conditions at Lomita, where a small room furnished with a single army cot cost $15 per month, were even worse than the hastily thrown up Assembly Centers to which the Nikkei had originally been sent. The Japanese American Citizens League (JACL) reported at the January 1946 Conference on Resettlement in New York City that it had received numerous complaints about the insanitary conditions at Lomita. A critical problem was that only "three latrine units" were provided to the 600 residents.

> There are 6 toilets and 6 laundry tubs to one unit. No disinfectants are provided for the latrines. The laundry tubs are used by the people to wash clothes, wash dishes, baby bottles, baby chambers, bathe babies, etc., as no other facilities are provided for this need. (p. 2)

Winona trailer camp in Burbank was another temporary facility established with WRA funding, "then run as a regular FPHA project" for approximately 1,000 needy families (War Relocation Authority, 1946g). According to the California State Department of Social Work (CSDSW, 1946b), "the trailers were so filthy that an animal should not have been expected to live in them. Undoubtedly it was worse than any housing the Japanese had to put up with during the evacuation" (p. 1). Some were not lucky enough to have access to even these inadequate facilities. Yasumura (1945) also reported that his organization had heard from individuals who "slept in the railroad stations, in the parks and under culverts and bridges" (p. 8). The WRA's own report noted that "in the outlying farm regions, many are sleeping in barns and garages, and there is very little hope of having the situation ease up in the next few years" (Sasaki, 1946b, p. 15). In late January 1946, according to the CSDSW (1946a), there were still:

> 4000 persons in temporary housing projects in San Francisco and Los Angeles. There are an additional 1700 in hostels through the state. . . . The FPHA in Los Angeles reports that only 146 families and 67 individuals have found other housing to date. There are 630 welfare cases in the 8 projects in Los Angeles County. People are moving out of the San Francisco housing project at the rate of about 50 per month (p. 1).

The YWCA (1945) considered the efforts of the WRA, which "does not consider a housing problem existing when evacuees say that they have a place to go" (p. 2), no matter where and in what condition such a place might be, an entirely inadequate response to the problem at hand. It found the WRA employment services equally lacking. The reality in many areas of resettlement was that while there were plentiful openings for manual and service labor—for domestics servants, janitors, caretakers, etc.—jobs in professional fields and high-paying positions in industry were not open to the Nikkei (Committee on Resettlement of Japanese Americans, 1945a; Nishi, n.d.). Many of those who returned to the West Coast were unable to return to their former jobs and industries. First, in many locales, union members and other organized groups opposed the return of Nikkei workers. Organized boycotts blocked the sale of Nikkei-produced farm goods. Contract gardeners were in high demand in urban California, but so many who had done such work prior to the war no longer had the necessarily equipment, which had been sold for trifling sums on the eve of removal or stolen or damaged during their absence.

The YWCA's National Board (1943) resolved to tackle the two pressing problems of housing and employment by urging local chapters in resettlement areas to both hire and house Nikkei women. Local associations were to lay an "increasing emphasis" on the issue of employment of women of "other races" in professional capacities, "thus removing race as a barrier to employment" (p. 1). Many local associations were, however, less resolved than the national leadership for such immediate desegregation, conflicted about "the whole question as to whether the YWCA should actively participate in the resettlement program to the extent of opening up housing in the local residence and employing Japanese-American girls as stenographers or in food service departments" (Briesemeister, 1946, p. 43). Caucasian YWCAs generally did not share their facilities with minority groups, and many such branches had never employed minority staff except perhaps as domestics. In one Association, "the question as to whether the YWCA residence would accept Japanese-American girls was discussed over a period of three months and a positive decision was finally reached with quite a strong minority viewpoint being presented" (Briesemeister, 1946, p. 43). Another Association, in which "there began to be feeling that the saturation point" (Briesemeister, 1944b, p. 2) on the hiring of Nikkei staff had been reached wondered if there should be a limit to the number of Nikkei employed by a chapter at any one time. Should the Nikkei be allowed to use the pool facilities? If so, can they do so "at the time white people swam?" (Briesemeister, 1944b, p. 2). Such questions were "not so different from those that arise around Negro–white relationships" (Briesemeister, 1944b, p. 2). While there was "decidedly not as much feeling about the Japanese-Americans as there is about the Negroes" (Briesemeister, 1944b, p. 2), they were, nevertheless, difficult and divisive issues for the Associations. Some local Associations took it for granted "that to actively aid the resettlement program is the responsibility of a YWCA" (Watson, 1942, p. 1). Others did not, opined Annie Clo Watson; "If the Y.W.C.A. leadership in Akron properly reflects the attitudes of the city, resettlement there would be difficult" (p. 1).

References

Alissi, A. S. (2001). The social group work tradition: Toward social justice a free society. *Social Group Work Foundation Occasional Papers.* Retrieved from http://digitalcommons.uconn.edu/sw_op/1

Alway, L. (1943). Travel Report, Tule Lake Relocation Center, August 2–4, 1943, dated August 25, 1943, pp. 1-1-8. Folder 3, Box 724. YWCA of the U.S.A. Records, Sophia Smith Collection. Northampton, MA: Smith College.

Amache Young Women's Christian Association. (1942). Matron's Group meeting, Amache Young Women's Christian Association, Amache, Colorado, November 24, 1942, 7–10:00 P.M., pp. 1–2. Folder 9, Box 724. YWCA of the U.S.A. Records, Sophia Smith Collection. Northampton, MA: Smith College.

Amache Young Women's Christian Association. (1943). Report of the Amache YWCA, Granada Relocation Center, Amache, Colorado, June, 1943, pp. 1–7. Folder 9, Box 724. YWCA of the U.S.A. Records, Sophia Smith Collection. Northampton, MA: Smith College.

Andrews, J. (2001). Group work's place in social work: A historical analysis. *Journal of Sociology and Social Welfare, 28*(4), 45–65.

Bird, E. (1942). International Institutes—Philosophy and Point of View: Source Material provided by Ethel Bird, September, 1934, pp. 1–6. Folder 4, Box 521. YWCA of the U.S.A. Records, Sophia Smith Collection. Northampton, MA: Smith College.

Breton, M. (1990). Learning from social group work traditions. *Social Work with Groups*, *13*(3), 21–34.

Briesemeister, E. (1942). Report on Interviews with Center Administration, Granada Relocation Center, Amache, Colorado, November 22, 1942, pp. 1–4. Folder 9, Box 724. YWCA of the U.S.A. Records, Sophia Smith Collection. Northampton, MA: Smith College.

Briesemeister, E. (1943). Report on Jerome Relocation Center, January 6, 1943, pp. 1–3. Folder 10, Box 723. YWCA of the U.S.A. Records, Sophia Smith Collection. Northampton, MA: Smith College.

Briesemeister, E. (1944a). Report on Granada Relocation Center, Amache, Colorado, March 26-April 2, 1944; report filed May 17, 1944, pp. 1–3. Folder 13, Box 724. YWCA of the U.S.A. Records, Sophia Smith Collection. Northampton, MA: Smith College.

Briesemeister, E. (1944b). Resettlement: The way local Associations have approached work with Japanese-Americans, an attachment to the Progress report of the Organization of Community Committees to Aid in the Resettlement of Japanese Evacuees, dated June 19, 1944, pp. 1–3. Folder 3, Box 720. YWCA of the U.S.A. Records, Sophia Smith Collection. Northampton, MA: Smith College.

Briesemeister, E. (1946). America's children—what happened to us?: Summary report of the Japanese Evacuee Project, January 1942–September 1946, pp. 1–54. Folder 3, Box 721. YWCA of the U.S.A. Records, Sophia Smith Collection. Northampton, MA: Smith College.

Butler, L. E. (1943). Letter No. 2. Round Robin from Colorado River WRA Project, Poston, Arizona, March 11, 1943, pp. 1–2. Folder: Copies of Circular Letters (1–9) Feb. 28, 1943–Dec. 1945 Box 3. Records of the War Relocation Authority, 1941–1989, Record Group 210, Office Files of Miss Lou Butler, Head Counselor of the Welfare Section of the Community Management Division at the Colorado River Relocation Center, compiled 1942–1945. ARC Identifier 5752763/MLR Number UD 6. Washington, DC: National Archives and Records Administration.

California State Department of Social Welfare. (1946a). Conference with Social Security Board, January 23, 1946, pp. 1–3. Box Social Welfare—War Services—Resettlement Assistance, General, 1942–48 (F3729:110). Department of Social Welfare Records, War Services Bureau. Sacramento: California State Archives.

California State Department of Social Welfare. (1946b). Conference with Social Security Board, May 24, 1946, pp. 1–2. Box Social Welfare—War Services—Resettlement Assistance, General, 1942–48 (F3729:110). Department of Social Welfare Records, War Services Bureau. Sacramento: California State Archives.

Christensen, E. (1944). Report on visit to Hearts Mountain Relocation Center, Heart Mountain, Wyoming, October 25–November 1, 1944, pp. 1–14. Folder 24, Box 724. YWCA of the U.S.A. Records, Sophia Smith Collection. Northampton, MA: Smith College.

Committee on Resettlement of Japanese Americans. (1945a). Hardships of Scheduled Relocation: Background material for the national conference on Japanese Americans, November 8, 1945, pp. 1–3. Folder 158—SWD4, NSWA; NSWA—Relocation and Resettlement of Japanese-Americans, 1942–1947, Box 16: Folders 158–169. National Social Welfare Assembly Records—SW0004, Social Welfare History Archives. Minneapolis: University of Minnesota.

Committee on Resettlement of Japanese Americans. (1945b). Registration list: National Conference of Japanese Americans, November 8, 1945, pp. 1–3. Folder 158—SWD4, NSWA; NSWA—Relocation and Resettlement of Japanese-Americans, 1942–1947, Box 16: Folders 158–169. National Social Welfare Assembly Records, National Social Welfare Assembly Records—SW0004. Minneapolis: University of Minnesota.

Committee on Resettlement of Japanese Americans. (1945c). Relocating the dislocated: First Aid for wartime evacuees (Japanese Americans), January 1945, pp. 1–11. Folder 6, Box 721. YWCA of the U.S.A. Records, Sophia Smith Collection. Northampton, MA: Smith College.

Committee on Resettlement of Japanese Americans. (1946a). Home for minority groups, prepared from material submitted by the National Housing Authority: A bulletin of the Committee on Resettlement of Japanese-Americans & National Social Welfare Assembly, November 1946 (pp. 1–6). Folder 160—SWD4, NSWA; NSWA—Relocation and Resettlement of Japanese-Americans, 1942–1947, Box 16: Folders 158–169. National Social Welfare Assembly Records—SW0004, Social Welfare History Archives. Minneapolis: University of Minnesota.

Committee on Resettlement of Japanese Americans. (1946b). Notes on meeting of staff representatives of national agencies called by The Committee on Resettlement of Japanese-Americans, National Social Welfare Assembly, April 16, 1946. Prepared by Jean M. Hall, pp. 1–4. Folder 160—SWD4, NSWA; NSWA—Relocation and Resettlement of Japanese-Americans, 1942–1947, Box 16: Folders 158–169. National Social Welfare Assembly Records—SW0004, Social Welfare History Archives. Minneapolis: University of Minnesota.

Committee on Resettlement of Japanese Americans. (1946c). Organizing your community to meet the needs of Japanese-Americans: A bulletin of the Committee on Resettlement of Japanese-Americans & National Social Welfare Assembly, June 1946, pp. 1–4. Folder 161, Box 16: Folders 158–169. National Social Welfare Assembly Records—SW0004, Social Welfare History Archives. Minneapolis: University of Minnesota.

Committee on Resettlement of Japanese Americans (n.d.). Untitled document containing the organizational history of the Committee on Resettlement of Japanese Americans with Outline of the functions and services of the Committee on Resettlement of Japanese Americans, pp. 1–3. Folder 158—SWD4, NSWA; NSWA—Relocation and Resettlement of Japanese-Americans, 1942–1947, Box 16: Folders 158–169. National Social Welfare Assembly Records—SW0004, Social Welfare History Archives. Minneapolis: University of Minnesota.

Coyle, G. L. (1952). PART I: Social group work: An aspect of social work practice. *Journal of Social Issues, 8*(2), 23–34. doi: 10.1111/j.1540-4560.1952.tb01601.x

Cozzens, R. B. (1974). Assistant National Director of the War Relocation Authority: An oral history conducted in 1974 by Rosemary Levenson. *Japanese American Relocation Reviewed, Volume II: The Internment* (pp. 1–105). Berkeley: Regional Oral History Office, Bancroft Library, University of California.

Crawford, J. D. (1942). Testimony of Tom Matsubara and Bill Honda of Poston regarding conditions at Lewes, Delaware: Memo to Moris Burge, Acting Project Director, from James D. Crawford, Relocation Program Officer, March 17, 1944, pp. 1–9. Folder 030.11 Relocation, Box 106: Subject-Classified General Files—Colorado River Central Files—020.31 to 030.32. Records of the War Relocation Authority, 1941–1989, Record Group 210, Subject-Classified General Files of the Relocation Centers—compiled

1942–1946. ARC Identifier 1544889/MLR Number PI-77 48. Washington, DC: National Archives and Records Administration.

Daniels, R. (1972). *Concentration camps U.S.A.: Japanese Americans and World War II.* New York: Holt, Rinehart and Winston.

Ellis, M. B. (1942a). Confidential letter written May 8, 1942 by Mabel Ellis, marked Copy of handwritten letter received Saturday morning, May 9, 1942 air-mail special delivery, to Miss Stuff from Miss Ellis, pp. 1–3. Folder 22, Box 719. YWCA of the U.S.A. Records, Sophia Smith Collection. Northampton, MA: Smith College.

Ellis, M. B. (1942b). Interview with Mr. John Bird, Director, Public Relations, War Relocation Authority, May 11, 1942, Washington, DC: Memorandum to YWCA Consulting Group on West Coast Situation, from Mabel B. Ellis, pp. 1–2. Folder 22, Box 719. YWCA of the U.S.A. Records, Sophia Smith Collection. Northampton, MA: Smith College.

Ellis, M. B. (1942c). Report of conference with Grace Coyle, July 24, 1942: Memorandum to West Coast Consultants from Mabel Brown Ellis, July 30, 1942, pp. 1–2. Folder 23, Box 719. YWCA of the U.S.A. Records, Sophia Smith Collection. Northampton, MA: Smith College.

Ellis, M. B., & Wilkins, H. J. (1942). The West Coast evacuation in relation to the struggle for freedom: Public Affairs News Service, Bulletin No. VI—(Series No. 6), May 12, 1942, pp. 1–16. Folder 22, Box 719. YWCA of the U.S.A. Records, Sophia Smith Collection. Northampton, MA: Smith College.

Ernst, C. F. (1943). Community problems in Relocation: Summary of a report presented at the Regional Conference—American Public Welfare Association, Salt Lake City, Thursday, October 21, 1943, pp. 1–5. Box Social Welfare—War Services—Resettlement Assistance, General, 1942–48 (F3729:110). Department of Social Welfare Records, War Services Bureau. Sacramento: California State Archives.

Flack, H. N. (1943). YWCA World Emergency Fund: Japanese Evacuees Report 1942, dated February 5, 1943, pp. 1–2. Folder 1, Box 720. YWCA of the U.S.A. Records, Sophia Smith Collection. Northampton, MA: Smith College.

Germain, C. B., & Gitterman, A. (1980). *The life model of social work practice.* New York: Columbia University Press.

Graebner, W. (1986). The small group and democratic social engineering, 1900–1950. *Journal of Social Issues, 42*(1), 137–154.

Hall, J. M. (1946). Our attitudes!, prepared by Miss Jean M. Hall, Secretary: Bulletin on problems relating to the resettlement of Japanese-Americans, by The Committee on Resettlement of Japanese-Americans & National Social Welfare Assembly, August 1946, pp. 1–4. Folder 161, Box 16: Folders 158–169. National Social Welfare Assembly Records—SW0004, Social Welfare History Archives. Minneapolis: University of Minnesota.

Hartford, M. E. (1983). Group work today—through a rear view mirror, or issues in work with groups in a historical perspective. In N. C. Lang & C. Marshall (Eds.), *Patterns in the mosaic: proceedings of the 4th annual symposium for the advancement of social work with groups* (pp. 737–763). Toronto, Ontario: Committee for the Advancement of Social Work with Groups.

Hayashi, D. (1942). Organizational meeting of the YWCA: Second meeting, Topaz, November 14, 1942, pp. 1–2. Folder 20, Box 724. YWCA of the U.S.A. Records, Sophia Smith Collection. Northampton, MA: Smith College.

Height, D. I. (1945). The Adult Education Program of the YWCA among Negroes. *The Journal of Negro Education, 14*(3), 390–395.

Japanese American Citizens League. (1946). JACL objectives: A national program of reconversion and rehabilitation of Japanese Americans—presented to New York Conference on Japanese American Resettlement, pp. 1–5. Folder 12—Wartime Problems—Japanese Relocation, Box 37—Wartime Problems: Japanese Relocation. Family Service Association of America—SW076, Social Welfare History Archives. Minneapolis: University of Minnesota.

Kikuchi, M. (1942). Letter from Mrs. Miya Kikuchi, Chairman of the Board, Manzanar YWCA to Miss Helen N. Flack, dated November 3, 1942, pp. 1–9. Folder 14, Box 723. YWCA of the U.S.A. Records, Sophia Smith Collection. Northampton, MA: Smith College.

Kimmerling, C. (1945). Personal narrative report of the Welfare Section by Constance Kimmerling, Head Counselor, April 13, 1945 to November 1, 1945, dated November 15, 1945 *War Relocation Authority, Minidoka Relocation Center* (Calisphere, Japanese American Relocation Digital Archives ed., pp. 1–8). Berkeley: Bancroft Library, University of California.

Kimmerling, C., Fite, A. L., & Abbott, C. W. (1945). Report of the Welfare Section, August 1942 to November 1945 *War Relocation Authority, Minidoka Relocation Center* (Calisphere, Japanese American Relocation Digital Archives ed., pp. 1–69). Berkeley: Bancroft Library, University of California.

Lane, M. D. (1946). Japanese resettlement. *Public Welfare, 4,* 127–130.

Lewis, A. S. (2008). *The barrier breaking love of God: The multicultural activism of the Young women's Christian Association, 1940s to 1970s.* PhD, Rutgers University, New Brunswick, New Jersey.

Lyle, B. (1943). Summary Report of the Japanese American Project, August 1942–September 1943, pp. 1–7. Folder 2, Box 720. YWCA of the U.S.A. Records, Sophia Smith Collection. Northampton, MA: Smith College.

Manzanar Relocation Center. (1944). Minutes of the meeting of the Coordinating Council Meeting, November 28, 1944, pp. 1–3. Folder: 60.120 Youth Coordinating Council, Box 225: Manzanar Relocation Center Central Files 50.026 to 62.014 (1942 to 1943). Records of the War Relocation Authority, 1941–1989, Record Group 210, Subject-Classified General Files of the Relocation Centers—compiled 1942–1946. ARC Identifier 1544889/MLR Number PI-77 48. Washington, DC: National Archives and Records Administration.

Marks Jr., E. B. (1943). Memorandum to John H. Provinse, Chief, Community Services Division, WRA, Washington, DC, April 2, 1943, pp. 1–3. Folder: Provinse, John—Jan-April, 1943, Box 35: Washington Office Records—Chronological File; General—Alphabetical—PF-John Provinse. Records of the War Relocation Authority, 1941–1989, Record Group 210, General Outgoing Correspondence, compiled 1942–1946. ARC Identifier 1534421/MLR Number PI-77 18. Washington, DC: National Archives and Records Administration.

Matsumoto, T. (1945). Report of visits to four Relocation Centers (Granada, Minidoka, Heart Mountain & Rohwer), March 9–April 1, 1945, pp. 1–21. Folder 11—Japanese, Americans Relocation Centers and Resettlement, correspondence, reports, brochures, regulations, etc. . . 1942–1945 Box 222. Immigration & Refugee Services of America: Common Council for American Unity Collection, Immigration History Research Center. Minneapolis: University of Minnesota.

Meyer, D. S. (1944). Annual Report of the Director of the War Relocation Authority: Reprinted from the Annual Report of the Secretary of the Interior for the

Fiscal Year ended June 30, 1944, pp. 279–293. Folder: Annual Report of the Director of the War Relocation Authority. Fiscal yr. June 30, 1944, Box 3: Washington Office Records—Documentary Files: Semi-Annual Reports—1943 & 1944; Semi-Annual Reports—Evacuee Employment; Annual Reports—1943 & 1944; History or WRA—Ruth KcKee; Annual Report of the Director of WRA; Semi-Annual Reports—Owego 1944. Records of the War Relocation Authority, 1941–1989, Record Group 210, Headquarters Basic Documentation Reports, compiled 1942–1946. ARC Identifier 1526983/ MLR Number PI-77 3. Washington, DC: National Archives and Records Administration.

Meyer, D. S. (1945). Annual Report of the Director of the War Relocation Authority: Reprinted from the Annual Report of the Secretary of the Interior for the Fiscal Year ended June 30, 1945, pp. 275–290. Folder: Annual Reports—War Relocation Authority—1944–1945, Box 4: Washington Office Records—Documentary Files—Semi-Annual Reports, 1944 & 1945: Semi-Annual Reports 1946 (Final), War Records Project Report, 19944 & 1945; Semi-Annual reports, Legal Division. Records of the War Relocation Authority, 1941–1989, Record Group 210, Headquarters Basic Documentation Reports, compiled 1942–1946. ARC Identifier 1526983/ MLR Number PI-77 3. Washington, DC: National Archives and Records Administration.

Meyer, D. S. (1974). War Relocation Authority, the Director's account: An oral history conducted in 1974 by Amelia R. Fry. *Japanese American relocation reviewed, Volume II: The internment* (pp. 1a–55a). Berkeley: Regional Oral History Office, Bancroft Library, University of California.

Minneapolis Relocation Committee. (1943). Letter from the Chairman addressed to Dear Friends, dated December 30, 1943, p. 1. Folder 9—Y.W.C.A. MPLS Committee, Japanese Resettlement, Box 238—Agencies: YMCA. United Way of Minneapolis Records—SW070, Social Welfare History Archives. Minneapolis: University of Minnesota.

Miyamoto, S. F. (1942). A brief analysis of the relocation program and its problems, July 23, 1943, pp. 1–21. Folder T1.840, Box BANC MSS 67/14 c. Japanese American Evacuation and Resettlement Study, Japanese American Evacuation and Resettlement records. Berkeley: Bancroft Library, University of California.

Morimitsu, A. T., & Waller, T. (1942). Tule Lake Relocation Center Community Activities Report, for the period May 27, 1942 to July 20, 1942, dated July 25, 1942, pp. 1–13. Folder 1, Box 724. YWCA of the U.S.A. Records, Sophia Smith Collection. Northampton, MA: Smith College.

Mukaye, K. (1942). Report on Granada Relocation Center, Granada, Colorado, October 11, 1942, pp. 1–4. Folder 9, Box 724. YWCA of the U.S.A. Records, Sophia Smith Collection. Northampton, MA: Smith College.

Myer, D. S. (1971). *Uprooted Americans: The Japanese Americans and the War Relocation Authority during World War II.* Tucson: University of Arizona Press.

Nakamura, M. L. (1942). Letter from Mary Lucy Nakamura, Girls Clubs, Heart Mountain, Wyoming, to Miss Esther Briesemeister, dated November 5, 1942, pp. 1–3. Folder 23, Box 724. YWCA of the U.S.A. Records, Sophia Smith Collection. Northampton, MA: Smith College.

National Social Case Work Council. (1943). Resettlement of Japanese Americans by the War Relocation Authority: Memorandum to member agencies, from the National Social Case Work Council Sub-committee on Japanese Resettlement, January 6, 1943, pp. 1–4. Folder 1, Box 720. YWCA of the U.S.A. Records, Sophia Smith Collection. Northampton, MA: Smith College.

National Social Welfare Assembly. (1946). Proceedings of the Working Conference on Problems Relating to Resettlement of Japanese-Americans held under the auspices of National Social Welfare Assembly, January 17, 1946, pp. i–173. Folder 159—SWD4, NSWA; NSWA—Relocation and Resettlement of Japanese-Americans, 1942–1947, Box 16: Folders 158–169. National Social Welfare Assembly Records—SW0004, Social Welfare History Archives. Minneapolis: University of Minnesota.

Newstetter, W. I. (1935). What is social group work. In H. R. Knight (Ed.), *Proceedings of the National Conference of Social Work at the sixty-second annual session held in Montreal, Canada, June 9–15, 1935* (Vol. 62, pp. 291–299). Chicago, Illinois: University of Chicago Press.

New York School of Social Work. (1947). *Bulletin of the New York School of Social Work, Columbia University: Report for the year October 1, 1946–September 30, 1947* (Vol. 16). New York: Community Service Society of the City of New York.

Niiya, B., & Robinson, G. (July 1, 2015). Escheat suits. *Densho Encyclopedia of the Japanese American Incarceration.* Retrieved from http://encyclopedia.densho.org/Escheat suits/

Nisei Student Relocation Commemorative Fund. (n.d.) Our origins: The National Japanese American Student Relocation Council (NJASRC). Retrieved from http://www.nsrcfund.org/our-history-our-stories/our-origins

Nishi, S. F. (n.d.). Report on trip to West Coast and Relocation Centers (Poston, Gila, Topaz, Heart Mountain), submitted by Rev. Shunji F. Nishi, pp. 1–20. Folder 5, Box 720. YWCA of the U.S.A. Records, Sophia Smith Collection. Northampton, MA: Smith College.

North, L. (1942). The educational system at Granada Relocation Center, Amache, Colorado, November 23, 1942, pp. 1–4. Folder 9, Box 724. YWCA of the U.S.A. Records, Sophia Smith Collection. Northampton, MA: Smith College.

Okazaki, M. (1946). Group work and recreation for Japanese-Americans, prepared by Miss Mari Okazaki, Social Worker, International Institute, San Francisco California: A bulletin of the Committee on Resettlement of Japanese-Americans & National Social Welfare Assembly, June 1946, pp. 1–4. Folder 161, Box 16: Folders 158–169. National Social Welfare Assembly Records—SW0004, Social Welfare History Archives. Minneapolis: University of Minnesota.

Park, Y., & Kemp, S. P. (2006). Little Alien Colonies: Representations of immigrants and their neighborhoods in social work discourse, 1875–1924. *Social Service Review, 80*(4), 705–734

Payne, V. (1944). Weekly report—week ending March17, 1944: Memorandum to Reports Division from Social Service Department, Heart Mountain Relocation Project, Heart Mountain, Wyoming, pp. 1–5. Folder: Welfare—General, Box 159: Heart Mountain Relocation Center—Central Files—Hearings and Reports to Community Activities (General). Records of the War Relocation Authority, 1941–1989, Record Group 210, Subject-Classified General Files of the Relocation Centers—compiled 1942–1946. ARC Identifier 1544889/MLR Number PI-77 48. Washington, DC: National Archives and Records Administration.

Powell, J. W. (1943). America's refugees: Exodus and diaspora. In C. Trumble (Ed.), *Proceedings of the National Conference of Social Work: selected papers, Seventieth Annual Meeting, War Regional Conferences, New York, St. Louis, Cleveland, 1943* (Vol. 70, pp. 301–309). New York: Columbia University Press.

Provinse, J. H. (1943). Letter to Miss Grace Coyle, School of Applied Social Sciences, Western Reserve University, Cleveland, Ohio, from John H. Provinse, Chief, Community Management Division, WRA, Washington, DC, November 10, 1943, pp. 1–2. Folder: WELA-WEZ, Box 48: Washington Office Records—Chronological File; General—Alphabetical—War Refugee Board—Wilson. Records of the War Relocation Authority, 1941–1989, Record Group 210, General Outgoing Correspondence, compiled 1942–1946. ARC Identifier 1534421/MLR Number PI-77 18. Washington, DC: National Archives and Records Administration.

Provinse, J. H. (1944). Letter to Miss Grace Coyle, School of Applied Social Sciences, Western Reserve University, Cleveland, Ohio, from John H. Provinse, Chief, Community Management Division, WRA, Washington, DC, February 15, 1944, p. 1. Folder: WELA-WEZ, Box 48: Washington Office Records—Chronological File; General—Alphabetical—War Refugee Board—Wilson. Records of the War Relocation Authority, 1941–1989, Record Group 210, General Outgoing Correspondence, compiled 1942–1946. ARC Identifier 1534421/MLR Number PI-77 18. Washington, DC: National Archives and Records Administration.

Provinse, J. H. (1945). Letter from John Provinse, Acting Director, to Miss Esther Briesemeister, pp. 1–2. Folder 4, Box 723. YWCA of the U.S.A. Records, Sophia Smith Collection. Northampton, MA: Smith College.

Reith, M. B. (1943). Report on Topaz WRA Project, Topaz, Utah, June 7–10, 1943, pp. 1–6. Folder 21, Box 724. YWCA of the U.S.A. Records, Sophia Smith Collection. Northampton, MA: Smith College.

Roe, C. (1944). YWCA Serves Evacuees in Resettlement Bulletin Vol. II, No. 8, July 1944, pp. 1–2. Folder 4, Box 720. YWCA of the U.S.A. Records, Northampton, MA: Smith College.

Sakoda, J. M. (1989). The "Residue": the unsettled Minidokans, 1943–1945. In Y. Ichioka (Ed.), *Views from within: the Japanese American Evacuation and Resettlement Study* (pp. 247–279). Los Angeles: University of California Press.

Sasaki, T. S. (1946a). Daily report #47: Orientation—integration, August 22, 1946, pp. 1–3. Folder: 15.101 Los Angeles, CA, Daily Reports, #1-50, Box 1: Washington Office Records—Liquidation Files—Special Studies—15.100 Santa Clara Area thro 15.101.B L.A. Area Records of the War Relocation Authority, 1941–1989, Record Group 210, Liquidation Files—Special Studies—General Files Relating to the Resettlement Study, compiled 1946–1947. ARC Identifier 1566649/MLR Number PI-77 64. Washington, DC: National Archives and Records Administration.

Sasaki, T. S. (1946b). Monthly report on Los Angeles, September 1st to 30th, 1946, pp. 1–17. Folder: 15.101.B Los Angeles, CA, Final Reports, Box 1: Washington Office Records—Liquidation Files—Special Studies-15.100 Santa Clara Area thro 15.101.B L.A. Area Records of the War Relocation Authority, 1941–1989, Record Group 210, Liquidation Files—Special Studies—General Files Relating to the Resettlement Study, compiled 1946–1947. ARC Identifier 1566649/MLR Number PI-77 64. Washington, DC: National Archives and Records Administration.

Schwartz, W. (2006). The group work tradition and social work practice. *Social Work with Groups, 28*(3/4), 69–89.

Spickard, P. R. (1986). Injustice compounded: Amerasians and Non-Japanese Americans in World War II concentration camps. *Journal of American Ethnic History, 5*(2), 5–22.

Tozier, M. M. (1945). Roundtable Conference of Building Better Race Relations: Education of public opinion toward Minority groups, November 24, 1945, pp. 1–16. Folder

13, Box 537. YWCA of the U.S.A. Records, Sophia Smith Collection. Northampton, MA: Smith College.

Underhill, B. S. (1945). California State Department of Social Welfare Office Memorandum to Perry Sundquist, October 24, 1945, p. 1. Box Social Welfare—War Services—Resettlement Assistance, General, 1942–48 (F3729:110). Department of Social Welfare Records, War Services Bureau. Sacramento: California State Archives.

United States Army. (1943). *Final report, Japanese evacuation from the West Coast, 1942.* Washington, DC: U.S. Government Printing Office.

United States Civil Service Commission. (1943). United States Civil Service Commission Classification Sheet: Associate Public Welfare Consultant (P-3), War Relocation Authority, Office for Emergency Management, pp. 1–2. Folder: Welfare Section, Box 2. Records of the War Relocation Authority, 1941–1989, Record Group 210, Job Descriptions—compiled 1942–1946. ARC Identifier 1543527/MLR Number PI-77 36. Washington, DC: National Archives and Records Administration.

War Relocation Authority. (1943a). Community Activities semi-annual report: July through December 1943, pp. 1–6. Folder: Semi-Annual Reports—Community Management Division Reports of Health Section & Reports of Welfare Section, Box 5: Washington Office Records—Documentary Files—Semi-Annual Reports: Operation D Division, Community Mgmt. Div, Administrative Mgmt. Division. Records of the War Relocation Authority, 1941–1989, Record Group 210, Headquarters Basic Documentation Reports, compiled 1942–1946. ARC Identifier 1526983/ MLR Number PI-77 3. Washington, DC: National Archives and Records Administration.

War Relocation Authority. (1943b). Cue Sheet for Community Activities Leaders, No.1, pp. 1–4. Folder: Community Activities—Community Management Division, Box 1: Administrative Mgmt. Evacuee Property thru Estimate of Appropriations. Records of the War Relocation Authority, 1941–1989, Record Group 210, Washington Office Records—Washington Documents. ARC Identifier 1519285/MLR Number PI-77 2. Washington, DC: National Archives and Records Administration.

War Relocation Authority. (1943c). Evacuee resistance to relocation—reasons for the Relocation Program: Community Analysis Report No. 5, June 1943, marked "not for publication," pp. 1–9. Folder 16, Box 722. YWCA of the U.S.A. Records, Sophia Smith Collection. Northampton, MA: Smith College.

War Relocation Authority. (1943d). Guidelines of Community Activities—some suggestions for the organization of the development of C.A. program at relocation centers, especially in relation to the project objectives (dated February, 1943), pp. 1–17. Folder: Community Activities—Community Management Division, Box 2: Administrative Mgmt.—Estimate of Approp.; Community mgmt.—Community Activities, Business Enterprise, Educational Activities, Community Government. Records of the War Relocation Authority, 1941–1989, Record Group 210, Washington Office Records—Washington Documents. ARC Identifier 1519285/MLR Number PI-77 2. Washington, DC: National Archives and Records Administration.

War Relocation Authority. (1943e). Project Analysis Series No. 9, June 23, 1943: Preliminary Survey of Resistances to Resettlement at the Tule Lake Relocation Center, pp. 1–15. Folder 3, Box 724. YWCA of the U.S.A. Records, Sophia Smith Collection. Northampton, MA: Smith College.

War Relocation Authority. (1943f). *The relocation program: A guidebook for the resident of relocation centers, May 1943.* Washington, DC: War Relocation Authority.

War Relocation Authority. (1944a). Conference of Community Management—Report of the Summarizing Committee, May 13, 1944, pp. 1–6. Folder: Conference of Community Management—Denver, Colorado—May 13, 1944, Box 8: Meetings and Conferences 1943–1945. Records of the War Relocation Authority, 1941–1989, Record Group 210, Washington Office Records—Washington Documents. ARC Identifier 1519285/MLR Number PI-77 2. Washington, DC: National Archives and Records Administration.

War Relocation Authority. (1944b). Report of Community Activities July through December 1944, pp. 1–4. Folder: Semi-Annual Reports—Community Management Division Reports of Health Section & Reports of Welfare Section, Box 5: Washington Office Records—Documentary Files—Semi-Annual Reports: Operation D Division, Community Mgmt. Div, Administrative Mgmt. Division. Records of the War Relocation Authority, 1941–1989, Record Group 210, Headquarters Basic Documentation Reports, compiled 1942–1946. ARC Identifier 1526983/ MLR Number PI-77 3. Washington, DC: National Archives and Records Administration.

War Relocation Authority. (1944c). Report of Community Activities, January to July 1944, pp. 1–8. Folder: Community Activities—Community Management Division, Box 2: Administrative Mgmt.—Estimate of Approp.; Community mgmt.- Community Activities, Business Enterprise, Educational Activities, Community Government. Records of the War Relocation Authority, 1941–1989, Record Group 210, Washington Office Records—Washington Documents. ARC Identifier 1519285/MLR Number PI-77 2. Washington, DC: National Archives and Records Administration.

War Relocation Authority. (1944d). Semi-Annual Reports—WRA—Printed—July 1 to Dec. 31, 1944, pp. 1–80. Folder: Semi-Annual Reports—WRA—Printed—July 1 to Dec. 31, 1944, Box 4: Washington Office Records—Documentary Files—Semi-Annual Reports, 1944 & 1945: Semi-Annual Reports 1946 (Final), War Records Project Report, 19944 & 1945; Semi-Annual reports, Legal Division. Records of the War Relocation Authority, 1941–1989, Record Group 210, Headquarters Basic Documentation Reports, compiled 1942–1946. ARC Identifier 1526983/ MLR Number PI-77 3. Washington, DC: National Archives and Records Administration.

War Relocation Authority. (1946a). Directory of organizations maintaining programs for Japanese Americans, pp. 1–35. Folder 12—Wartime Problems—Japanese Relocation, Box 37—Wartime Problems: Japanese Relocation. Family Service Association of America—SW076, Social Welfare History Archives. Minneapolis: University of Minnesota.

War Relocation Authority. (1946b). Final Report of the Los Angeles, CA District War Relocation Authority, January 31, 1946, p. 1. Folder: Final Reports—Los Angeles District WRA, January 31, 1946, Box 11: Final Reports—Northern and Southern California. Records of the War Relocation Authority, 1941–1989, Record Group 210, Field Basic Documentation—Relocation Center Records—compiled 1942–1946. ARC Identifier 1532647/MLR Number PI-77 4C. Washington, DC: National Archives and Records Administration.

War Relocation Authority. (1946c). Hostels: Relocation Division Memorandum No.92, June 4, 1945, pp. 1–7. Folder 158—SWD4, NSWA; NSWA—Relocation and Resettlement of Japanese-Americans, 1942–1947, Box 16: Folders 158–169. National Social Welfare Assembly Records—SW0004, Social Welfare History Archives. Minneapolis: University of Minnesota.

War Relocation Authority. (1946d). Hostels: Relocation Division Memorandum No.92, Supplement 1, June 18, 1945, p. 1. Folder 158—SWD4, NSWA; NSWA—Relocation and Resettlement of Japanese-Americans, 1942–1947, Box 16: Folders 158–169. National Social Welfare Assembly Records—SW0004, Social Welfare History Archives. Minneapolis: University of Minnesota.

War Relocation Authority. (1946e). Hostels: Relocation Division Memorandum No.92, Supplement 2, July 7, 1945, p. 1. Folder 158—SWD4, NSWA; NSWA—Relocation and Resettlement of Japanese-Americans, 1942–1947, Box 16: Folders 158–169. National Social Welfare Assembly Records—SW0004, Social Welfare History Archives. Minneapolis: University of Minnesota.

War Relocation Authority. (1946f). *Impounded people, Japanese Americans in the relocation centers*. Washington: U.S. Government Printing Office.

War Relocation Authority. (1946g). Semi-annual report: January 1 to June 30, 1946, pp. 1–29. Folder 12—Wartime Problems—Japanese Relocation, Box 37—Wartime Problems: Japanese Relocation. Family Service Association of America—SW076, Social Welfare History Archives. Minneapolis: University of Minnesota.

War Relocation Authority (n.d.-a). Community Activities, pp. 1–4. Folder: Community Activities—Community Management Division, Box 2: Administrative Mgmt.— Estimate of Approp.; Community mgmt.—Community Activities, Business Enterprise, Educational Activities, Community Government. Records of the War Relocation Authority, 1941–1989, Record Group 210, Washington Office Records— Washington Documents. ARC Identifier 1519285/MLR Number PI-77 2. Washington, DC: National Archives and Records Administration.

War Relocation Authority (n.d.-b). Resettlement program (compiled), pp. 1–65. Folder E8.00, Box BANC MSS 67/14 c. Japanese American Evacuation and Resettlement Study, Japanese American Evacuation and Resettlement records. Berkeley: Bancroft Library, University of California.

War Relocation Authority (n.d.-c). When You Leave the Relocation Center, pp. 1–7. Folder 13, Box 722. YWCA of the U.S.A. Records, Sophia Smith Collection. Northampton, MA: Smith College.

Watson, A. C. (1942). Notes on Japanese Resettlement, December 1–15, 1942: Memorandum from Annie Clo Watson to Thomas W. Holland, War Relocation Authority, and George E. Rundquist, Federal Council of Churches, December 17, 1942, pp. 1–4. Folder 23, Box 719. YWCA of the U.S.A. Records, Sophia Smith Collection. Northampton, MA: Smith College.

Watson, A. C. (1943a). From evacuation to resettlement: A page from history. *Woman's Press, 37*, pp. 198–199, Smith College, YWCA of the U.S.A.—Bound Periodicals. Northampton, MA: Smith College.

Watson, A. C. (1943b). Japanese Resettlement, Aug. 1, 1943: Summary report for approximately one year—beginning September, 1942: For official files of the YWCA; not for distribution, pp. 1–3. Folder 2, Box 720. YWCA of the U.S.A. Records, Sophia Smith Collection. Northampton, MA: Smith College.

Wilson, G. (1976). From practice to theory: A personalized history. In R. W. Roberts & H. Northen (Eds.), *Theories of social work with groups* (pp. 1–44). New York: Columbia University Press.

Woodsmall, R. L. (1942). Impressions of the Japanese Relocation Center at Manzanar, California: World's YWCA, Washington, DC, dated December 1, 1942, pp. 1–5. Folder

14, Box 723. YWCA of the U.S.A. Records, Sophia Smith Collection. Northampton, MA: Smith College.

Wygel, W. (1943). Report on Manzanar, July 22–27, 1943, pp. 1–11. Folder 16, Box 723. YWCA of the U.S.A. Records, Sophia Smith Collection. Northampton, MA: Smith College.

Yasumura, J. (1945). Report on the closing of Minidoka Relocation Center by Jobu Yasumura, Department of Cities, American Baptist Home Mission Society, dated November 5, 1945, pp. 1–9. Folder 17, Box 724. YWCA of the U.S.A. Records, Sophia Smith Collection. Northampton, MA: Smith College.

Yatsushiro, T. (1946). Daily report #12: Nisei organizations—YWCA Young People Society, August 29, 1946, pp. 1–6. Folder: 15.103 Denver, Colorado, Daily Reports 1–40, Box 2: Washington Office Records—Liquidation Files—Special Studies—15.102 Chicago, Illinois—15.103 Denver, Colorado. Records of the War Relocation Authority, 1941–1989, Record Group 210, Liquidation Files—Special Studies—General Files Relating to the Resettlement Study, compiled 1946–1947. ARC Identifier 1566649/MLR Number PI-77 64. Washington, DC: National Archives and Records Administration.

YWCA National Board. (1942). A proposal for work which the National Board of the Young Women's Christian Association might assume in relation to Japanese reception and resettlement areas in the Western Defense Command, prepared by Helen Flack, Nationality Secretary, Western Region, San Francisco, pp. 1–3. Folder 20, Box 719. YWCA of the U.S.A. Records, Sophia Smith Collection. Northampton, MA: Smith College.

YWCA National Board—Community Division Committee. (1943). Minutes of the Community Division Committee Meeting, Tuesday, May 4, 1943, p. 1. Folder 20, Box 719. YWCA of the U.S.A. Records, Sophia Smith Collection. Northampton, MA: Smith College.

YWCA National Board—Race Relations Subcommittee of the National Public Affairs Committee. (1944). Minutes of Meeting of Race Relations Sub-Committee of the Public Affairs Committee, April 19, 1944, pp. 1–4. Folder 1, Box 395. YWCA of the U.S.A. Records, Sophia Smith Collection. Northampton, MA: Smith College.

YWCA National Board—Race Relations Subcommittee of the National Public Affairs Committee. (1945). Minutes: Race Relations Subcommittee, October 17, 1945, pp. 1–4. Folder 2, Box 395. YWCA of the U.S.A. Records, Sophia Smith Collection. Northampton, MA: Smith College.

9

Resettlement

Part II: The Work of the Welfare Sections

Relocation of Minors

Unattached Children

The most willing resettlers were, unsurprisingly, "young adults between 18–25—representing the venturesome leadership type" (YWCA National Board—Race Relations Subcommittee of the National Public Affairs Committee, 1944, p. 1), who tended to be better educated and more employable than their older counterparts. They were "generally the men and women with professional background or the young people who were eager to obtain a university education or specialized skills" (Choda, 1946, p. 141). By May of 1945, the bulk of that segment of the camp population was resettled across "44 states and the District of Columbia" (Lane, 1946, p. 127). While these young adults could, despite vehement opposition from their parents, legally make the decision to leave the camps without their families, a number of much younger, minor children also left the camps for resettlement unaccompanied by a parent or a legal guardian. According to the War Relocation Authority (WRA, 1944c), it was "comparatively simple" (p. 14) to develop resettlement policies and procedures for school boys" and "school girls," high school-aged children who were "placed in homes where they could work for their maintenance" (p. 14) as domestic laborers in Caucasian households while attending school.[1] Poston Welfare Head Lou Butler (1945b) reported that the placements and conditions of work within them "were approved by the appropriate child welfare agency before leave was arranged for the minor" (p. 14), though whether such arrangements included follow-up visits by those agencies to ensure that the living and working conditions remained acceptable was not specified.

The WRA's (1944b) overall policy for unaccompanied minors was that welfare staff and relocation officers in the camps worked together to create a plan

---

[1] See Richard Nishimoto's monograph "Domestic Service," which provides a brief history of the Nikkei in domestic service in the prewar year and includes a section on this practice of school children working in Caucasian households (Nishimoto, 1943).

Facilitating Injustice: The complicity of social workers in the forced removal and incarceration of Japanese Americans, 1941–1946. Yoosun Park, Oxford University Press (2020). © Oxford University Press.
DOI: 10.1093/acprof:oso/9780199765058.001.0001

"to assure appropriate state and community assistance" (p. 2). Approval from the Washington headquarters for the resettlement plan for unaccompanied minors was required before any such children could be released from the camps. As the year 1944 ended, however, the policy was changed to forego headquarters approval when there was "assurance form the Relocation Officer or Supervisor that the plan was approved by the appropriate state child welfare agency" (p. 2). This was, clearly, a shift motivated by the resettlement push. By the WRA's own admission, the views of the Welfare Sections and the Relocation Sections differed on the need for headquarters approval. The two sections did work together—in better harmony in some camps than others—but Relocation Sections tended to deem headquarters approval inessential and delay-causing; Welfare Sections, on the other hand, insisted that "speed was not essential in the relocation of minors" (p. 2). Welfare Sections argued for more oversight, at least "until it was demonstrated that both the centers and the field offices fully understood the steps necessary to protect children relocating without parental protection" (p. 2). The determination of the adequacy of care planning for the resettlement of unaccompanied minor children was given ultimately to the relocation office; the WRA's priority was speed rather than protection.

To be clear, the gaps in child protection were a problem that predated the resettlement push. Minidoka Welfare department (Kimmerling, Fite, & Abbot, 1945) noted that it discovered through the "Daily Departure Notices" section of the camp newspaper and from "occasional complaints from the field" that hundreds of children as young as 10 and 12 had regularly been "allowed to leave the Center for various types of leave without adequate planning" (p. 27). They went out on seasonal leaves, for example, to labor in canneries and farms.

> Parental approval of these departures was presumed to have been obtained when the children brought back to the Relocation Office a form containing the parents' names. The parents were not interviewed, and no other attempt was made to determine whether or not they understood the child's plans or approved them. It was frequently reported, and later definitely ascertained by investigation, that the living conditions on some of the farms were far from desirable, that the children had no supervision after working hours, and that frequently they got into difficulty in the nearby towns. The children were given no help in budgeting their incomes and parents were disappointed when many of them returned to the Center without any money. (p. 27)

Prompted by the Welfare Section, the Washington headquarters eventually "clarified this situation" (p. 27), and Seasonal Leave Clearance procedures began to include Welfare Section oversight in cases of "unattached" children. In the 1944 spring planting season, approximately 150 children and parents were interviewed by the Minidoka welfare staff to counsel the families and to obtain parental approval before seasonal leave clearance was granted to the children. According to Kimmerling, while some of the "children showed annoyance at being obliged to come in for a discussion of their plans," their parents" were very expressive of their appreciation at being consulted. (p. 27). Permissions for Indefinite Leave or resettlement were, however, still being granted minors by the relocation division without advanced planning or parental permission. "Some Middle Western cities reported difficulties resulting from such placements" (p. 27). Welfare and relocation divisions were deadlocked on the issue, with the former pressing for more oversight and the latter seeing only delays in doing so; it took the intercession of the camp's director backing the necessity of Welfare Section consultation to finally establish advance planning procedures for resettlement of unattached children. Rohwer Welfare Head Wilma Dusseldorp (1945) reported, similarly, that her department "gradually" (p. 4) discovered that many minors had applied for and received permission for resettlement from the Relocation Section without the consent or even the knowledge of their parents. Rohwer also eventually instituted a new policy to make permission for resettlement conditional upon parental consultation and approval.

Dusseldorp, like others, usually characterized the conflict between Nisei children wanting to leave the camps and Issei parents who did not want their children to leave without them as another facet of the oft-cited acculturation gap.

> The parents' refusal to allow the children to relocate many times meant that the parents were trying to hold their children to old customs which the children, could not fully accept. The function of the Welfare Section at times took the form of helping the children continue in their obligations toward their parents, and at other times, helping the parents to accept the Americanized ways and ideas of their children. (p. 20)

Berta Choda (1946) described that many of the younger generation "had to struggle with themselves and their families before they could break away from the age-old rule of maintaining unity in family life and the ipso facto infallibility of their elders" (p. 141). While the WRA as a whole, and social workers in particular, tended to exoticize the divergence of will between the parents and the children as a cultural gap, it is difficult to imagine any parent, regardless of race or culture, who would not be reluctant to send a child out alone into a world whose antipathy toward them was substantiated in the fact of their incarceration. It was a world which, moreover, the parents could not easily visit, send aid to, or intervene in should any harm befall their children. The following death notice send out by Relocation Officer Prudence Ross (1945), of an unaccompanied 17-year-old boy resettled in Chicago, was found in Poston's archived records.

For your information seventeen year old H.T. whose parents are still at Poston was killed July twentieth when he fell down shaft of freight elevator at Continental Plastics, 314 E. West Erie, Chicago, where he was employed as handyman, coroner's jury gave verdict of accidental death. Funeral arrangements being made at Poston. (p. 1)

The Manzanar Children's Village

As the WRA's plan to push resettlement and clear out the camps for closure became increasingly more strident, the need to find permanent placements for the children in the Manzanar Children's Village became urgent. While the majority of the children at the Village had come from California orphanages, the Village also housed children newly orphaned since the removal, as well as "temporary orphans" (Nobe, 1999, p. 66) who needed temporary care while parents were ill, interned, or otherwise unable to provide care. They could not be returned to existing Californian orphanages; the military exclusion blocking their return to the West Coast was still in place, and those institutions did not, in any case, want Nikkei children. Neither did orphanages in eastern parts of the United States: anti-Nikkei racism was not an exclusively West Coast phenomenon. The Japanese Children's Home, the all-Nikkei orphanage which had been housed in Los Angeles, could not be easily replicated elsewhere; it had been licensed only in California and Joy. R. Kusumoto, its founder and director, had returned to Japan in one of the earliest waves of repatriation (Manzanar Public Welfare Department, 1943b). Fostering children in the camps was also a difficult proposition given the overcrowded quarters in which all families already struggled to manage. Suitable families willing to foster or adopt Nikkei children on the outside were scarce. The WRA's warning that interracial adoption or foster care was inadvisable since the "child's future happiness depends on compete acceptance by foster-relatives and their community, as well as by the foster-parents" (Merritt, 1944b, p. 1) provides a sense of the hostile environment in which the Welfare Sections were working to find caretakers.

Even aside from all of the preceding problems, a major stumbling block to adoption or any long-term planning for the future of the children was the issue of legal guardianship, which in most cases remained unresolved even when Manzanar was decommissioned in late October of 1945. In a letter to Margaret D'Ille, Martha Chickering, the outgoing Head of the California State Department of Social Work (CSDSW) who had overseen the removal of the bulk of the children in the Village, regretted that the issue of guardianship had not been resolved prior to their removal from California.[2]

---

[2] She left the CSDSW to become the new head of the UC Berkeley School of Social Work.

The question you raise in regard to the children in the Children's Village is a very serious one and I will pass it on to the chief of our Division of Child Welfare to follow up. We tried very hard to get those children made wards of a court before they went to Manzanar, because we thought that would assure them some continuing legal protection. However, this did not prove possible. As I will be leaving the Department within the next day or two, I am not trying myself to do anything about this, but will pass it on, as I say, to Miss Lucille Kennedy, who will follow it up. (Chickering, 1943b, p. 1)

Resolution of the matter from within the camps proved even more difficult (Kuramoto, 1976). To what and whose jurisdiction did the child belong? Was it the state the child came from, the state in which the child was incarcerated, the Bureau of Public Assistance regional division, or the WRA resettlement regional catchment area? The WRA itself, seeing itself as a temporary agency intent on shutting its doors as soon as possible, clearly was not interested in taking on the responsibility for guardianship.

Adoption was also made difficult by the fact that only two agencies were licensed to place children for adoption in California: the Children's Home Society and the Native Sons and Native Daughters Central Committee on Homeless Children (Chickering, 1943a). In addition to all the usual procedural complications involved in any adoption proceedings, a great barrier to the adoption of Nikkei children was, of course, "their racial inheritances, and the present war situation" (D'Ille, 1943, p. 2). One of the agencies, an arm of the Native Sons and Native Daughters of the Golden West, was a blatantly racist organization which had carried out some of the most vicious campaigns against the Nikkei in California for decades and was unlikely to aid the WRA in its efforts to place Nikkei children. The second agency, the Children's Home Society, also exhibited a "certain amount of anti-Japanese bias and prejudice on the part of some of the members of the board" (Glick, 1944, p. 3). A privately funded organization supported by contributions from the general public, the Society averred that the "agreement of their constituency in any plan of importance undertaken" was necessary; aiding Nikkei children in need of adoptive homes was considered such a plan.

At this present time, because of the war feeling, many contributors might be very conservative at the suggestion that the Children's Home Society help out with adoptions of Japanese children. On their board, there had been a division of opinion. Some members of the board, who had sons now fighting in the South Pacific, were loath to do anything that would help any person of Japanese ancestry and found it hard to distinguish between a Japanese in this country, even American citizens, and the military in Japan. (Manzanar Public Welfare Department, 1943a, p. 1)

On December 16, 1943, after months of correspondence and in-person discussions, a multiagency meeting to work out the problems in adoption finally came together. Manzanar Welfare Section Head Margaret D'Ille met with representatives of the CSDSW and the Children's Home Society to discuss four possible scenarios for arranging adoptions for the Village children. The first scenario was that the Children's Home Society would, as was its remit, "take responsibility as one of the licensed agencies of California" (Manzanar Public Welfare Department, 1943b, p. 1) and arrange adoptions. The second scenario was that the Manzanar Welfare Section would become a licensed adoption agency under the CSDSW and be allowed to organize the necessary adoptions. The third possibility was that the Children's Home Society would be the responsible body, with the Welfare Section officially involved in some manner. The final possibility was that CSDSW would directly oversee adoption of Nikkei children in the camps with the assistance of the Welfare Section (Manzanar Public Welfare Department, 1943b, p. 1). Given that the WRA was a temporary wartime agency, whereas adoptions "are not temporary but involve the whole life of a child" (Manzanar Public Welfare Department, 1943b, p. 3), assigning control over adoption to the Children's Home Society or the CSDSW made sense. Conversely, given that the WRA was a federal agency with the ability to act in many states, assigning control of adoptions to the WRA also made some sense. The meeting ended inconclusively with no plan adopted; it was more than six months later, on June 29, 1944, two years after the establishment of the Children's Village, that the Board of Directors of the Children's Home Society of California (CHSC) finally notified Manzanar of its decision to provide adoption services to Nikkei children (Merritt, 1944a, p. 1).[3] The espoused willingness on the part of CHSC, however, produced few results. By the time the Village was shuttered on July 31, 1944, approximately four months prior to the closing of the Manzanar itself, only a few children had been adopted or placed in foster care (Kuramoto, 1976; Nobe, 1999). About half the children housed at the Village had been returned to their parents; a few considered "old enough to relocate on their own" (Kuramoto, 1976, p. 47) had been resettled. The remaining 26 children "were left to the care

---

[3] The CHSC letter arrived just as a management shift of the Village had taken place; a new Caucasian superintendent named Eva Robbins was replacing Lilian and Harry Matsumoto who were leaving Manzanar for resettlement. Eva Robbins, the Caucasian social worker appointed as superintendent in 1944 had no prior experience working with the Nikkei community (Nobe, 1999). How much of the failure of the WRA to find permanent homes for the children of the Village was due to her inadequacies as a social worker is impossible to reconstruct, but it seems unlikely that the failure was due to disinterest. Annie Sakamoto, one of the young children sent at the end of the war to foster care in California, remembered Robbins with fondness (Irwin, 2008). She recalled that during her time at the Village, she would visit Eva Robbins in her quarters; "I used to go to her house, sit on her lap, play the piano, or the typewriter" (Irwin, 2008, p. 221). Robbins would travel from her home in Indiana to visit her in California in the years after the war; they remained in touch until Robbin's death in her nineties.

of various county welfare departments as the war ended" (Kuramoto, 1976, p. 47). The Semi-Annual Report of the Welfare Section for the period between January 1 and June 30, 1945, includes a brief note that a "summary on each resident in the Village" was prepared by the Welfare Section and sent to the "appropriate" county agency in which the child was determined to have legal residence. "That agency will assume responsibility for placing the child" (War Relocation Authority, 1945c, p. 3).

In historian Lisa Nobe's (1999) view, just as the "government agents had not given much thought to individual orphans when it came to internment, they were just as negligent about their dispersal from the Children's Village when the war ended" (p. 70). As unsuccessful as the social work efforts might be judged in the final analysis, the archived records of the Manzanar welfare department do indicate that attempts to secure permanent resolutions for the children had been made years prior to the closure of the camps. The case of S., an 11-year-old girl incarcerated with her grandparents at Gila River, provides a glimpse into the jurisdictional confusion and other complexities involved in the handling of child custody in the camps and illustrates that child custody was not a matter taken lightly by the WRA officials. The young girl had been under her maternal grandparents' care since her mother's death six years prior to removal. Her father and his new wife were residents of a mountain state outside the exclusion zone at the time of the West Coast clearing, and thus had not been incarcerated in the camps. Their wish to gain custody of the child, communicated by letter to the camp administration at Gila River, was vehemently opposed by the grandparents and the girl herself who had "considerable resentment directed towards her father" (Thunder, 1943, p. 1) for his long absence from her life. The custody tangle, difficult under any circumstances, was confounded not only by the fact that the child was in Arizona and under WRA jurisdiction but because the grandparents had indicated their decision to be transferred to Tule Lake and to be repatriated to Japan from there, with every intention of taking the girl with them.[4] The camp Welfare Section was initially quite unsympathetic to the father's request, unimpressed by "his seeming lack of foresight" (Thunder, 1944b, p. 2) about the impact that a sudden separation from the grandparents would have on the child. Social workers involved were uncertain that he was motivated by "a real desire for the child" (Thunder, 1944b, p. 2) rather than "a sense of duty and guilt plus community criticism" (Thunder, 1944b, p. 2). The Section was adamant that, without a court order, it could not hold the child at the camp when the grandparents

---

[4] This was in the aftermath of the loyalty questionnaire debacle, often referred to by the social welfare departments as the "registration crisis." The grandparents had opted for a transfer to Tule Lake, at which those who had registered their decision to be repatriated to Japan would be segregated prior to their departure (see next section for further details).

were segregated to Tule Lake. But the WRA's Denver Relocation Officer's testament that the father was quite well-off financially and, in stark contrast to the "intensely Japanese nationalistic" (Thunder, 1944a, p. 1) grandparents, was socially "accepted not only by the best people in Denver of Japanese ancestry but by many Caucasians" (Curtis, 1943, p. 1), had an ameliorating effect on the Welfare Section's stance. The office did, nevertheless, do its due diligence and contact the Denver Children's Aid Society to investigate the father and the suitability of his home. In the final analysis, after much correspondence and discussion, it was determined that the grandparents had never been granted legal custody of the girl, which had always resided with the father. The camp director made the ultimate decision to release the girl to her father.

Dependency: "New Habits of Idleness"

At least in its public recounting, the WRA demonstrated an in-depth and often sympathetic knowledge of the losses suffered by the Nikkei as well as the difficulties they would encounter in resettlement. It acknowledged that the Nikkei had suffered "a considerable amount of property damage and loss as a result of the evacuation" (War Relocation Authority, 1946d, p. 18). Most had exhausted any savings in supplementing the subsistence wages paid for work in the camps. Those few who had homes to return to found them vandalized and stored furniture and equipment stolen or damaged (War Relocation Authority, 1946d). Robert Cozzens (1974), one-time Assistant Director of the WRA, recalled one such home he saw in 1945.

> In Auburn, Washington, we went in to check the property of people who had left everything stored there. It was next door to a laundry and the people in the laundry were supposed to look after it. But people had been permitted to get in there or had broken in. We could see no place where they got in except with keys. The girls' clothes—dress uniforms and party dresses and formals— were taken and hung and slit with razor blades top to bottom. The ashes of the deceased—and they had many urns there—were poured all over everything. All the furniture that was stored in there was slit with knife blades or razor blades across the chairs and up and down the backs. The vandalism was unbelievable. (p. 45)

But such knowledge was profoundly at odds with the organization's primary mandate for clearing out the camps. The organizational rhetoric tended, therefore, to elide its sympathies and veer toward interpretations that portrayed the reluctance of the Nikkei to leave the camps as moral and psychological degeneration rather than judicious concern about real circumstances. First, the plight of the Nikkei was identified not as displacement and poverty produced by forced removal and incarceration, but as a problematic rise in dependency and the erosion of self-sufficiency; they had developed "new habits of idleness" (Hoey, 1942, p. 196). The locus of the problem lay within the people, rather than with the external forces that created the problem. While the WRA acknowledged that "the shock of evacuation" had had great impact, it also characterized the Nikkei's unwillingness to leap into resettlement with enthusiasm (and even gratitude) as a problematic attrition of will and resilience, attributed to the "fact that all recent decisions of a similar nature have been made for him by the government" (War Relocation Authority, 1943a, p. 5). The experience of being "wards of the government" had "halted the assimilation process and stunted initiative" (War Relocation Authority, 1943a, p. 3). Resettlement, as the process of Americanization intended by the WRA, promised to revive that lost sense of independence and enterprise. The Nikkei's troublesome willingness and ability to continually critique, resist, and protest administrative policies and practices, including resettlement, did not, of course, count as evidence of initiative or independence.

Many social workers shared this tendency for moralizing judgment. Social work organizations had from the start feared the possibility of "the chance that evacuation may cause the re-establishment of acute race consciousness together with the multitude of social problems which arise from periods of enforced idleness" (California State Department of Social Welfare, 1942–43, p. 8). The YWCA's main motivation for establishing its Japanese American Evacuation Project (JAEP)—through which it ran its camp programs and aided the WRA's resettlement efforts—had been to ameliorate the negative psychological effects that mass living in the "abnormal communities" (Briesemeister, 1946, p. 21) of incarceration would have on the Nikkei. JAEP fieldworker Marian Brown Reith (1943) reported in 1943 that an "adjustment to a state of dependency" (p. 2) was one of the factors that "militate against" (p. 1) resettlement. Berta Choda (1946) of the Bureau of Public Assistance, one-time Assistant Counselor at the Heart Mountain Welfare Section, described the condition thus:

> Surrounding the center was a fence that closed out freedom, it is true, but also the worry, pain, and struggle for survival experienced by the Japanese in the hostile competitive society "outside." Institutional psychology had developed out of this "security" derived from center living, and was probably the most significant reason for the resistant attitude toward leaving. Here was a mass regression to dependency rationalized as hostility to the government, and expressed in a "sit-down" response toward the efforts of the government representatives— the WRA personnel in the relocation program. (p. 142)

Social worker and Community Analysis Division employee Anne Freed (1944) explained in the social work journal *Survey Midmonthly*: "Instead of seizing the opportunity to leave, they build up a resistance to resettlement. Many have become suspicious. They fear the unknown. They prefer to sit and wait. They fail to recognize resettlement as a practical opportunity to regain their democratic rights" (p. 118).

Robert George (1946) surmised in the same publication that the Nikkei were reluctant to leave because they preferred the camps over the homes they left behind:

> The centers seemed very comfortable places to many of these people. The older men and women, in particular, felt even more at home there than they had in the West Coast communities from which they came. Their experiences at camp brought them closer together. They began to lose the sense of time; present day happenings were lost in the roseate hue of the past. Compact social groupings, comparative comfort and security came as a blessing in disguise. (p. 292)

This view aligned with the WRA (1943e) contention that the Issei, in particular, were reluctant to be dislodged from "the keen enjoyment experienced through participation in group cultural and recreational activities at the center" (p. 5). WRA director Dillon Meyer (cited in Rowe, 1971) explained that some of the "older Japanese" had never been "happier" than in the camps.[5] The approximately 8,000 older men "who had worked up and down the coast as migrant labor" (p. 40) were weary. Similarly, "old ladies, who had worked on farms throughout all these years, had the first leisure they had in their life" (p. 40). Neither group wanted to go home. The WRA had eventually "to pick them up by the seat of the pants and the scruff of the neck and put them on the trains to get them relocated" (p. 40).

From the point of view of the incarcerated, the resettlement decision posed complex questions without clear answers. All choices were fraught: Should they go? Where was it safe to go? What locale might have reasonable housing and employment? Was it better to wait until the war ended? Did it make sense to hold out for the West Coast to reopen? Should the family stay together or separate to find better opportunities? According to Nisei writers of the period, many, especially the immigrant Issei, were indeed "extremely reluctant to resettle and begin life anew" (Yatsushiro, Ishino, & Matsumoto, 1944, p. 193). But their explanation for the reluctance was qualitatively different:

---

[5] Dillon Meyer took part in this conversation, which was an oral history interview with James H. Rowe Jr., Assistant to the US Attorney General and a critic of the internment.

One must remember that most of the Issei had come to the United States in their early twenties and had found work on the railroads and farms. By toiling long hours and living frugally they had managed to establish businesses and farms of their own. Now at their advanced age, which averaged around sixty years, evacuation had swept away the accomplishments of the past thirty and forty years. (p. 193)

If the camps represented security, it was not because they were such congenial places of leisure and entertainment but because all other sources of security had been taken away. The camps were "for those who had remained in them, the only security in a world that had been made completely insecure as a result of the evacuation" (United States Civil Service Commission, 1943, p. 200). One of the true ironies of this situation was the fact that the "evacuation" had originally been justified as a measure to "safeguard" (War Relocation Authority, 1943d, p. 7) the Nikkei from the inevitability of violence and discrimination that the war would spur in their neighbors. As the Nikkei resistance to the resettlement project became ever more evident, however, the WRA ruled that "the relocation Center as a protective buffer against the outside world was over-emphasized in the minds of evacuees" (War Relocation Authority, 1943d, p. 7).

The Nikkei's supposed slide from independence into dependence was a contradictory, if established, discourse which problematized the population for both their reluctance to accept assistance *and* their willingness to do so. The Nikkei's reluctance for government aid in the camps, attributed "primarily on certain attitudes held by them, rather than on lack of need of such assistance" (War Relocation Authority, 1945a, p. 1), was a quality that was, to some degree, lauded by the social workers given their horror of fostering dependency. But the exhibition of "pretty strong scruples against taking public aid" (Pratt, 1945, p. 9) on the part of the camp inmates was also a distinct practical problem for social workers who found that the Nikkei did not behave as aid recipients should: they avoided direct contact with the Welfare Section and its personnel, preferred the use of go-betweens, were reluctant to disclose financial information, resented questions about private matters. The Nikkei had to be taught to accept the aid social work was dispensing; "many who were in need because of age and infirmity had to be more or less convinced that there was nothing degrading or disgraceful about taking such assistance if one were in need" (Pratt, 1945, p. 9).

Their willingness to accept public assistance and to gain facility in using it was, moreover, not only necessary for their subsistence in the camps, but also to the resettlement endeavor. The success of the resettlement project depended, according to a 1945 Community Analysis report, "heavily on the readiness of evacuees to learn the use of the various agencies which can help them in their adjustment to normal living (War Relocation Authority, 1945a, p. 1). The more facile the Nikkei were in accessing government assistance, the more willing they were to accept it, the easier they would be to convince to leave the camps. The availability of public aid in resettlement was touted by the WRA as an incentive to the reluctant and uncertain. Marie Dresden Lane assured camp social workers that when news of the "actual receipt of rent, cash for food, a bed, stove, etc. gets back to the Center" from those resettled on the outside, the hold-outs in the camps would be more likely to opt for resettlement. To this end, the Nikkei's transformation from unwilling clients to compliant aid recipients accomplished over years of poverty in the camps and continued "acquaintance with the Welfare Section" (Kell, 1945, p. 6), was to be considered an shift in orientation that would prove to be of "value to them" (Kell, 1945, p. 6) in resettlement.

This official thrust toward public assistance, as well as the professional ethos that held that need itself was not pathological, did not entirely mitigate the deeply seated belief of many social workers and other WRA personnel that, no matter the reason for the need, willing acceptance of aid was a moral failure. The line between having the initiative to seek and obtain needed aid, willing and able to properly function as a social work client, and becoming the dreaded dependent lacking the will and enterprise to live an independent life was razor thin. Too much reluctance to receive aid made the social worker's task difficult; not enough reluctance was an indication of moral degeneration. While the availability of aid had been touted as an incentive to resettle, their use of it quickly became problematized. The line had clearly been crossed by the Nikkei; there was "too much leaning on the various agencies" (quoted in Sasaki, 1946, p. 2) by the resettled Nikkei, according to Beryl Cox of the Bureau of Public Assistance. While their numbers on the welfare rolls were decreasing as time passed, still too many "preferred to remain on relief until forced to get a job" (p. 2). In some families with multiple children, there was "little tendency to go out to shift for themselves" (p. 2) since the amount of aid was greater than what the parents could earn. The population as a whole had lost "their pre-war pride of having only a few on the relief rolls" (p. 2).

The Nikkei's supposed slide from upstanding though exasperating independence to a state of dependency was all the more problematic because, when they sought and accepted aid, they did not do so as acquiescent clients who displayed humility and gratitude. Instead, as a December 1943 document called "Requests Made by Camp Residents of Poston, Arizona" (Residents of Colorado River Relocation Center, 1943, p. 2) demonstrated, assistance was understood by Nikkei clients as a form of compensation for losses incurred. The Poston document outlined the position that "the United States government has put them in a position of dependency. Therefore, whatever WRA may offer is a proper return for the action taken by the government" (War Relocation Authority, 1945a, p. 2). This, of course, was a perspective that WRA leadership vehemently opposed. To understand public assistance as compensation or reparation was tantamount to admitting that the removal and incarceration was a wrong that needed to be righted. A report entitled "Evacuee Attitudes Towards Public Assistance" (War Relocation Authority, 1945a) prepared by the combined forces of Poston's Welfare and Community Analysis Sections, identified this stance as a fundamental problem. The report construed that while the incarcerated Nikkei had "learned in the course of two years to use the available machinery" (p. 2) of aid, they had not concurrently developed a proper understanding of the nature of their role as aid recipients. The "prevailing attitude" (p. 2) among the Nikkei that public assistance was something to which they had "a just right" (p. 2) was an erroneous "evacuee view of evacuation" (p. 2), a perspective that served the Nikkei "as a satisfactory rationalization" (p. 2) for their growing dependency.

The Family Counseling Program

To combat the newly wrought culture of dependency at the heart of Nikkei resistance to resettlement, the WRA created a new program in November of 1943, variously called Family Counseling Program, Special Counseling, Family Counseling, and even "Family Discussion" (Pratt, 1945, p. 5) at one camp. The Welfare Section at each camp was called to establish a separate unit "which would assist families and individuals in developing a plan, including plans to relocate, for the future of the total family" (War Relocation Authority, 1943f, p. 3); social workers from the Welfare Section would meet with each family "thus giving them opportunities to discuss individual attitudes, fears, and needs" (Freed, 1944, p. 118), but doing so "with a view both to breaking down the rationalizations of reluctant families and to gathering information which would enable WRA to plan realistically its future program" (War Relocation Authority, 1946c, p. 38). The Family Counseling Program was, in other words, a "massive persuasion program" (Spicer, Hansen, Luomala, & Opler, 1969, p. 190) designed "to convince Japanese-Americans that it would be to their advantage to leave the centers and relocate in the Midwest and East before the end of the war" (Spicer et al., 1969, p. 190).

According to Community Analyst Edward Spicer (1952), "the family was not urged to resettle" (p. 255) by the social workers during these interviews.[6] But as he also observed, follow-up meetings were conducted "[w]henever definite or tentative plans to resettle came to light" (p. 255) at the initial interview, and even when the families resisted any planning, the program required social

---

[6] An anthropologist specializing in the Yaqui people of the U.S. Southwest and Mexico, Spicer began as a community analyst at Poston (1942–1943) and became the second head of the Community Analysis Section at the WRA's Washington headquarters (Niiya, May 6, 2015).

workers to persist in maintaining "successive contacts with each family, spaced a month or more apart" (p. 255). Pressure was applied, if not directly through explicit statements made at such meetings, then through the sheer relentlessness of the ongoing "contacts"; the end goal of the meetings and the program that organized them was clear to all. The Washington Headquarters described the role of the Welfare Sections in frank terms: since the "knowledge that the welfare counselor often turned up key problems which were retarding relocation" (War Relocation Authority, 1944c, p. 13), the meetings served resettlement goals by "revealing and studying these problems" (War Relocation Authority, 1944c, p. 13). According to Lucy Adams, social worker and Manzanar's head of Community Services, several attendees at the all-centers staff conference in 1944 attested that the Family Counseling Program had "been the most effective means of direct contact and influence upon the individuals in the center" (War Relocation Authority, 1944a, p. 4).

Like most programs and projects instituted by the WRA, the mandate to create Family Counseling Programs was taken up differently across the ten camps. For many of the camp Welfare Sections, already struggling with insufficient staff and resources to manage its existing programs, the headquarters' call to establish a separate unit for resettlement counseling was infeasible to accomplish. Poston, instead, "began the special counseling in a small way" (Butler, 1945b, p. 13) by interviewing those families already involved with the department. Minidoka, similarly, began by adding relocation planning to its existing roster of work; "all cases interviewed for other purposes were approached with the possibilities of relocation. Their plans, whether definite or tentative, were entered in the case records and followed up in subsequent interviews" (Kimmerling et al., 1945, p. 26). This slow approach, shaped by necessity, was congruent with the Welfare Sections' desire to avoid the appearance of compulsion. The Minidoka Welfare Section, like others, lacked the personnel to staff a separate program, but its approach also stemmed from the belief that it was better not to create "an intensive counseling program, which might give the impression that we were again trying to force evacuees into relocation" (Kimmerling et al., 1945, p. 11). A slower paced, "longer range program" was predicted to be more effective in the long run.

> This would dispose of any indication that there was a great haste, or that a big "push" was on and would give time for counselors to become acquainted with, and efficient in the type of approach which must be used in order to gain the confidence of the people involved. (p. 11)

To this end, the title "Family Discussion Program" was deliberately chosen at Topaz, "since it was determined that the word 'discussion' when translated into Japanese described more nearly the friendly non-coercive kind of interviews intended by this program" (Pratt, 1945, p. 5). The intent, according to Head Counselor Pratt, was to engage in careful discussion with reluctant families, resulting in "interviewer and interviewee working out a solution together" (p. 5). Jerome's Head Counselor J. Lloyd Webb's (1943) view was that it would be counterproductive to compel people who "were not psychologically prepared to discuss their reactions to relocation" (p. 3) to have to do so. He was, moreover, unconvinced "that adequate counseling and recording for all families and persons in the center can be accomplished within a period of three or four months" (p. 1) allocated by the WRA for the task.

From the perspective of the Relocation Division, created for the explicit purpose of pushing the Nikkei out as fast as it could manage, the Welfare Sections' insistence on caution was an impediment. Victor Mclaughlin (1945), the head of the Minidoka Relocation Section, averred that the Welfare Section "never quite seemed to fall in line with the service organization set up in relocation" (p. 4). In his view, the Welfare Section's assertions for "professionalism" was a continuing problem for an endeavor that had no time for such niceties; staff involved in relocation had been "instructed to retain a sympathetic attitude toward the residents, but not to 'drool' over them" (p. 4). Social workers were "forgetting entirely that there was a task to be accomplished" and that "these people" must be handled "on a basis which they could understand" (Mclaughlin, 1945, p. 4). That this methodological conflict was not specific to Minidoka is attested by the vituperations of William Huso, the Gila Relocation Head and perhaps the severest critic of Welfare Sections' running of the Family Counseling Program. According to William Tuttle, head of Gila's Welfare Section, it was necessary to use time and resources on "publicizing the program in order that it be accepted by the people in the community" (Tuttle, 1945, p. 3) because a "good deal of resentment had to be overcome inasmuch as the residents were bound to believe that this was just another way of trying to force relocation" (Tuttle, 1945, p. 3). Huso disagreed.

> The fundamental premise upon which Washington planning of the counseling program was constructed was that if a person had managed to acquire a master's degree from an acceptable school of social work, that person, ipso facto, was capable, solely through the use of tried and tested counseling techniques, of molding another human being's will in such a way that the latter would voluntarily embark upon a course of action which would have been contrary to his personal disposition and in conflict with all the socio-economic forces as he felt them working on him before the grace of the counselor was shed upon them. On the other hand, as a corollary, any person who had not attended a school offering post-graduate degrees in social work, regardless of his education, experience and personal attributes, would be totally incapable of accomplishing results comparable to those of the specialized social worker. (Huso, 1945, p. 79)

Washington headquarters apparently agreed. According to Huso, the Family Counseling Program's only utility had been "to open the eyes of some of the key Washington officials" (Huso, 1945, p. 79) to their error in putting social workers in charge of the endeavor. Indeed, the program's lack of speedy returns on investment resulted in a policy shift that removed Welfare as the division holding central responsibility for relocation counseling and empowered instead the Relocation Division. The dates reported by the various camp Welfare Sections on this shift differ: at Topaz, the "Family Relocation Unit," which had initially been set up within the Welfare Section, was transferred to the "newly created Relocation Office, formerly the Employment Office" (Pratt, 1945, p. 4) at the end of June 1943. At Minidoka, the cautious approach adopted by the Welfare Section was abandoned in April when Washington "announced a deadline date on which all families on the Center were to be interviewed for the purpose of determining 'future outlook'" (Kimmerling et al., 1945, p. 26), and the task of relocation counseling became divided between Welfare and Relocation, with the former responsible only for cases already known to them.

Welfare Section social workers were clearly unhappy about the numbers-driven methods that increasingly directed resettlement efforts. The Minidoka Welfare Section disapproved of the mass registration process adopted by the camp's Relocation Section.

> Although instructions stated specifically that the counseling was to be done on a case-by-case basis that gave no appearance of "another survey," the Relocation Division felt that they could not meet the deadline by any other means. They planned to open the mess halls daily, and send notices to the residents in the respective blocks to report for interviews. The Welfare Section suggested less obvious and more reassuring methods, such as beginning with families whose plans were incomplete, those who had relocated members, etc. and working gradually through the whole group. Welfare also pointed out that the information desired could not be elicited by mere questioning. But the Relocation Division was adamant in its plan to conduct a Survey, and since they intended to call the Welfare Cases (about 400) along with all the other people living in the blocks, Welfare had no alternative to cooperating in the Survey. Accordingly, several staff members, appointive and evacuee, from the Welfare Section went to the mess halls daily, for the next six weeks, and interviewed the Welfare cases (about 400) and as many others as possible. The Relocation Division estimated that about eighty percent of the residents called for interviewing responded (but they also recognized the fact that the information obtained was of very doubtful value). Many of the residents who had expressed intentions to relocate at an early date refused to consider specific plans when approached later, and many who admitted no plans when interviewed left the Center soon afterward.

The Survey fostered feelings of suspicion and resentment among evacuees, who regarded it as an evidence of coercion on the part of the Authority. They felt that they were being forced out of the Center before they were ready to go. (Kimmerling et al., 1945, p. 26)

Jerome's J. Lloyd Webb (1943) argued that the Family Counseling Program should be run on the "basis of voluntary application by family heads and adult individuals in so far as possible" (p. 3). Topaz Head Counselor Claud Pratt (1945) opined that Family Counseling interviews were only useful when they "were conducted by experienced counselors, and under proper conditions" (p. 6) and, it was "better not to attempt such a program if well-qualified persons were not available" (p. 6). But while the social workers registered their disapproval of Relocation's heavy-handed methods, they did so only on the basis that the methods lacked viability. The social workers argued that a hasty, compulsory program would backfire and be likely to kindle rather than mitigate resistance against resettlement; they did not fundamentally disagree with the plan that the Nikkei inmates should to be persuaded to leave the camps. The bureaucratic language of the reports is often difficult to penetrate. Webb's (1943) statement that the Family Counseling Program was instituted for the purpose of "obtaining an understanding of the objectives on the part of the residents" (p. 3) does, however, read as an indication that the counseling sessions were designed to convince the Nikkei of the need for and the benefits of leaving the camps for resettlement. Similarly, Pratt's (1945) assessment that the counseling sessions "helped many to think about their problem in more realistic terms" (p. 6) can be deciphered as an admission that the counseling was done to aid the Nikkei in coming to terms with the immovable fact that they needed to leave the camps. However more carefully, slowly, and professionally these social workers approached the counseling sessions, there is no doubt that the "welfare counselors were assigned to interview families with a view to breaking down the rationalizations of reluctant families" (Meyer, 1944, p. 281) and that those workers carried out those interviews to do so.

The control shifted further toward Relocation in the following months, and the slower paced casework-based counseling program that most Welfare Sections had been running were replaced by a much more hard-nosed, and indeed less "professional," interviewing program run by the camps' relocation divisions. The transition methods differed across the camps.

At Colorado River [Poston] and Central Utah [Topaz] the Welfare Section and Relocation Division were merged into a new Relocation Division, with a District plan of operation. At Gila, Rohwer, and Minidoka a closer cooperation and clearance between the two units was brought about and procedures set up for a District plan in which a counselor and a relocation interviewer would work in teams in specifically assigned districts. Under this plan, the counselor handles all welfare cases and the interviewer, all cases not involving any welfare problems. (War Relocation Authority, 1945d, pp. 3–4)

Consistent across the different formulations, however, was the result that, by the Winter of 1944, a new program of Relocation Counseling—a titular as well as a methodological shift replacing the opaquely named "Family Counseling" program—appears to have been formally instituted under the aegis of the Relocation Section. Under its structure, the Welfare Sections' purview was limited to "dependency cases," those individuals and families identified as "in need of public assistance and/or case work services when they resettled in normal communities" (Kell, 1945, p. 9). The Welfare Sections reviewed existing case and health records, and, when they found "typical factors of dependency, such as old age, dependent children, and physical handicaps" (War Relocation Authority, 1944c, p. 13), interviewed those individuals and families, as well as their neighbors "in order to gather material for an index of those who would probably need public assistance for relocation" (p. 13). The files on these dependency cases allowed the camps to estimate the numbers who would need welfare aid and were eventually used to inform localities about resettling individuals and families requiring services. From the time of this shift of control from Welfare to Relocation, an intensive program of resettlement planning became "the chief function" (Kell, 1945, p. 9) of the Welfare Sections. Social workers in the Welfare Sections were exhorted to think and function as workers in "referral agencies rather than 'case work' agencies" (Lane, 1945, p. 1). In the months following, the Welfare Sections themselves were "discontinued" and folded into the camp relocation divisions. Heart Mountain reported that Relocation, Health, and Welfare Sections at that camp "joined forces" (Choda, 1946, p. 141) in January of 1945. Poston reported that its Welfare Section's "staff, records, and equipment became a part of the Relocation Division" (Butler, 1945b, p. 15) in May of 1945.

In the initial stages of the resettlement process, the YWCA had unquestioningly supported the resettlement program and had worked to both promote it within the camps and in the communities of resettlement outside. Its endorsement of the resettlement project had, however, distinctly waned by the Spring of 1945. The Race Relations Subcommittee (1945b) of the YWCA National Board concluded that the WRA "should no longer urge people out until the government or some outside people guarantee some sort of housing. Many of them are better off there [in the camps], than moving out and moving to slum areas" (p. 1). The YWCA argued that the "bottleneck between the Washington office of WRA and local offices" (YWCA National Board—Race Relations Subcommitee of the National Public Affairs Committee, 1945a, p. 1) placed an unmanageable burden on local social service organizations. The WRA should create instead a temporary agency to "coordinate the related work of social security, housing, employment" (p. 1), work that the WRA's resettlement offices were responsible for doing but were doing inadequately: "The WRA program is good on paper. Reports sound wonderful. But the program has broken down; the people are not relocating; they're being dislocated" (p. 1). The Board voted in October of 1945 to request that the WRA "revise its schedule for closing the centers taking into consideration the aged and unemployable and others for whom it would be very difficult to resettle" (YWCA Race Relations Sub-Committee of the Public Affairs Committee, 1945, p. 2). The requests probably would have made no difference even if they had been made earlier. That they were 11th-hour appeals ensured that they did not.

The camps were set to close. Whatever their professional concerns and personal distaste might have been, social workers worked within given parameters, without radical protest or significant contestation, as they did throughout this history. One CSDSW field supervisor had observed during the removal phase that social work's task was "to do a difficult job in as decent a manner as possible" (Sundquist, 1942, p. 1); social workers did their best to do so also in the resettlement phase. Jobu Yasumura (1945) of the American Baptist Home Mission Society, generally an observer highly critical of the WRA's resettlement measures, noted that the return of "welfare cases" to Washington state, where the Welfare Department was "unusually cooperative," went smoothly in part "due to the fact that the one section of the Minidoka Project that almost 'defied' the administration in their efforts to help the people was the Welfare Section" (p. 8) headed by Constance Kimmerling. The social workers did not, however, desist from the work or make any discernible protests about the nature of the work. What actual impact the Family Counseling and other social worker endeavors had on the resettlement project is impossible to gauge. Topaz Head Counselor Claud Pratt (1945) held even at the time that "there is no way of knowing to what extent a discussion with a family or a person caused them to relocate earlier than they might otherwise have done" (p. 5). Whether or not the counseling programs were successful in convincing the reluctant population to change their minds, and whatever benefit the families might have gained through the counseling sessions, Topaz Relocation Officer Leah K. Dickinson's (1945) statement that the Family Counseling interviews served as "an entering wedge into the confidence of center residents" (p. 2) is a chilling judgment of the role of social workers in the resettlement push. No matter how decently they attempted to carry out their assigned tasks, the very purpose of those tasks was, at best, to perpetrate intrusive surveillance and, at worst, coerce families into compliance.

Evictions of the Recalcitrant

The impressions, inklings, and confidences social workers garnered through the counseling interviews and passed on to the administration was "information which would help the War Relocation Authority to plan its future course of action more realistically" (Meyer, 1944, p. 281). It is likely that such social work data informed the administration of the needs of the Nikkei, resulting, for example, in the increased relocation grants and greater aid in transporting household goods which did emerge. It is equally likely, also, that social work data helped shape the administration's conclusion that drastic measures "emphasizing the finality of center closure" (War Relocation Authority, 1946e, p. 3) were needed to empty the camps. The WRA mandated that "services or operations that interfere with the relocation of the residents, or that postpone such relocation, shall be curtailed or eliminated as soon as possible," whereas those "that advances relocation may be continued as long as they are necessary" (War Relocation Authority, 1946e, p. 3). On the ground, actualization of that mandate was often fueled by a "Get 'em out at any cost" (War Relocation Authority, 1943b, p. 7) philosophy which insisted on a corrective "policy of making center life as tough as possible" (War Relocation Authority, 1943b, p. 6). A Community Analysis report on Jerome noted:

> Caucasian staff become profane when they talk about how much the people here are babied. They say you will never get people to leave until you cut out a lot of the pampering here. (War Relocation Authority, 1943c, p. 3)

In his damning first-hand account of the closing of Minidoka, Jobu Yasumura (1945) detailed what "can only be described as Gestapo methods" (p. 1) used by the WRA to end such pampering, which apparently included the availability of basic facilities.

> Part of the pressure was the decision to shut off and lock up sanitary facilities (one building to each block housing, laundry, bath and toilet facilities) in what was termed "orderly" fashion. It was orderly, certainly, in terms of pressure— the first block to suffer closing of facilities were those that had the greatest numbers of residents and the more articulate and, therefore, to the administration, the "agitators." (p. 1)

The move to make the camp as unpleasant a place to be as possible also included the closure of most of the remaining mess facilities days before the camp itself went out of business. The WRA "did not operate to keep the residents well fed"

(p. 5), according to Yasumura, who witnessed "quite a number of people" (p. 5) turned away from one of the remaining mess halls, which had run out of food.

> This happened on a Sunday and of those turned away, ten hungry residents walked to the administration area to protest and to seek food, but could find no responsible person that could help them. Fortunately, two or three sympathetic A.P.'s [Appointed Personnel] heard their plight and scurried around and raided personal cupboards and supplied bread and jams and canned meats to tide them over. (p. 5)

While a number of Caucasian workers who "possess and radiate warmth and were trying to under extreme pressure to be human" (p. 1), their efforts did not wield much impact in the context of the all-out institutional pressure to clear out the camps.

> The Welfare Section was particularly embarrassed by the fact that it could not apply good social techniques nor be lenient in special hardship cases because of limitations imposed by a "streamlined, economy-minded" regime. (p. 2)

The final blow for many families was the closure of all camp schools (except those in Tule Lake where Nikkei awaiting deportation to Japan were held) at end of the 1945 Spring term. In so far as advancing the resettlement push, it was "without doubt one of the most significant and successful moves made by WRA in a long time" (Nishi, n.d., p. 8). Lou E. Butler (1945a) the Welfare Head of Poston, which closed its schools in June, noted that as "education is highly rewarded by the group, this fact gave them additional reason to try to get settled elsewhere before September" (p. 1); August and September saw the largest numbers of departures since the inception of the resettlement push (Butler, 1945b).

What remained in the "streamlined" camps in the final months before the disbanding of the WRA was a population least willing and least able to leave; the poorest and the most vulnerable: the elderly non-English speakers, single mothers, and others with questionable likelihood of finding sufficient employment, housing, and support on the outside (War Relocation Authority, 1943a, 1943e). According to social worker Berta Choda (1946), however, they were the most aggrieved, "were evacuees whose dominant feeling was bitterness toward the government for removing them from their homes and depriving them of their hard- and long-earned goods" (p. 141). Headquarters Administrative Order 289 set "drastic procedures for the movement of recalcitrant residents" (Yasumura, 1945, p. 2) who were still refusing to make departure plans despite all the different pressures, including repeated interviews with the Relocation and Welfare Sections. Notwithstanding Dillion Meyer's insistence that "[a]ll terminal departures have been orderly and without incident" (Meyer, 1945, p. 1), evictions and forced removal of these "die hards" (Lane, 1946, p. 127), "bitter-enders" (Huso, 1945, p. 142), and "recalcitrants" (Huso, 1945, p. 142) would mark the end of the WRA tenure in the camps. Under Administrative Order 289, remaining individuals and families were given eviction notices, known as "three-day notices of departure." Minidoka still had 2,258 inmates on September 15, 1945, when such "scheduled departures" (Meyer, 1945, p. 1) began.

The "scheduled departures" for removal at the start of the "evacuation" process had often been changed at the last moment, leaving many individuals and families less than a day to settle their affairs and report for their indefinite incarceration. Yasumura (1945) reported that many at Minidoka suffered a similar fate at this other end of the process.[7] A particularly egregious example of the "notorious three-day notice case" was that of a 74-year-old man whose departure had been originally set for September 22, 1945. Because his old-age pension was not due to arrive at the camp until after that date, however, his departure was rescheduled with approval from the Relocation Section for October 16.

> On October 10, however, at the request of the Welfare Section a 3-day notice was served on him to be out of the Center by the 12th. It was later explained by the project attorney that the date set was less than 3 days from the time of the notice because his old-age pension acceptance had come through, and anyway he was on the list leave a month previous. (It should be said that the project attorney is essentially a fair person and was acting on orders.) On the 12th an Internal Security man and the project attorney went to the barrack of the old

---

[7] Just as the entrainment process at the front end of the internment had often been, the departure from the back end of the internment was also chaotic and unaided. Yasumura observed:

> The day following my arrival I went to Shoshone from whence the residents were leaving on the trains. On that day there were some 80 persons leaving, mostly for Seattle and Portland and a few were headed East. There were no A.P. at the station and the people were left to shift for themselves, as far as the WRA was concerned. I had a job immediately, interpreting for a number of the old men and women lined up to get their tickets and later to get their baggage checked. That day and on subsequent days when I went to the station, particularly when there were large numbers leaving, I found that there were always matters arising the required the services of someone that could interpret for the people. There were also situations and problems cropping up that required that a WRA official be present. It was only after talking to the Welfare Section supervisor and pointing out to her the need for some WRA official capable of answering questions, and able to decide matters that she finally decided to send someone to the station every day. She was actually overruling the decision of the acting project director not to send anyone. He had claimed that WRA officials could do very little and would only stand around to be useless. (Yasumura, 1945, p. 6)

man and picked him up, dressed as he was in dirty jeans and other old clothes.
Minus baggage or any of his personal belongings he was taken to Shoshone and
put out onto the station platform. (Yasumura, 1945, p. 7)

The elderly man thus evicted refused to comply with the order to leave, declining
to accept the train ticket and the $37 in cash thrust upon him by the worker who
brought him to the station. The town sheriff was eventually called in to put him
on the train bound for Seattle.

The final narrative reporting of W. E. Rawlings (1946), Minidoka Project
Director during the last six months of the camp's operations, begins with the
defense of "the so called 'three day notice" (p. 2). They could not be called
"forced relocation at Minidoka" (p. 2), in his view, since most people complied and the notices were useful to many; some who "were aged, infirm or
so bewildered by events that they welcomed assistance in making a decision"
(p. 2). "Assistance" provided included "packing, care of children, transportation, securing ration books, grants and leave documents and boarding buses
and trains" (p. 2). While the declining availability of workers was cited for the
reduction of essential services and the closure of facilities such as the mess
hall, "personnel seemed always available when recalcitrant families were to
be picked up and evicted" (Yasumura, 1945, p. 1). In Rawlings's view, such
"assistance" to speed people of out of the camps "may or may not be considered forced relocation depending on the hue of the glasses through which it
is viewed" (p. 2). The hue of Rawlings's glasses showed only a few cases which
could be considered forced relocation.

Three able bodied batchelors [sic] were selected as the first recipients for departure notices. One agreed to go, one hid out and one refused and resisted.
The one hiding out was located by the Council Chairman and left voluntarily
the following day. The one resisting was evicted. The pattern had been cut and
no more evictions were necessary until the closing date, October 23, when one
family consisting of parents and three children refused to leave. They were
evicted. (p. 2)

Minidoka closed on October 28, 1945, and its 1,116 acres of farm land
cleared and cultivated by the Nikkei were leased out to "private farm operations" (Meyer, 1945, p. 1). Jerome, the first camp to do so, had ceased operations more than a year before, on June 30, 1944, a handful of months
after the start of the Family Counseling Program. Eight others shut down
between October and November of 1945. Tule Lake, the last, closed its doors
on March 20, 1946.

Resettlement Assistance

Leave Assistance Grants

Financial aid programs for those leaving the camps for resettlement was as confusing, complicated, and unsettled as any program the WRA had devised and run. The Leave Assistance cash grant instituted in late March of 1943 by the WRA was designed to function as an incentive to promote resettlement. It initially paid out $50 for those without dependents, $75 for those with one dependent, and a maximum of $100 for those with two or more dependents. Since there were many large families with multiple children for whom the $100 cap per family did not work, the grant amounts were increased later that year to $25 per individual. The money to be used "to meet initial expenses at the point of relocation" (Social Security Board, 1945, p. 24) was to cover the first month's budget and the cost of transportation to the destination, supplemented by an additional grant of $3 per person per diem while in route to their destination. In 1944, as a further incentive, the WRA lifted the limitation it had initially set on the amount of personal property that it would pay to ship to the resettlement destination and instituted the provision of Pullman accommodations for the ill and infirm (Sakoda, 1943). Even in their increased form, however, these small grants were in no way sufficient to allow individuals and families to reestablish themselves out in the world. Minidoka Welfare (Kimmerling et al., 1945) underlined the fact that it was "difficult to meet the needs of certain relocating families" (p. 47) with the limited funding the Welfare Section had on hand. A CSDSW memorandum reported from the other end of resettlement that "there were not sufficient funds on hand at Topaz" (Underhill, 1945c, p. 1) to provide the grants for those headed to California. Poston and Manzanar also ran out of funds before the camps were empty; Heart Mountain was quickly reduced to only granting relocation funds to families of three or more. The ill-funded Leave Assistance Grant never functioned as an effective incentive.

Like all other programs of the WRA, moreover, the grant program was poorly planned, hastily rolled out, and implemented differently across the camps. Some relocation officers, "feeling that it saves the government money to give a small grant even if this results in slowing down relocation and so perpetuating the cost of maintaining evacuees who do not relocate" (War Relocation Authority, 1943a, p. 2) appear to have begrudged every dollar granted. At Topaz, according to its Head Relocation Officer Leah Dickinson (1945), the "control of these grants and the adjustment of problems arising from this Assistance program" (p. 7) was handled by the Assistant Relocation Program Officer Claud Pratt, the erstwhile Head Counselor of the Welfare Section prior to the merger of the two sections. Pratt was said to have done "an exceptionally fine job in working out an equitable distribution of the available funds" (p. 7) while staying within the allotted budget. Constance Kimmerling (1945) reported that it was difficult for her staff to make decisions about how to allocate aid at Minidoka. They did not know how to calculate a month's budget since it was impossible to know the "particular circumstances into which the families would be plunged when they left the Center and dispersed to various parts of the country" (p. 47). The Relocation Field offices in resettlement areas could have provide guidance had "proper machinery and staff "(p. 47) been obtained, but since they had not, relevant local information was unavailable to the staff making decisions in the camps. Kimmerling noted that it "is always difficult for beginners to make decisions regarding assistance which is less than actual need" (p. 45), and especially so for her staff, used to a more liberal aid environment.

Two of the assistant supervisors had recently been in psychiatric and child welfare work, handling long-time care cases in programs where adequate relief is most important. The other supervisor had been on the State staff of a public agency which was notably liberal in granting public assistance according to need. (p. 45)

The Leave Assistance Grants were not so liberal.

"Assistance to Enemy Aliens"

The WRA's original plan was that those needing assistance for longer than the single month the Leave Assistance Grant was to cover would be aided through local agencies in the community of resettlement. It soon realized, however, that there was an inevitable time gap between the limits of its assistance and the actualization of local aid, the result of inevitable bureaucratic hurdles involved in getting the resettled onto local aid rolls. The second plan put in place was to fill that time gap with funds from the Bureau of Public Assistance (BPA) of the Social Security Board (SSB). The BPA program called "Services and Assistance to Enemy Aliens and Others Affected by Restrictive Governmental Action" had been available to the Nikkei at the beginning of the war during the removal phase. On January 13, 1944, the WRA requested the SSB to extend the services in aid of its resettlement program. Six months later, in July of 1944, once negotiations with Congress finally resulted in the appropriation of $50,000 for the purpose, SSB agreed to expand the program to the resettled Nikkei (War Relocation Authority, 1945c). Often referred to as the "Resettlement Assistance Program" (Leahy, 1946) and more usually as "Assistance to Enemy Aliens"—despite the fact that most incarcerated and now resettling Nikkei were U.S. citizens—the program was "primarily designed" (War Relocation Authority, 1945d, p. 1) to provide assistance to those Nikkei resettling in new locales where they had no previous history and thus no claim to legal residence. [8] Once the West Coast exclusion was rescinded in December of 1944, however, the program had to be expanded to cover those who returned to their community of legal residence but were still "pending the determination of their eligibility for one of the permanent welfare programs" (War Relocation Authority, 1945d, p. 1) in their locality. In certain circumstances, the aid was used to supplement local aid. Many Nikkei, for example, were unable to find housing upon their return and had to resort to living in "special housing projects" (Aaron, 1945, p. 1)—such as barracks and dormitories—without facilities for cooking, and they incurred costs in excess of "county general relief allowances for food" (p. 1). In those instances where the County "finds it impossible to increase their standards in order to meet total need" (p. 1), resettlement assistance could be used to supplement the aid. The program also covered death and burial costs, including cremation and transportation of remains to relatives, whether still in camps or in a resettlement locale, and these could be used to pay for temporary foster care placement for unattached children until they could be put into regular mechanisms for foster care services.

The BPA program was also a temporary measure designated only to "provide basic items of the budget" (War Relocation Authority, 1945c, p. 2) such as rent and food, and it did not include the provision of funds for "re-establishing households" (War Relocation Authority, 1945c, p. 2), which so many resettling Nikkei needed. Most had been forced to give away or sell furniture and other household goods for paltry sums in the haste of the removal, and what was left behind was stolen or vandalized during the years of incarceration. In June of 1945, the WRA further modified its own aid program to provide funds for the purchase of "minimum household equipment" (War Relocation Authority, 1945d, p. 2). Given that the grants were to be made to people who had already left the camps, funneling the funds through local welfare agencies would have been a sensible measure. County and local welfare agencies did not, as a rule, provide aid for household goods and had no established procedures for handling such funds. Even if those agencies were willing to administer such funds, making an exception to do so would, in the WRA's view, make it "difficult not to considers

---

[8] A CSDSW internal memo explained that Charles Wollenberg, the head of the CSDSW who took over the role from Martha Chickering, had "requested that the term Enemy Alien be dropped as far as possible, and either the whole correct title of the Program with the latter part which is '. . . Other persons affected by restrictive action of the Government' used since he finds, in interpreting it to the outside world, increasingly difficult to talk about caps on enemy alien program in connection with the Japanese most of whom are citizens. Therefore, the new fiscal procedure forms will carry the total title" (MacLatchie, 1945, p. 1).

grants for the purchase of furniture as restitution" (War Relocation Authority, 1945d, p. 2) rather than aid. The WRA thus decided to distribute such funds through its own welfare offices in the camps, adding it as one more additional line item to its existing aid expenditures. In practice, however, such funds did not always materialize. A series of correspondence made in mid-December 1945 between the CSDSW and the WRA reveal that an urgent request for the purchase of stoves for eighteen families with children was denied; the WRA stated it had "no funds whatsoever for such purchases as this" (California State Department of Social Welfare, 1945a, p. 1). The families had resettled from Gila Camp to Costa, California, to work as sharecroppers and were living in "6 unheated barracks" (Dumble, 1945, p. 1). A request for a grant to buy basic items such as a refrigerator, a crib, tables, and chairs by a man living with his family in a bare one-room shack was similarly denied by Tule Lake's Finance Officer who wrote that there were "no funds available at the center for payment of furniture inasmuch as this office is closing in a few days" (Gorton, 1946, p. 1).

Establishing Residency

As the reluctant were encouraged, persuaded, coerced, and eventually forced to leave the camps to join the movement back west, "major emphasis was placed on working out dependency summaries and attempting to obtain acceptance of financial responsibility for dependent persons from their State of residence" (Pratt, 1945, p. 7). The "dependency summaries" put together by camp Welfare Sections contained a great deal of information compiled in part from materials which had been gathered at the initial family registration at the Wartime Civil Control Administration (WCCA) control stations at the time of removal and had tracked them through their incarceration in the Assembly Center then to the current camp. Case notes of whatever contact the family might have had with the Welfare Section during these years, information from relocation interviews conducted as part of the Family Counseling program, and records of the family's contact with other sections of the camps provided the rest. The "Basic Family Face Sheet" detailed the family's composition and the facts of the family's incarceration history; the "Statement of Economic Resources," completed by the head of household, had to account for the resources of every member of the given household; and the "Social Facts and Requirement for Resettlement" form contained the department's summary of the family's medical, financial, educational, religious, and employment history and identified the family's "social adjustment needs." The summaries also included information—records of pre-removal residence and references from people in that community who could attest to residency—to be used by the local welfare offices in verifying residence. The administration of both the BPA "Enemy Aliens" assistance and the existing welfare mechanisms were the purview of local—County level, in the case of California—welfare departments; eligibility for both was contingent on the establishment of residency—a legal claim to access services in that locality. The dependency summaries thus compiled were sent to area resettlement offices where an Area Adjustment Advisor, a "social worker with community organization experience" (War Relocation Authority, 1945d, p. 1), was tasked with channeling the information to the appropriate local welfare offices. The local welfare office would then determine whether or not the family or individual was considered to have legal residency in that community and if "that community accepts them as residents and will provide assistance in accordance with their needs" (War Relocation Authority, 1945d, p. 1).

In the post-exclusion period, all Nikkei leaving the camps were theoretically free to go and settle anywhere in the country. According to Section 30.4.66.B of WRA Handbook Release No. 184 sent out to camp administrators in January 1945, "absolute and complete freedom of choice shall be assured each family" (War Relocation Authority, 1945b) in its resettlement procedures. In actuality, the "dependent" families were not afforded such freedom of choice. The WRA's Semi-Annual Report for July 1 to December 31, 1945, stipulated, in contradistinction to the policy stated in the Handbook:

> Dependent families who refuse to indicate choice of location, or to discuss relocation, will have to make their relocation plans by a certain date or plans will be made for them. No transportation or other financial assistance shall be provided to dependent persons who depart for States in which they have no legal residence, without assumption of responsibility for their support by other members of the family and without approval of public welfare agencies in the community of destination. (War Relocation Authority, 1946e, p. 4)

Rohwer Welfare head Wilma Dusseldorp (1945) explained that if the social workers in her department deemed that the desire of "dependency cases" to resettle in locations where they did not have legal residency was "justified, considering family complications and the person's own desires and needs" (p. 34), the office made efforts to accomplish such a move. Most such efforts did not ultimately work out, however, because of "residence complications" (p. 34); localities were unwilling to extend their welfare benefits to those without the legal weight of established residency. Since most states required one to three years of continuous residence as a requirement for public welfare assistance eligibility (War Relocation Authority, 1946c), this made the return to former communities from which they were removed the only real option for many.

The end of the West Coast Exclusion in December 1945 spurred large numbers of the Nikkei to move back to their former communities in the three coastal states. Those states, from which the majority of the Nikkei had been removed, had agreed to discount the years of incarceration in the camps in calculating residency (War Relocation Authority, 1945c).[9] Washington and Oregon, according to WRA Welfare Head Marie Dresden Lane (1945), were "not interested in County residence; they are interested in knowing whether there is a socially desirable reason for the family returning" (p. 2). Oregon State archives do not contain records on the resettlement procedures, and Lane's claim for that state cannot be verified. A memorandum sent to county welfare departments in March 1945 by Washington State Department of Social Security director Kathryn E. Malstrom (1945) does lend support for Lane's characterization of that state. In it, Malstrom directs the counties for "full use of community resources" in assisting the "resettlement of persons of Japanese ancestry either in their old place of residence or to join their family in a new place" (p. 6). Though Washington counties did verify residency, it seems that county-level residency status mattered less in comparison to California, where "general assistance is provided from county funds only" (Lane, 1945, p. 1) and counties routinely required stringent qualification checks for aid eligibility.

California law stipulated three years residence within the state, with one year of continuous and self-supporting residence within the county (Dusseldorp, 1945). In that state, from which the vast majority of the incarcerated Nikkei had originated, the 58 counties were "individually and solely responsible for the administration of general relief" (War Relocation Authority, 1946f, p. 4) and for the determination of eligibility. Eligibility verification procedures and standards, consequently, differed greatly among the counties (Wollenberg, 1945). The only way a person without legal residence could receive general relief in a nonresident county was if an intercounty agreement between the county of legal residence and the county of desired residence could be effected. According to the WRA, however, some counties never entered into "such agreements" (War Relocation Authority, 1946f, p. 11) as a general rule and were unlikely to do so for the Nikkei, specifically. There were, nevertheless, many families whose resettlement depended precisely on solving the complicated issues of residency in counties hostile to their return. Howard Hollenbeck, on the Relocation Section staff at Poston, recorded one such case presented for joint discussion by the Welfare and Relocation Sections. The father of the family was confined to a tuberculosis

[9] The states in which the Nikkei had been incarcerated did not, for most purposes, consider them residents and refused, for example, to provide long-term care for individuals needing institutionalization in state medical facilities (see Chapter 6 for a discussion of Colorado's deportation of mentally ill patients back to California).

sanitarium; one son was resettled in California. The mother and the other children comprising the rest of the family unit wished to leave Poston to join the son working in California and to have the father moved to a facility nearby. None of them, however, could claim official residency in that county. In so far as the WRA and state welfare agencies were concerned, family reunification, the major factor in this case, was a "socially desirable" (Lane, 1945, p. 3) and valid rationale for families to resettle outside of residence-established counties; counties did not often agree. Because the state's relationship to counties in these matters was advisory "rather than supervisory" (War Relocation Authority, 1946f, p. 4), and the WRA had no standing at all with the counties, neither had the power to force intercounty agreements or to compel acceptance by counties, no matter how socially desirable plans seemed to be (Wollenberg, 1945).[10] The county's willingness to accept responsibility for the tubercular father's care in its public facility was a definite necessity (Hollenbeck, 1945). Housing and employment—the possibility for the family to be self-supporting—for the family members seemed feasible to find in that locale, but was not a certainty. Both were precisely the kinds of factors that triggered county refusal; few counties were willing to add names to their relief rolls in any circumstance, and even fewer were willing to do so when those names were Japanese.

The dependency summaries constructed by camp social workers were an important factor in this matter, according to Marie Dresden Lane. The summaries provided the information used by county officials in determining a family's or an individual's acceptability for entry into the county. In an uncharacteristically heated missive sent to camp Welfare Sections on May 21, 1945, Lane (1945) exhorted social workers to refrain from including certain kinds of information which was "definitely prejudicial to county acceptance" (p. 2) and had "no bearing on eligibility for assistance and residence requirements" (p. 2). That a client had "drank up $750 in liquor and now needs assistance" (p. 3) was an example of one type of prejudicial information which should not be included. She also warned against any and all commentary about the clients' consideration of a "return to Japan" or connection to "Japanese culture" (p. 2). "He wants to return to Japan, but needs assistance until he can" and "has taken four trips to Japan and wishes to return when the war is over" and "he is fearful of returning to _____ County because of prejudice against Japanese in this county,

---

[10] California was not the only state to have such county-level independence. WRA records cite New Jersey as another state in which this kind of decentralization resulted in resettlement problems: "New Jersey State Welfare work is carried on by individual County agencies of varying standards. This has made for unevenness of operation between counties, and the success of the results obtained frequently depended upon the closeness of the War Relocation Authorities relationship to the individual County Board, the welfare standards in individual County, and the amount of pressure that Mr. Dowdell could bring to bear on the County" (War Relocation Authority, 1946b, p. 167).

but he is an accepted resident of _____ County and is totally dependent and has been accepted by the county but he prefers to move where there are Buddhists" (p. 3) were examples Lane had seen in summaries sent to California and Washington State and found problematic. Portraying individuals as "undeserving" dependents whose need for aid was caused by their own bad behaviors was counterproductive to securing aid for any population. Given the active opposition to the return of the Nikkei, any commentary which painted the individuals as Japanese by inclination and behavior was even more "prejudicial." Not only were both types of representations "inaccurate, misleading, [and] show personal prejudice" (p. 3) on the part of the writer, they were antithetical to furthering the WRA's resettlement goals.

A central component of the dependency summary was the list of references to be used for residence verification. The construction of that list was, however, no simple matter: references could only be provided by in-person interview, and, more importantly, only Caucasians were considered valid referees (California State Department of Social Welfare, 1945b). Given the enforced residential and economic segregation in which so many Nikkei had lived, "many had no Caucasian contacts" to offer, and even those who had some limited contact "could not remember names and addresses" (War Relocation Authority, 1946f, p. 4) of those acquaintances. Predictably, older, non–English-speaking Issei had most trouble in identifying "Caucasian references" (War Relocation Authority, 1945d, p. 2) of any kind—even less, those who were willing to extend themselves to be interviewed by the local welfare agency. This was particularly true for those single men who had worked as "itinerant farm laborers" (Dusseldorp, 1945, p. 33) and had no fixed abodes and little meaningful contact with Caucasians. Given these difficulties, and the not inconsiderable labor involved in tracking down references who had been identified incorrectly or insufficiently or had relocated from identified addresses, the Caucasian reference requirement was eventually discarded in most locales. As CSDSW War Services Supervisor Bertha Underhill observed, most counties that had been "unwilling to accept residence affidavits signed by Japanese" (Underhill, 1946a, p. 1) eventually relaxed the stipulation for both in-person interview confirmations and the Caucasian-only bar. The initial system of verification had, however, entailed a mountain of work for all involved and created such long delays that, for many "potential dependency cases" (Dusseldorp, 1945, p. 34), camp closures came before eligibility was ascertained. In the end, families and individuals had to leave the camps and head to localities without knowing whether or not assistance of any kind would be extended to them.

To be clear, not all residency claims were accepted. Martha Dusseldorp (1945) noted that, in some cases, obtaining verification to "the satisfaction of the California county" (p. 34) was an impossibility despite a great deal of effort exerted by her staff and the client concerned. A CSDSW internal memorandum notes the county rejection of the case of a "single Japanese man" who had "worked as a migratory farm labor in several Western states" and for whom "only 2-plus years California residence could be verified" (Taylor, 1946, p. 1). A family who had been incarcerated at Heart Mountain was rejected first by the state of Wyoming, where they had resided for four years prior to moving to California in 1941. Wyoming considered that the family's move to California had been a permanent departure and deemed the family ineligible. Then, Los Angeles County, to which the family had relocated prior to their removal, also deemed them ineligible because they had only one year's residency in the state (Brown, 1945, p. 1).

The underlying factor accounting for much of the delay in residence verification was, of course, that many counties in California were opposed to the return of the Nikkei. As Marie Dresden Lane explained in a retrospective article published in 1946, early in the resettlement process, the WRA, the Social Security Board, and the public welfare departments of California, Oregon, and Washington formulated an agreement on the structures and procedures for the various aid programs.

> The WRA agreed on its side not to assist a family to resettle unless and until the community had received a copy of the family's case summary and had accepted it either as having legal residence (and therefore entitled to assistance under the state programs), or for care under the "aid to enemy aliens and others" program. Each state, on its side, agreed to investigate the claim to legal residence, to accept the family if the legal residence was established, or to accept it without legal residence if the plan for its care seemed a socially desirable one—and in that case to assist it from state funds, from "aid to enemy aliens and others" funds or from private funds. The Social Security Board approved this arrangement. (p. 129)

What they apparently had not fully anticipated was the county-level obstruction they encountered in California. Only five counties (Sutter, Santa Barbara, Monterey, San Luis Obispo, and Los Angeles) were cooperative. Monterey County received fulsome praise.

> Their investigations are made very promptly—responses to requests for residence verifications frequently forwarded the day following receipt of the request. Arrangements were made to assure admittance to the county hospital without difficulty. Whenever verification of residence and authority to return was forwarded for a possible hospital patient, the WRA was requested to inform the CWD [County Welfare Department] of the date of arrival in order that they may notify the hospital. In one case, a letter was written by the county

hospital and given to a WRA representative, meeting the patient, to be used as an introduction upon arrival at the hospital. In several cases, in which the WRA indicated that the individual might be self-supporting upon return, the County, in giving authority to return, asked that the person be advised to call at their office if in need after arrival. (Billings, 1946a, p. 1)

Sutter County was "liberal in accepting various forms of evidence in determining residence" (Roddy, 1946b, p. 3). Housing for single men was secured by the county, and allowances for rent, fuel, and utilities were readily granted (Roddy, 1946a). In Santa Barbara County, similarly, the verification work was done as "expeditiously as possible, delays occurring only when the Japanese, due to language handicap, had not been able to give sufficient information regarding past employment references" (Parmley, 1945, p. 1). Despite staff and housing shortages and some indication of suspicion and hostility from the community, San Luis Obispo County was prompt in its responses and willing in its attitude. The worker assigned to the task, moreover, took the initiative to contact former employers to ask them to take back returning Nikkei workers and met with other area employers to request that they provide new jobs, all in "an effort to assist returning Japanese to reestablish their former lives" (Taylor, 1946, p. 2). Los Angeles County, despite being "one of the slowest to get started in handling dependency summaries" (War Relocation Authority, 1946f, p. 8) because of its massive caseload and staff shortages, had a contingent of workers who appeared "at all times to be sympathetic to the problems of the WRA [and] cooperated as fully as possible" (War Relocation Authority, 1946f, p. 8).

Far more numerous were the counties reluctant to provide assistance despite the clear legal responsibility they had for indigent care (Miller, 1945). Many counties used delaying tactics, putting off acceptance "for long periods by continually asking for more information" (War Relocation Authority, 1946f, p. 10). San Joaquin, Stanislaus, and Merced refused even to start the verification process unless the client was physically present in the county (War Relocation Authority, 1946g, p. 5). Others declared an outright refusal to administer aid to resettling Nikkei (Esgar, 1945), despite the fact that funds came from federal coffers rather than county budgets.[11] Fresno and Merced counties were two example of the latter (MacLatchie, 1945). County Boards of Supervisors, comprised of individuals who were "definitely antagonistic," as in the case of Merced, or the San Joaquin County Board Chairman who "while pretending not to be

---

[11] The Arizona State Department of Social Security and Welfare (ASDSSW) also refused to administer federal resettlement assistance. The ASDSSW maintained that the WRA and state governor had forged an agreement at the start of the incarceration that no nonresident Nikkei would be resettled in the State (War Relocation Authority, 1946f).

so, nevertheless, was prejudiced against any minority race" (War Relocation Authority, 1946g, p. 14), were often responsible for the refusals. Placer County Board of Supervisors, for example, passed a resolution prohibiting the provision of any and all aid to "indigent Japanese returned from relocation centers" (Underhill, 1945b, p. 1), including federal funds from the SSB, though the county had received only two applications, one from an aged Issei man who was "told that no aid could be given him" and a woman with children eligible for "Aid to Needy Children" (Underhill, 1945b, p. 1) residing in a temporary hostel. The Board in Tulare County blocked the dispensing of aid which had already been authorized by the welfare director (Miller, 1945), and it could not "be said that any degree of cooperation was derived from any Board of Supervisors" (War Relocation Authority, 1946g, p. 14) in Stockton County.

In Imperial County, said to be the "most difficult county in the area to cope with" (War Relocation Authority, 1946f, p. 11), the Board of Supervisors "met the entire problem with complete silence" (War Relocation Authority, 1946f, p. 11) and simply refused to respond to the WRA and the CSDSW. "The dependency summaries were ignored as were follow-up letters . . . no replies to cases referred were ever obtained" (War Relocation Authority, 1946f, p. 11). The county welfare department was instructed by the Supervisors to "refer all cases pertaining to Japanese to them" (War Relocation Authority, 1946f, p. 11) and to refrain from making any decisions (Underhill, 1945b). During the removal phase in 1942, approximately 100 tubercular patients had been left behind in Hillcrest Sanatorium in Los Angeles County, exempt from the removal by the fact of their institutionalization. With the WRA scheduled to be dissolved with the closure of the camps, the hospital expenses paid by the WRA for the duration needed to be picked up by other sources. Patients without Los Angeles County residency were scheduled to be transferred out to facilities in the county of their legal residence. All counties but Imperial accepted their patients. "The Imperial County health physician replied that they had no beds available and that they would not be willing to pay for care elsewhere" (War Relocation Authority, 1946f, p. 16).

The bigoted attitudes of the county boards "were not always reflected in the activities of the welfare departments" (War Relocation Authority, 1946g, p. 14). The records indicate, however, that welfare departments and their personnel in several counties did exhibit similarly racist attitudes. Yolo County Welfare Department had "consistently refused to grant any assistance to Japanese-Americans" (Underhill, 1945b, p. 3). It was unwilling even to administer federal resettlement funds allotted to them from the SSB and declined to enter into an intercounty agreement with another county caring for its residents (Underhill, 1945b). Correspondence from the department made clear that the Nikkei "were unwelcome in the county and that it would be advisable for them to go elsewhere" (Underhill, 1946b, p. 2). A "considerable hardship to Japanese in the County" (Underhill, 1945b, p. 2) was noted in San Benito County, where the Welfare Department "did not wish to accept responsibility for administration of assistance of any kind" (Billings, 1946b, p. 1), and letters requesting residence verification went unanswered. The CSDSW's Bertha Underhill recounted a conversation she had with the director of that County Welfare Department.

> [A]lthough she states that it is true the hostel is running out of funds, contends that the Japanese are still eating. She will discuss with her Board of Supervisors this week the possibility of accepting a revolving fund, but she expressed her doubt it would be approved, and it is clear she will make little effort to persuade the Board to accept it. There was also a serious problem in this county in regard to care of a group of Japanese suffering from tuberculosis. The county had consistently refused to accept the cases. It is our understanding that some of these cases were returned to the hospital without authority of the County. (Underhill, 1945b, p. 2)

The San Joaquin County Welfare Department also evinced hostility to the return of the Nikkei, whom they considered the problem of the federal government. Its Welfare Director refused to administer the federal resettlement funds "on the premise that such aid might establish an undesirable precedent" (War Relocation Authority, 1946g, p. 13). Those funds were time-limited, and the returnees would ultimately become the responsibility of the county.[12]

In many cases of county obstructions and outright refusals, the WRA's only option was to turn to private organizations to fill the gaps in services. In the case of San Joaquin County, for example, the Salvation Army and the Tuberculosis Association provided emergency aid to 20 urgent cases (War Relocation Authority, 1946g). Some organizations, such as the YWCA, as discussed previously, had been involved on multiple fronts from the start of the war. The American Friends Service Committee had also been involved throughout the war, leading the push to move students out of the camps and into colleges in the East and the Midwest, and had developed "a definite procedure for helping to find employment" for the Nikkei (American Friends Service Committee, 1942,

---

[12] San Joaquin had a relatively large caseload, with 325 total referrals, comprised of 144 "aged and indigent single men"; 4 were blind individuals; 55 dependent families; 21 hospitalized patients; and 24 cases of "needy children" (War Relocation Authority, 1946g, p. 13). Of these, only about 240 ever applied for and received aid. In comparison, Stanislaus County had a total of 13 referrals, 10 of whom never actually appeared for aid; Merced County had a total of 14 referrals, 8 of whom never asked for aid (War Relocation Authority, 1946g, p. 13). Placer County Welfare Department received only two applications (Underhill, 1945b).

p. 2) in those areas. The International Institute, which had offered some crucial services in the removal phase, became more seriously involved in the resettlement period.

> Besides offering continued casework service, arrangements have been made for a staff person to act as an interpreter to accompany the Issei to the American Red Cross, the Bureau of Public Assistance and hospitals. Furthermore, financial assistance of temporary nature has been made available to individuals and families. (War Relocation Authority, 1946a, p. 15)

In the beginning of the resettlement period, the Travelers Aid Society had volunteered its services to meet trains and greet and aid the individuals and families arriving in unfamiliar locations of resettlement. In Los Angeles, "a rather well-defined program of cooperation resulted" (War Relocation Authority, 1946a, p. 20) between the WRA and the Society, which allowed its offices in railroad stations to be used by WRA relocation staff so they could provide services to returnees at the point of arrival. The Salvation Army "cared for single men in need of clothing or transportation to jobs" (War Relocation Authority, 1946a, p. 15) and aided families ineligible for grants from the WRA with the purchase of furniture. The Church Welfare Bureau of the Church Federation in California operated a casework department which made home visits and intervened with employers and schools on behalf of Nikkei clients.

In the end, all California counties but Imperial, which held out till the end, granted/administered some assistance to the returning Nikkei (War Relocation Authority, 1946f). The reversals in attitude was credited to the CSDSW which, through phone calls, letters, in-person meetings, and, in the case of Tulare County, an appeal to the State Attorney General and the Governor (Underhill, 1945a), was "usually able to convince the county departments of the necessity for granting assistance" (War Relocation Authority, 1946f, p. 10). The nonresponsive, noncooperative, and preemptive blocking tactics deployed by the various counties meant, however, that those in need suffered long periods of uncertainty and deprivation. As Rohwer Welfare Head Wilma Dusseldorp (1945) put it:

> If the county welfare boards had been prepared to give more assurance about the availability of public assistance for those in need, or if they had acted faster on the cases that had been submitted as applications for public assistance, prior to relocation, the results would have been realized by less fear and greater stability on the part of these individuals who doubted their ability to be self supporting after relocation. (p. 34)

Tule Lake, the final camp to close, did so on March 20, 1946. The Los Angeles Area Relocation Office closed on May 15, 1946 (LeHane, 1946). Executive Order 9742, signed by President Harry S. Truman on June 26, 1946, officially terminated the WRA.

References

Aaron, A. H. (1945). Letter to Mr. Charles M. Wollenberg, Director, California State Department of Social Welfare, from Azile Aaron, Public Assistance Representative, Social Security Board, San Francisco, CA, November 26, 1945, pp. 1–2. Social Welfare—War Services—Resettlement Assistance, Assistance Standards, 1942–1946 (F3729:107). Department of Social Welfare Records, War Services Bureau. Sacramento: California State Archives.

American Friends Service Committee. (1942). Bulletin on Minorities in the United States: Japanese and Japanese-Americans; Bulletin 2, November 25, 1942, pp. 1–3. Folder 1–3—Bulletins on Minorities, Box 16—Pamphlets: Major. American Friends Service Committee—SWPO1, Social Welfare History Archives. Minneapolis: University of Minnesota.

Billings, M. (1946a). War Service Review—Monterey County: California State Department of Social Welfare Office Memorandum to War Services Division, January 10, 1946, pp. 1–3. Social Welfare—War Services—Federal Review, 1945–46 (F3729:131). Department of Social Welfare Records, War Services Bureau. Sacramento: California State Archives.

Billings, M. (1946b). War Service Review—San Benito County: California State Department of Social Welfare Office Memorandum to War Services Division, January 9, 1946, pp. 1–2. Social Welfare—War Services—Federal Review, 1945–46 (F3729:131). Department of Social Welfare Records, War Services Bureau. Sacramento: California State Archives.

Briesemeister, E. (1946). America's children—what happened to us?: Summary report of the Japanese Evacuee Project, January 1942–September 1946, pp. 1–54. Folder 3, Box 721. YWCA of the U.S.A. Records, Sophia Smith Collection. Northampton, MA: Smith College.

Brown, L. W. (1945). Letter to Jane Hoey, Director, Social Security Board, from Lucy Williams Brown, Acting Head of Welfare Section, War Relocation Authority, dated September 24, 1945, p. 1. Folder: Social Security Board, Box 40: Washington Office Records—Chronological File; General—Alphabetical—SN-STATE DEPT. Records of the War Relocation Authority, 1941–1989, Record Group 210, General Outgoing Correspondence, compiled 1942–1946. ARC Identifier 1534421/MLR Number PI-77 18. Washington, DC: National Archives and Records Administration.

Butler, L. E. (1945a). Letter No. 9. Round Robin from Colorado River WRA Project, Poston, Arizona, December, 1945, pp. 1–3. Folder: Copies of Circular Letters (1–9) Feb. 28, 1943–Dec. 1945 Box 3. Records of the War Relocation Authority, 1941–1989, Record Group 210, Office Files of Miss Lou Butler, Head Counselor of the Welfare Section of the Community Management Division at the Colorado River Relocation Center, compiled 1942–1945. ARC Identifier 5752763/MLR Number UD 6. Washington, DC: National Archives and Records Administration.

Butler, L. E. (1945b). Story of the Family Welfare Section, May 1942 to May 1945, pp. 1–17. Calisphere, Japanese American Relocation Digital Archives, Box Poston, Arizona. Berkeley: Bancroft Library, University of California.

California State Department of Social Welfare. (1942–43). Evacuation of Japanese in California *Social Welfare—War Services—WCCA—Reports, General, 1942–43 (F3729-146)*. Department of Social Welfare Records, War Services Bureau. Sacramento: California State Archives.

California State Department of Social Welfare. (1945a). Resettlement Assistance—purchase of stoves, December 19, 1945, p. 1. Social Welfare—War Services—Resettlement Assistance, Assistance Standards, 1942–1946 (F3729:107). Department of Social Welfare Records, War Services Bureau. Sacramento: California State Archives.

California State Department of Social Welfare. (1945b). Review of War Services cases in Kings County, December 28, 1945, pp. 1–2. Social Welfare—War Services—Federal Review, 1945–46 (F3729:131). Department of Social Welfare Records, War Services Bureau. Sacramento: California State Archives.

Chickering, M. A. (1943a). Letter to Mrs. Margaret DIlle, Counselor, Manzanar Relocation Center, Manzanar, California, from Martha A. Chickering, Director, State Department of Social Welfare, Sacramento, California, October 22, 1943, pp. 1–2. Folder: 61.520—Child Welfare—Children's Village, Box 224: Manzanar Relocation Center—Central Files—50.026 to 62.014. Records of the War Relocation Authority, 1941–1989, Record Group 210, Subject-Classified General Files of the Relocation Centers—compiled 1942–1946. ARC Identifier 1544889/MLR Number PI-77 48. Washington, DC: National Archives and Records Administration.

Chickering, M. A. (1943b). Letter to Mrs. Margaret D'Ille, Counselor, Manzanar Relocation Center, Manzanar, California, from Martha A. Chickering, Director, State Department of Social Welfare, Sacramento, California, October 27, 1943, p. 1. Folder: 61.520—Child Welfare—Children's Village, Box 224: Manzanar Relocation Center—Central Files—50.026 to 62.014. Records of the War Relocation Authority, 1941–1989, Record Group 210, Subject-Classified General Files of the Relocation Centers—compiled 1942–1946. ARC Identifier 1544889/MLR Number PI-77 48. Washington, DC: National Archives and Records Administration.

Choda, B. (1946). A counseling program in a relocation center. *The Family, 27*(4), 140–145.

Cozzens, R. B. (1974). Assistant National Director of the War Relocation Authority: An oral history conducted in 1974 by Rosemary Levenson. *Japanese American Relocation Reviewed, Volume II: The Internment* (pp. 1–105). Berkeley: Regional Oral History Office, Bancroft Library, University of California.

Curtis, J. H. (1943). Letter to Mr. Leroy H. Bennett, Project Director, Gila River Project, Rivers, Arizona, from James H. Curtis, Relocation Officer, WRA Denver, Colorado, October 15, 1943, p. 1. Folder: 580—Community Service and Welfare, Box 144: Gila River Relocation Center—Central Files—571 to 580. Records of the War Relocation Authority, 1941–1989, Record Group 210, Subject-Classified General Files of the Relocation Centers—compiled 1942–1946. ARC Identifier 1544889/MLR Number PI-77 48. Washington, DC: National Archives and Records Administration.

D'Ille, M. (1943). Memorandum to Mrs. Lucy W. Adams, Chief of Community Services Division, from Margaret D'Ille, Counselor, Community Welfare, Manzanar Relocation Center, Manzanar, California, March 9, 1943, pp. 1–2. Folder: 18.200—Social Welfare

Cases, Box 220: Manzanar Relocation Center—Central Files—50.026 to 62.014. Records of the War Relocation Authority, 1941–1989, Record Group 210, Subject-Classified General Files of the Relocation Centers—compiled 1942–1946. ARC Identifier 1544889/MLR Number PI-77 48. Washington, DC: National Archives and Records Administration.

Dickinson, L. K. (1945). Closing report, Relocation Division. War Relocation Authority, Central Utah Project, Topaz, Utah, dated November 1, 1945, pp. 1–7. Retrieved from http://content.cdlib.org/ark:/13030/ft0f59n5mr/?query=miss%20leah%20k.%20 dickinson&brand=calisphere

Dumble, M. F. (1945). Teletype to Bertha S. Underhill, December 19, 1945, 1:19 P.M, p. 1. Social Welfare—War Services—Resettlement Assistance, Assistance Standards, 1942–1946 (F3729:107). Department of Social Welfare Records, War Services Bureau. Sacramento: California State Archives.

Dusseldorp, W. V. (1945). Historical Statistical—Functional Report of Welfare Section, Wilma Van Dusseldorp—Head Counselor. War Relocation Authority, Rohwer Relocation Center, McGehee, Arkansas (Calisphere, Japanese American Relocation Digital Archives ed.). Berkeley: Bancroft Library, University of California.

Esgar, M. H. (1945). Notes by Mildred H. Esgar, Assistant Secretary, National Social Welfare Assembly, on meeting re: Japanese-Americans, National Social Work Office, November 1, 1945, pp. 1–5. Folder 158—SWD4, NSWA; NSWA—Relocation and Resettlement of Japanese-Americans, 1942–1947, Box 16: Folders 158–169. National Social Welfare Assembly Records—SW0004, Social Welfare History Archives. Minneapolis: University of Minnesota.

Freed, A. O. (1944). Our racial refugees. The Survey, 80(4), 117–119.

George, R. C. L. (1946). Our Japanese Americans now. The Survey, 81(11), 291–294.

Glick, P. M. (1944). Adoption matters at Manzanar: Memorandum to John H. Provinse, Chief, Community Services Division, from Philip M. Glick, Solicitor, WRA, Washington, DC, January 13, 1944, pp. 1–4. Folder: Provinse, John—3—November 1943–May 1944, Box 35: Washington Office Records—Chronological File; General—Alphabetical—PF-John Provinse. Records of the War Relocation Authority, 1941–1989, Record Group 210, General Outgoing Correspondence, compiled 1942–1946. ARC Identifier 1534421/MLR Number PI-77 18. Washington, DC: National Archives and Records Administration.

Gorton, E. K. (1946). Letter to G. M. Ikeda from E. K. Gorton, Finance Officer, Tule Lake Relocation Center, April 26, 1946, p. 1. Social Welfare—War Services—Resettlement Assistance, Assistance Standards, 1942–1946 (F3729:107). Department of Social Welfare Records, War Services Bureau. Sacramento: California State Archives.

Hoey, J. M. (1942). Mass relocation of aliens II. In A. Dunham (Ed.), Proceedings of the National Conference of Social Work: Selected papers, Sixty-Ninth Annual Conference, New Orleans, Louisiana, May 10–16, 1942 (Vol. 69, pp. 194–199). New York: Columbia University Press.

Hollenbeck, H. (1945). Joint Case Review meeting: Relocation Division Unit II, Welfare Section Unit II, February 14, 1945, pp. 1–3. Folder 040.46 Welfare, Box 108: Subject-Classified General Files—Colorado River Central Files—040.22 to 050.11. Records of the War Relocation Authority, 1941–1989, Record Group 210, Subject-Classified General Files of the Relocation Centers—compiled 1942–1946. ARC Identifier 1544889/MLR Number PI-77 48. Washington, DC: National Archives and Records Administration.

Huso, W. (1945). A history of Relocation at the Gila River Relocation Center. War Relocation Authority, Gila River Relocation Center, Rivers, Arizona, dated December 21, 1945 (Calisphere, Japanese American Relocation Digital Archives ed., pp. 1–148). Berkeley: Bancroft Library, University of California.

Irwin, C. (2008). *Twice orphaned: Voices from the Children's Village of Manzanar*. Fullerton, CA: Center for Oral and Public History.

Kell, A. S. (1945). Welfare Section Final Report by Adeline S. Kell, Counselor, Term of Service August 28, 1944 to Center closure. War Relocation Authority, Heart Mountain Relocation Center, Heart Mountain, Wyoming (Calisphere, Japanese American Relocation Digital Archives ed., pp. 1–12). Berkeley: Bancroft Library, University of California.

Kimmerling, C., Fite, A. L., & Abbott, C. W. (1945). Report of the Welfare Section, August 1942 to November 1945. War Relocation Authority, Minidoka Relocation Center (Calisphere, Japanese American Relocation Digital Archives ed., pp. 1–69). Berkeley: Bancroft Library, University of California.

Kuramoto, F. (1976). *A History of the Shonien, 1914–1972: An account of a program of institutional care of Japanese children in Los Angeles*. San Francisco: R and E Research Associates.

Lane, M. D. (1945). Memo to all Projects from Mrs. Marie D. Lane, Head, Welfare Section, WRA, May 21, 1945, pp. 1–3. Folder: Welfare Handbook—Butler, Box 5. Records of the War Relocation Authority, 1941–1989, Record Group 210, Office Files of Miss Lou Butler, Head Counselor of the Welfare Section of the Community Management Division at the Colorado River Relocation Center, compiled 1942–1945. ARC Identifier 5752763/MLR Number UD 6. Washington, DC: National Archives and Records Administration.

Lane, M. D. (1946). Japanese resettlement. *Public Welfare, 4*, 127–130.

Leahy, M. (1946). Public assistance for restricted persons during the Second World War. *Social Service Review, 19*(1), 24–47.

LeHane, M. (1946). Closing dates of WRA LA Area Office—District Office: California State Department of Social Welfare Office Memorandum from Mary LeHane to Bertha Underhill, April 3, 1946, p. 1. Social Welfare—War Services—Resettlement Assistance, General, 1942–48 (F3729:110). Department of Social Welfare Records, War Services Bureau. Sacramento: California State Archives.

MacLatchie, E. B. (1945). State Department. of Social Welfare Office Memorandum to Bertha Underhill from Elizabeth B. MacLatchie, May 1, 1945, p. 1. Social Welfare—War Services—Resettlement Assistance, Assistance Standards, 1942–1946 (F3729:107). Department of Social Welfare Records, War Services Bureau. Sacramento: California State Archives.

Malstrom, K. E. (1945). Resettlement of persons of Japanese ancestry: Memorandum No. 45-34 from Kathryn E. Malstrom, Director of the Washington State Department of Social Security to county administrators and state staff, dated March 28, 1945, pp. 1–7. Director's memoranda, 1945, Box A6. Public Welfare and Social Security Departments Collection. Olympia: Washington State Archives.

Manzanar Public Welfare Department. (1943a). Memorandum of a talk between Mrs. D'Ille, Counselor, Manzanar Relocation Center and Miss Ellen Marshall, Acting Director of Social Work for Children's Aid Society of California, pp. 1–2. Folder: 61. 520—Child Welfare—Children's Village, Box 224: Manzanar Relocation Center—Central Files—50.026 to 62.014. Records of the War Relocation Authority, 1941–1989,

Record Group 210, Subject-Classified General Files of the Relocation Centers—compiled 1942–1946. ARC Identifier 1544889/MLR Number PI-77 48. Washington, DC: National Archives and Records Administration.

Manzanar Public Welfare Department. (1943b). Memorandum of an interview in Los Angeles at the office of the State Welfare Board, Los Angeles, California, December 16, 1943, pp. 1–4. Folder: 61. 520—Child Welfare—Children's Village, Box 224: Manzanar Relocation Center—Central Files—50.026 to 62.014. Records of the War Relocation Authority, 1941–1989, Record Group 210, Subject-Classified General Files of the Relocation Centers—compiled 1942–1946. ARC Identifier 1544889/MLR Number PI-77 48. Washington, DC: National Archives and Records Administration.

Mclaughlin, V. V. (1945). Personal Narrative Report of Relocation Program Officer. War Relocation Authority, Minidoka Relocation Center, Hunt, Idaho, pp. 1–5. Retrieved from http://content.cdlib.org/ark:/13030/ft0d5n98hz/?query=minidoka%20relocation%20program&brand=calisphere

Merritt, R. P. (1944a). Letter to Clyde Getz, Executive Secretary, Children's Home Society, Los Angeles, CA, from Mr. Ralph P. Merritt, Project Director, Manzanar Relocation Center, June 29, 1944, p. 2. Folder: 61.520 Child Welfare—Children's Village, Box 225: Manzanar Relocation Center Central Files 50.026 to 62.014 (1942 to 1943). Records of the War Relocation Authority, 1941–1989, Record Group 210, Subject-Classified General Files of the Relocation Centers—compiled 1942–1946. ARC Identifier 1544889/MLR Number PI-77 48. Washington, DC: National Archives and Records Administration.

Merritt, R. P. (1944b). Letter to Harry E. Titus, War Relocation Officer, War Relocation Officer, from Mr. Ralph P. Merritt, Project Director, Manzanar Relocation Center, August 28, 1944, p. 1. Folder: 61.520 Child Welfare—Children's Village, Box 225: Manzanar Relocation Center Central Files 50.026 to 62.014 (1942 to 1943). Records of the War Relocation Authority, 1941–1989, Record Group 210, Subject-Classified General Files of the Relocation Centers—compiled 1942–1946. ARC Identifier 1544889/MLR Number PI-77 48. Washington, DC: National Archives and Records Administration.

Meyer, D. S. (1944). Annual Report of the Director of the War Relocation Authority: Reprinted from the Annual Report of the Secretary of the Interior for the Fiscal Year ended June 30, 1944, pp. 279–293. Folder: Annual Report of the Director of the War Relocation Authority. Fiscal yr. June 30, 1944, Box 3: Washington Office Records—Documentary Files: Semi-Annual Reports—1943 & 1944; Semi-Annual Reports—Evacuee Employment; Annual Reports—1943 & 1944; History or WRA—Ruth KcKee; Annual Report of the Director of WRA; Semi-Annual Reports—Owego 1944. Records of the War Relocation Authority, 1941–1989, Record Group 210, Headquarters Basic Documentation Reports, compiled 1942–1946. ARC Identifier 1526983/MLR Number PI-77 3. Washington, DC: National Archives and Records Administration.

Meyer, D. S. (1945). Memorandum from Dillon S. Meyer, Director, War Relocation Authority, to Washington Staff, October 24, 1945, p. 1. Folder: Internal Security Section—Community Management Division, Box 4: Community Management Division—Monthly Vocational Training (1944–45), Education, Welfare and Housing, Health, Internal Security, Religion. Operational Division—Engineering and Agriculture. Records of the War Relocation Authority, 1941–1989, Record Group 210,

Washington Office Records—Washington Documents. ARC Identifier 1519285/MLR Number PI-77 2. Washington, DC: National Archives and Records Administration.

Miller, C. F. (1945). Letter to Hon. Robert Kenny, Attorney General, San Francisco, California, from Charles F. Miller, Area Supervisor, WRA, San Francisco, California, November 16, 1945, pp. 1–2. Social Welfare—War Services—Resettlement Assistance, General, 1942–48 (F3729:110). Department of Social Welfare Records, War Services Bureau. Sacramento: California State Archives.

Niiya, B. (May 6, 2015). Edward Spicer. *Densho Encyclopedia of the Japanese American Incarceration*. Retrieved from http://encyclopedia.densho.org/Edward Spicer/

Nishi, S. F. (n.d.). Report on trip to West Coast and Relocation Centers (Poston, Gila, Topaz, Heart Mountain), submitted by Rev. Shunji F. Nishi, pp. 1–20. Folder 5, Box 720. YWCA of the U.S.A. Records, Sophia Smith Collection. Northampton, MA: Smith College.

Nishimoto, R. S. (1943). Domestic Service, pp. 1–35. Folder W 1.85, Box BANC MSS 67/14 c. Japanese American Evacuation and Resettlement Study, Japanese American Evacuation and Resettlement records. Berkeley: Bancroft Library, University of California.

Nobe, L. N. (1999). The Children's Village at Manzanar: The World War II Eviction and Detention of Japanese American Orphans. *Journal of the West, 38*(2), 65–71.

Parmley, E. (1945). War Services Cases—Santa Barbara County: California State Department of Social Welfare Office Memorandum to Bertha Underhill, December 17, 1945, p. 1. Social Welfare—War Services—Federal Review, 1945–46 (F3729:131). Department of Social Welfare Records, War Services Bureau. Sacramento: California State Archives.

Pratt, C. H. (1945). Closing report of the Welfare Section, from Sept. 11, 1943 to Center Closing, dated December 20, 1945 *War Relocation Authority, Central Utah Project, Topaz, Utah* (Calisphere, Japanese American Relocation Digital Archives ed., Vol. The Bancroft Library, pp. 1–10): University of California, Berkeley.

Rawlings, W. E. (1946). Project Director's narrative: Minidoka Relocation Center, Hunt, Idaho, September 1, 1945 to February 6, 1946 *War Relocation Authority, Minidoka Relocation Center* (Calisphere, Japanese American Relocation Digital Archives ed., pp. 1–4). University of California, Berkeley: The Bancroft Library.

Reith, M. B. (1943). Report on Tule Lake Visit, March 1, 11–12, 1943, pp. 1–14. Folder 3, Box 724. YWCA of the U.S.A. Records, Sophia Smith Collection. Northampton, MA: Smith College.

Residents of Colorado River Relocation Center. (1943). Requests made by Camp residents of Poston, Arizona, December 21, 1943, pp. 1–3. Folder 120.1 Complaints and Criticism, Box 112: Subject-Classified General Files—Colorado River Central Files—110.41 to 130. Records of the War Relocation Authority, 1941–1989, Record Group 210, Subject-Classified General Files of the Relocation Centers—compiled 1942–1946. ARC Identifier 1544889/MLR Number PI-77 48. Washington, DC: National Archives and Records Administration.

Roddy, M. (1946a). Review of War Services cases in Sutter County, January 14, 1946, pp. 1–2. Social Welfare—War Services—Federal Review, 1945–46 (F3729:131). Department of Social Welfare Records, War Services Bureau. Sacramento: California State Archives.

Roddy, M. (1946b). Review of War Services cases in Tulare County, January 15, 1946, pp. 1–3. Social Welfare—War Services—Federal Review, 1945–46 (F3729:131).

Department of Social Welfare Records, War Services Bureau. Sacramento: California State Archives.

Ross, P. (1945). Teletype to all Project Directors, from Prudence Ross, Relocation Supervisor, Chicago Office, July 23, 1945, p. 1. Folder: 543.1—Individual Burial, Box 99: Central Utah Relocation Center—Central Files—543 to 583. Records of the War Relocation Authority, 1941–1989, Record Group 210, Subject-Classified General Files of the Relocation Centers—compiled 1942–1946. ARC Identifier 1544889/MLR Number PI-77 48. Washington, DC: National Archives and Records Administration.

Rowe, J. H. (1971). The Japanese Evacuation Decision: An oral history conducted in 1971 by Ameila Fry. *Japanese American Relocation Reviewed, volume I: Decision and exodus* (pp. i–45). Berkeley: Regional Oral History Office, Bancroft Library, University of California.

Sakoda, J. M. (1943). The Relocation Program at Tule Lake, Part II, pp. 1–174. Folder R 20.84:2, Box BANC MSS 67/14 c. Japanese American Evacuation and Resettlement Study, Japanese American Evacuation and Resettlement records. Berkeley: Bancroft Library, University of California.

Sasaki, T. S. (1946). Daily Report, September 30, 1946, pp. 1–4. Folder: 15.101 Los Angeles, CA, Daily Reports, 1-50, Box 1: Washington Office Records—Liquidation Files—Special Studies—15.100 Santa Clara Area thro 15.101.B L.A. Area Records of the War Relocation Authority, 1941–1989, Record Group 210, Liquidation Files—Special Studies—General Files Relating to the Resettlement Study, compiled 1946–1947. ARC Identifier 1566649/MLR Number PI-77 64. Washington, DC: National Archives and Records Administration.

Social Security Board. (1945). Agency services 3/5/45: XIII. cooperation with the War Relocation Authority, Part One—Background of Relocation Program for persons of Japanese ancestry, pp. 21–28. Folder: Welfare and Housing—Community Management Division, Box 4: Washington Office Records—Washington Document: Community Management Division—Monthly Vocational Training (1944–45); Education, Welfare and Housing, Health, Internal Security, Religion; Operational Division—Engineering and Agriculture. Records of the War Relocation Authority, 1941–1989, Record Group 210, Headquarters Basic Documentation Reports, compiled 1942–1946. ARC Identifier 1519285/MLR Number PI-77 2. Washington, DC: National Archives and Records Administration.

Spicer, E. H. (1952). Resistance to freedom: Resettlement from the Japanese relocation centers during World War II. In E. H. Spicer (Ed.), *Human problems in technological change: A casebook* (pp. 245–256). New York: Russell Sage Foundation.

Spicer, E. H., Hansen, A. T., Luomala, K., & Opler, M. K. (1969). *Impounded people: Japanese Americans in the Relocation Centers*. Tucson: University of Arizona Press.

Sundquist, P. (1942). Letter to Mr. C.A. Stuart, Director, San Joaquin County Welfare Department, from Perry Sundquist, Public Assistance Supervisor, Lodi Control Station, May 22, 1942, pp. 1. *Social Welfare—War Services—WCCA—Reports, General, 1942–43 (F3729-146)*. Department of Social Welfare Records, War Services Bureau. Sacramento: California State Archives.

Taylor, E. H. (1946). Review of War Services cases in San Luis Obispo County: California State Department of Social Welfare Office Memorandum to Bertha Underhill from Elizabeth H. Parmley, by Edna H. Taylor, December 20, 1946, pp. 1–3. Social Welfare—War Services—Federal Review, 1945–46 (F3729:131). Department of Social Welfare Records, War Services Bureau. Sacramento: California State Archives.

Thunder, M. E. (1943). Letter to Mr. Jacob Gerrild, Director of Case Work, Colorado Children's Aid Society, Denver, Colorado, from Margaret E. Thunder, Assistant Counselor, Social Service Department, Gila River Project, Rivers, Arizona, November 10, 1943, pp. 1–2. Folder: 580—Community Service and Welfare, Box 144: Gila River Relocation Center—Central Files—571 to 580. Records of the War Relocation Authority, 1941–1989, Record Group 210, Subject-Classified General Files of the Relocation Centers—compiled 1942–1946. ARC Identifier 1544889/MLR Number PI-77 48. Washington, DC: National Archives and Records Administration.

Thunder, M. E. (1944a). Letter to Miss Zella Allred, Case Worker, Colorado Children's Aid Society, Denver, Colorado, from Margaret E. Thunder, Assistant Counselor, Social Service Department, Gila River Project, Rivers, Arizona, March 14, 1944, pp. 1–3. Folder: 580—Community Service and Welfare, Box 144: Gila River Relocation Center—Central Files—571 to 580. Records of the War Relocation Authority, 1941–1989, Record Group 210, Subject-Classified General Files of the Relocation Centers—compiled 1942–1946. ARC Identifier 1544889/MLR Number PI-77 48. Washington, DC: National Archives and Records Administration.

Thunder, M. E. (1944b). Letter to Mr. Jacob Gerrild, Director of Case Work, Colorado Children's Aid Society, Denver, Colorado, from Margaret E. Thunder, Assistant Counselor, Social Service Department, Gila River Project, Rivers, Arizona, February 10, 1944, pp. 1–2. Folder: 580—Community Service and Welfare, Box 144: Gila River Relocation Center—Central Files—571 to 580. Records of the War Relocation Authority, 1941–1989, Record Group 210, Subject-Classified General Files of the Relocation Centers—compiled 1942–1946. ARC Identifier 1544889/MLR Number PI-77 48. Washington, DC: National Archives and Records Administration.

Tuttle, W. K. (1945). History of Gila Welfare Section by W. K. Tuttle, Head, Welfare Section. War Relocation Authority, Gila River Relocation Center, Rivers, Arizona (Calisphere, Japanese American Relocation Digital Archives ed., pp. 1–10). Berkeley: Bancroft Library, University of California.

Underhill, B. S. (1945a). California State Department of Social Welfare Office Memorandum to Perry Sundquist, October 24, 1945, p. 1. Social Welfare—War Services—Resettlement Assistance, General, 1942–48 (F3729:110). Department of Social Welfare Records, War Services Bureau. Sacramento: California State Archives.

Underhill, B. S. (1945b). Confidential Report on Resettlement Assistance, November 29, 1945, pp. 1–3. Social Welfare—War Services—Resettlement Assistance, General, 1942–48 (F3729:110). Department of Social Welfare Records, War Services Bureau. Sacramento: California State Archives.

Underhill, B. S. (1945c). Discussions with War Relocation Authority, October 19, 1945, p. 1. Social Welfare—War Services—Resettlement Assistance, General, 1942–48 (F3729:110). Department of Social Welfare Records, War Services Bureau. Sacramento: California State Archives.

Underhill, B. S. (1946a). War Services Review schedules—San Luis Obispo County: California State Department of Social Welfare Office Memorandum to Mary LeHane, January 3, 1946, p. 1. Social Welfare—War Services—Federal Review, 1945–46 (F3729:131). Department of Social Welfare Records, War Services Bureau. Sacramento: California State Archives.

Underhill, B. S. (1946b). Yolo County War Services Review, January 17, 1946, pp. 1–2. Social Welfare—War Services—Federal Review, 1945–46 (F3729:131). Department of Social Welfare Records, War Services Bureau. Sacramento: California State Archives.

United States Civil Service Commission. (1943). United States Civil Service Commission Classification Sheet: Associate Public Welfare Consultant (P-3), War Relocation Authority, Office for Emergency Management, pp. 1–2. Folder: Welfare Section, Box 2. Records of the War Relocation Authority, 1941–1989, Record Group 210, Job Descriptions—compiled 1942–1946. ARC Identifier 1543527/MLR Number PI-77 36. Washington, DC: National Archives and Records Administration.

War Relocation Authority. (1943a). Evacuee resistance to relocation—reasons for the Relocation Program: Community Analysis Report No. 5, June 1943, marked not for publication pp. 1–9. Folder 16, Box 722. YWCA of the U.S.A. Records, Sophia Smith Collection. Northampton, MA: Smith College.

War Relocation Authority. (1943b). Evacuee resistance to relocation: War Relocation Authority Community Analysis Report No. 2, June 1943, pp. 1–9. Folder: Administrative Notices (6 of 7), Box 1: Administrative Notices. Records of the War Relocation Authority, 1941–1989, Record Group 210, Washington Office Records—Washington Documents. ARC Identifier 5634012/MLR Number P 4 (formerly UD 5). Washington, DC: National Archives and Records Administration.

War Relocation Authority. (1943c). Preliminary evaluation of the Resettlement Program at Jerome Relocation Center: Project Analysis Series No. 5, Community Analysis Section, May 1943, pp. 1–4. Folder 10, Box 723. YWCA of the U.S.A. Records, Sophia Smith Collection. Northampton, MA: Smith College.

War Relocation Authority. (1943d). Preliminary Survey of Resistances to Resettlement at the Tule Lake Relocation Center, June 23 1943, pp. 1–15. Folder 3, Box 724. YWCA of the U.S.A. Records, Sophia Smith Collection. Northampton, MA: Smith College.

War Relocation Authority. (1943e). Project Analysis Series No. 9, June, 23, 1943: Preliminary Survey of Resistances to Resettlement at the Tule Lake Relocation Center, pp. 1–15. Folder 3, Box 724. YWCA of the U.S.A. Records, Sophia Smith Collection. Northampton, MA: Smith College.

War Relocation Authority. (1943f). Report of the Welfare Section, July 1- December 31, 1943, pp. 1–6. Folder: Semi-Annual Reports—Community Management Division— Reports of Health Section & Reports of Welfare Section, Box 5: Washington Office Records—Documentary Files—Semi-Annual Reports: Operation D Division, Community Mgmt. Div, Administrative Mgmt. Division. Records of the War Relocation Authority, 1941–1989, Record Group 210, Headquarters Basic Documentation Reports, compiled 1942–1946. ARC Identifier 1526983/MLR Number PI-77 3. Washington, DC: National Archives and Records Administration.

War Relocation Authority. (1944a). Conference of Community Management—Report of the Summarizing Committee, May 13, 1944, pp. 1–6. Folder: Conference of Community Management—Denver, Colorado—May 13, 1944, Box 8: Meetings and Conferences 1943–1945. Records of the War Relocation Authority, 1941–1989, Record Group 210, Washington Office Records—Washington Documents. ARC Identifier 1519285/MLR Number PI-77 2. Washington, DC: National Archives and Records Administration.

War Relocation Authority. (1944b). Report of the Welfare Section, July 1—December 31, 1944, pp. 1–6. Folder: Semi-Annual Reports—Community Management Division Reports of Health Section & Reports of Welfare Section, Box 5: Washington Office Records—Documentary Files—Semi-Annual Reports: Operation D Division, Community Mgmt. Div, Administrative Mgmt. Division. Records of the War Relocation Authority, 1941–1989, Record Group 210, Headquarters Basic

Documentation Reports, compiled 1942–1946. ARC Identifier 1526983/MLR Number PI-77 3. Washington, DC: National Archives and Records Administration.

War Relocation Authority. (1944c). Semi-Annual Reports—WRA—Printed—July 1 to Dec. 31, 1944, pp. 1–80. Folder: Semi-Annual Reports—WRA—Printed—July 1 to Dec. 31, 1944, Box 4: Washington Office Records—Documentary Files—Semi-Annual Reports, 1944 & 1945: Semi-Annual Reports 1946 (Final), War Records Project Report, 19944 & 1945; Semi-Annual reports, Legal Division. Records of the War Relocation Authority, 1941–1989, Record Group 210, Headquarters Basic Documentation Reports, compiled 1942–1946. ARC Identifier 1526983/MLR Number PI-77 3. Washington, DC: National Archives and Records Administration.

War Relocation Authority. (1945a). Evacuee attitudes towards public assistance: Prepared by the Welfare and Community Analysis Sections, February 28, 1945, pp. 1–3. Folder: Welfare Handbook—Butler, Box 5. Records of the War Relocation Authority, 1941–1989, Record Group 210, Office Files of Miss Lou Butler, Head Counselor of the Welfare Section of the Community Management Division at the Colorado River Relocation Center, compiled 1942–1945. ARC Identifier 5752763/MLR Number UD 6. Washington, DC: National Archives and Records Administration.

War Relocation Authority. (1945b). Handbook release No. 184, dated January 20, 1945, pp. 1–13. Folder: Japanese Internment, Box A8. Public Welfare and Social Security Departments Collection. Olympia: Washington State Archives.

War Relocation Authority. (1945c). Semi-Annual Reports: Report of the Welfare Section, January 1– June 30, 1945, pp. 1–4. Folder: Semi-Annual Reports—Community Management Division—Reports of Health Section & Reports of Welfare Section, Box 5: Washington Office Records—Documentary Files—Semi-Annual Reports: Operation D Division, Community Mgmt. Div, Administrative Mgmt. Division. Records of the War Relocation Authority, 1941–1989, Record Group 210, Headquarters Basic Documentation Reports, compiled 1942–1946. ARC Identifier 1526983/MLR Number PI-77 3. Washington, DC: National Archives and Records Administration.

War Relocation Authority. (1945d). Semi-Annual Reports: Welfare Section, January 1—June 30, 1945, pp. 1–6. Folder: Semi-Annual Reports—Community Management Division Reports of Health Section & Reports of Welfare Section, Box 5: Washington Office Records—Documentary Files—Semi-Annual Reports: Operation D Division, Community Mgmt. Div, Administrative Mgmt. Division. Records of the War Relocation Authority, 1941–1989, Record Group 210, Headquarters Basic Documentation Reports, compiled 1942–1946. ARC Identifier 1526983/MLR Number PI-77 3. Washington, DC: National Archives and Records Administration.

War Relocation Authority. (1946a). Final Report of the Los Angeles, CA District War Relocation Authority, January 31, 1946, p. 1. Folder: Final Reports—Los Angeles District WRA, January 31, 1946, Box 11: Final Reports—Northern and Southern California. Records of the War Relocation Authority, 1941–1989, Record Group 210, Field Basic Documentation—Relocation Center Records—compiled 1942–1946. ARC Identifier 1532647/MLR Number PI-77 4C. Washington, DC: National Archives and Records Administration.

War Relocation Authority. (1946b). Final Report of the Philadelphia, PA District Office, War Relocation Authority final report, February 4. 1946, p. 1. Folder: Final Reports—Final Reports—Philadelphia, PA District Office, WRA, February 4, 1946, Box 5: Final Reports—East Coast Area—Philadelphia District (Vol. 6); Washington District (Vol.

7). Records of the War Relocation Authority, 1941–1989, Record Group 210, Field Basic Documentation—Relocation Center Records—compiled 1942–1946. ARC Identifier 1532647/MLR Number PI-77 4C. Washington, DC: National Archives and Records Administration.

War Relocation Authority. (1946c). *The relocation program*. Washington, DC: U.S. Government Printing Office.

War Relocation Authority. (1946d). Semi-annual report: January 1 to June 30, 1946, pp. 1–29. Folder 12—Wartime Problems—Japanese Relocation, Box 37—Wartime Problems: Japanese Relocation. Family Service Association of America—SW076, Social Welfare History Archives. Minneapolis: University of Minnesota.

War Relocation Authority. (1946e). Semi-annual report: July 1 to December 31, 1945, pp. 1–51. Folder 12—Wartime Problems—Japanese Relocation, Box 37—Wartime Problems: Japanese Relocation. Family Service Association of America—SW076, Social Welfare History Archives. Minneapolis: University of Minnesota.

War Relocation Authority. (1946f). Southern California area War Relocation Authority final report, p. 1. Folder: Final Reports—Southern California Area WRA, March 1, 1946, Box 11: Final Reports—Northern and Southern California. Records of the War Relocation Authority, 1941–1989, Record Group 210, Field Basic Documentation—Relocation Center Records—compiled 1942–1946. ARC Identifier 1532647/MLR Number PI-77 4C. Washington, DC: National Archives and Records Administration.

War Relocation Authority. (1946g). Stockton District War Relocation Authority final report, p. 1. Folder: Final Reports—Northern California Area WRA, May 15, 1946, Box 11: Final Reports—Northern and Southern California. Records of the War Relocation Authority, 1941–1989, Record Group 210, Field Basic Documentation—Relocation Center Records—compiled 1942–1946. ARC Identifier 1532647/MLR Number PI-77 4C. Washington, DC: National Archives and Records Administration.

Webb, J. L. (1943). Reactions to Mr. Barrow's letter of November 9 and Draft of Procedure on Special Counseling, November 26, 1943, pp. 1–7. Folder: 61.510—Welfare (General), Box 198: Jerome Center, Denson, Arkansas—Central Files—61.310 to 61.510. Records of the War Relocation Authority, 1941–1989, Record Group 210, Subject-Classified General Files of the Relocation Centers—compiled 1942–1946. ARC Identifier 1544889/MLR Number PI-77 48. Washington, DC: National Archives and Records Administration.

Wollenberg, C. M. (1945). Letter to Mr. Charles F. Miller, relocation Supervisor, WRA, San Francisco, CA, from Charles M. Wollenberg, Director, California State Department of Social Welfare, July 24, 1945, pp. 1. Social Welfare—War Services—Resettlement Assistance, Assistance Standards, 1942–1946 (F3729:107). Department of Social Welfare Records, War Services Bureau. Sacramento: California State Archives.

Yasumura, J. (1945). Report on the closing of Minidoka Relocation Center by Jobu Yasumura, Department of Cities, American Baptist Home Mission Society, dated November 5, 1945, pp. 1–9. Folder 17, Box 724. YWCA of the U.S.A. Records, Sophia Smith Collection. Northampton, MA: Smith College.

Yatsushiro, T., Ishino, I., & Matsumoto, Y. (1944). The Japanese-American looks at resettlement. *The Public Opinion Quarterly, 8*(2), 188–201.

YWCA National Board—Race Relations Subcommittee of the National Public Affairs Committee. (1944). Minutes, Race Relations Subcommittee, September 27, 1944, pp. 1–3. Folder 1, Box 395. YWCA of the U.S.A. Records, Sophia Smith Collection. Northampton, MA: Smith College.

YWCA National Board—Race Relations Subcommittee of the National Public Affairs Committee. (1945a). Race Relations Subcommittee Meetings, November 14, 1945, pp. 1–4. Folder 2, Box 395. YWCA of the U.S.A. Records, Sophia Smith Collection. Northampton, MA: Smith College.

YWCA National Board—Race Relations Subcommittee of the National Public Affairs Committee. (1945b). Race Relations Subcommittee Minutes, May 9, 1945, pp. 1–5. Folder 2, Box 395. YWCA of the U.S.A. Records, Sophia Smith Collection. Northampton, MA: Smith College.

YWCA Race Relations Sub-Committee of the Public Affairs Committee. (1945). Minutes, Race Relations Subcommittee, October 17, 1945, pp. 1–4. Folder 2, Box 395. YWCA of the U.S.A. Records, Sophia Smith Collection. Northampton, MA: Smith College.

10

Conclusion

The "Value of a Social Work Staff in a Mass Evacuation Program"

Complicity

The urge to speculate on how the history of the removal and incarceration might have played out differently without, as one California State Department of Social Work (CSDSW) social worker described, the "splendid part in the program played by the Social Worker" (Marcom, 1942, p. 1) is irresistible. What might have happened had social workers and social work organizations definitively opposed mass incarceration, refused, comprehensively, to facilitate the process? Would the Nikkei have fared worse in this wartime history without the "ready cooperation of the agencies" (DeWitt, 1942, p. 1)? Many social workers involved in the events did, no doubt, do their best. Katherine Day (1942a), reported on the Wartime Civil Control Administration (WCCA) Fresno station during the removal period.

> Regardless of the amount of work involved, the public assistance staff willingly made changes at the request of the evacuees up to and including last depar-ture day—realizing that even these seemingly insignificant (with relation to the amount of work involved in changing records and statistics) requests might mean the difference between the personal happiness or unhappiness of the in-dividual evacuee at a particularly distressing time in his life. (p. 3)

Despite being thrown into the work "with very little instruction" (Pigatti, 1942, p. 2), given "[c]onstant changes in instructions and new instructions" (Irvin, 1942, p. 2), as well as "false information" and "having their work invalidated" (Barry, 1942, p. 1) by military and other officials, social workers quickly and efficaciously "adjusted to the program" (Pigatti, 1942, p. 2), to carry out their assigned tasks not only in the removal process but in the concentration camps and on into resettlement.

Ruth Kingman (1974), reminiscing about her work as the Executive Secretary of the Pacific Coast Committee on American Principles and Fair Play, contended that "almost all of the evacuation was carried out in less than the distasteful way

Facilitating Injustice: The complicity of social workers in the forced removal and incarceration of Japanese Americans, 1941–1946. Yoosun Park, Oxford University Press (2020). © Oxford University Press.
DOI: 10.1093/acprof:oso/9780199765058.001.0001

it might have been" because of those who were "trying to do an inhumane thing in a humane way" (p. 12b). There is little doubt that—less carefully, earnestly, and sympathetically—some other government employees without casework skills and social work sensibilities would have performed the tasks that social workers took on. Without social workers "experienced in dealing with human beings faced with problems," as Katherine Day (1942b) conjectured, "the effect on the evacuees might well have had far more serious consequences" (p. 2). The recorded history of conflict between the relocation and welfare divisions in the camps supports her assertion. The Minidoka Relocation Section's criticism of the social workers' insistence on "professionalism" in planning resettlement, its reproach that staff had been "instructed to retain a sympathetic attitude toward the residents, but not to 'drool' over them" (Mclaughlin, 1945, p. 4), as social workers apparently did in its view, serves to applaud rather than demean social work as it was meant.

But can social work count on the credit side of its ledgers of professional history the commendation of the Western Defense Commander Lieutenant General John L. DeWitt's (1942) that "the successful accomplishment of this unprecedented task would not have been possible" (p. 1) without its participation? Katherine Day (1942b), Public Assistance Supervisor reporting on the Sacramento and Florin WCCA Stations, asserted that the "value of a social work staff in a mass evacuation program was significantly demonstrated" (p. 2). But should social work ever have demonstrated its value in the execution of such injustice? Whom did social workers serve: the Nikkei, their clients, or the government, their employer? The historian and social work scholar David Wagner (2000) asks, are "the manifest claims of people to be charitable and well-meaning an assurance that they are indeed *helping people*?" (p. 6, emphasis in original). Did social work's efforts in allaying the impact of the forced removal and incarceration balance out its role in facilitating the injustice of internment? How do we understand its responsibilities? How should we weigh social work's deeds?

In "trying to make sense" (p. 702) of the involvement of members of his discipline in the wartime history of removal and incarceration, the anthropologist Orin Starn (1986) observed that the standard explanation "downplays the broad ethical issues and political implications of their participation, asserting that anthropologists eased the relocation process for both Japanese Americans and WRA [War Relocation Authority] administrators" (p. 702). The converse argument is the "radical position that ethnographers were essentially accomplices of the government in relocation" (p. 702). Characterizing both views as essentially unsatisfying, Starn argues that the first perspective "minimizes the fact that WRA ethnographers were part of the administrative apparatus that enforced an executive order publicly denounced even at the time as racist and unconstitutional; it does not adequately address the questions about science, power, and politics that the internment episode so sharply poses" (p. 702). The second perspective, however, "fails to consider the good intentions of WRA anthropologists or their reasons for involvement" (p. 702). Whatever motivations and intentions drove the anthropologists, ultimately, Starn concludes, "their unquestioning adoption of contemporary anthropological interpretive strategies and their unwillingness to take a public stand against internment metamorphized the aim of advocacy into legitimation of domination" (p. 716). Social work's involvement in this history must be similarly understood.

Social work equivocated. As discussed at length in Chapter 1, social work organizations did not support mass removal, landing mostly on the stance that individual adjudication of loyalty rather than wholesale removal was the preferable course. But neither, on the whole, did they oppose wholesale removal, abdicating their right to and responsibility for contesting the wisdom of the government at war. Neither the disciplinary publications nor the archival records of workers in the field provide an unmitigated critique of the events. Social work organizations cooperated with the government organs that built and maintained the mass incarceration. In a 1942 article in the *Compass*, Frank Bruno, the American Association of Social Workers (AASW) President, pondered "What is the place of a professional association in a complex and complicated project such as this war and its aftermath?" (p. 19). The answer, at least for the AASW, did not include attention to the plight of the Nikkei. The wholesale uprooting and removal of the population garnered scant and inconsistent attention from the profession as a whole. Various private social service agencies, such as the Jewish Social Service Bureau and the National Refugee Service, did attempt to aid the Nikkei during the removal process. But such efforts were discouraged by the SSB because they hampered the smooth progress of the removal (see Chapter 1). The efforts seem to have dissolved without much struggle. The Committee on Resettlement of Japanese Americans, originally organized by the American Baptist Home Mission, included multiple social welfare organizations. It was a group, however, organized specifically to deal with the issues of resettlement; that is, with issues that brought the plight of the Nikkei into their own backyards (see Chapter 6).

Philip Schafer (1943), a social worker who worked as a supervisor under the aegis of the BPA during the removal phase and as an officer in the Chicago resettlement office under the WRA, commented that, overall, "social workers throughout the country, outside of the relocation centers, have not been adequately aware of these new people coming into their communities, nor have they interested themselves in the problems which this group presents" (p. 19). The historian Robert Shaffer (1998), calling for a kinder judgment of the liberal response to the internment than has been given, argues that many such organizations did shift their perspective later in the war to become "energetic critics" (p. 103). Shaffer insists, moreover, that, on the whole, social service organizations did successfully provide "material support for the internees, campaigns against harassment of resettled Japanese Americans" and these along with their "low-key community organizing to prepare people in the West for the return of their exiled neighbors" should be understood to as "a creative spirit of resistance which yielded some measure of success" (p. 110).

The YWCA's wartime work with the Nikkei could indeed be counted as an example of such work. In the context of its times and in comparison to other social work organizations, the YWCA was progressive in its vision of racial equality and courageous in its proactive, vocal consistency. It was unique among social work organizations in seeing the interment—the wholesale alienation and criminalization of a population *qua* its race—for the "immense" (Ellis, 1942, p. 9) ethical, moral, and political implication it posed for the national democracy. Perhaps most importantly, the YWCA was there in the fray throughout, with vocal protests against the "evacuation" at the beginning, as a steadfast and savvy presence in the camps, and as unflagging advocates and facilitators in the end as the WRA emptied its camps and thrust the plight of the Nikkei out into new communities of resettlement east and return west. The YWCA's Japanese American Evacuation Project (JAEP) provided valuable services to the Nikkei. "From my brief visit in Manzanar it is very clear that the YWCA fills a unique place in the life of the community" (p. 4) commented Ruth Woodsmall (1942), a visitor from the World YWCA, the umbrella organization of the international network of YWCAs. "The eager responsiveness to all of these different gatherings planned by the YWCA was an evidence of the loneliness of the life of Manzanar in the reaching out for contacts with the outside world" (p. 4). In a letter to the International Institute's Annie Clo Watson in July 1943, Harry Mayeda, a Nisei supervisor of Community Activities at Tule Lake, conveyed a similar message.

> I like to say very frankly that many of the Nisei in the relocation centers are disillusioned and disheartened over the Supreme Court's decision upholding the evacuation orders. Then too, with the unjustifiable persecution of the Nisei by the American Legion, Native Sons of the Golden West, Associated Farmers of California, Hearst Press, and the Dies Committee is not adding to faith on the part of the Nisei in this country. However, persons like yourself, Mrs. Marian Brown-Reith, Bruce McGuire, Essie McGuire, Catherine MacArthur, and many others too numerous to add have certainly been of enormous help in assisting the naysayers retain their faith in America. I, for one, am deeply grateful to such a splendid organization as the YWCA for their contribution to more sympathetic understanding of the Nisei by Americans. (p. 2)

The WRA Director Dillon Meyer's February 1946 letter of commendation to the YWCA highlighting Esther Briesemeister's "outstanding" work in the camps described the JAEP fieldworkers' visits to the camps as having "maintained an outside contact for many evacuees that could not be supplied in any other way" (p. 1). The letter also paid particular "tribute to the YWCA for its courageous and progressive position in many communities where it has assumed a leadership of an interracial program on a thoroughly democratic basis, and for its consistently fair treatment of all minority groups" (p. 1).

The YWCA's endeavors on behalf of the Nikkei indeed must be counted as having been helpful in many ways. The progressivism of the YWCA did not preclude, nevertheless, the fundamentally racist belief that being Japanese and being American were mutually exclusive states. The YWCA's well-intended and earnestly executed programs of integration, both in and outside of the camps followed the same racist schema that undergirded the Army's policy for exempting from incarceration certain mixed-race individuals who, having lived exclusively among Caucasians, "had not developed Oriental thought patterns or been subjected to so-called Japanese culture" (United States Army, 1943, p. 145). The history presented here is all the more disturbing because it is that of social workers, like those of the JAEP, doing what seemed to them to be more or less right and good. The past should not be judged by today's standards. Professional and humane standards shift over time and must be understood within their particular context. The actions and motivations described here occurred in a period rife with fear and propaganda. Undergoing a major shift from its private charity roots into its public sector future, social work bounded with the rest of society into "a patriotic fervor supporting the total mobilization of resources to fight World War II" (Specht & Courtney, 1994, p. ix). The profession's disinclination to forthrightly oppose the removal can be understood in part as an understandable reluctance to oppose the actions of the democratic FDR administration, the architect of the New Deal (Shaffer, 1998) in whose creation it had been instrumental (Abramovitz, 1998). "For better or worse, social work had become a part of the machinery of the state" (Abramovitz, 1998, p. 516) during the 1930s, establishing a major professional foothold in public sector work arising from those policies and programs, and its disinclination to publicly challenge the policies of that state and its inability to defy the mandate to participate in state actions is fathomable, if lamentable. BPA head Jane Hoey's (1942), statement at the 69th National Conference of Social Work, that social workers could both "minimize hardship" for the Nikkei and improve the Nikkei by helping "to make loyal Americans appreciative of democratic ideals" (p. 199) can perhaps be interpreted as the public face of a state official working within that professional bind between social work ideals and bureaucratic constraints.

While policies of a government at war, intractable bureaucratic structures, tangled political alliances, and complex professional obligations all may have mandated compliance to some degree, it is, nevertheless, difficult to deny that social work and social workers were also willing participants, informed about and aware of the implications of that compliance. Not all social workers, it must be said, saw the forced removal and mass incarceration of the Nikkei as a particularly troubling issue. Many were indeed conflicted. They were sympathetic to "a community being torn literally apart from its roots" (Simmons, 1942, p. 2) and discomfited by their participation in the process of that destruction. The sociologist Pierre Bourdieu (1993) argues that it is necessary to study "what informants don't say, or say only by omission, in their silences," and he argues that it is "important to wonder about these things that no one says" (p. 52).[1] The social workers' unease—their ambivalence and their need for rationalization—is perhaps most clearly represented in the actions recorded but not discussed: in, for example, the scrupulousness with which the social workers in the removal phase obtained permission from family members for institutionalization and other such actions leading to separation, in full knowledge that no family could alter or refuse any part of the decision. But social workers also saw merit in their work: their participation would serve as "valuable and unique experience" for their own professional development, prove significant to the nation as a "war measure" (Copland, 1942, p. 2), and ultimately be of benefit to the community undergoing demolition. A CSDSW (1942-43) report on the Santa Anita assembly center opined, for example, that "this evacuation may be a social asset rather than a social liability for America" (p. 8).

> The administration of this camp is keenly aware of the things which camp life may be able to do for the evacuees as well as being cognizant of the things that it may do to them. Possible good things to come out of the evacuation include lessons in actual self-government, improvement in general health conditions and possible reduction of hard feelings between the Nisei (American-born Japanese) and the Issei ("the older generation"). (p. 8)

The same report quoted the words of "one social worker who had spent a life time of work bringing the foreign-born into citizenship and partnership in American life" who opined that the internment was both necessary and just.

> It is a tragic thing to see the machinery of freedom in reverse, and to have a part in the deprivation of any group of American citizens or of foreign-born of the liberty America has always stood for—but it is part of the bitter necessities of war. War *is* [emphasis in the original] tragedy and any pretense that the grim necessities of war can be handled in a way which removes the tragedy is, of

[1] Lane Hirabayashi (1999) cites Bourdieu to make a similar point in his critique of Anthropology's use of resident Nikkei researchers.

course, failure to face reality. But when an Army, in the midst of war, under the direction of a government prosecuting a war, can deal with its potential enemies with emphasis upon humanness and the protection of human values to the utmost possible in war times, then the American experiment in democracy has demonstrated its enduring strength in a way which justifies all it has ever cost us, or will cost us in the days to come. (pp. 9–10)

In an article published in May of 1942, at the start of the JAEP's foray into the camps, Mabel Ellis and Helen Wilkins of the YWCA pondered that, on the problem of racism, "[p]erhaps the most difficult problem to face is our own attitude" (p. 9). The history of the YWCA, arguably the best of social work's wartime work with the Nikkei, makes clear that even the most conscientious and courageously undertaken deeds carried out by responsible individuals with both skill and training are not free of the pitfalls of bias and partiality. The materials analyzed throughout the preceding chapters indicate that the social workers involved believed, at least in part, in the ideas and ideals that made internment not only a possibility but an inevitability. The history traced here highlights the simple but oft-ignored reality, in other words, that social work and social workers do not practice outside the discursive confines of the society in which they live and work. Social workers share and practice the biases of their social and historical contexts; the dominant mores and ethos of the times in which ingrained racism and casual xenophobia was standard were reflected in their beliefs and carried out in their choices. An apt assertion is made by the historian and social work professor James Leiby (1983), who critiques "law-like generalizations" (p. 93) about human behavior in models that explain social workers as hapless handmaidens of the government.

I think that the best way, the historical way to explain social action—that is, people acting together in some mutual relation—is the way we ordinarily explain our own acts and those of people we know as well, as more or less conscious, deliberate, and voluntary responses to circumstances and contingencies. The observable regularities appear because people in life more or less willingly follow rules that they have learned more or less well ("socialization") and that seem to them more or less right and good ("values"). (p. 94)

History of the Present

The choices taken and enacted by the profession and professionals in this history underscore the explanatory inadequacy of the trope of social control versus social service applied so often to social work. It is entirely insufficient to dichotomize social workers either as agents of social control, practicing the "penetration, disruption, and policing of working-class communities" (Ehrenreich, 1985, p. 52) and other vulnerable populations, or as altruistic individuals who have stepped up to do the unenviable task of carrying out the dirty work of society. The control–service (or care–justice) dichotomy is built upon a positivist fallacy: the assumption that there is a clear demarcation between the virtue of service and the iniquity of control and, more importantly, that social work and social workers can objectively distinguish and choose between the two. The more complex and, indeed, uncomfortable reality is that "social control refers to the entire range of actions and pressures which are designed to lead the individual to function within society without threatening to disrupt the social order" (Goroff, 1974, p. 20), rather than only those actions explicitly intended to do so. The control–service dichotomy, in other words, occludes the discomfiting possibility that social control is immanent in all good social service practice. Had social work refused to participate in the work of the removal and incarceration, the suffering of the Nikkei indeed may have been greater. Both its professional commitments and its vocational ethos to do what it can to ameliorate social ills argued against a refusal to participate. But in carrying out those "willingly accepted" (DeWitt, 1942, p. 1) tasks, social work enacted and thus legitimized the bigoted policies of racial profiling en masse. In social work's unwillingness to take a resolute stand against the removal and incarceration—motivated by the need to fend off accusations of "coddling," as well as by the desire to protect the professional footholds it had gained in the federal welfare machinery—the well-intentioned profession, doing its conscious best to do good, enforced the existing social order and did its level best to keep the Nikkei from disrupting it. As Mimi Abramovitz (1998) averred, "Silence and tolerance of actions that violate professional or humane standards only bolster society's more conservative forces" (p. 524). Social work was silent; social workers tolerated.

The profession's role in carrying out problematic policies and, in doing so, upholding systems and institutions that it identifies as being responsible for creating those problematic policies in the first place is neither unique to this particular event nor this particular time. In his study of the community development movement in the 1950s, Robert Fisher (1985) has critiqued the actions of social workers and social work organizations for "the misuse of community developments to further cold war objectives" (p. 116). Amy LaPan and Tony Platt (2005) traced the complicity of social work and social workers in the American eugenics movement. Historian Linda Gordon has documented the repressive maternalism of social work and social workers in the context of domestic violence (1988) and welfare provisions for single mothers (1994). Other, broader examinations of such structures as American charity (Wagner, 2000), welfare provision (Piven & Cloward, 1993), and social reform (Ehrenreich, 1985) have also included the specific criticism of social work and social workers facilitating unjust government policies and actualizing social biases while striving to mitigate the consequences of those policies.

CSDSW field supervisor Perry Sundquist's conclusion that the "use of trained social workers enabled a difficult job to be done as decently as possible" (Sundquist, 1942, p. 1) cannot be wholly accepted. In multiple arenas throughout the history outlined in these chapters, social workers clearly could have acted more decently. Perhaps most crucially, social work and social workers could have done far, far more to push the possibilities of that which counted as decency. The political, ethical, and methodological stances of social workers in the Welfare Sections were derided by other Caucasian workers in other divisions in the camps as being too soft, too "sentimentalist" (War Relocation Authority, 1943, p. 12). Those professional stances were, on the other hand, seen by the Sections' "evacuee workers" as misguided, oppressive, and unjust measures that failed to put the welfare of their community as its primary objective. The much hated Mrs. Halle, erstwhile head of the Tule Lake Welfare Section, was said to have been able to "only think in terms of rules set up by the WRA, and did not attempt to see problems in terms of the needs of the people" (Sakoda, 1942, p. 3). But even those social workers who did attempt to do so and regretted the paucity of the available aid did not seem to have ever understood the fundamental misalignment between their view of aid as charity and that of the Nikkei, who saw it as a right to which they were entitled because their need for it was created by the very government that begrudgingly doled out the meager aid.

This misalignment is also not a singular problematic specific to those circumstance but a fundamental one in social work, evident across the span of its existence and the range of its roles. Underlying James Sakoda's observation that the Caucasian social workers did not realize "that social work in the Project might possibly be different from social work being practiced on the outside" (Sakoda, 1942, p. 3) was a demand to differentiate the Nikkei from ordinary relief recipients and entitlement from charity—bifurcations that remain intact today. But what might social work look like if it could imagine its practices beyond those dichotomies, to look instead to the systems of injustice rather than the individuals who suffer from them; to work to address instead the structures that create the call to distinguish the deserving from the undeserving rather than endeavor to adjust the undeserving so that they might someday become deserving? What might social work in the camps have looked like had it, instead of urging caution to deflect attention to its work, instead of denying that its work was coddling the Nikkei, have attempted, at the very least, to challenge the very logic that made—and continues to make—assisting the needy and caring for the vulnerable actions to be mistrusted, defended, and justified?

A provocative counterpoint to the social workers in the Welfare Sections who took the usual path of cooperation with administrative policies, whatever their personal views on the debacle might have been, was a number of "pacifistically inclined" (Billigmeier, 1943, p. 115) teachers at Tule Lake who refused to administer the so-called loyalty questionnaires or participate in the registration process in any way. Initially threatened with termination from their jobs, they were eventually allowed to take leaves of absence for the duration. No similar protests appear to have been made by social workers. The two Tule Lake school teachers who requested to live in camp housing among the inmates and to be paid the same nominal salary also come to mind (cited in Glick, 1943). Expelled from the WRA and banished from the camps in disgrace, their singular protest ensured that they were no longer on hand to be of help to the inmates. Perhaps, as the camp administration disdained, theirs was a hollow gesture. But from this far end of history, it also looks like a courageous one, a type of radical action few imagined and fewer took, however ineffectual it may have proved. Did social work and social workers lack equal courage? Was it the better part of valor to stay in and do what one can, as the social workers opted to do? Or was it a lack of imagination that prevented social work from doing so, stopped it from pushing the limits of how decency was conceptualized and operationalized in the camps and in the world outside? In their critique of the U.S. welfare system, Frances Fox Piven and Richard Cloward (1993) averred, "[t]hose who write about relief are usually enmeshed in the relief system, either as its ideologues or as its administrators. Understandably enough, they are strained to justify the system, although they may identify flaws in it" (p. xviii). How then can social work, a profession dedicated to ameliorating the ills of society ever do radical, progressive work to change that society if it cannot see with clarity and analyze with a skeptic's eye the work in which it is embroiled?

In her final recounting of the work of the JAEP, Esther Briesemeister (1946) explained that not all parts and members of the YWCA were "in accord with the emphasis given the work with evacuees (p. 53). Despite this lack of agreement, however, "intrepid souls went on with services in behalf of the Japanese" (p. 53). This was possible, in Briesemeister's view, because the YWCA was made up of "a pioneering group of women in many fields oftentimes controversial and explosive" and unafraid to face conflict out in the world *and* among its ranks. Critique and disagreement was "a healthy sign," Briesmeister opined, for the organization would become "too cloistered and too insulated were we not faced with dissension within our own ranks" (p. 53). If social work is truly invested in the formulation of present stances and future goals that seek, at least, to avoid past mistakes, it must actively seek and support such dissensions and disagreements among its ranks. The need for critique and self-scrutiny cannot be celebrated rhetorically only so that it can be shunted aside, but invited, cultivated, and applied.

Critical disciplinary history, the reflexive study of past actions in order to write the history of the present, is one method of dissension. Knowledge of social work's past, however discomfiting such knowledge may be, and clear-eyed analysis of its past actions and inactions, however chastening such endeavor might prove, are the necessary work of critique. The study of disciplinary history in social work, unfortunately, has long been in decline. The "history of social work has virtually disappeared from the curriculum in many schools" (1998, p. 524), Mimi Abramovitz noted two decades ago, and this absence in curricula as well as in scholarship has only become more profound in the ensuing years. History as an arena of study, and, more importantly, history as a modality of inquiry to illuminate the social problems of the present, has nearly disappeared in social work. Many reasons, including the neoliberalization of universities and the growing instrumentalization of social work scholarship, could be cited to explain this phenomenon. Whatever the cause, the profession's willing ignorance of its past actions belies its avowed commitment for social justice and social change. The profession cannot hope to identify the fault lines within its work or reasonably assess their implications without the study of its public past—the articulation of the forces that have constituted and continue to shape the society and the profession in which it is embedded.

The purpose of a disciplinary history is not to judge past deeds but to analyze them to inform present efforts and forge future paths. The intent of this study was to do "something more than distribute praise and blame" (Bourdieu, 1993, p. 52) by highlighting, through the tracing of an occluded history, the continued need to examine how social work makes sense of its professional obligations in relation to its professional ethics; to deliberate how this value-driven profession should, today, conceptualize its role as contemporary facilitators of problematic social policies from immigration restrictions to welfare reform. An examination of the profession's past responses may help it better understand how it should respond to the current crises of war and conscience. This history of the intersecting discourses of race, racism, and culture, as well as the issues of legal and social citizenship, may be helpful to the necessary task of examining the profession's current approaches, practices, and policies regarding newcomers and minority populations and the concepts of diversity and citizenship within which they are framed. Has the profession's views and practices around the problematic of race and racism, theories of culture and community, shifted sufficiently from the days of the internment? Is social work's current ideal of acculturative integration radically different from the YWCA's vision of assimilationist integration? Does acculturation contest the primacy of the "Caucasian community," entertain the kinds of inclusion that allow for the radical reshaping of the community by those who are so acculturated and integrated? To what thorny events and problematic tangles does the contemporary profession—as did the AASW of the wartime period—remain oblivious today? Which complex challenges has it—like the YWCA—found solutions for without sufficient soul-searching? What should, as a profession and as its practitioners, social work and social workers promote, argue to protect, or to protest and defy colluding in? How will we know the difference?

The history presented here occurred in a nation at war, in which the rights of a discrete population were abrogated to ensure, allegedly, the security of the nation. The events of a nation in crisis in a century past may seem to be of marginal relevance today, but the issues clearly remain unchanged. Questions of loyalty, patriotism, and citizenship; of race, culture, ethnicity; of belonging, assimilation, and integration are still linked to visible minority populations whose political, civil, and human rights are similarly threatened. Another "mass evacuation" or some other catastrophic government action is all too feasible in today's toxic, frightening, sociopolitical environment. A rekindled permissiveness for open displays of white supremacy, xenophobia, anti-Semitism, Islamophobia, homophobia, and misogyny is evident in the strident nativist discourses calling for the creation of a southern border wall, the recreation of the World War II "internment camps," and the total exclusion of all Muslims from entry into the United States. The Trump administration's policy for separating children from families entering the U.S.United States at the southern border has been likened to "Japanese American internment camps of World War II" (Takano, 2018; Waxman, 2018). The National Association of Social Workers (NASW) has denounced the administration's plans as "malicious and unconscionable" (National Association of Social Workers, 2018b) and has offered suggestions to social workers on ways they can "volunteer to help immigrant children separated from family" (National Association of Social Workers, 2018a). What no social work organization has done is question whether social workers should be participating in the government actions. Is social work once again facilitating injustice by staffing agencies and organizations carrying out the separations? Is it better to have social workers staff the facilities in which the children are incarcerated since there is little doubt that some others without social work skills and sensibilities would do so, less carefully, earnestly, and sympathetically? Or should the profession, as the Tule Lake teachers did, refuse to participate in carrying out this new injustice? What should today's social workers do?

Attorney General Francis Biddle told the wartime nation in 1942 that "[e]very man who cares about freedom, about a government by law—and all freedom is based on fair administration of the law—must fight for it for the other man with whom he disagrees, for the right of the minority, for the chance for the underprivileged with the same passion of insistence as he claims for his own rights" (United States Congress—House Select Committee Investigating National Defense Migration, 1942, p. 11044). His own initial opposition to the internment eroded ultimately under multiple pressures. How should social work, caught in the conflicting pressures of government policies, public accountability, professional viability, and its own cherished yet troublesome value base, realize such ideals today? Especially in light of its troubled past, how should a profession dedicated to the ideals of social justice and service on behalf of the vulnerable make sense of its role in *these* dangerous times?

References

Abramovitz, M. (1998). Social work and social reform: an arena of struggle. *Social Work*, 43(6), 512–526.

Barry, E. C. (1942). Elk Grove Civil Control Station: State Department of Social Welfare Office Memorandum to Margaret S. Watkins, from Edwina C. Barry, Sacramento, July 8, 1942, p. 1. Social Welfare—War Services—WCCA—Reports—Control Stations—Anaheim-Isleton, 1942 (F3729:147). Department of Social Welfare Records, War Services Bureau. Sacramento: California State Archives.

Billigmeier, R. H. (1943). Diary 2, Sept. 1942-Feb. 1943, Mar. 20, 1943, Tule Lake Relocation Center, pp. 1–122. Folder R 20.03:2, Box BANC MSS 67/14 c. Japanese American Evacuation and Resettlement Study, Japanese American Evacuation and Resettlement records. Berkeley: Bancroft Library, University of California.

Bourdieu, P. (1993). *For a sociology of sociologists: Sociology in question.* London: Sage.

Briesemeister, E. (1946). America's children—what happened to us?: Summary report of the Japanese Evacuee Project, January 1942–September 1946, pp. 1–54. Folder 3, Box 721. YWCA of the U.S.A. Records, Sophia Smith Collection. Northampton, MA: Smith College.

Bruno, F. J. (1942). The AASW as a means of helping professional social workers meet their wartime responsibilities. *Compass*, 23(5), 19–20.

California State Department of Social Welfare. (1942–43). Evacuation of Japanese in California. Social Welfare—War Services—WCCA—Reports, General, 1942-43 (F3729-146). Department of Social Welfare Records, War Services Bureau. Sacramento: California State Archives.

Copland, B. G. (1942). On Alien Control Centers: State Department of Social Welfare Office Memorandum to Miss Margaret S. Watkins, Los Angeles, May 9, 1942. Social Welfare—War Services—WCCA—Control Stations—May, 1942 (F3729:139). Department of Social Welfare Records, War Services Bureau. Sacramento: California State Archives.

Day, K. (1942a). Report of the Operation of the Fresno WCCA Station, May 12 through May 17, 1942, pp. 1–3. Social Welfare—War Services—WCCA—Reports—Control Stations—Anaheim-Isleton, 1942 (F3729:147). Department of Social Welfare Records, War Services Bureau. Sacramento: California State Archives.

Day, K. (1942b). Supplemental Report of Fresno WCCA Station: State Department of Social Welfare Office Memorandum to Margaret S. Watkins from Katherine Day Public Assistance Supervisor, WCCA Station, Sacramento, Report on Alien Control Stations, Sacramento and Florin, June 23, 1942. Social Welfare—War Services—WCCA—Reports—Control Stations—Sacramento—Yuba City, 1942 (F3729:149). Department of Social Welfare Records, War Services Bureau. Sacramento: California State Archives.

DeWitt, J. L. (1942). Letter to Richard M. Neustadt, Regional Director, Federal Security Agency, November 26, 1942. Social Welfare—War Services—WCCA—Control Stations—July, 1942–Jan., 1943 (F3729:141). Department of Social Welfare Records, War Services Bureau. Sacramento: California State Archives.

Ehrenreich, J. H. (1985). *The altruistic imagination: A history of social work and social polity in the United States.* Ithaca, NY: Cornell University Press.

Ellis, M. B. (1942). Confidential letter written May 8, 1942 by Mabel Ellis, marked Copy of handwritten letter received Saturday morning, May 9, 1942 air-mail special delivery, to Miss Stuff from Miss Ellis, pp. 1–3. Folder 22, Box 719. YWCA of the U.S.A. Records, Sophia Smith Collection. Northampton, MA: Smith College.

Ellis, M. B., & Wilkins, H. J. (1942). The West Coast evacuation in relation to the struggle for freedom: Public Affairs News Service, Bulletin No. VI—(Series No. 6), May 12, 1942, pp. 1–16. Folder 22, Box 719. YWCA of the U.S.A. Records, Sophia Smith Collection. Northampton, MA: Smith College.

Fisher, R. (1985). Community development and the Cold War: Lubricating the social machine. *Journal of the Community Development Society, 16,* 107–120.

Glick, P. M. (1943). Minor crime wave : memorandum to John H. Provinse, Chief, Community Services Division, from Philip M. Glick, Solicitor, WRA, Washington, DC, October 11, 1943, pp. 1–2. Folder: Provinse, John—#2—May-October, 1943, Box 35: Washington Office Records—Chronological File; General—Alphabetical—PF-John Provinse. Records of the War Relocation Authority, 1941–1989, Record Group 210, General Outgoing Correspondence, compiled 1942–1946. ARC Identifier 1534421/MLR Number PI-77 18. Washington, DC: National Archives and Records Administration.

Gordon, L. (1988). *Heroes of their own lives: The politics and history of family violence: Boston, 1880–1960.* New York: Viking.

Gordon, L. (1994). *Pitied but not entitled: Single mothers and the history of welfare, 1890–1935.* New York: The Free Press.

Goroff, N. N. (1974). Social welfare as coercive social control. *Journal of Sociology & Social Welfare, 2*(1), 19–26.

Hirabayashi, L. R. (1999). *The politics of fieldwork: research in an American concentration camp.* Tucson: University of Arizona Press.

Hoey, J. M. (1942). Mass relocation of aliens II. In A. Dunham (Ed.), *Proceedings of the National Conference of Social Work: Selected papers, Sixty-Ninth Annual Conference, New Orleans, Louisiana, May 10–16, 1942* (Vol. 69, pp. 194–199). New York: Columbia University Press.

Irvin, B. C. (1942). Alien Evacuation, Arroyo Grande Station, April 24–30, 1942: State Department of Social Welfare Memorandum to Miss Margaret S. Watkins, from Gladys C. Johns, by Bessie C. Irvin, filed May 14, 1942, pp. 1–3. Social Welfare—War Services—WCCA—Reports—Control Stations—Anaheim-Isleton, 1942 (F3729:147). Department of Social Welfare Records, War Services Bureau. Sacramento: California State Archives.

Kingman, R. (1974). The Fair Play Committee and Citizen Participation: An oral history conducted in 1974 by Rosemary Levenson. *Japanese American Relocation Reviewed, Volume II: The Internment* (pp. 1b-97q). Berkeley: Regional Oral History Office, Bancroft Library, University of California.

LaPan, A., & Platt, T. (2005). To stem the tide of degeneracy: The eugenic impulse in social work. In S. A. Kirk (Ed.), *Mental disorders in the social environment* (pp. 139–164). New York: Columbia University Press.

Leiby, J. (1983). Social control and historical explanation: historians view the Piven and Cloward thesis. In W. I. Trattner (Ed.), *Social welfare or social control? Some historical reflections on Regulating the Poor* (pp. 90–113). Knoxville: University of Tennessee Press.

Marcom, M. K. (1942). Report of Area Supervisor on the Stockton Control Station, May 20, 1942. Social Welfare—War Services—WCCA—Reports—Control Stations—Sacramento—Yuba City, 1942 (F3729:149). Department of Social Welfare Records, War Services Bureau. Sacramento: California State Archives.

Mayeda, H. (1943). Letter from Harry Mayeda, supervisor of Community Activities at Tule Lake to Annie Clo Watson, Secretary, Division of Community YWCA, July 1, 1943, pp. 1–2. Folder 3, Box 724. YWCA of the U.S.A. Records, Sophia Smith Collection. Northampton, MA: Smith College.

Mclaughlin, V. V. (1945). Personal Narrative Report of Relocation Program Officer. *War Relocation Authority, Minidoka Relocation Center, Hunt, Idaho*, 1–5. Retrieved from http://content.cdlib.org/ark:/13030/ft0d5n98hz/?query=minidoka%20relocation%20program&brand=calisphere

Meyer, D. S. (1946). Letter to Mrs. Harrison S. Elliott, General Secretary of the YWCA from Dillon S. Myer, Director of the War Relocation Authority, February 26, 1946, p. 1. Folder 4, Box 723. YWCA of the U.S.A. Records, Sophia Smith Collection. Northampton, MA: Smith College.

National Association of Social Workers. (2018a). How to volunteer to help immigrant children separated from family. Retrieved from http://www.socialworkblog.org/advocacy/2018/06/how-to-volunteer-to-help-immigrant-children-separated-from-family/

National Association of Social Workers. (2018b). NASW says plan to separate undocumented immigrant children from their parents is malicious and unconscionable. Retrieved from https://www.socialworkers.org/News/News-Releases/ID/1654/NASW-says-plan-to-separate-undocumented-immigrant-children-from-their-parents-is-malicious-and-unconscionable

Pigatti, F. G. (1942). Report of Operation of WCCA Station No. 32 at 822 E. 20th Street, L.A., May 15 1942, pp. 1–2. Social Welfare—War Services—WCCA—Reports—Control Stations—Lawndale-Riverside, 1942 (F3729:148). Department of Social Welfare Records, War Services Bureau. Sacramento: California State Archives.

Piven, F. F., & Cloward, R. A. (1971/1993). *Regulating the poor: The functions of public welfare*. New York: Vintage Books.

Sakoda, J. M. (1942). Social Welfare Department, Tule Lake Relocation Center, November 11, 1942, pp. 1–130. Box BANC MSS 67/14 c. Japanese American Evacuation and Resettlement Study, Japanese American Evacuation and Resettlement records. Berkeley: Bancroft Library, University of California.

Schafer, P. (1943). A War Relocation Authority community. *Compass, 25*(1), 16–19.

Shaffer, R. (1998). Cracks in the consensus: Defending the rights of Japanese Americans during World War II. *Radical History Review, 72*(3), 84–120.

Simmons, H. (1942). Letter to Martha Chickering, Director, State Department of Social Welfare, Sacramento, California, from Helen Simmons, Pittsburgh, Contra Costa County, California, February 12, 1941, p. 1. Box Social Welfare—War Services—WCCA—Control Stations—May, 1942 (F3729:139). Department of Social Welfare Records, War Services Bureau. Sacramento: California State Archives.

Specht, H., & Courtney, M. E. (1994). *Unfaithful angels: How social work has abandoned its mission*. New York: The Free Press.

Starn, O. (1986). Engineering internment: Anthropologists and the War Relocation Authority. *American Ethnologist, 13*(4), 700–720.

Sundquist, P. (1942). Letter to Mr. C.A. Stuart, Director, San Joaquin County Welfare Department, from Perry Sundquist, Public Assistance Supervisor, Lodi Control Station, May 22, 1942. Social Welfare—War Services—WCCA—Reports, General, 1942-43 (F3729-146). Department of Social Welfare Records, War Services Bureau. Sacramento: California State Archives.

Takano, M. (2018). Trump's family separation policy echoes my family's World War II internment. That damage lasted decades. *NBC News.* Retrieved from https://www.nbcnews.com/think/opinion/trump-s-family-separation-policy-echoes-my-family-s-world-ncna885021

United States Army. (1943). *Final report, Japanese evacuation from the West Coast, 1942.* Washington, DC: U.S. Government Printing Office.

United States Congress—House Select Committee Investigating National Defense Migration. (1942). *National Defense Migration. Part 29, San Francisco Hearings: Problems of Evacuation of Enemy Aliens and Others from Prohibited Military Zones [microform]: Hearings before the United States House Select Committee Investigating National Defense Migration, Seventy-Seventh Congress, second session, on Feb. 21, 23, 1942.* Washington, DC: U.S. Government Printing Office.

Wagner, D. (2000). *What's love got to do with it? A critical look at American charity.* New York: The New Press.

War Relocation Authority (1943). Project Analysis Series No. 9, June 23, 1943: Preliminary Survey of Resistances to Resettlement at the Tule Lake Relocation Center, pp. 1–15. Folder 3, Box 724. YWCA of the U.S.A. Records, Sophia Smith Collection. Northampton, MA: Smith College.

Waxman, O. B. (2018). Family separation is being compared to Japanese internment. it took decades for the U.S. to admit that policy was wrong. *Time.* Retrieved from http://time.com/5314955/separation-families-japanese-internment-camps/

Woodsmall, R. L. (1942). Impressions of the Japanese Relocation Center at Manzanar, California: World's YWCA, Washington, DC, dated December 1, 1942, pp. 1–5. Folder 14, Box 723. YWCA of the U.S.A. Records, Sophia Smith Collection. Northampton, MA: Smith College.

Glossary of Terms

Terms	Definition
American Association of Social Workers (AASW)	Founded in 1921, the AASW was a national membership organization with local chapters; its divisions included personnel practices, government and social work, employment practices, and personnel standards. The AASW was disbanded in 1955, when several organizations consolidated to form the National Association of Social Workers (NASW).
Alien Assistance Services/ Social Assistance Program	Part of a federal effort overseen by the Social Security Board and administered by county social welfare departments to provide information, referrals, financial assistance and other "contingency" services on an emergency basis to those "enemy aliens and their families" who had been disrupted by internment and incarceration (California State Department of Social Welfare, 1942, p. 1 of Part II).
Alien Enemy Control Unit	A U.S. Department of Justice program established in 1942 responsible for the management, control, and, ultimately, internment and incarceration of those deemed enemy aliens.
Alien Enemy Evacuation Program	A federal program overseen by the Federal Security Agency's Bureau of Public Assistance and administered through state social welfare departments, responsible for overseeing and conducting interviews to combat problems associated with the removal of the Nikkei during the so-called "voluntary" phase of evacuation.
American Council for Nationalities Service (ACNS)	A merging of the American Federation of International Institutes and the Common Council for American Unity. This entity remains in operation today as the Immigration and Refugee Services of America. The ACNS was charged, in part, with providing information to foreign language news outlets, including press and radio.

American Federation of International Institutes (AFII)	Grown from YWCA's Immigration Institutes movement, and previously known as the National Institute of Immigrant Welfare, the AFII was formed to provide educational services and to assist in the adjustment of immigrant populations, but also to resist the doctrine of assimilation and to encourage and celebrate cultural pluralism.
Appointed Personnel (AP)	The camp/prison staff's official title. APs were commonly referred to as, simply, the "Caucasians." APs provided services to evacuees and maintained the status quo set forth in the camps, often working alongside evacuees to provide services.
Bureau of Public Assistance (BPA)	A section of the Federal Security Agency under the Social Security Board, the BPA provided extremely limited cash assistance and in-kind benefits—known as basic items of the budget—to those unable to provide for their needs as a result of working and living restrictions and internment imposed by the U.S. government. The BPA program called "Services and Assistance to Enemy Aliens and Others Affected by Restrictive Governmental Action" had been available to the Nikkei at the beginning of war during the removal phase and, during resettlement, the "Assistance to Enemy Aliens" program was enacted.
Civilian Assembly Centers	The temporary detention centers were also called Reception Centers, built on fairgrounds or sites usually used for other purposes where Nikkei were held before they were moved to more permanent incarceration camps operated by the War Relocation Authority.
California State Department of Social Work (CSDSW)	In California, responsible for coordinating the provision of financial aid to the expelled Terminal Islanders as well as the Nikkei who "voluntarily" removed themselves from prohibited areas, known as both Alien Assistance Services and the Social Assistance Program. It was estimated by then director of the CSDSW, Martha Chickering, that more than 300 social caseworkers would be drawn from their "regular duties" to work in various Civil Control Stations.
Department of Justice Internment Camps	The Issei arrested as dangerous enemy aliens in the immediate aftermath of the Pearl Harbor attack were held in Department of Justice internment camps, which also held Italian and German nationals deemed security risks.
Enemy Alien Assistance Program (EAAP)	Part of the Bureau of War Services, the EAAP provided unemployment compensation to eligible individuals.

Family Welfare Association of America (FWAA)	Also known as the Family Services Association of America (FSAA), the FWAA was so named from 1930 to 1946 and was part of the charity organization movement. The organization also engaged in research and casework on a predominantly voluntary basis and was involved in issues including "Wartime WWII Problems."
Farm Security Migratory Labor Camps	Farm Security Migratory Labor Camps contracted nearly 33,000 Nikkei to work as seasonal farm laborers, many in the sugar beet industry. The Nikkei often took the place of American workers who were doing other things related to the war effort at the time. The Nikkei were relocated from Civilian Conservation Corps Camps to complete these agricultural "assignments."
Federal Security Agency (FSA)	The federal agency responsible for overseeing the Nikkei removal via their Bureau of Public Assistance and providing aid to enemy aliens via their Social Security Board.
Japanese American Evacuation and Resettlement Study (JERS)	Led by UC Berkeley sociologist Dorothy Swaine Thomas, JERS was one of three in situ studies of the events undertaken by social scientists. JERS hired multiple, mostly Nisei, fieldworkers to gather data on the individual and institutional processes of mass incarceration.
Japanese American Evacuation Project (JAEP)	A YWCA program, On April 1, 1942, the National Board of the YWCA voted to establish and finance the Japanese American Evacuation Project (JAEP); major concerns the JAEP were to address were (1) "the psychological effect upon the Japanese who have been forced to leave their homes, businesses, friends, etc., and the effect upon American citizens of Japanese parentage who have been uprooted, despite their loyalty to the United States" and (2) "the ultimate concern of living re-adjustments after war, for the Japanese" (YWCA National Board— Race Relations Subcommittee of the National Public Affairs Committee, 1942, p. 1).
Japanese Emergency Relief Committee (JERC)	An independent Nikkei organization prior to incarceration and internment, the JERC sought the help of the San Francisco International Institute in an effort to have the Nikkei's frozen funds be released to the San Francisco Community Chest so that those funds could be funneled into the Institute and distributed to assist the Nikkei during their incarceration. These funds were ultimately not released.

National Institute of Immigrant Welfare	Founded by Edith Terry Bremer in 1933, the National Institute of Immigrant Welfare was the national umbrella organization for independent International Institutes. The National Institute of Immigrant Welfare sponsored yearly conferences and advised individual international institutes on specifics of immigration and naturalization. Bremer believed in the reformation and humanization of immigration laws in the United States.
Office of Defense Health and Welfare Services	According to President Roosevelt, the Office of Defense Health and Welfare Services was to serve as the "center for coordination" of the defense program, to make specialists in health and welfare available to assist in planning and execution of the removal, to complete studies and surveys designed to, "assure the provision of adequate defense health," and to keep the President informed of progress (*Science Magazine*, 1941). The Office was an attempt to use public health planning and research to aid the war effort.
Social Security Board (SSB)	An agency created in 1935 by the Social Security Act, under the Bureau of Public Assistance, the SSB was the part of the Federal Security Agency (FSA) charged with providing aid to enemy aliens and others affected by government action. The SSB refused to accept money proffered from social work agencies and private institutions despite the extreme need of the people during removal, incarceration, and resettlement—the focus was on efficiency of removal, not the fallout. The SSB became part of the newly created Federal Security Agency in 1939 and was renamed the Social Security Administration in 1946.
U.S. Employment Services	The U.S. Employment Service assisted in locating workers for "critical war industries" and also recruited evacuees to that end. The U.S. Employment Service was one of the agencies enlisted to assist the Wartime Civil Control Administration in setting up and running assembly centers. The Employment Services were responsible for approving both housing facilities and minimum wage standards.
U.S. War Relocation Authority (WRA)	Formed on March 18, 1942, the WRA built and operated the ten relocation camps that interned and incarcerated Japanese Americans, with the ultimate goal of settling those interned outside of "excluded zones." The WRA also operated a camp for European refugees in Oswego, New York.

Wartime Civil Control Administration (WCCA)	Responsible for the logistics of removing the 110,000 Nisei from the West Coast, the WCCA opened seventeen makeshift camps called "Assembly Centers" meant to hold detained individuals before their transfer to more permanent—and marginally better equipped—relocation camps.

WRA Incarceration Camps

Camp Name	Other Name	Nearby town/settlement	Location	Open	Closed	1st Arrival	Last Departure	Peak Pop.
Granada	Amache	Granada, CO	Powers County, southeastern Colorado	24-08-42	15-10-45	27-08-42	15-10-45	7,318
Gila River	Rivers	Rivers, AZ	Gila River Pima Indian Reservation, Pinal County, southern Arizona	20-07-42	10-11-45	20-07-42	10-11-45	13,348
Heart Mountain		Cody, WY	Park County, northwest Wyoming	12-08-42	10-11-45	12-08-42	10-11-45	10,767
Jerome	Denson	Jerome, AK	Drew and Chicot Counties, southeastern Arkansas	06-10-42	20-06-44	06-10-42	30-06-44	8,497
Manzanar	Owens Valley	Owens Valley, CA	Inyo County, east-central California	21-03-42	28-10-45	21-03-45	21-11-45	10,046
Minidoka	Hunt	Jerome and Twin Falls, ID	Jerome County, south-central Idaho	10-08-42	28-10-45	10-08-42	28-10-45	9,397
Colorado River	Poston	Parker, AZ	Colorado River Indian Reservation, La Paz (previously Yuma) County, western Arizona	08-05-42	28-11-45	08-05-42	28-11-45	17,814
Rohwer		Rohwer, AR	Desha County, southeastern Arkansas	18-09-42	30-11-45	18-09-42	30-11-45	8,475
Central Utah	Topaz	Delta and Abraham, UT	Millard County, central Utah	11-09-42	31-10-45	11-09-42	31-10-45	8,130
Tule Lake		Newell, CA	Klamath Reclamation Project, Modoc County, northern California	27-05-42	20-03-46	27-05-42	20-03-46	18,789

Assembly Centers	Other Name	Original Use	Location	Opened	Closed	Max Pop	Primary Destination
Fresno		Big Fresno Fairgrounds, CA	Fresno, CA	06-May	30-Oct	5120	Jerome, Gila River
Owen's Valley		Civilian Conservation Corp Camp	Owen's Valley, CA	21-Mar	31-May	9666	transferred to WRA
Marysville		Migrant Workers' Camp	Arboga, CA	08-May	29-Jun	2451	Tule Lake
Mayer		Civilian Conservation Corp Camp	Mayer, AZ	07-May	02-Jun	245	Poston
Merced		County Fairgrounds	Merced, CA	06-May	15-Sep	4508	Granada
Parker Dam	Colorado River		Parker Dam, AZ	08-May	31-May	11738	transferred to WRA
Pinedale		Warehouses	Fresno, CA	07-May	23-Jul	4792	Tule Lake, Poston
Pomona		LA County Fairgrounds	Pomona, CA	07-May	24-Aug	5434	Heart Mountain
Portland	Camp Harmony	Fairgrounds racetrack stables	Portland, OR	02-May	10-Sep	3676	Heart Mt., Poston
Puyallup		Fairgrounds racetrack stables	Puyallup, CA	28-Apr	12-Sep	7390	Tule Lake, Minidoka
Sacramento	Walerga	Migrant Workers' Camp	Walerga Park, Sacramento, CA	06-May	26-Jun	4739	Tule Lake
Salinas		Rodeo grounds	Salinas, CA	27-Apr	04-Jul	3594	Poston
Santa Anita		Racetracks stables	Arcadia, CA	27-Mar	27-Oct	18719	Poston, six others
Stockton		San Joaquin County Fairgrounds	Stockton, CA	10-May	17-Oct	4271	Rohwer, Gila River
Tanforan		Racetracks stables	San Bruno, CA	28-Apr	13-Oct	7816	Central Utah
Tulare		County Fairgrounds	Tulare, CA	20-Apr	04-Sep	4978	Gila River
Turlock		Stanislaus County Fairgrounds	Turlock, CA	30-Apr	12-Aug	3662	Gila River

APPENDIX C

WCCA Station List

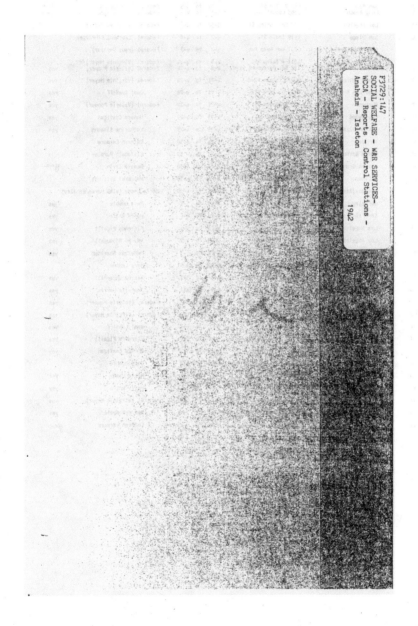

TABULATION OF CONTROL STATIONS - PUBLIC ASSISTANCE SUPERVISORS - SUMMARY REPORTS

Military Area # I

.0.	PLACE		DATES	PA SUPERVISOR	SUMMARY REPORT REC'D.BY SS BD.
2	San Pedro	362 W. 7th St.	3-31 to 4-5	Federal (Maurice Bobb)	yes
2	Long Beach	1333 Locust Ave.	3-31 to 4-5	Federal (Mary Bragman)	yes
3	Los Angeles	707 So. Spring St.	3-30 to 4-2	Federal (Winifred Ryder)	yes
4	San Diego	1919 India St.	4-2 to 4-8	Federal (Laurabel Ethridge)	
5	San Francisco	1731 Van Ness Ave.	4-2 to 4-7	Federal (Paul Vernier)	
6	Los Angeles	4311 - 147th St.	4-8 to 4-14	Federal (Virginia Meyer)	
6	Downey	112 So. Paramount Blvd.	4-8 to 4-14	Federal (Valerie Popper)	yes
7	Santa Monica	2422 Lincoln Blvd.	4-21 to 4-28	Federal (Virginia Meyer)	yes
8	West Los Angeles	2110 Corinth St.	4-21 to 4-28	Opal Cundiff	yes
9	Burbank	151 Magnolia St.	4-21 to 4-28	Federal (Valerie Popper)	yes
10	Hollywood	1157 N. LaBrea	4-23 to 4-29	Honora Costigan	yes
11	Los Angeles	961 S. Mariposa	4-23 to 4-29	Katherine Simmons	yes
12	Ventura	322 So. Calif. St.	4-24 to 4-30	Kathryn Larmore	
13	Santa Barbara	112 W. Cabrillo	4-24 to 4-30	Elizabeth Pemley	
14	Arroyo Grande	Hi School Gym	4-24 to 4-30	Bessie Irvin	yes
15	Salinas	Nat'l. Guard Armory	4-24 to 4-30	Margaret Billings	
16	Watsonville	Vet. Memorial Bldg.	4-24 to 4-30	Merle Leedy (also Norma Bentley)	
	Berkeley	2345 Channing Way	4-25 to 5-1	Mary Dumble	yes
20	San Francisco	2031 Bush St.	4-25 to 5-1	Harry White	yes
21	Los Angeles	3500 S. Normandie	4-25 to 5-1	Florence Pigatti	yes
22	Los Angeles	2514 S. Vermont	4-25 to 5-1	Wm. R. McDougall	yes
23	Vacaville	American Legion Hall	4-27 to 5-3	Madeline Sheridan	yes
24	Byron	Odd Fellows Hall	4-27 to 5-3	Mary LeHane	
27	Oakland	530 - 18th St.	5-1 to 5-7	Bertha Underhill	yes
28	Oakland	1117 Oak St.	5-1 to 5-7	Jeanette Harris	yes
29	Torrance	16522 S. Western Ave.	5-1 to 5-7	Federal (Valerie Popper)	yes
30	Los Angeles	7412 S. Broadway	5-1 to 5-7	Federal (Virginia Meyer)	yes
31	Los Angeles	859 S. Central	5-1 to 5-7	Opal Cundiff	yes
32	Los Angeles	822 E. 20th St.	5-4 to 5-9	Florence Pigatti	yes
33	Los Angeles	120 N. San Pedro	5-4 to 5-9	Honora Costigan	yes
34	Hayward	920 C St.	5-4 to 5-9	Mary Dumble	
35	San Mateo	Masonic Temple	5-4 to 5-9	Merle Leedy	yes
41	San Francisco	1550 Buchanan	5-6 to 5-11	Harry White	yes
42	Los Angeles	4527 Lexington	5-6 to 5-11	Federal (Virginia Meyer)	yes
43	Los Angeles	360 So. Westlake	5-6 to 5-11	Wm. McDougall	yes
44	Tulare	Civic Memorial Bldg.	5-7 to 5-13	Kathryn Larmore	yes

C.E.O. No.		PLACE	DATES			PA SUPERVISOR	SUMMARY REPORT REC'D.BY SS Bd
46	Hanford	Civic Auditorium	5-7	to	5-13	Warren Webb	yes
47	Loomis	Union Grammar School	5-8	to	5-14	Madeline Sheridan	yes
48	Newcastle	Community Hall	5-8	to	5-14	Helen Clauson	yes
50	Modesto	1125 - 10th St.	5-8	to	5-13	Mercedes Davis	yes
51	Merced	Vet. Memorial Hall	5-8	to	5-13	Jack Snow	yes
52	Sacramento	Civic Memorial Auditorium	5-8	to	5-16	Alfred Knight	yes
53	Stockton	1420 N. California	5-8	to	5-13	Perry Sundquist	yes
54	Pasadena	58 E. California	5-9	to	5-14	(Federal)	yes
55	Covina	American Legion Hall	5-10	to	5-15	Florence Pigatti	yes
56	Monterey Park	804 W. Garvey	5-10	to	5-15	Opal Cundiff	yes
59	Oceanside	Japanese School	5-11	to	5-17	Frances Wallace	yes
60	Anaheim	249 E. Center St.	5-11	to	5-17	Mary LaHane	yes
61	Huntington Beach	Memorial Hall	5-11	to	5-17	Bessie Irvin	yes
62	Selma	American Legion Hall	5-12	to	5-17	Bertha Underhill	yes
63	Madera	G & 6th Sts.	5-12	to	5-17	Lexie Cotton	yes
64	Fresno	2107 Inyo St.	5-12	to	5-17	Katherine Day	yes
65	Santa Rosa	201 B St.	5-12	to	5-17	Jeannette Harris	yes
(	Los Angeles	Old S.P. Station, 5th & Central	5-12	to	5-17	(Federal) (Virginia Meyer)	yes
69	Yuba City	State Armory	5-13	to	5-18	Eileen Ryan	yes
70	Lodi	State Guard Armory	5-14	to	5-21	Perry Sundquist	yes
71	Brawley	336 N. 7th St.	5-15	to	5-21	Helen Frankl	yes
72	El Centro	455 Commercial St.	5-15	to	5-21	Elizabeth Parmley	yes
73	Indio	City Hall	5-15	to	5-19	Honora Costigan	yes
75	Isleton	Odd Fellows Hall	5-15	to	5-20	Edwina Barry	yes
76	Chico	334 Broadway	5-15	to	5-19	Helen Clauson	yes
77	Gilroy	Hi School Gym.	5-16	to	5-21	Margaret Billings	✓
78	Woodland	American Legion Hall	5-16	to	5-21	Helen Stebbins	yes
81	San Francisco	1501 O'Farrell	5-16	to	5-20	Harry White	yes
82	Ukiah	Palace Hotel Bldg.	5-19	to	5-23	Doris Todd	yes
83	Riverside	3557 Main St.	5-20	to	5-25	Bessie Irvin	yes
84	Palmdale	522 Sierra Highway	5-21	to	5-25	(Federal)	yes
84	Needles	719 Front St.	5-21	to	5-25	(Federal)	yes
85	Bakersfield	County Fair Grounds	5-20	to	5-25	Kathryn Larmore	yes
86	Los Angeles	2925 E. 2nd St.	5-23	to	6-6	(Federal) (Valerie Popper)	yes
92	Elk Grove	Masonic Hall	5-24	to	5-30	Edwina Barry	yes
9.	Florin	Red Men's Hall	5-24	to	5-30	Alfred Knight	yes
94	Walnut Grove	Walnut Grove Hotel	5-24	to	5-30	Helen Clauson	yes

C.E.O. No.		PLACE	DATES	PA SUPERVISOR	SUMMARY REPORT REC'D.BY SS Bd.
95	Perkins	Washington School	5-24 to 5-30	Lexie Cotton	yes
96	San Jose	State College	5-24 to 5-30	Margaret Billings	yes
97	Manteca	Legion Memorial Hall	5-24 to 5-30	Jack Snow	yes
99	Clarksburg	Grammar School	5-31 to 6-6	Madeline Sheridan	yes

TABULATION OF CONTROL STATIONS - PUBLIC ASSISTANCE SUPERVISORS - SUMMARY REPORTS

MILITARY AREA No. II

C.E.O. No.	PLACE		DATES	PA SUPERVISOR	SUMMARY REPORT REC'D.BY SS BD.
100	GHICO	509 MAIN ST.	7-4 TO 7-13	BERTHA UNDERHILL	YES
101	MARYSVILLE	319 C STREET	7-5 TO 7-13	JACK SNOW	YES
102	LINCOLN	CIVIC AUDITORIUM	7-5 TO 7-13	ALFRED KNIGHT	YES
103	CLOVIS	UNION HIGH SCHOOL	7-8 TO 7-18	WARREN WEBB	YES
104	LINDSAY	JUNIOR HI SCHOOL	7-8 TO 7-18	KATHRYN LARMORE	YES
105	NEEDLES	719 FRONT STREET	7-11 TO 7-18	FEDERAL (MISS POPPER)	YES
106	SANGER	UNION HI GYM	7-27 TO 8-11	WARREN WEBB	YES
107	REEDLEY	JR. COLLEGE GYM	7-27 TO 8-11	KATHERINE DAY	YES
108	VISALIA	MUNICIPAL AUDITORIUM	7-27 TO 8-11	KATHRYN LARMORE	

Civilian Exclusion Orders & Control Stations, By Counties

Alameda County

       CEO #19 - 2345 Channing Way, Berkeley   April 25, 1942 to May 1, 1942
        " #24 - See Contra Costa County
        " #27 - 530 - 18th Street, Oakland   May 1, 1942 to May 7, 1942
        " #28 - 1117 Oak Street, Oakland   May 1, 1942 to May 7, 1942
        " #34 - 920 C Street, Hayward   May 4, 1942 to May 9, 1942
        " #81 - See San Francisco County

Alpine County - Not affected - Outside Military Area No. 1

Amador County

       CEO #92 - See Sacramento County
        " #95 - "   "   "

Butte County

       CEO #76 - 334 Broadway Street, Chico   May 15, 1942 to May 19, 1942

Calaveras County

       CEO #50 - See Stanislaus County
        " #95 - See Sacramento   "

Colusa County

       CEO #69 - See Sutter County

Contra Costa County

       CEO #19 - See Alameda County
        " #24 - Odd Fellows Hall, Byron   April 27, 1942 to May 3, 1942
        " #28 - See Alameda County
        " #81 - See San Francisco County

Del Norte County

       CEO #82 - See Mendocino County

El Dorado County

       CEO #95 - See Sacramento County

Fresno County

       CEO #62 - American Legion Hall, Selma   May 12, 1942 to May 17, 1942
        " #63 - See Madera County
        " #64 - 2107 Inyo Street, Fresno   May 12, 1942 to May 17, 1942

Glenn County

CEO #76 - See Butte County

Humboldt County

CEO #82 - See Mendocino County

Imperial County

CEO #71 - 336 N. 7th Street, Brawley   May 15, 1942 to May 21, 1942
"   #72 - 455 Commercial Street, El Centro   May 15, 1942 to May 21, 1942

Inyo County - Not affected - Outside Military Area No. 1

Kern County

CEO #84 - See Los Angeles and San Bernardino Counties
"   #85 - County Fair Grounds, Bakersfield   May 20, 1942 to May 25, 1942

Kings County

CEO #45 - Civic Auditorium, Hanford   May 7, 1942 to May 13, 1942

Lake County

CEO #82 - See Mendocino County

Lassen County - No affected - Outside Military Area No. 1

Los Angeles County

CEO #2 - 362 W. 7th Street, San Pedro   March 31, 1942 to April 5, 1942
"   #2 - 1333 Locust Avenue, Long Beach   March 31, 1942 to April 5, 1942
"   #3 - 707 S. Spring Street, Los Angeles   March 30, 1942 to April 2, 1942
"   #6 - 4311 - 147th St., Los Angeles (Lawndale) April 8, 1942 to April 14, 1942
"   #6 - 112 S. Paramount Blvd., Downey   April 8, 1942 to April 14, 1942
"   #7 - 2422 Lincoln Blvd., Santa Monica   April 21, 1942 to April 28, 1942
"   #8 - 2110 Corinth Street, West Los Angeles   April 21, 1942 to April 28, 1942
"   #9 - 131 Magnolia Street, Burbank   April 21, 1942 to April 28, 1942
"   #10 - 1157 N. La Brea Avenue, Hollywood   April 23, 1942 to April 29, 1942
"   #11 - 961 S. Mariposa Avenue, Los Angeles   April 23, 1942 to April 29, 1942
"   #21 - 3500 S. Normandie Avenue, Los Angeles   April 25, 1942 to May 1, 1942
"   #22 - 2314 S. Vermont Avenue, Los Angeles   April 25, 1942 to May 1, 1942
"   #29 - 16522 S. Western Avenue, Terrance   May 1, 1942 to May 7, 1942
"   #30 - 7412 S. Broadway, Los Angeles   May 1, 1942 to May 7, 1942
"   #31 - 839 S. Central Avenue, Los Angeles   May 1, 1942 to May 7, 1942
"   #32 - 822 E. 20th Street, Los Angeles   May 4, 1942 to May 9, 1942
"   #33 - 120 N. San Pedro Street, Los Angeles   May 4, 1942 to May 9, 1942
"   #42 - 4525 Lexington Avenue, Los Angeles   May 6, 1942 to May 11, 1942
"   #43 - 360 S. Westlake Avenue, Los Angeles   May 6, 1942 to May 11, 1942

- 2 -

Los Angeles County - Continued

    CEO #54 - 38 E. California Street, Pasadena   May 9, 1942 to May 14, 1942
    " #55 - American Legion Hall, Covina   May 10, 1942 to May 15, 1942
    " #56 - 804 Garvey Blvd., Monterey Park   May 10, 1942 to May 15, 1942
    " #66 - Old S. P. Depot, Los Angeles   May 12, 1942 to May 17, 1942
    " #84 - 522 Sierra Highway, Palmdale   May 21, 1942 to May 25, 1942
    " #86 - 2923 E. 2nd Street, Los Angeles   May 23, 1942 to June 6, 1942

Madera County

    CEO #63 - Memorial Hall, Madera   May 12, 1942 to May 17, 1942

Marin County

    CEO #65 - See Sonoma County

Mariposa County

    CEO #51 - See Merced County

Mendocino County

    CEO #82 - 181 Smith Street, Ukiah   May 19, 1942 to May 23, 1942

Merced County

    CEO #51 - Veterans' Memorial Hall, Merced   May 8, 1942 to May 13, 1942

Modoc County - Not affected - Outside Military Area No. 1

Mono County - Not Affected - Outside Military Area No. 1

Monterey County -

    CEO #15 - National Guard Armory, Salinas   April 24, 1942 to April 30, 1942

Napa County

    CEO #65 - See Sonoma County

Nevada County - Not affected - Outside Military Area No. 1

Orange County

    CEO #59 - See San Diego County
    " #60 - 249 E. Center Street, Anaheim   May 11, 1942 to May 17, 1942
    " #61 - Memorial Hall, Huntington Beach   May 11, 1942 to May 17, 1942

Placer County

    CEO #47 – Union Grammar School, Loomis   May 8, 1942 to May 14, 1942
    "   #48 – Community Hall, Newcastle   May 8, 1942 to May 14, 1942
    "   #95 – See Sacramento County

Plumas County – Not affected – Outside Military Area No. 1

Riverside County

    CEO #73 – City Hall, Indio   May 15, 1942 to May 19, 1942
    "   #83 – 3557 Main Street, Riverside   May 20, 1942 to May 25, 1942

Sacramento County

    CEO #52 – Civic Memorial Auditorium, Sacramento   May 8, 1942 to May 16, 1942
    "   #75 – Odd Fellows Hall, Isleton   May 15, 1942 to May 20, 1942
    "   #92 – Masonic Hall, Elk Grove   May 24, 1942 to May 30, 1942
    "   #93 – Red Men's Hall, Florin   May 24, 1942 to May 30, 1942
    "   #94 – Walnut Grove Hotel, Walnut Grove   May 24, 1942 to May 30, 1942
    "   #95 – Washington School, Perkins   May 24, 1942 to May 30, 1942

San Benito County

    CEO #77 – See Santa Clara County

San Bernardino County

    CEO #83 – See Riverside County
    "   #84 – 719 Front Street, Needles   May 21, 1942 to May 25, 1942

San Diego County

    CEO #4 – 1919 India Street, San Diego   April 2, 1942 to April 8, 1942
    "   #59 – Japanese School House, Oceanside   May 11, 1942 to May 17, 1942

San Francisco County

    CEO #5 – 1701 Van Ness Avenue, San Francisco   April 2, 1942 to April 7, 1942
    "   #20 – 2031 Bush Street, San Francisco   April 25, 1942 to May 1, 1942
    "   #41 – 1530 Buchanan Street, San Francisco   May 6, 1942 to May 11, 1942
    "   #81 – 1501 O'Farrell Street, San Francisco   May 16, 1942 to May 20, 1942

San Joaquin County

    CEO #24 – See Contra Costa County
    "   #53 – National Guard Armory, Stockton   May 8, 1942 to May 13, 1942
    "   #70 – State Guard Armory, Lodi   May 14, 1942 to May 21, 1942
    "   #97 – Union High School, Manteca   May 24, 1942 to May 30, 1942

San Luis Obispo County

      CEO #13 - See Santa Barbara County
       " #14 - High School Gym, Arroyo Grande   April 24, 1942 to April 30, 1942

San Mateo County

      CEO #35 - Masonic Temple Building, San Mateo   May 4, 1942 to May 9, 1942

Santa Barbara County

      CEO #13 - 112 W. Cabrillo Blvd., Santa Barbara   April 24, 1942 to April 30, 1942
       " #14 - See San Luis Obispo County

SantaClara County

      CEO #77 - High School Gym, Gilroy   May 16, 1942 to May 21, 1942
       " #96 - State College, San Jose   May 24, 1942 to May 30, 1942

Santa Cruz County

      CEO #16 - Veterans' Memorial Building, Watsonville April 24, 1942 to April 30, 1942

Shasta County

      CEO #76 - See Butte County

Sierra County - Not affected - Outside Military Area No. 1

Siskiyou County

      CEO #76 - See Butte County

Solano County

      CEO #23 - American Legion Hall, Vacaville   April 27, 1942 to May 3, 1942

Sonoma County

      CEO #65 - 201 B Street, Santa Rosa   May 12, 1942 to May 17, 1942

Stanislaus County

      CEO #50 - 1125 - 10th Street, Modesto   May 8, 1942 to May 13, 1942

Sutter County

      CEO #69 - State Guard Armory, Yuba City   May 13, 1942 to May 18, 1942

Tehama County

      CEO #76 - See Butte County

Trinity County

    CEO #82 — See Mendocino County

Tulare County

    CEO #44 — Civic Memorial Building, Tulare   May 7, 1942 to May 13, 1942

Tuolumne County

    CEO #50 — See Stanislaus County

Ventura County

    CEO #12 — 322 S. California Street, Ventura   April 24, 1942 to April 30, 194

Yolo County

    CEO #78 — American Legion Hall, Woodland   May 16, 1942 to May 21, 1942
    CEO # ? — Grammar School, Clarksburg   May 31, 1942 to June 6, 1942
        199

Yuba County

    CEO #69 — See Sutter County

APPENDIX D

Relocation Offices

As of 2/10/45

UNITED STATES DEPARTMENT OF INTERIOR
War Relocation Authority

Washington

Relocation Offices

INTERMOUNTAIN AREA

Ray B. Haight, Acting
Relocation Supervisor
234 Atlas Building
Salt Lake City 1, Utah

LeGrand Dunkley, Act'g
Relocation Officer
234 Atlas Building
Salt Lake City 1, Utah

Ernest J. Palmer
Relocation Officer
328 Idaho Building
Boise, Idaho

William C. Moore
Relocation Officer
515 Realty building
Spokane 8, Washington

WESTERN PLAINS AREA

Everett R. Lane, Acting
Relocation Supervisor
Midland Savings Building
Denver 2, Colorado

James H. Curtis
Relocation Officer
Midland Savings Building
Denver 2, Colorado

C. Fred Lane
Relocation Officer
116 Park Place Bldg.
827 8th Avenue
Greeley, Colorado

Edmund Baklor
Relocation Officer
324 Central Block
Pueblo, Colorado

Cecil Morgan
Relocation Officer
243 Old Post Office Bldg.
Amarillo, Texas

NORTH CENTRAL AREA

Prudence Ross, Acting
Relocation Supervisor
226 West Jackson Blvd.
Room 204
Chicago 6, Illinois

Wayland Lessing, Reloc. Officer
Chicago Metropolitan District
226 West Jackson Blvd.
Chicago 6, Illinois

Milton C. Geuther
Relocation Officer
Greater Ill. District
226 West Jackson Blvd.
Chicago 6, Ill.

Norwood Dillman
Relocation Officer
Room 634
Circle Tower bldg.
Indianapolis 4, Indiana

Joseph Hansen, Act'g.
Relocation Officer
Room 7083, Plankinton bldg.
161 West Wisconsin Ave.
Milwaukee 1, Wisconsin

Elmer B. Isaksen
Relocation Officer
Room 548
Midland Bank Bldg.
Minneapolis 1, Minn.

Frances O'Malley
Acting Relocation Officer
1510 Fidelity Bldg.
Kansas City 6, Missouri

Mary Elizabeth Brooks
Relocation Officer
1415 Paul Brown Bldg.
St. Louis, Missouri

William K. Holland
Relocation Officer
City National Bank Bldg.
Omaha, Nebraska

Frank E. Gibbs
Relocation Officer
520 Liberty Bldg.
Des Moines, Iowa

GREAT LAKES AREA

Robert M. Cullum
Relocation Supervisor
960 Union Commerce
Bldg.
Cleveland 14, Ohio

Dorothy G. Berber
Acting Relocation Off.
509 Ninth Chester bldg.
Cleveland 14, Ohio

Carl L. Spicer
Relocation Officer
3660 A.I.U. Bldg.
Columbus 15, Ohio

Harry E. Titus
Relocation Officer
1005 Union Trust Bldg.
Cincinnati 2, Ohio

Wendell P. Gee
Relocation Officer
1417 Penobscot bldg.
Detroit 26, Michigan

George Graff
Relocation Officer
1126 Rand Bldg.
Buffalo 3, N. Y.

Howard Mather
Relocation Officer
429 Fulton Bldg.
Pittsburgh 22, Pa.

OM-134

as of 2/10/45

MIDDLE ATLANTIC AREA

Leo T. Simmons, Acting
Relocation Supervisor
Room 5516, 350 Fifth Ave.
New York 1, New York

E. Price Steiding
Relocation Officer
Room 5516, 350 Fifth Ave.
New York 1, New York

Herman L. Yager
Relocation Officer
902 Stephen Girard Bldg.
21 South 12th St.
Philadelphia 7, Pa.

Claude C. Cornwall
Relocation Officer
313 Terminal Building
Rochester, New York

Emery Fast
Relocation Officer
Barr Bldg.
910 17th St., N. W.
Washington 25, D. C.

Relocation Officer
1322 O'Sullivan Bldg.
Baltimore 2, Maryland

Edward V. Berman
Relocation Officer
20 Washington Place
Newark, New Jersey

NEW ENGLAND AREA

Roger F. Clapp
Relocation Supervisor
1700 Federal P. O. Bldg.
Boston 9, Mass.

Charles G. McCallister
Relocation Officer
804 American Industrial Bldg.
983 Main St.
Hartford, Connecticut

SOUTHERN AREA

Jesse H. Lewis
Relocation Supervisor
238 Saratoga St.
Industries Bldg.
New Orleans, La.

R. E. Arne
Relocation Officer
238 Saratoga St.
Industries Bldg.
New Orleans, Louisiana

Robert Taylor
Relocation Officer
Room 415, Realty Bldg.
24 Drayton St.
Savannah, Georgia

W. Homer Hill
Relocation Officer
434 Mercantile Bldg.
Dallas, Texas

Absolom N. Ragon, Jr.
Relocation Officer
Pyramid Bldg.
Little Rock, Ark.

NORTHERN CALIF. AREA

Relocation Supervisor
690 Market St.
San Francisco 4, Calif.

Fred Ross
Relocation Officer
690 Market St.
San Francisco, Calif.

Theodore R. E. Lewis
Relocation Officer
Ford and Walker
Watsonville, Calif.

Paul J. Fischer
Relocation Officer
3208 Hamilton Ave.
Fresno, Calif.

Wayne Phelps
Relocation Officer
1709 21st St.
Sacramento, Calif.

SOUTHERN CALIF. & ARIZONA AREA

Paul G. Robertson
Relocation Supervisor
1031 South Broadway
Los Angeles 15, Calif.

G. Raymond Booth
Relocation Officer
1031 South Broadway
Los Angeles 15, Calif.

PACIFIC NORTHWEST AREA

Harold S. Fistere
Relocation Supervisor
Room 309, Walker Bldg.
1306 Second Ave.
Seattle 1, Wash.

Sheldon Hagan
Relocation Officer
1331 Third Ave. Bldg.
Seattle 1, Wash.

Clyde Linville
Relocation Officer
836 American Bank Bldg.
Portland, Oregon

Murray Stebbins
Relocation Officer
Room 439, Liberty Bldg.
416 East Yakima Ave.
Yakima, Wash.

WRA Eligibility for Unrestricted Residence

A. Criteria for classifying evacuees into groups

Group I. Eligible for unrestricted residence anywhere in the
United States.

A. CITIZENS, who

1. Have no parents, children, brothers, or sisters now in Japan.

2. Have not attended school in Japan for longer than one year
above the elementary level and not at all since January 1, 1940.

3. (a) Have made no visits at all to Japan since January 1, 1940.

   (b) Have made no more than two visits to Japan since birth.

   (c) Have not resided in Japan longer than a total of three
   years after reaching twelve years of age.

4. Have never been employed by the Japanese government.

5. Have not been employed by a semi-official Japanese firm
(Mitsubishi, Mitsui, Domei) since January 1, 1940; and have
not been employed by a semi-official Japanese firm prior to
that date for longer than a total of one year.

6. Have never been employed as a Japanese language school
instructor.

7. Have never been employed as a Japanese sports instructor
(Kudo, Judo, Kendo).

8. Have not been employed since January 1, 1936, as a writer
or correspondent for a Japanese language periodical published
in Japan or as writer or broadcaster for Japanese radio.

(War Relocation Authority, 1943, p. 22)
War Relocation Authority (1943). "General information (Segregation Program)."
pp. 1–72, folder E6.00, box BANC MSS 67/14 c. Federal Government Records, Japanese
American Evacuation and Resettlement records. Berkeley: Bancroft Library, University
of California.

WRA Administrative Manual—Welfare

NARA   2/10/11

E 29 — Headquarter Records
          Management files
          WRA Administrative Manuals
                              (2 sets)

Box 1

ff: WRA Administrative Manual
                    (Set 1)
          Index, Table of Contents, 1030

.1 The Welfare Section at WRA centers operates as a part of the Community Management Division. The head of the Section, known as Counselor, is administratively responsible to, and comes under the supervision of, the Assistant Project Director in charge of the Community Management Division. From the standpoint of the techniques to be applied, the Counselor is responsible to the Head of the Welfare Section in Washington.

Organization at Centers

.2 Policies, procedures and regulations governing the operation of the Welfare Section are determined and issued by the Director of the War Relocation Authority. It is the administrative responsibility of the Project Director to see that such policies, procedures and regulations are carefully adhered to. The application of these policies, procedures and regulations will, from time to time, be further augmented by technical instructions and advice with regard to method and technique by the Washington Welfare Section.

Policies, Procedures and Regulations

.3 The general functions of the Center Welfare Section are:

A. To establish and maintain such practices as will effectuate the general public welfare policies established by the War Relocation Authority, allowing — within the general principles established — for such adaptation as local conditions may require.

B. To assist families and individuals through such services as will develop and make use of their own capacity in meeting difficult personal and environmental problems. This will mean counseling with individuals and families on problems such as delinquency, personal maladjustment, family difficulties, and broken homes.

C. To provide child welfare services. Such services would include:

(1) Consultative services to working mothers;

(2) Services relating to day care, and foster care;

Functions at Centers

(3) Treatment for dependent and neglected children, and for children with special problems;

(4) Child placement;

(5) A program of counseling for youth.

D. To establish and maintain cooperative relations with public and private social, health and welfare agencies

11/18/43
Supersedes A.I. # 91

C-0734 F3 bu

WRA   Welfare 30.4

(.3D)

and institutions. Such assistance would be in the
form of advice, counsel and other services dealing
with specialized problems such as psychiatric case
work, child guidance and child welfare.

E. To administer a program of clothing allowances.

F. To administer public assistance grants to those individuals and families whose income is inadequate to
meet minimum needs.

G. To cooperate with the Relocation Division in planning
for individuals and families who are relocating.

H. To assign living quarters to individuals and families,
other than appointed personnel, with consideration giv-
en to the size of the family, the family's preference
as to location; and, in the case of individuals, if advisable, an opportunity to select those individuals
with whom they would prefer to live. To concern itself
with other problems pertaining to the social aspects of
housing.

I. To establish and maintain records essential to the operation of the Section; and to prepare periodic reports
of the work of the Section.

**Functions
(cont'd.)**

J. To plan and effectuate a program of in-service training
for evacuee case aides in the functions of individual
and family counseling services.

K. To coordinate the Welfare program with that of other
Sections of the Community Management Division and with
the activities of the other Divisions at the Center.

L. To counsel with and to assist individuals and families
with their repatriation plans; to refer to and cooperate with the Project Attorney on all matters pertaining
to the legal aspects of repatriation; to cooperate with
the Statistician regarding the maintenance of the official records of requests for repatriation and cancella-
tions.

M. To recommend to the Project Director approval or disapproval of requests of evacuees to transfer residence
to another Center; and, in the case of approved cases,
to make all the necessary arrangements for the transfer
to the second Center.

11/18/43
Supersedes A.I. # 91

C-0754 P4 bu-final

.10 Project Directors are authorized to make public assistance grants to evacuees whose income is inadequate to
meet minimum needs.

.11

A. Those persons shall be eligible for grants who are
without adequate means of support for themselves and
their dependents and who are in need of public assistance, including the following:

    (1) Single individuals and heads of families who are
unable to work because of illness or incapacity.
Eligibility under this classification shall not
exist until after all rights to illness compensation under regulations of the War Relocation
Authority have expired.

    (2) Children without support under 16 years of age.

    (3) The heads of families which have a total net in-
come (from all sources) that is inadequate to
meet their needs.

B. Eligibility shall not exist for employable persons
who refuse to work.

.12

A. The amounts of grants for needs other than clothing
shall not exceed the following except as provided in
D below:

    (1) For men - $4.75 per month

    (2) For women - $4.25 per month

    (3) For children (13-17) - $2.50 per month

    (4) For children (under 13) - $1.50 per month

B. The nearest age at the beginning of the fiscal year
shall determine the age throughout the year, for the
purposes of the preceding paragraph.

C. The grant for any family shall be the total of the
grants for which the individual members are eligible.

D. In addition to the amounts stated above in A, the
Project Director is authorized to make special grants
to meet cases of critical need. Each such case shall
be approved by the Project Director.

E. Grants for clothing may be made in particular cases,
in addition to other public assistance grants, in accordance with need. However, such grants shall not

Policy on
Issuance of
Public Assistance
Grants

Eligibility

Amounts
of
Grants

12/16/43
Supersedes A.I. # 35

C-0797 P3 bu

WRA   Welfare 30.4

(.12E)

exceed the rates for clothing allowances set forth in Section 30.4.51.

F. The total grant in any instance shall not exceed the applicant's needs.

Approval of Vouchers for Grants

.13 Grants will be payable on the basis of vouchers approved by the Project Director or his authorized representative, and certified by the Project Certifying Officer.

Responsibility for Receipt and Investigation of Applications for Assistance

.14 It shall be the responsibility of the Welfare Section of the Community Management Division to receive and investigate all applications for public assistance grants, and to render such follow-up service and perform such other services as are necessary to good family case work.

.15

Regulations

A. No assistance shall be extended for a longer period than 30 days at one time. The circumstances of each recipient shall be reviewed or reinvestigated at least once each 30 days before further assistance is approved. For continuing cases, however, a new application will not be required for each grant payment. The original application will be sufficient unless the case has been inactive for at least 30 days.

B. Public assistance grants must be used for the purposes for which they have been made. Any misuse of public assistance funds shall be sufficient reason for discontinuance of further assistance.

C. No assistance grant shall be made where the applicant is eligible for the same or equivalent assistance from another agency, or where another type of assistance will better enable the applicant to meet his real needs.

.16

A. All applications for public assistance grants shall be made on Form WRA-76, entitled "Application for Public Assistance Grant". This form shall be prepared in duplicate. The original shall be retained in the Welfare Section, and the copy shall be forwarded immediately to the center files.

Procedure

B. The Welfare Section shall promptly investigate the need of each applicant for assistance. On the basis of such investigation the Section shall determine whether a grant is necessary and the amount of grant required.

12/16/43
Supersedes A.I. # 35

C-0797 P4 bu

(.16)

C. If it is determined that a grant is necessary, the
    Welfare Section shall assign a case number to the ap-
    plication from a register kept for that purpose, and
    shall prepare Form WRA-77, entitled "Voucher for Pub-
    lic Assistance Grant". It shall fill out each voucher
    completely with the exception of the WRA and D. C.
    Voucher Number. Vouchers shall be prepared in quin-
    tuplicate for distribution as hereinafter prescribed.
    (Note that more than one grant can be listed on one
    voucher form). The Head or the Assistant Head of the
    Welfare Section shall sign the original of each vouch-
    er in the space indicated for verification. The
    voucher shall then be forwarded with the original ap-
    plication (or applications) containing the facts con-   **Procedure**
    cerning the case and the recommendations to the Chief   (cont'd.)
    of the Division of Community Management for approval.
    (If the Project Director so desires, he may require
    each voucher to be approved by himself.)

D. Approved vouchers shall be forwarded to the Project
    Finance Officer, who will examine them to determine
    that they are properly made out but will not pass on
    the recipient's eligibility for assistance. Payment
    will be made in cash by the Agent-cashier on the bas-
    is of approved and audited vouchers. The Project
    Director may if he wishes have the grants paid by
    check issued by the Assistant Regional Disbursing Of-
    ficer-in-Charge, rather than in cash. This may be
    done only if the evacuees are able to cash the check
    easily and without the payment of a service charge in
    excess of five cents (5¢) per check.

.17 Grants made shall be reported to Washington monthly on   Reports
     Form WRA-243.

.50   A.   Each evacuee who is employed or who is eligible for
           extended illness compensation shall receive a supple-
           mentary allowance for clothing for himself and each
           of his dependents. Clothing allowances shall also be
           paid to dependents of employees of Business Enterprises
           and to dependents of evacuee religious workers whose
           compensation from a congregation or denomination does
           not exceed $19. per month (30.5.24 C and 30.7.8 B).

      B.   An evacuee shall be eligible for a clothing allowance   **Eligibility**
           at the end of each monthly pay period if he has been   **for**
           employed for at least one-half the monthly scheduled   **Clothing**
           hours or has received extended illness compensation   **Allowance**
           during at least 15 days of that month.

      C.   The clothing allowance shall be paid to the head of the
           family for himself and all dependents who are not em-
           ployed or receiving extended illness compensation. All
           other members of the family who are employed or who
           are receiving extended illness compensation shall re-
           ceive their clothing allowances as individuals.

.51
      A.   The following schedule for clothing allowances shall
           apply to the Tule Lake, Minidoka, Heart Mountain,
           Central Utah, Manzanar, and Granada Relocation Centers:

	Annually	Monthly
Persons 16 yrs. of age or over	$45.00	$3.75	**Clothing**
Persons 8 to 16 yrs. of age	39.00	3.25	**Allowance**
Persons under 8 yrs. of age	27.00	2.25	**Rates**

      B.   The following schedule for clothing allowances shall
           apply to the Colorado River, Gila River, Rohwer, and
           Jerome Relocation Centers:

	Annually	Monthly
Persons 16 yrs. of age or over	$42.00	$3.50
Persons 8 to 16 yrs. of age	36.00	3.00
Persons under 8 yrs. of age	24.00	2.00

.52
      A.   The Welfare Section in each Relocation Center shall   **Certification**
           prepare Basic Family Card, WRA-95. One of the pur-   **for Clothing**
           poses of this card is to make available to the   **Allowance**

9/29/44
Supersedes Issuance of 11/25/43
Release # 123

C.1670 PB bu

(.52A)

Welfare Section necessary information for fulfilling its responsibility for preparation of clothing allowance orders and certification thereof. These cards shall be prepared for all basic family units now in Relocation Centers, and a new card shall be made as new families or individuals arrive at the Center.

B. After the face of the form has been completed the back shall be properly set up, and the cards filed alphabetically.

C. The Finance Section will provide the Welfare Section with a copy of payrolls and all grant vouchers for each month and these shall be posted on the backs of the cards. The Personnel Management Section will route a copy of WRA-92, "Application for Extended Illness Compensation", to the Welfare Section for all persons eligible for extended illness compensation. Information from these forms shall be noted immediately on the back of the card.

Certification for Clothing Allowance (cont'd.)

D. Computations shall then be made of the amount of clothing allowances due to individuals, or to heads of families with dependents, in accordance with the conditions of eligibility specified in Section 30.4.50.

E. When the computations have been completed on the backs of the Basic Family Cards the pertinent information shall be transcribed to Clothing Allowance Order, Form WRA-93. These orders shall then be routed to the Finance Section following proper approval by the Welfare Section.

F. It is imperative that all of the data on the Basic Family Card be kept current. Changes in family composition and in dependency status due to birth, marriage, death, relocation, unemployment, or other reason must be promptly recorded.

G. If there are omissions or other errors they shall, upon the securing of adequate information, be corrected in the next allowance. However, corrections cannot be made if the error is not discovered within a two month period. In case of errors discovered within the two month period, a memorandum shall be addressed to the Finance Section giving an explanation of the circumstances.

9/29/44
Supersedes Issuance of 11/25/43
Release # 123

C-1870-p4-bu-final

WRA   Welfare 30.4

(.52)

    H. Basic Family Cards shall be kept in alphabetical
       file at all times when not in actual use.

    I. Copies of the payroll shall be maintained in a
       chronological file.

.53 In order to have uniformity in terminology and in
    application of policy, the following guides should be
    used in determining basic family units.

    A. A family in most instances consists of father,
       mother, and unmarried children. For all such
       units a Basic Family Card should be prepared.

    B. In instances where there are deviations from the
       normal family group the following suggestions are
       made:

       (1) A married son of an evacuee, his wife, and
           children if any, should be considered a basic
           family unit and a card should be prepared for
           them.

       (2) A married daughter of an evacuee, her husband,
           and children if any, should be considered a
           basic family unit and a card should be pre-
           pared for them.

       (3) A married son who is a widower, and his un-
           married children, should be considered a
           basic family unit and a card should be pre-
           pared for them.

       (4) A married daughter who is a widow, and her
           unmarried children, should be considered a
           basic family unit, and a card should be pre-
           pared for them.

       (5) Children who are without parents and who are
           living with relatives should be considered
           a part of the basic family unit of the rela-
           tive.

Guides for Determining the Basic Family Unit

11/25/43
Supersedes A.I. # 103

WRA   Welfare 30.4

(.53B)

   (6) Children who have been adopted, whether legally
     or otherwise, even though their own families
     may be living should be considered a part of
     the basic family unit of the foster parents.

   (7) Single unattached individuals should in most
     instances be considered a basic unit.

   (8) In the case, however, that an elderly relative
     of either the man or woman of a basic family
     unit is living with the basic family, he or she
     should be considered a part of the basic family
     unit. This might be a parent, grandparent,
     aunt, uncle, or some other close relative.

Clothing Allowance Order

.54 At the end of each month the Welfare Section shall prepare in triplicate (from Family Record Cards) Clothing
Allowance Order, Form WRA-93. The original and first
copy will be forwarded to the Project Finance Section;
the second copy will be retained in the files of the
Welfare Section. Form WRA-93 will be signed by the
Project Director unless he delegates the authority to
sign to the Head of the Welfare Section.

Issuance of Grants

.55 The Finance Section will be responsible for determining
the accuracy of all extensions and totals, and will prepare Grant Vouchers on the basis of Clothing Allowance
Orders. After preparation, the Grant Voucher will be
approved by the Project Director or Head of the Welfare
Section and then forwarded to the Agent-Cashiers for payment. Agent-Cashiers will pay clothing allowances on the
basis of approved, audited clothing allowance orders, and
only the amounts shown in columns 8 and 9. The Project
Director, in his discretion, may have clothing allowances
paid by checks issued by the Assistant Regional Disbursing Officer-in-Charge rather than in cash paid by the
Agent-Cashier. This may be done only if the evacuees are
able to cash the checks easily and without the payment of
a service charge in excess of five cents (5¢) per check.
(See Finance Handbook, page G-36).

11/25/43
Supersedes A.I. # 103

C-0747 P6 bu-final

Job Descriptions

Public Welfare Consultant

Form 2931
January

UNITED STATES CIVIL SERVICE COMMISSION

CLASSIFICATION SHEET

C.S.C. No. ....

Bureau No. ....

Code ....

CHECK TO INDICATE WHETHER SHEET IS FOR—		GIVE FOLLOWING INFORMATION FOR ITEM CHECKED	CLASSIFICATION			
			Service	Grade	Class	Initials
New position	X	Indefinite (Temporary or permanent)	Recommended by Bureau	P	4	180
Vice change		(Name and C.S.C. number on sheet of position into which viced)	Allocation by head of Department	P	4	180
Identical additional position		(Name and C.S.C. number on sheet of position with which identical)	Allocation by Civil Service Commission	P	4	180
Material modification of duties		(Mention nature of modification)	Action No.			
Other change		(Explain reason for submission of sheet)	Date JUL 1 5 1943			

1. Name ......Vacancy......
   (Surname)   (Given name)   (Initial)

2. C.S.C. number of last sheet for this employee ....

3. Employee's present basic annual salary rate ....

4. Allowances (deduction for Q.S.L., etc.) ....
   (Character and value)

5. Department ..Office for Emergency Management..

6. Bureau ..War Relocation Authority..

7. Division ..Community Management..

8. Section or unit ..Welfare..

Title of position ..Public Welfare Consultant..
   (Usual departmental or organizational title)

10. Description of the duties and responsibilities of the position: (Describe, as objectively and concretely as possible, the duties and responsibilities of the position in question, following this order: (1) Kind and extent of supervision or direction under which the work is performed; (2) the major, regular, periodic, or more important tasks, indicating proportion of time; (3) the tasks of lesser frequency or importance, indicating proportion of time; (4) any supervisory responsibility, showing the number of employees in each grade supervised; and (5) any other facts or figures bearing upon the characteristics of the position from the standpoint of difficulty, complexity, responsibility, independence of action or decision, or any other allocation factor.)

Under the general supervision of the Public Welfare Consultant, participates in the formulation and revision of policies and procedures for the administration of the welfare program of the Authority; through correspondence and individual and group conferences, interprets policies, standards, and procedures to the staff of several relocation centers; and through consultation and technical advice, assists center personnel in the establishment and maintenance of acceptable standards of public welfare administration.

Adapts to the needs of the welfare program standard-setting material in various aspects of social work, such as standards of assistance, prevention and treatment of juvenile delinquency, illegitimacy, and adoption, and makes available to the centers such material in the form of manuals or handbooks. Participates in the development and revision of uniform recording and reporting procedures for the several centers. Analyzes reports and special studies and makes recommendations to the Public Welfare Consultant regarding significant problems, developments, and trends in the various aspects of the welfare program at each center. Prepares selected bibliographies for use by the center welfare sections in staff development or in-service training programs. Advises the Project Director, Assistant Project Director in charge of Community Management, and welfare staff regarding standards of public welfare administration and assists center personnel in the development and maintenance of acceptable standards for the granting of financial assistance, treatment and prevention of

(CONTINUE STATEMENT OF DUTIES ON REVERSE OF SHEET)

16—2002

Head Counselor

10. Description of the duties and responsibilities of the position (continued):

juvenile delinquency, care of dependent and neglected children, services for physically and mentally handicapped persons and other individuals and families in need of social services.

Through consultation with center personnel, study of records, and personal observation evaluates the effectiveness of the welfare program in each center and its relation to other phases of center administration. Makes recommendations to the center administration and to the Public Welfare Consultant regarding needed changes in any phase of the operation of the welfare program including personnel needs.

Consults with representatives of Federal and state agencies regarding the development of policies and procedures relating to the functions of the Authority's welfare program. Advises with center personnel in the development of cooperative relationships and agreements with state and local public and private agencies, such as state departments of public welfare, juvenile courts, family societies and child guidance clinics for the provision of needed social services.
(Continued on attached sheet)

11. (a) For what purpose is any part of the work described above reviewed within the same organizational subdivision or unit?

(b) Give the usual organizational title of the reviewer or reviewers.

12. Give name and usual organizational title of employee's immediate supervisor. Principal/Welfare Consultant, P
Public

13. Give actual qualifications (education, training, experience, etc.) of employee; or, if the position is a vacancy, the qualifications necessary for the work.

EDUCATIONAL TRAINING	EXPERIENCE AND OTHER SPECIAL QUALIFICATIONS
Indicate by an "X" the highest grade or year. Elementary school: ... 1 2 3 4 5 6 7 8 ☐ ☐ ☐ ☐ ☐ ☐ ☐ ☐ High school: ... 1 2 3 4 ☐ ☐ ☐ ☐ College: ... 1 2 3 4 ☐ ☐ ☐ ☐ Name ... Technical or post graduate: Kind and extent...	

14. Date when employee entered upon the duties and assumed the responsibilities described above ...

(Signature of preparing officer)

Date July 7, 1943

(Signature of reviewing officer)
Gladys Pearlson, Classification Officer

U.S. GOVERNMENT PRINTING OFFICE   16—2008

Assistant Counselor

Makes regular and special reports to the Public Welfare Consultant in
connection with field visits. Participates in staff meetings of the
Welfare Section and the Community Management Division. Aids in the recruitment of welfare personnel for relocation centers by interviewing
applicants for positions, and performs other responsibilities as assigned.

Minimum Qualifications

Education: Certificate or degree from a recognized school of social work,
          or the equivalent.

Experience: At least five years' employment of increasing responsibility
           in recognized public or private social welfare agencies, at
           least one year of which shall have been in case work in a
           family or children's agency with recognized standards, and at
           least two years of which shall have been in responsible super-
           visory or administrative capacities with a state or Federal
           agency.

vet

Counseling Aide

P-4-180

Office for Emergency Management   T.10-11,025
War Relocation Authority
San Francisco Region
Relocation Project
Community Service Division
Community Welfare Section
November 4, 1942

Head Counselor (CAF-11)

Under the supervision of the Chief of Community Services, CAF-13, is responsible for establishing, directing, and maintaining a complete counseling and individual and family welfare program, including the selection and training of Japanese Counseling Aides.

Supervises the activities of a counselor, an assistant counselor, and a housing superintendent.

Plans and supervises the selection and training of a number of Japanese Aides in the functions of individual and family case work, counseling, and the like; supervises the administration of public-assistance grants to unemployed Project personnel, including the receiving and investigation of requests for public assistance and for recommending to the Chief of Community Services and the Fiscal Office the disposition of such requests; supervises the counselor in the solution by Counseling Aides of such social and individual problems as delinquency, family difficulties, problems of foster care, broken homes, and the like, by means of interviewing, obtaining personal and family histories, and investigating the complete background and present situation; counsels individuals or families; supervises the Assistant Counselor in the establishment of a plan for administering a Clothing Allowance Program; maintains liaison with the employment and other divisions within the Project for the purpose of securing complete records of backgrounds and present situations of the cases within the jurisdiction of the section.

Contacts both private and public social agencies outside the Project, and secures cooperation and assistance from these agencies in the form of advice, counseling, and actual personnel time in the fields of psychiatric case work, child guidance and child welfare work and other needed services.

The incumbent receives general technical instructions from the Assistant Regional Director's Office, and receives administrative direction and policy instructions from the Chief of Community Services. Because of the paucity of trained Japanese Counselors and social workers, the incumbent will be largely responsible for the supervision of a complete training program of personnel assisting in the above functions. The incumbent is responsible for adapting standardized and accepted techniques, procedures, and principles to the peculiar circumstances existing within the Project among the Japanese residents.

Superintendent of Children's Village

<u>Head Counselor (CAF-11)</u>

<u>Minimum Qualifications</u>

<u>Education</u>: Bachelor's Degree from an accredited university, college, or state teachers college, and one year of study in an acceptable school of Social Work. Eudcation must include courses in Social Welfare Case Work, Family Problems, Social Adjustment, and in Public Welfare organization and Administration.

<u>Experience</u>: Four years of successful experience, one of which is in a supervisory capacity in Social Welfare work where a thorough working knowledge of Government aid, family problems, and social adjustment has been gained, and two years of which are in a responsible administrative capacity.

STANDARD POSITION DESCRIPTION

Department of the Interior
War Relocation Authority
Relocation Center
Community Management Division
Welfare Section   Date Allocated: 10-1-44

Title: ASSISTANT COUNSELOR   P-3

Description:

    Under the supervision of the Counselor, assists in
the establishment, direction, and maintenance of the welfare
program at the center. Supervises the family counseling
program in relation to relocation and/or other individual or
family plans. Supervises a program of financial assistance
and other welfare services. Is particularly responsible for
a program of staff-development or in-service training.

    Selects from among the residents of the center a
number of case aides and trains them in the functions of
individual and family counseling. Instructs case aides in
methods of interviewing, obtaining personal and family history
in relation to background and present situation of individuals
and families; case recording, etc. Plans and conducts staff
meetings, orientation program for Junior Counselors and evacuee
case aide staff.

    Supervises a number of Junior Counselors and evacuee
case aides in a family counseling program for relocation.
Establishes and maintains good working relationships with other
divisions and sections. Develops and maintains an organized
plan for referral of families planning relocation to the
Relocation Division.

    Assists in the administration of the financial assist-
ance program, including the review of applications for financial
assistance and recommends the disposition of such applications. Supervises a staff of Junior Counselors and evacuee
case aides in a program of counseling and other services needed
in case of delinquency, dependency, and neglect, foster home
finding, and supervision of foster home placements. Assists
the Counselor in the direction and supervision of the functions
of housing assignments and clothing allowances.

    Upon assignment by the Counselor, contacts both private
and public social agencies outside the center to secure the

(over)

(continued)

cooperation and assistance in the form of advice and counseling, case work service in the fields of psychiatric case
work, child guidance, foster care and other needed services
for residents of the center.

Desirable Qualifications:

Education: Bachelor's degree from an accredited university,
college, or state teachers' college, and one year
of study in an recognized school of social work.
Education should include courses in social welfare
case work, family problems, social adjustment,
and in public welfare organization and administration.

Experience: Two years of successful experience, one of which
has been in supervisory capacity in social welfare
work where a thorough working knowledge of government aid, family problems, and social adjustment
has been gained.

OM-1526

STANDARD POSITION DESCRIPTION

Department of the Interior
War Relocation Authority
Relocation Center
Community Management Division
Welfare Section   Date Approved: 7-1-44

Title: COUNSELING AIDE   SP-6

Description:

Under the supervision of the Counselor, makes
investigations by interviews, correspondence, home visits,
and other means available to determine the facts in cases
of delinquency, domestic difficulties, financial distress,
and other maladjustments of individuals and groups within the center.

Under the supervision of the Counselor, assembles
the data collected as described above into a report; keeps
a record of contacts concerning each case; prepares case
histories on the basis of these facts and interviews according to standard case work procedure.

Under the direction of the Counselor, recommends
utilization of the various resources within the center to
correct these problems, namely, health facilities, cash
grants, school, recreation, housing adjustments, etc.;
or recommends institutionalization or carries through
treatment agreed upon with the Counselor and other officers
of the center.

Desirable Qualifications:

Education: A. B. degree from an accredited college or
            university. Speaking knowledge of Japanese
            language.

Experience: Five years' successful experience in work relat-
            ing to individuals such as teaching, or work in
            a public or private agency which provides services
            for people.

OM-1533

p-1-180

Position #T.10-5048
Revised 6-23-42

Office for Emergency Management
War Relocation Authority
San Francisco Region
Relocation Project
Community Services Division
Community Welfare Section

Counseling Aide

Under the supervision of the Counselor, performs counseling service and social case work within the Project.

Investigates cases of social maladjustment, family difficulties, delinquency, and the like; interviews Japanese residents who have problems of the above nature; suggests solutions and counsels the Japanese in methods of alleviating their situation; obtains complete personal and family histories by contacting personal friends, relations, or such divisions within the Project as the Employment and Housing Division; writes case histories; investigates requests for public assistance and reports the findings to the Counselor; works and advises with juveniles within the Project who have become delinquent, and suggests methods of eliminating the predisposing factors of such delinquency; suggests educational and leisure-time programs which will fit the individual needs of the person.

The incumbent receives complete training from the Counselor and works under the direct supervision of the Counselor. Case summaries and recommendations are reviewed by the Counselor.

DI-88
(Approved July 1942)

CLASSIFICATION SHEET—ORIGINAL

P.3-180

UNITED STATES
DEPARTMENT OF THE INTERIOR

FIELD SERVICE—REGULAR ROLLS

CLASSIFICATION			
	Grade	Salary	Initials
Recommended by field station	P	3	
Recommended by Bureau	P	3	MW 6/29/44
Allocation by Department			

1. Bureau War Relocation Authority
   (a) Name of field unit Manzanar Reloc. Center(only
   (b) Field station Manzanar State California

2. Name VACANCY
   (Surname first) Age Proposed position Supt. Of Children's $ 3200
   (Number and title) Village (Salary)

   (a) Previous incumbent No. Field unit
   Grade Salary, $

3. Duties { ☐ the same as those of   ☐ similar to those of } No. Field unit
   Grade Salary, $

4. Number of regular working hours; per day 8 ; per week 48
   (a) If this is not a full-time position, give full details

5. Title of appropriation or fund from which salary is paid

6. Allowances (deductions for quarters, heat, light, subsistence, etc.)
   (Character and value)

7. Present position Service or field unit Grade Salary, $
   (Number and title)

8. Description of work: (Follow instructions carefully.)
   Describe explicitly each task performed, giving first the regular and more important tasks and second the less important and incidental duties. Use a separate paragraph for each task and number the paragraphs. In the column at the right state the estimated percentage of the total time required for each task.

   Percentage of time given to each task.

Under the general direction of the Counselor, is responsible for the administration of the Children's village. As a specialist in child care and child placement is not subject to technical supervision. Resident children range in age from under one year old to High School age.

Is responsible for the development of complete and comprehensive plans and programs for the management of the Children's Village, including plans for adoption, foster-home care, regulations and procedures for admissions and discharges and plans for the care of children while in residence at the Village. Is required to be informed of current developments in field of child welfare and child placement.

Performs research into the laws, regulations and procedures of various state and local jurisdictions in order, properly to arrange adoption and foster-home placements. Develops standards for adoption and foster-home placements and follow-up.

Reviews applications from persons desiring to adopt or to provide foster-home care to children in the Village. Reviews various factors in the family background of applicants and of the children to determine advisability of approval. Makes recommendations to superiors, which are subject to

(CONTINUE STATEMENT OF DUTIES ON REVERSE OF SHEET)

16—59807-1

8. Description of work: (Continued)

only cursory review. Contacts the Childrens Bureau and other
public and private social agencies to secure their cooperation and
services.

In cooperation with specialists in other divisions and sections
develops plans and programs for the care and welfare of children
at the Village; for example, cooperates with the Health Section in
obtaining needed medical care and with the Education Section in the
education of school age children, providing information and
assistance in working out their adjustments. Personally supervises
the operation of a nursery school for Village children of pre-school
age. As required, arranges for psychiatric and psychological
examinations for the children.

Compiles histories of the children, including habits, behavior
problems, attitudes, school progress, etc. Maintains records and
provides data regarding residents of the Village. Supervises
personnel employed in the Children's Village, including Junior

9. How long have the duties of the individual named been substantially as described above? ....

10. Does the employee work under immediate supervision, or to a large extent on his own responsibility? (Describe fully.)

11. What part of the employee's work is reviewed and for what purpose? ....

12. Does the position involve supervision over other employees? Yes .... No ...... If the answer is "Yes," give names, titles, and grades of employees supervised ....

13. Give name, title, and grade of employee's immediate superior .... Counselor, CAF-11 ....

14. Give actual qualifications (education, training, experience, etc.) of employee; of if the position is a vacancy, the qualifications necessary for the work:

Educational training	Experience and other special qualifications
Indicate by an "X" the highest grade or year. Elementary school .... 1 2 3 4 5 6 7 8 ☐☐☐☐☐☐☐☐ High school .... 1 2 3 4 ☐☐☐☐ College .... 1 2 3 4 ☐☐☐☐ Name .... Technical or post-graduate: Kind and extent........	

Date .... June 28, 1944 .... Preparing officer ....
~~Gladys Pearlson, Classification Officer~~ (Title)

Date .. June 29, 1944 .... Approved by Bureau ....
Meyer Weinger, (Signature) Classification Officer (Title)

U. S. GOVERNMENT PRINTING OFFICE

Counselors assigned on a temporary basis, and evacuee personnel
employed in its operation. Establishes rules and regulations
for the operation of the Village. Prepares quarterly
and annual budget requests and justifications for submission
to superior.

Performs related work as required.

Index

For the benefit of digital users, indexed terms that span two pages (e.g., 52–53) may, on occasion, appear on only one of those pages.